HUMAN GROWTH AND DEVELOPMENT ACROSS THE LIFESPAN

HUMAN GROWTH AND DEVELOPMENT ACROSS THE LIFESPAN

Applications for Counselors

Edited by

David Capuzzi

Walden University, Johns Hopkins University

Mark D. Stauffer

Walden University

Mary, So glad you have interest in this topic! Best wishes for continued personal and professional success. I hope your retirement planning goes well. David C.

WILEY

Library of Congress Cataloging-in-Publication Data

Names: Capuzzi, Dave, editor. | Stauffer, Mark D., editor.
Title: Human growth and development across the lifespan : applications for counselors / edited by David Capuzzi and Mark D. Stauffer.
Description: Hoboken, New Jersey : John Wiley & Sons, Inc., [2016] | Includes bibliographical references and index.
Identifiers: LCCN 2015042772 | ISBN 9781118984727 (cloth) | ISBN 9781118984758 (ePDF) | ISBN 9781118984741 (epub)
Subjects: LCSH: Counseling psychology. | Counseling. | Developmental psychology.
Classification: LCC BF636.6 .H86 2016 | DDC 158.3—dc23 LC record available at http://lccn.loc.gov/2015042772

Cover Design: Wiley

Printed in the United States of America

FIRST EDITION

HB Printing 10 9 8 7 6 5 4 3 2 1

Contents

Acknowledgments

We would like to thank the authors who contributed their expertise, knowledge, and experience in the development of this textbook. We would also like to thank our families, who provided the freedom and encouragement to make this endeavor possible. Our thanks are also directed to members of the Wiley production team: Rachel Livsey as Acquisition Editor and Patricia Rossi as Executive Sponsoring Editor, for their encouragement and assistance with the publication of the book; Kristi Bennett for copyediting; and to Maria Sunny Zacharias our Production Editor.

Special thanks are extended to Stephanie Scott, core faculty of clinical mental health counseling at Walden University, for review and suggestions of our content areas when we were developing this book. Additionally, thanks go out to Kakumyo-Lowe Charde for his review of chapter components on spiritual development.

About the Editors

David Capuzzi, PhD, NCC, LPC, is a counselor educator and member of the core faculty in clinical mental health counseling at Walden University and professor emeritus at Portland State University. Previously, he served as an affiliate professor in the Department of Counselor Education, Counseling Psychology, and Rehabilitation Services at Pennsylvania State University and scholar in residence in counselor education at Johns Hopkins University. He is past president of the American Counseling Association (ACA), formerly the American Association for Counseling and Development, and past chair of both the ACA Foundation and the ACA Insurance Trust.

From 1980 to 1984, Dr. Capuzzi was editor of the *School Counselor*. He has authored a number of textbook chapters and monographs on the topic of preventing adolescent suicide and is coeditor and author with Dr. Larry Golden of *Helping Families Help Children: Family Interventions With School Related Problems* (1986) and *Preventing Adolescent Suicide* (1988). He coauthored and edited with Douglas R. Gross *Youth at Risk: A Prevention Resource for Counselors, Teachers, and Parents* (1989, 1996, 2000, 2004, 2008, 2014); *Introduction to the Counseling Profession* (1991, 1997, 2001, 2005, 2009, 2013); *Introduction to Group Work* (1992, 1998, 2002, 2006; with Mark Stauffer, 2010); and *Counseling and Psychotherapy: Theories and Interventions* (1995, 1999, 2003, 2007, 2011; coauthored and edited with Mark Stauffer, 2016). Other texts are *Approaches to Group Work: A Handbook for Practitioners* (2003), *Suicide Across the Life Span* (2006), and *Sexuality Issues in Counseling*, the last coauthored and edited with Larry Burlew. He has also coauthored and edited with Mark Stauffer *Career Counseling: Foundations, Perspectives, and Applications* (2008, 2012) and *Foundations of Addictions Counseling* (2008, 2012, 2016). He has authored or coauthored articles in a number of ACA-related journals.

A frequent speaker and keynoter at professional conferences and institutes, Dr. Capuzzi has also consulted with a variety of school districts and community agencies interested in initiating prevention and intervention strategies for adolescents at risk for suicide. He has facilitated the development of suicide prevention, crisis management, and postvention programs in communities throughout the United States; provides training on the topics of youth at risk and grief and loss; and serves as an invited adjunct faculty member at other universities as time permits.

An ACA fellow, he is the first recipient of ACA's Kitty Cole Human Rights Award and also a recipient of the Leona Tyler Award in Oregon. In 2010, he received ACA's Gilbert and Kathleen Wrenn Award for a Humanitarian and Caring Person. In 2011, he was named a Distinguished Alumni of the College of Education at Florida State University.

Mark D. Stauffer, PhD, NCC, is a counselor educator and member of the core faculty in mental health counseling at Walden University. He specialized in couples, marriage, and family counseling during his graduate work in the counselor education program at Portland State University, where he received his master's degree. He received his doctoral degree from Oregon State University, Department of Teacher and Counselor Education.

As a clinician, Dr. Stauffer has worked in the Portland Metro Area in Oregon at crisis centers and other nonprofit organizations with low-income individuals, couples, and families. He studied and trained in the Zen tradition and presents locally and nationally on meditation and mindfulness-based therapies in counseling. His research focus centers on Eastern methods and East–West collaboration.

Dr. Stauffer was a Chi Sigma Iota International fellow and was awarded the American Counseling Association's (ACA) Emerging Leaders Training Grant. He recently served as cochair of the American Counseling Association International Committee.

In addition to the present counseling textbook with Dr. Capuzzi, Dr. Stauffer has coedited several textbooks in the counseling field: *Introduction to Group Work* (2010); *Career Counseling: Foundations, Perspectives, and Applications* (2006, 2012); *Foundations of Addictions Counseling* (2008, 2012, 2016); and *Foundations of Couples, Marriage and Family Counseling* (2015). Drs. Stauffer and Capuzzi are currently working on *Counseling and Psychotherapy: Theories and Interventions* (6th ed., 2016) with the American Counseling Association.

About the Contributors

Eric D. Anderson, PhD, is an instructor with the College of Education and Human Services at Wright State University. Dr. Anderson earned his bachelor's in history and psychology from Capital University, his master's in rehabilitation counseling from The Ohio State University, and his doctorate from the University of Wisconsin–Madison in rehabilitation psychology.

Dr. Anderson's teaching specialty is rehabilitation services, and his research interests include rehabilitation counseling and neuropsychology.

Jeff Cook, PhD, is assistant professor in the graduate counseling program at University of Wisconsin–Whitewater. He received his doctorate in counselor education from Oregon State University.

Dr. Cook is a licensed professional counselor (Wisconsin and Oregon) and a national certified counselor with the National Board of Certified Counselors. His academic focus is in family systems, intercultural counseling, professional orientation, and supervision. Prior to full-time academic work, Dr. Cook worked in private practice with a focus on trauma, shame, and couples and also as a school counselor and career counselor.

Nazak Dadashazar, MA, LPC-S, NCC, received her master's in counseling psychology at the University of Mary Hardin-Baylor (Belton, Texas) and is currently pursuing her doctorate in counselor education and supervision from Walden University. Ms. Dadashazar currently works for the U.S. Department of Justice as a federal law enforcement officer and as a military and family life consultant with Mental Health Network, Government Services, an organization employed by the U.S. Office of the Secretary of Defense.

Her counseling experience includes working extensively with the veteran population, men and women of the active armed forces, adolescents, children, domestic violence victims, sex offenders, inmates, and culturally diverse populations in the areas of assessment, diagnosis, treatment planning, crisis management, and intervention. Through her work as a federal hostage negotiator and critical incident stress debriefer, Ms. Dadashazar's research interests include the psychology of criminal and serial offenders, trauma and posttraumatic stress disorder, and social justice issues.

Darcie Davis Gage, PhD is an associate professor at the University of Northern Iowa and teaches in the CACREP accredited clinical mental health and school counseling programs. She received her graduate education in counseling at Pittsburg State University and the University of Iowa. Dr. Davis-Gage's research interests are in the areas of group counseling, creativity and flow theory, and diversity issues related to counselor education and practice. Her current research agenda includes examining the how popular media can be used to train counselors.

Dr. Davis Gage brings 15 years of various counseling experiences to the classroom. She worked as a counselor in a variety of mental health agencies which included a partial hospitalization program, a women's mental health agency, a college counseling and advising center, and private practice. Dr. Davis Gage is an active member of the American Counseling Association, the Association of Counselor Education and Supervision, and the North Central Association for Counselor Education and Supervision.

Kerrie R. Fineran, PhD, is assistant professor in the counselor education program at Indiana University–Purdue University, Fort Wayne, and also serves as coordinator of school counseling for the program. She earned her BS from the College of William and Mary in Williamsburg, Virginia, where she was also an NCAA Division I student athlete (swimming). Dr. Fineran obtained her MEd in counseling from Shippensburg University in Pennsylvania and her PhD in counselor education and supervision from the University of Toledo in Ohio.

Dr. Fineran's passion is preparing master's-level students to be competent, compassionate scholar practitioners who endeavor to serve individuals, couples, families, and communities in a variety of capacities. Her research and writing interests include best practices in counselor preparation; suicide assessment, prevention, and postvention; and working with individuals with substance and behavioral addictions, including reducing the stigma associated with these types of disorders. She is a member of and serves on various committees for professional organizations, including the American Counseling Association, Association for Counselor Education and Supervision, International Association of Addictions and Offender Counselors, Association for Specialists in Group Work, Chi Sigma Iota International Counseling Honor Society, and numerous state and local organizations.

Brandé Flamez, PhD, NCC, LPC, is a licensed professional counselor and clinical professor in the counseling and special populations department at Lamar University. Dr. Flamez is also the CEO founder of the nonprofit SALT (Serving and Learning Together) World, Inc., which provides volunteer services to developing countries. Her clinical background includes working with children, adolescents, and families in community-based and private counseling settings both nationally and internationally. In addition, Dr. Flamez helped design an outpatient program for court-referred adolescents and specializes in diagnosing and assessment. Dr. Flamez is active in the counseling profession. Currently, she serves on the American Counseling Association (ACA) Governing Council for the International Association of Marriage and Family Counselors, ACA Finance Committee, and ACA Investment Committee and is chair of the ACA Publications Committee. She is also past-president of the Association for Humanistic Counseling.

Dr. Flamez is on the editorial board for the *Family Journal* and *Journal of College Counseling*. She has presented over 100 times nationally and internationally and has authored or coauthored more than 30 book chapters and articles. Dr. Flamez is coauthor of the assessment textbook *Counseling Assessment and Evaluation: Fundamentals of Applied Practice* (2015), *Diagnosing Children and Adolescents: Guide for Mental Health Practitioners* (2015), and the upcoming textbook *Introduction to Marriage, Couples, and Family Counseling: Applied Practice* (2017). She is the recipient of numerous national awards, including the 2015 Counselor Educator Advocacy Award, the 2014 ACA Kitty Cole Human Rights Award, the 2012 ACA Gilbert and Kathleen Wrenn Award for a Caring and Humanitarian Person, and the 2012 IAMFC Distinguished Mentor Award.

Amy E. Ford, PhD, is a clinical core faculty member at Oregon State University (OSU)–Cascades in Bend, Oregon. She received her MS (2001) and PhD (2005) in counseling from OSU, and she has worked full time as a counselor educator since 2004. She joined the OSU faculty full time in 2012. Dr. Ford holds national credentials as an approved clinical supervisor and nationally certified counselor. She is a licensed professional counselor in Oregon and a certified compensation and pension examiner with the U.S. Department of Veteran's Affairs.

Dr. Ford's professional interests are trauma, posttraumatic stress disorder, veterans, humanitarian work, best practices in counselor education, and parental alienation. She has volunteered with Medical Teams International (MTI) since 2005 and has been on international assignment with MTI to Banda Aceh, Indonesia, and Chisinau, Moldova. One of her current projects at OSU is developing a counseling practicum outreach that offers low-cost mental health services to the Central Oregon community.

Leif A. Ford, PhD, earned his doctorate in psychology from Walden University in 2015. His dissertation researched the effects of emotional intelligence within the American workplace. He has a diverse professional background, including 8 years working in an international corporation and more than 20 years of experience in education and pastoral/community care.

Dr. Ford specializes in providing interventions and care for individuals and organizations challenged by relationship dysfunction and individuals with cognitive development issues resulting from family or substance abuse. He is passionate about contributing to positive social change through holistic human development.

Juliana J. Forrest-Lytle, MS, received her bachelor's in psychology and a certificate in women's studies from the University of Central Florida and her master's in mental health counseling from Walden University. Ms. Forrest-Lytle is currently completing her doctorate at Walden University in counselor education and supervision specializing in counseling and social change. While working toward her PhD, Ms. Forrest-Lytle is a teaching assistant to faculty in Walden's clinical mental health counseling program and works as a counselor for children in foster care.

Ms. Forrest-Lytle has applied experience working with adults in individual and couples counseling and with adolescents and children. She has also designed and led psychosocial education groups for adolescents and taught anger management and stress management classes within her community.

Her research interests include burnout, self-care, work–life balance and stress management, multiculturalism in counseling, communication in marriage and other relationships, family dynamics, and parenting concerns.

Matt Glowiak, PhD, NCC, LPC, is assistant professor of the master's of clinical psychology program at Benedictine University and contributing faculty in the bachelor's of human services program at Walden University. Dr. Glowiak also cofounded Counseling Speaks, a practice in Chicago, Illinois, focused on clinical counseling, consultation, coaching, supervision, crisis intervention, and psychoeducational services and products. Dr. Glowiak completed his doctorate in counselor education and supervision at Walden University, where his dissertation focused on veteran educators' perceptions of the Internet's impact on K–8 learning and social development. He served as Chi Sigma Iota (CSI) president of the Omega Zeta Chapter and was selected by CSI International as a leadership fellow. Currently, he is serving the profession as president of the Chicago Counseling Association.

Dr. Glowiak is committed to counselor and client advocacy as evidenced through his leadership roles but also through community and clinical service. He counsels children, adolescents, and adults in a variety of settings. He has diverse contributions to the field through publication and continues to pursue his research interests in the areas of childhood development, technology use in counseling, and leadership.

Janet Froeschle Hicks, PhD, is associate professor of counseling and chair of the educational psychology and leadership department in the College of Education at Texas Tech University. She is both a licensed professional counselor and a certified school counselor in Texas.

Dr. Froeschle Hicks worked many years in the public school system as a teacher and school counselor as well as in the community before earning her doctorate in counseling and becoming a professor. She currently specializes in working with families, children, and adolescents.

Melinda Haley, PhD, received her master's in counselor education at Portland State University in Oregon and her doctorate in counseling psychology from New Mexico State University in Las Cruces. She was assistant professor at the University of Texas–El Paso in the counseling and guidance program for 5 years before transitioning to her current work as a core faculty member in the counselor education and supervision doctoral program at Walden University. She has written numerous book chapters and journal articles on diverse topics related to counseling.

Dr. Haley has extensive applied experience working with adults, adolescents, children, inmates, domestic violence offenders, and culturally diverse populations in the areas of assessment, diagnosis, treatment planning, crisis management, and intervention. Dr. Haley's research interests include multicultural issues in teaching and counseling, personality development over the life span, personality disorders, the psychology of criminal and serial offenders, trauma and posttraumatic stress disorder, bias and racism, and social justice issues.

Brooks Bastian Hanks, PhD, LCPC, is a core faculty member at Walden University in the clinical mental health counseling program. Dr. Bastian Hanks's scholarly interests include child sexual abuse, forensic interviewing, vicarious trauma, mental health accessibility, and professional development within the counseling and counselor education fields. She is a member of the American Counseling Association and the Association of Counselor Education and Supervision Council for the Acreditation of Counseling and Related Educational Programs and their Idaho branches. Dr. Bastian Hanks values the development of a strong professional identity and is an advocate for the counseling profession.

Clinically, since 2005 Dr. Bastian Hanks has been working with children who have been sexually abused and their families. She also works as a forensic interviewer and victim advocate. Dr. Bastian Hanks has worked in the field of substance abuse counseling with adolescent and adult clients and is a counseling supervisor for both master's-level and postmaster's-level counselors and enjoys being part of the growth process of her clients, supervisees, and students.

Nicole R. Hill, PhD, LPC, is professor and chair of the Department of Counseling and Human Services at Syracuse University. Dr. Hill's scholarly interests include working with children and adolescents, multicultural counseling competencies, professional development of faculty and graduate students, and mentoring. She currently serves as doctoral program co-coordinator and the Council for the Accreditation of Counseling and Related Educational Programs liaison. She is committed to leadership and professional engagement that strengthen counseling, counselor education, and supervision as a discipline. Her participation on the executive boards of Chi Sigma Iota, the Association for Counselor Education and Supervision, and Counselors for Social Justice has contributed to a broader understanding of how to advance the profession through service and advocacy.

Before joining the faculty at Syracuse University, Dr. Hill served as interim dean of the graduate school and chair of the Department of Counseling at Idaho State University. Her clinical experience is focused on counseling children and adolescents.

Brian Hutchison, PhD, LPC, NCC, is assistant professor, international studies fellow, and coordinator of the school counseling program at the University of Missouri–St. Louis. Dr. Hutchison received his doctorate in counselor education and supervision from Pennsylvania State University. He is the founding president of the Missouri Career Development Association, has served 3 years on the American Counseling Association of Missouri Executive Board, currently sits as co-chair of the Global Connection Committee for the National Career Development Association, and is an active member in several national counseling organizations. Currently, he serves on the editorial board of the *Journal of Counseling & Development*, *Journal of Humanistic Counseling*, and *Asian Pacific Education Review* and sits as an ad hoc reviewer for *Career Development Quarterly*.

Dr. Hutchison's scholarship can be broadly described as focused on career development and counseling within two primary counseling domains: school counseling and career counseling. This broad theme is infused into three primary scholarship areas: social class issues in counseling; international, multicultural, and social justice issues in counseling; and counselor education broadly defined. To this end, he has more than two dozen publications pertaining to social class bias in school counseling, career theory, career counseling, school counseling, academic advising, and specific counseling interventions. Recent publications include peer-reviewed articles in the *Journal of Counseling & Development, Journal of Humanistic Psychology, Equity & Excellence in Education*, and *Career Development Quarterly* and textbook chapters in seven books published by professional organization presses.

Kim Lee Hughes, PhD, LAPC, is assistant professor in the Department of Counseling at the University of Texas–San Antonio. She received her doctorate in counseling and student personnel services from the University of Georgia in 2015. She is coauthor of several book chapters on cross-cultural counseling.

Her clinical, research, and advocacy interests include queer college youth of color and empowerment, LGBTQQ youth in school settings, qualitative research, social justice, and multicultural training. Dr. Hughes was the 2014 chair of the Georgia Gay-Straight Alliance Summit and 2012 presidential fellow for the Association of Counselor Educators and Supervisors.

Andrew J. Intagliata, MA, is a doctoral student and graduate assistant in the counselor education program at the University of Toledo. He is the current president of the Alpha Omega chapter of Chi Sigma Iota. He earned both his MA and BA from the University of Toledo. Currently, he teaches undergraduate counseling courses at the University of Toledo as part of his graduate assistantship.

Mr. Intagliata is a PC/CR in Ohio. He has experience working in community mental health counseling and currently works with children and adolescents who have experienced abuse. His areas of clinical interest are domestic violence and child abuse.

Christie Jenkins, PhD, is a core faculty member at Walden University in the clinical mental health counseling program. Dr. Jenkins has been with Walden for more than 5 years teaching a variety of courses but finding her passion in the field experience classes. She has also been serving in the social service field for more than 19 years and as a counselor for more than 10 years. She began working in domestic violence safe houses as a child advocate, life skills trainer, crisis intervention specialist, and court advocate. She is independently licensed in two states and has a supervisory designation in the state of Ohio. She has been CEO, associate director, and supervisor for the Family and Child Abuse Prevention Center and the Children's Advocacy Center. She has over 10 years of experience working with a vast array of clientele in inner-city Toledo.

Dr. Jenkins has presented locally and at the state and national levels on various topics affecting counselors and their clients. She is also very active in professional organizations for counselors. Dr. Jenkins's primary research interests are in animal assisted therapy and domestic violence. She was just awarded the Ohio Counselor of the Year (2014) award by the Ohio Counseling Association. She was previously awarded the 2012 Clinical Supervisor of the Year and the 2012 Clinical Counselor of the Year from the Northwest Ohio Counseling Association. She is currently the president of the Ohio Association for Counselor Education and Supervision. She will be president of the Ohio Association for Spiritual, Ethical, and Religious Values in Counseling (OASERVIC) in 2015–2016.

Adrianne L. Johnson, PhD, is assistant professor in the clinical mental health counseling program at Wright State University. She earned her doctorate in counselor education from the University of Arkansas in 2007. Dr. Johnson's research interests and professional experience include clinical mental health counseling, addictions, crisis intervention, and diversity issues in counseling and counselor education.

She is active in various organizations committed to mental health advocacy and strongly promotes excellence in counselor education through teaching and supervision, scholarly publication, and international presentations.

Amber Lange, PhD, is a licensed professional counselor, a certified advanced alcohol and drug counselor, and national certified counselor. She has been providing counseling services since 2005. Before her counseling career she was the creator and director of a drop-in, part-time, child-care center. She has extensive training and experience in treating adults and youth. Her expertise includes trauma, grief, and loss; chemical dependency; infidelity; and work–life balance. Her experience includes both community counseling and private practice work.

Dr. Lange is an active participant within her counseling association and is an advocate for the counseling profession. Additionally, she has been teaching in higher education since 2004 and currently teaches master's-level students the skills necessary for becoming a professional counselor. Dr. Lange is a known speaker. She speaks on topics such as relationships, divorce, alcoholism, domestic violence, and addiction. She has researched, published about, and utilized a therapy dog in counseling. She also is working with several school counselors on utilizing dogs in schools.

John M. Laux, PhD, is a professor of counselor education and the current chair of the Department of School Psychology, Higher Education, & Counselor Education at the University of Toledo. He earned his PhD from the University of Akron, MA from West Virginia University, and BA from Ambassador University. He teaches courses in research, internship, psychopathology, and personality assessment.

Dr. Laux is a PCC-S in Ohio, a licensed independent chemical dependency counselor in Ohio, and a psychologist. His areas of clinical interest include substance use disorders and personality disorders. He has clinical experience in a variety of treatment settings including the Cincinnati VAMC, community mental health, a university counseling center, an inpatient chemical dependence treatment center, and private practice. His wife, Audrey, and two sons are the source of his support.

Elsa Soto Leggett, PhD, is associate professor with the University of Houston–Victoria (UHV) in Sugar Land, Texas. She is also program coordinator of the counselor educator program. She is a licensed professional counselor, board approved supervisor, and registered play therapist–supervisor as well as a certified school counselor. Her clinical experience, research, and advocacy have concentrated on mental health work with children and adolescents. Her work focuses on counseling with children and adolescents, school counseling, solution focused counseling, creative integration, and play therapy with a strong interest in services provided in school settings.

Dr. Leggett was a founding board member of the newest American Counseling Association division, the Association of Child and Adolescent Counseling (ACAC). She was the president of ACAC from 2013 to 2015. She has also served as president of the Texas Association of Counselor Education and Supervision in 2012–2013 and UHV Faculty Senate in 2014–2015. She has provided numerous publications and presentations at international, national, state, and local levels.

Katheryne T. Leigh, MEd, is a currently a second-year doctoral student at the University of Missouri–St. Louis in the counselor education and supervision program. She graduated from the University at Buffalo in 2012 with an MEd in school counseling and holds provisional school counseling certification in New York and Missouri. Ms. Leigh has experience working with several diverse populations of students and educational settings. These experiences include work with students living with developmental disorders, emotional disorders, and issues stemming from poverty and oppression. Having the opportunities to be immersed within different populations and ages encouraged Ms. Leigh to expand her education to include critical theory and critical consciousness within diverse experiences and contribute to the field of counselor education.

While at the University of Missouri–St. Louis, Ms. Leigh has taken steps toward her goals of becoming a counselor educator specializing in school counseling and critical counselor education pedagogy including social justice and advocacy work within the community and in the schools. Some of her research interests include cultural competency, critical school counseling pedagogy, social justice work, and advocacy within the school counseling profession. Additional interests include relational-cultural and critical race theories in counseling research. Upon graduation from the PhD program, Ms. Leigh plans on working in academia as a counselor educator further contributing to the profession through critical scholarship and advocacy for school counselors and students alike.

Mark Aaron Mayfield, MA, NCC, LPC, is assistant professor of counseling at Colorado Christian University. Mr. Mayfield is currently in the dissertation stage of his doctorate, pursuing a PhD in counselor education and supervision at Walden University. His clinical, research, and advocacy interests include exploring experiential therapeutic alternatives for active duty military and veteran survivors of posttraumatic stress disorder (specifically equine-facilitated and -assisted psychotherapy), bullying prevention, professional identity development through the enhancement of quality supervision, and the advocacy for marginalized populations.

Mr. Mayfield is an active member of the American Counseling Association (AHC, IMFCA, ACES, and several other divisions of ACA) and serves on the Association for Humanistic Counseling's Empty Plate Project Committee. He is also an active member of the Chi Sigma Omega Zeta Chapter and the Golden Key Honor's Society. Mr. Mayfield's early counseling work focused on in-home family therapy, court-ordered drug rehabilitation therapy, family therapy, adolescent substance abuse treatment, group therapy, and equine-facilitated psychotherapy. Mr. Mayfield currently lives in Colorado, where he also maintains a supervision practice and an equine-facilitated psychotherapy practice.

Taryne M. Mingo, PhD, is assistant professor at Missouri State University and has a career background as an elementary professional school counselor for rural student populations in Georgia. Her research interests include advocating for marginalized student populations across P–16 settings; using intersectionality theory to support marginalized student populations, womanist theory, and supervision; and incorporating a social justice lens within school counseling programs.

Dr. Mingo has served as a member on the Georgia School Counselor Association leadership team and was invited to participate in White House convening for school counselors as part of the Reach Higher Initiative, which encouraged an increase in postsecondary education for all high school graduates across the nation. Dr. Mingo identifies as a social justice change agent who seeks to find new and innovative methods toward accessing education, to support student learning, and to promote every student reaching his or her highest potential.

Tammie O'Neil, MS, is a member of the American Counseling Association. She is currently working as a licensed mental health counselor in private practice at Karner Psychological Associates. She has previously worked with at-risk youth and families with two agencies. She was able to assist families in attaining appropriate mental health care as well as community services to mitigate their psychosocial difficulties.

Ms. O'Neil is currently working on her PhD in counselor education and supervision at Walden University. She will use this degree to assist student counselors in developing the skill sets necessary to facilitate changes associated with individual, family, and couples counseling.

Ann Ordway, JD, EdS, is distance clinical professor in the counseling and special populations department at Lamar University in Beaumont, Texas. She holds her Juris Doctor from Seton Hall University and has been a licensed attorney in New Jersey for nearly 25 years, where she has practiced exclusively in the field of family law. Ms. Ordway currently practices parenting coordination, provides supervision for parenting time, and serves as a child advocate.

Ms. Ordway is a doctoral student at Walden University, where she is completing her dissertation toward a PhD in counselor education and supervision. She is a frequent regional and national presenter, and she has authored and coauthored several articles related to high-conflict divorce, parental alienation, and parenting coordination. Ms. Ordway's areas of interest include the preparation of counselors for court testimony and court-involved roles, multicultural competence, and various aspects of human development.

Dilani M. Perera-Diltz, PhD, is associate professor of counseling at Lamar University in Beaumont, Texas. She is a licensed professional clinical counselor, professional school counselor, and a licensed independent chemical dependency counselor in Ohio. She has worked in a variety of clinical settings including a prison, a hospital, and private practice.

Her research interests include assessment, social justice, and counselor education. She is coeditor of *The Counselor Educator's Survival Guide: Designing and Teaching Outstanding Courses in Clinical Mental Health Counseling and School Counseling* (2011), a reference for all counselor educators to find resources for teaching courses in counselor education. She has more than 20 peer-reviewed articles and book chapters. Outside of work, she enjoys listening to her 11-year-old's stories on life and spending time with her pets.

Torey Portrie-Bethke, PhD, NCC, is a core faculty member for the master's program in clinical mental health counseling at Walden University. Dr. Portrie-Bethke holds a PhD in counselor education and counseling; MCoun in couples, marriage, and family counseling; and a BS in communication disorders and hearing sciences. Dr. Portrie-Bethke specializes in providing counseling services for children, adolescents, and families using experiential counseling methods such as adventure-based counseling, play therapy, and sandplay. Her scholarly interests include counseling supervision, adventure-based counseling, online counselor education, childhood sexual abuse, vicarious trauma, and experiential teaching methods.

Dr. Portrie-Bethke is dedicated and enthusiastic in her role as a counselor educator and as a mental health and family counselor working toward empowering students and clients in the direction of positive growth and development. She provides clinical supervision for master's practicum and internship students. In her strength-based supervision role, she works to enhance students' self-efficacy through creating a bridge between counselor development and emerging counseling skills, techniques, and theory. She promotes students' professional identity and advocates for the profession by utilizing networking techniques such as student inclusion in presentations and professional publications. Dr. Portrie-Bethke is a frequent presenter in the areas of adventure-based counseling, abuse/trauma, play therapy, counseling supervision, and group counseling.

Gail K. Roaten, PhD, is associate professor in the Clinical Counseling and Marriage and Family Therapy Program at Hardin-Simmons University. She also chairs that graduate program and serves as the clinic director. Gail has been a counselor educator for 11 years, serving previously at Texas State University as the school counseling coordinator. Over many semesters, Dr. Roaten has taught the life span development class and focused on development as it relates to counseling in numerous other classes. One of her focused areas of research and publication is counseling children and adolescents.

Dr. Roaten is an active member of numerous professional organizations. She has been a part of a group of counselor educators and clinicians in the recent formation of the Association for Child and Adolescent Counseling; she will serve as president of that organization for the next 2 years. She is actively involved in the American Counseling Association, the Association for Counselor Education and Supervision, the Texas Counseling Association, and the Texas Association of Counselor Educators and Supervisors.

Tiffany Rush-Wilson, PhD, is the skill development coordinator for the counseling unit at Walden University with a focus on both the online classrooms and in-person residencies. She has taught a variety of courses in the clinical mental health counseling and psychology programs.

Professionally, Dr. Rush-Wilson is independently and dually licensed and certified as a counselor in the United States and Canada. She is interested in the impact of language and communication on mental health and body image and has worked in community mental health, children's services, and extensively in private practice. She is a member of both the American and Canadian Counseling Associations and the Academy for Eating Disorders and has participated in community outreach and presented on women's issues, scope of practice, and eating disorders at local, national, and international venues.

Kelli A. Saginak, PhD, serves as professor and the school counseling program coordinator in the Department of Professional Counseling at the University of Wisconsin–Oshkosh. She has worked in the field of education as a teacher, counselor, prevention specialist, and consultant for more than 20 years. In her university role, she strives to educate and train counselors to serve the needs of today's youth as advocates, leaders, and experts in child and adolescent development.

Dr. Saginak's passion for youth inspires her writing, scholarship, and teaching in the areas of school counseling, counseling process, counseling with children and adolescents, life span development, and addictions counseling. She presents on a variety of counseling-related topics and enjoys collaborating with students, colleagues, community partners, and school districts. She has served on her community's board of education and continues to support the district's focus on student development. Dr. Saginak's recent endeavors have inspired her to travel abroad with graduate students to Malaysia, where the group serves refugee children and adolescents and provides education and training to counselors, social workers, and human services professionals in Kuala Lumpur.

Stephanie K. Scott, PhD, is a core faculty in the clinical mental health counseling program at Walden University. She has her doctorate in human services, with a specialization in marriage and family therapy, which she earned at Capella University. Dr. Scott is a licensed mental health counselor in Florida, and her clinical work includes individuals, couples, and families. Much of her clinical work focuses on adolescents and young adults, with special attention to trauma, identity, and developmental considerations.

Dr. Scott's areas of research include affective training both in counselors and in clients, cultural diversity and conceptualization, systemic family issues, and standards of practice. She is also founder of a local teen advocacy organization that supports adolescent health and wellness. Dr. Scott has worked extensively in inpatient and outpatient settings and currently maintains a small private practice in Florida.

Anneliese A. Singh, PhD, LPC, is associate professor in the Department of Counseling and Human Development Services at the University of Georgia. Her clinical, research, and advocacy interests include investigating the resilience and coping of transgender survivors of trauma, LGBTQQ bullying and violence prevention, and South Asian American survivors of child sexual abuse. Dr. Singh has particular expertise in qualitative methodology with historically marginalized groups and is the author of *Qualitative Inquiry in Counseling and Education* (2012).

Dr. Singh is past president of the Association of Lesbian, Gay, Bisexual, and Transgender Issues in Counseling, a division of the American Counseling Association, where her presidential initiatives included the development of counseling competencies for working with transgender clients, supporting queer people of color, and ensuring safe schools for LGBTQQ youth. She has received numerous awards for her scholarship and community activism on violence prevention and intervention, including American Counseling Association awards (O'Hana Social Justice and Kitty Cole Human Rights) and the Ramesh and Vijaya Bakshi Community Change Award. Dr. Singh is a founder of the Georgia Safe Schools Coalition, an organization that works at the intersection of heterosexism, racism, sexism, and other oppressions to create safe school environments in Georgia; and of the Trans Resilience Project, which works on increasing knowledge and awareness of transgender resilience.

Robyn Trippany-Simmons, EdD, received her doctorate in counselor education from the University of Alabama. She serves as residency coordinator and core faculty in the master's in counseling programs at Walden University. Dr. Trippany-Simmon's research and clinical interests include sexual trauma, vicarious trauma, play therapy, spirituality in counseling, and professional identity issues. She serves on the editorial review board for the *Journal of Mental Health Counseling, Association for Play Therapy Magazine*, and *Tennessee Counseling Association Journal*.

Dr. Trippany-Simmons is a licensed professional counselor in Alabama and a registered play therapist. She also maintains a small counseling practice, where she works with individuals and couples in a faith-based counseling setting. She lives in north Alabama with her family.

Javier Cavazos Vela, PhD, is assistant professor of counseling and guidance at University of Texas Rio Grande Valley. He obtained a doctorate in counselor education from Texas A&M University–Corpus Christi. His research interests include Latina/o students' educational and mental health experiences.

He has published 34 peer-reviewed articles and book chapters on topics ranging from higher education to counselor education and supervision. His work has appeared in journals such as *Professional School Counseling, Counselor Education and Supervision, Journal of School Counseling*, and *Journal of Hispanic Higher Education*.

When he is not writing, he enjoys spending time with family, running, and watching sports.

Ann Vernon, PhD, is professor emerita at the University of Northern Iowa, where she was coordinator of the school and mental health programs for many years. In addition, she had a large private practice, specializing in applications of rational-emotive and cognitive behavior therapy with children and adolescents as well as adults. Presently, she works pro bono at a low-income clinic in Tucson, primarily treating anxiety and depression.

Dr. Vernon has written more than 20 books and many chapters and articles on a variety of topics related primarily to counseling children and adolescents. She is recognized as leading expert in applications of rational emotive and cognitive behavioral therapy with young clients and has presented trainings and workshops throughout the United States and Canada as well as in Romania, South America, Singapore, Australia, Mexico, and Europe. She is visiting professor in counseling at the University of Oradea in Romania, where she teaches courses on counseling children and adolescents. Dr. Vernon is president of the Albert Ellis Institute and a member of the International Standards Training and Review Committee, which sets policies for rational emotive and cognitive behavioral therapy training programs throughout the world.

Holly H. Wagner, PhD, is assistant professor at the University of Missouri–St. Louis. She graduated from Idaho State University in May 2014 with a PhD in counselor education and counseling. Dr. Wagner's specialty area is school counseling, with areas of concentration including career development, human growth and development, helping relationships, and professional orientation and ethics. She is a certified school counselor in Montana, a nationally certified counselor, a licensed professional counselor in Missouri and Idaho, and a certified family life educator. Dr. Wagner has previous work experience as a professional school counselor in a K–8 school setting from 2006 to 2009 and as the school counseling program leader at Montana State University from 2009 to 2011. Her teaching and counseling experience over the years has enhanced her ability to work with individuals at a variety of developmental levels. Whether teaching at the kindergarten level as a school counselor or the master's level as a counselor educator, she discovered her true passion for education and the process of learning along a broad continuum of development and life stages.

At University of Missouri–St. Louis, Dr. Wagner is continuing to enhance her teaching, research, and supervisory skills. Her research interests include school counseling, counselor development, feminist pedagogy, cultural competence, LGBTQQIA competence and advocacy, and social justice issues in counselor education. She looks forward to continued research and scholarship that impact clinical, programmatic, pedagological, and supervisory domains within the field of counseling and counselor education.

Kathy Ybañez-Llorente, PhD, LPC-S, is associate professor of counseling at Texas State University. She holds a doctorate in counselor education and is licensed as a professional counselor and board approved supervisor in her state. Dr. Ybañez-Llorente teaches foundational and clinical counseling courses to graduate students across all degree tracks and also serves as the professional counseling program's practicum and internship clinical coordinator.

Professionally, Dr. Ybañez-Llorente has provided counseling services to children, adolescents, and families in a variety of settings, from private practice, community counseling agencies, and foster care and state contract settings to inpatient psychiatric settings. She has also worked with elementary-age students, where she provided year-long anxiety reduction classroom guidance interventions.

Preface

The profession of counseling can be described as one in which counselors and counselor researchers assist individuals, families, and communities with positive change and best care in meeting developmental needs and goals. Counselors in school, mental health, rehabilitation, hospital, private practice, and a variety of other settings must be thoroughly prepared to support clients in their capacities to develop as healthy, productive, happy individuals. Professional organizations, accrediting bodies, licensure boards, and graduate preparation programs and departments are charged with making sure that counselors are able to serve the public through best-care practices and to avoid harming clients. Counselor education and supervision standards require a background in human development theories and key research findings and an ability to describe and explain human phenomena that are universal, cultural, and individual in nature. As professionals, counselors must also be able to apply the knowledge base of key areas of study, offering a holistic approach with their clients as they search for growth and maturity and face the unexpected transitions in life.

Counselors can expect clients to want to address issues connected to the transition from one developmental stage to the next. This book is written for use in graduate-level counseling programs, but it can also be used in undergraduate and community college programs because of the case studies, suggestions for counseling practice, and the clear writing style. The Council for the Accreditation of Counseling and Related Educational Programs (CACREP) and other certification association requirements demand that most university programs in counselor education offer a course in human development for all students regardless of specialization (e.g., school, clinical mental health, rehabilitation, couples, marriage and family, student personnel). This book is therefore written and geared toward the mental health worker. Throughout this text, readers will find that core material is covered, but, in keeping with the aim of supporting counselors in training, human development is addressed in relation to counselor job requirements.

Although the text addresses history, theory, and research related to human development, emphasis is also given to practitioner techniques and skills. Each chapter infuses material on how issues of human development impact clients' lives and the realm of counseling. Writers, experienced in counseling with a holistic approach to human development, were asked to contribute to the text so that readers will not only understand the foundations of human development study but also apply these foundations to their roles as practicing, licensed, and certified counselors. Each chapter covers application points and also contains a Key Pointers section to provide additional insights.

The book is unique in both content and format. Contributing authors—experts nationally recognized for their expertise, research, and publications—provide state-of-the-art information. Readers are thus provided with content in areas not always addressed in introductory human development texts. Examples of this include Chapter 19, which covers grief and loss as it relates to human development, and Chapter 3, which is focused on spiritual and moral development. Because counselors are called to be competent in cross-cultural issues and advocacy, Chapter 4 goes beyond discussing broad cultural issues and delves into the importance of cross-cultural competency in working with clients.

The book is designed for students who are taking a preliminary course in human development from a life span perspective. We know that one text cannot adequately address all the factors that comprise the complex and holistic aspects of assisting clients who present with issues related to specific developmental stages. We have, however, attempted to provide our readers with a broad perspective based on current professional literature and the rapidly changing world in which we live at this juncture of the new millennium. The following overview highlights the major features of the text.

OVERVIEW

As previously noted, the format for the co-edited textbook is based on the contributions of authors who are recognized for their expertise, research, and publications. With few exceptions, each chapter contains case studies that illustrate the practical applications of the concepts presented. Most chapters refer the reader to websites for additional, supplemental information. Professors may want to use the PowerPoint presentations that go along with each chapter. There is also a test manual, which can be used to develop quizzes and exams on the book's content.

The book is divided into key developmental stages by age range. Part 1, Essential Concepts (Chapters 1–4), is an introduction and discusses the qualities, processes, and influences on human development. Key pointers for studying human development are provided. Chapters 2 and 3 cover key theories for understanding development from biopsychosocial standpoints and also from theorists covering moral and spiritual development. Because counseling is focused on working with diverse clients and because counselors need to understand how sociocultural influences affect human development, Chapter 4 is devoted to unpacking this for the reader.

Parts 2–8 contain two chapters each: one on physical and cognitive aspects of development and one on social and emotional aspects. The stages covered in these sections are birth and infancy, early childhood, middle childhood, adolescence, young adulthood, middle adulthood, and late adulthood. The aim of each section is to provide a holistic perspective by adding to concepts developed in Part 1.

Part 9, which contains the final chapter of the book, deals with end of life and related issues such as bereavement. Because human development is multidirectional and includes gain and loss, a discussion of how counselors can best work with clients in this final stage of development thus provides good closure to the book.

Every attempt has been made to provide current information in each area of focus. It is our hope that this first edition of *Human Development Across the Life Span: Applications for Counselors* will provide the beginning student counselor with the basics needed for follow-up courses and supervised practice in the arena of counseling clients across the life span.

HUMAN GROWTH AND DEVELOPMENT ACROSS THE LIFESPAN

PART 1

Essential Concepts

Human Development: Counseling the Ever-Changing Person in Context

Mark D. Stauffer and David Capuzzi

In reflecting on one's own life, readers may recognize many examples of physical, psychological, social, and cognitive development that are shared by nearly all. The facts of birth and death and constant change are central to the processes of human development. Without constant change, how could one develop? To develop, something must leave a current form and transition to a new one, even if the change is imperceptibly small. Ask yourself, how different from my present form was I at the time of my first explicit memory? Explicit memories are long-term recallable images and words from earlier periods in life. How have your physical body, mental capabilities, or identity changed since that time?

Both context and time are important to developmental change. If one examined deeply to find a way in which a person has developed without dependence on anything else, there would be no evidence. From a simplistic view we are reliant on air, water, and the many influencing physical systems of life. But if we are not isolated, meaning we are not in some type of developmental vacuum, then an individual is who he is because of the context he is embedded in. Because the world is different as a totality at each moment, each of us is also unique at each given time because of this embedded quality. For example, what changes do you notice in yourself and your context from 1 hour ago, 1 day ago, 1 month ago, 1 year ago? The greater gap between two comparative times makes it easier to recognize the differences accumulated by change, the differences that have cascaded from one time of life to another.

Each time period of a person's life is unique, and, at the same time, one can notice commonalities shared with other time periods. As this chapter will also explore, some changes are unique and personal, whereas others are shared as a result of sociocultural, historical, hereditary, and environmental influences. There are also certain qualities or characteristics about development itself as a change process. This chapter will explore how development is continuous, discontinuous, multidimensional, multidirectional, and plastic. In addition to examining growth, maturation, and learning as critical developmental processes, this chapter will examine key points for how counselors can approach human development across the lifespan.

ORIENTATION TOWARD THE STUDY OF HUMAN DEVELOPMENT FOR COUNSELORS

As a convenient definition, human development is the physical, cognitive, emotional, and social changes that occur in a person's life. Readers should note three important ways that human development occurs. First, what aspects of development are universal in nature? Another way to word this question is what aspects of human development can be generalized across humanity with some level of accuracy and consistency? Counselors must understand universal aspects of development. Because of the high similarity of genetic makeup between humans and other species, some of those universal aspects can be understood as part of the web of life.

Second, at a more differentiated level than the universal level, counselors must examine what elements vary by culture, race, and ethnicity. Do people in Papua New Guinea vary from one another because of difference in ethnicity (i.e., there are many variations in culture in Papua New Guinea)? How might they vary from those in Chile across the Pacific Ocean? Because humans are highly social and place a lot of awareness and attention on social cues and conditions, the assumption might be that there is a great difference between cultures. However this may seem, modern research efforts, such as the Human Genome Project from 1990 to 2003, have suggested that cultural differences, though important in making us unique, represent fractional differences between groups (Chial, 2008). "Chimpanzees and humans share 99.0% of the same genes, and humans share 99.9% of the same genes with each other" (Berninger, 2015, p. 173).

Genetic variation demonstrates fractional differences between different world ethnic groups. "Modern humans (*Homo sapiens*) are a recently appearing and homogenous species regardless of ancestral geographic origins. Admixture, even among and between highly isolated populations, has resulted in widespread, worldwide distribution of genes and thus human variation" (American Anthropological Society, 1997, p. 1). There are just as great, if not greater, differences within as between groups; for example, there is greater genetic variation found within all women than between men and women. Furthermore, "the proportion of human genetic variation due to differences between populations is modest, and individuals from different populations can be genetically more similar than individuals from the same population" (Witherspoon et al., 2007, p. 352).

Third, counselors must understand development that is unique and personal to the individual. As this chapter will examine, development of the individual is marked by nonnormative influences. The way that each person traverses through life creates a unique footprint. The following box better illustrates the connection between what is person specific, what is cultural, and what is universal.

BOX 1.1   THE HAND AS AN ILLUSTRATION OF DEVELOPMENT

The hand provides an illustration of the different levels of development. The hand is universal. Universal does not mean that all people have hands, however; it is our genetic inheritance. Looking at various hands, one can see different sizes as a result of genetic variation and stages of growth (e.g., the size of an infant's hands compared with an adult's) and different skin pigmentations reflecting diversity of genetics. Some hands will reveal sociocultural variation because of wedding bands, decorative nails, or jewelry, suggesting some type of status. The hand has nonnormative features, such as scars, which signify the wear and tear from hard work. Fingers and fingertips are universally part of the hand, but each fingerprint is unique to the person. Finally, you get to determine what to do with those hands.

At its most basic level, the study of human development across the lifespan must first help the practitioner more accurately describe human development. In addition to being able to take inventory and name phenomena through description, it is important for a counselor to consider the context of human development. Part of being able to explain human development, or why X phenomena happen, is to explain human development from a systemic perspective. Counselors need to be able to move beyond Cartesian or linear understandings of development to systemic understanding of human development. As the field gains greater understanding of human development in general, and as the counselor works with a client and gains an understanding of the client as embedded in a context, the clinician can help modify development trajectories and improve subjective and objective outcomes through various modalities of learning. Counselors can also help clients adapt and transition through the ever-changing landscape of life. For example, a client at any age will process grief and loss due to the death of a close person, but the counselor will understand how development has impacted cognitive and behavioral understandings and responses to grief and loss. Finally, as a profession, our study of human development includes research to help better predict human development.

CONCEPTUALIZING HUMAN DEVELOPMENT

This chapter covers some of the fundamental concepts about human development and describes key themes about the nature of human development. Many of the concepts for deliberation show up in how clients come to examine their own problems and life experiences. Some of the concepts will promote the integration of theoretical concepts discussed later in the text.

Continuity Versus Discontinuity

The continuity or discontinuity of development has been a longstanding field debate. Continuity refers to successive lifespan development, where development in childhood and adolescence are formative and relate to outcomes in later life (Schulenberg & Zarrett, 2006, p. 150). Consider how the forming of bones, healthy parental attachment, or progression from gross to fine motor skills early in life emergee in a relatively predictable trajectory toward long-term skeletal strength, a host of biopsychosocial benefits from stable attachments, and better coordination in adulthood. Theorists who focus on continuity in child development point to research focused on the impact of early environmental enrichment with later life outcomes.

Discontinuity refers to significant shifts in development. Early developmental scientists suggested that development was discontinuous because sudden shifts in development would vault an individual out of a period of relative stability, such as at puberty. From this perspective, some shifts might come in noticeable stages that one may or may not mature through—for example, the stages related to the developmental theories of such theorists as Erikson, Piaget, and Kohlberg (covered in chapters 2 and 3 and infused throughout this book).

That continuity versus discontinuity is placed in dynamic tension using the word *versus* may be misleading since these two do not need to be exclusive. Others have used continuity *and* discontinuity, rather than *versus*, to suggest that the two seemingly antithetical qualities can be observed and even play off each other. The subtle changes and the sudden changes are complementary.

Multidirectional

Discontinuity also is noticed when early developmental trends are reversed or disrupted or do not follow the previously causal developmental course. The ability for development to increase and decrease at different stages points to the multidirectional quality of development. For example, a major transformation of a person's life at a key life stage might redirect preceding course of development. When considering the lifespan, what comes to mind as evidence for discontinuous development?

Critical Periods

With an examination of early childhood development in such areas as language acquisition, attachment, and brain development, researchers examined *critical periods*, of which there are various definitions. "One definition is the period in which a subject is particularly susceptible to damage (i.e., 'period of suscepti-bility'). Another definition of critical period is the restricted period in which recovery or a flexible response occurs (i.e., a 'period of plasticity' or 'sensitive period')" (Uylings, 2006, p. 69). Harsh environments, for example, might deny important touch and warmth necessary for long-term social attachment. In addition, critical periods provide an opportunity to maximize development. For example, a pregnant woman would want to refrain from harmful influences such as drugs, alcohol, and tobacco and would want to enhance prenatal care by exercising, getting enough sleep, having regular medical visits, and taking prenatal supplements.

Counselors also consider interventions that are developmentally possible and appropriate for clients. For example, an adept counselor would not try to discuss psychological concepts with a 5-year-old because they require abstract thinking skills that will not be available until a later stage due to brain development. A coun-selor working with the late adult population would understand and normalize that, in general, older adult goal setting is geared toward loss prevention, unlike with younger adults, who are oriented toward growth (Ebner, Freund, & Baltes, 2006). Interestingly enough, Ebner and colleagues found that "orientation toward pre-vention of loss correlated negatively with well-being in younger adults" (p. 666). Interventions should be culturally appropriate to the stage.

Nature Versus Nurture

Another dynamic theme in developmental science is nature versus nurture, also expressed as genetics versus environment. It can be challenging to deter-mine what is genetic and what is environmental since children receive 50% of their genes from parents but also are *embedded* in the environment strongly mediated by the family. The word embedded is often used because it more adequately describes the interdependence of a person with the environ-ment. This is similar to Heidegger's (1962) descriptions of people as being in the world, a mutuality where the individual being is continually making, changing, and influencing the world and conversely the environment is mak-ing, changing, and influencing the individual. The environmental–genetic interaction is hard to pull apart because the two things are not separate. For example, in addictions treatment, primary and secondary are tightly con-nected. As another example, connection between parent behavior and child behav-ior (i.e., anxious parent and anxious child) may just as readily reflect a "genetic transmission as well as or instead of an environmental affect" (McAdams et al., 2014, p. 1139).

Counselors should cautiously examine assumptions when making causal attri-butions for a client issue on either the nature or nurture side. Are Martha's eat-ing disorder and her academic giftedness due to heredity or the environment? How much is Harry's heart attack due to "bad" genes or "bad" health behaviors? Counselors examine the evidence-based material and realize that problems have biopsychosocial origins and solutions. Whole sections on fitness, psychology, and nutrition attest to the consumer's intrinsic motivation to develop in some way. Consider that many people never learn to read, swim, play the piano, sing in tune, cook, and accurately draw without books or instruction on reading, swimming, music, voice, cooking, and drawing. Our heredity comes with capacities for wonderful skills, but they must be nurtured by the environment.

Multidimensional and Systemic

Human development is multidimensional and systemically oriented. Depending on how one conceptualizes the nature of humanity, there are many dimensions to human development. A teacher once suggested that there are many ways to slice a tomato, equating this to the idea that there are innumerous ways to examine a person's life or the nature of reality (Carlson, personal communication). For example, this book is organized around four dimensions: physical, emotional, social, and emotional. One could also examine the biopsychosocial label, which suggests that human development is a combination of biological, psychological, and social elements. Within specific dimensions, there are yet other developmental dimensions. These dimensions appear different at distinct periods of life from infancy to late adulthood.

For counselors, it is most helpful to view the developing self and lived experience from a systemic perspective. Development is influenced by circular causality. Beyond linear cause and effect notions, circular causality suggests that development happens in a contextual and cyclical manner. Most often, counselors consider that A (e.g., pregnant teen abuses alcohol) causes B (e.g., fetal alcohol syndrome), or that A can cause B, which will keep having repetitive effects over time, or that A causes B, which causes then causes C (e.g., child is socially bullied for strange facial features and outbursts of anger), which then causes D (e.g., poor self-esteem when she grows up as a pregnant teen) in a chain of cause and effect. Additionally, clients grasp that A causes more of B and then B causes more of A (the child with fetal alcohol syndrome might continue the pattern of alcohol abuse in adolescence). A *positive feedback loop* is where the pattern promotes the pattern at greater intensity levels. *Negative feedback* is the process by which the system does not circularly reinforce some particular phenomenon.

Adept counselors go beyond linear models of causality and see the reciprocal and multidimensional interactions of development. Counselors can inadvertently overfocus on certain dimensions to the detriment of the systemic view. This can happen with a patterned approach or narrow lens toward the issue. To further explain this point, the examination of the definition of mindlessness is useful. Mindlessness is an attention to a subset of contextual cues that "trigger various scripts, labels and expectations, which in turn focus attention on certain information while diverting attention away from other information" (Nass & Moon, 2000, p. 83). Such overfocus does not mean lack of awareness; it means the focus is limited.

Not only is development multidimensional, but also these dimensions are interrelated. Like a ball of knotted yarn, how can one pull a string from one side without untying another part? One aspect of development influences other aspects of development, so in classic coming-of-age stories one sees the physical transitions of the person arising with or causing emotional, cognitive, and social blossoming; noted by self-consciousness and interpersonal insecurity the desire to move toward independence from family, and beginnings of existential contemplations and angst.

Development is systemically interrelated across dimensions and is also related to other processes of development. An individual's development over time is interrelated to the development of families, groups, or species (Badcock, 2012). Development also relates to previous development, suggesting that the interrelationship spans time. Development in one area might speed or slow the development in other areas, suggesting that timing and severity are connected in development. Where do you notice or not notice this?

The process of mutual selection reinforces the person and environment interdependence. The process of selection is subject to reinforcing feedback loops; Schulenberg and Zarrett (2006) suggested that "through a process of niche selection, individuals select available environments and activities on the basis of personal characteristics, beliefs, interests, and competencies; selected ecological niches then provide further opportunity for socialization and further selection" (p. 140).

Plasticity

Plasticity is the ability of an organism, in this case the developing human or some part of an organism (e.g., brain), to change in response to positive and negative environmental experiences. Environments influence the biopsychosocial dimensions of self, and people influence their environment. Plasticity occurs across multiple dimensions of development and throughout the lifespan (e.g., personality; Mroczek, 2014). As an example, neural plasticity is the "ability of the central nervous system to change in response to experience" (Vida, Vingilis-Jaremko, Butler, Gibson, & Monteiro, 2012, p. 357). Despite older notions of a peak to decline brain development scenario, researchers began to discover that the physical regions of the brain exhibited lifelong plasticity (e.g., brain synaptic organization; Kolb & Teskey, 2012). Counselors can help clients learn to take advantage of the person–environment relationship. Neuroscientific research has shown structural brain changes as a result of behavior modification; for example, Kang and colleagues (2013) found that "meditators, compared with controls, showed significantly greater cortical thickness in the anterior regions of the brain, located in frontal and temporal areas, including the medial prefrontal cortex, superior frontal cortex, temporal pole and the middle and interior temporal cortices" (p. 27). Plasticity is also demonstrated through the process of compensation.

BOX 1.2 COMPENSATION

Early notions of development held that development was a straight trajectory to a peak point, at which a developmental skill or quality was at its optimal state and thereafter would decline over time. Though compensation has been viewed and studied by various scientific disciplines, generally it is the ability to use a resource to diminish the impact of a decline in an area of performance. For example, one error in seeing this as a linear peak to valley experience is that it misses the dynamic quality of humans. Compensation may help a person who has functional impairment by employing new and novel strategies or perhaps by employing assistance from additional brain regions to perform tasks lost as a result of damage (Vida et al., 2012).

PROCESSES OF HUMAN DEVELOPMENT

When examining the biopsychosocial development of a person over a lifespan, a counselor will note the variation of influences that have affected development. The key processes related to development are growth, maturation, and learning. In some ways, the aspects of human development that are most shapeable are key to the counselor's job because clients come to counseling in efforts to change their lives. Counselors must have expertise, defined as complex, domain-specific skills. Expertise, or complex and rich knowledge in an area or domain, allows one to add to and adapt the knowledge and skills of that area of expertise more rapidly (O'Byrne, Clark, & Malakuti, 1997; Skolvholt, Rønnestad, & Jennings, 1997).

Experts are able to more easily add new information and make sense of how it fits into the larger picture of that domain of knowledge. Consider that, compared with an intern, an experienced heart surgeon better understands how a new tool on the table might be used. Another key characteristic of being an expert is that experts are more easily able to sort and understand the value of information within their areas of expertise, for example, rapidly determining and acting confidently on intake data in a crisis situation. In addition, expertise allows professionals to sort between relevant and irrelevant materials and stimuli (O'Byrne et al., 1997; Skolvholt et al., 1997). Consider how developing assessment skills can be likened to developing the skill base of being a professional taster. Professional tasters, whether with mustard, wine, cheese, soda, or potato chips, are able to distinguish variations in quality and characteristics because they (a) have increased domain-specific knowledge (variations in mustard), (b) have heightened awareness on the domain (i.e., mindfulness of color, taste, texture, smell), and (c) use a mechanism to categorize and quantify data. Time and time again, people fail taste tests with beverages they drink on a daily basis, often because they have never spent time developing expertise. This may be similar to how some of your clients experience their interpersonal and intrapersonal mental health.

One area where counselors-in-training often need help is during intake. Without expertise in the field, they often probe for less relevant material, which has an impact on the counseling and the client. On the flip side, beginners can find a fresh, out-of-the-box idea because they may be less biased toward certain solution possibilities. For example, sometimes seasoned workers in social settings may overly adhere to protocols because they have learned from difficult experience and mistakes not to break such protocols; however, there are often clients who would grow more and have better outcomes if protocols were not adhered to. To help the counselor sort between the most relevant materials, the counselor will want to know how key processes of development are at play in the context of a client's life. Three processes discussed in this chapter are growth, maturation, and learning.

Growth

Growth is the process of physical development, often specifically related to the quantifiable measurement of growing larger. For example, Baby Zander is born at Humanity Hospital and comes in for regular pediatric checkups where height and weight are measured. The medical team often communicates the results in relation to age-related norms and discusses any implications with the family. At the 1-month checkup, Dr. Wayum assures the family that Zander is within developmental range for height and weight and is growing appropriately: he has grown 1.5 inches since birth and is now 21 inches long, he has gained about 1 ounce per day in weight, and he has added 1 inch in head size.

Counselors and other health professionals examine growth because research has correlated cognitive and learning deficits and other important life variables with stunted stature. For example, deficits in growth may signal an examination of malnutrition or the presence of disease or disorder. For example, McCoy, Zuilkowski, and Fink (2015) studied 2,711 Zambian 6-year-olds and found that height for age, which they used as a proxy for overall health and nutritional status, was predictive of children's cognitive skills. Across the globe, some of the key elements that affect growth in the early years are malnutrition, poverty, sickness, and parenting practices that do not respond to a child's needs for development. School counselors and teachers often know that when children are sick, hungry, or dealing with family problems they just don't have the energy and attention to focus on learning. Whether one, is examining growth, maturation, or learning, counselors examine how they those areas of development impact and are impacted by well-being and health.

Maturation

Maturation is at times used synonymously with *growth*; however, from a human development studies perspective, maturation is different from growth because it refers to physical, intellectual, and psychological development. Counselors are concerned with maturation, which may occur across dimensions and mutually influencing phenomena. For example, when Kiasha comes of age, her physical, cognitive, social, and emotional self goes through a maturation process. This is noted by physical changes like breast development and menstruation; by the ability to think in abstract ways; by concern about world affairs, social justice, and women in politics; and by increased attention to peer input and romantic "love" while pushing for independence from parents.

Learning

Much time is spent discussing the importance of and process of learning in human development. To realize developmental capacity, people need opportunities for learning. This has been the major call to action of the equality and justice movement. Given the same relative capacities, the development of two people will vary based on what resources a person is provided. Generally speaking, people must be exposed to and taught to read to harness the capacity for written language. Other skills may be present in a person's life, but without learning, level of proficiency and mastery are limited. Consider what it takes to move a person from basic knowledge and skills in cooking, music, woodwork, caregiving, or computer use to becoming a master chef, great composer, high-end furniture maker, psychiatric nurse, or a securities software programmer.

BOX 1.3   SOME KEY TYPES OF LEARNING THAT INFLUENCE DEVELOPMENT

Behavioral learning: People develop through behavioral conditioning that relates to environmental incentives and consequences.

Social learning: Development occurs through interactions with others. One can learn from peers, those that are slightly more developed in an area, or someone with a novel approach.

Cognitive learning: Through cognitive processing and inherent biological mechanisms for complex cognitive skills, people can grow through cognitive learning.

Mirror-neuron copy process learning: Through a perception–action coupling mechanism, mirror neurons help people see a skill and copy it (see Turati et al., 2013).

Scaffold learning: Learning is built on previous learning and development.

Scaffolded Learning

Because learning enhances development, scaffolded learning is important. Just as one might climb a scaffold, a type of ladder, a person creates new learning by building off previous learning. Counselors and educators alike are alert to the developmental importance of scaffolded learning (Belland, Kim, & Hannafin, 2013). For example, emotion-focused therapy (EFT) and emotional intelligence rest on the notion that individuals can develop into more sophisticated emotional beings. An emotion-focused therapist might scaffold learning over the course of therapy to help clients learn how to bring awareness to emotions in session; then identify emotions; experience emotions that have been avoided; understand about emotional schemes; examine the idiosyncratic nature of emotional response; understand primary adaptive, secondary reactive, and instrumental emotions; then work with dsyfuntional themes; and so on (Goldman & Greenberg, 2015). As another pertinent example, researchers have found that to work with depressive thoughts within cognitive therapy, one can increase the skills of metacognition through watching thoughts (Kerr, Sachhet, Lazar, Moore, & Jones, 2013). A person can cognitively work with depression much better by first leaning the skill of mindfulness to increase awareness of depressive thoughts (i.e., metacognition around depressive thoughts). If you are a counselor-in-training, consider how your learning toward working with clients will be scaffolded.

BOX 1.4   SCAFFOLDED LEARNING EXERCISES FOR COUNSELORS-IN-TRAINING

How will the previous learning step help with the subsequent steps?

1. Read about it.
2. Examine cases.
3. Formulate ideas and write responses to written cases.
4. Watch video recordings of practicing counselors and therapists.
5. Understand the behaviors and processes of therapy.
6. Apply learning by role playing.
7. Work with clients in practicum and internship under supervision.
8. Record and transcribe sessions for review in individual supervision.
9. Process cases together under group supervision.
10. Counsel clients and learn from mistakes, ruptures, and successes in session.
11. Teach and supervise others in counseling.

INFLUENCES ON DEVELOPMENT

The many qualities that mark the nature of change over a lifespan provide a window into how development is influenced and how, as a professional, a counselor can influence the maturation and learning of a person. In the middle of a counselor's work, there is a paradox: the client and counselor have to accept circumstances while also cultivating change; the person has to accept himself or herself while changing to be successful. This brings up another contrasting theme in the study of human development: passivity versus activity of the person. This tug-of-war has been captured throughout literature, for example, in Virgil's Aeneid, where fate versus will or the will of the gods were juxtaposed (Virgil, 2003). Client narratives may resemble the stories of protagonists in age-old stories because the human themes reflect key existential struggles. From a scientific standpoint, developmental influences are often viewed as falling into the following categories: hereditary, normative history graded, normative age graded, normative sociocultural graded, nonnormative, and environmental–contextual.

BOX 1.5   VARIOUS INFLUENCES IN VICKI'S LIFE

Age Graded	History Graded	Sociocultural	Nonnormative
Late adulthood			
Middle adulthood 2000–current Menopause	2008 recession	Children boomerang	Develops cancer Earns bachelor's degree
Young adulthood 1979–1999 Career launch	Gulf War	Marriage/divorce	Enters counseling 1995
Adolescence 1972–1978 Puberty	Vietnam War ends	Graduates high school with cohort	Posttraumatic stress disorder from sexual assault
Middle childhood 1966–1971	Hippie movement	Enrolls in public school	Mother leaves father and church
Early childhood 1962–1965	Equal rights movement Kennedy assassination	Irish Catholic Boston	Grandparents live in the house, provide nurturing additional child care
Birth and infancy 1959–1961		Low socioeconomic status	Born with cleft palate
Victoria "Vicky" Long, born 1959			

Heredity

Human development is influenced by heredity. Species *heredity* is the genetic inheritance that we have in common as a human species. Humans are uniquely upright in posture, hairless creatures that blush and have remarkable brains that allowing for advanced cognitive skills. "We speak language, routinely cooperate with others to reach complex shared goals, engage in abstract reasoning and scientific inquiry, and learn a rich set of sophisticated cultural behaviors from others" (Rosati, Wobber, Hughes, & Santos, 2014, p. 449). Species heredity influences which traits are universal to all humans as compared with other species. Just as there is plasticity in the individual, the species can influence and be influenced by the environment. Will the changes in climate influence heredity of the human species on physical, social, cognitive, and psychological levels? What are examples of plasticity as climate change science begins to unfold a picture of a changing landscape?

The understanding of individual heredity is intimately tied to the multidisciplinary study of genetics. With a high-powered microscope and the introduction of dye, one can view chromosomes along with other fundamental building blocks. Humans have two pairs of 23 chromosomes (22 autosomes with one pairing linked to sex, either XY male or XX female), totaling 46 chromosomes (Berninger, 2015). Missing chromosomes, extra chromosomes, and chromosomal abnormalities are among the variations in chromosomes that are correlated with various syndromes important to mental and physical health. For example, Down syndrome is associated with an extra 21st chromosome (Figure 1.1). Each chromosome has hundreds

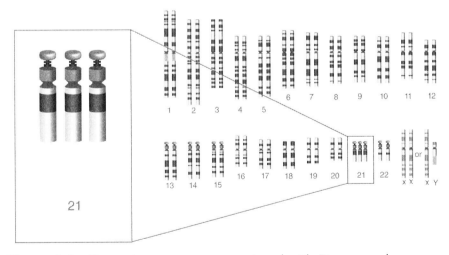

Figure 1.1 Extra chromosomes associated with Down syndrome.
Courtesy of National Human Genome Research Institute and the Smithsonian National Museum of Natural History.

of genes that provide instructions for how a person will develop. *Genotype* is a term used to describe the inherited genes that make up the underlying possibility for expression. *Phenotype* is a term used to describe the genetic manifestation, or how genes are expressed. Phenotypes are influenced though not dependent on genes. As an example, a person's genetic heredity may include schizophrenia, but it may not be expressed in that person's life. "Genotyping allows the maximum of structural and functional properties, but the eventual outcome is under the influence of the environment in positive or negative directions" (Uylings, 2006, p. 16). Development of the human cortex may be maximized by prenatal care and a healthy mother but may be negatively influenced by prenatal drug use (Silva, Villatoro Velázquez, Oliva Robles, Hynes, & de Marco, 2014), environmental toxins, disease, ill health, and malnutrition. In addition, some genes are regulatory genes and control the developmental activation and deactivation of other genes, a process that impacts the developmental onset of critical periods and events in development (Berninger, 2015).

Normative History Grade Influences

Certain influences impact development for the individual and his or her cohort. A cohort is a group that shares a specific set of circumstances over time. When a cohort shares certain historical circumstances or events that influence development, we call these influences *normative history grade influences*. Consider how development might be influenced by surviving the Chernobyl nuclear disaster in 1986. How would this be different from someone exposed to radiation in a university lab? Consider how being part of a civil war and genocide event (e.g., Rwanda), living with drug wars along the border between the United States and Mexico, or the great 2008 recession might impact different people within those historical cohorts. Even when members of a cohort share historical circumstances, there are variations in how the circumstances are experienced and influence development for its members.

Social science researchers categorize groups (cohorts) into variously defined normative historical influences. Consider the generational categorization of the silent generation (1925–1945), baby boomers (1946–1964), Generation X (1965–1981), and millennials, also referred to as Generation Y (1982–present). Generations share years of birth and therefore similar social and historical atmospheres, such as wars, catastrophes, and technological innovations (Amayah & Gedro, 2014). These labels are associated with eras of American history; for example, baby boomers were born at the tail end of WWII and matured in the Vietnam War and equal rights movement era. As other examples, consider the categorization of digital natives, or those who grew up with widespread digital technology, computers, and mobile smartphones, versus a digital immigrant, or someone born before this type of technology was pervasive (Kirk, Chiagouris, Lala, & Thomas, 2015). How does exposure to technology or lack thereof affect development in positive and negative ways? It is important to note that the literature has cautioned against the use of generational stereotypes promoted in popular culture (Amayah & Gedro, 2014).

Normative Age-Graded Development

Age-graded developments are influences shared by people across times but at a particular stage in life; for example, this book focuses on the following age-graded periods: birth and infancy; early childhood; middle childhood; adolescence; young adulthood; middle adulthood; and late adulthood. When considering the life of your extended family, what developmental changes occurred for each member during infancy?

Counselors regularly treat client stress or grief and loss connected to age-graded milestones that are not achieved by clients or the members of a client's family. For families with members who have lifelong developmental disabilities, grief and loss are common when there are delays or blocks to some type of development (Carroll, 2013; O'Brien, 2007). Inasmuch as some age-graded developments have been prized, others have been taboo. As an example, consider how menopause was not often discussed in American culture, although this period clearly is critical for the developing middle adult woman.

Normative Sociocultural-Graded Influences

Normative sociocultural-graded influences are shared by others of the same sociocultural group. Consider the impact that cultural rites of passage or even socioeconomic status have on a person's ongoing development. The quinceañara has been traditionally held in Latin America as a coming-of-age event celebrated on the 15th birthday, which marks a transition for girls from childhood into womanhood. Many such sociocultural rituals are marked by change in adult responsibilities, the ability to do religious ceremonies, and often the start of coupling and marriage. Other examples of coming-of-age ceremonies are Jewish bar mitzvahs and bat mitzvahs, Sikh amrit sanchar, the Catholic sacrament of confirmation, the Hindu ritushuddi, and kovave in Papua New Guinea. Depending on the culture, it may signify a change in dress and haircut, may mark a physical maturation, or may change where one sleeps at night. Regardless, these influence development and affect those of a similar sociocultural cohort.

In the United States and Canada, counselors often pay attention to the influence of socioeconomic status on individual development. So how does being raised in an affluent home compare with growing up with few economic resources? Decades worth of research in the United States suggests that socioeconomic status and socioeconomic adversity can affect the development of children. Enriching environments, caregiver time and energy, and early investment such as preschool attendance may mediate the negative effects of socioeconomic adversity (McCoy et al., 2015). Also consider other types of groups that share normative sociocultural-graded influences on development (e.g., immigrant, refugee).

Family Life Cycle

Family culture is one of the primary sociocultural influences. Family development is directly tied to the nature and composition of the family (Del Corso & Lanz,

2013). When discussing the family, counselors who work in mental health, family, school, and rehabilitation settings refer to family based on the reality of family composition in today's society. This goes beyond ideal notions of the family and includes same-sex-parented families, single-parent families, blended families, families headed by grandparents, and other close social groups where family care, responsibility, and identity reside regardless of blood relations. The family life cycle examines development of the family as a unit moving through key developmental periods (Figure 1.2). The family life cycle is systemically connected to the individual's development. When success, harm, loss, change, and maturation happen to one member or subgroup of the family, they influence the development of the rest of the family. Some transitions in family are more challenging than others. The family life cycle model first introduced by Carter and McGoldrick (1980) in their seminal work *The Family Life Cycle: A Framework for Family Therapy* suggested that families can get stunted when transitioning through stages of the cycle and that counselors can directly help families make sense of and negotiate a functional way forward.

Some family transitions come with increased stress and also with expanded opportunities. Just as with individual development, counselors help clients sort between distress and eustress. Eustress is stress that is seen as necessary and part of maturation. What stressors did you experience as an adolescent as being beneficial to your life? Challenges and mistakes can be converted to positive outcomes. Counselors help clients sort through and walk through the fear and discomfort of making positive developmental gains that are frightening. These feelings can at times emotionally and physically present in a similar way to real threats to safety and self-esteem. For example, a person may have an upset stomach, increased psychomotor agitation, and clammy palms when sharing deep convictions with a new group or when robbing a store.

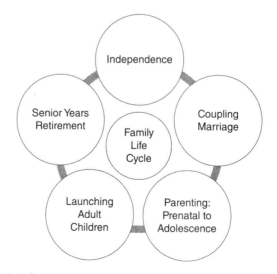

Figure 1.2 The family life cycle (basic).

Consider the challenges for a middle-aged couple launching their last child during his or her early adult years. What struggles might they face in their own development? Or consider Felicia and Jen, a married couple in their late 30s who have matured in their psychosocial development. Up until now they have been aunts to many nieces and nephews, and they are now looking to start a family. Felicia is now pregnant through a close family donor process. How might this life cycle change for this new family provoke individual development on multidimensional biopsychosocial levels?

Nonnormative Influences

Nonnormative influences do not adhere to a particular time frame, nor are they common across a predictable cohort. Because illness is often unpredictable, it often falls into this category of developmental influences. For example, Jose could contract, malaria at age 5, 15, or 65. Regardless of the age at which malaria is contracted, but especially during a critical development period, Jose's development path would be influenced in both positive (e.g., shapes career toward helping the ill and vulnerable) and negative ways (e.g., loss of hearing from treatment).

BOX 1.6   HOW WOULD YOU CATEGORIZE EACH ONE OF THESE INFLUENTIAL EVENTS?

Death of a close family member
Marital separation
Serve on a 2-year religious mission abroad
Injured at work
Marriage at age 18
Retirement at 65
Family member contracts terminal illness
Pregnancy at age 40
Selected to carry on family business
Bankruptcy
Imprisonment
Foreclosure of mortgage or loan
Significant change in responsibilities at work
Youngest child leaves home for college
Graduation from school
Eviction
Increase to unhealthy body mass index
Cohabitation with partner
Hurricane destroys neighborhood
City police prejudice, profiling, and excessive force with minorities
Change in schools
Move to new residence
Riots disenfranchise neighborhood
Develop anorexia

Environment

A cohort may be affected by environmental influences on development (e.g., shared neighborhood, workplace, presence of wild areas, quality of resources). For example, in a study of 3,965 middle-age Australians, Van Dyck, Teychenne, McNaughton, De Bourdeaudhuij, and Salmon (2015) found that mental health-related quality of life was not only associated with social support for physical activity from family and neighborhood social cohesion, but also with the neighborhood physical activity environment and personal safety.

KEY COUNSELING POINTERS FOR HUMAN DEVELOPMENT

- The counseling relationship is dynamic and influences the development of clients. Because of the irreversible quality of time, counseling is strongly tied to the behaviors, thoughts, communications, and feelings that occur in session with the client (Salvatore & Tschacher, 2012).
- Counselors must think in a multidimensional and systemic way, but most people do not habitually view the world in a systemic way. As a mental practice, examine the systems and subsystems of your current circumstance as a habit so it becomes natural when working with clients.
- Popular ideas of development suggest that development is static and only growth related. Counselors who want to serve clients well will be versed in human transition, grief, and loss. Death is a developmental process (Kubler-Ross, Kessler, & Shriver, 2014).
- During critical periods, counselors must be as concerned about maximizing developmental outcomes as they are about minimizing stunting or unnecessary decline.
- Because learning is so important to a variety of developmental steps and outcomes, counselors need to be aware of how people learn differently and how disability can influence the process of learning. Instruction, process work, and psych education in the counseling setting should fit with a person's optimal learning format.
- Whether development reflects continuity or discontinuity, clients often look for coherence through meaning making and life narratives. For children, global narratives are not present, but as a person moves into adolescence and again into young and middle adulthood, life narratives become helpful to a host of life processes (Köber, Schmiedek, & Habermas, 2015). Life review has been shown to be of particular use to older adults (Lewis, 2001).
- Advocacy is important so people can get the opportunities and resources to develop to capacity. Learn how to advocate for clients and how to help clients advocate for themselves on microsystemic (e.g., individual) and macrosystemic (e.g., institutional, societal) levels.
- When examining nonnormative influences, use stressful events inventories such as the 43-point Social Readjustment Rating Scale by Holmes and Rahe (1967).

- The competencies endorsed by the American Counseling Association in the realms of (a) multicultural counseling, (b) advocacy, (c) cross-cultural counseling, (d) LGBTQQ, and (e) working with multiracial clients are each vital guides and aspirational motivators for counselors.

SUMMARY

Human development as a study, like human life, is ever-changing. Some key concepts that apply to human development were explored in the chapter, and these set the stage for other chapters in this book. Development is continuous, discontinuous, multidimensional, multidirectional, and plastic. Modern science has uncovered important findings about how humans change over a lifespan and how some changes are unique and personal, whereas others are shared in common as a result of sociocultural, historical, hereditary, and environmental influences. There are also human development processes that are important to counseling: growth, maturation, and importantly, learning.

USEFUL WEBSITES

Human Connectome Project
http://www.humanconnectome.org/
Smithsonian: National Museum of National History
Genome: Unlocking Life's Code (Smithsonian: National Museum of National History)
http://www.unlockinglifescode.org
Counseling Today Articles: Human Development Across the Lifespan
http://ct.counseling.org/tag/topic-ct-human-development-across-the-lifespan/
American Counseling Association Counselor Competencies Page
http://www.counseling.org/knowledge-center/competencies

REFERENCES

Amayah, A. T., & Gedro, J. (2014). Understanding generational diversity: Strategic human resource management and development across the generational "divide." *New Horizons in Adult Education & Human Resource Development*, *26*(2), 36–48.

Badcock, P. B. (2012). Evolutionary systems theory: A unifying meta-theory of psychological science. *Review of General Psychology*, *16*(1), 10–23. http://doi.org/10.1037/a0026381

Belland, B. R., Kim, C., & Hannafin, M. (2013). A framework for designing scaffolds that improve motivation and cognition. *Educational Psychologist*, *48*(4), 243–270.

Berninger, V. W. (2015). A genetics primer and brain primer for interdisciplinary frameworks. In *Interdisciplinary frameworks for schools: Best professional practices for serving the needs of all students* (pp. 171–196). Washington, DC: American Psychological Association. Retrieved from http://ezp.waldenulibrary.org/login?url=http://search.ebscohost.com/login.aspx?direct=true&db=psyh&AN=2014-08456-007&scope=site

Carroll, D. W. (2013). Death and bereavement. In *Families of children with developmental disabilities: Understanding stress and opportunities for growth* (pp. 135–148). Washington, DC: American Psychological Association. Retrieved from http://ezp.waldenulibrary.org/login?url=http://search.ebscohost.com/login.aspx?direct=true&db=psyh&AN=2013-03465-010&scope=site

Carter, E., & McGoldrick, M. (1980). *The family life cycle: A framework for family therapy*. London, England: Karnac Books.

Chial, H. (2008). DNA sequencing technologies key to the Human Genome Project. *Nature Education, 1*(1), 219.

Del Corso, A. R., & Lanz, M. (2013). Felt obligation and the family life cycle: A study on intergenerational relationships. *International Journal of Psychology, 48*(6), 1196–1200. http://doi.org/10.1080/00207594.2012.725131

Ebner, N. C., Freund, A. M., & Baltes, P. B. (2006). Developmental changes in personal goal orientation from young to late adulthood: From striving for gains to maintenance and prevention of losses. *Psychology and Aging, 21,* 664–678.

Greve, W., Thomsen, T., & Dehio, C. (2014). Does playing pay? The fitness-effect of free play during childhood. *Evolutionary Psychology, 12*(2), 434–447.

Goldman, R. N., & Greenberg, L. S. (2015). Fundamentals of emotion-focused therapy. In *Case formulation in emotion-focused therapy: Co-creating clinical maps for change* (pp. 21–42). Washington, DC: American Psychological Association. doi:10.1037/14523-002

Heidegger, M. (1962). *Being and time*. Oxford, England: Blackwell Publishing.

Holmes, T. H., & Rahe, R. H. (1967). The social readjustment rating scale. *Journal of Psychosomatic Research, 11,* 213–218

Kang, D.-H., Jo, H. J., Jung, W. H., Kim, S. H., Jung, Y.-H., Choi, C.-H.,… Kwon, J. S. (2013). The effect of meditation on brain structure: cortical thickness mapping and diffusion tensor imaging. *Social Cognitive and Affective Neuroscience, 8*(1), 27–33. http://doi.org/10.1093/scan/nss056

Kerr, C. E., Sacchet, M. D., Lazar, S. W., Moore, C. I., & Jones, S. R. (2013). Mindfulness starts with the body: Somatosensory attention and top-down modulation of cortical alpha rhythms in mindfulness meditation. *Frontiers in Human Neuroscience, 7,* 12. http://doi.org/10.3389/fnhum.2013.00012

Kinsley, C. H., Bardi, M., Karelina, K., Rima, B., Christon, L., Friedenberg, J., & Griffin, G. (2008). Motherhood induces and maintains behavioral and neural plasticity across the lifespan in the rat. *Archives of Sexual Behavior, 37*(1), 43–56. http://doi.org/10.1007/s10508-007-9277-x

Kirk, C., Chiagouris, L., Lala, V. & Thomas, J. (2015, March 1). How Do Digital Natives and Digital Immigrants Respond Differently to Interactivity Online? *Journal of Advertising Research*, *55*(1), 1–14.

Köber, C., Schmiedek, F., & Habermas, T. (2015). Characterizing lifespan development of three aspects of coherence in life narratives: A cohort-sequential study. *Developmental Psychology*, *51*(2), 260–275. http://doi.org/10.1037/a0038668

Kolb, B., & Teskey, G. C. (2012). Age, experience, injury, and the changing brain. *Developmental Psychobiology*, *54*(3), 311–325. http://doi.org/10.1002/dev.20515

Kubler-Ross, E., Kessler, D., & Shriver, M. (2014). *On grief and grieving: Finding the meaning of grief through the five stages of loss*. New York, NY: Scribner.

Lewis, M. M. (2001). Spirituality, counseling, and elderly: An introduction to the spiritual life review. *Journal of Adult Development*, *8*(4), 231–240. doi:10.1023/A:1011390528828

McAdams, T. A., Neiderhiser, J. M., Rijsdijk, F. V., Narusyte, J., Lichtenstein, P., & Eley, T. C. (2014). Accounting for genetic and environmental confounds in associations between parent and child characteristics: A systematic review of children-of-twins studies. *Psychological Bulletin*, *140*(4), 1138–1173. http://doi.org/10.1037/a0036416

McCoy, D. C., Zuilkowski, S. S., & Fink, G. (2015). Poverty, physical stature, and cognitive skills: Mechanisms underlying children's school enrollment in Zambia. *Developmental Psychology*, *51*(5), 600–614. http://doi.org/10.1037/a0038924

Mroczek, D. K. (2014). Personality plasticity, healthy aging, and interventions. *Developmental Psychology*, *50*(5), 1470–1474. http://doi.org/10.1037/a0036028

Nass, C., & Moon, Y. (2000). Machines and mindlessness: Social responses to computers. *Journal of Social Issues*, *56*(1), 81–103.

Natalie, C. E., Alexandra, M. F., & Paul, B. B. (2006). Developmental changes in personal goal orientation from young to late adulthood: From striving for gains to maintenance and prevention of losses. *Psychology and Aging*, *21*(4), 664–678. http://dx.doi.org/10.1037/0882-7974.21.4.664

O'Brien, M. (2007). Ambiguous loss in families of children with autism spectrum disorders. *Family Relations: An Interdisciplinary Journal of Applied Family Studies*, *56*(2), 135–146. http://doi.org/10.1111/j.1741-3729.2007.00447.x

O'Byrne, K., Clark, R. E., & Malakuti, R. (1997). Expert and novice performance: Implications for clinical training. *Educational Psychology Review*, *9*(4), 321–332. http://doi.org/10.1023/A:1024742505548

Rosati, A. G., Wobber, V., Hughes, K., & Santos, L. R. (2014). Comparative developmental psychology: How is human cognitive development unique? *Evolutionary Psychology*, *12*(2), 448–473.

Salvatore, S., & Tschacher, W. (2012). Time dependency of psychotherapeutic exchanges: The contribution of the theory of dynamic systems in analyzing process. *Frontiers in Psychology*, *3*. http://doi.org/10.3389/fpsyg.2012.00253

Schulenberg, J. E., & Zarrett, N. R. (2006). Mental health during emerging adulthood: Continuity and discontinuity in courses, causes, and functions. In J. J. Arnett & J. L. Tanner (Eds.), *Emerging adults in America: Coming of age in the 21st century* (pp. 135–72). Washington DC: American Psychological Association.

Silva, F. S., Villatoro Velázquez, J. A., Oliva Robles, N. F., Hynes, M., & de Marco, M. (2014). Relationship between human development and drug use: Human development index and drug use. *Salud Mental, 37*(1), 35–39.

Skovholt, T. M., Rønnestad, M. H., & Jennings, L. (1997). Searching for expertise in counseling, psychotherapy, and professional psychology. *Educational Psychology Review, 9*(4), 361–369. http://doi.org/10.1023/A:1024798723295

Turati, C., Natale, E., Bolognini, N., Senna, I., Picozzi, M., Longhi, E., & Cassia, V. M. (2013). The early development of human mirror mechanisms: Evidence from electromyographic recordings at 3 and 6 months. *Developmental Science, 16*(6), 793–800.

Uylings, H. B. M. (2006). Development of the human cortex and the concept of "critical" or "sensitive" periods. *Language Learning, 56*, 59–90. doi: 10.1111/j.1467-9922.2006.00355.x

Van Dyck, D., Teychenne, M., McNaughton, S. A., De Bourdeaudhuij, I., & Salmon, J. (2015). Relationship of the perceived social and physical environment with mental health-related quality of life in middle-aged and older adults: Mediating effects of physical activity. *PLoS ONE, 10*(3), 1–16. Retrieved from http://ezp.waldenulibrary.org/login?url=http://search .ebscohost.com/login.aspx?direct=true&db=psyh&AN=2015-13375-001& scope=site

Van Geert, P. (2011). The contribution of complex dynamic systems to development. *Child Development Perspectives, 5*(4), 273–278. http://doi.org/10.1111/j .1750-8606.2011.00197.x

Vida, M. D., Vingilis-Jaremko, L., Butler, B. E., Gibson, L. C., & Monteiro, S. (2012). The reorganized brain: How treatment strategies for stroke and amblyopia can inform our knowledge of plasticity throughout the lifespan. *Developmental Psychobiology, 54*(3), 357–368. http://doi.org/10.1002/dev .20625

Virgil. (2003). *The Aeneid* (D. West, Trans.). London, England: Penguin Books.

Witherspoon, D. J., Wooding, S., Rogers, A. R., Marchani, E. E., Watkins, W. S., Batzer, M. A., & Jorde, L. B. (2007). Genetic similarities within and between human populations. *Genetics. 176*(1): 351–359. doi:10.1534/ genetics.106.067355

Theories of Human Development

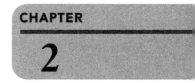

David Capuzzi, Mark D. Stauffer, and Tammie O'Neil

WHY STUDY PSYCHOLOGICAL THEORIES OF DEVELOPMENT?

This book is about human development across the lifespan, and it addresses physical, cognitive, social, and emotional development from birth to the end of life. Understanding the development and the changes that take place in all of us in these four domains is critical to the work of the counselor. The reason that the study of psychological theories in the context of human growth and development is important is because these theories provide models for viewing personality development across the lifespan. These models explain past behavior, help with understanding current behavior, predict future behavior, and provide parameters for assessing an individual's motivations, needs, and unresolved issues. As noted by Capuzzi and Gross (2011), "The greater a counselor or therapist's awareness of the strengths and possibilities inherent in numerous theoretical frames of reference, the greater the potential for understanding the uniqueness of a particular client and for developing the most effective treatment plan" (p. v).

This chapter provides an overview of the psychoanalytic, behavioral, cognitive, developmental, sociocultural, ecological, attachment, and phenomenological theoretical frameworks for understanding human growth and development across the lifespan.

THEORIES AND THEIR IMPACT ON UNDERSTANDING HUMAN GROWTH AND DEVELOPMENT ACROSS THE LIFESPAN

Psychoanalytic Theory

Regarding psychoanalytic theory, Adrianne Johnson (2011, p. 60) aptly noted:

Psychoanalytic theory suggests that behavior is largely determined by irrational forces, unconscious motivations, and biological, or instinctual, drives (Bush, 1978). Humans are conceptualized largely in terms of biology, and maladaptive behaviors are symptomatic of a subconscious response to social interactions which the mind interprets as unsafe, thereby threatening the stability of the human personality structure.

Terminology and concepts linked to classical psychoanalysis have become inherent aspects of our culture, with terms such as *Freudian slip, repression*, and *denial* used regularly in the everyday language of those around us. For at least 100 years psychoanalytic theory, as conceptualized by Sigmund Freud (1856–1939), has been pivotal to the work of counselors and therapists around the globe. It is based on the concept that individuals are unaware of the many factors that cause their maladaptive behaviors and discomforting emotions. Psychoanalytic treatment is highly individualized and seeks to show how early childhood experiences have impacted the formative aspects of our personality development (Thomas, 2008). To understand contemporary psychoanalytic approaches to theory, it is important to be conversant with five theoretical directions: Freudian drive theory, ego psychology, object relations, self psychology, and relational psychoanalysis (Sharf, 2008).

Freudian Drive Theory

One of the best known constructs of psychoanalytic theory is that of the interactive system comprising and influencing the human personality. As conceptualized by Freud, the inherently instinctual and biological drives of the psyche are referred to as the *id*, the *superego* (i.e., the critical, moralizing function), and the *ego* (i.e., the organized, realistic part that mediates and seeks a balance between the instinctual nature of the id and the critical, moralizing function of the superego; Johnson, 2011; Sharf, 2008). The id, the ego, and the superego are used to describe the structural model of the personality that drives and guides an individual's behavior across the lifespan.

Freud theorized that human personality develops through a series of childhood stages during which the pleasure-seeking energies of the id become focused on certain erogenous areas (Dimen, 1999). A child at a given stage of development has certain needs, and if these psychosexual stages are successfully experienced the result is a healthy personality. Frustration occurs when these needs are not met, and if certain issues are not resolved during a given stage, the individual will become fixated and will persistently focus on an earlier psychosexual stage. Such fixations often provide the substance for follow-up counseling.

Freud believed that psychosexual energy, or libido, is the driving force behind behavior and that, at certain points in the developmental process, a single body part is sensitive to sexual, erotic stimulation (Johnson, 2011; Sharf, 2008). These *erogenous zones* are the mouth, the anus, and the genital region.

Freud suggested five psychosexual stages. The first is the oral stage, experienced during the first year of life. During this stage, the infant's primary source of gratification occurs through the mouth, and the sucking reflexes are especially important (Heimann, 1962). Since the infant is dependent on caretakers to satiate these needs, the infant develops a sense of trust and comfort through oral stimulation. The primary conflict at the oral stage is the weaning process; the infant must become less dependent on the caretakers and more self-reliant to meet his or her own needs. If fixation occurs at this stage, Freud believed the individual might have issues with dependency or aggression later in life and may experience an emphasis on oral stimulation, such as drinking, eating, smoking, or nail biting (Nevid, 2009).

The second stage is the anal stage (1–3 years of age). The major conflict during this stage is toilet training; the child has to learn to control his or her bodily needs. Developing this control leads to a sense of accomplishment and independence (Gabbard, 1979). Success at this stage is dependent on the way parents approach toilet training. Freud believed that positive experiences during this period of human development were the basis for adults to become competent, productive, and creative and that negative experiences result in two primary negative outcomes. If parents are too lenient, Freud suggested that an anal-expulsive personality could develop in which the individual has a messy, wasteful, or destructive personality. If parents are too strict or begin toilet training prematurely, an anal-retentive personality develops, in which the individual is stringent, orderly, rigid, and obsessive (Heimann, 1962).

The phallic stage, in which the libido is focused primarily on the genitals, occurs between ages 3 and 6 years. Children also notice the differences between males and females. Freud believed that at this stage boys begin to see their fathers as rivals for their mothers' affections (the Oedipus complex; Howes, 1997). Simultaneously, the child fears that he will be punished by the father for these feelings, a fear Freud termed *castration anxiety*. The term *Electra complex* was used to describe a similar set of feelings experienced by young girls and was derived from what Freud believed was penis envy. He theorized that eventually the girl begins to identify with the same-sex parent as a means of vicariously possessing the other parent. For girls, however, Freud believed that penis envy was never fully resolved and that all women remain somewhat fixated on this stage (Fuchsman, 2001).

The latency stage (ages 6–12 years) is the time in which the id, the ego, and the superego develop the foundation for the adult's instinctual drives and behavioral responses. This fourth stage is a time of exploration in which sexual energy is directed into other areas such as intellectual pursuits and social interactions. The stage begins about the time children enter school and become more concerned with peer relationships, extracurricular activities, and personal interests. The development of the ego and superego contribute to this period of calm since the id and libido are suppressed (Schneider, 1988).

The final stage, the genital stage, begins after age 12 years and continues through adulthood. During this stage, the individual develops strong sexual interests, drives, and desires; an interest in the welfare of others also grows during this stage. If the other stages have been positively experienced, the individual is well balanced, warm, and caring. The outcome of this stage is to establish a balance between the various life areas. This is the stage in which the ego fully emerges to mediate conflict between the id and superego regarding social and sexual interactions with others (Carducci, 2007).

BOX 2.1 PSYCHOANALYSIS TODAY

Even though the number of practitioners who subscribe to and practice classical psychoanalysis has diminished as time has passed and counselors and therapists have adopted cognitive, behavioral, brief, and other modalities for working with clients, there are many practitioners who currently use the theory as developed by Freud and his followers. This usually means that such a practitioner serves a very affluent clientele since the number of sessions, sometimes more than one per week, makes the therapeutic experience costly and of longer duration than managed care providers will fund.

Freud also proposed a class of drives known as the *life instincts* (those that deal with basic survival, pleasure, and reproduction) and *death drives* (an unconscious desire to die). The energy created by the life instincts became known as the libido. Behaviors commonly associated with life instincts include love, cooperation, and other pro-social actions. Self-destructive behavior is an expression of the energy created by the death instincts. When this energy is directed inward, it manifests as masochism and self-loathing. If directed outward, it is expressed as aggression and violence (Jaffe, 1982). If counselors and therapists subscribe to these concepts of life instincts and death drives, exploration of how they are manifested in the life of a client can provide substance for exploration during the process of counseling and psychotherapy.

Freud's concept of defense mechanisms can be observed daily even among those who are not familiar with psychoanalytic theory. These mechanisms are functions of the ego, which strive to protect individuals from experiencing the anxiety and guilt provoked by discord between the id and superego. These coping strategies safeguard the psyche against feelings and thoughts that are too difficult for the conscious mind to cope with, such as inappropriate or unwanted thoughts and impulses, and prevent them from entering the conscious mind. Excellent descriptions of these defense mechanisms can be found in Corey (2013) and Sharf (2008).

Two of very important concepts associated with psychoanalysis were the ideas of transference, or the process that occurs when the client attributes feelings about another person onto the counselor, and countertransference, or the emotional responses to a client that are determined by the counselor's own unconscious conflict rather than by the client's personality traits and experiences. Transference exposes the unconscious motivation behind the individual's defense mechanisms by reenacting the attitudes, feelings, impulses, and desires that were generated in early life in relation to important figures in the client's development. The counselor's awareness of countertransference can provide important insight into the client's inner world and into the emotions and reactions the client often induces in others (Johnson, 2011) and can be used in the development of counseling and treatment plans on behalf of the client.

Ego Psychology: Anna Freud and Erik Erikson

Anna Freud (1895–1982) studied preschool children and provided psychoanalytic counseling and therapy at her clinic in London. When considering child development, she focused on the aggressive and sexual drives of children as well as on measures of maturation such as progressing from dependence to self-mastery. Anna Freud emphasized developmental lines as she provided explanations of how children move from an egocentric focus, during which they do not notice or attend well to other children, to a more other focused attitude toward their peers to whom they begin to relate to as real people (Freud, 1965). Anna Freud believed that as time passes these developmental lines show an increasing emphasis on the ego and that the ego, as well as the id, should be the focus of psychoanalytical treatment. In her writings about defense mechanisms (Freud, 1936) she added the *defenses identification with the aggressor* and *altruism*. When employing identification with the aggressor, a person assumes a role that he or she has been passively traumatized by, and, in altruism, a person becomes helpful to avoid being helpless. Anna Freud's contributions to the understanding of human development (child development) described how a variety of defense mechanisms develop and how some are maladaptive but others are adaptive and very normal ways of dealing with the external world (Sharf, 2008).

Erik Erikson (1902–1994) was a student of Anna Freud's and made a number of additional contributions to ego psychology, especially his explanation of psychosocial stages of human development that included stages of adult as well as child development (Hoare, 2005). Erikson proposed eight stages of human development (and later a ninth was added) that focused on crises that must be addressed at significant times in a person's life. If these crises are not properly negotiated, there could be difficulty negotiating other developmental crises, and counselors using Erikson's concepts about this aspect of human development would likely want to assist clients with the resolution of unresolved crises. Unlike Freud, Erikson believed that these stages are not completed during a prescribed time period but remain active throughout life and can affect relationships at any time.

Erikson described the following nine stages (the ninth published posthumously) that were characterized by a positive view of human development across the lifespan:

1. *Infancy: trust versus mistrust* (birth to 1 year). During this stage the infant either learns to trust or mistrust others and themselves. Ideally, this stage results in ability to place trust in oneself, parents, and the world. Counselors who work with clients who have trust issues may suspect that during this stage of development the client was not able to count on basic needs being met.

2. *Early childhood: autonomy versus shame and doubt* (2 to 3 years). Because of increasing mobility, the child must decide whether to assert his or her will. The best outcome of this stage, according to Erikson, is that the child learns to develop self-control when needed without experiencing a loss of self-esteem. Sometimes counselors need to explore early childhood memories with clients who experience shame and doubt as they review their life paths.

3. *Preschool age: initiative versus guilt* (4 to 5 years). During this stage, the preschool child is curious about many things, observations, and experiences and develops more ability to manipulate objects. Hopefully, the child develops direction and purpose in the activities that he or she pursues so that the same thing occurs later in life.

4. *School age: industry versus inferiority* (6 to puberty). During this stage, the child develops more curiosity about how things are made and how they work. It is important for the child to develop a sense of mastery and competence during this stage. If this does not occur, the child, and later the adolescent or adult, may have difficulty taking needed problem-solving steps or making decisions.

5. *Adolescence: identity versus role confusion* (teens). The question "Who am I?" is characteristically asked and thought about during this stage. This is important since it helps a young person begin to develop a better sense of self and a stronger ego-identity. Counselors who have adult clients who do not have a solid sense of self and ego-identity may need to assist the client with what many clients develop at a younger age.

6. *Young adulthood: intimacy versus isolation* (early adulthood). The outcome of this stage is the development of enhanced ability to reach out and connect with others and is the key to being able to be intimate with another and successfully build a career. The implications for counseling become apparent when this stage has not been successful.

7. *Middle age: generativity versus stagnation* (middle adulthood). During this stage the individual should be able to look beyond self-fulfillment and embrace the needs of society and future generations. Hopefully, the mature adult has the capacity to start a family, if desired, and be concerned about others outside of the family.

8. *Later life: integrity versus despair* (late adulthood). This stage is often characterized by doing a life review and developing a sense of satisfaction from looking at the past.

9. *Very old age: hope and faith versus despair* (late 80s and beyond). This stage was published by Erikson's wife (Joan) after Erikson's death (Crandell, Crandell,

& Vander Zanden, 2012) in 1994 and is based on what Erikson thought about and experienced during his later years. This stage involved facing a new sense of self connected with failing bodies and the need for the care of others. The hoped for outcome is a sense of wisdom and a feeling of transcendence.

Erikson's stages encompass the lifespan, but, interestingly, Erikson was affirmed by his peers in counseling and psychology for his work with children and adolescents. He was an innovative play therapist and promoted understanding of the identity crisis that usually occurs at the time an individual is an adolescent.

Object Relations Psychology: Donald Winnicott and Otto Kernberg

Object relations psychology provides an additional perspective on human development and how early mother–child relationships affect later personality development (Shulman, 2010). The focus of the theory is on how the child views or internalizes the relationship and how these views affect individuals as they become adults (Sharf, 2008). Object relations theorists are interested in how people separate from their mothers via a process termed *individuation*. The emphasis is on internalized relationships and differs from Freud's focus on internal drives and the manner in which they manifest in the psychosexual stages Freud described. There are many writers and theorists who have addressed object relations theory, and their contributions are described by St. Clair (2004) and Greenberg and Mitchell (1983).

BOX 2.2 PSYCHOANALYTIC THEORY AND DIVERSITY

Interestingly, because of the perceived elitist view of the use psychoanalytic theory, scholars and practitioners, including those who subscribe to object relations theory, have considered the unique experiences of gender, racial, cultural, and power dynamics inherent in mainstream society and why such factors must always be considered when applying psychoanalytic concepts and techniques. Psychoanalytic ideas on diversity have been further developed by scholars who would consider themselves psychodynamic feminist thinkers.

Donald Winnicott (1896–1971) was probably as influential as Sigmund Freud on how counseling and therapy should be facilitated. His concepts of the *transitional object*, the *good-enough mother*, and the *true self* and *false self* were influential in the development of understanding how early attachment to the mother impacts later life (Mellier, 2014; Sharf, 2008). Winnicott observed and pointed out that infants move from feeling like they control all aspects of the world they live in to an awareness of the existence of others. Winnicott (Greenberg & Mitchell, 1983) believed that a transitional object, such as a stuffed toy, baby blanket, or similar object, is instrumental in helping an infant move from experiencing himself as the center of the universe to experiencing himself as one person among other objects or persons that are not fully under his control. Central to the healthy development of the child and movement from dependence to independence is parental involvement. Winnicott (1965) used the term *good enough* to describe a mother who could respond to and meet the needs of the infant early in life and then gradually let the infant develop more and more independence. If the mother does not readily or easily respond to the infant, a true self may not develop. The *true self*, according to Winnicott, precipitates an ability to be spontaneous and real and make the distinction between himself and his mother. The *false self* can develop when there is not adequate mothering and, as a result, infants become compliant and do not separate as they should from their mothers; this can lead to many relationship problems later in life that need addressed in the process of counseling psychotherapy.

Otto Kernberg, born in Austria in 1928, has attempted to integrate object relations theory and drive theory. Much of Kernberg's work has focused on how borderline personality disorders develop. Kernberg explained the concept of *splitting* or the process of separating incompatible feelings from each other. Kernberg saw this as a normal developmental process as well as a defensive process. As noted by Sharf (2008), a child may see someone as all bad when that other person does not behave the way that is desired and does not meet expectations; the person is seen as only bad rather than as a total person with specific traits. A personality disorder develops when someone has experienced frustration when being parented and becomes angry and begins to see his mother as not good enough and may focus on feelings of anger and being threatened. As adults, such individuals find it difficult to integrate feelings of love and anger in images of themselves and others, which leads to relationship disturbances later in life.

Heinz Kohut's Self Psychology

Heinz Kohut (1913–1981) elicited reaction from both critics and followers. Kohut's self psychology emphasized narcissism as a partial description of human development rather than as a pathological condition. Kohut saw narcissism as an organizer of development so that love for self precedes love for others; this contrasted with Freud's viewpoint that narcissism was an inability to love or relate to others. As noted by Sharf (2008, p. 40), "Crucial to understanding Kohut's theory are concepts of self, object, and selfobject. Self-absorption (the grandiose self) and the attention of the powerful parent (the idealized selfobject) occur in the course of child development before the age of four. Difficulty with early developmental stages has an impact on how individuals relate to others and how they view themselves." As Kohut's work developed, he emphasized the concept of self more and more and made less and less reference to the id, ego, and superego and therefore became more and more removed from the conceptualizations of other ego and object relations psychoanalysts. Kohut believed that that a state of tension may exist between the grandiose self (the expectation of being able to get whatever is desired) and the idealized parental image (the belief that parents are wonderful and the best), which results in the development of the bipolar self. The child chooses between doing what he or she wants to do (the grandiose self) and what parents expect (the idealized selfobject). When children do not get what they want, they may have a tantrum (narcissistic rage). Kohut believed that such outbursts were normal, especially if mirroring has occurred in the context of the parent–child relationship. (Mirroring occurs when the parent shows the child she is happy with the child, thus supporting the grandiose self so that the child feels understood.) Kohut assumed that that problems developing adequate selfobjects and a strong self-concept were the reason for later disorders and appropriate topics for the counseling process.

Relational Psychoanalysis

Greenberg and Mitchell (1983) saw drive theory as very different from the views of relational theories such as object relations and self psychology. Relational therapists (Bowers & Lerner, 2013) examined their own contributions to the reactions of clients and reacted to client statements rather than just observing them (Katz, 2013):

- Each therapist will have will have an impact on the client based on his or her personality.
- Each client or therapist pairing will be unique.
- What happens in the counseling or therapy process is unpredictable.
- The therapist is a subjective rather than an objective participant.

These premises result in a less authoritarian approach to counseling and psychotherapy on the part of the counselor or therapist than what usually takes place in most of the drive, ego, object relations, and self approaches previously described (Cirio, 2012). Counselors subscribing to this theory learn how clients, past and current relationships have impacted them across the lifespan (Rothschild, 2010).

Counselors and therapists do not agree about which of these five approaches to use (drive, ego, object relations, self, or relational) to work with clients and to understand the parameters of development across the lifespan; more and more practitioners use a combination of psychoanalytic theories. In part, this is because of differences in the views of human nature and the concepts of Freud and other psychoanalytic theorists and practitioners and other theoretical frameworks, such as behavior theory, that attracted the attention of those engaged in the helping professions.

Behavioral Theories

Early forms of psychology assumed that mental life was the appropriate subject matter for psychology, and introspection was an appropriate method to engage that subject matter. In 1913, John B. Watson proposed an alternative: classical S–R behaviorism. According to Watson, behavior was a subject matter in its own right, to be studied by the observational methods common to all sciences. (Moore, 2011, p. 49)

John B. Watson and Behavioral Theory

As noted by Kalodner (2011), early behaviorism was connected to learning theory, the development of clearly defined techniques, and systematic, well-designed research. Behaviorism was developed, in part, because of a reaction against the Freudian emphasis on the unconscious as the subject matter of psychology and introspection as the method of its investigation (Moore, 2011, 2013). Emphasis was placed on observable behaviors that could be tracked and used as the basis for understanding and changing behavior as counseling and therapy progressed. John B. Watson (1878–1958) was an experimental psychologist at Johns Hopkins University and is generally recognized as one of the most influential individuals in the development of behaviorism (Kalodner, 2011).

BOX 2.3 THE FIRST PSYCHOLOGY DEPARTMENT IN THE US

The first university psychology department in the United State was located at Johns Hopkins University on the Homewood campus. Established in 1883, this department, now known as the Department of Psychological and Brain Sciences, is dedicated to research rather than clinical training and is one of the top-ranked psychology departments in the world.

The contributions of Ivan Pavlov, Edward L. Thorndike, B. F. Skinner, and Albert Bandura were also instrumental in bringing concepts of behavioral counseling to the forefront (Sharf, 2008).

Ivan Pavlov and Classical Conditioning

Classical conditioning (or respondent conditioning) explains what takes place prior to learning through the mechanism of pairing (Corey, 2013). Ivan Pavlov (1849–1936) was the point person in providing an explanation of what happens in pairing and classical conditioning through his experiments with dogs. He knew that placing food in a dog's mouth leads to salivation (respondent behavior). He noticed and recorded what happened when the food was repeatedly presented with some neutral stimulus (a stimulus that did not result in the respondent behavior of salivation). He used the pairing of the sound of a bell with food and eventually the dog would salivate to the sound of the bell alone. This, and other similar experiments, informed the process of classical conditioning, which eventually was applied to how people develop responses to the stimuli in the environment during the passage of time.

Using Pavlov's principles of classical conditioning, in which unconditioned stimuli (loud bell) paired with conditioned stimuli (white rat) lead to a conditioned response (startle), Watson trained a child named Albert (age 11 months) to fear a white rat, white cotton, and even Watson's white hair! This demonstration was important because it indicated that human emotions can be learned and modified using learning principles as a part of a counseling or treatment plan.

Thorndike, Skinner, and Operant Conditioning

Unlike classical conditioning, which emphasized the antecedents of behavior, operant conditioning (also known as instrumental conditioning) focuses on both the antecedents and consequences of behavior as a way of explaining how individuals develop behaviors across the lifespan (Sharf, 2008).

E. L. Thorndike (1874–1949) studied how people learn using controlled experimental procedures at about the same time Pavlov conducted his research. Instead of observing and learning about reflex behavior as Pavlov had done, Thorndike was interested in learning about how new behavior was learned. Thorndike used cats as subjects and placed food outside their cages and watched to see how the cats would try to get to the food by pressing a latch to escape the cage. The first escape was achieved through trial and error, but over time and through additional attempts, the escapes occurred more and more quickly. Based on these experiments, Thorndike developed the law of effect, which essentially stated that the consequences that follow behavior precipitate new learning. Thorndike identified this learning process as operant conditioning (Sharf, 2008).

The person most closely associated with the concept of operant conditioning, however, was B. F. Skinner (1904–1990), who conducted experiments similar to those of Thorndike (Holcutt, 2013) and wrote extensively about extending the principles of operant conditioning to the way people learn. Skinner was a prolific writer and wrote about applying the principles of operant conditioning to government, education, business, religion, and psychotherapy. His well-known (and much disputed) novel *Walden Two* (1948) showed how operant conditioning could provide the basis for an ideal community.

In addition to the aforementioned concepts and principles, there are many other explanations of how individuals learn and develop coping strategies across the lifespan connected with behavioral theory. The impact of positive reinforcement, extinction, generalization, discrimination, shaping, and observational learning have all been studied and analyzed as means of understanding human growth and development and as cues to how to help clients change their behavior. Readers can learn more about these concepts by reading journals such as *Behavioral Disorders*, *Behavioral Technology Today*, *Behavior Modification*, *Behavior Therapist*, and *Behavior Therapy*.

BOX 2.4 SKINNER'S SUPPORT OF FREUD

It is a little publicized fact that Skinner agreed with Freud on a number of concepts. For example, like Freud, Skinner believed that human behavior was influenced by the unconscious (the unconscious impact of environmental events rather than the impact of the Freudian constructs of the id, ego, and superego). In addition, Skinner cited Freud more than any other author and believed that psychoanalysis may have come closest to providing a unified theory of man.

Cognitive Theories

Although cognitive processes are not considered to be the cause of psychological disorders, they are a significant component. In particular, automatic thoughts that individuals may or may not be aware of can be significant in personality development. (Sharf, 2008, p. 337)

Cognitive theory and therapy are often associated with the work of Aaron Beck, born in 1921 (Giacomantonio, 2012), and they stress the importance and impact of belief systems and thinking on impacting and understanding the development of a person's behavior and emotions. Although a person's thoughts are not considered to be the sole cause of dysfunctional behaviors, they are considered to be a significant component connected with personality development across the lifespan. In addition to Beck's contributions, those of Albert Ellis and Donald Meichenbaum played major roles in the use of cognitive theories by counselors and therapists (Corey, 2013; Sharf, 2008).

Beck's Influence

Aaron Beck was dissatisfied with psychoanalysis and behavior therapy (Kalodner, 2011). Although he was originally schooled in psychoanalysis, Beck objected to the unconscious aspects of Freud's theory and believed that people can be aware of their own internal thoughts and be responsible for them. Additionally, he found behavioral explanations for human behavior to be too limited to adequately explain human emotional difficulties. For Beck, psychological disturbances may be the result of "faulty learning, making incorrect inferences on the basis of inadequate or incorrect information, and not distinguishing adequately between imagination and reality" (1976, pp. 19–20). Beck's work in cognitive therapy has been extremely influential in the treatment of depression (Pössel & Black, 2014) and has been expanded to other psychological problems.

Interestingly, Beck developed and wrote about cognitive theory and therapy at about the same time as Ellis was describing the constructs connected with rational emotive behavior therapy even though he and Beck were not working collaboratively (Corey, 2013). While working with depressed clients, Beck noticed that these clients were very negative about the way they interpreted certain life events and seemed to be guilty of engaging in cognitive distortions, which formed a set of core beliefs about themselves and others. The major cognitive distortions that Beck identified as in need of modification during counseling and psychotherapy were as follows (Corey, 2013):

- *Arbitrary inferences*: or the tendency to form conclusions without needed and supporting evidence. This includes what Beck termed *catastrophizing*, or assuming that the worst possible outcomes imaginable would occur in response to something that the individual had done or as the result of a situation the individual had created.
- *Selective abstraction*: the proclivity to form conclusions based on an isolated event or detail. For example, someone who is depressed might select only the most negative aspects of an event thus supporting the depression. When this occurs, the individual ignores all other aspects of the situation and the context in which the event occurred.
- *Overgeneralization*: the process of holding on to extreme beliefs on the basis of just one incident and applying them to other incidents or situations that are very dissimilar to the original incident.
- *Magnification or minimization*: usually means the individual views a situation to be much more or much less important than it really is given the circumstances. Operating on the basis of such viewpoints supports inaccurate conclusions.
- *Personalization*: the tendency to apply certain events or statements to themselves even though there is no basis for making such a connection.
- *Labeling and mislabeling*: the predisposition to focus one's identity on imperfections or mistakes and allowing these labels and mislabels to become the primary focus of one's identity.
- *Dichotomous thinking*: classifying experiences or other people as good or bad or as either–or extremes with no ability to see anything in between.

Cognitive theory holds that if someone has developed this way of thinking during their life course, it is possible to change such distortions and avoid engaging in dysfunctional behavior as a result.

BOX 2.5   CRITICISMS OF COGNITIVE THERAPY

Although no one disputes the fact that cognitive therapy can work, the theory underpinning this therapy is criticized because it does not provide an explanation of the causes of cognitive distortions or dysfunctional beliefs, and there is no emphasis on what mechanisms are keeping therapeutic change in place or undermining progress. In addition, the theory behind cognitive therapy is also criticized because no identified causal mechanisms can be measured before and after counseling or therapy has taken place.

Ellis, Rational Emotive Behavior Therapy, and Cognitive Behavioral Theory

As mentioned already, avoiding cognitive distortions can lead to more functional behavior. Thus, the term *cognitive behavioral* is used in conjunction with discussing cognitive theory. Albert Ellis (1913–2007) was the first of the well-known cognitive behavioral theorists. Founder of the Albert Ellis Institute in New York City, he was originally a practitioner of traditional psychoanalysis but became discouraged with the slow progress of clients. In the mid 1950s he began developing and practicing rational emotive behavior therapy, which continues to be a major cognitive behavioral approach to working with clients (Corey, 2013; Sharf, 2008). The core theory underpinning Ellis's contributions is that emotions stem mainly from beliefs and that human beings are born with potential for both rational and irrational thinking. Irrational beliefs stem from what we learn from significant others during childhood and can be recreated throughout the lifespan through repetition of early indoctrinated irrational beliefs. An individual's beliefs precipitate emotions and subsequent behaviors; rational beliefs precipitate appropriate emotions and functional behavior; and irrational beliefs precipitate inappropriate emotions and dysfunctional behavior.

Central to Ellis's theory were the concepts of responsible hedonism and humanism (Sharf, 2008). Hedonism is usually viewed as being connected with seeking pleasure and avoiding pain. According to Ellis, however, responsible hedonism is connected with maintaining pleasure over the long term by avoiding short-term pleasures that lead to pain (e.g., addictions). Ellis believed that enjoyment was a major goal in life but that individuals with a responsible view of hedonism think through the consequences of their behavior when making decisions. Ellis also believed in the humanist perspective that human beings are holistic and goal directed and are important just because they are alive; unconditional self-acceptance was essential to happiness and the realization that, although certain behaviors may have been less than ideal, these behaviors should not be viewed as the basis for questioning their worth or essence.

BOX 2.6   ALBERT ELLIS'S PRODUCTIVITY

Ellis was an extremely productive person and, until he was hospitalized with pneumonia at the age of 92 in 2006, typically worked at least 16 hours a day, writing books in longhand on legal tablets, visiting with clients, and teaching. Even after the onset of his illness and despite his profound hearing loss, Ellis kept working with the assistance of his wife, Australian psychologist Debbie Joffe. Even though Ellis spent more than a year moving back and forth between a hospital and a rehabilitation facility, he eventually returned to his residence on the top floor of the Albert Ellis Institute, where he died on July 24, 2007, in his wife's arms. Ellis authored and coauthored more than 80 books and 1,200 articles (including 800 scientific papers) during his lifetime. He died at age 93 years.

As noted earlier, even though Ellis and Beck did not collaborate and develop their theories conjointly, their notions of cognitive distortions were almost identical. In addition to the major distortions listed in the discussion of Beck's work, Ellis (1962) also emphasized musts or shouldisms such as the following:

- I must be loved by everyone I know.
- I must be entirely competent, adequate, and all achieving to have any worth.
- Since some people are wicked, they must be continuously blamed for what they do and have done.
- It is awful and terrible when things don't go the way I planned or want them to go.
- I must worry about danger and dangerous things that I cannot control.
- I must rely on someone other than myself who is stronger than I am.
- I must worry about other people's problems.
- I must find the right, correct solutions to my problems.

Ellis developed the term *musterbation* for the aforementioned types of statements and held that it leads to irrational beliefs and emotional and behavioral difficulties throughout the lifespan. Concrete application of Ellis's theory for the role of the counselor is consistently used by contemporary practitioners.

Donald Meichenbaum's Cognitive Behavior Modification

Another alternative to the cognitive theories discussed is Donald Meichenbaum's cognitive behavior modification, which focuses on client's self-verbalizations. According to Meichenbaum, a person's self-statements affect his or her behavior in much the same way as statements made by another person (Corey, 2013). The basic premise of Meichenbaum's theory is that individuals, as a precursor to changed behavior, must notice how they think, feel, and behave and the impact they have on others and learn to interrupt think, feel, and behave the scripted nature of their behavior so they can implement change. Although Meichenbaum's theory shares the same assumptions made by Beck and Ellis that upsetting emotions are the result of irrational thoughts, his theory emphasizes helping individuals become more aware of their self-talk and the stories they tell about themselves (Corey, 2013). In addition, Meichenbaum suggests that it may be more effective to behave our way into new thinking than to think our way into new behavior. According to Meichenbaum, the only way a person can change what has become habitual during the course of a lifetime is to engage first in self-observation, then in starting a new internal dialogue, and finally in learning new skills (Meichenbaum, 2007).

Bandura and Social Cognitive Theory

Social cognitive theory, formerly known as social learning theory, was developed by Stanford University psychologist Albert Bandura (born in 1925). Bandura believed that people are cognitive beings and that their processing of information plays a central role in the way they learn, behave, and develop over a lifetime (Gilson, Chow, & Feltz, 2012). Bandura agreed with Skinner that operant conditioning is an important aspect of learning, but he also believed that people think ahead to the consequences of their behavior, are able to anticipate those consequences, and are often more influenced by what they think will happen than the consequences they actually experience (Sigelman & Rider, 2012). Bandura also believed that people learn to reinforce or punish themselves using their thoughts and these reinforcements or punishments also affect their behavior. Interestingly, Bandura wanted his theory to be called social cognitive theory instead of social learning theory because he wanted to separate his ideas from those of Watson and Skinner because his theory is about the motivating and self-regulating role of cognition in human behavior (Heydari, Dashtgard, & Moghadam, 2014).

BOX 2.7 BANDURA'S BOBO DOLL EXPERIMENT

Bandura's most famous experiment was the 1961 Bobo doll experiment, in which he filmed a woman beating up a Bobo doll and shouting aggressive words. After the film was then shown to a group of children, the children were allowed to play in a room that contained a Bobo doll. The children immediately began to beat the doll and imitated the actions and words of the woman in the film. The study was significant because it departed from the behavioral position that all behavior is controlled by reinforcement or rewards. Since the children received no encouragement or incentives to beat up the doll, they were simply imitating the behavior they had observed. Bandura termed this phenomenon *observational learning* and characterized the elements of effective observational learning as attention, retention, reciprocation, and motivation.

Bandura also emphasized that observational learning was the most important mechanism through which human behavior changes. By making this point, Bandura made his cognitive emphasis very clear as well as the power of observing models (other people) and imitating their behavior (Sharf, 2008). As time passed, Bandura began studying human agency (or the ways people exert cognitive control over themselves, their environments, and their lives) in addition to the study of observational learning. Bandura noted that even infants learn to make things happen in their worlds. As time passes, individuals develop high or low senses of self-efficacy in certain areas of activity (Yiu, Cheung, & Siu, 2012). (Self-efficacy is the belief that a person can successfully achieve desired outcomes in a specified area, e.g., completing an advanced degree, applying for a promotion at work, learning a foreign language.) Although Watson and Skinner believed that people are more or less passively influenced by the environment, Bandura believed that people are active, cognitive beings and that human development occurs because of continuous reciprocal interaction among the person, his or her behavior, and his or her environment (Sharf, 2008). Bandura did not believe that the environment ruled; rather, he believed that people choose, build, and change their environments through a process he called *reciprocal determinism*. In a sense, people's traits and behaviors influence the people around them just as the people around an individual exert influence on the individual (Oppong, 2014). Bandura also believed that human development is context specific, can proceed among many alternative paths, and is continuously developing throughout a lifetime.

Piaget and Cognitive Developmental Theory

Jean Piaget (1896–1980), a Swiss psychologist who began to study children's intellectual development during the 1920s, has also had a profound effect on how we view human growth and development across the lifespan (Sigelman & Rider, 2012). Piaget's interest in cognitive development began to take shape while he worked at the Alfred Binet laboratories in Paris, where the first standardized IQ test was developed. In the process of testing children, Binet became interested in why children answered questions incorrectly rather than correctly. He began to interview children about why they answered certain questions as they did and noted the similarities of answers among children of approximately the same age and how these answers were different from the answers of older children. He concluded that the differences were not because younger children knew less than older children but that younger children think in a qualitatively different way than older children. As a result of Binet's influence Piaget developed a developmental theory that described changes in the way individuals think from infancy to adolescence (Sigelman & Rider, 2012):

- The *sensorimotor* stage is from birth to 2 years, and, at first, infants use their senses and motor actions to begin to explore and understand the world. At the beginning of this stage, they use only innate reflexes, but by the end of the stage they are beginning to be capable of symbolic thought using images or words to problem solve.
- The *preoperational* stage is from 2 to 7 years, and individuals use the ability for symbolic thought to develop language capacity, participate in pretend play, and problem solve. During this stage thinking is not logical; the child is very egocentric and is easily fooled by perceptions.
- The *concrete operations* stage is from 7 to 11 years, and during this stage children acquire concrete operations that enable them to mentally classify, add, and act on concrete objects in their heads. They can solve practical and real-world problems but experience difficulty understanding hypothetical and abstract situations and problems.
- The *formal operations* stage develops at 11 or 12 years of age and older. During this stage adolescents can understand and address abstract concepts and hypothetical possibilities and can anticipate long-range consequences of possible behaviors. As time passes and experience accumulates, they can develop hypotheses and systematically evaluate them employing scientific methods.

BOX 2.8 CHALLENGES TO PIAGET'S THEORY

Piaget's theory, though vital in understanding child psychology, did not go without criticism. A main figure whose ideas contradicted Piaget's ideas was the Russian psychologist Lev Vygotsky, who stressed the influence a child's cultural background has on the stages of development. Because different cultures stress different social interactions, he challenged Piaget's idea that the hierarchy of learning development had to develop in succession.

Counselors can use Piaget's theory to better understand how clients of a certain chronological age think and act and inform what they might need to do in the process of developing a counseling or treatment plan.

Vygotsky's Sociocultural Viewpoint

Lev Vygotsky (1896–1934) was a Russian psychologist who was born in 1896, the same year at Piaget (Sigelman & Rider, 2012). He was an active scholar at about the same time as Piaget, but his work was banned for political reasons in Russia. Americans did not initially embrace his work due to lack of translations into English. Vygotsky's main message was that cognitive development occurs in the context of his or her culture and develops based on a child's social interaction in that culture (Sigelman & Rider, 2012). It is interesting to note that, even though Vygotsky died at the age of 38, he wrote more than 200 scientific publications and was even later referred to as the Mozart of psychology (Salonen, 2013).

BOX 2.9 MORE ABOUT VYGOTSKY

Zone of proximal development (ZPD) and *scaffolding* were two terms coined by Vygotsky. ZPD was Vygotsky's term for the range of tasks that a child is in the process of learning to complete. The lower limit of ZPD is the level of skill reached by the child working independently (also referred to as the child's actual developmental level). The upper limit is the level of potential skill that the child is able to reach with the assistance of a capable instructor.

Scaffolding is a concept closely related to the idea of ZPD. Scaffolding refers to changing the level of support to match the cognitive potential of the child. Over the course of a teaching session, one can adjust the amount of guidance to fit the child's potential level of performance. More support is offered when a child is having difficulty with a particular task, and, over time, less support is provided as the child makes gains on the task. Ideally, scaffolding works to maintain the child's potential level of development in the ZPD.

Vygotsky believed that the group or culture is closely tied to the way a child's cognitive growth occurs and that a child's social interaction affects how thinking occurs. Moreover, the development of personality is closely tied to cultural context (Christy, 2013). As noted by Crandell et al. (2012), the major premises of Vygotsky's work are as follows:

- The way an individual develops is tied to early formative years and has historical characteristics depending on when and where the individual grew up.
- As changes occur in a person's social situation and activities, the development of the individual reflects these changes.
- As a person observes what someone is doing or saying, these activities and language characteristics are likely to become internalized.
- A systematic use of signs and symbols (language) must be available for a person to internalize activities and communication patterns.
- An individual assimilates the values of a culture by being part of the culture and interacting with others who are part of the culture.

The implications of the aforementioned premises emphasize how important it is for all counselors to be culturally sensitive and to avoid imposing their own values and outlooks on clients who grew up in a different context. Alexander Luria (1902–1977), a colleague of Vygotsky's, provided additional credence to Vygotsky's theory when he tested groups of children ages 9 to 12 years who grew up in very different (rural vs. urban) environments by giving them key or target words to respond to with the first thing that came to mind (Sigelman & Rider, 2012). Luria discovered that children growing up in rural communities with more limited social experience gave very similar responses to one another, but that these responses were very different from those of children residing in urban areas (who also gave very similar responses to one another). Luria concluded and agreed with Vygotsky that knowledge depends on social experience as well as a variety of tools. These tools are things like spoken language, writing, and problem solving, and they are culturally embedded, transmitted through social interaction, and influence how a person understands the world and interacts with others.

Urie Bronfenbrenner's Ecological Theory

An important viewpoint that also considers human development as related to the culture and environment is the ecological theory of Urie Bronfenbrenner (1917–2005). Bronfenbrenner wanted to move away from the outlook of traditionalists, who focused on either the environment or the person to understand human development and the relationship between them, since people do not develop in a vacuum but rather they grow up embedded in a particular environment.

Bronfenbrenner examined the mutual accommodation that occurs between the developing person and the changing contexts of four levels of environmental influence: the *microsystem*, the *mesosystem*, the *exosystem*, and the *macrosystem* (Figure 2.1). The microsystem consists of the network of social systems and physical settings a person is part of every day. It might include parents and grandparents,

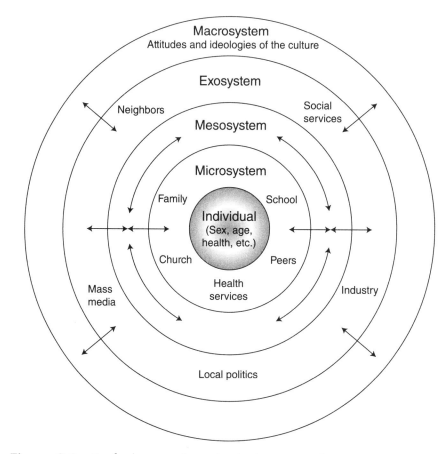

Figure 2.1 Brofenbrenner's ecological systems theory.

extended family members, siblings, neighbors, peers, school, and church. The mesosystem consists of the interrelationships between the social systems and physical settings in which the person is immersed and how they affect the development of the person. For example, one child's parents may value academic achievement, be involved in their child's educational experience, and stress the importance of college, whereas the parents of a peer may see schooling as positive because it provides daily structure so the parents can be at work while their child is in school. The environment that is external to the developing person is the exosystem and consists of social structures that directly or indirectly affect a person's life. This could be the church, the school, the government, mass media, and a variety of social networks. The macrosystem consists of broad patterns that are expressed in a culture. For example, some countries emphasize paternity as well as maternity leaves or automatic access to health care or post–high school education more than what exists in the United States.

Bronfenbrenner recognized the simultaneous impacts of these nested environments on a person's development and encouraged researchers and clinicians to view people in the context of these four environments to understand why people may react differently to the same situation. Bronfenbrenner also increased awareness of the fact that, as time passes and environments change, the same phenomenon may be viewed differently at a subsequent age or stage of development. For example, advancing age and the meaning of life may be viewed one way at age 22 years and quite differently by the same person at age 62 years.

John Bowlby's Attachment Theory

John Bowlby (1907–1990) was a British psychologist well known for his interest in child development and for his seminal writing and research on attachment theory (Slater, 2007). Bowlby was very dissatisfied with traditionally accepted theories and sought answers from such fields as evolutionary biology, ethology, developmental psychology, cognitive science, and control systems theory, and he drew upon them to formulate new insights about infant attachment (Stroebe & Archer, 2013). Bowlby really did not agree with Freud's drive theory and wanted to develop a more up-to-date theory. Attachment theory is the dominant theory used today in the study of infant and toddler behavior, infant mental health, counseling, and therapy with children, and Bowlby's theory was complemented and supplemented by a colleague, Mary Ainsworth, a Canadian-American psychologist.

As noted by Mercer (2006), Bowlby's theory emphasizes four areas:

1. Children between the ages of 6 months and about 30 months usually develop emotional attachments to familiar caregivers (who may or may not be the parents), especially if the adults recognize and respond to child communications.
2. Young children reveal their emotional attachments by their preferences for particular familiar people, their tendencies to want to be in close proximity to those people, especially in times of distress, and their desires to use these adults as secure bases from which to explore the environment.
3. The early formation of emotional attachments contributes to the foundation of later emotional and personality development, and the kinds of behaviors shown by toddlers to familiar adults have some continuity to the social behaviors they will show later in life.
4. Events that interfere with attachment, such as abrupt separation of the toddler from familiar people or the inability of caregivers to be sensitive, responsive, or consistent in their interactions, have short-term, and possible long-term, negative impacts on the child's emotional and cognitive life.

Four different attachment classifications have been identified in children: secure attachment, anxious-ambivalent attachment, anxious-avoidant attachment, and disorganized attachment. All four of these classifications have implications for counselors working with both children and adults. *Secure attachment* is thought to be the best attachment style. Secure attachment occurs when children feel secure in the presence of their caregivers. A toddler who is securely attached to his or her parent (or other caregiver) will usually explore freely while the caregiver is present, typically engages with strangers, is often visibly upset when the caregiver departs, and is generally happy to see the caregiver return. *Anxious-ambivalent attachment* takes place when the infant experiences separation anxiety when separated from the caregiver and does not feel reassured when the caregiver returns. In general, a child with an anxious-ambivalent attachment style will typically explore little and is often wary of strangers, even when the parent is present. When the mother or caregiver departs, the child is often highly distressed. *Anxious-avoidant attachment* is characterized by the infant avoiding parents or caregivers. A child with an anxious-avoidant attachment style often shows little emotion when the caregiver departs or returns. The child will not explore very much regardless of who is there. *Disorganized attachment* occurs when there is a lack of attachment behavior. Infants experiencing disorganized attachment exhibit overt displays of fear; contradictory behaviors, or affects occurring simultaneously or sequentially; stereotypic, asymmetric, misdirected, or jerky movements; or freezing and apparent dissociation. In the 1980s, the theory was extended to attachment in adults. Attachment applies to adults when adults feel close attachment to their parents and their romantic partners.

Carl Rogers's Phenomenological Worldview

The person-centered theory of Carl Rogers (1902–1987) was, and still is, one of the most popular in the psychology, counseling, and education professions. His perceptions of people and the way a supportive environment assists in their development across the lifespan have had an impact on a wide variety of the helping professions (Hazler, 2011). His view of human nature was a major deviation from the psychoanalytic and behavioral models for working with people and understanding personality development that were predominant in the early part of the 20th century.

BOX 2.10   CARL ROGERS'S INFLUENCE

Carl Ransom Rogers was an extremely influential American counselor and therapist and among the founders of the humanistic approach to working with clients. Rogers is widely considered to be one of the founding fathers of psychotherapy research and was honored for his pioneering research with the Award for Distinguished Scientific Contributions by the American Psychological Association (APA) in 1956.

Rogers viewed individuals as possessing inherent qualities that made growth possible; he believed that attempting to change basic personality characteristics or behaviors was not necessary. He maintained that people viewed the world and people around them from their own unique perspective; this perspective is referred to as a *phenomenological* perspective. In addition, Rogers believed that, no matter what that phenomenological view of the world was, all people are continually attempting to actualize their best and most productive selves. As noted by Hazler (2011), such a positive and optimistic view was often challenged by those who called attention to the fact that there are unlimited opportunities to observe people thinking and acting in ways that are harmful to themselves and others. But Rogers believed such thoughts and actions were reflections of a distorted view of oneself and the world caused by trying to meet the expectations of others rather than trying to actualize one's own self.

BOX 2.11　THE EVOLUTION OF ROGERS'S THINKING

Rogers originally developed his theory to be the foundation for a system of therapy. He initially called this *nondirective therapy* but later replaced the term nondirective with *client centered* and then later *person centered*.

Rogers's person-centered view of people is based on four key beliefs: 1) people are trustworthy; 2) people innately move toward self-actualization and health; 3) people have the inner resources to move themselves in positive directions; and 4) people respond to their uniquely perceived world (phenomenological world). The activation of these characteristics within a person's external environment brings about the most desirable aspects of development across the lifespan. The foundation of person-centered theory is anchored in a set of beliefs about people and relationships rather than a series of programmable verbal and behavioral techniques (Hazler, 2011). Rogers believed:

- *No two people see the world exactly alike.* According to the phenomenological approach, no two individuals can be expected to view things in exactly the same way. Counselors and therapists must recognize that whatever their clients personally believe reality is will be different and that each client will have a unique perspective.
- *People make simple mistakes in judgment.* People make choices that appear to be the correct ones for them, but they are ineffective because the choices match the perceived world of those around them rather than being based on an individual's own best judgment. People are attempting to act in ways they believe others would have them act (conditions of worth) rather than trusting their own positive, growth-oriented nature.
- *The client has the ability to actualize potential.* Person-centered counselors place tremendous confidence in clients even though they know that they will make mistakes in judgment. Such confidence is based on the belief that people are innately good and always seek a fully functioning experience in the world

even though they make mistakes. People's tendency to actualize potential in positive ways is the driving force recognized by the person-centered counselor who seeks to free the client from self-induced constraints.

• *The perceived world of the client may not approximate the world sought.* People experience difficulties because sometimes the world they perceive is not congruent with the world they would naturally seek for themselves. The natural, growth-oriented, self-trusting nature of these people collides with their chosen world, because they continually look outside their true selves for decisions. Their behavior is based on perceptions of what other people think is right and this results in decisions and actions that are not personally fulfilling. This conflict is termed *incongruence.*

• *Congruent individuals trust their worldview.* Congruent people trust their view of the world and their ability to act on their basic positive nature and generally gain the acceptance they expect. They feel confident about reacting spontaneously because of they believe they can differentiate between appropriate and inappropriate behaviors.

BOX 2.12 ROGERS AND CROSS-CULTURAL RELATIONS

During the latter part of Rogers's life, he began to apply his theory to cross-cultural relations and facilitated workshops in highly stressful situations and global locations including conflicts and challenges in South Africa, Central America, and Ireland. Along with Alberto Zucconi and Charles Devonshire, he cofounded the Istituto dell' Approccio Centrato sulla Persona (Person-Centered Approach Institute) in Rome, Italy.

Rogers's international work for peace culminated in the Rust Peace Workshop, which took place in November 1985 in Rust, Austria. Leaders from 17 nations convened to discuss the topic "The Central America Challenge." The meeting was notable for several reasons: it brought national figures together as people (not as their positions), it was a private event, and it was an overwhelmingly positive experience during which participants heard one another and established personal connections. It was very different than stiffly formal and regulated diplomatic meetings.

Rogers's theory maintains that people develop in self-fulfilling ways when the process of change is facilitated through a helping relationship guided by the presence of three basic conditions: genuineness, acceptance and caring, and empathic understanding.

THEORIES AND THEIR APPLICATION
TO COUNSELING CLIENTS

This chapter provides thumbnail sketches of theoretical frameworks that can be used as points of departure for counseling clients. These brief theory overviews serve only as an introduction to the more thorough study of theories of counseling and psychotherapy that are always components of master's and doctoral programs in counseling, counseling psychology, and counselor education, and they are not meant to be to take the place of more careful consideration and study. They are meant, however, to convey the idea that inherent in each theory there are constructs that can be used to illuminate human growth and development across the lifespan. In addition, each theoretical framework provides practicing counselors with insight about what to listen for and emphasize during the counseling process and, in many instances, the kinds of techniques that can be used to precipitate change. The challenge for beginning and practicing counselors and therapists is to develop a preferred way of working or a personal theory of counseling and psychotherapy based on a psychological theory or theories.

How can counselors develop a preferred way of working with clients? The answer to this question is complex and is not one that most counselors answer until they have done considerable introspection and have accumulated experience with a variety of clients. In fact, it often takes years of introspection, counseling experience, and supervised practice to formulate a personal theory. Many counselors and therapists continue to revise their conceptualizations of the best way to approach the therapeutic alliance throughout their tenures as practicing counselors for a number of reasons. For example, the personality traits of the counselor or therapist have a definite impact on what theory or theories are of high interest to the counselor or therapist in search of a conceptual frame of reference. The value a counselor places on early childhood experience; observable versus non-observable elements or behavior in the life of a client; and the role of cognitions, culture, or a supportive environment all become parameters for consideration in the counselor's search for the most meaningful way to approach the therapeutic alliance. As subsequent chapters of this textbook are read and considered, it is our hope that the reader will be able to address the physical, cognitive, social, and emotional needs of a given client at a specific stage of his or her development through the application of the theory or theories that inform a preferred way of working with clients.

SUMMARY

This chapter provided an overview of psychological theories that can be used to develop perspective on how human growth and development occur across the lifespan. Freud's drive theory; the ego psychology of Anna Freud and Erik Erikson; the object relations psychology of Donald Winnicott and Otto Kernberg;

Heinz Kohut's self psychology; the relational psychology and perspectives of Greenberg and Mitchell; the behavioral theories of John Watson, Ivan Pavlov, E. L. Thorndike, and B. F. Skinner; the cognitive theories of Aaron Beck, Albert Ellis, and Donald Meichenbaum; Albert Bandura's social cognitive theory; Jean Piaget's cognitive developmental theory; Lev Vygotsky's sociocultural viewpoint; Urie Brofenbrenner's ecological theory; John Bowlby's attachment theory; and Carl Rogers's phenomenological worldview were all selected and presented as examples of theoretical perspectives available to enhance understanding of human development. The chapter concluded with a brief discussion of theories and their application to counseling clients.

USEFUL WEBSITES

Freudian Drive Theory
http://www.personality-development.org/theories-personality-development/sigmound-freud
Freud's Psychoanalytic Theory of Personality
https://www.boundless.com/psychology/textbooks/boundless-psychology-textbook/personality-16/psychodynamic-perspective-on-personality-77/freud-s-psychoanalytic-theory-of-personality-304-12839/
Anna Freud
http://www.annafreud.org/
Erik Erikson
http://www.erikson.edu/about/history/erik-erikson/
Otto Kernberg
http://www.psybc.com/pdfs/library/KERNBERG.pdf
Heinz Kohut
http://www.practicalphilosophy.net/?page_id=426
John Watson
http://www.lifecircles-inc.com/Learningtheories/behaviorism/Watson.html
Ivan Pavlov
http://education-portal.com/academy/lesson/ivan-pavlov-and-classical-conditioning-theory-experiments-contributions-to-psychology.html#lesson
E. L. Thorndike
http://www.lifecircles-inc.com/Learningtheories/behaviorism/Thorndike.html
B. F. Skinner
http://www.instructionaldesign.org/theories/operant-conditioning.html
Aaron Beck
http://www.beckinstitute.org/history-of-cbt/
Albert Ellis
http://www.albertellis.org
Albert Bandura
http://www.instructionaldesign.org/theories/social-learning.html.

Jean Piaget
http://www.icels-educators-for-learning.ca/index.php?option=com_
    content&view=article&id=46&Itemid=61
Urie Bronfenbrenner
http://www.mentalhelp.net/poc/view_doc.php?type=doc&id=7930
John Bowlby
http://www.psychology.sunysb.edu/attachment/online/inge_origins.pdf
Carl Rogers
http://www.newworldencyclopedia.org/entry/Carl_Rogers

REFERENCES

Beck, A. T. (1976). *Cognitive therapy and emotional disorders*. New York, NY: International Universities Press.

Bowers, E. P., & Lerner, R. M. (2013). Familial and nonfamilial relationships as ecological sources of health and positive development across the life span: A view of the issues. *Research in Human Development, 10*(2), 111–115. doi:10.1080/15427609.2013.786535

Bush, M. (1978). Preliminary considerations for a psychoanalytic theory of insight. *International Review of Psycho-Analysis, 5*(1), 1–13.

Capuzzi, D., & Gross, D .R. (Eds.). (2011). *Counseling and psychotherapy: Theories and interventions* (5th ed.). Alexandria, VA: American Counseling Association.

Carducci, B. J. (2007). *The psychology of personality: Viewpoints, research, and applications* (2nd ed.). Hoboken, NJ: Wiley.

Christy, T. C. (2013). Vygotsky, cognitive development and language. *Historiographia Linguistica, 40*(1–2), 199–227. doi:10.1075/hl.40.1.07chr

Cirio, P. A. (2012). Impact and influence of relational psychoanalysis. *International Journal of Psycho-Analysis, 93*(3), 495–497. doi:10.1111/j.1745-8315.2012.00569.x

Corey, G. (2013). *Theory and practice of counseling and psychotherapy* (9th ed.). Belmont, CA: Brooks/Cole, Cengage Learning.

Crandell, T. L., Crandell, C. H., & Vander Zanden, J. W. (2012). *Human development* (10th ed.). New York, NY: McGraw-Hill.

Dimen, M. (1999). Between lust and libido: Sex, psychoanalysis, and the moment before. *Psychoanalytic Dialogues, 9*, 415–440.

Ellis, A. (1962). *Reason and emotion in psychotherapy*. Secaucus, NJ: Lyle Stuart.

Erikson, E. H. (1963). Childhood and Society (2nd ed.). New York: Norton.

Freud, A. (1936). *The ego and mechanisms of defense*. New York, NY: International Universities Press.

Freud, A. (1965). Normality and pathology in childhood: Assessments of development. In *Writings* (Vol. 6.). New York, NY: International Universities Press.

Fuchsman, K. (2001). What does Freud mean by the oedipus complex? *Free Associations, 9A*, 82–118.

Gabbard, G. O. (1979). Stage fright. *International Journal of Psychoanalysis, 60*, 383–392.

Giacomantonio, S. G. (2012). Three problems with the theory of cognitive therapy. *American Journal of Psychotherapy, 66*(4), 375–390.

Gilson, T. A., Chow, G. M., & Feltz, D. L. (2012). Self-efficacy and athletic squat performance: Positive or negative influences at the within- and between-levels of analysis. *Journal of Applied Social Psychology, 42*(6), 1467–1485. doi:10.1111/j.1559-1816.2012.00908.x

Greenburg, J. R., & Mitchell, S. A. (1983). *Object relations in psychoanalytic theory.* Cambridge, MA: Harvard University Press.

Hazler, R. J. (2011). Person-centered theory. In D. Capuzzi & D. Gross (Eds.), *Counseling and psychotherapy: Theories and interventions* (pp. 143–166). Alexandria, VA: American Counseling Association.

Heimann, P. (1962). Notes on the anal stage. *International Journal of Psychoanalysis, 43*, 406–414.

Heydari, A., Dashtgard, A., & Moghadam, Z. E. (2014). The effect of Bandura's social cognitive theory implementation on addiction quitting of clients referred to addiction quitting clinics. *Iranian Journal of Nursing & Midwifery Research, 19*(1), 19–23.

Hoare, C. H. (2005). Erikson's general and adult developmental revisions of Freudian thought: "Outward, forward, upward." *Journal of Adult Development, 12*(1), 19–31. doi:10.1007/S10804-005-1279-0

Holcutt, M. (2013). The fruits and fallacies of Fred Skinner on freedom. *Independent Review, 18*(2), 263–278.

Howes, D. (1997). Oedipus out of the Trobriands: Sensory order, erotogenic zones, and psychosexual development in the Massim region of Papua New Guinea. *Psychoanalytic Psychology, 14*, 43–63.

Jaffe, D. S. (1982). Aggression: Instinct, drive, behavior. *Psychoanalytic Inquiry, 2*, 77–94.

Johnson, A. (2011). Psychoanalytic theory. In D. Capuzzi & D. Gross (Eds.), *Counseling and psychotherapy: Theories and interventions* (pp. 59–76). Alexandria, VA: American Counseling Association.

Kalodner, C. R. (2011). Cognitive-behavioral theory. In D. Capuzzi & D. Gross (Eds.), *Counseling and psychotherapy: Theories and interventions* (pp. 193–214). Alexandria, VA: American Counseling Association.

Katz, S. (2013). General psychoanalytic field theory: Its structure and applications to psychoanalytic perspectives. *Psychoanalytic Inquiry, 33*(3), 277–292. doi:10.1080/07351690.2013.779894

Meichenbaum, D. (2007). Stress inoculation: A preventive and treatment approach. In P. M. Leher, R. L. Woolfolk, & W. Sime (Eds.), *Principles and practices of stress management* (3rd ed., pp. 497–518). New York, NY: Guilford Press.

Mellier, D. (2014). The psychic envelopes in psychoanalytic theories of infancy. *Frontiers in Psychology, 5*, 1–16. doi:10.3389/fpsyg.2014.00734

Mercer, J. (2006). *Understanding attachment.* Westport, CT: Praeger.

Moore, J. (2011). Behaviorism. *Psychological Record, 61*(3), 449–465.

Moore, J. (2013). Three views of behaviorism. *Psychological Record, 63*(3), 681–691. doi:10.11133/j.tpr.2013.63.3.020

Nevid, J. S. (2009). *Essentials of psychology: Concepts and applications* (2nd ed.). Belmont, CA: Wadsworth.

Oppong, S. (2014). Between Bandura and Giddens: Structuration theory in social psychological research? *Psychological Thought, 7*(2), 111–123. doi:10.5964/psyct.v7i2.104

Pössel, P., & Black, S. W. (2014). Testing three different sequential mediational interpretations of Beck's cognitive model of the development of depression. *Journal of Clinical Psychology, 70*(1), 72–94. doi:10.1002/jclp.22001

Rothschild, D. (2010). Partners in treatment: Relational psychoanalysis and harm reduction therapy. *Journal of Clinical Psychology, 66*(2), 136–149. doi:10.1002/jclp.20670

Salonen, L. (2013). L. S. Vygotsky's psychology and theory of learning applied to the rehabilitation of aphasia: A developmental and systemic view. *Aphasiology, 27*(5), 615–635. doi:10.1080/02687038.2013.780284

Schneider, M. (1988). Primary envy and the creation of the ego ideal. *International Review of Psychoanalysis, 15*, 319–329.

Sharf, R. S. (2008). *Theories of psychotherapy and counseling: Concepts and cases* (4th ed.). Belmont, CA: Brooks/Cole, Cengage Learning.

Shulman, G. (2010). The damaged object: A "strange attractor" in the dynamical system of the mind. *Journal of Child Psychotherapy, 36*(3), 259–288. doi: 10.1080/0075417X.2010.523814

Siegelman, C. K., & Rider, E. A. (2012). *Lifespan human development* (7th ed.). Belmont, CA: Wadsworth, Cengage Learning

Skinner, B. F. (1948). *Walden two*. New York, NY: Macmillan.

Slater, R. (2007). Attachment: Theoretical development and critique. *Educational Psychology in Practice, 23* (3), 205–219.

St. Clair, M. (2004). *Object relations and self psychology: An introduction* (4th ed.). Belmont, CA: Wadsworth.

Stroebe, M. S., & Archer, J. (2013). Origins of modern ideas on love and loss: Contrasting forerunners of attachment theory. *Reviews of General Psychology, 17*(1), 28–39. doi:10.1037/a0030030

Thomas, B. (2008). Seeing and being seen: Courage and the therapist in cross-racial treatment. *Psychoanalytic Social Work, 15*(1), 60–68.

Winnicott, D. W. (1965). *The maturational processes and the facilitating environment*. New York, NY: International Universities Press.

Yiu, T. W., Cheung, S. O., & Siu, L. Y. (2012). Application of Bandura's self-efficacy theory to examining the choice of tactics in construction dispute negotiation. *Journal of Construction Engineering & Management, 138*(3), 331–340. doi:10.1061/(ASCE)CO.1943-7862.0000403

The Many Facets of Human Development: Spiritual and Moral Developmental Theories

Mark D. Stauffer, Jeff Cook,
Robyn Trippany-Simmons, and
Tiffany Rush-Wilson

When asked about the best and worst of what humanity has to offer, a continuum would emerge along the lines of moral and spiritual development. The great leaders of our time were more than moral, ethical, and political change agents; they were spiritual leaders from various cultural backgrounds. Although constructs such as spirituality are hard to define and religious and moral development can be sensitive areas of cultural difference, spiritual and moral development should not be overlooked. This chapter does not cover all of the models for spiritual development and moral development. World cultures are rich in the ways and means of moral, spiritual, and religious development. This chapter provides an introduction, some additional resources on the topic, and some of the most noted theories in the field of counseling.

SPIRITUAL DEVELOPMENT

For decades, the counseling professional deemphasized spirituality and religion in counseling, perhaps relegating it to the realm of personal belief or faith, because spirituality deals with transcendence. It may reflect a cultural rift or taboo in higher education, which separated what was scientific and political from what was religious (Love, 2001). Indeed, the topics of spirituality and religion are rarely part of the required counseling curriculum. Coverage of the topics may at times be infused in courses, or perhaps focused on because they are part of an explicit faith-based counseling or pastoral counseling program. With transitions toward multicultural and social justice orientations, the field has moved closer to acknowledging that spirituality and religion should not be ignored in coursework, let alone in counseling sessions. Furthermore, it is desirable and useful to address this realm in counseling.

BOX 3.1   HOW WOULD YOU HANDLE THESE SCENARIO?

Consider these scenarios and how you might handle these as a counselor:

- In group, a client expresses anger and hurt and defames a religious tradition based on past traumas. Another member of the group has mentioned how much they value and grow from that same religious tradition.
- A 7-year-old child recently lost a parent during a violent crime and asks you, "Why did God do this?"
- A client has intense euphoria and unusual bodily sensations after a weeklong meditation retreat. She asks whether this is a spiritual experience or something wrong with her mind.
- A client states that he is a devout observer of his religion and wants to know if you share his belief.
- A client believes that she is not growing in her religious and spiritual tradition, and she asks you what to do, knowing that you do not share her religious background.
- A client asks you whether he can come to counseling to focus on spirituality.
- A client claims an uncommon, possibly supernatural, experience derived from her religious and spiritual practice, one that you have not had and have a hard time understanding.

Do counselors have a choice about whether or not they address spirituality in counseling? The research suggests that clients will bring issues of religion and spirituality into counseling and that counselors need to be skilled helpers in this realm (Pargament, Loman, McGee, & Fang, 2014; Plumb, 2011; Post, Wade, & Cornish,

2014). Issues of religion and spirituality enter the counseling session and directly relate to mental health and wellness outcomes (Exline & Rose, 2013). Counselors help clients make positive developmental changes in all aspects of life, so they must become comfortable and competent to be of use. One central competency of the spiritual competencies endorsed by the American Counseling Association (ACA) and the Association for Spirituality, Ethical, and Religious Values in Counseling (ASERVIC) stresses that the professional counselor be able to "describe and apply various models of spiritual and/or religious development and their relationship to human development" (ASERVIC, 2009, Competency 6). Being comfortable and competent does not mean that one needs to perform spiritual counseling or have a theoretical orientation that focuses on spirituality. Often a clinical mental health counselor may refer a client to a pastoral counselor, spiritual director, or appropriate clergy for religious direction. It does, however, mean that religion and spirituality are integrated into counseling to meet the client's worldview and counseling-related concerns.

Spirituality has been defined in various ways as a scientific construct, but in short it relates to those elements of experience that may be attributed to what is transcendent, ultimate in meaning, and is divine and may or may not relate to religiosity. Generally defined, religion refers to the traditions and institutions arranged around spirituality and spiritual development. So the field differentiates between spirituality and religion; they are not mutually exclusive (Exline, Pargament, Grubbs, & Yali, 2014). All clients are considered to have spiritual elements, even when they are not religious, as they wrestle with questions such as: Who am I? What happens when I die? What is my life about? Is there life beyond this world? How did we get here? Why do I feel disconnected from my life and world? Is my religion correct? At other times clients will have spiritual questions that relate to their religious affiliation or context. Regardless of whether religion is part of a client's spiritual experience, counselors must be ready and competent to help clients with spirituality and questions that arise. They work with clients on spiritual development because spiritual development reflects a "dimension of human life and experience as significant as cognitive development, emotional development or social development" (Roehlkepartain, King, Wagner, & Benson, 2006, p. 9). It is a universal human process affecting multidimensional domain of self and context.

The professional fields have conceptualized development with stage-based linear approaches as well as approaches based on constructivism. Stage-based models point toward spiritual development as qualitative changes over time in a person's life ending up in some type of final stage of development. Constructivism encourages interpretive approaches to development. From this lens, researchers and clinicians are concerned about how the client with a given context understands certain phenomena. For example, they might examine how cultural identity development and meaning making occur for different members of a Catholic, Filipino immigrant family to Vancouver, British Columbia, a culturally diverse, Beta global city. Importantly, counselors must understand and apply both stage-based and constructivist views of spiritual and moral development because both lenses are helpful in their own way. For example, stage-based models can provide forward leaning motivation, directionality, and a clearer picture of how one's capacity to grow can be influenced by opportunity and context.

FAITH DEVELOPMENT THEORY

For more than three decades, James Fowler's *faith development theory* (FDT) has impacted the fields of religious education, pastoral education, and psychology (Parker, 2010). Fowler earned his PhD in religion and society from Harvard University in 1971 and has taught at Emory's Chandler School of Theology since 1977. FDT developed out of Fowler's attempt to merge practical theological experience and developmental psychology. In this attempt, Fowler draws from the psychosocial psychology of Erik Erikson, the cognitive-structural psychologies of Jean Piaget and Lawrence Kohlberg, and the theology and philosophies of Paul Tillich and Richard Niebuhr (Fowler, 1981; Parker, 2010). The result is a linear, seven-stage, developmental model that Fowler called faith development theory.

As Fowler wove together developmental psychology and theology, he concluded that the best term to use was faith rather than religion or spirituality (Fowler, 1981; Parker, 2009). Fowler (1981) argues that faith is universal, whereas religious experience is more culturally nuanced. Faith is a person's or group's way of "finding coherence in and giving meaning to the multiple forces that make up our lives. Faith is a person's way of seeing him- or herself in relation to others against a background of shared meaning and purpose" (p. 4). In defining faith, Fowler drew from Tillich (1957), who writes of faith as that which holds a person's ultimate concern in life and the beliefs and values that then emerge. The notion of ultimate concern is more robust than simply belief as an intellectual pursuit of doctrine or creed; rather faith is viewed more as a state of being, a way in which each person makes meaning out of daily experience. Faith defined in this manner then takes up residence in the earliest relationships of the infant, prompting Fowler to consider faith or meaning making as both a developmental and relational process that spans a lifetime. Therefore, faith is not to be compartmentalized as a separate dimension; rather, "faith is an orientation of the total person, giving purpose and goal to one's hopes and strivings, thoughts and actions" (Fowler, 1981, p. 14). Though Fowler defined the word *faith* as applicable across cultures (e.g., atheist, Buddhist, Hindu), faith itself comes from a specific cultural background and would unlikely be the best word to use in a counseling session for many populations. Other words might be more useful here; for example, English-speaking Buddhists would use *practice*. Defined in this manner, it has far-reaching implications for the development of culturally competent counselors.

In this manner, the helping professional is challenged not only to understand how race, gender, ability, status, age, and sexual orientation impact the helper and the helping relationship but also to consider how a helper's faith impacts the helping relationship. Stated more directly, for a helper to meet the standards of cultural competence, a helper must explore the role of faith in order to help clients explore faith (ASERVIC, 2009). Fowler's work creates a platform for helpers to understand the process of faith development and the crisis that propels a person from one stage of development to another. A crisis, often characterized by doubt, pain, risk, and loss, around a person's ultimate concern, is necessary so that a more robust faith system can arise.

BOX 3.2 WHAT IS FAITH?

The helping profession has made significant strides in the areas of multiculturalism and social justice, embracing and affirming diversity in ethnicity, culture, gender, sexual orientation, religion, and spirituality. Faith (defined by Fowler) is a universal human activity of meaning making, and a part of our cultural competence is naming and articulating our faith so that we might work with others in their faiths. How would you describe your faith or ultimate concern to a close friend? Class? Client?

Undifferentiated Faith (Stage 0)

Fowler suggested that the first stage is more of a prestage, which starts in utero and continues for months after birth. This stage is the *undifferentiated faith stage*. This stage is initially characterized by primal feelings, perhaps by an attitude of pervading hopefulness about self and environment. It is felt more than communicated through the use of words (Parker, 2010). Fowler suggested that the baby's experiences (though undifferentiated) of love, courage, and hope are fused yet still very much experienced by the infant as the infant begins to experience the world as safe and predictable or unsafe and chaotic. Feelings shape the infant's ultimate concern as the world is experienced as safe or unsafe, trustworthy or untrustworthy (Erikson, 1980; Fowler, 1981). Fowler referred to this early stage as the experience of *mutuality*, or the relational dance between caretaker and infant. The challenge during this prestage is the development of trust with the potential of mistrust developing in one of two directions: in one direction is the development of an excessive narcissism that distorts the infant's relational experience; in the other direction is a neglect that leaves the infant with an experience of isolation. Potential long-term effects may result in a lack of confidence in others and self, thereby making it difficult to move into the additional stages—stages that depend on safe relational encounters (Fowler, 1981).

Intuitive-Projective Faith (Stage 1)

With the development of thought and language the child is now capable of using symbols and ritual play to express her ultimate concern. The intuitive-projective

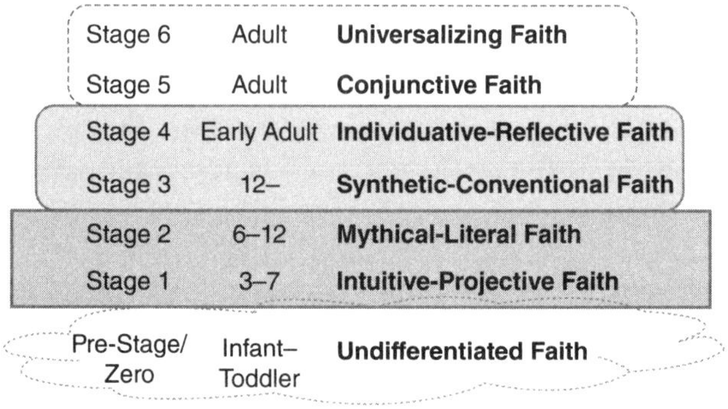

Figure 3.1 Fowler's stages of faith.

stage generally spans the ages of 3 to 7 years. This stage is characterized by fantasy and imagination. It is marked by a fluidity of thought as the child is constantly engaging new information without a basis (consistent with Piaget's preoperational stage of egocentrism) for where such information is formed. This fluidity creates an unrestrained flow of thought and fantasy for the child. Consequently, children are powerfully influenced by the examples, moods, actions, and stories of their caregivers. Thus, both the gift of this stage and the danger of this stage is the birth of imagination. Imagination brings with it powerful images and stories that impact the child's intuitive understanding and feelings about existence and meaning making. This developmental period is a time of constant integration of knowledge collected from the child's environment without filter and in an egocentric manner. Consequently, the potential danger exists for stories of damnation, shame, or an angry deity to take up residence within the child's imagination and for the development of a worldview based in fear, guilt, and shame (Fowler, 1981).

As relational experiences characterized by power, powerlessness, imagination, and fantasy shape the child's worldview, the stage naturally leads to a totemic connection with a person or object in a manner that concretizes the child's ultimate concern or faith development. For example, a teddy bear or a blanket may represent the security and safety the child feels (Kropf, 1990). Wounding in this stage can lead to adolescents and adults who present as either overly rigid and controlling in an effort to protect against a dangerous world or who present as brittle and vulnerable to the views and criticisms of others (Fowler, 1981).

Counseling Application

Helpers working with a client who experienced wounding in the intuitive-projective stage will benefit from having an awareness of FDT, and of the impact that a loss of trust may have in shaping the individual's worldview, and of the likelihood to present externally (controlling) or internally (shame). The building of the therapeutic alliance is an essential part of treatment and healing. The client who presents on either side of the controlling or shame-based spectrum will often find vulnerability to be scary and may require more time for the development of the therapeutic relationship.

Mythical-Literal Faith (Stage 2)

The mythical-literal stage (ages 7–12) is best described as the period in which a child creates meaning from the information flow of stage 1 and grasps the importance of reciprocity as a way of governing divine-human (human-human) relationships. This developmental process of making sense of the unrestrained, fluid flow of images and messages from stage 1 is an attempt by the child to bring order to his or her world (Fowler, 1981; Parker, 2010). The beliefs and symbols of the intuitive-projective stage now begin to take on a literal meaning. In contrast to the egocentrism of stage 1, which limited children's ability to differentiate between God's (i.e., caregiver's) perspective and their own, stage 2 children begin to build an ability to differentiate and to embrace the meaning for themselves. A sense of belonging emerges as the child identifies with stories that connect community and family. The gift of this stage is the gift of consciousness and the ability to make meaning of experience that connects the child to others outside of self. This ordering of stories coincides with Piaget's concrete operation stage of development. Furthermore, this stage is typified by the child's sense of reciprocal justice paralleling Kohlberg's conventional morality that leads a child to view the world from a lens of justice: what one person is entitled to the other is entitled to (Fowler, 1981).

Fowler suggested that the moral reciprocity that defines this stage creates the basis for a construction of God seen in anthropomorphic terms (having human characteristics). The child's emphasis on reciprocity creates data for the child's construction of faith development at this stage, or the continued development of the child's ultimate concern in life (Kelliher, 2011). Because meaning in this stage is both made and trapped (Fowler, 1981, p. 149), caregivers significantly shape the child's faith development. For example, a caregiver who is experienced as strong, powerful, and just helps to develop a system of faith that is just and secure. Conversely, serious deficiencies within a caretaker can lead to a child whose ultimate concern is "over-controlling, stilted perfectionism or 'works righteousness' or in their opposite, an abasing sense of badness embraced because of mistreatment, neglect or the apparent disfavor of significant others" (Fowler, 1981, p. 150). As the child enters what Piaget labeled as the formal operational stage, she begins to think in abstract terms and is therefore able to question the stories of authority figures that have helped to shape her faith—thus prompting movement into stage 3.

Counseling Application

Important for the helper working with an individual wounded in this stage of development is the counselor's ability to help the client recapture the reciprocal relationships and the meaning that emerged from these relationships. As these relational narratives emerge, helpers have the opportunity to empathize with emerging feelings of injustice and painful unmet longings.

Synthetic-Conventional Faith (Stage 3)

The synthetic-conventional stage (adolescence), as with earlier stages, is embedded in the context of interpersonal relationships. Experience now extends beyond the family as the adolescent seeks to develop a sense of identity through peers, school, work, social media, and, for some, religion. Fowler suggested that some individuals may remain in this stage for a lifetime because it is characterized by a focus on strong interpersonal relationships and a respect for leaders who reinforce the system of faith thus far embraced (Fowler, 1981; Parker, 2011). The burden of this stage is self-consciousness. Self-consciousness in this stage is experienced as a deeply personal awareness of the self in relationship to others, and it may be expressed as discomfort with self in relationship to others. Therefore, the individual's ultimate concern seeks to find a coherent narrative in the complexity of environments and relationships. Drawing from Harry Stack Sullivan's concept of a *chum relationship*, Fowler (1981) suggested that adolescents look for a close other to mirror or reflect the emerging self. This chum relationship looks for a friend who has similar gifts, interests, and needs and who meets the adolescent's need to be known and accepted in a developmental stage of self-consciousness. Fowler (1981), drawing from Erikson, further reinforced that the identity crisis of adolescence is found in the discrepancies between the adolescent's (adult's) self-image and the image of the adolescent that is reflected by others. Homeostasis within this stage emerges when the adolescent both conforms to her environment and becomes comfortable with an identity that is mediated by significant others, and, for some, mediated by the decisive other, or God, who can exert a powerful ordering of one's identity (Fowler, 1981).

The ultimate concern during this stage of faith development is conformity. It is this conformity and the equilibrium that eventually results that causes many adults to stay firmly planted in this stage, holding beliefs tacit (unevaluated) to maintain this equilibrium. Often these beliefs may be held strongly and felt deeply, and to evaluate them would serve only to threaten the individual's important spheres of belonging.

BOX 3.3   WHAT STAGE ARE YOU IN?

Fowler indicated that many remain in stage 3, which is characterized by interpersonal relationships that are in many ways similar to what Harry Stack Sullivan referred to as chum relationships. Both the environment and the relationships create a level of comfort and homeostasis that supports one's faith stage, and without a crisis, the person will be tempted to remain in such comfort. Reflecting on your own faith journey, what stage are you in?

Transition and Crisis

Because many adults remain in this stage of faith development, it is important to give consideration to factors that prompt movement toward stage 4. Factors contributing to movement from stage 3 to stage 4 often include significant clashes that impact the person's faith, events that lead the individual to question her ultimate concern and the beliefs and values that ensue. Often these clashes may arise from tragedy and loss. Significant loss that leads to critical reflection of an individual's faith may be triggered by the death of a loved one; the loss of a job or marriage or partnership; a clash with authority figures, such as officially sanctioned leaders (e.g., priest); or a clash with practices that were previously considered sacred (communion or baptism). This transition is often both painful and scary and may endure for 5 to 7 years if the person moves on to stage 4 (Fowler, 1981; Kelliher, 2011).

Counseling Application

Many areas of importance emerge when considered clinically. Two primary areas are the depth to which one internalizes the expectations and evaluations of others and the loss of identity and relationships that often result as a person transitions from stage 3 to stage 4. Fowler (1981) indicated that "the expectations and evaluations of others can be so compellingly internalized that later autonomy of judgment and action can be jeopardized; or interpersonal betrayals can give rise either to nihilistic despair about a personal principle of ultimate being or to a compensatory intimacy with God" (p. 173). In addition, movement from this stage may result in changes of community. For example, individuals may leave their original faith community during this transition. This transition can occur when a faith community discourages members to think beyond conventional boundaries (Kelliher, 2011). Further, this transition is often in early adulthood to midlife and may coincide with additional developmental changes or the loss of a significant other, which can further intensify the experience of guilt and shame. Parker (2011) wrote, "The counsellor should be able to help the client sort out what belongs to these two losses, making the whole experience less confusing" (p. 115).

Individuative-Reflective Faith (Stage 4)

If stage 4 is to emerge, it generally does so in early adulthood to midlife. The later a person enters this stage, the more difficult the transition, because others are also impacted by this period of reflection, such as a spouse and children. In this stage the tacit (unevaluated) faith begins to be replaced by a system of belief that is more explicit, and with this comes a return to a more robust sense of internal security and knowingness. Whereas the person still values the input and judgments of others, she is less bound to the judgments characteristic of the stage 3 person and ultimately submits her faith to what Fowler (1981) referred to as an "internal panel of experts," or what Fowler called the executive ego (p. 179).

A gift of this stage is the process of coming to see faith as embedded in a particular cultural context. Specific to this stage is a growing awareness of social systems and institutions. While maintaining the interpersonal perspective of stage 3, the person is now able to draw on a system of faith that has been formed and reformed over the course of time and reflection, and she is able to differentiate her experience of faith from that of others in the culture within which she is embedded (Fowler, 1981; Parker, 2010).

Counseling Application

Clinically, keep in mind that some clients may be grieving the loss of the more simplistic stage 3 faith and some of the relationships that were lost in this development. Although the stage 4 person witnesses the implicit faith becoming explicit, this process can result in an overreliance on the rational mind in an effort to resolve relational issues. And, helpers may quickly find themselves hooked in a battle of wits (Parker, 2009).

Conjunctive Faith (Stage 5)

Fowler believes that it is unusual for the conjunctive-faith stage to emerge prior to midlife. Stage 5 arrives on the scene as the individual reflects on the past and the pain of personal limitation, defeat, and the reality of irrevocable life decisions. Reflecting on such life experience prompts a hunger for reclaiming the past in a manner that reinforces the individual's faith in light of contradiction, disillusionment, and paradox (Fowler, 1981). In an effort to integrate conscious and unconscious life experience, the individual thirsts to understand what is different, including new experiences in other faith systems. This process is once again scary because the person risks a changing worldview, and this crisis of faith prompts the working out of opposites and polarities as the person moves toward a more holistic faith experience. The adaptive feature of this stage rests in the ability to embrace paradox and mystery and the ability to contribute to humanity without a need for preconceived responses (Fowler, 1981). The danger inherent within this stage is the temptation to become passive, withdrawn, or cynical in the face of relativism (Parker, 2009). According to Kelliher (2011), "With this growth comes a synthesis of opposites, for example, an appreciation and acceptance that each person is both feminine and masculine, young and old, constructive and destructive" (pp. 8–9). This stage of faith development leads to a personal readiness to be *spent for* others—in an effort to help others cultivate a greater sense of meaning and identity.

This stage brings with it a readiness "for significant encounters with other traditions than its own, expecting that truth has disclosed and will disclose itself in those traditions in ways that may complement or correct its own … that no interfaith conversation is genuinely ecumenical unless the quality of mutual sharing and receptivity is such that each party makes him- or herself vulnerable to conversion to the other's truth. This would be stage 5 ecumenism" (Fowler, 1981, p. 186). This development does not suggest a lack of commitment to a worldview;

rather, it embraces an openness to truth and a confidence that with "each genuine perspective will augment and correct aspects of the other, in a mutual movement toward the real and the true" (Fowler, 1981, p. 187).

Counseling Application

A potential threat to the person in stage 5 is a withdrawal or a cynicism that may develop in response to an experience of relativism as other worldviews are known and appreciated (Parker, 2009). The helper for the stage 5 individual will likely need to be a stage 5 individual, who is able to reinforce a strong faith identity that without weakening serves as a catalyst to other's worldviews.

Universalizing Faith (Stage 6)

Transition into this stage, if and when it occurs, is in midlife and beyond. Transition to stage 6 occurs as the person is able to reconcile paradox through universalizing aspirations. This genuine reconciliation of faith systems leads an individual to incarnate his or her faith with no regard for the self, living to be *spent* for *the other*. Fowler suggested that Mother Teresa, Gandhi, Martin Luther King Jr., and Thomas Merton are persons who represent this stage, though many others exist within and across cultures. The criteria that shape this stage are considered to be an "inclusiveness of community, of radical commitment to justice and love and of selfless passion for a transformed world, a world made over not in their images, but in accordance with an intentionality both divine and transcendent" (Fowler, 1981, p. 201). Persons entering this stage of development can best be described as having generated a faith composition that is inclusive of all; they live and dwell as incarnations of a faith (ultimate concern) that is strong, kind, inclusive, and just. Such persons are contagious as they transcend categories that often create *the other*, as often common in social, political, economic, and ideological realms. Universalizers are often experienced as subversive in their engagement of the world, and they often die at the hands of those they are seeking to liberate (Fowler, 1981). Their faith leads them to embrace the sacredness of life while living deeply aware of the brevity of life, further prompting them to embrace service and care for those at any place along the faith stages and of any faith tradition. Parker (2011) indicated that counselors do not need to consider how to work with the stage 6 individual, as they do not present for counseling.

Concluding Remarks on Fowler's Theory for Counseling

James Fowler's faith development theory has important implications for those in the helping profession. The importance of cultural competence has been well established within the counseling profession, and also well established are the different parts of ethnicity, including race, gender, age, ability status, sexual orientation, and spirituality or religion. Two spiritual competencies are as follows:

1. "The professional counselor recognizes that the client's beliefs (or absence of beliefs) about spirituality and/or religion are central to his or her worldview

and can influence psychosocial functioning" (ASERVIC, 2009, Competency 2, p. 1).

2. "The professional counselor actively explores his or her own attitudes, beliefs, and values about spirituality and/or religion" (ASERVIC, 2009, Competency 3, p. 1).

Fowler's seminal work strongly states that faith is a universal human concern and is an orientation of the total person—an orientation that gives purpose and meaning to life.

Eastern Models of Spiritual Development

It would be remiss to discuss spiritual development without providing some alternative to Western notions of spiritual development. This is especially important as a number of theories and founding clinicians of counseling therapies were influenced by and drew from Eastern philosophy and practice (e.g., dialectical behavior therapy, transpersonal psychotherapy), so the underpinning tenets reflect an Eastern approach. Various cultures focus on spiritual development as a process of coming into proper relationship with universal nature; for example, in Taoism it is harmony with the Dao, transliterated often as "the way." "This coming into harmony is not viewed as a matter of progressive, individual development, but an emergent, transitory, and intrinsically relational quality" (K. Lowe-Charde, personal communication, May 11, 2015). Eastern spirituality aims beyond the self-centric and toward an awakened self in harmony with absolute and relative truths. For example, Tozan's (ninth-century) five ranks or stages and the ancient 10 oxherding (Suzuki, 1994) pictures are descriptions of spiritual development from an Eastern perspective, connecting (examples where spiritual development connects) around the path of realization of self in relation to absolute and relative truth. Within the context of Eastern notions of interdependence and impermanence of all phenomena, such developmental models are not conceptualized as a soul climbing a staircase but rather as a transitory being connected to the essential from various vantage points much like spokes to a wheel or viewpoints on a mountain. The absolute realm is the undifferentiated aspect of reality, the ultimate realm empty of the concrete and particular, "no differentiation can be found between the many phenomena" (Bolleter, 2014); the world is (what it is) complete and whole. The relative relates to the concrete, the specific manifestations of life, (i.e., a tree is a tree and not a dog), when the light shines the many phenomena are illuminated. From a relative perspective, humans grow, change in willful directions, experience grief and loss, and find a self within values, traits, and culture.

MORAL DEVELOPMENT THEORIES

Jill, a 55-year-old mother of two, shows up for her weekly appointment and appears to be in emotional distress. She tells her counselor that she is unsure about how to approach the new concern in her life. Single for 20 years, Jill is now involved in her first, serious, postdivorce relationship with a new man. This relationship has taken place over the last 4 months and is now becoming more intense. Jill is very concerned because her new partner frequently spends the night at her home. As a mother of two young adult children and a woman who describes her upbringing and current worldview as deeply religious, Jill is now struggling with cohabitating with her boyfriend, which is not consistent with her religious beliefs. She is also experiencing residual guilt over her divorce from several years ago. She questions her own morality.

WHAT IS MORAL DEVELOPMENT?

Moral development is the study of how people's ideas and behaviors regarding the social, ethical, and judicial treatment of others evolve over the lifespan. It has been a widely discussed topic predating the beginning of the field now known as psychology and studied by some of the founders of the study of human behavior. Freud (1936) and Skinner (1953) helped to lay a foundation for the study of moral behavior, and the field was expanded by the works of Piaget (1926, 1965), Kohlberg (1973), and Gilligan (1990), who were among the earliest theorists to examine moral development.

Piaget and Moral Development

Although Jean Piaget (1896–1980) studied cognitive development, which included thinking and how one perceives the world, he did not specifically study morality. His work introduced, and confirmed, much of what a lot of what we as counselors understand about children and counseling children. According to Piaget, children between the ages of 5 to 10 have heteronomous (i.e., other-driven) thinking and value following rules because they are *supposed* to do so and fear consequences of not doing so. Morality is based on whether rules are followed. Followed by this, the development of autonomous thought (i.e., self-directed) begins around age 11 years and continues through adolescence, which allows one to analyze situations differently and apply reasoning and judgment to whether or not a rule should be broken and why. With this new capacity, humans are less absolute in their beliefs and begin to understand that moral decisions are often made on a case-by-case basis (Piaget, 1932). Lawrence Kohlberg and Carol Gilligan, researchers who studied moral development after the works of Piaget, adopted several aspects of Piaget's original work. Both researchers found that logic and morality develop through a stage process in which each stage is more stable and more sophisticated in its approach than the previous stages (Kohlberg, 1973). Meeting clients where they are at in their developmental level is important. For example, counselors might help family members or school staff to develop consistent rules based on what is concrete rather than processes that require cause and effect or abstract thinking prior to the development of those skills.

Kohlberg's Theory of Moral Development

Lawrence Kohlberg (1927–1987) was a psychologist and researcher who studied moral development, expanding the thinking beyond that of Piaget. He embarked on a cross-sectional study using 72 children between the ages of 10 and 16 years in Chicago, the city where he lived and worked (McLeod, 2011). A longitudinal study conducted in 1983 by Colby, Kohlberg, Gibbs, and Lieberman, in which researchers followed 58 of the original participants at regular intervals for 20 years, lent further support for Kohlberg's findings. Both Kohlberg and Colby, Kohlberg, Gibbs, and Lieberman (1983) found that each person passes through particular stages of moral development in a predictable, sequential order. As a person advances through moral development, his or her moral decision making becomes more sophisticated. Cognitions at each advancing stage replace the less developed cognitions of the previous stage. To assess the level of moral thinking, Kohlberg presented participants with several narratives with follow-up questions. The most famous of these vignettes is the Heinz dilemma. After the children responded to the vignette, Kohlberg classified responses into three different levels, or stages, with two substages within each: preconventional, conventional, and postconventional (Table 3.1).

Heinz's wife was dying from a particular type of cancer. Doctors said a new drug, discovered by a local chemist, might save her. Heinz tried desperately to buy some, but the chemist was charging 10 times the money it cost to make the drug, which was much more than Heinz could afford.

Heinz could raise only half the money, even after help from family and friends. He explained to the chemist that his wife was dying and asked if he could have the drug cheaper or pay the rest of the money later. The chemist refused, saying that he had discovered the drug and was going to make money from it. The husband was desperate to save his wife, so later that night he broke into the chemist's store and stole the drug.

1. Should Heinz have stolen the drug?
2. Would it change anything if Heinz did not love his wife?
3. What if the person dying was a stranger, would it make any difference?
4. Should the police arrest the chemist for murder if the woman died?

In the preconventional stage, the respondents evidenced thinking in which a personal moral code had not yet been adopted. At this point in development, thinking was hallmarked by rules imposed by others, known as heteronomous thinking. In this stage there were two categories: (1) obedience and punishment and (2) individualism and exchange.

Substage 1: Obedience and Punishment

Children reported viewpoints consistent with a belief in absolute rules and power of authorities. The children who were interviewed did not give responses that

Table 3.1 Kolhberg's Stages of Moral Reasoning		
Levels of Moral Reasoning	**Stages Within Levels of Moral Reasoning**	**Application of Stages to Heinz Dilemma**
Level 1: Preconventional morality The rules are something outside of oneself; following the rules results in avoiding punishment and gaining rewards.	Stage 1: Punishment and obedience orientation Stage 2: Naïve hedonism	The decision to steal or not steal the drug is based on whether Heinz would get into trouble. Heinz's decision is based on the reward that Heinz or the chemist would obtain.
Level 2: Conventional morality Rules and expectations are internalized; following the rules results in being accepted and maintaining the good within society.	Stage 3: Good boy/girl orientation Stage 4: Social order maintaining	Heinz's decision is based on how others would perceive him. Heinz's decision is based on how he or the chemist is upholding the law and maintaining allegiance to societal expectations.
Level 3: Postconventional morality Rules must be examined for underlying beliefs, philosophies, and reasoning; following the rules is important but making certain that the rules align with personal beliefs, philosophies, and reasoning is of most importance.	Stage 5: Social contract orientation Stage 6: Individual ethical principles of conscious orientation	Heinz's decision is based on a broader concept of justice related to social consensus and idealism. Heinz's decision is based on his personal beliefs and principles regarding the rightness or wrongness associated with stealing the drug.

showed an appreciation, or understanding, of different viewpoints. Rather, they gave answers that described Mr. Heinz's actions in terms of *right is right* and *wrong is wrong*. The primary motivation for the responses was the avoidance of punishment and the salient goal for the respondents in this age group, who almost unanimously said that Heinz was wrong for breaking in and stealing the medicine, was that he should not steal because stealing is wrong and bad. Sometimes they made it clear that there are negative consequences of stealing. The moral thinking at this stage is consistent with a belief that if you were punished you must have done something wrong.

Substage 2: Individualism and Exchange

During this stage children understand that the rules are not the only way to see things and that each person has an idea about how they want to conduct themselves. They also understand that punishment may result from a person's actions and that sometimes taking the risk of potential punishment could make sense. At this stage, a person understands that punishment is something people still want to avoid when breaking the rules established by authority figures. In response to the Heinz dilemma, Kohlberg found that children at this stage reported that Heinz was thinking about himself when he stole the drug to take care of his wife. They also described the chemist as protecting his own self-interest, which was met by charging a hefty, profitable sum for the drug he invented. Children at this stage often did note that the chemist was being unfair for the high price he charged for the medicine, which made it unattainable to someone who needed it to save a life. Children understand that different people may have differing viewpoints.

The next two categories fall within the second stage of moral development, the conventional level. At this stage values and standards of society begin to emerge and are internalized by the individual. Because this study was both longitudinal and cross-sectional, as previously noted, the respondents to the same Heinz dilemma were older and thus provided slightly different responses. Here, authority has become internalized and moral reasoning is guided largely by one's understanding of the norms of the groups to which they claim strong affiliation or membership. The two substages in this category are (1) good interpersonal relationships and (2) maintaining social order.

Substage 3: Good Interpersonal Relationships

In this stage, moral decision making is connected with abiding by the values established by family and the community. People need to have compassion, trust, and empathy for others. People at this stage of moral development understand that although technically *wrong*, there may be a valid reason for violating the rules in favor of benefitting people considered personally important like a loved one or someone in need. It is important, here, to be viewed by others as a *good* person and gain their approval (Kohlberg, 1973).

Substage 4: Maintaining Social Order

Society as a whole is the focus of moral thought in this stage. There is an expectation that citizens uphold the laws and rules established for everyone. This is similar, in some ways, to the obedience and punishment stage; however, children at that stage are unaware of laws. People at this stage identify the *wrongness* of Heinz's behavior. The goal at this stage is avoid guilt more so than punishment.

Postconventional morality, the final stage, also has two substages. Justice and the rights of individuals are primary concerns at this stage. However, this level is thought to be attainable by only 10–15% of people who are at least in middle adulthood (Kohlberg, 1973). The two substages in this level are (1) social contracts and individual rights and (2) universal principle.

Substage 5: Social Contracts and Individual Rights

The task is defining one's own idea of a functional society. With many ideas of what a *good society* means, there is an understanding that there is more than one way for society to function. Human rights are compared to the law and are theoretical about how the world *should* be. It is clear that although rules are important, even necessary, they do not always *work* for everyone in society as intended. At this stage of moral development, people are usually not in favor of breaking the law and can distinguish between a real and ideal society, embrace the sanctity of human life, and rationalize and justify why valuing human life over profit is a moral decision. Laws do not always deliver the greatest good for all human beings and may need to be broken.

Substage 6: Universal Principles

Kohlberg's final stage challenged his own thinking. He believed that very few, if any, would reach this stage. At this level of moral development, larger scale morals are the focus. Issues such as global human rights, civil rights for a given group, social justice, and broad equality are salient. Morals around these issues are so developed and strong that the person is willing to risk facing consequences, such as disapproval of loved ones or society in defense of their beliefs. This stage requires that the person be able to see situations through the eyes of another (Kohlberg, 1984).

Table 3.2 outlines the cognitions associated with each substage of Kohlberg's model.

Limitations of Kohlberg's model

Several concerns have been noted with Kohlberg's model. A primary concern was that the sample was biased. An all-male sample was used and then normalized for everyone. The criticism is that males have approaches to moral dilemmas that are distinct from females. In fact, Kohlberg (1984) claimed that the moral reasoning of men and boys is superior to that of women and girls. It further brings into question issues of how factors such as culture, race, sexual orientation, socioeconomic status, personal history, past trauma, and other factors may influence how people resolve issues. The validity of Kohlberg's theory is questionable (i.e., would the respondent answer the same way in a real-life situation). Other concerns include whether or not moral development is always forward moving and if someone who provides a postconventional response once would give a postconventional response in every situation; if so, does this response actually match a person's moral behavior?

Table 3.2   Typical Expressed Motives for Action in the Case of Heinz's Dilemma

	Should Take the Drug	Should Not Take the Drug
Stage 1	Can't let her die—that's bad and you will get in trouble.	If you steal the medicine for your wife you will get caught and then you will go to prison.
Stage 2	If someone finds out that you took the drug, but you apologize and give it back it might not be so bad.	While her dying would be bad, you didn't make her get sick so it's not your fault.
Stage 3	If you let her die you should be ashamed of yourself. How can you face anyone if you let her die?	How will you feel later if you take something that did not belong to you, regardless of the circumstances? Do you want to be known as a thief to everyone?
Stage 4	You'll always feel terrible and guilty she died—and you did not do what you could to stop that. You owe it to her.	You really don't want her to die and feel like you have no choice but you will feel terrible once you stop and think about what you did and what that makes you.
Stage 5	If you let her die because you were too cowardly to get her some help, you will not be able to respect yourself. Think this through. Is letting her die the best decision?	Do you want to see yourself as a thief? Do you want others to see you this way? You do not want to see any harm come to a anyone, including financial harm.
Stage 6	You will never forgive yourself, or have peace, if you don't do what you can to stop her death.	Although everyone would understand why you did this, there are many people who also need this drug. Why should you steal the drug rather than them?

Source: Modified from Kohlberg (1969, pp. 380–381).

Gilligan's Ethics of Care

Carol Gilligan studied under Lawrence Kohlberg. She disagreed with aspects of his theory and identified the sex bias present in this theory. Gilligan posited that men and women have different orientations toward resolving moral decisions. She noted that the *ethics of justice* (i.e., androcentric) values that are socially expected and sanctioned for males (and, according to Kohlberg, set the standard for what is moral) are inconsistent with the *ethics of care* approach to moral issues more commonly used by women.

Gilligan identified boys as having an orientation toward justice. In the book *Mapping the Moral Domain*, Gilligan, Ward, and Taylor (1988) defined a justice orientation as "draw[ing] attention to the problems of inequality and oppression and hold[ing] up an ideal of reciprocity and equal respect" (p. 73). For Gilligan, this orientation is typical of men and is the basis for Kohlberg's six-stage theory.

Although a justice-seeking orientation can apply to both sexes, women are more likely to process information differently (Gilligan, 1982). Gilligan conducted her research in a similar way to that of Kohlberg. Instead of using scenarios, like that of securing life-saving medicine for one's dying spouse, Gilligan's scenarios had a different element. Her scenarios were related to contemporary issues, such as abortion decisions during a time when this was a socially charged political topic. Women, according to Gilligan, have a care orientation that "draws attention to problems of detachment or abandonment and holds up an ideal of attention and response to need" (Gilligan et al., 1988, p. 73). She believed that women gravitate toward the concepts of feelings, needs, and care. Gilligan also noted that women approach moral decision making from a relational perspective focused on issues such as abandonment, attachment, and connection. Further, she espoused that for women, two moral edicts exist: treating others fairly and not ignoring the needs of others. Using a generalization about how women conceptualize morality, women are more likely to value and demonstrate relational, connected orientations to decision making. Universal statements to describe men and women are often used, but Gilligan asserted that there are differences in moral decision making.

Just like Kohlberg, Gilligan's model also included three stages: preconventional, conventional, and postconventional. Gilligan's model, however, focused explicitly on what she identified as the ethics of care with no substages. During the preconventional stage, a person aspires to survive as an individual. After this stage is resolved this person enters a transitional stage during which the person begins to transition from a place of self-centeredness to a place of responsibility to other people. As a result of this transition the person enters the second, or conventional, stage of moral development. During this stage of moral development the person believes that self-sacrifice is rewarded. As the person continues to develop beyond the conventional level she enters the transition from focusing on striving for goodness to striving for truth.

In the final stage, identified as the postconventional stage, a person internalizes principles of nonviolence and nonmaleficence toward the self and others. The person also is able to both make a decision and take responsibility for that decision.

Challenges to Gilligan's Model

Gilligan's model is not without controversy. Challenges have been made to both the need for a separate theory of moral development for women and to the veracity of the research on which this theory was built. Nunner-Winkler (1984), for example, raised the concern that Gilligan's model does not provide solid evidence for women typically choosing moral results that favor a caring position over one of justice as compared to men. Gilligan (1990) answered this criticism by pointing out that her findings are not presented as prescriptive or universal. Further, it was noted that perhaps Gilligan *misunderstood* Kohlberg's model by presenting justice and care as dichotomous positions and that conceptualizing *a voice* for women ignores the differences among women, including those related to racism, classism, and lesbophobia. It is interesting that these criticisms are similar to those originally raised by Gilligan of Kohlberg (Tong, 1993).

Table 3.3 Gilligan's Stages of Moral Reasoning		
Three Levels of Moral Reasoning	**Transitions Between Levels**	**Factors That Facilitate Transition**
Level 1: Orientation to individual survival	Level 1.5: From selfishness to responsibility: "I love me" changes to "I love you."	Through attaching and connecting with others, self-interest is redefined into what one "should" do.
Level 2: Goodness as self-sacrifice	Level 2.5: From goodness to truth: "I love you more than me."	Responsibility to and for others becomes equal to goodness, self is defined by goodness through sacrificing for the sake of others.
Level 3: Morality of nonviolence	From conformity to choice: "I love myself and you."	Concern for self is balanced with concern for others.

Case Study Application

Let's consider the previously mentioned case of Jill. How might you, as her counselor, approach the presenting concern over her morality? Certainly you would allow her to process through her concern and, from that processing, have an idea of where Jill might fall in Gilligan's or Kohlberg's model. But what then? How would you use this information to inform your counseling sessions with Jill?

As Gilligan indicated, Kohlberg's model seems geared toward justice. With Jill's self-report of being deeply religious, justice could be a very relevant factor. She certainly seems to be struggling with her thoughts regarding the *rightness* or *wrongness* of her relationship. As a counselor, you could use a Socratic approach in which you had her identify what feels right or wrong in the relationship and with her divorce 20 years ago. From a more relationally oriented perspective, as with Gilligan's model, a discussion of Jill's circumstances within the context of herself, her partner, her ex-spouse, and her daughters is reasonable. Additionally, a counselor could also provide psychoeducation on Gilligan's model along with subsequent processing of how Jill believes she fits within the stages is appropriate.

Values Clarification

Counselors foster moral development through *values clarification*, i. e., helping client's identify, understand, choose, and live according to values. "Values are our standards and principles for judging worth. They are the criteria by which we judge 'things' (people, ideas, situations) to be good or desirable; or on the other hand bad, worthless or despicable; or, of course, somewhere in between these extremes. We may apply our values consciously or they may function unconsciously, as part of the influence of our frame of reference, without our being aware of the standards implied by our decisions" (Rath, Harmon, & Simon, 1966, p. 129). Whether conscious or not, values are constantly informing decision making processes and behavior. To aid personal development, counselors help clients explore the values they inherited from familial, peer, and cultural sources while also exploring those values that are different than the values of their past context. Along this path, clients often struggle between competing values because life is full of choices and dilemmas. For example, a middle-aged woman may struggle with the choice of taking a career opportunity that takes time from family. In this case she may struggle as, on one hand, self-sufficiency, independence, and creativity are valued, and on the other hand, loyalty, and time with family are emphasized. The client feels the struggle of competing values though each of these sets of values is excellent; however, what clients often enter counseling with is a sense of failure; being a bad mother because familial values are not fully realized and being a "bad" worker because work values are not fully realized. The mature person comes to terms with such limitations and excels at the navigation of dilemmas. Above and beyond a first order change, where counselors help clients affect a given situation or problem, counselors create second order change by helping clients change the way they view, consider, and act on values; they cultivate a way of being where clients become aware of and intentional about their values. Rath et al. (1966) proposed a developmental model of fully developed values. As with other models of spiritual and moral development, as a person develops he or she moves from contemplative stages around values to action and commitment.

BOX 3.4 CRITERIA FOR A FULLY DEVELOPED VALUE LEADING TO GROWTH

Explores and selects the value

> First: A value is freely chosen.
> Second: A value is chosen from alternatives.
> Third: A value is chosen after considering the consequences.

Internal and external honoring of the value

> Fourth: A value is publicly affirmed.
> Fifth: A value is cherished.

Living out or embodying the value

> Sixth: A value must be performed.
> Seventh: A value becomes a pattern of life.

Outcome requirement: The fully developed value enhances growth.

KEY COUNSELING POINTERS FOR MORAL AND SPIRITUAL DEVELOPMENT

Having a counseling plan to best support clients at their developmental levels is crucial. As development inevitably shifts, so does the approach. It is not uncommon to hear parents say that the second you get used to a child, they change. One counselor educator remarked that it is the parent and not the teen that is truly rebellious as the parents often refuse to accept the natural developmental process of independence and the increasing importance of peers in adolescent years.

Counselors create systemic change with development in mind when a client is highly embedded and vulnerable. As examples, family counselors enhance the early childhood environment and assist the family in providing rich and supportive experiences because spiritual development is relational, and moral development starts early. Gerontological counselors advocate for vulnerable elders in care systems to meet later life spiritual needs such as life review, as well as the refinement and dissemination of wisdom within community. School counselors institute comprehensive school counseling plans that are developmental in nature so that social/emotional, career, and academic needs of various students along the K–12 educational path, impact the moral development of children.

To encourage sophisticated moral development in children, counselors help caregivers move from power-over models of discipline to inductive models of discipline. Inductive models of discipline focus on understanding best discipline practices. They support children with clear, appropriate, and consistent responses along the developmental spectrum with continual and repeated investment of time and energy. This leads to a sense of safety and relaxation in the environment and importantly the internalization of a prosocial and developed sense of morality (Passini, Pihet, & Favez, 2013). Counselors new to discipline should take up further readings on evidence-based discipline practices or examine discipline practices such as positive discipline, the IRIS training module, and positive behavioral interventions and supports (PBIS), which focus on positive reinforcement of behaviors.

Counselors must work to understand the variations of religious and spiritual developmental paths. This also includes clearly knowing one's own background and biases. Many times counselors will need to do their own personal work and resolve woundedness around spirituality and religion in order to work unimpaired with clients. Consider examining the professional tab at http://www.tolerance.org for training such as their antibias modules.

Counselors must integrate issues of spirituality and religion into counseling. Integration into one's practice is different from spiritual counseling or religious counseling. Cashwell and Young (2010) suggested that clients can gain substantially when spirituality and religion are integrated into counseling when they are brought forward by the client, rather than the counselor imposing his or her own views and beliefs on the client.

Counselors may often have to use the skill of reframing to expand definitions and conceptualizations around spirituality and religion. This should be done in a way that is positive. For example, a counselor prompts a couple with, "Tell me about your spirituality?" One of the partners says, "I really have no spirituality and don't go to church." The counselor then normalizes the experience, provides a broad definition and examples of how different people experience spirituality, and explores ways that the client experiences this in his or her life.

Counselors can help heal clients from harmful group and leader experiences affecting their spiritual identity and development. As spirituality is relational, counselors can help distinguish between helpful and harmful group processes and practices in the client's spiritual well-being and identity. Counselors can validate spiritual identity, the pain of trauma, and the residual effects of group traumatization. Consider referring clients to an exit counselor if they have recently left a group exhibiting strong cult-like behaviors, if you do not have the training to deal with this (Szimhart, 2009). Sometimes negative group processes have been referred to as *toxic spirituality or religion*. Counselors may also have to assist client growth and advocate when groups contribute to rather than counteract prejudice (Doehring, 2013).

Counselors also help clients deal with *spiritual bypass*. Spiritual bypass occurs when a person uses spiritual and religious practices to stave off healthy emotions or to ignore important realities. Mathieu (2011) suggested that "spiritual bypass shields us from the truth, it disconnects us from our feelings, and helps us avoid the big picture. It is more about checking *out* than checking *in*—and the difference is so subtle that we usually don't even know we are doing it" (p. 1). This can happen at various stages of psychospiritual development.

SUMMARY

Counselors must pay attention to the spiritual and moral development of clients, though at times these realms may be hard to navigate. Spirituality and religion are not synonymous but are often connected. Spiritual development is different from religious development, though such development may overlap. Though spirituality is hard to define, it is of utmost importance for the counselor to understand the many cultural expressions of spirituality. The Association for Spiritual, Ethical, and Religious Values in Counseling (ASERVIC) and the American Counseling Association (ACA) have endorsed the spiritual competencies for integrating spirituality into counseling. Competent practice suggests that counselors know and apply various models of spiritual and moral development. Several models were highlighted in this chapter, including those of Piaget, Kohlberg, Gilligan, and Fowler. Finally, the chapter presented material on fully developed values as well as key pointers for counselors on this chapter's topic.

USEFUL WEBSITES

Association for Spiritual, Ethical, and Religious Values in Counseling (ASERVIC)

http://www.aservic.org
Teaching Tolerance: Project of the Southern Poverty Law Center
http://www.tolerance.org/ (see professional development)
International Cultic Studies Association (ICSA)
http://www.icsahome.com/
Positive Behavioral Interventions and Supports (PBIS)
https://www.pbis.org/

REFERENCES

Association for Spiritual, Ethical, and Religious Values in Counseling (ASERVIC). (2009). *Spiritual competencies for addressing spiritual and religious issues in counseling*. Retrieved from http://www.aservic.org

Bolleter, R. (2014). *Dongshan's five ranks: Keys to enlightenment*. Somerville, MA: Wisdom Publications.

Cashwell, C., & Young, S. (2011). *Integrating spirituality and religion into counseling* (2nd ed.). Alexandria, VA: American Counseling Association Publishing.

Colby, A., Kohlberg, L., Gibbs, J., & Lieberman, M. (1983). A longitudinal study of moral judgment. *Monographs of the Society for Research in Child Development*, *48*(1–2, Serial No. 200). Chicago, IL: University of Chicago Press.

Doehring, C. (2013). An applied integrative approach to exploring how religion and spirituality contribute to or counteract prejudice and discrimination. In K. I. Pargament, A. Mahoney, E. P. Shafranske, K. I. Pargament, A. Mahoney, & E. P. Shafranske (Eds.), *APA handbook of psychology, religion, and spirituality (Vol. 2): An applied psychology of religion and spirituality* (pp. 389–403). Washington, DC: American Psychological Association.

Erikson, E. H. (1980). *Identity and the life cycle*. New York, NY: W.W. Norton.

Exline, J. J., Pargament, K. I., Grubbs, J. B., & Yali, A. M. (2014). The Religious and Spiritual Struggles Scale: Development and initial validation. *Psychology of Religion and Spirituality*, *6*(3), 208–222.

Exline, J. J., & Rose, E. D. (2013). Religious and spiritual struggles. In R. F. Paloutzian & C. L Park (Eds.), *Handbook of the psychology of religion and spirituality* (2nd ed., pp. 380–398). New York, NY: Guilford Press.

Fowler, J. (1981). *Stages of faith: The psychology of human development and the quest for meaning*. New York, NY: HarperOne.

Freud, S. (1936). *The ego and mechanisms of defense*. New York, NY: New York International University Studies.

Gilligan, C. (1982). *In a different voice: Psychological theory and women's development*. Cambridge, MA: Harvard University Press.

Gilligan, C. (1990). Joining the resistance: Psychology, politics, girls and women. *Michigan Quarterly Review*, *24*(4), 501–536.

Gilligan, C., Ward, J. V., & Taylor, J. M. (1988). *Mapping the moral domain: A contribution of women's thinking to psychological theory and education*. Cambridge, MA: Harvard University Press.

Kelliher, A. (2011). Spirituality, a faith development approach: Implications for practice. *Irish Association of Humanistic and Integrative Psychology*, *65*. Retrieved from http://www.iahip.org

Kohlberg, L. (1969). Stage and sequence: The cognitive developmental approach to socialization. In D. A. Goslin (Ed.), *Handbook of socialization theory and research* (pp. 347–380). Chicago, IL: Rand McNally.

Kohlberg, L. (1973). The claim to moral adequacy of a highest stage of moral judgment. *Journal of Philosophy*, *70*(18), 630–646.

Kohlberg, L. (1984). Essays on moral development: Vol. 2. The psychology of moral development. *Moral stages, their nature and validity*. New York, NY: Harper & Row Publishing

Kropf, R. W. (1990). *Faith: Security and risk*. Mahwah, NJ: Paulist Press.

Love, P. G. (2001). Spirituality and student development: Theoretical connections. *New Directions for Student Services*, *95*, 7.

Mathieu, I. (2011). *Recovering spirituality: Achieving emotional sobriety in your spiritual practice*. Center City, MN: Hazelden Publishing.

McLeod, S. (2011). *Kohlberg*. Retrieved from http://www.simplypsychology.org/kohlberg.html

Nunner-Winkler, G. (1984). Two moralities? A critical discussion of an ethic of care and responsibility versus an ethic of rights and justice. In W. M. Kurtines & J. L. Gewirtz (Eds.), *Morality, moral behavior, and moral development* (pp. 348–361.) New York, NY: Wiley & Sons.

Pargament, K. I., Lomax, J. W., McGee, J. S., & Fang, Q. (2014). Sacred moments in psychotherapy from the perspectives of mental health providers and clients: Prevalence, predictors, and consequences. *Spirituality in Clinical Practice*, *1*(4), 248–262. doi:10.1037/scp0000043

Parker, S. (2009). Faith development theory as a context for supervision of spiritual and religious issues. *Counselor Education & Supervision*, *49*, 39–53.

Parker, S. (2010). Research in Fowler's faith development theory: A review article. *Review of Religious Research*, *51*(3), 233–252.

Parker, S. (2011). Spirituality in counseling: A faith development perspective. *Counseling and Development*, *89*(1), 112–119.

Passini, C. M., Pihet, S., & Favez, N. (2014). Assessing specific discipline techniques: A mixed methods approach. *Journal of Child and Family Studies*, *23*, 1389–1402. doi:10.1007/s10826-013-9796

Piaget, J. (1926). *The language and thought of the child*. New York, NY: Harcourt Brace & Company.

Piaget, J. (1932). *The moral judgement of the child*. New York, NY: Free Press.

Plumb, A. M. (2011). Spirituality and counselling: Are counsellors prepared to integrate religion and spirituality into therapeutic work with clients? *Canadian Journal of Counselling and Psychotherapy*, *45*(1), 1–16.

Post, B. C., Wade, N. G., & Cornish, M. A. (2014). Religion and spirituality in group counseling: Beliefs and preferences of university counseling center clients. *Group Dynamics: Theory, Research, and Practice*, *18*(1), 53–68. doi:10.1037/a0034759

Rath, L., Harmon, M., & Simon, H. (1966). *Values clarification*. New York, NY: Grand Central Publishing.

Roehlkepartain, E. C., King, P. E., Wagner, L., & Benson, P. L. (2006). *The handbook of spiritual development in childhood and adolescence*. Thousand Oaks, CA: SAGE.

Skinner, B. F. (1953). *Science and human nature*. New York, NY: Free Press.

Suzuki, D. T. (1994). *A manual of Zen Buddhism*. New York, NY: Grove Press.

Szimhart, J. (2009). Razor's edge indeed: A deprogrammer's view of harmful cult activity. *Cultic Studies Review, 8*(3), 231–265.

Tillich, P. (1957). *Dynamics of faith*. New York, NY: HarperCollins.

Tong, R. (1993). *Feminine and feminist ethics*. Belmont, CA: Wadsworth.

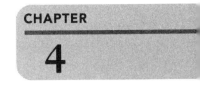

Cross-Cultural Counseling and Human Development

Anneliese A. Singh, Kim Lee Hughes, and Taryne M. Mingo

INTRODUCTION

For the past four decades (Sue & Sue, 2013; Sue et al., 1998), attention to cross-cultural counseling and human development has not only increased, but also has become a benchmark competency in the counseling field in the United States (Sue, Arredondo, & McDavis, 1992). Cross-cultural counseling has been defined as including the awareness, knowledge, and skills related to counseling clients from diverse backgrounds (Sue et al., 1992) and worldviews. The terms *cross-cultural counseling* and *multicultural counseling* are often used as interchangeable terms, just as *culturally responsive counseling* or *culturally relevant counseling* also refer to the same practice. A foundational component of cross-cultural counseling entails counselor development of multicultural counseling competence in an ongoing way across professional development, beginning in counselor training and supervision and situated as a proactive aim throughout a counselor's career. The current chapter discusses the history of cross-cultural counseling, key multicultural concepts and ideas, important social justice and advocacy concerns, and gives a brief description of the lifespan of human development. Interactive boxes and case studies are shared throughout the chapter, and website resources for further learning are provided at the end of the chapter.

History of Cross-Cultural Counseling

In 1992, the Association of Multicultural Counseling and Development developed competencies to guide the professional development of culturally responsive counseling. They were published in various formats (Arredondo et al., 1996; Sue et al., 1998) to increase the integration of multicultural counseling in cross-cultural counseling practice. In doing so, the field moved from a diversity focus on the numbers of various diverse social identities and groups present in a given context (e.g., number of Latino/as accessing a counseling center) to a multicultural focus on the social identities and related experiences of both the client and the counselor (e.g., how clients' cultural backgrounds influence their well-being) and the cross-cultural transactions between them in the counseling relationship (e.g., how counselor and client cultural backgrounds influence the therapeutic relationship).

As cross-cultural counseling scholars began to research the development of multicultural counseling competence, much attention was given to the counseling transactions between counselors and clients based on their mutually shared or dissimilar social identities (Burkard, Ponterotto, Reynolds, & Alfonso, 1999; Cook & Helms, 1988). During the two decades of this research, there was a simultaneous increase in the attention to issues of advocacy and social justice related to multicultural counseling. This movement was described as a return to the roots of counseling, where social justice was an integral aspect (Kiselica & Robinson, 2001; Singh & Salazar, 2010). For instance, Kiselica and Robinson (2001) asserted that "the purposes of advocacy counseling, social action, and social justice interventions are to increase a client's sense of personal power and to foster sociopolitical changes that reflect greater responsiveness to the client's personal needs" (p. 387), citing DuBois and other historical figures within and outside of the counseling profession who engaged in mental health advocacy. In addition, the roots of social justice in group counseling reach back to the founding of the Hull House by feminist Jane Addams, who developed groups for immigrants experiencing health disparities (Singh & Salazar, 2010).

The initial focus of cross-cultural counseling research focused on the influence of discrimination and prejudice on mental health, but it has recently begun to examine constructs such as wellness, resilience, and strengths-based approaches. Resilience has historically been defined as how well clients navigate adversity in their lives, or how they "bounce back" from difficult times in their lives (Masten, 2001). However, research has recently begun to investigate how clients are resilient in the face of oppression (Singh, 2012) and how to enhance this in counseling with historically marginalized groups (Hendricks & Testa, 2012).

In addition, identity intersectionality has also gained more importance in cross-cultural counseling; counselor and client social identities do not exist in isolation but rather have a complex intersection. For instance, an African American man experiences not only discrimination in society related to his race/ethnicity, but also oppression related to his gender identity. In this example, then, multiple societal oppressions position African American men as "dangerous" or "criminal." These societal stereotypes and oppressions influence the mental and physical health of African American men, so a counselor working with African American men should explore these impacts. However, the counselor should also holistically explore both the potential resilience and trauma related to these experiences.

> ## BOX 4.1 THE INFLUENCE OF RACISM AND OTHER OPPRESSIONS ON THE LIVES OF BLACK MEN
>
> You are working with a client named Jamal, an African American who is 18 years old and beginning college. Jamal attended predominantly Black schools growing up and is currently in a predominantly White context for the first time in college. Jamal presents for counseling, describing feeling "out of sorts and kind of depressed." He describes having a hard time relating to his professors and fellow students. As you conduct the counseling intake with Jamal, answer the following questions:
>
> - What are the key social identities and experiences of oppression and resilience you migth explore with Jamal?
> - What is the self-reflection you would need to do as a counselor who shares a racial/ethnic identity with Jamal or as a counselor who does not share a similar racial/ethnic identity?
> - How might you use the ACA Multicultural and Social Justice Competencies (2015) to guide the development of your knowledge related to providing culturally responsive counseling with Jamal?
> - How might you use the ACA Advocacy Competencies (Lewis, Arnold, House, & Toporek, 2003) to guide the development of your knowledge related to providing culturally responsive counseling with Jamal?

Multicultural Competence: Key Terms, Ideas, and Concepts

Because the U.S. population has rapidly diversified, multicultural counseling education and practice have become a growing concern (Nadal, Griffin, Wong, Hamit, & Rasmus, 2014). All individuals are multicultural, which means they have a combination of privileged and oppressed identities that construct their social identities. Master identities are evident and less mutable (i.e., race/ethnicity), and emergent identities may be fluid (i.e., gender expression) (Warner, 2008). These identities combine and develop over time, and different identities may be more salient at various points across the lifespan. For instance, an individual's religious affiliations may change dramatically over the lifespan from practicing Christianity as a young adult to converting to Buddhism as a result of experiences during middle adulthood. Or someone could be an officer in the military during middle adulthood and require extensive care in late adulthood due to a mental illness like Alzheimer's disease. We maintain multiple identities of oppression and privilege over a lifetime, yet the balance of those identity categories is subject to change based on context (Jones, Kim, & Skendall, 2012).

Counselors are trained to understand the importance of cross-cultural competence and the influence of diversity on the counseling relationship, yet fewer counselors understand how to develop and implement cross-cultural interventions (Knox, Burkhard, Johnson, Suzuki, & Ponterotto, 2003). Multicultural counseling competence begins with an understanding of key terms, ideas, and concepts, including intersectionality. Intersectionality examines the way social identities of privilege and oppression play out for various groups across various social systems (i.e., how individuals from diverse backgrounds interact and navigate in various social systems; Ramsay, 2014). The theory of intersectionality originated in the field of public policy in relation to the experiences of African American women who were negatively affected in the legal system based on the intersections of their gender and race/ethnicity (Crenshaw, 1991). Feminist theorists in counseling adopted intersectionality theory because this theory challenged assumptions of essentialism of social identities (i.e., instead of using race/ethnicity as a sole focus of intervention for women of color; Warner & Shields, 2013). Intersectionality theory is gaining new applications that expand beyond race/ethnicity and gender to include class, ability, sexual orientation, immigration status, marital status, mental health status, nationality, occupation, religion, and other ways of categorizing individual difference (Gopaldas, 2013). The expansion of the definition of intersectionality to include multiple social identities means that everyone is intersectional and experiences unique social privileges and oppressions every day (Ramsay, 2013).

Social identities are interdependent with issues of mental health (Wilson, Okwu, & Mills, 2011). All individuals have multiple intersections of identity, including privileged and oppressed identities. A preponderance of privileged identities may lead to increased access without merit, whereas a preponderance of oppressed identities may lead to decreased access without cause (Shields, 2008). The study of intersectionality examines the way multiple marginalized identities render individuals invisible and disempowered in social systems at the micro, meso, and macro levels (Crenshaw, 1991; Purdie-Vaughns & Eibach, 2008). An imbalance in privileged and oppressed identities for some individuals may cause mental health distress due to limited access and participation, which results in unjust and inequitable systems like schools, employment, and government agencies (Ramsay, 2014). A move toward social justice requires consideration for ways to increase access for individuals with multiple marginalized identities while striving for equity across multicultural identities (Goodman et al., 2004).

Social identities are socially constructed and may be based on an individual's physical characteristics, such as race/ethnicity or sex (Ingram, Chaudhary, & Jones, 2014; Warner, 2008). Social identities may also highlight less visible attributes like sexual orientation and mental ability (Bowleg, 2008). In each case, these social identities are contextual or fluid, not fixed and socially defined (Ben-Moshe & Magaña, 2014). As such, aspects of an individual's social identity transform and change over the course of the lifespan based on context (Jones et al., 2012). For example, a mixed-race person assigned the female sex in the Midwest who is placed into the foster care system may graduate from an Ivy League university and join the upper middle class as an educated stay-at-home mother in a heterosexual marriage. In this case, the individual's intersectionality changed in multiple ways as she moved over the life cycle in terms of education, class privilege, and family experiences.

Cross-cultural counseling is concerned about the way an individual's identities of privilege and oppression come together to influence his or her overall well-being and experiences in social systems like school, the justice system, and various community contexts (Nadal et al., 2014). Multiple identities of privilege may converge to produce unfair and unearned advantage, whereas multiple identities of oppression may limit access and engagement (Kohl, 2006). When multiple identities of privilege are systemically arranged to promote advantage for one group over another, there may be evidence of discrimination in the form of a particular system of oppression or -ism (e.g., classism, heterosexism, racism; Gopaldas, 2013). Awareness around the existence of -isms and the way that they join and affect the mental health of intersectional clients is an essential multicultural counseling competence. Identities of privilege and oppression are constructed by society in the context of history and are maintained by the status quo. This means that all advantages related to social identities of privilege exist in tandem with disadvantages related to social identities of oppression (Ben-Moshe & Magaña, 2014). Oppressed social identities are most commonly related to discriminatory social practices targeted at particular identity markers: racial/ethnic discrimination is called racism; gender discrimination is called sexism; sexual orientation discrimination is called heterosexism; discrimination against persons with disabilities is called ableism (2013). Essentially, people with social identities related to oppression are subject to discrimination on the basis of an -ism (e.g., racism, sexism, adultism), whereas people with social identities related to privilege are generally associated with maintaining the status quo. Table 4.1 presents an example of how social identities are related to privilege and oppression experiences.

Intersectionality plays an important role in cross-cultural counseling because social identities define and shape an individual's development and sense of self in society (Nadal et al., 2014). Cross-cultural counseling requires that counselors raise their awareness around their own identities of privilege and oppression and how these influence clients from diverse cultural backgrounds

Table 4.1   Social Identities of Privilege and Oppression

Social Identity	Privilege	Oppression
Race/ethnicity	White	Latino/a
Gender	Male	Transgender
Sexual orientation	Straight	Queer
Age	45 years old	78 years old
Ability	Gifted student	Student with attention-deficit/ hyperactivity disorder
Education	Doctoral degree	GED
Class	Upper middle class	Poverty
Religion	Christian	Muslim
Regionality	Beverly Hills	Compton

(Sue, Capadilupo, & Holder, 2008; Tomko & Munley, 2012). This may be particularly important for White counselors working with clients of color because there may be systemic barriers to building trust in the counseling dyad (Knox et al., 2003). Beyond issues of race/ethnicity, counselors must understand their privilege in the counseling relationship due to the power differential inherent in all counseling (Buser, 2009). Counselor self-awareness is particularly important in cross-cultural counseling because experiences of discrimination from the larger society can show up in the counseling dyad and cause client distress (Owen, Tao, Imel, Wampold, & Rodolfa, 2014). As such, counselor transparency around issues of cultural difference including race/ethnicity (Knox et al., 2003), sexual orientation (Shelton & Delgado-Romero, 2013), and ability (Ben-Moshe & Magaña, 2014) have been shown to facilitate trust in the counseling relationship. For instance, during the introductory session, mental health counselors may want to explore issues of intersectionality directly with their clients by discussing obvious differences and similarities. A White counselor may want to discuss issues of racial/ethnic difference and similarity with their clients to develop more transparency and authenticity in the counseling dyad. The same is true for counselors with varying intersections; the idea is to bring the obvious into the therapeutic process.

Research also suggests that counselors of color are more willing than their White counterparts to openly discuss cross-cultural differences such as oppression in the counseling dyad (Knox et al., 2003; Owen et al., 2014), which is one way to demonstrate multicultural competence (Sue et al., 1992). A study by Knox et al. (2003) showed that White counselors experienced hesitancy and fear broaching issues of cultural difference in session unless directed by the client despite understanding the multicultural relevance of discussing cultural differences like race (also see Owens et al., 2014). Therefore, multiculturally competent counselors should be prepared to discuss issues of intersectionality and the ways multiple marginalized identities negatively affect their clients' mental health and also to explore the ways these experiences influence and shape the counseling relationship (Lambert, Herman, Bynum, & Ialongo, 2009; Nadal et al., 2014). This process can begin in the rapport-building stages during the counseling intake and assessment session and continue throughout the course of counseling. Discussing issues of cross-cultural context early in the counseling alliance may increase trust and improve outcomes for clients across difference (Owen et al., 2014).

Micro- and Macroaggressions

Multiple oppressed identities subject individuals to discrimination in large and small ways and are therefore important for counselors to assess and understand in cross-cultural counseling. Oppression enacted through the enforcement of unjust policy and inequitable application of the law is called a macroaggression(s) (Donovan, Galban, Grace, Bennett, & Felicié, 2012). Macroaggressions are overt forms of discrimination that are systemic and difficult to transform due to a history of social inequity (Reid & Knight, 2006). Macroaggressions are pervasive and tend to be quantifiable. An example of a macroaggression is the school-to-prison pipeline for young men of color or the recently overturned "Don't Ask, Don't Tell" policy related to lesbian, gay, bisexual, transgender, and queer (LGBTQ) people serving in the U.S. Armed Forces. Quiroga, Medina, and Glick (2014) discussed the negative influence of changing immigration policies in Arizona on Latino adults despite their immigration status (U.S. or foreign born). Recently, an Alabama chief justice instructed probate court judges not to issue same-sex marriage licenses despite a federal court ruling. A look at the statistics on men in prison between the ages of 18 and 25 years would be a way to prove the existence of inequitable treatment in the judicial system for men of color. Conversely, microaggressions may be hard to quantify and even more pervasive than macroaggressions (Nadal et al., 2014).

Microaggressions are subtle acts of discrimination perpetrated by an individual with a privileged identity against someone with an oppressed identity (Owen et al., 2014; Sue et al., 2008). They are harmful in cross-cultural counseling because they minimize the client to a stereotype or an exception to an unstated rule (Franklin, Boyd-Franklin, & Kelly, 2006; Gassner & McGuigan, 2014). The term *microaggressive* was coined in the late 1970s toward the end of the Civil Rights era and was used to describe ways that racial/ethnic inequities are intricately woven into social systems (Pierce, Carew, Pierce-Gonzalez, & Willis, 1978). The term is used by social justice scholars and advocates to examine multiple identities of oppression including sexual orientation, mental health, ability, and race/ethnicity. Unlike the more overt acts of discrimination associated with macroaggressions, microaggressions are defined to include micro insults, micro assaults, and micro invalidations that may be unconscious to the microaggressor because of the normalization of systems of inequity (Sue, 2010). For example, a Latino human resource director in a hospital setting may address all of the male interns as doctor while addressing all the female interns as miss or missus, according to their marital status. He may believe that he is addressing the women appropriately, and may be unconscious of the fact that his behavior is demeaning and microaggressive.

Pascoe and Richman (2009) found that perceived discrimination has a significant impact on mental and physical health outcomes, particularly for people of color, who have multiple marginalized identities. For individuals with multiple intersections of oppression, there may be benefit in discussing macro- and microaggressions in the counseling relationship to assist clients with feelings of shame, guilt, regret, and remorse associated with the daily navigation of continual discrimination (Sue et al., 2008). Engaging in honest dialogue about discrimination in cross-cultural counseling may increase client retention and improve the counseling relationship by building trust and rapport (Knox et al., 2003; Nadal et al., 2014; Sue et al., 1992). Counselors should carefully balance open dialogue about difference with a focus on the needs of the client as opposed to disclosing their own intersectional identities, which can undermine credibility in cross-cultural dyads (Nadal et al., 2014; Owen et al., 2014).

BOX 4.2 MICROAGGRESSION EXPERIENCES

Lisa is an Asian Pacific Islander senior partner at a financial brokerage firm that hires graduate-level interns. She manages a multicultural division of employees and holds a weekly staff meeting with her direct reports. Upon entering a staff meeting, Lisa overhears several White male employees talking to a Native American female intern. Lisa can hear their conversation and is alarmed when she overhears one of the men ask the intern, "Why do you want to work here? Don't you own some equity in a tribal casino?" Lisa is more alarmed when the intern attempts to answer the question to a round of laughter from the group. Lisa clears her throat to let the group know that she is in the room; she then calls the meeting to order, shifting the focus away from the intern and onto the purpose of the meeting. After the meeting, Lisa speaks with the intern to see if she is doing okay. Lisa explains that she overheard the conversation and found it inappropriate and that the intern had a right to be offended, too.

- What could Lisa have done differently in this situation?
- Are you guilty of microaggressive behavior? If so, under what circumstances?
- Have you been a victim of microaggression? How did you know?
- How might microaggression look in a counseling session?

Counselor Use of Language in Developing Multicultural Competence

An essential component of cross-cultural counseling is to use language that empowers clients as opposed to language that disempowers or reinforces systems of oppression (Warner & Shields, 2013). The words that counselors use with clients can facilitate a working alliance or reinforce the status quo, causing a rupture (i.e., discrimination and oppression; Buser, 2009; Sue et al., 2008). The language that counselors use in counseling settings also demonstrates their values around issues of difference. Therefore, word choice is one way to show respect for a client's cultural positionality (Buser, 2009). Conversely, when working with diverse cultures, insensitive use of language may lead to misunderstanding and disconnections in the counseling alliance (Knox et al., 2003; Owens et al., 2014).

The following are a few examples of ways that cross-cultural counselors can use language that demonstrates their commitment to client advocacy:

- A couples counselor who refers to all clients as *partners* instead of using limited language like *husband* and *wife*, which may be discriminatory toward couples who choose not to marry

- A high school counselor who addresses all of her adolescent clients with the title of miss or mister to counter adultist assumptions in the counseling relationship
- A White Jewish counselor who openly discusses issues of cultural difference with clients of color as a part of the client assessment process, as opposed to ignoring obvious difference, which may be misinterpreted as indifference or insensitivity by clients of color
- A straight African Amerian male mentoring gay African American adolescents on safe sexual practices in a way that engages and empowers the group, as opposed to using language that stigmatizes

For counselors with multiple privileged identities, it may be difficult to challenge language that reinforces their privilege in the current social system. For instance, it may be difficult for an upper-middle-class White female counselor to recognize the housing implications for individuals from lower socioeconomic backgrounds. As such, the counselor may make assumptions about the living conditions and lifestyle of the clients she serves. If she is a school counselor working with undocumented families from South Korea, she may not understand that economic status influences multiple aspects of her clients' lives, such as their ability to access quality housing. An approach involving courageous conversations (i.e., difficult dialogues) is one way that social justice advocates, including feminist scholars, have tried to broach charged social topics (Sue et al., 2008). It is one way to discuss privilege and oppression openly without making assumptions about the experiences of the other (Collins, 2002).

Research showed that clients of color perceived counselors who actively acknowledged the importance of cultural differences as being more credible (Knox et al., 2003). On the other hand, failure to address issues of cultural difference between the counselor and client may perpetuate societal patterns of discrimnation by imposing a dominant cultural imperative on diverse clients (Granello & Wheaton, 1998). Counselors working with culturally diverse clients in cross-cultural relationships should be intentional with the language they use when exploring various topics with their clients to increase their credibility. Counselors can demonstrate cultural competence by using intentional language and effective broaching with diverse client populations (Day-Vines et al., 2007). This means that counselors are aware of and use proactive language in and outside of the counseling relationship by actively engaging in cross-cultural relationships personally and professionally (Arrendondo et al., 1996; Knox et al., 2003).

In accordance with the 2014 ACA Code of Ethics, counselors promote social justice cross-culturally when they embrace the unique dignity and worth of all clients and support the development of their unique potential. One way to credibility is through affirmative and informed language inside and outside of the counseling relationship. The counselor may be seen as more authentic, trustworthy, and competent when using language that demonstrates sensitivity for diversity (Owens et al., 2014).

Using the ACA Advocacy Competencies to Enhance Crosscultural Counseling Competence Multicultural Competence Through Social Justice Advocacy

Multicultural counseling is responsible for bringing awareness to counselors about the cultural variables present within the counseling relationship (Ratts, 2011) and for acknowledging the social influences that impact the lives of students and clients every day. Counselors who practice from a social justice framework are knowledgeable about client issues and intervene with or on behalf of their clients to promote social justice, equity, and access to resources (Ockerman & Mason, 2012). Counselors operating from a social justice framework can have a significant impact on the human development of marginalized persons, particularly as it relates to having an ally listen to their experiences and advocate on their behalf. Professional school counselors, for example, can address equity and access gaps in academic achievement among marginalized student populations and can advocate for additional opportunities and resources that will ensure every student reaches his or her maximum potential for academic, social, and personal growth (Singh, Urbano, Haston, & McMahon, 2010). Unfortunately, the national media seems to continuously report a significant number of victims impacted by social injustices throughout the country. Leelah Alcorn, a transgender teen from Ohio, committed suicide after feeling she could not live in a world that was unaccepting of her true identity (Fantz, 2015). Trayvon Martin, another victim of social injustice, was walking home through a nearby neighborhood community and was shot and killed by one of the neighborhood residents who perceived him, an unarmed Black teenage male, as threatening and dangerous (Botelho, 2012). These are just a few examples of marginalized persons who lost their lives as a result of an unjust system that does not embody a multicultural perspective. Their stories convey how the lack of a multicultural perspective promotes a broken system that protects only privileged individuals. Therefore, counselors are called to increase their multicultural competence and to advocate for marginalized persons and communities impacted by oppression as change agents and advocates for social justice.

Defining Social Justice

Social justice refers to the way privilege and oppression impact the well-being of individuals and communities (Singh et al., 2012). Counseling and social justice advocacy are intertwined; each is necessary to help students and clients reach their full potential and achieve mental well-being (Chang, Crethar, & Ratts, 2010). This includes environmental factors within the education system that are believed to have a negative impact on learning and academic performance (Ratts & Hutchins, 2009). For example, school counselors may notice a disproportionate number of African American male students being referred to the counselor or principal for classroom misconduct. Recognizing the negative impact on students' academic performance when they are consistently removed from the classroom, the school counselor can address environmental factors that are contributing to these students' removal from the classroom from a social justice approach. Counselors should also become aware of the ways their attitudes, beliefs, and values may promote or maintain injustices to marginalized groups of people by recognizing the privileges afforded to them as helping professionals.

Privilege is defined as unearned benefits systemically given to specific members of society (Crethar, Rivera, & Nash, 2008). Becoming multiculturally competent is important because many well-meaning counselors and counselor educators are unaware of their own privileged status and how systemic injustice affects the mental well-being of their students and clients (Comstock et al., 2008). Systemic injustice can also affect the human development of students and clients specifically as it relates to their beliefs about their own potential to be successful in their endeavors. Privilege is maintained by social injustices that prevent equitable opportunities and access to resources and contribute to the oppression of marginalized groups of people. Counselors must be intentional in remaining self-reflective about their privileges to ensure they are not portraying the same attitudes or beliefs that contribute to a systematically unjust system that promotes some and devalues others.

Counselors who operate from a framework that incorporates multiculturalism and social justice recognize oppression as the foundation of mental health problems. They attempt to advocate for a society that is liberated from systemic barriers (Ratts, 2011) that prevent individuals from living full lives. Oppression gives power to some while disempowering others and is presented in various forms of injustice such as classism, heterosexism, ableism, racism, and sexism. Therefore, counselors need to begin a combined approach toward helping marginalized persons by recognizing cultural variables within the counseling relationship and by advocating against social injustices that continue to negatively impact students and clients outside the counseling environment.

Increasing multiculturalism and social justice competence are critical in training and supervising future counselors (Malott & Knoper, 2012). A number of scholars suggest counselor educators incorporate social justice advocacy training into their academic programs (Bemak, Chung, Talleyrand, Jones, & Daiquin, 2011; Brubaker, Puig, Reese, & Young, 2010). This training would entail discussions surrounding social justice, privilege, oppression, and student engagement in political activism. Arranging future counseling professionals to work with diverse students and clients as a means of building multicultural competence is not enough. Training future counseling professionals on culturally and contextually appropriate interventions and strategies, however, can further extend their ability to help marginalized persons from a social justice framework.

Multicultural competence is recognized as interwoven with a social justice framework designed to advocate on behalf of students and clients (Malott & Knoper, 2012). The ACA Advocacy Competencies (Lewis et al., 2003) were designed to educate counselors to become knowledgeable and aware of social injustice in their work with clients and to be intentional in creating systemic change by reducing social inequity (Toporek, Lewis, & Crethar, 2009). The use of these competencies is especially beneficial for helping counselors support their clients from within their specific contextual environments as opposed to supporting their clients as entities with needs functioning outside that environment. Counselors should use the ACA Advocacy Competencies to advocate for positive change at the micro and macro levels and to promote change within institutional and public arenas (Brady-Amoon, 2011). Therefore, incorporating a social justice lens to advocate for clients and students is not an alternative or different perspective of multicultural competence but extends multicultural competence by acknowledging the various levels of advocacy. As mentioned earlier, multicultural competence is not enough to support and advocate on behalf of a diverse clientele population, especially if the counselor remains focused at the client (micro) level. Counselors trained to operate from a social justice lens, a reflection of ACA Advocacy Competencies, not only advocate for clients at the micro level, but also on behalf of their clients by promoting change within their contextual environments, institutions, and public arenas (macro level).

There is certainly a need for professional counselors to advocate at the micro and macro levels of their clients. Micro level advocacy includes supporting the client's needs directly by working with the client in his or her present state of need. Macro level advocacy includes recognizing external factors that may have contributed to the client's need to seek counseling, such as frustrations of living up to social expectations or inability to find employment, and taking steps to address those external factors directly by writing letters to community stakeholders, providing information at community events or conferences, or building a network of allies interested in a collaborative effort to address situations that affect their community. These are a few examples of direct macro level advocacy. In addition, advocacy at the macro level is particularly important in recognizing systemic barriers that oppress or marginalize certain groups of people, and it may significantly contribute toward the aforementioned external factors. Having a social justice mindset on both levels is essential to understanding the interdependence of micro and macro systems in the lives of clients and students (Singh et al., 2010). Advocating at the micro and macro levels can posivitely impact clients' human development by empowering them to become change agents within their own environments. The goal of advocacy at the client level is to help them access resources, to inform privileged groups about barriers affecting client well-being, to find potential allies, and to create a plan to address barriers affecting clients (Toporek et al., 2009). Advocacy on behalf of clients can be used to increase equity and access for clients of marginalized groups and can help members of privileged groups recognize how they may be unintentionally maintaining a society that marginalizes groups of people.

Using the ACA Advocacy Competencies to Practice Cross-Cultural Counseling

Each level of the ACA Advocacy Competencies (Lewis et al., 2003) is explored in the following section as an example of practicing cross-cultural counseling. It is organized as two approaches of advocacy: with the client and on behalf of the client. Advocating with the client and on behalf of the client will be different across

each competency level. Advocacy with the client involves more direct intervention that impacts the client within the cultural context of his or her environment.
Advocacy on behalf of the client involves intercession of contributing factors that
influence the client's environment.

The Micro Level

Empowering the client is an approach toward advocating with the client at
the micro level. The goal of empowerment at the micro level is to help clients
recognize their strengths and external factors that contribute to their development
and to build self-advocacy (Toporek et al., 2009). A culturally competent social
justice school counselor can practice cross-cultural counseling by empowering an
African American male student who has been referred to counseling for consistently falling behind in class and failing to complete homework through positive
self-fulfillment practices that address his needs from within his cultural context.
Some children may not have support in their home environments that would
facilitate homework completion and may need an advocate to work with them in
finding alternative approaches to academic success. The school counselor can also
help students understand how external influences can contribute to their academic
struggles and empower them beyond those limitations by acknowledging their
resiliency and strength. By helping the student understand his capabilities outside
his situation, the culturally competent school counselor can help him develop a
sense of empowerment in knowing which school faculty to seek for assistance
or knowing additional allies he can go to when he lacks resources, guidance, or
support. Empowering the individual through practicing cross-cultural counseling
involves helping the student identify his or her strengths, talents, and skills
(Goodman et al., 2004). The goal of cross-cultural counseling at the micro level is
to provide the student access to resources, inform faculty and staff about barriers
affecting student performance, find potential allies, and create a plan to address
barriers affecting the student (Toporek et al., 2009).

Advocacy on behalf of students can be used to increase equity and access for
marginalized students. Practicing cross-cultural counseling on behalf of students
can involve the school counselor seeking additional resources within the school
and nearby community to provide support, such as organizing in-home tutoring
for the student. Counselors can practice cross-cultural counseling by advocating
on behalf of clients through collaborating with various organizations interested
in social justice advocacy, which, through combined efforts, promotes systemic
change within the community (Toporek et al., 2009). School counselors can collaborate with community members about the needs of students within the community, the effects of poverty among adolescents, and how this population affects
the community (Ratts & Hutchins, 2009). To know how to collaborate with the
community, school counselors need to be able to identify environmental barriers
that affect students and to educate community stakeholders about the effects of
these barriers so they may join the schools in implementing positive change for students and families. School counselors can address the equity and access gaps within
the community by acting on behalf of students and families through leadership to

illuminate problems and by collaborating with others to envision and work toward change (Toporek et al., 2009). School counselors may also want to incorporate statistics that make student issues more personal to the community. Some schools have organized a committee composed of business partners and agencies to address the issues that impact the lives of students and their ability to succeed in school, such as poor housing conditions, rates of violence in certain neighborhoods, and drug usage. Incorporating a cross-cultural counseling approach toward advocating with and on behalf of students in educational settings at the micro level may prevent institutional discrimination and work against a larger system of injustice.

The Meso Level

Advocating with clients at the meso level involves collaborating with organizations that are already dedicated to assisting the client's needs and environmental concerns. Counselors can practice cross-cultural counseling by connecting clients to organizations that support their needs and also informing organizations of their availability to assist clients who are already receiving support from their organization. This may involve a counselor joining the governing board of a local sexual assault center for children and using his or her position to inform parents and educators on recognizing the signs of abuse and where to find support for children who have been abused. The goal of cross-cultural counseling includes the counselor serving as an ally for clients and as a resource connecting them to opportunities for support. Collaboration is the focus of cross-cultural counseling and advocating with the client at the meso level and can foster a genuine relationship between counselor and client.

Systems advocacy involves the counselor going beyond assisting the client in coping with stressors within his or her environment and taking on roles of leadership, systems analysis, and a desire to address the factors that create stressors for clients. Advocating on behalf of clients at the meso level involves recognizing how systemic oppression contributes to the lived experiences of clients. Practicing a cross-cultural approach on behalf of clients at the meso level may begin with counselors conducting research on the number of sexual assault cases toward children as a means to provide awareness of an overlooked problem within their community. If counselors are truly concerned about the welfare of their clients and helping them overcome personal barriers, they must also be committed to taking an active role toward removing systemic barriers that were specifically designed to keep certain clients from overcoming them. Therefore, counselors need to be willing to advocate beyond the counseling room and into leadership roles within the community.

The Macro Level

When practicing a cross-cultural counseling approach with clients at the macro level, providing information to the public is essential in empowering these individuals because it enables those impacted by oppression to have their voices heard by a wider audience. For example, in some communities there has been an increase in the number of governmental housing and mobile home communities being demolished to build luxurious apartment buildings and condominiums. These projects are sometimes constructed to bring in more money from college students and other privileged groups. These renovations often displace families of economic disadvantage, leaving them homeless or temporarily living with family members or in homeless shelters. An example of cross-cultural counseling practices with clients at the macro level could involve the counselor hosting a nonviolent demonstration to protest renovations that displace families while also providing the community with information about the impact of renovations on families of economic disadvantage. A cross-cultural approach toward social justice advocacy means advocating for change within the community. Recognizing the lived experiences of marginalized clients and sharing their experiences with the general public can provide awareness about the impact government decisions have on individuals within the community. Advocating with marginalized groups allows their voices to be heard and can also provide awareness to stakeholders involved in governmental policy. Including the voices of marginalized populations is essential when advocating for change within a community setting because, unfortunately, their experiences are oftern overlooked or ignored when certain community decisions are made.

Cross-cultural counseling, or advocating for systemic change on behalf the larger public arena, involves bridging allies, students, parents, educators, and community stakeholders to address systemic issues that should be resolved through political action (Lewis, Ratts, Paladino, & Toporek, 2011). Providing information about the problems that impact one's community to state and national legislators who make decisions that ultimately impact students is advocating on behalf students at the macro level. For example, school counselors can practice a cross-cultural approach on behalf of their students at the macro level by reaching out to lobby leaders to advocate on behalf of undocumented students and partner with allies who recognize the injustice of preventing undocumented students an opportunity to seek post-secondary education. Additional examples of a cross-cultural approach on behalf of students at the macro level include partnering with community and business organizations. These partnerships can be used to begin a dialogue about how children of undocumented families are further disadvantaged in accessing educational opportunities and how this maintains a cycle of inequitable opportunities to be academically successful. School counselors can inform political leaders how systemic barriers are environmental factors that inhibit academic success, and, as a result, prevent students from accessing the resources and support systems necessary to foster their future career aspirations (Butler, 2012).

As mentioned previously, counseling and social justice are intertwined, and true advocacy involves counselors advocating for their students and clients beyond the counseling office (Malott & Knoper, 2012). It is unfortunate that many students and clients are born in situations that prevent them from realizing their strengths and capabilities. As a result, these students grow up to become adults who were never able to reach their full potential due to their circumstances and limited resources, and they will be eventually blamed, due to a socially unjust structure, by society for their failure to do so. In the next section of the chapter, we briefly discuss what cross-cultural counseling may look like across the lifespan.

Cross-Cultural Counseling in Childhood and Early Adolescence

Understanding the contextual factors that influence the well-being of children and adolescents is an important aspect of cross-cultural counseling. Childhood reflects a time when individuals are most enthusiastic about learning and direct their energy toward mastering knowledge and skills (Santrock, 2006). This is also a time when they are likely to experience a sense of inferiority as a result of feeling incompetent or less productive than other children (Santrock, 2006). According to Erikson's industry versus inferiority stage of development, the adults in a child's life have a responsibility to encourage him or her to explore and discover aspects of himself or herself that he or she may have never realized before (Erikson, 1968), so the child may recognize his or her capabilities for success. Some children, due to systemic oppression, may not have opportunities to explore those skills as a result of early exposure to marginalization and oppression. This can have a significant impact on their development as they move into adulthood and could potentially inhibit their abilities to self-actualize or live fulfilling lives based on their future aspirations.

For example, an African American female student who attends a predominantly White elementary school may experience isolation due to a lack of representation of African American students and faculty. This could result in the student encompassing feelings of self-hatred due to her hypervisibility in the classroom setting and the development of social assumptions that only White people can become teachers and administrators. Not seeing oneself represented in successful and authoritative positions might lead the student to begin questioning her abilities to be successful in a predominantly White educational setting. Returning to the LGBTQ example, in addition to employment discrimination, anti-LGBTQ laws and internalized heterosexism may have influenced clients' exploration of or access to family building resources, information, and options. Therefore, counselors employing a cross-cultural approach to support this student will need to understand the importance of her ability to see herself as academically capable and successful in taking on new tasks. According to Sue (2003), all forms of examination related to supporting ethnic student populations should incorporate the ethnicity of the individual within the design. Having a positive perception of one's ethnic group identity has been found to be an important predictor for future psychological outcomes (Phinney & Ong, 2007).

Cross-Cultural Counseling in Late Adolescence and Early Adulthood

The challenges for the late adolescent and early adult are the mastery of connection and the establishment of meaningful relationships (Beaumont & Pratt, 2011). These relationship patterns start in the home environment and are fostered by successes or failures to develop healthy connections at schools and in the community at large. Specifically, this developmental stage is associated with graduating from high school and the movement toward contextual environments outside of the family, like college or employment (Wickrama, Conger, Lorenz, & Martin, 2012). These new environmental contexts call for new skills and new ways to navigate and transition into adulthood (Melchior et al., 2014).

BOX 4.3 EXPLORING AND ADDRESSING THE ISSUES OF ECONOMIC DISADVANTAGE AND OTHER OPPRESSIONS ON STUDENTS WHO SPEAK ENGLISH AS A SECOND LANGUAGE

You are working with a second-grade Latina student, Sylvia, who recently immigrated to the United States with her family, speaks limited English, and whose family has very few resources. Sylvia and her family are considered undocumented citizens within the state, and as a result, her family must always fear the possibility of being deported. Sylvia has a difficult time adjusting to the classroom setting, and her teacher describes her as being socially withdrawn. She does not understand the assignments given by her teacher, and she usually responds by crying until she is removed from the classroom and sent to the counseling office. Sylvia's academic and social experiences are likely to have a significant impact on her future development as a student and female of color. If Sylvia is unable to access an equitable learning environment that is available in her native language, it is likely she will fall further behind academically. This can lead to gaps in academic achievement compared with other students, future possibility of special education services, and an inability to see herself as academically capable. If Sylvia is unable to fully engage in her social environment without fear of deportation or deportation of her family members, she is likely to miss valuable opportunities (i.e., field trips, postsecondary options, and driving tests) that will assist her development in reaching her full potential.

- What social barriers do you recognize that are presenting this student from being successful?
- How could you advocate with Sylvia? On behalf of Sylvia?
- How do you see yourself advocating for Sylvia at the meso and macro levels of the ACA Advocacy competencies (Toporek et al., 2009)?

BOX 4.4 EXPLORING CROSS-CULTURAL CONCERNS IN CHILDHOOD AND EARLY ADOLESCENCE

A teacher escorts a 7-year-old African American male student named Phillip to the school counselor's office for bullying behavior and acts of defiance. He is the only African American student in his class at a predominantly White, rural elementary school. He has been sent to the principal's office four times this month for refusing to complete homework and not following directions in the classroom. Phillip's teacher acknowledges to the school counselor that he has become a disruption to the class and his behaviors are preventing the other students from learning. She then turns to Phillip and instructs him not to return to her class until he is prepared to behave himself in the classroom and then leaves him with the school counselor. Still looking at the floor, Phillip says quietly, "I hate school."

- What systemic issues might be influencing Phillip's behavior?
- How might you begin the counseling session with Phillip from a cross-cultural counseling framework?
- How could you encourage future success at Phillip's school?
- How could you advocate for Phillip's academic experience?
- What are the knowledge and skills you will need to work with Phillip in a culturally responsive manner?

Young adults deal with a multitude of sociopolitical factors based on their intersectionality. Nadal and colleagues (2014) found that intersectional microaggressions based on race/ethnicity may be particularly harmful when they occur in the context of school or employment settings, which are fundamental development transitions for this age group. Young adults with multiple marginalized identities may need greater support navigating various contextual environments because of the mental health implications of discrimination (Torres, Driscoll, & Burrow, 2010). For many young adults, moving beyond the context of their community of origin may mean encountering cultural difference for the first time, particularly in the areas of race/ethnicity, sexual orientation, and gender identity. For youth from privileged backgrounds, young adulthood may be their first encounter with individuals with multiple marginalized identities (Poteat & Spanierman, 2012). These encounters may lead to greater awareness about oppression, or they may lead to an insistence that society is based on merit, or what is called a *color-blind approach* (Poteat & Spanierman, 2012). The color-blind approach is based in dichotomized thought processes that may reinforce steoreotypes that promote discrimination and prejudice around difference (Gassner & McGuigan, 2014). For instance, a White male from an upper-class background at a midwestern university may assume that his African American roommate was accepted as an extension of an affirmative action program or that he is a first-generation college student.

BOX 4.5   CASE STUDY WITH CHICANA STUDENT IN LATE ADOLESCENCE

Angelica, an 18-year-old Chicana high school student, has been awarded a scholarship to a woman's college in the northeast. Angelica has a diagnosis of Asperger's syndrome and has attended private schools, where her middle-class parents are active members of the educational community. Her parents have a strong value for education and close ties to the Catholic Church. Angelica is the eldest of four sisters, and her parents want her to attend the state university and live in the family residence. Angelica recently started dating and has become more social during her senior year, which has changed her perspective on family and her role with her sisters. Angelica has been referred to the school counselor because she shared her dilemma with a trusted teacher, who wrote the recommendation to the women's college.

For individuals from collaborative cultures (e.g., Asian-Pacific Islanders or Central Americans), it may be difficult to translate personal progress into measurable success. Maturity may be measured by the way an individual can promote the collective success of the family or community. In these cases, individuals may forego the Western concept of self-actualization in favor of community advancement and shared resources. Issues of personal intersectionality may be less important than issues of familial progress. In this case, Angelica's disability has little influence on the expectations of her family that she be a caregiver for her sisters, whereas her teacher is encouraging her to pursue individual excellence, perhaps in light of her disability.

- Should Angelica take the scholarship? Why or why not?
- What role does her diagnosis have in the decision-making process? As her counselor, how would you approach her intervention?
- What are the cultural implications for Angelica if she decides to take the scholarship?
- What possible barriers may Angelica face as a Chicano woman with a disability if she decides to attend a college away from her home community?

On the other hand, individuals with multiple marginalized intersections of identity, who are vulnerable to more discrimination, may experience increased stress and lower self-esteem, which may have an impact on their academic performance and, more importantly, their mental health (Solorzano, Ceja, & Yosso, 2000; Sue, Lin, Torino, Capodilupo, & Riveria, 2009). The primary purpose of college is to become academically prepared for the workforce, yet the social component is vital to persistence rates and may be impacted by issues of cross-cultural identity and goodness of fit in the campus environment (Petty, 2014; Schultz, 2012). While college campuses may not have overt or macroaggressive discriminatory policies, colleges and universities are a microcosm of society and therefore students, faculty, and administrators are subject to cross-cultural discrimination and microaggression based on differences like race/ethnicity, social class, and ability (Gassner & McGuigan, 2014; Stebleton & Soria, 2012). Students with multiple marginalized identities may feel a lack of connection to campus organizations, may feel isolated in residence halls, or may feel isolated because they are commuter students (Lightweis, 2014).

Young adulthood is a critical time for understanding cross-cultural difference and developing acceptance across differences. Culturally competent counselors have an opportunity to work with young adults toward acceptance for diversity by facilitating an atmosphere of acceptance and celebration of difference in their educational environments. High school counselors can assist students with multiple marginalized identities to assess their strengths and needs before entering college for adequate preparation (Pham & Keenan, 2011). Once students have enrolled in college, counselors and adminstrators can assist students in developing cross-cultural competence by developing programming and training around difference and incorporating issues of diversity into the core curriculum (Gassner & McGuigan, 2014).

BOX 4.6   ADDRESSING INTERSECTING MARGINALIZED IDENTITIES IN EARLY ADULTHOOD

Seth is a graduating senior and the only child of a White single mother. Seth is blond with blue eyes, like his mother, even though his biological father is Cuban. Seth is exploring ways to fund his college education when he discovers a scholarship for first-generation Latino males to attend historically Black colleges and universities. Seth currently attends a predominantly White high school, where his friends and associates assume he is White. If he receives the scholarship, it will be awarded at a schoolwide honors ceremony and everyone will know about his background. Seth is unsure how to handle the situation and makes an appointment with his school counselor to discuss his options.

- What are some of the questions you might have for Seth if you were handling his intake session?
- In your opinion, what does race/ethnicity have to do with college choice?
- What challenges might Seth face accepting a scholarship to a historically Black college and university?
- Are the challenges greater than the possible rewards?

Cross-Cultural Counseling in Middle and Late Adulthood

Cross-cultural counseling in middle and late adulthood naturally has a major focus on end-of-life concerns. When working with clients in middle adulthood, there is a generativity (versus stagnation) of focus that typically follows identity development models (Erikson, 1968). However, as noted in earlier stages of development, experiences of social injustice and oppression can delay this development milestone, and various cultures may diverge from typically White and Western identity development models.

For instance, LGBTQ clients in middle adulthood may have experienced significant employment discrimination in their careers, resulting in a wide variety of impacts from losing employment to job changes to homelessness related to a lack of financial resources. These experiences impinge on the hallmark aspects of middle adulthood asserted in the counseling and psychological literature, which indicates that clients in this stage deepen their contributions to their work and family and develop feelings of accomplishment and that their lives have meaning. Returning to the LGBTQ example, in addition to employment discrimination, anti-LGBTQ laws and internalized heterosexism may have influenced clients' exploration or access to family building resources, information, and options. Therefore, LGBTQ clients may be exploring family building later in life, and counselors should be prepared not only to have these discussions with their LGBTQ clients but also to be able to process the grief experienced or self-advocacy needed related to family building.

BOX 4.7 EXPLORING CROSS-CULTURAL CONCERNS IN MIDDLE ADULTHOOD

Tommy, a 50-year-old client who identifies as a gay Filipino man, presents for counseling with family building concerns. His partner has recently decided he would like to have children. Tommy shares he is experiencing stress related to his partner's decision. Tommy shares that he "never wanted to have kids," because he thought as a gay man it would never be possible. Tommy also says his partner was fired from his job a month ago because his boss "found out he was gay." Tommy shares that his partner "can't prove" he was fired for being gay, but "it doesn't matter because there are no employment protections" for sexual orientation in his state.

- What are the major counseling concerns that are important to explore with Tommy?
- How might you explore the intersection of his sexual orientation, race/ethnicity, and gender identity with Tommy?
- What are the knowledge and skills you will need to work with Tommy in a culturally responsive manner?

In late adulthood, concerns about maturity become important in terms of experiencing ego integrity versus despair (Erikson, 1968). In this stage of life, clients typically reflect on their lives and the meaning they have had, and they feel a sense of satisfaction in lives well lived and in good decision making. This is also a time of life where feelings of regret and despair are relevant and may need exploration as clients look back on their lives. Late adulthood is also a time of addressing end-of-life issues such as health care, family concerns, and hospice. In terms of cross-cultural counseling practice, it is vital that counselors not only clearly assess cultural identities and salient oppression and resilience experiences but also explore needed advocacy for the clients with whom they work.

BOX 4.8 CASE STUDY OF TRANSGENDER IDENTITY IN LATE ADULTHOOD

Bella is a 79-year-old transgender woman. Her sex assigned at birth was male; however, she has been living in her current gender identity for the past 40 years. When Bella came out as a transgender person, her family disowned her, and she has not been in touch with them since. At that time, Bella moved to an urban city to have access to better medical resources and social support. About 3 years ago, Bella lost her job due to downsizing. Because of the loss of income, Bella had to move in with her sister (who was still not supportive of Bella's gender identity). While separated from her social support group and experiencing significant stress related to loss of income, Bella's health began to fail. She was diagnosed with chronic fatigue syndrome, which affects her to the degree that she has had to move into an assisted living residence. Bella's doctor at this residence refuses to prescribe her hormone therapy, although there are no other medical complications with hormones related to her current health condition. Bella wants to move back to the city where she once lived, but there are no affordable assisted living residences there. Bella begins to wonder if she should just "detransition," even though she strongly identifies as a woman. She worries what might happen to her not only in her current assisted living residence but also as a transgender woman in her future interactions with her doctors.

KEY COUNSELING POINTERS FOR CROSS-CULTURAL COUNSELING

When developing multicultural and social justice competence in counseling, counselors should keep the following key counseling pointers in mind:

- Understand key terms and concepts associated with intersectionality or the way multiple identities come together to define an individual over the life span.
- Intentional cross-cultural counseling requires an understanding of the counselor's identities of privilege and oppression and the intersectional identities of their clients.
- The use of language is a powerful tool in the counseling relationship and can solidify the counseling alliance when done to empower the client.
- Microaggressive behavior is pervasive and happens in cross-cultural counseling dyads, with or without intention. Culturally competent counselors address these issues with clients in the context of trust building.
- Cross-cultural counseling requires intentional immersion in diverse contexts inside and outside of the counseling relationships.
- Be prepared to hold courageous conversations (Singh & Salazar, 2010) on social justice issues within your counseling settings to develop a network of allies and support.
- Educate counselors and mental health professionals about the multicultural and social justice competencies as well as the systemic oppression that impacts clients and students within your community.
- Develop an action plan on how to support and advocate for students and clients across levels of the ACA Advocacy competencies (Lewis et al., 2003) (i.e., micro, meso, and macro).
- Write letters to stakeholders about the issues your clients and students face in your community.
- Become actively involved in a community event that promotes social justice for marginalized groups, and encourage other members of the mental health profession to become involved as social justice allies.

SUMMARY

This chapter defined key components of cross-cultural counseling and also discussed the connection between multicultural counseling competence and advocacy competence as foundational components of cross-cultural counseling. Major benchmark competency documents that undergird cross-cultural counseling were described, including the ACA Multicultural and Social Justice Competencies (2015) and the ACA Advocacy Competencies (Lewis et al., 2003). The authors reviewed the importance of client and counselor social identities (e.g., racial/ethnic, sexual orientation, disability) in the practice of cross-cultural counseling. In addition, the role that social justice concerns (e.g., racism, heterosexism, classism, transphobia) have in influencing mental and physical health disparities was also discussed. Therefore, in addition to counselors developing awareness, knowledge, and skills in their counseling practice with clients from diverse backgrounds and worldviews, counselors must also be prepared to conduct a thorough initial cultural and social justice assessment with clients and to continue to maintain this focus throughout the counseling process.

USEFUL WEBSITES

ACA Multicultural and social justice counseling competencies
http://www.counseling.org/das
Association of Multicultural Counseling and Development
http://www.multiculturalcounseling.org
National Disabilities Institute
http://www.realeconomicimpact.org/

RESOURCES

Association of LGBT Issues in counseling
http://www.algbtic.org
Counselors for Social Justice
http://www.counseling-csj.org

REFERENCES

Adams, M. (2013). Conceptual frameworks. In M. Adams, W. Blumenthal, C. R. Castaneda, H. W. Hackman, M. L. Peters, & X. Zuniga (Eds.), *Readings for diversity and social justice* (3rd ed., pp.1–5). New York, NY: Routledge.

Arredondo, P., Toporek, R., Brown, S. P., Sanchez, J., Locke, D. C., Sanchez, J., & Stadler, H. (1996). Operationalization of the multicultural counseling competencies. *Journal of Multicultural Counseling & Development*, *24*(1), 42–78. doi:10.1002/j.2161-1912.1996.tb00288.x

Beaumont, S. L., & Pratt, M. M. (2011). Identity processing styles and psychosocial balance during early and middle adulthood: The role of identity in intimacy and generativity. *Journal of Adult Development*, *18*(4), 172–183. doi: 10.1177/2158244013518053

Bemak, F., Chung, R. C. Y, Talleyrand, R. M., Jones, H., & Daiquin, J. (2011). Implementing multicultural social justice strategies in counselor education training programs. *Journal for Social Action in Counseling and Psychology*, *3*, 1–43.

Ben-Moshe, L., & Magaña, S. (2014). An introduction to race, gender, and disability: Intersectionality, disability studies, and families of color. *Women, Gender, and Families of Color*, *2*(2), 105–114. doi:10.5406/womgenfamcol.2.2.0105

Botelho, G. (2012, May 12). *What happened the night Trayvon Martin died*. Retrieved from http://www.cnn.com/2012/05/18/justice/florida-teen-shooting-details/index.html

Bowleg, L. (2008). When Black + lesbian + woman ≠ Black lesbian woman: The methodological challenges of qualitative and quantitative intersectionality research. *Sex Roles, 59*(5–6), 312–325. doi:10.1080/13691058.2011.556201

Brady-Amoon, P. (2011). Humanism, feminism, and multiculturalism: Essential elements of social justice in counseling, education, and advocacy. *Journal of Humanistic Counseling, 50*(2), 135–148. doi:10.1002/j.2161-1939.2011 .tb00113.x

Brubaker, M. D., Puig, A., Reese, R. F., & Young, J. (2010). Integrating social justice into counseling theories pedagogy: A case example. *Counselor Education & Supervision, 50,* 88–102. doi:10.1002/j.1556-6978.2010.tb00111.x

Burkard, A. W., Ponterotto, P. G., Reynolds, A. L., & Alfonso, V. C. (1999). White counselor trainees' racial identity and working alliance perceptions. *Journal of Counseling and Development, 77,* 324–329. doi:10.1002/j.1556-6676.1999. tb02455.x

Buser, J. K. (2009). Treatment-seeking disparity between African Americans and Whites: Attitudes toward treatment, coping resources, and racism. *Journal of Multicultural Counseling and Development, 37*(2), 94–104. doi: 10.1002/j.2161-1912.2009.tb00094.x

Butler, S. K. (2012). Issues of social justice and career development. *Career Planning & Adult Development Journal, 28*(1), 140–151.

Chang, C. Y., Crethar, H. C., & Ratts, M. J. (2010). Social justice: A national imperative for counselor education and supervision. *Counselor Education & Supervision, 50*(2), 82–87. doi:10.1002/j.1556-6978.2010.tb00110.x

Collins, P. H. (2002). *Black feminist thought: Knowledge, consciousness, and the politics of empowerment.* New York, NY: Routledge.

Comstock, D. L., Hammer, T. R., Strentzsch, J., Cannon, K., Parsons, J., & Salazar, G. (2008). Relational-cultural theory: A framework for bridging relational, multicultural, and social justice competencies. *Journal of Counseling & Development, 86,* 279–287. doi:10.1002/j.1556-6678.2008.tb00510.x

Cook, D. A., & Helms, J. E. (1988). Visible racial/ethnic supervisees' satisfaction with cross-cultural supervision as predicted by relationship characteristics. *Journal of Counseling Psychology, 35*(3), 268–274. doi:10.1037/0022–0167.35.3.268

Crenshaw, K. (1991). Mapping the margins: Intersectionality, identity politics, and violence against women of color. *Stanford Law Review, 6,* 1241–1299. doi:10.2307/1229039

Crethar, H. C., Rivera, E. T., & Nash, S. (2008). In search of common threads: Linking multicultural, feminist, and social justice counseling paradigms. *Journal of Counseling & Development, 86*(3), 269–278. doi:10.1002/ j.1556-6678.2008.tb00509.x

Day-Vines, N. L., Wood, S. M., Grothaus, T., Craigen, L., Holman, A., Dotson-Blake, K., & Douglass, M. J. (2007). Broaching the subjects of race, ethnicity, and culture during the counseling process. *Journal of Counseling & Development, 85*(4), 401–409. doi:10.1002/j.1556-6678.2007.tb00608.x

Donovan, R. A., Galban, D. J., Grace, R. K., Bennett, J. K., & Felicié, S. Z. (2013). Impact of racial macro-and microaggressions in Black women's lives: A preliminary analysis. *Journal of Black Psychology, 39*(2), 185–196. doi: 10.1037/a0037537

Erikson, E. H. (1968). *Identity, youth, and crisis.* New York, NY: Norton.

Fantz, A. (2015, January 4). *Ohio transgender teen's mom: "He was an amazing boy."* Retrieved from http://www.cnn.com/2014/12/31/us/ohio-transgender-teen-suicide/index.html

Franklin, A. J., Boyd-Franklin, N., & Kelly, S. (2006). Racism and invisibility: Race-related stress, emotional abuse and psychological trauma for people of color. *Journal of Emotional Abuse, 6*(2–3), 9–30. doi:10.1300/j135v06n02_02

Gassner, B., & McGuigan, W. (2014). Racial prejudice in college students: A cross-sectional examination. *College Student Journal, 48*(2), 249–256.

Goodman, L. A., Liang, B., Helms, J. E., Latta, R. E., Sparks, E., & Weintraub, S. R. (2004). Training counseling psychologists as social justice agents: Feminist and multicultural principles in action. *Counseling Psychologist, 32*(6), 793–836. doi:10.1177/0011000004268802

Gopaldas, A. (2013). Intersectionality 101. *Journal of Public Policy & Marketing, 32,* 90–94.

Granello, D. H., & Wheaton, J. E. (1998). Self-perceived multicultural competencies of African American and European American vocational rehabilitation counselors. *Rehabilitation Counseling Bulletin, 42,* 2–15.

Hendricks, M. L., & Testa, R. J. (2012). A conceptual framework for clinical work with transgender and gender nonconforming clients: An adaptation of the minority stress model. *Professional Psychology: Research and Practice, 43,* 460–467.

Ingram, P., Chaudhary, A. K., & Jones, W. T. (2014). How do biracial students interact with others on the college campus? *College Student Journal, 48*(2), 297–311.

Jones, S. R., Kim, Y. C., & Skendall, K. C. (2012). (Re-) framing authenticity: Considering multiple social identities using autoethnographic and intersectional approaches. *Journal of Higher Education, 83*(5), 698–724. doi: org/10.1353/jhe.2012.0029

Kiselica, M. S., & Robinson, M. (2001). Bringing advocacy counseling to life: The history, issues and human dramas of social justice work in counseling. *Journal of Counseling & Development, 79,* 387–397.

Knox, S., Burkard, A. W., Johnson, A. J., Suzuki, L. A., & Ponterotto, J. G. (2003). African American and European American therapists' experiences of addressing race in cross-racial psychotherapy dyads. *Journal of Counseling Psychology, 50*(4), 466. doi:10.1037/0022-0167.50.4.466

Kohl, B. G., Jr. (2006). Can you feel me now? Worldview, empathy, and racial identity in a therapy dyad. *Journal of Emotional Abuse, 6*(2–3), 173–196. doi:10.1300/j135v06n02_11

Lambert, S. F., Herman, K. C., Bynum, M. S., & Ialongo, N. S. (2009). Perceptions of racism and depressive symptoms in African American adolescents: The role of perceived academic and social control. *Journal of Youth and Adolescence, 38*(4), 519–531. doi:10.1007/s10964-009-9393-0

Lewis, J. A., Arnold, M. S., House, R., & Toporek, R. L. (2003). *Advocacy competencies*. Retrieved from http://www.counseling.org/resources/competencies/advocacy_competencies.pdf

Lewis, J. A., Ratts, M. J., Paladino, D. A., & Toporek, R. L. (2011). Social justice counseling and advocacy: Developing new leadership roles and competencies. *Journal for Social Action in Counseling & Psychology, 3*(1), 5–16.

Lightweis, S. (2014). The challenges, persistence, and success of White, working-class, first-generation college students. *College Student Journal, 48*(3), 461–467.

Malott, K. M., & Knoper, T. (2012). Social justice in application: Counselor training in a legal context. *Journal for Social Action in Counseling & Psychology, 4*(2), 23–40. doi:10.1300/J135v06n02_11

Masten, A. (2001). Ordinary magic: Resilience processes in development. *American Psychologist, 56*(3), 227–238: doi:10.1037//0003-066X.56.3.227.

Melchior, M., Touchette, É., Prokofyeva, E., Chollet, A., Fombonne, E., Elidemir, G., & Galéra, C. (2014). Negative events in childhood predict trajectories of internalizing symptoms up to young adulthood: An 18-year longitudinal study. *PloS One, 9*(12), e114526. doi:10.1371/journal.pone.0114526

Nadal, K. L., Griffin, K. E., Wong, Y., Hamit, S., & Rasmus, M. (2014). The impact of racial microaggressions on mental health: Counseling implications for clients of color. *Journal of Counseling & Development, 92*(1), 57–66. doi:10.1002/j.1556-6676.2014.00130.x

Ockerman, M. S., & Mason, E. C. M. (2012). Developing school counseling students' social justice orientation through service learning. *Journal of School Counseling, 10*(5), 1–26.

Owen, J., Tao, K. W., Imel, Z. E., Wampold, B. E., & Rodolfa, E. (2014). Addressing racial and ethnic microaggressions in therapy. *Professional Psychology: Research and Practice, 45*(4), 283. doi:10.1037/a0037420

Pascoe, E. A., & Richman, L. (2009). Perceived discrimination and health: A meta-analytic review. *Psychological Bulletin, 135*(4), 531–554. doi:http://dx.doi.org/10.1037/a0016059

Petty, T. (2014). Motivating first-generation students to academic success and college completion. *College Student Journal, 48*(2), 257–264.

Pham, C., & Keenan, T. (2011). Counseling and college matriculation: Does the availability of counseling affect college-going decisions among highly qualified first-generation college-bound high school graduates? *Journal of Applied Economics & Business Research, 7*(1), 12–24.

Phinney, J., & Ong, A. (2007). Conceptualization and measurement of ethnic identity: Current status and future directions. *Journal of Counseling Psychology, 54,* 271–281. doi:10.1037/0022-0167.54.3.271

Pierce, C., Carew, J., Pierce-Gonzalez, D., & Willis, D. (1978). An experiment in racism: TV commercials. In C. Pierce (Ed.), *Television and education* (pp. 62–88). Beverly Hills, CA: Sage.

Poteat, V. P., & Spanierman, L. B. (2012). Modern racism attitudes among White students: The role of dominance and authoritarianism and the mediating effects of racial color-blindness. *Journal of Social Psychology*, *152*(6), 758–774. doi:10.1080/00224545.2012.700966

Purdie-Vaughns, V., & Eibach, R. P. (2008). Intersectional invisibility: The distinctive advantages and disadvantages of multiple subordinate-group identities. *Sex Roles*, *59*(5–6), 377–391. doi:10.1007/s11199-008-9424-4

Quiroga, S. S., Medina, D. M., & Glick, J. (2014). In the belly of the beast: Effects of anti-immigration policy on Latino community members. *American Behavioral Scientist*, *58*(13), 1723–1742. doi:10.1177/0002764214537270

Ramsay, N. J. (2014). Intersectionality: A model for addressing the complexity of oppression and privilege. *Pastoral Psychology*, *63*(4), 453–469. doi:10.1007/s11089-013-0570-4

Ratts, M. J. (2011). Multiculturalism and social justice: Two sides of the same coin. *Journal of Multicultural Counseling & Development*, *39*(1), 24–37. doi:10.1002/j.2161-1912.2011.tb00137.x

Ratts, M. J., & Hutchins, A. M. (2009). ACA advocacy competencies: Social justice advocacy at the client/student level. *Journal of Counseling & Development*, *87*(3), 269–275. doi:10.1002/j.1556-6678.2009.tb00106.x

Reid, D. K., & Knight, M. G. (2006). Disability justifies exclusion of minority students: A critical history grounded in disability studies. *Educational Researcher*, *35*(6), 18–23. doi:10.3102/0013189x035006018

Schultz, D. (2012). Blue-collar teaching in a white-collar university. *Journal of Public Affairs Education*, *18*(1), 67–86.

Shelton, K., & Delgado-Romero, E. A. (2013). Sexual orientation microaggressions: The experience of lesbian, gay, bisexual, and queer clients in psychotherapy. *Journal of Counseling Psychology*, *58*(2), 210–221. doi:10.1037/a0022251

Shields, S. A. (2008). Gender: An intersectionality perspective. *Sex Roles*, *59*(5–6), 301–311. doi:10.1007/s11199–008–9501–8

Singh, A. A. (2012). Transgender youth of color and resilience: Negotiating oppression, finding support. *Sex Roles: A Journal of Research*, *68*, 690–702. doi:10.1007/s11199–012–0149–z

Singh, A. A., Merchant, N., Skudrzyk, B., Ingene, D., Hutchins, A. M., & Rubel, D. (2012). Association for specialists in group work: Multicultural and social justice competence principles for group workers. *Journal for Specialists in Group Work*, *37*(4), 312–325. doi:10.1080/01933922.2012.721482

Singh, A. A., & Salazar, C. F. (2010). Process and action in social justice group work: Introduction to the special issue. *Journal for Specialists in Group Work*, *35*(2), 93–96. doi:10.1080/01933922.2010.492908

Singh, A. A., & Salazar, C. F. (2010). The roots of social justice in group work. *Journal for Specialists in Group Work*, *35*(2), 97–104.

Singh, A. A., Urbano, A., Haston, M., & McMahon, E. (2010). School counselors' strategies for social justice change: A grounded theory of what works in the real world. *Professional School Counseling*, *13*(3), 135–145. doi: 10.5330/psc.n.2010–13.135

Smith, L., Foley, P. F., & Chaney, M. P. (2008). Addressing classism, ableism, & heterosexism in counselor education. *Journal of Counseling & Development*, *86*, 303–309. doi:10.1002/j.1556–6678.2008.tb00513.x

Solorzano, D., Ceja, M., & Yosso, T. (2000). Critical race theory, racial microaggressions, and campus racial climate: The experiences of African American college students. *Journal of Negro Education*, *69*(1-2) 60–73. doi: 10.1080/13613324.2014.885422

Stebleton, M., & Soria, K. (2012). Breaking down barriers: Academic obstacles of first-generation students at research universities. *Learning Assistance Review (TLAR)*, *17*(2), 7–19.

Sue, D. W. (2010). *Microaggressions in everyday life: Race, gender, and sexual orientation*. New York, NY: Wiley.

Sue, D. W., Arredondo, P., & McDavis, R. J. (1992). Multicultural counseling competencies and standards: A call to the profession. *Journal of Counseling & Development*, *70*(4), 477–486. doi:10.1002/j.1556-6676.1992 .tb01642.x

Sue, D. W., Capodilupo, C. M., & Holder, A. (2008). Racial microaggressions in the life experience of Black Americans. *Professional Psychology: Research and Practice*, *39*(3), 329. doi:10.1037/0735-7028.39.3.329

Sue, D. W., & Constantine, M. (2003). Optimal human functioning in people of color in the United States. In B. Walsh (Ed.), *Counseling psychology and optimal human functioning* (pp. 151–169). Mahwah, NJ: Earlbaum.

Sue, D. W., Lin, A. I., Torino, G. C., Capodilupo, C. M., & Rivera, D. P. (2009). Racial microaggressions and difficult dialogues on race in the classroom. *Cultural Diversity and Ethnic Minority Psychology*, *15*(2), 183. doi:10.1037/ a0014191

Sue, S. (1998). In search of cultural competence in psychotherapy and counseling. *American Psychologist*, *53*, 440–448.

Sue, D. W. & Sue, D. (2013). *Counseling the Culturally Diverse: Theory and Practice*. (6th edition). Hoboken, New Jersey: John Wiley & Sons.

Tomko, J. K., & Munley, P. H. (2013). Predicting counseling psychologists attitudes and clinical judgements with respect to older adults. *Aging & Mental Health*, *17*(2), 233–241. doi:10.1080/13607863.2012.715141

Toporek, R. L., Lewis, J. A., & Crethar, H. C. (2009). Promoting systemic change through the ACA advocacy competencies. *Journal of Counseling & Development*, *87*(3), 260–268. doi:10.1002/j.1556–6678.2009.tb00105.x

Torres, L., Driscoll, M. W., & Burrow, A. L. (2010). Racial microaggressions and psychological functioning among highly achieving African-Americans: A mixed-methods approach. *Journal of Social and Clinical Psychology*, *29*(10), 1074–1099. doi:10.1521/jscp.2010.29.10.1074

Warner, L. R. (2008). A best practices guide to intersectional approaches in psychological research. *Sex Roles*, *59*(5–6), 454–463. doi:10.1007/s11199-008- 9504-5

Warner, L. R., & Shields, S. A. (2013). The intersections of sexuality, gender, and race: Identity research at the crossroads. *Sex Roles, 68*(11–12), 803–810. doi:10.1007/s11199-013-0281-4

Wickrama, K. A. S., Conger, R. D., Lorenz, F. O., & Martin, M. (2012). Continuity and discontinuity of depressed mood from late adolescence to young adulthood: The mediating and stabilizing roles of young adults' socioeconomic attainment. *Journal of Adolescence, 35*(3), 648–658. doi:10.1016/j.adolescence.2011.08.014

Wilson, B. D., Okwu, C., & Mills, S. A. (2011). Brief report: The relationship between multiple forms of oppression and subjective health among Black lesbian and bisexual women. *Journal of Lesbian Studies, 15*(1), 15–24. doi:10.1080/10894160.2010.508393

PART 2

Birth and Infancy

Birth and Infancy: Physical and Cognitive Development

Christie Jenkins, Kerrie R. Fineran, and Amber Lange

INTRODUCTION

For the past 6 years, I have watched my twin daughters grow and develop at a rapid pace. It is fascinating to watch both of them achieve milestones at different paces in completely different ways. How can two children split from the same egg be so different? As the information progresses through the chapter, it will become clear how multiple factors impact the physical and cognitive development of children.

This chapter begins by exploring physical growth and advancements in motor dexterity. It is important to look at not only the genetic components of growth but also the environmental factors that can help or hinder progress. The intricacies of language development in early childhood will be explored. The next step is to investigate early childhood cognition through the lens of Piaget and Vygotsky. The chapter ends by looking at how information is stored and processed. This will happen through the unique perspective of a counselor.

PHYSICAL DEVELOPMENT

Physical development refers to the organic changes that occur in children as they mature. Some of the imperative characteristics that establish optimal physical development during birth and infancy are changes in physical and brain growth, motor skills, health issues, and learning skills.

During the first 2 years of development, children are growing and changing at an exponential rate. Each year, a child can grow 2 to 3 inches in height and put on an additional 5 pounds in weight. Girls tend to be smaller than boys on average.

Girls continue to retain body fat as they age while boys tend to be more muscular. As their bodies continue to grow and change, better motor coordination develops.

SKELETAL DEVELOPMENT

The skeletal system is made of cartilage and bone. It is the framework of the body and determines movement while protecting vital organs. The ages from 2 to 6 years bring a large boost in skeletal changes. Growth centers (epiphyses) are hard at work changing cartilage into bone. These are found throughout the skeletal system. Doctors often use these growth centers to predict and diagnose growth disorders in children.

As children end their preschool years and enter into ages 5 and 6 years, many begin to lose their baby teeth. Tooth loss can be greatly influenced by genetic components. Hilgers, Akridge, Scheetz, and Kinance (2006) contended that children who are overweight or obese tend to lose their teeth quicker and children who are malnourished for extended periods of time may wait longer for their adult teeth to appear.

It is estimated that 30% of U.S. children have tooth decay (U.S. Department of Health and Human Services, 2007). One of the biggest issues at this age is that those diseased primary teeth can affect the health of the child's permanent teeth. It is imperative that children not only brush their teeth but also avoid sugar and drink water with fluoride.

BRAIN DEVELOPMENT

The skill levels of children ages 2 to 6 years improve greatly in regard to coordination, perception, attention, memory, language, thinking, and imagination. The actual size of the brain increases from 70% to 90% of its adult weight (Nelson, Thomas, & de Haan, 2006). Most children between the ages of 3 and 6 years experience an active period within their left cerebral hemisphere. The right hemisphere increases at a constant pace throughout early and middle childhood (Thompson et al., 2000).

In early to middle childhood, the frontal lobe areas that are devoted to inhibiting impulses and organizing behavior experience rapid growth in various cortical regions (Diamond, 2004). This goes hand in hand with a child's ability to control his or her behavior in conjunction with his or her newfound greater command of the language. In comparison, a child's spatial ability (e.g., directions, drawing, shape recognition) develops over time into adolescence. These spatial skills are typically found in the right hemisphere. This shows the difference between the regions and how complex cognitive functions work together to anticipate increased developmental needs.

One area that shows this complexity is handedness. A child's dominant cerebral hemisphere will determine skilled motor activity. Right-handed people typically house language in the left hemisphere. However, left-handed individuals may have language housed in the right hemisphere or even shared between the two hemispheres (Szaflarski et al. 2002). A child's preference for the right or left hand is evident by the child's first birthday (Hinojosa, Sheu, & Michael, 2003).

Although there is a slight tendency for a left-handed parent to have a left-handed child, it may be due to the environmental impact of having a left-handed parent. For example, twins are more likely to prefer a different hand. Derom, Thiery, Vlietinck, Loos, and Derom (1996) proposed that this may be due to the positioning of the twins in utero. The positioning of a single birth may lead to advancements in movement on the right side (Previc, 1991).

In some parts of Africa, children are punished for preferring their left hand. In Tanzania, 99% of adults are right-handed (Provins, 1997). According to Flannery and Liederman (1995), left-handed individuals have a knack for developing enhanced verbal and mathematics skills. With this being said, there is a large population of left-handed individuals with severe retardation and mental illness. This may be due to an injury to the left hemisphere (Powls, Botting, Cooke, & Marlow, 1996).

Specific Areas of Brain Development

The brain is affected by intricate connections meant to increase the central nervous system functioning. The cerebellum helps with control of body movement and balance. Motor growth begins at birth. By the end of preschool, most children have a good sense of movement, can play ball, and begin writing. Children who have experienced trauma to this region typically have a motor and cognitive decline. This can include issues with language and memory (Noterdaeme, Mildenberger, Minow, & Amorosa, 2002).

The hippocampus plays an integral role in memory and the ability to navigate images. During the preschool and school years, the hippocampus and cerebral cortex are developing at a rapid pace in conjunction with the frontal lobes (Nelson et al. 2006). The corpus callosum provides even bodily movements and contributes to different portions of thinking, attention, perception, problem solving, and language development (Thompson et al. 2000). This interaction between the hemispheres becomes increasingly important as the complexity of the task escalates.

Counselors also need to be aware of the importance placed on secure attachment and bonding as the brain continues to develop. Children need to have emotional exchanges with their primary caregivers especially before language develops to ensure that children feel secure and their needs are met. Children who do not have this emotional connection can grow up confused, misconstrued, and self-doubting. Because these attachment patterns are relatively stable by 12–18 months of age, unless different incidents change them, these patterns will indicate how well someone will relate to others in adulthood.

Also up for consideration are mirror neurons. Mirror neurons get their name from the process of firing when there is an action or when someone simply watches an action. This is thought of as mirror movement, because it is as if the observer is actually acting. The speculation is that this mirror movement is our foundation to be social, imitate others, acquire language, and be empathic. When this system is impaired by having fewer mirror neurons or less functioning ones, we may be able to understand issues like autism more readily.

INFLUENCES ON PHYSICAL AND GROWTH AND HEALTH

There is a vast array of contributing influences on growth and development; it begs the universal theme of nature versus nurture. In the next section, it will become clear how heredity and hormones, emotional well-being, nutrition, and infectious disease play an important role on physical growth and development.

Heredity and Hormones

Bogin (2001) contended that physical stature and the growth rate of children are related to their parents. The pituitary gland plays an integral role in release of hormones. Genes guide this piece by directing the manufacturing of these hormones.

Two hormones create growth in individuals. Growth hormone (GH) plays a role in the development of body tissue with the exception of the genitals and central nervous system. Saenger (2003) purported that children with a GH deficiency tend to reach a maximum height of 4 feet, 4 inches tall. However, when they are treated with injections of GH at an early age, they can grow at a normal pace. Thyroid-stimulating hormone (TSH) stimulates the thyroid gland in the release of thyroxine. This works in conjunction with the GH to increase the impact of brain development and body mass. According to Salerno and colleagues (2001), children who do not have enough thyroxine have to receive it immediately or they will end up with mental retardation. These children also grow at a limited rate. With appropriate intervention, these children can ultimately grow normally.

Emotional Well-Being

Emotional well-being is a vital part of physical growth and health. Kemeny (2003) suggested that children in homes with emotional and financial issues were more likely to suffer respiratory and intestinal problems and unintentional injuries. Deltondo et al. (2008) contended that GH is suppressed in children with high levels of stress. For example, psychosocial dwarfism can be a result of extreme emotional deprivation. The symptomology includes extremely short stature, serious adjustment issues, immature skeletal age, and decreased levels of GH (Tarren-Sweeney, 2006). To ensure that these problems do not remain constant, children need to be removed from their emotionally deprived environments.

Nutrition

Preschool children tend to have a love–hate relationship with food. This can present a problem for parents who want to ensure that their child is receiving proper nutrition. Hursti (1999) purported that preschoolers tend to eat more at some meals and less at others and that this should not be an area of concern. Modeling food choices can be a great start to increase a child's willingness to try healthy foods that may appear out of his or her comfort zone (Fuller, Keller, Olson, Plymale, & Gottesman, 2005). Birch, Fisher, and Davison (2003) believed that parental control of food has been linked to the child's inability to discover his or her own sense of self-control.

Another factor greatly impacting children is not only lack of access to healthy food but also lack of food altogether. In 2002, 15.8 million children in the United States lived in food insecure households (U.S. Department of Agriculture, 2007). Many families need to make the heart-wrenching decision between shelter and food. This causes families to buy food that may be cheap and therefore lack the nutrients necessary for proper development. The most common deficiencies are iron, calcium, vitamin A, and vitamin C (Ganji, Hampl, & Betts, 2003). Children from these households can be a half to 1 inch shorter than children living in a food secure household (Cecil et al., 2005).

INFECTIOUS DISEASE

Physical growth and cognitive development are greatly impacted by disease. When children are not receiving proper nutrition, infection and malnutrition create a perfect storm. The body cannot readily absorb nutrients with a diminished appetite and intestinal fluctuations like diarrhea. According to the World Health Organization (2008a), 2 million children die each year due to the unsafe water and contaminated food sources that cause widespread diarrhea. This coupled with the fact that these children living in poverty do not receive proper immunizations puts them at an even greater risk for disease.

Childhood diseases have greatly decreased over the past 50 years due to the immunization of infants and young children. In 1994, the United States guaranteed free immunizations to all children. Although there is much debate in the United States regarding immunizing children, we have seen an upsurge of whooping cough and rubella in children without immunizations. The end result can be life threatening (Kennedy & Gust, 2008).

CHILDHOOD INJURIES

Accidents are the leading cause of death to children in industrialized nations. Almost 35% of childhood deaths and 50% of adolescent deaths are the result of preventable injuries like automobile accidents, burns, and drowning (Children's Defense Fund, 2008).

Risk Factors

Gender should be factored into the risk for childhood injuries. National Safe Kids Campaign (2005) reported that boys are 1.5 times more likely to be injured due to their increased activity, impulsivity, and risk-taking behaviors. Children who struggle with issues associated with attention-deficit disorder and attention-deficit/hyperactivity disorder (ADD/ADHD) are defiant or aggressive and also pose a greater safety challenge (Schwebel & Gaines, 2007). These children may lack the self-regulation and ability to follow instructions intended to keep themselves safe. According to the World Health Organization (2008b), parents in poverty who are single and have low educational levels may have too many additional stressors to ensure the continued safety of their children.

Prevention

Kendrick, Barlow, Hampshire, Stewart-Brown, and Polnay (2008) reported that one of the greatest indicators for prevention of home accidents is parental involvement and the modeling of safety practices. Today we have laws meant to ensure the safety of children in the United States. We make sure that our children are in proper car seats and they are appropriately installed. We make sure that our medicine bottles have childproof caps. We place fences around our backyard pools. With this being said, many parents follow their own rules and feel overwhelmed by the plethora of safety suggestions (Damashek & Peterson, 2002). Parents may rely too heavily on their children's knowledge of personal safety and the lessons taught at home and school. Morrongiello, Midgett, and Shields (2001) reported that parental supervision is a key component as older preschoolers typically remember only half of the safety rules taught to them by their parents.

MOTOR DEVELOPMENT

Early childhood brings on new motor skill growth for children that matches their increase in size and strength. This coupled with the continued development of the central nervous system makes their environment ripe with new challenges to undertake.

Gross Motor Development

Children begin to find their balance as their bodies become less top heavy and their center of gravity shifts to their trunk. This allows them to begin the more advanced motions of running, jumping, hopping, and eventually skipping. With these new skills come the ability to utilize their arms in a more advanced manner. They can now do activities such as play catch or ride a bike with training wheels. With each year that passes, children increase their physical stamina and ability to master more advanced pieces.

Fine Motor Development

The preschool years bring about new growth in fine motor skills. As children gain more control of their extremities, it lends to a greater command of more intricate work like puzzles, cutting and pasting, and more advanced crafting projects. Parents see a markedly significant different in children's abilities to care for themselves and their abilities to express their thoughts through their artwork.

Children begin to feed themselves, dress themselves, and brush their teeth, although in the younger stages they may need prompting and greater direction. One of the biggest milestones during this early development is learning to tie shoes. This a complex balance of motor skills and cognitive development coming together to achieve a goal.

Drawing is another area where we can see increased growth with young children. At first a child may scribble on paper to represent a scene that is not easily identifiable. Around the age of 3 years, children begin to formulate pictures that can be understood and have meaning (Braswell & Callanan, 2003). Between the ages of 3 and 4 years, children begin to understand the use of lines to represent objects. They incorporate this knowledge into the stick figure drawings prevalent at this age. Toomela (2002) suggested that the drawings develop as a gradual progression due to an increase in language, perception, memory, and fine motor skills.

It takes years for children to understand that writing and drawing are two different entities. This is usually solidified between the ages of 4 and 6 years. Before this period of time, children use more symbolic pictorial references meant to speak for the image. For instance, most children will draw some semblance of a circle to represent the sun (Levin & Bus, 2003). Older preschool children begin to learn to write letters and their names. However, these letters and names may be less than perfect as some of the print may be backward, extremely large or small, or sloppy.

Gender Differences in Motor Skills

There is an evident difference in motor skills depending on gender. Boys tend to excel in skills that involve strength and control. They can, on average, run faster, jump farther, and throw a ball a greater length than their female counterparts. Girls, however, have an edge in the fine motor skills required for more intricate detail and gross motor skills that command a combination of movements like skipping (Haywood & Getchell, 2005).

Societal gender roles also affect this piece. Boys and girls tend to be segregated into categories based on their abilities to perform certain physical activities. For example, boys may be expected to play football, whereas girls may be expected to take gymnastics or dance lessons. It is important to note that the parental response to these activities can greatly influence the child's ability to further develop his or her motor skills. When parents are too critical, force activities, or have a win-at-all-cost attitude, their children may not be as self-confident as the children of other parents who allow this piece to unfold naturally (Berk, Mann, & Ogan, 2006).

LANGUAGE DEVELOPMENT

As we have moved throughout this chapter, we have no doubt seen how connected each skill set is with the next. Language is no exception to this rule. When children move through ages 2–6 years, their language skills develop at an exponential rate. Their successes and challenges pave the way for their own command of language.

VOCABULARY, GRAMMAR, AND COMMUNICATION

A child's vocabulary develops from 200 words at age 2 years to approximately 2,000 words at age 6 years. Parents who work with their children on vocabulary have preschoolers with bigger vocabularies (Callanan & Sabbagh, 2004). Naigles and Swenson (2007) reported that children ascertain the meaning of words by hearing their placement in sentences. This also allows children to figure out a speaker's intention and perspective (Akhtar & Tomasello, 2000).

Information-processing theorists support the notion that children are keen to discover word placement and how the combination of words is meaningful in the sentence. Children are on a mission to find reliability and patterns in language (Chang, Dell, & Bock, 2006). Through the process of learning vocabulary and grammar, children begin to engage in rich communication with others. Pan and Snow (1999) contended that at the age of 2 years children are already taking turns and responding appropriately to other's conversations. With this being said, children's communication declines when children cannot see their partners' reactions or a visual reference (Cameron & Lee, 1997).

One of the greatest indicators of how well children develop language is their engagement with adults in conversation (NICHD Early Child Care Research Network, 2000). Children who are encouraged to develop their language skills with appropriate feedback and freedom from criticism tend to develop a better skill set (Saxton, Backley, & Gallaway, 2005). We can see how each skill builds on the next skill throughout the learning stages; Piaget's work also reinforces this.

PIAGET'S THEORY OF COGNITIVE DEVELOPMENT: BIRTH THROUGH INFANCY

Piaget was born in 1896 in Switzerland. His early interest was biology, and he completed a doctorate thesis on the topic of mollusks. Piaget's interests in biological processes led him to France, where he was eventually introduced to Alfred Benet and was part of Benet's team that studied and researched intelligence in the 1920s. Piaget was intrigued by how children answered questions on the tests of intelligence and suspected that there were qualitative differences in children's abilities based on age and maturation. After a time, he returned to Switzerland as the director of the Rousseau Institute. It was during these years that he began his own studies on cognitive development. Piaget wanted to understand how children know and develop the ability to think. As part of acquiring this knowledge, Piaget originally observed his own three children (son and two daughters) and the children of his friends. It was from these original observations that Piaget deduced that children think qualitatively differently from adults. In wanting to understand how children construct knowledge, he came to believe that children's thinking and reasoning development occurred in natural and sequential stages with later stages integrating materials from earlier stages. He also believed that initial stage mastery was mandatory to move to more developmentally complex stages and that all children passed through a universal sequence of four stages. He believed that maturation and experience were necessary for transcendence to the next stage (Mooney, 2013).

COGNITIVE THEORY OF DEVELOPMENT

Piaget's theory of cognitive development is built on four stages: sensorimotor, preoperational, concrete operational, and formal operational. Piaget believed these were based loosely on age and acquired experience and that children begin building knowledge structures, which continue to be validated or challenged as thinking matures. Material that is challenged affords a child the opportunity to create, change, or expand his or her knowledge structure.

Sensorimotor Stage of Development

The sensorimotor stage occurs from birth to approximately 2 years of age. During this time, behavior changes from completely unintentional to willful. Behavior begins with involuntary reflexes such as sucking, grasping, and looking; continues toward intentional behaviors with goal-directed actions, such as shaking a rattle or throwing a stuffed animal; continues with the use of repetition, (see box 5.1) such as continually dropping a plate off a high chair; and ends with imitation and manipulation, such as dress-up and make-believe play. These prior examples coincide to the six substages within the sensorimotor stage (Table 5.1).

BOX 5.1   SENSORIMOTOR DEVELOPMENT IN ACTION

"If he dumps that bowl of cereal over one more time, I am going to pull my hair out!" Marissa was sitting in my office lamenting about her recent experience of attempting to get her son, Nathan, to eat with a plate, a bowl, and forks and spoons. Nathan is a 12-month-old active merrymaker. "He seems to get into everything" she says, "and some days I feel so exhausted. My partner comes home from work and asks what I did all day, and even I'm not sure how to answer that question! It feels like all I've done is repeatedly clean up messes, change diapers, and talk baby talk. When is this all going to end?"

- How do you explain Nathan's development from a Piagetian perspective?
- What advice do you have for Marissa?
- What can you do to help Nathan?
- What might Piaget say to Marissa?

Table 5.1 Substages Within the Sensorimotor Stage of Development

Reflexes	Birth to 1 month	Reflexive behaviors without volition including sucking, following objects with eyes, and grasping.
Primary circular reactions	1–4 months	Reflexive behaviors become more voluntary. Habits and reproduction of actions occur, for example, reaching and grasping toward a mother's face.
Secondary circular reactions	4–8 months	Objects are utilized with intention and purpose. Repetition and understanding means and ends occur, for example, turning on and off the TV remote.
Coordination of secondary circular reactions	8–12 months	Expectations are placed on objects with increased coordination of vision and touch. Logic and coordination of means and ends occur; for example, if a button is pushed on the toy it rings. Object permanence also occurs during this stage.
Tertiary circular reaction	12–18 months	Trial and error is used to solve problems and experimentation occurs. Attempts at new behaviors occur.
Symbolic thought	18–24 months	Thinking about information occurs with the ability to have insight and creativity. For example, the child can think about wanting a cookie although one is not present.

It is during the sensorimotor stage that object permanence takes place. Object permanence is the understanding that an object continues to exist even when the object is no longer present. This understanding occurs in children around 8–12 months of age. Before this time the idiom out of sight, out of mind applies see box 5.2. For example, if a caregiver hides a stuffed animal underneath a blanket before a child masters object permanence, the child will believe the stuffed animal is gone from existence and no longer attends to the missing object. As mastery of object permanence is occurring, the child is aware that the stuffed animal is under the blanket and may actively engage and try and secure the toy from under the blanket. As the child matures (about 18–24 months) and object permanence is mastered, the child is aware that even if the object is not found under the blanket he or she can begin looking in other places the animal may be hiding.

BOX 5.2   OBJECT PERMANENCE IN ACTION

"I can't even take a shower by myself anymore!" says Lena. "Every time I try to leave the room Maria starts crying; even if I try to keep talking from another room, she still cries. I am very frustrated. The same thing happens when I try to put her to bed at night or try to lay her down for a nap. Unless I am sitting there and she can see me, Maria cries. I'm not sure what to do any longer." Lena presents in my office with her 6-month-old daughter, Maria. Maria is sleeping quietly in her car sleeper, and Lena appears tired and unkempt. Lena reports that she cannot leave Maria or she cries. She reports that Maria is her first child and that she does not feel like she gets a break. She states that anytime she tries to leave Maria, Maria begins crying and does not stop. Lena states that the crying makes her feel guilty. She says the separation problem has gotten so bad that she can't even close the shower curtain or Maria starts to cry.

- What information does Lena need to understand about child development?
- How can Lena care best for herself and her daughter during this phase of development?
- What might Piaget say to Lena?

Preoperational Stage of Development

The preoperational stage of development occurs from approximately ages 2 through 7 years and includes two substages (Table 5.2). During this time, children focus on language acquisition and learning to communicate. It is during this stage that most children experience egocentrism. Egocentrism is the inability to see a viewpoint other than one's own (for example, see box 5.3). Piaget's most famous experiment to demonstrate egocentrism was called the three-mountain problem (Piaget & Inhelder, 1956), where men were placed at various spots on a pretend Swiss mountain model. Children in the preoperational stage do not understand

Table 5.2 Substages of the Preoperational Stage of Development		
Symbolic function	2–4 years	Children begin to play with others via imaginary play. Egocentrism and cause and effect thinking occur.
Intuitive thought	4–7 years	Curiosity and logical reasoning emerge. The arrival of the question "Why?", centration, conservation, and irreversibility are characteristics of this stage.

how someone viewing the mountain from the other side cannot see the men the same way the child can see the men. Piaget believed that not until a child reached the concrete operational phase could he or she successfully master the idea that there are several possibly perspectives. Additionally, this concept of egocentrism can be witnessed if you ask a child why it is raining outside and he or she responds, "So I can get wet?"

BOX 5.3 PREOPERATIONAL CONCEPTS IN ACTION

Candace and Kurt, 4-year-old twins, are playing make-believe in my office. Candace is happily chatting about breakfast and pretending to cook bacon and eggs while Kurt is pretending to shave. The counselor is meeting with Candace, Kurt, and their mother, Carla, because Carla is worried that something is wrong with the twins. She states that no matter how hard she tries to encourage cooperation and friendship between the twins, she cannot figure out successful ways to help them get along. She states that Candace and Kurt are fighting nonstop and that when Kurt behaves badly Candace responds by behaving badly. Whether Carla uses discipline or reinforcement does not seem to matter as Kurt and Candace are hitting, pulling hair, yelling, and kicking each other. Both will repeatedly say, "If you hit me, then I get to hit you back" in a singsong tone. Carla is asking for help to teach them how to get along. Carla, a nurse practitioner, and I talk about parenting and boundaries when suddenly Candace screams, "Give that bacon back!" and throws the pan at Kurt. Before either I or Carla can get up, Kurt stuffs the plastic bacon in his mouth and says, "No, I'm gonna eats this first!" and runs to the corner of the room chewing all the way. Carla sighs, and I jump up to make sure Kurt does not swallow plastic bacon. While I am making my way toward Kurt, he picks up the frying pan and throws it at Candace. Carla scolds Kurt for taking the bacon and making Candace throw the pan. Kurt responds and says, "She threw it at me, so I can throw it at her." Suddenly, I am standing in the middle of the playroom with a frying pan and plastic bacon wondering if these children have mastered a quid pro quo relationship.

- What techniques might you implement with the twins?
- What does empathy mean at this point in development?
- What might Piaget say to Carla?

Centration is another concept requiring mastery during the preoperational phase of development. Centration is the fixation on one feature of an object to the exclusion of all other features. In the following example see box 5.4, Bogart can see only the amount of coins and not the coins' worth. Piaget's famous experiment to demonstrate centration was to pour equal amounts of fluid into varying sized jars and ask children to pick which jar had more fluid. Although the jar widths varied, equal amounts of fluid were poured in front of the child, yet the child was unable to identify that each jar contained an equal volume of liquid. It was not until a child had mastered the preoperational phase of development that he could correctly answer that all jars had the same amount of fluid.

BOX 5.4   CENTRATION IN ACTION

"It's not fair!" screamed Bogart at the top of his lungs. Immediately his father tries to shush him. Even I am surprised that such a small boy can scream so loudly and wonder if my colleagues might wonder what kind of strange things were happening in my office. Bogart is a 4-year-old boy with a 6-year-old sister, Brianna. They are playing with their father's loose change, and Brianna splits the change monetarily equally. Bogart receives only two coins, and she receives six coins. Bogart insists that she is cheating and that she has to share. When Brianna does not give him any coins because they both have an equal amount, Bogart drops to the ground and starts to have a temper tantrum. Bogart's dad sighs and states, "This happens all the time. He gets stuck on something and no matter how hard I try to explain it, he just doesn't listen. What am I supposed to do about this?"

- What might you say to Bogart's dad about his development?
- What principles of cognitive development can the counselor share with the father?
- What might Piaget say to Bogart, Brianna, and their dad?

There are two additional stages of cognitive development created by Piaget. These are the concrete operational stage and the formal operational stage. During the concrete operational stage children between the ages of 6–12 years begin to think logically and problem solve. During the formal operational stage, children around the age of 12 (and through adulthood) utilize logic and abstract thinking to understand and problem solve.

Additional Key Concepts From Piaget

Schemas: both a category for knowledge and a process of knowing. These may also be thought of as cognitive structures.

Assimilation: the process of taking in information from the environment so that it can be incorporated into a schema. Information is used to interpret the world. Thus, when a child sees a dog and labels it a dog, assimilation has occurred.

Adaptation to assimilated information: occurs when the process of modifying information and experiences to fit an already created schema happens (Piaget, 1971). Thus, when the child sees a puppy, labels it a dog, is corrected, and now calls the dog a puppy, adaptation has occurred.

Accommodation: the process of adjusting and changing to already acquired information. This process is about adjusting schemas to better fit already acquired information or to create a new one. This happens because the current way of thinking does not adequately or correctly capture the phenomenon. Thus, if the child sees a horse and calls it either a puppy or a dog, the child is corrected and now calls the dog a dog and the horse a horse because accommodation has occurred.

Benefits of Piaget's Work

Piaget's theory encouraged generations of research on cognition, development, and the study of young children. Before Piaget published his research, it was commonly believed that children's thinking was simply a less complex form than adults. His greatest contribution was to show that children actually think differently and not in less complex ways than adults. His studies have been replicated around the globe and it is not uncommon to find his experiments as homework assignments in both undergraduate and graduate level cognitive and lifespan development courses. He can be credited with contributing to educational philosophies as well as helping to develop an understanding about children contributing to their own learning and development. His research spurred cognitive development research toward creation of the information processing theory.

Limitations of Piaget's Work

Many of Piaget's original ideas have been challenged and some of his work is no longer considered the standard in cognitive development. We now know that adult teaching may have a significant impact on Piagetian problem solving over pure children's discovery (Siegler & Svetina, 2006) and that the age at which children are able to acquire intellectual thinking is much lower than Piaget originally thought. Additionally, strict stage-like cognitive development does not appear accurate with a better understanding being that humans acquire knowledge in a more gradual and continuous way (Bjorklund, 2012; Thompson & Goodman, 2011). Researchers now believe that knowledge acquisition continues far beyond the adolescence period of development (Labouvie-Vief, 2006; Moshman, 2011), and neuroimaging serves to be more promising than strict reliance on observational procedures for studying cognitive development in children as well as adults. Piaget also has been criticized for not addressing culture in the unique capacity that Vygotsky does in his theory.

VYGOTSKY'S SOCIAL CULTURAL THEORY

It has been said that the most important scientific advances are born of necessity and revolution. In the case of Vygotsky, a new way of understanding human cognitive development was born out of social revolution, inspired by deep philosophy, and repressed by a political regime. His writings were discovered by the Western world after the end of the Cold War, have since contributed significantly to the understanding of cognitive development, and have become foundational aspects of many education-, psychology-, and counseling-oriented textbooks. Vygotsky's story is psychological, educational, political, historical, and cultural; this narrative inspired a theory that truly embodies these themes in a way that is complex but also clearly observable and distinctly practical.

Core to Vygotsky's perspective is that knowledge and development are co-constructed and that the human mind evolves only as it internalizes what is experienced through social interaction. As such, Vygotsky developed a theory of cognitive development that more fully integrates the impact of culture, society, and interpersonal interaction than do many other theories of intellectual development. He emphasized language as a tool that assists learners to advance cognitively through interactional processes. His collection of ideas is often known as *social cultural theory*, *sociocultural theory*, or *cultural-historical activity theory* (CHAT). Because they were both noted theorists in human cognitive development, Vygotsky is often compared to Jean Piaget. Although Piaget is often cited as believing that learning occurs as a reaction to development, Vygotsky believed that social learning actually precedes and drives cognitive development.

Biographical Sketch of the Theorist

Lev Semenovich Vygotsky was born in 1896 (the second of eight children) in the Russian province of Belorussia (Belarus today) to what were considered to be middle-class and well-educated parents. His family was actively Jewish, and his place in time and history had a significant impact on his adult theoretical work. In the late 1800s, Russia was in transition. Serfdom had been abolished, some power was given to localities, the legal system was becoming separated from government control, required military service was reduced, and finances were reformed, leaving room for industrial expansion. When Alexander III ascended to the throne of Russia after the assassination of his father, Alexander II, in 1881, he promoted a link between Jewish people and the assassination and put into place an emphasis on the endorsement of Russian culture above all others. The Orthodox Church was allowed to grow and became a significant presence in schools, voting rights were restricted, and access to higher education was strongly controlled. Vygotsky was born soon after Tsar Nicolas II ascended to the throne of Russia.

During Vygotsky's youth, the Russian Revolution came to fruition, and Nicolas II abdicated his throne, ending a 1,000-year-old monarchy and leaving room for Vladimir Lenin's return to Russia as leader of the Bolshevik wing of Russia's socialist movement in 1917. The years before, during, and after World War I were all characterized by unrest in Vygotsky's country. His father became a prominent banker in the town of Gomel (about 4 hours by car to Minsk and 8.5 hours to Moscow), where Vygotsky would spend much of his life. He graduated from a Jewish primary school in 1913 and wished to pursue teaching, like his mother who was trained as an educator but who had chosen to stay home with her eight children. However, this career path was prohibited for Jewish students pursuing a degree at a government-sponsored university. Instead, Vygotsky chose to study medicine but later changed to law. He simultaneously enrolled in a Jewish university where he studied history and philosophy (although Jewish universities were not recognized and were unable to grant degrees).

He graduated from Moscow University in 1917, the year of the Russian Revolution, and returned to Gomel. He began teaching, studying psychology, and writing. He was often in poor health and had the first of his experiences with tuberculous in 1920. He married his wife, Roza, in 1924, and they later had two daughters. He began teaching in Moscow at the Institute of Psychology and continued to publish writings on psychology and pedagogy. He was joined by numerous students and scholars, leading to the development of the Vygotsky Circle. He died of tuberculous in 1934 at the age of 37 years. By 1936, his writings were banned with the rise of Stalin under the Soviet rule. After Stalin's death in 1953, the ban was lifted. Scholars began to see Vygotsky's work as providing a unique view of cognitive development that spoke to some of the critiques of Piaget's work, a lack of cultural consideration, and an emphasis on physical development as a precursor to cognitive development.

BOX 5.5   THE VYGOTSKY CIRCLE

Do you find it helpful to talk about things you are learning with your friends, peers, and colleagues? Have new ideas, interesting questions, or different ways of thinking emerged from these conversations? Also known as the Vygotsky cult or the Vygotsky boom, the Vygotsky circle was an informal group of academics and scholars who gathered together to share and consider their ideas and theories. When Lev Vygotsky moved to Moscow, he and a few other graduate students began meeting to discuss various concepts; the group grew slowly and eventually included the noted developmental psychologist Alexander Luria and the man known as the father of social psychology, Kurt Lewin. The circle was known for emphasizing the interrelation between theory, research, history, and practice. What interesting ideas and scientific breakthroughs might come from the conversations you have with your peers?

Development of a Theory

It is undeniable that Vygotsky's work has had a significant impact on the understanding of cognitive development. His contributions, especially as related to the impact of social interaction and culture, have revolutionized how counselors and educators view development, encouraging a more systemic view rather than an intrapersonal one. When considering the sociopolitical climate of the world in which he lived, it is not hard to conceptualize the reasons behind his emphasis on culture and social interaction in his work. He was influenced greatly by the German philosopher and social change agent Karl Marx. Vygotsky actually witnessed and lived through the powerful changes espoused by Marxist doctrine. Part of the revolution was the transformation of academic disciplines to reflect the new philosophy of the day. It was based in this climate of transformation that Vygotsky developed CHAT, which is often narrowly defined as a cognitive theory of development but, when considered more broadly, actually encompasses many internal aspects of the human animal, including cognition, motivation, need, desire, preference, and affect.

Influence of Philosophy

Vygotsky was known to be an avid reader, and he studied numerous philosophies extensively. It is clear that his work and ideas were heavily inspired by the philosophies of Karl Marx, the German philosopher Georg Wilhelm Friedrich Hegel, and Dutch philosopher Benedict Spinoza, among others. According to Margaret Gredler (2009), examples of these influences include the Vygotskian ideal that perception is the precursor to conscious awareness and is one of the great tasks of early childhood. This is based on Hegel's triad, where thesis is an intellectual proposition, antithesis is a rejection of the thesis, and synthesis is a solution to the conflict of thesis and antithesis by finding common factors and developing a new thesis. Hegel himself did not use these terms, but they are most often used to describe his work. The ideas are somewhat similar in form to Piaget's assimilation, adaptation, and accommodation. Separating Vygotsky's theory and associated concepts from the philosophical roots from which they stem is a disservice and an oversimplification. However, to avoid a lengthy foray into deep layers of sociological and philosophical thought (though as a reader you are encouraged to take that journey at some point), it may be prudent to simply highlight that Vygotsky's writings exemplify socialist ideals of co-construction and co-ownership. Marx wrote, "Human essence is no abstraction inherent in each individual. In its reality it is the ensemble of the social relations" (1845/1978, p. 145). This focus on the social nature of humanity was the basis for Vygotsky's assertion that cognitive development is not something that happens within an individual but rather occurs between individuals who are immersed in various contexts.

Key Concepts From Vygotsky

Through CHAT, Vygotsky (1978) posited that human activity is the result of interplays between ontogeny (physical development), phylogeny (human evolution), and changing social and cultural conditions or interactions, which then impact cognitions and consciousness. Therefore, Vygotsky argued that social interaction plays a foundational role in cognitive development. He suggested a two-stage process to development: first interpsychological (between people), and then later intrapsychological (inside the developing person). He noted that all higher cognitive functions originate through relationships between people, which include memory, attention, and the cognitive understanding.

Because growth is a collaborative process in Vygotsky's view, others who are more cognitively advanced must assist developing children in their learning processes. He suggested that because language is the main way that humans communicate with one another, it therefore has a significant impact on human cognitive development. Vygotsky believed that language is a tool that develops from social interactions for the purpose of communication. Later, language ability becomes internalized as thought and inner speech. Hence, individual thought is actually the result of language.

Speech and Metacognition

Because language is a tool that mediates the development of knowledge in Vygotsky's view, it is transformed throughout the process of development in a strategic manner. This is in direct opposition to Piaget's suggestion that children babble and talk to themselves (egocentric speech) in an incoherent way for no specific purpose, and this eventually disappears as higher cognitive functions evolve. In the Vygotskian perspective, egocentric speech, which was instead termed *private speech*, eventually transforms into *inner speech*, the kind of internal dialogue that makes possible higher order thinking. This process is divided into three distinct phases. The first occurs when children (at approximately 3 years of age) begin to give running commentary on their actions, tracking their own activities, irrespective of the presence of another person who may be observing or with whom they could interact ("Henry going outside now," "Putting on shirt," "Where is doggie?"). There is no expectation of interaction necessarily, but the language tool helps children to identify their actions and stay focused on what they are doing. As children mature and reach the age of 6 or 7 years, the private speech becomes less overt. Children may move their lips without actually speaking or may only speak out loud part of an idea. Later, around age 8 years, the private speech becomes more fully internalized, and children are able to use inner speech to self-regulate, direct their actions, and organize knowledge.

Once children have developed inner speech, they are able to think through their experiences in a new way. Rather than simply accepting what they are told or what they observe, they become able to unconsciously compare new information with what is already known. By processing information in a new way and observing this process, children become able to think about how they are thinking. Therefore, *metacognition* is essentially thinking about how one thinks. Changes in thinking occur when new information is compared to old information in an inner debate, and understanding emerges when the conflict is resolved. Others (e.g., parents, siblings, teachers, peers, counselor) can interact with children in specific ways to help facilitate this assimilative process.

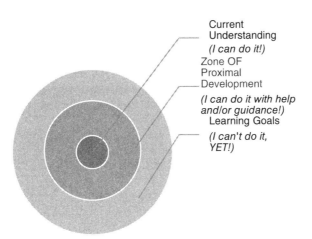

Current
Understanding
(I can do it!)
Zone OF
Proximal
Development

*(I can do it with help
and/or guidance!)*
Learning Goals

*(I can't do it,
YET!)*

Figure 5.1   Zone of proximal development.

Zone of Proximal Development

The *zone of proximal development* (ZPD) is the distance between the developing learner's ability to perform a task (under guidance from a more knowledgeable other [MKO] or with peer collaboration) and the ability to solve the problem independently (see Figure 5.1). The MKO refers to anyone who has a better understanding or a higher ability level than the developing learner with respect to a particular task, process, or concept. The general idea is that when learners work with others (MKOs) who are, at a minimum, at least somewhat more advanced than the learners are on an activity that is just slightly more difficult than their current abilities allow, more learning occurs. Although learning is highly likely to occur in this zone, one must be mindful of the caveat that developmental advancement at any given time during the developmental process is limited by the learner's individual inherent potential. However, the basic foundation is that individuals learn more when they have others guiding them; therefore, full development of the ZPD depends on social interaction.

Scaffolding

To help a developing learner move through the ZPD from what is unknown to what is known, or from what one cannot do to what one can do, a *scaffolding* strategy may be employed. Jerome Bruner, a noted educational psychologist, was directly inflected by Vygotsky and emphasized the importance of discovery learning in which learners construct their own knowledge through activity rather than by having information relayed to them. Therefore, a teacher or other MKO can best assist learners by helping to facilitate this investigative discovery process through providing information and assistance, but not organizing the material or doing tasks for them. Bruner (1978) said that the term scaffolding "refers to the steps taken to reduce the degrees of freedom in carrying out some task so that the child can concentrate on the difficult skill she is in the process of acquiring" (p. 19). Essentially, scaffolding is a support and challenge process that sustains a child's current state of learning while challenging a step beyond the current state to promote more advanced learning or skill, which in turn facilitates cognitive development.

BENEFITS AND APPLICATIONS FOR COUNSELORS

For his eleventh thesis on Fuerbach (1845), Karl Marx wrote, "The philosophers have only *interpreted* the world, in various ways; the point, however, is to *change* it." This is not to say that theory and rational discourse do not have a place, but that meaning is lost without action and practical application. How then might Vygotsky's concepts, which can appear abstract in nature, be applicable to counselors working directly with clients? First, one of the great strengths of Vygotsky's theory is that it is a model not limited to cognitive development in the very young. We can observe how children learn in relationship with others, but we can also observe how others, regardless of stage of life, may also learn in this way.

Additionally, Vygotskian concepts can also be clearly tied to some of the most influential counseling theories that are frequently utilized today. For example, parallels to Vygotsky's ideas can be made to well-known learning theories such as Alfred Bandura's social learning theory (1976), in which society provides the foundation for the development of thought and action (i.e., modeling is a significant factor in the acquisition of skills). The frameworks associated with private speech and metacognition have clear equivalents in techniques used by cognitive counselors including promoting positive, affirming self-talk and the process of reflecting on one's thinking patterns. Examining distorted thoughts and generating alternative rational thoughts is a process facilitated by metacognition. Like many of these techniques, Vygotskian ideas can be effectively integrated with most major counseling theories, both individually oriented approaches and perspectives that are more systemic in nature, which are often a focus of training for couple and family counselors.

One of the most influential aspects of Vygotsky's vision is that, for counselors, his theory emphasizes the impact of culture on cognitive development. Our view of child development, and therefore our own development as humans, is shaped by culture in its many various forms: racial and ethnic identity; religion and spiritual beliefs; gender; sociopolitical, economic, and historical trends; and family-based traditions and values. When it is recognized that culture impacts development, even cognitive development at early ages, counselors can be reminded that developmental goals of clients may be different from those of the counselor. Thus, conversations regarding expectations and goals related to cognitive growth can be more productive, increasing the likelihood of treatment that is based on a foundation of cultural competence.

Four-Step DCHAT Counseling Framework

Vygotsky's work is rarely considered practically significant for the clinical practice of counseling. However, Kathryn Douthit (2008) proposed a step-by-step strategy for working with clients who have problems related to developmental issues from a Vygotskian perspective that she called developmental cultural-historical theory (DCHAT) counseling (see box 5.3). She identified a few key concepts from his work that may have a significant impact on the work counselors engage in with clients and that serve as a foundation for her four-step model. First, she noted that changes in how people think and engage with the world are facilitated by use of, as Vygotsky would call it, a *tool*, which in the case of counseling is language (or other communicative activity). This concept is exemplified in helping a client to develop a vocabulary to more fully identify and express emotion, which is a common task in counseling sessions. Helping clients learn to effectively communicate their needs and wants and to give verbal expression to abstract feelings are often core tasks in counseling.

Second, Douthit (2008) noted that changes in thinking and interaction are often spurred on by understanding how society, culture, and history impact us, which when reflected on is an example of the concept of metacognition. When clients are unsure of the impetus for disagreeable states of being, counselors often work to help them identify what changed in their lived experiences and ask them to think about how they perceived and interpreted those events. Even when using a theoretical intervention like identifying distorted thinking patterns and establishing alternative, realistic beliefs (as in a cognitive-behavioral technique), counselors are asking clients to engage in metacognition by thinking about how they think.

Another applicable concept put forth by Douthit (2008) is that dialectical processes are particularly suited to helping clients resolve disequilibrium (conflict, dissonance, or incongruence) by integrating new understanding with previous understandings. Most clients who present to counseling experience some kind of disequilibrium or challenge to their homeostasis. For example, a client who is feeling depressed and guilty about wanting to leave an abusive partner may have trouble reconciling this type of choice with moral beliefs about vows and marriage. In this case, the counselor and client may engage in a dialectical process to work though this incongruence to develop a new schema that values the client's initial perspective but allows for flexibility in beliefs based on previously unconsidered factors.

Last, the concept of scaffolding within the ZPD is something that likely can apply to all types of counseling, regardless of theory and interactional style. Counselors often help clients make changes by encouraging development through using scaffolding techniques to support and challenge clients within the ZPD. Counselors are encouraged to meet clients where they are by being observant, staying present in the moment, providing normalization and validation, and considering stages of change (Prochaska & DiClemente, 1986). Counselors begin building a scaffold from this place of joining with clients and then pushing and challenging them in incremental ways to take steps toward their therapeutic goals. Although at first glance it may seem difficult to apply Vygotsky's notions regarding cognitive development to the actual practice of counseling, it seems clear that these concepts may assist counselors in case conceptualization and intervention planning in many stages of human growth rather than limiting their use to understanding early cognitive development.

In Douthit's (2008) counseling strategy, she outlined four steps that may facilitate client growth in working with a developmental issue. The first step is to work through discourse with clients with the goal of identifying the specific aspects of development that are most relevant to their concerns. This would likely involve a thorough exploration of client concerns, including the cognitive, affective, and behavioral impacts of the presenting issues. This extensive investigation will assist the counselor in identifying important developmental crises, tasks, or conflicts experienced by clients.

Second, Douthit (2008) suggested that the counselor might use some kind of scaffolding activity to foster clients' metacognitive insights into how developmental principles are impacting presenting problems. In fidelity with Vygotsky's view, the counselor would likely want to assist clients in exploring the influences of society, culture, and history on their lives. For example, if clients were to consider what aspects of life have really impacted how they see themselves (self-identify), this narrative may be made up of a number of factors including biological characteristics and predispositions. However, a greater majority of influential experiences would likely be interpersonal and sociocultural in nature: family-of-origin relationships; friendships and peer interactions; roles in frameworks such as education and faith communities; historical events; and cultural traditions and expectations. Helping clients to develop insight regarding the multidimensional nature of development and knowledge may help them to think about and manage conflicts in new ways.

In step three of Douthit's (2008) model, a counselor would help clients to explore their developmental paths using their newly acquired metacognitive insight from the previous stage. This would likely include examining the beginning of the current developmental crisis through the potential end point and identifying impacts of the resulting disequilibrium. The counselor would assist the client in fully exploring the conflict and connecting specific factors to the development of the current concern. Through a dialectal process involving support and challenge (scaffolding), the counselor can help the client see the multidimensional factors (e.g., social, political, relational, biological) impacting the conflict.

In step four of the model proposed by Douthit (2008), counselors and clients work together to take steps toward resolution of the conflict by identifying potential paths toward reestablished equilibrium. This may involve asking the client to deeply process in numerous ways, including expanding perspectives and cognitions, experiencing emotions and honoring those experiences, enhancing motivation and self-efficacy in relationship to potential action, and supporting behavioral changes. Table 5.3 provides a detailed example of how these steps may play out in an individual counseling session.

Table 5.3   Using DCHAT in Counseling With a Growing Family

Client Concern/Status	Counselor's Intervention With Basis in Four-Step DCHAT Counseling Model
Clients (two same-sex partners, Susan and Sarah; a 6-year-old son; and 2-year-old daughter) present to counseling with concerns about parenting and aggression of young son toward younger daughter.	**Step 1:** Counselor works to explore the concern with clients utilizing various assessment techniques, with a focus exploring developmental concerns.
During the process of exploring their developmental histories with counselor, Sarah reports that she is happy to be a parent of two young children but also feels lonely when left at home all day with them and is unsure what she wants to do with the rest of her life. She gave up a career in advertising to stay home with their son. She is concerned about their relationship now as she believes she and Susan are "in different places" because she is interested in going back to work but Susan prefers that she stay home with the children. In exploring the partner's histories, it is revealed that both partners had parents who worked outside the home when they were children, and rather than having a positive experience like Sarah, Susan felt neglected and abandoned by her parents, who rarely had time to spend with her when she was a child.	**Step 2:** Use scaffolding to assist client in gaining insight. Counselor chooses to have conversations with clients in a scaffolding-oriented way by meeting them where they are using validating, normalizing, and reflective techniques. Counselor then helps clients to process the impact of both personal and cultural expectations of "working parents" and the ways these impact their identities as women, mothers, lesbian partners, and employees. Using gentle reflections of discrepancy, the counselor encourages the client to identify areas of dissonance and incongruence. Counselor encourages metacognitive processing to assist clients in developing understanding about how they arrived at their current thoughts, feelings, and beliefs and how these impact the current concerns.
Additionally, the son shares that he doesn't like that his mom Susan isn't home as much as his mom Sarah and that when she is home his sister gets all the attention.	
Sarah is able to identify that she seeks to reclaim her identity as an employee because she believes this is the way she is expected to contribute to society beyond raising a family and that if she has an identity beyond being a parent, her children will admire her. She recognizes that she is attempting to define herself by standards that have little true intrinsic meaning for her. She identifies that being at home with her children has echoed an identity crisis similar to one she had when she was in her early 20s and was coming out to family and friends, feeling unsure of what career path to explore, and was debating moving away from her childhood	**Step 3:** Using developed insight, counselor helps clients to explore their personal developmental trajectory and sources of conflict. Counselor recalls that discrepancy can exist not only on cognitive but also on affective and motivational levels and brings this into the session by facilitating process-level discussion and emotional expression. Counselor assists clients in processing fear, shame, disappointment, loss, and resentment.

Table 5.3 *(Continued)*

Client Concern/Status	Counselor's Intervention With Basis in Four-Step DCHAT Counseling Model
home in the Midwest. Susan explores her fears around the changes that would have to occur in their schedules if Sarah went back to work. Their son examines how things have changed for him since his sister entered the family. He talked about how he used to be the first one his mom (Susan) said hello to when she got home from work and that his mom Sarah was always willing to play with him and make up new games with him before his sister was born.	
Clients are able to fully experience the impacts of their feelings of loneliness, loss, and fear. Sarah makes connections between the resolutions to her previous developmental crisis and things she may do to help herself as she experiences something similar in the present. She remembers specifically seeking out support from people experiencing similar challenges at that earlier time in her life and realizes that she does not currently have a lot of interaction with other same-sex couples or parents who stay home with their children. She believes that some of this isolation is contributing to the conflict she experiences regarding her role in society. She finds that she doesn't really desire to go back to work in a formal way but is instead seeking connection with others and a sense of purpose. She recalled that she used to be very involved in the LGBTQAA community, but since settling down with her partner and becoming invested in raising their children, political involvement lost a sense of immediacy for her, as she was content with their lifestyle. Client decides that she would like to work on ways to share her feelings more honestly with her partner, will attempt to reconnect with some old friends, and may look online for social and support groups in her community.	**Step 4:** Counselor assists clients in processing the conflict generated by the developmental concerns and uses strength-based interventions to help client to dialectically resolve the disequilibrium. Counselor encourages clients to develop change plans that involve steps to both understand the conflicts and work toward resolution. Here, some of the conflict was characterized by core beliefs associated with what Sarah saw as "typical" or "expected" developmental trajectories and loss of self-identity as both an employee and political advocate for equality issues. For Susan, some of the conflict was generated by lack of communication and by her focusing on helping her partner in the ways she assumed were helpful versus communicating about her partner's true needs. For the son, the conflict was between what he expected based on his experience and what he was actually experiencing in real time. He was not yet able to redefine himself in relationship to having a new sibling and the counselor used strengths-based interventions to help him grow in redefining his role. Additionally, communication strategies and skills were taught (using concepts of ZPD and scaffolding) to help him more effectively ask for what he needed versus acting out aggressively toward his sibling.

Table 5.3 (Continued)	
Client Concern/Status	**Counselor's Intervention With Basis in Four-Step DCHAT Counseling Model**
Susan realizes that in examining her interactions, she doesn't spend much time connecting with Sarah in a meaningful way as she attempts to help care for the children when she comes home from work. She becomes willing to examine the routine and look for ways to engage with the family as a whole, but also to spend quality adult time with her partner outside of the home. Their son works to explore the ways he can be a great big brother because he knows about fun games to play and things to do with younger children because his moms were able to teach him how to do those things. In working with him and his parents, he is given more (fun) responsibility in caring for his sister. The family works on ways to work together to teach the son developmentally appropriate ways of interacting with the daughter and in doing so, are able to give equal amounts of attention to the children at the same time. The counselor also works with the son developing skills to ask his parents for additional time when he is feeling lonely and scheduling one-on-one time with each of his moms on a weekly basis.	

Limitations and Criticisms of Vygotsky's Work

Vygotsky is not nearly as well known or as studied as Jean Piaget and other scholars of cognitive development, which is in large part due to the time-intensive difficulties associated with translating his writings from Russian fully and accurately (Van de Veer & Yasnisky, 2011). Therefore, compared with other theories, there is less empirical support associated with Vygotsky's. (See Hogan & Tudge, 1999, for a review of some relevant empirical studies.) This may be due to the fairly abstract nature of the concepts, lack of specific theoretical structure with testable hypotheses, and the broad scope of his assertions about human cognitive development. It is also important to note that his theory may not apply in all cultures and for all types of learning. Rogoff (1990) suggested that the concept of scaffolding in particular can be particularly problematic and that, in fact, there are many instances in which observation and practice may be significantly more effective ways to understand and utilize certain concepts and skills. This may be even more important when working with young children in a counseling capacity; many play therapy models emphasize the importance of observation and tracking when working with children rather than directive intervention. How children learn and process information may be important for counselors who work with clients in this age group to understand, but it may have less direct impact on the interventions chosen for implementation in session. We will investigate this notion by examining the intricacies of information processing.

EARLY CHILDHOOD CASE STUDY AND CLASS DISCUSSION

Bobby is an 8-year-old boy who presents to counseling at the insistence of his mother because of acting-out behaviors at home and school. He is refusing to follow instructions from his mother and teachers, his schoolwork is suffering, and he was recently in trouble on the school bus for kicking and punching another student who was trying to take his lunch bag. Bobby is also experiencing nightmares (sometimes wetting the bed) and is no longer interested in playing on his Little League baseball team, which he used to love. After talking things though with Bobby and his mother, you discover that Bobby's father left the family about 6 months ago. Bobby's mother reports that her husband calls weekly, and Bobby will hold the phone up to his ear but will not talk to his father. When she tries to talk with Bobby about what is happening, he seems to be reluctant to engage with her. She says that Bobby has two friends at school—one who had a father recently die and another who has parents currently in the process of divorce. She tells you that she is unsure of what will happen in the family in the future but suspects she will receive divorce papers from her husband soon. She reveals that she would like for Bobby to maintain some kind of relationship with his father but that the behaviors at home and school are what are most distressing to her at this time. Bobby is quiet in your initial session but tells you that he likes school and doesn't like it when his mom is "mad at him."

Class Discussion

1. What developmental issues are present in this case? What areas of counseling emphasis may require cognitive or skill development for Bobby or his mother?
2. How might you utilize the DCHAT counseling framework steps to work with Bobby? If you were to see his mother individually, how would you use the steps in your work with her? What about using the steps with them in a family session (maybe eventually including the father if possible)?
3. What societal, historical, and cultural issues impact this case? How would you go about processing these influences with the family?
4. Identify at least one area for growth and map it using the ZPD framework. What scaffolding activity can you work into your treatment plan to help promote growth in this area?

INFORMATION-PROCESSING THEORY

The information-processing theory is a conceptual way to understand how environmental stimuli are stored and retrieved in the mind with memory and cognition as primary components. It is a cognitive model likening memory to a computer with humans having the ability to process information by encoding, storing, and retrieving information (see Figure 5.2; Siegler, 2009). The model moves beyond the works of Piaget by proposing that memory development is a continuous ongoing process without stage-like progression. No one person is credited with the development of the information-processing model (Atkinson & Shiffrin, 1968; Gopnik & Tenenbaum, 2007; Johnson & Mareschal, 2001; Westermann, Sirois, Shultz, & Mareschal, 2006).

Similar to a computer, the mind is said to have both mental hardware and mental software. Mental hardware cognitive structures and places where memory is stored with mental software, including the organization of the information sensory stimuli, are ever present, and selected stimuli will enter the mind (input) and then be selectively stored to increase knowledge and understanding. Recall (output) of the sensory information depends on several components such as encoding, attention, habituation, storage, and retrieval. If the information is successfully recalled then the person is capable of a response.

Attention is the process of selecting environmental stimuli to receive additional processing with habituation occurring when the mind no longer holds that stimuli at the same degree of attention due to diminished exposure to the stimulus (Lamb, Bornstein, & Teti, 2002). Encoding describes how the information is categorized as it is entering the mind and how it is stored in long-term memory. The storage process describes how stimuli are held and kept in the mind with retrieval processes describing how the information is recalled after delayed periods of time.

Benefits of conceptualizing memory via the information-processing theory are that it operationalizes thinking and memory processes and gives researchers a way to study and compare differences in memory ability. Additionally, the information-processing theory has a good deal of empirical support (Birney & Sternberg, 2011). On the other hand, information-processing theory proponents are criticized for ignoring the role of emotions and the use of data from single-task experiments such as rote memorization of memory lists as evidence to support the theory. These data do not consider many complex real-world tasks. In the end, although the workings of a computer provide a good understanding for the

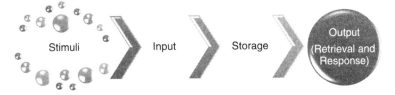

Figure 5.2 Information-processing model via the computer analogy.

basic concepts of information processing, memory and cognition may be more complicated, requiring a further comprehensive understanding of memory.

Memory

Memory processes significantly mature during the childhood years. Metamemory is the process of thinking about memories. It functions primarily by means of a child becoming more and more aware of his or her own thinking and includes an understanding of the function of memory, awareness of memory processes, the ability to remember, and the relationship between feelings and memories (Hertzog, 1992). These processes gradually develop and mature as a child ages and are involved in all three stages of memory.

Sensory Memory

Sensory memory is the repository for all incoming information. Humans are capable of processing and retaining incoming stimuli for $1/2$ to 5 seconds after stimuli are withdrawn. Humans also are capable of holding between 5 and 10 pieces of data in their mind at any one time. It is primarily believed that processing stimuli in sensory memory is more of an unconscious process, meaning that humans do not have the ability to selectively attend to many of the stimuli bombarding their senses. This concept helps explain why a parent cannot teach a child a second language by simply having an audio program on in the background. Without intentional and selective attention, the audio program is passive noise without retention.

BOX 5.6   EXPERIMENTING WITH SENSORY MEMORY

Try it and see: What happens when you try to think of two separate ideas at the exact same time? Is it possible? Try thinking about your last birthday AND what you ate for breakfast this morning. Interestingly enough, only one memory can be in conscious attention at any one time. Maybe you notice that you can think of these two memories with very little time in between? If so, notice that there is a switching back and forth; however, both cannot be thought about in the same moment. Also notice that thinking about both memories may cause you to feel overwhelmed and mentally taxed. This is called flooding and can occur when you become overstimulated.

The main purpose of sensory memory is to screen and select which information will be attended to for further consideration. Relevant and familiar stimuli tend to be the two types of information most likely to be further processed into the working or short-term memory. Other stimuli are processed too quickly and without consciousness. The mind does have the ability to selectively attend to a stimulus in sensory memory, but when doing this it is assumed that controlled attention to the stimuli further inhibits the ability to attend to other surrounding stimuli (see box 5.6).

BOX 5.7 UNDERSTANDING MEMORY: LEARNING A SECOND LANGUAGE

An English-speaking mother is interested in teaching her 5-year-old son to speak Spanish. Neither the mother nor the child is currently able to speak any Spanish. The mother purchases several CDs to play in the home and in the car. She also wants to use these CDs because she has heard that you can learn Spanish in your sleep if you set the tracks to repeat throughout the night. She also purchases flash cards and a Sesame Street video program with 10 bilingual episodes.

To help understand sensory memory, consider the story in box 5.7. The mother decides to play the audio sing-along language CD to her son. The mother sits on the floor with her child and sings along with the songs. She is concurrently saying Spanish words while singing the tune to the song. If the mother was encouraging the child to sing with her, then the words, the tune of the song, and the mother's voice and eye contact are all potential attending variables entering the sensory memory system. Other variables such as the feeling of sitting on the floor, the dog walking around in the room, or the sound of the furnace are passive variables without attention. These prior stimuli will leave sensory memory and be forgotten, whereas the former words to the song, the tune, and the presence of the mother will be forwarded in the information-processing pathway and enter short-term memory.

Short-Term Memory

If stimuli are not deleted or forgotten, the short-term memory system, otherwise known as working memory, further describes the memory process. The purpose of the short-term memory system is to help give meaning to stimuli while also making it available for further processing (Becker & Morris, 1999). Short-term memory processes include inference, linking to other information, reasoning, and perception. Two important features of short-term memory include organization and repetition. Organization includes the various ways the mind is able to categorize stimuli. Ways that information is categorized can include putting stimuli into parts and wholes, identifying relevance of information, and creating sequences to better understand the information. The human short-term memory spans a window of 15–30 seconds with the ability to hold somewhat small amounts of verbal and nonverbal information at any given time (Sternberg & Kaufman, 2011).

One popular technique for organizing data is chunking. Chunking is the process of grouping objects into data sets. This is one way for the mind to remember more information with less work. Originally, it was believed that individuals were able to chunk information into data sets of 7 ± 2 (Miller, 1956) with newer research indicating that humans actually chunk data into even smaller sets such as 5 ± 2.

The second process occurring in short-term memory is repetition. Repetition is the process of repeating information and also is called rote rehearsal. It is not uncommon for individuals to continuously repeat letters or numbers in order to accomplish a basic task such as remembering a phone number or completing a recipe. Sometimes people believe you can utilize a repetition technique to learn new information, but for the most part this is an unsuccessful practice because rote memorization does not lead to long-term learning. One way that rote memorization does seem to work for learning is after forgetting begins.

Let's return to our learning of a second language example. If a mother were to utilize rote memorization to teach her English-speaking child Spanish vocabulary words, she will need to repeat the words, have her child participate in an alternative task for a brief period of time with attention removed from the vocabulary words, and then to have her child selectively attempt to recall the words. This is one way rote rehearsal may be utilized as a successful technique leading to permanent learning (long-term memory).

Continuing with this example of teaching Spanish vocabulary words, a mother may decide to chunk words with similar relevance to help master memorization of these words. For example, the mother may pick the following words to learn together in a set: *knife, spoon, fork, plate, cup, napkin, table, chair, drink,* and *eat.* Presenting and then asking the child to recall these words at the same time is an example of utilizing the short-term memory process of chunking. In order to increase the probability of mastery of these words, a parent may want to stop repetition after a while and move to another task such as getting a drink of water. After the drink of water, returning to the vocabulary words and asking the child to recall the word set in both languages is an example of how short-term memory can be utilized for obtaining, processing, and remembering the vocabulary words. Even still, in order to permanently memorize both language versions of the words, all of the words will need to be stored in long-term memory. Long-term memory processes will require the boy to encode, store, and retrieve the words to be permanently stored.

Long-Term Memory

Long-term memory is the place where information is encoded, stored, and retrieved (World Health Organization, 2014). The long-term memory system is made up of two types of memories: implicit and explicit see box 5.8. Unconsciously recalled memories are called implicit memories, whereas intentionally recalled memories are called explicit or declarative memories and develop during childhood (Feldman, 2011). To permanently store information, processes such as utilizing selective attention, automaticity (Stanovich, 2003), and directing limited attention toward resources are necessary. Many believe that the capacity and ability of the long-term memory are limitless, with long-term memory holding millions of pieces of information (Anderson, 2000). Part of how the process of permanent learning occurs is by way of encoding and retrieval with a key concept being organization. The better an individual is able to organize information, the quicker he or she is able to transfer short-term memory stimuli into permanently learned variables.

BOX 5.8   EXPERIMENTING WITH IMPLICIT AND EXPLICIT MEMORY

Try it and see: What is the earliest memory you can recall? Usually people have memories from a very young age. Pause for a moment after you recall a memory and see if you can recall any earlier memories. Both of these memories are called explicit memories (consciously recalled). Now think about the steps necessary to get from home to work. There are many steps involved in this process. Do you find that you need to think of each step (implicit memory) in order to get yourself to work? Probably not. This is an example of implicit memory. After repeated attempts at successfully getting yourself to work, you are able to get there without mentally thinking of each step. Additionally, if you were to travel to work and accidently turn down the wrong street, that feeling of going the wrong way also is an example of implicit memory.

As information is being stored in long-term memory, humans are actively working to encode the data via models, words, personal experience, or pictures. Indeed, the largest limitation on long-term memory processing is an individual's ability to encode and retrieve large sums of information. Some examples of how humans make this encoding process easier include the use of imagery, rhyming, acronyms, peg words (information is connected to a word: three–me, four–door), and method of loci (information is connected to a location: purse–front door, cereal–cupboard). These methods help reduce cognitive load and allow successful long-term memory encoding and retrieval.

KEY COUNSELING POINTERS FOR PHYSICAL AND COGNITIVE DEVELOPMENT DURING BIRTH AND INFANCY

- Although there is leeway when assessing young children's physical and cognitive growth, it also is important to remember that developmental milestones exist. The extent to which a child does not appear to be meeting these milestones indicates the need for further cognitive or physical assessment.
- Empathizing with parents and caregivers about their frustrations regarding the day-to-day monotony of young children's behaviors may be helpful in developing rapport and creating a shared understanding of some of the difficulties involved in rearing small children.

- Patience is a key point for parents, caregivers, and counselors who are working with very young children.
- Since some parents' and caregivers' knowledge about rearing children may be deficient, the counselor should be prepared to provide psychoeducation on basic and more advanced child-rearing topics.
- Since it is not uncommon that parents and caregivers may disagree on specific ways to rear children, counselors may want to be prepared to address conflict in parenting while using research findings as a foundation for optimal development and health.

SUMMARY

The pace of childhood growth is fast and furious and begins to decline in the toddler years. Many parts of the brain are changing at a rapid pace. However, there is much more development to occur. Children who are in good health, have nutritious food to eat, and live in a healthy environment free of hazards have the best chance of favorable physical and cognitive growth.

Early childhood supplies a rich environment for children to make large strides in cognitive development. Theorists have examined how children conceptualize others' thoughts and how culture plays a role in learning. All these pieces work in concert to supply the unique foundation for children to process the overload of information that they receive each day and for us as counselors to do the most effective work with them.

USEFUL WEBSITES

Jean Piaget Society
https://www.piaget.org
PBS—Child Development
https://www.pbs.org/parents/child-development/
National Center for Infants, Toddlers, and Parents—Child Development
https://www.zerotothree.org/child-development/early-development/
Centers for Disease Control and Prevention—Child Development
https://www.cdc.gov/ncbddd/childdevelopment/
UNICEF—Child Development
https://www.factsforlifeglobal.org
U.S. Department of Health and Human Services—Child Development
https://www.acf.hhs.gov/programs/ecd/child-health-development/watch-
me-thrive

REFERENCES

Akhtar, N., & Tomasello, M. (2000). The social nature of words and word learning. In R. Golinkoff & K. Hirsh-Pasek (Eds.), *Becoming a word learner: A debate on lexical acquisition* (pp. 3–13) Oxford, UK: Oxford University Press.

Anderson, J. R. (2000). *Cognitive psychology and its implication* (5th ed.). New York, NY: Worth.

Atkinson, R. C., & Shiffrin, R. M. (1968). Human memory: A proposed system and its control processes. *Psychology of Learning and Motivation, 2,* 89–105.

Bandura, A. (1976). *Social learning theory*. Upper Saddle River, NJ: Prentice Hall.

Becker, J., & Morris, R. (1999). Working memory. *Brain and Cognition, 41,* 1–8.

Berk, L. E., Mann, T., & Ogan, A. (2006). Make believe play: Wellspring for development of self-regulation. In D. Singer, K. Hirsh-Pasek, & R. Golinkoff (Eds.), *Play = learning* (pp. 6–9). New York, NY: Oxford University Press.

Birch, L. L., Fisher, J. O., & Davison, K. K. (2003). Learning to overeat: Maternal use of restrictive feeding practices promotes girls' eating in the absence of hunger. *American Journal of Clinical Nutrition, 78,* 215–220.

Birney, D., & Sternberg, R. (2011). The development of cognitive abilities. In M. Bornstein & M. Lamb (Eds.), *Developmental science: An advanced textbook* (6th ed., pp. 353–388). New York, NY: Psychology Press.

Bjorklund, D. F. (2012). *Children's thinking* (5th ed.). Belmont, CA: Wadsworth Cengage Learning.

Bogin, B. (2001). *The growth of humanity*. New York, NY: Wiley-Liss.

Braswell, G. S., & Callanan, M. A. (2003). Learning to draw recognizable graphic representation during mother–child interactions. *Merrill-Palmer Quarterly, 49,* 471–494.

Bruner, J. S. (1978). The role of dialogue in language acquisition. In A. Sinclair, R. J. Jarvelle, & W. J. M. Levelt (Eds.), *The child's concept of language* (pp. 241–256). New York, NY: Springer-Verlag.

Callanan, M. A., & Sabbagh, M. A. (2004). Multiple labels for objects in conversations with young children: Parents' language and children's developing expectations about word meanings. *Developmental Psychology, 40,* 746–763.

Cameron, C. A., & Lee, K. (1997). The development of children's telephone communication. *Journal of Applied Developmental Psychology, 18,* 55–70.

Cecil, J. E., Watt, P., Murrie, I. S. L., Wrieden, W., Wallis, D. J., Hetherington, M. M., Bolton-Smith, C., & Palmer, C. N. A. (2005). Childhood obesity and socioeconomic status: A novel role for height growth limitation. *International Journal of Obesity, 29,* 1199–1203.

Chang, F., Dell, G. S., & Bock, K. (2006). Becoming syntactic. *Psychological Review, 113,* 234–272.

Children's Defense Fund. (2008). *Annual report 2007*. Washington, DC: Author.

Damashek, A., & Peterson, L. (2002). Unintentional injury prevention efforts for young children: Levels, methods, types and targets. *Developmental and Behavioral Pediatrics, 23,* 443–455.

Deltondo, J., Por, I., Hu, W., Merchenthaler, I., Semeniken, K., Jojart, J., & Dudas, B. (2008). Associations between the human growth hormone-releasing hormone and neuropeptide-Y-immunoreactive systems in the human diencephalons: A possible morphological substrate of the impact of stress on growth. *Neuroscience, 153,* 1146–1152.

Derom, C., Thiery, E., Vlietinck, R., Loos, R., & Derom, R. (1996). Handedness in twins according to zygosity and chorion type: A preliminary report. *Behavior Genetics, 26*, 407–408.

Diamond, A. (2004). Normal development of prefrontal cortex from birth to young adulthood: Cognitive functions, anatomy, and biochemistry. In D. T. Stuff & R. T. Knight (Eds.), *Principles of frontal lobe function* (pp. 466–503). New York, NY: Oxford University Press.

Douthit, K. (2008). Cognition, culture, and society: Understanding cognitive development in the tradition of Vygotsky. In K. L. Kraus (Ed.), *Lenses: Applying lifespan development theories in counseling* (pp. 83–118). Boston, MA: Lahaska Press.

Feldman, R. (2011). *Child development* (6th ed.). Upper Saddle River, NJ: Prentice Hall.

Flannery, K. A., & Liederman, J. (1995). Is there really a syndrome involving the co-occurrence of neurodevelopmental disorder, talent, non-right handedness and immune disorder among children? *Cortex, 31*, 503–515.

Fuller, C., Keller, L., Olson, J., Plymale, A., & Gottesman, M. (2005). Helping preschoolers become healthy eaters. *Journal of Pediatric Health Care, 19*, 178–182.

Ganji, V., Hampl, J. S., & Betts, N. M. (2003). Race-, gender- and age-specific differences in dietary micronutrient intakes of U.S. children. *International Journal of Food Sciences and Nutrition, 54*, 485–490.

Gopnik, A., & Tenenbaum, J. B. (2007). Bayesian networks, Bayesian learning and cognitive development. *Developmental Science, 10*, 281–287.

Gredler, M. E. (2009). Hiding in plain sight: The stages of mastery/self-regulation in Vygotsky's cultural-historical theory. *Educational Psychologist, 44*(1), 1–19. doi:10.1080/00461520802616259

Haywood, K. M., & Getchell, N. (2005). *Life span motor development* (4th ed.). Champaign, IL: Human Kinetics.

Hertzog, C. (1992). Improving memory: The possible roles of metamemory. In D. Herrmann, H. Weingartner, A. Searleman, & C. McEvoy (Eds.), *Memory improvement: Implications for memory theory* (pp. 61–78). New York, NY: Springer-Verlag.

Hilgers, K. K., Akridge, M., Scheetz, J. P., & Kinance, D. E. (2006). Childhood obesity and dental development. *Pediatric Dentistry, 28*, 18–22.

Hinojosa, T., Sheu, C.-F., & Michael, G. F. (2003). Infant hand-use preference for grasping objects contributes to the development of a hand-use preference for manipulating objects. *Developmental Psychobiology, 43*, 328–334.

Hogan, D. M., & Tudge, J. R. H. (1999). Implications of Vygotsky's theory for peer learning. In A. M. O'Donnell & A. King (Eds.), *Cognitive perspectives on peer learning* (pp. 39–65). Mahwah, NJ: Lawrence Erlbaum.

Hursti, U. K. (1999). Factors influencing children's food choice. *Annals of Medicine, 31*, 26–32.

Johnson, M. H., & Mareschal, D. (2001). Cognitive and perceptual development during infancy. *Current Opinion in Neurobiology, 11*, 213–218.

Kemeny, M. E. (2003). The psychobiology of stress. *Current Directions in Psychological Science, 12*, 124–129.

Kendrick, D., Barlow, J., Hampshire, A., Stewart-Brown, S., & Polnay, L. (2008). Parenting interventions and the prevention of unintentional injuries in childhood: Systematic review and mental analysis. *Child: Care, Health and Development, 34*, 682–695.

Kennedy, A. M., & Gust, D. A. (2008). Measles outbreak associated with a church congregation: A study of immunization attitudes of congregation members. *Public Health Reports, 123*, 126–134.

Labouvie-Vief, G. (2006). Emerging structures of adult thought. In J. J. Arnett & J. L. Tanner (Eds.), *Emerging adults in America: Coming of age in the 21st century* (pp. 59–84). Washington, DC: American Psychological Association.

Lamb, M. E., Bornstein, M. H., & Teti, D. M. (2002). *Development in infancy*. Mahwah, NJ: Erlbaum.

Levin, I., & Bus, A. G. (2003). How is emergent writing based on drawing? Analyses of children's products and their sorting by children and mothers. *Developmental Psychology, 39*, 891–905.

Marx, K. (1845/1978). Theses on Fruerbach. In R. C. Tucker (Ed.), *The Marx-Engles reader* (pp. 143–145). New York, NY: Norton.

Miller, G. A. (1956). The magical number seven, plus or minus two: Some limits on our capacity for processing information. *Psychological Review, 63*, 81–97.

Mooney, C. G. (2013). *Theories of childhood: An introduction to Dewey, Montessori, Erikson, Piaget and Vygotsky (2nd ed.)*. St. Paul, MN: Redleaf Press.

Morrongiello, B. A., Midgett, C., & Shields, R. (2001). Don't run with scissors: Young children's knowledge of home safety rules. *Journal of Pediatric Psychology, 26*, 105–115.

Moshman, D. (2011). *Adolescent rationality and development: Cognition, morality, and identity* (3rd ed.). New York, NY: Psychology Press.

Naigles, L. R., & Swenson, L. D. (2007). Syntactic supports for word learning. In E. Hoff & M. Shatz (Eds.), *Blackwell handbook of language development* (pp. 212–231). Malden, MA: Blackwell.

National Institute of Child Health and Human Development (NICHD) Early Child Care Research Network. (2000). The relation of child care to cognitive and language development. *Child Development, 71*, 960–980.

National Safe Kids Campaign. (2005). *Report to the nation: Trends in unintentional childhood injury mortality: 1987–2000*. Washington, DC: Author.

Nelson, C. A., Thomas, K. M., & de Haan, M. (2006). Neural bases of cognitive development. In D. Kuhn & R. Siegler (Eds.), *Handbook of child psychology: Vol. 2. Cognition, perception, and language* (6th ed., pp. 3–57). Hoboken, NJ: Wiley.

Noterdaeme, M., Mildenberger, K., Minow, F., & Amorosa, H. (2002). Evaluation of neuromotor deficits in children with autism and children with a specific speech and language disorder. *European Child and Adolescent Psychiatry, 11*, 219–225.

Pan, B. A., & Snow, C. E. (1999). The development of conversation and discourse skills. In M. Barrett (Ed.), *The development of language* (pp. 229–249). Hove, UK: Psychology Press.

Piaget, J. (1971). Mental imagery in the child: A study of the development of imaginal representation. London: Routledge and Kega Paul Ltd.

Piaget, J., & Inhelder, B. (1956). *The child's conception of space*. Boston, MA: Routledge & Kegan Paul.

Powls, A., Botting, N., Cooke, R. W. I., & Marlow, N. (1996). Handedness in very-low-birthweight (VLBW) children at 12 years of age: Relation to perinatal and outcome variables. *Developmental Medicine and Child Neurology*, *38*, 594–602.

Previc, F. H. (1991). A general theory concerning the prenatal origins of cerebral lateralization. *Psychological Review*, *98*, 299–334.

Prochaska, J. O., & DiClemente, C. C. (1986). Toward a comprehensive model of change. In W. R. Miller & N. Heather (Eds.), *Treating addictive behaviors: Processes of change* (pp. 3–27). New York, NY: Plenum Press.

Provins, K. A. (1997). Handedness and speech: A critical reappraisal of the role of genetic and environmental factors in the cerebral lateralization of function. *Psychological Review*, *104*, 554–571.

Rogoff, B. (1990). *Apprenticeship in thinking: Cognitive development in social context*. Oxford, UK: Oxford University Press.

Saenger, P. (2003). Dose effects of growth hormone during puberty. *Hormone Research*, *60* (Suppl. 1), 52–57.

Salerno, M., Micillo, M., Di Maio, S., Capalbo, D., Ferri, P., & Lettiero, T. (2001). Longitudinal growth, sexual maturation and final height in patients with congenital hypothyroidism detected by neonatal screening. *European Journal of Endocrinology*, *145*, 377–383.

Saxton, M., Backley, P., & Gallaway, C. (2005). Negative input for grammatical errors: Effects after a lag of 12 weeks. *Journal of Child Language*, *32*, 643–672.

Schwebel, D. C., & Gaines, J. (2007). Pediatric unintentional injury: Behavioral risk factors and implications for prevention. *Journal of Developmental and Behavioral Pediatrics*, *28*, 245–254.

Siegler, R. S. (2009). Improving the numerical understanding of children from lowincome families. *Child Development Perspectives*, *3*(2), 118–124.

Siegler, R. S., & Svetina, M. (2006). What leads children to adopt new strategies? A microgenetic cross sectional study of class inclusion. *Child Development*, *77*, 997–1015.

Stanovich, K. E. (2003). The fundamental computational biases of human cognition: Heuristics that (sometimes) impair decision making and problem solving. In J. E. Davidson & R. J. Sternberg (Eds.), *The psychology of problem solving* (pp. 291–342). New York: Cambridge University Press.

Sternberg, R., & Kaufman, S. (2011). *The Cambridge handbook of intelligence*. New York, NY: Cambridge University Press.

Szaflarski, J. P., Binder, J. R., Possing, E. T., McKiernan, K. A., Ward, B. D., & Hammeke, T. A. (2002). Language lateralization in left-handed and ambidextrous people: fMRI data. *Neurology*, *59*, 238–244.

Tarren-Sweeney, M. (2006). Patterns of aberrant eating among preadolescent children in foster care. *Journal of Abnormal Child Psychology*, *34*, 623–634.

Thompson, P. M., Giedd, J. N., Woods, R. P. MacDonald, D., Evans, A. C., & Toga, A. W. (2000). Growth patterns in the developing brain detected by using continuum mechanical tensor maps. *Nature, 404,* 190–192.

Thompson, R. A., & Goodman, M. (2011). The architecture of social developmental science: Theoretical and historical perspectives. In M. K. Underwood & L. H. Rosen (Eds.), *Social development: Relationships in infancy, childhood, and adolescence* (pp. 3–28). New York, NY: Guilford Press.

Toomela, A. (2002). Drawing as a verbally mediated activity: A study of relationships between verbal. Motor, visuospatial skills and drawing in children. *International Journal of Behavioral Development, 26,* 234–247.

U.S. Department of Agriculture. (2007). *Expenditures on children by families.* Miscellaneous Publication No. 1528-2007. Washington, DC: U.S. Government Printing Office.

U.S. Department of Health and Human Services. (2007, April). Trends in oral health status: United States, 1988–1994 and 1999–2004. *Vital and Health Statistics, 11* (248).

Van de Veer, R., & Yasnisky, A. (2011). Vygotsky in English: What still needs to be done. *Integrative Psychological & Behavioral Science, 45,* 475–493. doi:10.1007/s12124-011-9172-9

Vygotsky, L. S. (1978). *Mind and society: The development of higher mental processes.* Cambridge, MA: Harvard University Press.

Westermann, G., Sirois, S., Shultz, T. R., & Mareschal, D. (2006). Modeling developmental cognitive neuroscience. *Trends in Cognitive Sciences, 10,* 227–232.

World Health Organization. (2008a). *The global burden of disease: 2004.* Geneva, Switzerland: Author.

World Health Organization. (2008b). *The World Health Organization's infant feeding recommendation.* Retrieved from http://www.who.int/nutrition/topics/infantfeeding_recomendation/en/index.html

World Health Organization. (2008c). *World report on child injury prevention.* Geneva, Switzerland: Author.

World Health Organization. (2014). *ICF: International classification of functioning and disability.* Geneva, Switzerland: Author.

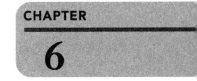

Birth and Infancy: Emotional and Social Development

Adrianne L. Johnson and Eric D. Anderson

INTRODUCTION

Baby Marcus is 8 months old. His foster parent, Juanita, appears frustrated and complains that "he doesn't seem right." You observe Marcus, but he will not meet your eyes, nor will he respond to cooing sounds. He starts to whimper, and Juanita, holding Marcus loosely in her arms, bounces him up and down to quiet him. She tells you that he doesn't appear to warm up to hugs and frequently ignores his toys. She tells you that when he cries at home she tries to comfort him but he won't look at her and continues to cry. He responds to strangers in a similar fashion and is often jittery and fussy. She tells you that she has two other foster children in the home and that his fussiness is "disruptive to the other children in the house." Juanita is home all day with the children while her husband, Roberto, is at work, and in the evenings the family has a meal together before what she calls "family time." During this time, she describes how she and her husband watch television, with Marcus on a blanket on the floor in front of them, while the other two school-aged children do homework on the computer or their iPads. You finally learn that Marcus was placed in foster care shortly after birth, and now his birth mother, Rochelle, has completed mandatory drug treatment and is seeking full custody of Marcus.

Infant mental health, which is an interdisciplinary field, is centered on the developing capacity of the child from birth to age 3 years to experience, regulate, and express emotions; form close and secure interpersonal relationships; and explore the environment and learn—all in the context of family, community, and cultural expectations for young children. Infant mental health evolves from healthy social and emotional development (Sampaio & Lifter, 2014). Today, this development is conceptualized as an amalgamation of genetics, environment, childrearing, and cultural influences, all of which contribute to the normative attributes of infant mental health.

Prenatal mental health may be of particular concern because of potential physiological effects on the developing fetus. Exposure to maternal stress during pregnancy has been hypothesized to exert a "programming influence" on fetal development that impacts birth outcomes, neonatal functioning, and later infant and child development (Sandman, Davis, Buss, & Glynn, 2012). Maternal anxiety, stress, and depression during pregnancy may increase fetal exposure to maternal and placental stress hormones that play a role in the organization of the developing fetal nervous system, leading to increased risk for subsequent disturbances in physiological and behavioral functioning in infants (Vedhara et al., 2012).

Recent research has found that the combination of depression and anxiety in pregnancy is associated with more severe symptomatology and more daily stress than having anxiety or depression alone, as well as poorer neonatal outcomes (Field et al., 2010), such as spontaneous preterm birth (Ibanez et al., 2012). A key example is the effect of maternal depression on child development. Not only is depression in children of depressed mothers more frequent and more severe than in children of nondepressed mothers, but also these children display more anxiety disorders, aggression, attention deficits, insecure attachment, poor self-esteem, and poor peer relations. The relation between psychopathology of parents and child development is not limited to the mother–child relationship. A father's postnatal depression has also been associated with child development such as excessive infant crying, child anxiety, and conduct problems. For instance, postnatal paternal depression was associated with a higher likelihood of a psychiatric diagnosis in children at the age of 7 years (Velders et al., 2011).

In addition, findings from research looking at associations between perinatal mental health and offspring emotional and behavioral problems that have examined both depression and anxiety indicate that the impact of postpartum depression on children's emotional/behavioral problems may be partly explained by prenatal maternal anxiety, making it important to consider both depression and anxiety during both the prenatal and postpartum periods. Exposure to elevated symptoms of maternal depression during pregnancy was associated with increased infant emotional and behavioral problems. Infants and children exposed to elevated symptoms of maternal anxiety during pregnancy tend to demonstrate emotional and behavioral problems in adolescence (Leis, Heron, Stuart, & Mendelson, 2014).

Research also suggests that being born preterm (less than 37 weeks of gestational age) is associated with adverse health and development outcomes for the infant that extend into the early childhood and beyond. These include neonatal morbidities; delays in motor, cognitive, and behavioral functioning during early childhood; and increased risk for chronic disease later in life. Recent trends have shown an overall increase in the preterm birth rate; especially conspicuous in the United States, the preterm birthrate has increased by 36% in 25 years (McDonald et al., 2013, p. 1468). Potential threats to development include poor nutrition, maternal and family health factors, and emotional responses of the mother to external stressors. These factors also compromise breastfeeding practices; mothers with reported elevated anxiety and depression also report problems with successful breastfeeding practices. This is of particular concern to infant and child development given the influence of mother–infant bonding, attachment, and brain-developing nutritional elements after birth (McDonald et al., 2013).

THEORETICAL FRAMEWORKS AND INFANCY

The practice of specifically studying infant emotional and social development was solidified in the 1950s when child development researchers Stella Chess and Alexander Thomas theorized that innate individual differences, what they called temperament, could be detected early in infancy and were shaped by the exchange of feedback between the infant and the caregiver. By 1970, it was widely accepted that an infant's emotional development was dependent upon a multitude of sources, including the complex interplay between both nature and nurture, and significantly influenced by the multidirectional transactions between infants and caregivers, as well as others (Sparrow, 2013). This understanding led to the development of several important theories about infant development.

Theories help the counselor articulate the exciting and rapidly changing emotional and developmental stages of infancy. Many theorists have suggested frameworks that may be used to understand age-appropriate development and to conceptualize appropriate interventions when appropriate development is interrupted. Each of these approaches explores the way infants and children develop emotionally, differing mainly on the question of whether emotions are learned or biologically predetermined and debating the way infants and children manage their emotional experiences and behavior.

Theories of Development

Hebb and Vygotsky

Two approaches to the development of the human mind have strongly influenced current psychology and cognitive neuroscience. The major idea of these approaches is that brains consist of cells and that, in the course of development, assemblies of cells, often called networks, are formed with repeated stimulation (Ghassemzadeh, Posner, & Rothbart, 2013; Johnson, 2011). This idea has led to significant developments in neuroscience and its applications to infant and child development.

Lev Vygotsky's main work was in developmental psychology, beginning in the 1930s. Vygotsky analyzed the role of speech in the development of higher cortical functions, which provided him with a methodology that he considered as an objective method in the study of psychology. He theorized that cognitive development in children emerged out of practical activity in a social environment. These ideas formed the basis of developmental plasticity, one of the most powerful concepts in developmental psychology. This idea has led to early-start programs to enrich the experiences of underprivileged children in reading, writing, and mathematical abilities and in music, sports, and art. It also led to studies on the effects of environmental stimulation on neural development that continue today (Ghassemzadeh et al., 2013).

Donald O. Hebb, psychologist and researcher, worked with rats as an animal model amenable to study psychology and behavior beginning in 1939. His research demonstrated that an enriched experience during development resulted in improved maze learning in adulthood. Hebb also showed that the effects of brain damage on the development of intelligence depended on the age when the damage occurred. Hebb and his student Kenneth Williams designed a variable path maze called the Hebb–Williams maze, which has since been used in numerous studies of learning in animals. Hebb's emphasis on the importance of experience for brain development led to the prolific study of brain plasticity in the following decades (Ghassemzadeh et al., 2013).

Erikson and Freud

According to Sigmund Freud's theory of psychosexual development (1905), the infant begins emotional and social development upon birth and continues this development throughout adulthood. The infant remains in the first stage of the five-stage model, known as the oral stage of psychosexual development, until approximately 12 months of age. The oral stage focuses on experiences of the mouth (e.g., sucking, eating, crying, biting), and Freud suggested that if an infant's needs were not met successfully at this stage, the infant would develop oral neuroses, or fixations, later in life, such as smoking, immaturity, and manipulative personality traits.

Alternatively, Erik Erikson's stages of psychosocial development (Erikson, Paul, Heider, & Gardner, 1959) proposed that the environment in which a child lived was crucial to providing growth, adjustment, a source of self-awareness, and identity. The first stage of his eight-stage model is the basic trust versus basic mistrust, which occurs from birth to 12 months of age. This stage emphasizes the quality of the maternal relationship for developing the trust that shapes the infant's basis for identity later in life. Thus, failure to develop this trust will result in a feeling of fear and a sense that the world is inconsistent and unpredictable. Erikson suggested that a crisis at this critical time would impact the infant's ability to engage in a trusting, gratifying adult relationship later in life.

Social Learning Theory

Albert Bandura suggested that infants come to control not only their behavior but also the behavior of other people around them. He proposed that entirely new behaviors could be acquired almost immediately through observational learning. Researchers and clinicians however have noted that this approach cannot comprehensively explain the sequence and timing of developmental stages, nor can it account for the spontaneous emergence of new behaviors (e.g., the infant develops stranger anxiety even when the infant has no experience with strangers, or an infant with a visual impairment learns to smile).

Table 6.1 Emotional and Social Milestones of Infants Through Age 12 Months	
Age	**Emotional and Social Milestones**
0–3 months	Smile and show pleasure in response to social stimulation Respond positively to touch
3–6 months	Give warm smiles and laughs Show excitement by waving arms and legs Cry when upset and seek comfort
6–9 months	Express several different clear emotions Show displeasure at the loss of a toy Respond to you when you talk to her or make gestures Start to understand your different emotions
9–12 months	Give affection and love Show happiness to see caregiver's face, toys, or a mirror Imitate some of your actions (e.g., waving, pretending to talk on the phone)

Behavior Ecology Theory

Also known as ecological systems theory, this approach emphasizes the goal of understanding developmental change within a holistic perspective. This emphasis on a system invites researchers and practitioners to focus on a set of interdependent components as a whole, since each of these components affects the others in reciprocal fashion. Simply, a caregiver and an infant develop together as a system in relationship with each other over time.

THEORIES OF ATTACHMENT AND CAREGIVING

Caregiving environments that do not provide the basic physical essentials of adequate food, water, sanitation, safety, and medical care are referred to as *globally deficient*, and those that are deficient in their socioemotional aspects of care are called *socioemotionally deficient* (McCall, Groark, & Rygaard, 2014, p. 88). Together, these environments typically do not support adequate caregiver–child interactions and relationships, and consequently, they lack warm, sensitive, and responsive interactions with children. This results in substantially delayed physical growth and mental and emotional development.

Ethological Theory

Ethological theory rose out of the work of John Bowlby after researching the impact of separation. Bowlby was a psychoanalyst who believed that mental health and behavioral problems could be attributed to early childhood. He theorized that children come into the world biologically preprogrammed to form attachments with others, because this will help them to survive. This suggests that attachment behaviors are instinctive and will be activated by any conditions that seem to threaten the achievement of proximity, such as separation, insecurity, and fear. Bowlby observed that when the individual to which the child has a primary attachment is present, they are the child's focus, but when the primary figure is present, the attachment is not active, allowing the child to separate and explore (Bowlby, 1951).

For a developing infant, the primary caretaker and protector quickly becomes also their main attachment (or primary attachment) out of necessity. The primary caretaker is usually observable by the child's behavior by roughly 6 months after birth. As the child completes their first year of life, with the attachment becoming more secure, the child is able to identify this primary figure from other people. Other individuals in the environment who provide care are referred to as secondary attachment figures and are those individuals who are in the child's life and assisted with care when the primary provider was unavailable. Further, attachment in infancy has a great impact on the formation of relationships later on in life (Bowlby, 2007).

Another important factor in the ethological theory of attachment is the concept of emotional communication, with easier emotional communication leading to more secure attachments and relationships later. This theory also suggests that the level of difficulty in communication between a caregiver and an infant can be observed and measured (Stevenson-Hinde, 2007). Psychologist Mary Ainsworth studied this concept by constructing the Strange Situation Classification (SSC). From this observational experiment, Ainsworth and Bell (1970) identified three main attachment styles:

1. Insecure-avoidant (type A): Within the first 12 months of life, children learn to think of themselves unworthy and unacceptable, caused by a rejecting primary caregiver. Insecure attachment styles are associated with an increased risk of social and emotional behavioral problems as children develop into their preschool years.
2. Secure (type B): As these infants grow into childhood, they develop a positive working model of themselves and have mental representations of others as being helpful while viewing themselves as worthy of respect.
3. Ambivalent-resistant (type C): Children have learned to view themselves with a negative self-image and exaggerate their emotional responses as a way to gain attention.

Group Discussion

According to the ethological theory, the baby, Marcus, whose story is given at the outset of the chapter, is preprogrammed to form an attachment with this biological mother, Rochelle. However, he was placed in foster care before this could happen. Juanita is now his caregiver, and she reports that there is little attachment between her and Marcus. What questions would you ask to learn how the attachment between Juanita and Marcus is being interrupted? What are the long-term implications of this lack of attachment?

BOX 6.1 AINSWORTH AND THE STRANGE SITUATION

Ainsworth developed the Strange Situation to observe the variety of attachment forms exhibited between mothers and infants. This experiment is set up in a small room with one-way glass so the behavior of the infant can be observed covertly. Infants were aged between 12 and 18 months. The sample comprised about 100 middle-class American families. Eight different observational scenarios were used: (1) mother, baby, and experimenter; (2) mother and baby alone; (3) stranger joins mother and infant; (4) mother leaves baby and stranger alone; (5) mother returns and stranger leaves; (6) mother leaves and infant is left completely alone; (7) stranger returns; and (8) mother returns and stranger leaves. Discuss in small groups: What are the cultural and ethical implications of this study? Are the results of this study still valid today?

BOX 6.2 SCREEN MEDIA AND DEVELOPMENT

The available literature suggests that screen media, in particular television, has a substantially disruptive effect on the quantity and quality of parent–child interactions, which are essential for developing secure attachments. Screen media use is largely a ubiquitous presence in the lives of young children and is continuing to rise with the proliferation of new forms of electronic media. It is suggested that adverse effects of media begin in infancy and the distraction caused by screen media can be harmful to children's development (Napier, 2014). Nathanson and Manohar (2011) recognized that the relationship between parents and media use is complex, suggesting that not only should the attachment between parent and child be considered but also that the parent's own attachment may have relevance to their media use. Richert, Robb, and Smith (2011) recognized the importance of social interaction in relation to overall healthy development and suggest that television reduces the quantity and quality of parent–child interaction.

Evolutionary Theory

Sigman (2012) suggested that infants are primarily social beings and that social and emotional skills, which are essential for mental health, are complex and technical and need to be learned person to person. And unlike behavioral or learning theories

Table 6.2   Attachment Styles and Interventions Based on Ainsworth's SCC Experiment

Attachment Style	Associated Behavior	Counseling Intervention
Insecure-avoidant (type A)	These infants are abnormally independent of the attachment figure both physically and emotionally and do not seek contact with the attachment figure when distressed.	Evaluate the infant and discuss with the caregivers how to respond to the needs of the infant in ways that do not result in rejection or insensitivity to the infant's needs. Stress management and coping skills may be a significant goal for caregivers since they may be emotionally unavailable to the infant when unable to manage their own stressors. Support groups may be a recommended strategy.
Secure type (type B)	These infants and children feel confident that the attachment figure will be available to meet their needs.	Encourage the caregivers to maintain sensitive and appropriate responses to exhibited needs of the infant or child, and focus on continued support for the caregivers.
Ambivalent-resistant (type C)	The infant or child will commonly exhibit clingy and dependent behavior, but will be rejecting of the attachment figure when they engage in interaction.	Assess the child's feelings of security and observe his or her behavior when in novel surroundings. Provide psychoeducation to the caregivers on how to appropriately soothe the infant and to maintain consistency in response to infant needs. Parenting classes may be a valuable recommendation.

that propose an infant would form an attachment with a caregiver that provides food, evolutionary theory suggests that infants have an innate biological need to touch and cling to something for emotional comfort.

To explore this, psychologist Harry Harlow studied attachment in rhesus monkeys during the 1950s and 1960s. Harlow theorized that maternal separation and deprivation had detrimental effects on infants. He separated eight infant monkeys from their mothers immediately after birth and placed them in cages with assess to two surrogate mothers—one made of wire and one covered in soft terry cloth. Four of the monkeys could get milk only from the wire mother and four only from the cloth mother. During the 165-day observation, he noticed that both groups of monkeys spent more time with the cloth mother, even if she had no milk. The infant would go to the wire mother only when hungry, and once fed it would return to the cloth mother for most of the day. Interestingly, the infants also displayed decreased fear in the presence of the cloth mother; the infant would explore the surroundings of the cage more when the cloth mother was present, and if a frightening object was placed in the cage the infants took refuge with the cloth mother, ignoring their need for milk altogether.

Harlow concluded that for an infant to develop normally, the infant must have some interaction with an object to which he or she can cling during the first months of life. He called this the *critical period*. He suggested that clinging is a natural response and noted from his experiments that in times of stress the infant monkeys ran to the object (in this case, the cloth mother) to decrease their stress. To further explore whether this was due to maternal deprivation or social isolation, he reared a separate group of monkeys in isolation for as long as 24 months. In contrast to the clinging behavior he observed in the first group, these monkeys either refused to eat and subsequently died or entered a state of emotional shock and exhibited autistic-like symptoms such as rocking and self-clutching and could not interact with other monkeys when they grew into adulthood (Harlow, 1958).

Harlow found, therefore, that it was social deprivation, rather than maternal deprivation, that the young monkeys were suffering from. In an effort to undo the social and emotional delays and social deficits in the monkeys, he exposed them to other infant monkeys for 20 minutes a day in a playroom with three other monkeys. These monkeys appeared uncertain about how to interact with their playmates and isolated themselves from the group for the duration of the experiment. As these monkeys grew into adulthood, they maintained moderate to severe social deficits and emotional delays.

To further study the parent–infant interaction in microscopic detail, Dr. T. Berry Brazelton and his colleagues created the face-to-face paradigm, in which infant and parent were seated closely facing each other and asked to interact as they usually would while separate video cameras for infant and parent recorded their microsecond-to-microsecond interactions. They found that as early as 8 weeks of age infants communicate with a broad repertoire of vocalizations, facial expressions, gestures, and changes in postural tone and body positioning and that these are used not only in specific responses to parental communications but also to initiate conversations with parents. From this study, the Neonatal Behavioral Assessment Scale (NBAS), also known as the Brazelton Neonatal Assessment Scale (BNAS), was developed to provide an index of a newborn's abilities and is usually given to an infant somewhere between the age of 3 days to 4 weeks old (Brazelton, 1978).

Goodness-of-Fit Model of Child-Rearing

The goodness-of-fit model focuses on the impact of the parent's way of interacting with a child (including punishment style), culture, and goals on the child's temperament. The combination of child needs and parenting styles can lead to a good fit, in which the two styles lead to positive interactions and development of a positive temperament. If there is not a good fit between parenting style and child needs, it can lead to negative consequences for the child (Lengua & Wachs, 2012). In terms of applications to counseling, the goodness-of-fit model can be used to find factors that may underlie problems in the parent–child relationship. Helping parents to adapt their style to the needs of the child can foster positive development and improve the relationship.

The goodness-of-fit model was initially designed through repeated assessments of children by Alexander Thomas and Stella Chess, child development researchers who concentrated on behavioral assessments instead of nonmeasurable markers of temperament such as cognitions. Through a longitudinal study of infant temperament and how temperamental qualities influence adjustment throughout life, the researchers theorized that infants could be categorized into one of three groups (Thomas & Chess, 1977, p. 24):

1. *The easy child:* This child shows regular eating patterns, elimination cycles, a positive approach response to new situations, and ability to accept frustration with little fuss. Maturation of sleep–wake patterns is one of the most important physiological developments during the first year of life (Cecchini et al., 2013); these infants are able to experience regulated sleep patterns easily and maintain these patterns over time.

    As infants, they adapt to change smoothly, smile easily, and demonstrate mood stability early in life. Most issues observed by counselors result from the infant being placed in more than one caregiving setting resulting in a disruption in predictable routine and social responses to needs and demands.

2. *The difficult child:* This child shows irregular eating, sleeping, and elimination cycles, which begins in infancy. These infants display a negative approach response to new situations (e.g., frequent and loud crying). They are slow to adapt to change, and as they grow into toddlerhood, they need more time to get used to novel things and environments. Counselors may observe frustrated responses from the infant upon interaction and may theorize that the issue arose in response to a disruption in socialization patterns.

3. *The slow-to-warm-up child:* This child shows negative responses of mild intensity when exposed to new situations, but slowly grows to accept them with repeated exposure beginning in infancy. These infants are born with the capacity to engage the environment, and in particular, to engage caregivers. The infant is able to focus and follow stimuli, being preferentially oriented toward human forms and sounds, when compared with nonsocially oriented stimuli (Legerstee, Anderson, & Schaffer, 1998). They have fairly regular biological routines that continue into the toddler years.

In the emotionally healthy infant, these qualities and patterns of behavior are nurtured and encouraged by a responsive caregiving environment. Studies conducted with infants who were maltreated, neglected, and abused show a deleterious impact in mental, emotional, and social development. Consequently, atypical rearing conditions are believed to hinder the development of stable relationships in later infancy (Bakermans-Kranenburg et al., 2011) and to inhibit the normative shift in socioemotional development during the first years of life. Additionally, difficulties with responsive caregiving often co-occur with other threats to family and community life (Murray et al., 1999).

BOX 6.3 DEVELOPMENT OF TEMPERAMENT

Research suggests that six key criteria are responsible for the development of temperament traits: (1) individual differences in normal behaviors pertaining to the domains of affect, activity, attention, and sensory sensitivity; (2) typically expressed formal characteristics such as response intensities, latencies, durations, thresholds, and recovery times; (3) appearance in the first few years of life (partial appearance in infancy, full expression by preschool age); (4) a counterpart that exists also in primates and certain social mammals (e.g., *Canis familiaris*); (5) closely, if complexly linked to biological mechanisms (e.g., neurochemical, neuroanatomical, genetic); and (6) relatively enduring and predictive of conceptually coherent outcomes (e.g., early inhibition predicting internalizing, early difficultness externalizing disorders) (Zentner & Bates, 2008, p. 15).

Group Discussion

Childrearing shapes how the child responds to novel and challenging situations. How would you classify baby Marcus from the opening story according to the goodness-of-fit model? What would your recommendations be for Juanita based on your classification?

Table 6.3 Stages of Healthy Attachment of Infants Through Age 12 Months

Age	Healthy Attachment Style
Birth–3 months	Indiscriminate attachments. The newborn is predisposed to attach to any human. Most babies respond equally to any caregiver.
4–7 months	Preference for certain people. Infants they learn to distinguish primary and secondary caregivers but accept care from anyone.
7–9 months	Special preference for a single attachment figure. The baby looks to particular people for security, comfort, and protection. It shows fear of strangers (stranger fear) and unhappiness when separated from a special person (separation anxiety).
9–12 months	Multiple attachments. The baby becomes increasingly independent and forms several attachments.

TEMPERAMENT AND DEVELOPMENT

Brains are shaped by relationships and experiences (Burns, 2006; Robinson, 2010), and most brain development occurs in the first 2 to 3 years of life (Balbernie 2013). Early experiences become the basis for relationships, self-control, a sense of coherence and future responses to anxiety and threat, and the ability to develop resilience (Zeedyk, 2013).

Nature and Nurture

As discussed in chapter 1, although there has been a long debate over whether nature or nurture has a greater impact on development, modern technology and research practice have led to the discovery that, in fact, both are important. Further, modern technology has led to better understanding of genetics, and researchers are investigating the impact of specific genetic sequences on behavior. In addition, better understanding of parenting and treatment of children along with the impact of a child's peers have all given us insight into how the environment influences development as well (Brendgen, 2014).

Though heritability is not a singularly defining feature of temperament, a recent development in molecular genetics is the understanding of *gene–environment interplay*. This is the idea that individuals can have a genetic predisposition that is impacted by certain environmental conditions, causing a specific developmental outcome that is a combination of both genetics and environment (Brendgen, 2014). Although both controllable and noncontrollable environmental conditions have been researched, studies have shown that it is the former conditions—those considered controllable—that impact genetic presentation (Johnson, Rhee, Whisman, Corley, & Hewitt, 2013). The impact of the environment on how a gene's phenotype expresses itself is referred to as developmental plasticity and can occur early on and impact not only social development but also physical development as well (LaFreniere & MacDonald, 2013).

Understanding and Responding to Emotions of Others

At birth, the infant is rapidly able to perceive emotions by selecting significant and important information from human faces and voices. Infants are able to learn about the other's emotion by integrating social-perceptual stimuli such as face and human voice in their internal states (O'Reilly & deHann, 2009) and by recognizing emotional states. From 3 to 6 months of age, infants begin expressing fear, disgust, and anger because of the maturation of cognitive abilities. Anger, often expressed by crying, is a frequent emotion expressed by infants. As is the case with all emotional expressions, anger serves an adaptive function, signaling to caregivers the infant's discomfort or displeasure and letting them know that something needs to be changed or altered. Although some infants respond to distressing events with sadness, anger is more common.

Some evidence suggests that ability to control distress via attention may be traced to early infancy. Despite the fact that central nervous system (CNS) development continues throughout life, the most evident changes occur during the first 2 years (Cecchini et al., 2013). Infants and children vary greatly in their responses to sensory stimuli. Some notice even very subtle changes in sound or sight, whereas others remain unaware of them. Some avoid certain kinds of sensory experience, whereas others are sensation seekers (Posner & Rothbart, 2007). Research supports that imitative learning plays a pivotal role in the acquisition of knowledge and abilities. Paulus (2014) suggested that an ideomotor approach to imitative learning (IMAIL) in infancy is the central mechanism of imitative and social learning. Specifically, the imitative behavior of infants begins a cascading bidirectional action–effect association through observation of the infant's own and others' actions. For example, for an infant to differentiate one emotion from another (e.g., happy vs. sad), the infant would imitate the visual appearance of an emotion and then would link the emotion to the action that directly follows. The infant would learn that a happy emotion is associated with tickling and giggling as observed and directly experienced, versus sadness, which is observed as frowning and lack of soothing touch.

Many studies have been conducted to assess the type and quality of emotional communication between caregivers and infants. Parents are one of the primary sources that socialize children to communicate emotional experience in culturally specific ways. Specifically through such processes as modeling, direct instruction, and imitation, parents teach their children which emotional expressions are appropriate to express within their specific subculture and the broader social context (Posner & Rothbart, 2007). The available literature suggests that screen media, in particular television, has a substantially disruptive effect on the quantity and quality of parent–child interactions, which are essential for developing secure attachments. Screen media use is largely a ubiquitous presence in the lives of young children and is continuing to rise with the proliferation of new forms of electronic media. It is suggested that adverse effects of media begin in infancy and the distraction caused by screen media can be harmful to children's development (Napier, 2014). Nathanson and Manohar (2011) suggested that the relationship between parents and media use is complex, suggesting that not only should the attachment between parent and child be considered but also that the parent's own attachment may have relevance to their media use.

Individual Reflection

Juanita has described their family's routine as including regular TV time. Since the importance of social interaction is key to overall healthy development, a counselor may need to assess the quantity and quality of parent–child interaction regarding screen media. For example, how does Juanita interact with Marcus during the evening routine? Is the screen media exposure child-friendly?

Shyness and Sociability

Socialization of emotion begins in infancy. Research indicates that when mothers interact with their infants they demonstrate emotional displays in an exaggerated slow motion, and that these types of display are highly interesting to infants.

It is thought that this process is significant in the infant's acquisition of cultural and social codes for emotional display, teaching them how to express their emotions, and the degree of acceptability associated with different types of emotional behaviors.

As infants become more aware of their environment, smiling occurs in response to a wider variety of contexts. They may smile when they see a toy they have previously enjoyed. They may smile when receiving praise for accomplishing a difficult task. Smiles such as these, like the social smile, are considered to serve a developmental function.

Human infants tend to engage in smiling involving mouth opening while gazing at their mothers' faces. Smiles involving both eye constriction and mouth opening tend to occur when human infants are gazing at their smiling mothers, when infants are being tickled, and in other rough-and-tumble games (Messinger, Cassel, & Acosta, 2008). These are called "duplay smiles" (p. 134). As in adults and children, infant smiles involving eye constriction tend to occur during emotionally positive events. Infants, for example, tend to engage in smiles involving eye constriction when they are being smiled at by their mothers. Infant smiles involving eye constriction also tend to involve mouth opening; these are called "Duchenne smiles" (p. 134).

Another process that emerges during this stage is social referencing. Infants begin to recognize the emotions of others and use this information when reacting to novel situations and people. As infants explore their world, they generally rely on the emotional expressions of their mothers or caregivers to determine the safety or appropriateness of a particular endeavor. The development of children's understanding of other people's actions is parallel to their own motor development. As infants become more proficient in the motor domain, they rapidly develop social skills requiring understanding of other people's actions. For example, infants toward the end of the first year of life will typically understand pointing, and from 6 months of age infants imitate other people's actions (Nyström, Ljunghammar, Rosander, & von Hofsten, 2011).

Rothbart's Three Dimensions of Temperament

Child development researcher Mary K. Rothbart proposed an alternative model for child temperament framework. This neurobiological developmental approach defines temperament as individual differences in reactivity and self-regulation that manifest in the domains of emotion, activity, and attention (Rothbart, 2004, p. 493). Moving away from classifying infants into categories, Rothbart suggested that individual personality differences in infants and young children that are present prior to the development of higher cognitive and social aspects of personality lead to the development of three underlying dimensions of temperament. Rothbart (2007) identified three underlying dimensions of temperament (p. 208):

1. *Surgency and extraversion:* This factor reflects the degree to which an infant is generally happy and active and enjoys vocalizing and seeking stimulation. This includes positive anticipation, impulsivity, increased levels of activity, and

a desire for sensation seeking. Increased levels of smiling and laughter are observed in babies high in surgency and extraversion. Infants who are high in this factor are less likely to develop shyness and low self-esteem later in life.

2. *Negative affect:* This factor reflects the degree to which an infant is shy and not easily calmed. This factor includes fear, frustration, sadness, discomfort, and anger. Anger and frustration are seen as early as 2 to 3 months of age. Anger and frustration, together, predict externalizing and internalizing difficulties. Anger, alone, is later related to externalizing problems, whereas fear is associated with internalizing difficulties. Fear as evidenced by behavioral inhibition is seen as early as 7–10 months of age and later predicts children's fearfulness and lower levels of aggression.

3. *Effortful control:* This factor reflects the degree to which an infant can focus attention, is not easily distracted, and can exercise restraint. This includes the focusing and shifting of attention, inhibitory control, perceptual sensitivity, and a low threshold for pleasure. Effortful control shows stability from infancy into the school years and also predicts conscience. Infants who are high in effortful control are more empathetic and have less aggression as children. Rothbart (2004) suggested that effortful control is dependent on the development of executive attention skills in the early years. In turn, executive attention skills allow greater self-control over reactive tendencies later.

KEY COUNSELING POINTERS FOR EMOTIONAL AND SOCIAL DEVELOPMENT DURING BIRTH AND INFANCY

Interventions begin with counselors being alert to threats to responsive care, which would include neglect and abuse by caregivers, depression and psychopathology of caregivers, a severe lack of resources for the family, and vulnerabilities imposed by the infants (e.g., prematurity, difficult temperaments; Fitzgerald, Weatherston, & Mann, 2011). Once families who are at risk are identified, interventions can be put into place (Sampaio & Lifter, 2014).

To develop a well-balanced sense of self and the ability to express emotions in healthy adaptive ways, infants need environments that make them feel safe and caregivers who give them consistent responses to their behavior and provide them with the consistent warmth and nurturing. These factors are important building blocks in the development of trust, healthy attachment, and reliable emotional regulation. When these factors are interrupted or lacking, the infant may exhibit any of the following symptoms: (a) does not show interest in others; (b) does not respond to caregivers in an age-appropriate predictable manner; (c) has extreme difficulty waiting for a need to be fulfilled; (d) is very rigid about such things as routine, food items, and clothing; (e) has limited or fleeting eye contact with others; (f) does not imitate the actions of others; and (g) does not respond to voice stimulation.

Assessment

It is essential for counselors to be knowledgeable about social-emotional development of infants and toddlers and trained in the administration of assessment tools before they begin to use social-emotional assessments. When appropriately administered, the results assist in developing appropriate intervention plans with parents and enhance the effectiveness of assessments and assist in forging collaborative parent–practitioner relationships.

The most widely used assessment measure in the evaluation of infant emotional and social development and disturbance is infant observation (Rustin, 2014). Traditionally, the infant is observed in a laboratory-based or video-recorded setting, and observed symptoms are compared with the age-appropriate norm to initially formulate a diagnosis for further exploration or rule-out. A more recent trend has been a request of clinicians to advocate for regular observations in the baby's own residence. This approach is intended to be friendly and nonintrusive and offers the observer a more comprehensive picture of the environmental and caregiving influences on the infants' behavior and development.

Currently, child–parent psychotherapy (CCP; Lieberman & Van Horn, 2009) is often utilized as a standardized assessment instrument to evaluate and promote wellness between the caregiver and the infant. CPP centers on the premise that "nurturance, protection, and culturally and age appropriate socialization from the attachment figure(s) comprise the cornerstone of mental health in infancy and early childhood and create interactive patterns that are internalized by the child in the forms of stable and lifelong psychological "structures" (Lieberman & Van Horn, 2009; p. 439).

Another empirically validated clinical model is the circle of security (Powell, Cooper, Hoffman, & Marvin, 2009), which is an attachment-based method to help caregivers provide a secure base for their infants. Still other interventions focus on the education of the caregivers, especially if they are compromised in some way (Suchman, DeCoste, & Mayes, 2009). Early identification and intervention with social-emotional delays will contribute to improved developmental trajectories and outcomes for young children and their family members. Infants' abilities to perceive, experience, and recognize emotions, which allows them to engage with caregivers, have been studied mainly through behavioral and EEG/ERP studies (Sampaio & Lifter, 2014).

The Social Emotional Assessment Measure (SEAM; Squires, Bricker, Waddell, Funk, & Clifford, 2014) is a tool for assessing and monitoring social-emotional and behavioral development in infants, toddlers, and preschoolers who are determined to be at risk for social-emotional delays or problems. This tool helps identify social-emotional concerns and can facilitate in-depth discussions between counselors and parents about difficulties in the home environment and available interventions. Another assessment tool designed to measure the development of infants' and toddlers' social and emotional health is the Devereux Early Childhood Assessment for Infants and Toddlers (DECA; Mackrain, LeBuffe, & Powell, 2007). This screening and assessment tool focuses on identifying key social and emotional strengths and the planning resources provide caregivers and parents with research-based strategies to promote children's resilience. It is designed for use with children 1 month through 36 months. Concurrently, the Checklist for Autism in Toddlers (CHAT) is highly effective in diagnosing the potential for an autistic diagnosis of the child at a later date.

Finally, the Parenting Interactions with Children: Checklist of Observations Linked to Outcomes (PICCOLO) is a 29-item measure used with families of children aged 10 months to 3 years to measure parenting strengths that have been shown to improve outcomes for children, including increased cognitive, language, and social emotional skills. The PICCOLO items are organized across four domain areas: affection, responsiveness, teaching, and encouragement. Parents are observed, and ideally videorecorded, playing with the infant or toddler for a 5- to 10-minute interval from which the items are scored. The videorecording and the scores then can be used with families to inform program interventions. The PICCOLO is a practical tool for programs providing services in the home because it can be used in various activities and settings and requires very little equipment and time to administer (Wheeler et al., 2013; Roggman, Cook, Innocenti, Jump Norman, & Christiansen, 2013).

Interventions for the Caregiver

Whether a counselor is observing the infant in an agency or in the infant's residence, caregiving dynamics should also be observed. Caregivers who are lacking in fundamental caregiving abilities may benefit from substance abuse process and education groups, individual and group counseling, health education, referrals and assessments, case management, life skills classes, interactive parenting classes, and family support groups. Parenting and support groups emphasize maximal parental participation and reinforce the necessity of secure emotional attachments between the infants and their caregivers.

BOX 6.4 TEMPERAMENT AND LATER CHILDHOOD BEHAVIOR

The specific kinds of behavior problems in later childhood appear to embody the specific temperament characteristics of early childhood. The two major dimensions of maladjustment or psychopathology are externalizing problems, such as aggression and rule-breaking, and internalizing problems, such as anxiety and depression. Research suggests that (a) temperamental tendencies to be unmanageable in the early years, which could have elements of either strong approach (positive emotionality) tendencies or weak effortful control, or both, tend to predict later externalizing problems more strongly than they predict internalizing problems; (b) temperamental fearfulness or inhibition tends to predict later internalizing problems more strongly than it predicts externalizing problems; and (c) temperamental negative emotionality or irritability tends to predict both internalizing and externalizing problems (Zentner & Bates, 2008).

Reorienting the caregivers to specific infant needs based on observable behavioral signals, these interventions have demonstrated increased nurturing in the caregivers as well as improved self-regulation and more organized attachment in the children (Dozier, Dozier, & Manni, 2002). More individual levels could include relationship-based support strategies that include the provision of general support and education to new parents, and additionally, it may be necessary to provide more intensive support that involves psychotherapeutic interventions for caregivers who are unable to provide responsive caregiving.

Individual Reflection or Group Discussion

The foster mother from the opening story, Juanita, seems frustrated and concerned. She may need help learning how to approach Marcus in a sensitive manner, which would convey her concern, such as holding him more closely or speaking with him while offering him a toy. She may also need support with her coping skills; a support group for foster parents would help her learn how to structure the family's time so that entertainment is age-appropriate, interactive, and engaging for all the children in the home. Has she tried playing peek-a-boo with him? Marcus may have special needs regarding abilities and limitations; how well does she know Marcus? What other interventions would you recommend for Juanita?

Interventions for the Infant

Infants engage in age-specific play behaviors that may indicate normal, or disrupted, emotional development. While traditional play therapy is prescribed for children as young as 3 years of age, the infant plays as well! Play for the infant is self-absorbed and based on exploration and assimilation. The healthy infant enjoys watching other members of the family, rocking and strolling, swinging, sitting and crawling on a blanket, being sung and read to, and walking with help. Infants are engaged in the vigorous process of self-discovery, learning their world by looking, listening, chewing, smelling, and grasping. It is important for counselors to educate caretakers on how this play behavior helps the infant learn, interact, and develop a healthy emotional response to the world around it. Caretakers may need to be educated on what toys are safe and age-appropriate and what games are safe and engaging for the infant (e.g., peek-a-boo, stuffed animals, rattles, mirrors, and musical toys; Encyclopedia of Children's Health, n.d.).

Individual Reflection or Group Discussion

The baby from the opening story, Marcus, appears to have disrupted attachment, and this could be caused by numerous factors. At 8 months old, he should be engaging with his toys, exploring his environment, and smiling in response to pleasurable caregiver actions such as cooing, facial expressions, and hugs. A counselor may need to observe Marcus while he and Juanita interact for an extended period of time, and may need to administer an assessment instrument to determine a specific identifiable cause. Modeling appropriate caregiving is essential for Marcus's emotional and social development; the counselor may need to demonstrate praise and soft talking with Marcus, both for Marcus and for Juanita. What other interventions would you recommend for Marcus?

SUMMARY

If infants do not have stimulating and safe caregiving environments, their emotional and social development require counseling interventions. When the caregiving environment offers a rich variety of developmentally appropriate attachment and stimulation, infants are more likely to become engaged in activities and show fewer challenging behaviors. Multidisciplinary infant mental health services are an emerging specialty in mental health designed to improve mother–infant outcomes and to identify risk factors early so that prevention and interventions are immediate.

These interventions are now seen to include the promotion of well-being, the prevention of risk in infancy and early childhood, intervention specific to relationship disturbances, and treatment of identified disorders of infancy within the context of relationship care (Fitzgerald et al., 2011). Infants at risk are those who are marginalized and disadvantaged by race and class. Counselors may define additional risk factors as infants and toddlers who are susceptible to abuse or neglect, have multiple caregivers or residential placements, or are genetically predisposed to mental, physical, or emotional dysfunction.

Perinatal and infant mental health counselors use a range of interventions, dependent on their training, such as assessment and evaluation, family-of-origin work and genograms with caregivers, home visits, coordination of services, and strategies to manage anxiety and depression in both the caregivers and the infants. Counselors often use intervention techniques and strategies within an attachment-based framework (Myors, Schmied, Johnson, & Cleary, 2014). By providing positive interactions and offering recommendations based on the infant's observed and assessed needs, counselors can collaborate with caregivers to provide the necessary tools and experiences to develop the infant's social skills and encourage emotional development.

USEFUL WEBSITES

Encyclopedia of Children's Health
http://www.healthofchildren.com
Child Care Services Association
http://www.childcareservices.org/
Floor Time Activities for Infants (0–17 Months)
http://www.earlychildhood.msstate.edu/resources/pdfs/floortime-0-17.pdf
HealthyChildren.org

http://www.healthychildren.org/English/ages-stages/baby/Pages/
Emotional-and-Social-Development-Birth-to-3-Months.aspx
PBS: Babies Are Children Too: Caring for Infants and Toddlers
http://www.pbs.org/wholechild/parents/babies.html
PBS: Social and Emotional Development
http://www.pbs.org/wholechild/abc/social.html
Zero to Three: Development of Social-Emotional Skills
http://www.zerotothree.org/child-development/social-emotional-
development/social-emotional-development.html

REFERENCES

Ainsworth, M. D. S., & Bell, S. M. (1970). Attachment, exploration, and separation: Illustrated by the behavior of one-year-olds in a strange situation. *Child Development*, *41*, 49–67.

Bakermans-Kranenburg, M. J., Steele, H., Zeanah, C. H., Muhamedrahimov, R. J., Vorria, P., Dobrova-Krol, N. A., & Gunnar, M. R. (2011). Attachment and emotional development in institutional care: Characteristics and catch up. *Monographs of the Society for Research in Child Development*, *76*, 62–91.

Balbernie, R. (2013). The importance of secure attachment for infant mental health. *Journal of Health Visiting*, *1*(4), 210–217.

Bowlby, J. (1951). *Maternal care and mental health*. New York, NY: Schocken.

Bowlby, R. (2007). Babies and toddlers in non-parental daycare can avoid stress and anxiety if they develop a lasting secondary attachment bond with one carer who is consistently accessible to them. *Attachment & Human Development*, *9*(4), 307–319.

Brazelton, T. B. (1978). The Brazelton Neonatal Behavior Assessment Scale: Introduction. *Monographs of the Society for Research in Child Development*, *43*(5–6), 1–13.

Brendgen, M. (2014). Introduction to the special issue: The interplay between genetic factors and the peer environment in explaining children's social adjustment. *Merrill-Palmer Quarterly*, *60*(2) 101–109.

Burns, H. (2006). Health in Scotland, 2006. *Annual report of the chief medical officer*. Scottish Government, Edinburgh.

Cecchini, M., Baroni, E., Di Vito, C., Piccolo, F., Aceto, P., & Lai, C. (2013). Effects of different types of contingent tactile stimulation on crying, smiling, and sleep in newborns: An observational study. *Developmental Psychobiology*, *55*(5), 508–517.

Dozier, M., Dozier, D., & Manni, M. (2002). Attachment and biobehavioral catch-up: The ABCs of helping infants in foster care cope with early adversity. *Zero to Three*, *22*, 7–13.

Encyclopedia of Children's Health. (n.d.). *Play*. Retrieved from http://www.healthofchildren.com/P/Play.html

Erikson, E. H., Paul, I. H., Heider, F., & Gardner, R. W. (1959). *Psychological issues* (Vol. 1). New York, NY: International Universities Press.

Evans, D., & Rothbart, M. (2007). Developing a model for adult temperament. *Journal of Research in Personality*, *41*, 868–888.

Evans, D., & Rothbart, M. (2009). A two-factor model of temperament. *Personality and Individual Differences*, *47*, 565–570.

Field, T., Diego, M., Hernandez-Reif, M., Figueiredo, B., Deeds, O., Ascencio, A., Schanberg, S., & Kuhn, C. (2010). Comorbid depression and anxiety effects on pregnancy and neonatal outcome. *Infant Behavior & Development*, *33*(1), 23–29.

Fitzgerald, H. E., Weatherston, D., & Mann, T. L. (2011). Infant mental health: An interdisciplinary framework for early social and emotional development. *Current Problems in Pediatric Adolescent Health Care*, *41*(7), 178–182.

Freud, S. (1905). *Three essays on the theory of sexuality*. London, UK: Hogarth Press.

Ghassemzadeh, H., Posner M., & Rothbart, M. K. (2013). Contributions of Hebb and Vygotsky to an integrated science of mind. *Journal of the History of the Neurosciences*, *22*(3), 292–306.

Gordon, S. (2000). *Attachment and development*. New York, NY: Oxford University Press.

Harlow, H. (1958). The nature of love. *American Psychologist*, *13*, 573–685.

Heffron, M. C. (2000). Clarifying concepts on infant mental health: Promotion, relationship-based preventive intervention, and treatment. *Infants & Young Children*, *12*, 14–21.

Ibanez, G., Charles, M. A., Forhan, A., Magnin, G., Thiebaugeorges, O., Kaminski, M., & Saurel-Cubizolles, M.J. (2012). Depression and anxiety in women during pregnancy and neonatal outcome: Data from the EDEN mother-child cohort. *Early Human Development*, *88*(8), 643–649.

Johnson, D., Rhee, S., Whisman, M., Corley, R., & Hewitt, J. (2013). Genetic and environmental influences on negative life events from late childhood to adolescence. *Child Development*, *84*(5), 1823–1839.

Johnson, M. H. (2011). *Developmental cognitive neuroscience* (2nd ed.). London, UK: Blackwell.

Lafreniere, P., & MacDonald, K. (2013). A post-genomic view of behavioral development and adaptation to the environment. *Developmental Review*, *33*, 89–109.

Legerstee, M., Anderson, D., & Schaffer, A. (1998). Five- and eight month-old infants recognize their faces and voices as familiar and social stimuli. *Child Development*, *69*, 37–50.

Leis, J. A., Heron, J., Stuart, E. A., & Mendelson, T. (2014). Associations between maternal mental health and child emotional and behavioral problems: Does prenatal mental health matter? *Journal of Abnormal Child Psychology*, *42*(1), 161–171.

Lengua, L., & Wachs, T. (2012). Temperament and risk resilient and vulnerable responses to adversity. In M. Zentner & R. Shiner (Eds.), *Handbook of temperament* (pp. 519–540). New York, NY: Guilford Press.

Lieberman, A. F., & Van Horn, P. (2009). Child-parent psychotherapy: A developmental approach to mental health treatment in infancy and early childhood.

In C. J. Zeanah (Ed.), *Handbook of infant mental health* (3rd ed., pp. 439–449). New York, NY: Guilford Press.

Mackrain, M., LeBuffe, P., & Powell, G. (2007). *Devereux early childhood assessment for infants and toddlers*. Lewisville, NC: Kaplan Early Learning Company.

Main, M., & Solomon, J. (1990). Procedures for identifying infants as disorganized/disoriented during the Ainsworth Strange Situation. In M. T. Greenberg, D. Cicchetti, & E. M. Cummings (Eds.), *Attachment in the preschool years* (pp. 121–160). Chicago, IL: University of Chicago Press.

McCall, R. B., Groark, C. J., & Rygaard, N. P. (2014). Global research, practice, and policy issues on the care of infants and young children at risk: The articles in context. *Infant Mental Health Journal, 5*(2), 87–93.

McDonald, S. W., Benzies, K. M., Gallant, J. E., McNeil, D. A., Dolan, S. M., & Tough, S. C. (2013). A comparison between late preterm and term infants on breastfeeding and maternal mental health. *Maternal and Child Health Journal, 17*(8), 1468–1477.

Mervielde, I., & De Pauw, S. (2012). Models of child temperament. In M. Zentner & R. Shiner, *Handbook of temperament* (pp. 21–37). New York, NY: Guilford Press.

Messinger, D. S., Cassel, T. D., & Acosta, S. I. (2008). Infant smiling dynamics and perceived positive emotion. *Journal of Nonverbal Behavior, 32*(3), 133–155.

Murray, L., Sinclair, D., Cooper, P., Ducournau, P., Turner, P., & Stein, A. (1999). The socioemotional development of 5-year-old children of postnatally depressed mothers. *Journal of Child Psychology and Psychiatry, 40*, 1259–1271.

Myors, K. A., Schmied, V., Johnson, M., & Cleary, M. (2014). Therapeutic interventions in perinatal and infant mental health services: A mixed methods inquiry. *Issues in Mental Health Nursing, 35*(5), 372–385.

Napier, C. (2014). How use of screen media affects the emotional development of infants. *Primary Health Care, 24*(2), 18–25.

Nathanson, A., & Manohar, U. (2011). Attachment, working models of parenting and expectations for using television in childrearing. *Family Relations, 61*(3), 441–454.

Nyström, P., Ljunghammar, T., Rosander, K., & von Hofsten, C. (2011). Using mu rhythm desynchronization to measure mirror neuron activity in infants. *Developmental Science, 14*(2), 327–335.

O'Reilly, H., & deHann, M. (2009). The neural basis of face processing in infancy and its relationship to the development of empathy. *Cognition, Brain, Behavior, 4*, 429–448.

Paulus, M. (2014). How and why do infants imitate? An ideomotor approach to social and imitative learning in infancy (and beyond). *Psychonomic Bulletin & Review, 21*(5), 1139–1156.

Posner, M. I., & Rothbart, M. K. (2007). *Educating the human brain*. Washington, DC: American Psychological Association.

Powell, B., Cooper, G., Hoffman, K., & Marvin, R. S. (2009). The circle of security. In C. H. J. Zeanah (Ed.), *Handbook of infant mental health* (3rd ed., pp. 450–467). New York, NY: Guilford Press.

Richert, R. A., Robb, M. B., & Smith, E. I. (2011). Media as social partners: The social nature of young children's learning from screen media. *Child Development*, *82*(1), 82–95.

Robinson, M. (2010). *Infant mental health: Effective prevention and early intervention*. London, UK: Unite the Union.

Roggman, L. A., Cook, G. A., Innocenti, M. S., Jump Norman, V., & Christiansen, K. (2013). Parenting interactions with children: Checklist of Observations Linked to Outcomes (PICCOLO) in diverse ethnic groups. *Infant Mental Health Journal*, *34*(4), 290–306.

Rothbart, M., Ahadi, S., & Evans, D. (2000). Temperament and personality: Origins and outcomes. *Journal of Personality and Social Psychology*, *78*(1), 122–135.

Rothbart, M. K. (2004). Temperament and the pursuit of an integrated developmental psychology. *Merrill-Palmer Quarterly*, *50*(4), 492–505.

Rothbart, M. K. (2007). Temperament, development and personality. *Current Directions in Psychological Science*, *16*(4), 207–212.

Rustin, M. (2014). The relevance of infant observation for early intervention: containment in theory and practice. *Infant Observation: International Journal of Infant Observation and Its Applications*, *17*(2), 97–114

Sampaio, A., & Lifter, K. (2014). Neurosciences of infant mental health development: Rrecent findings and implications for counseling psychology. *Journal of Counseling Psychology*, *61*(4), 513–520.

Sandman, C. A., Davis, E. P., Buss, C., & Glynn, L. M. (2012). Exposure to prenatal psychobiological stress exerts programming influences on the mother and her fetus. *Neuroendocrinology*, *95*(1), 8–21.

Sigman, A. (2012). Time for a view on screen time. *Archives of Disease in Childhood*, *97*(11), 935–942.

Sparrow, J. (2013). Newborn behavior, parent-infant Interaction, and developmental change processes: Research roots of developmental, relational, and systems-theory-based practice. *Journal of Child and Adolescent Psychiatric Nursing*, *26*(3), 180–185.

Squires, J., Bricker, D., Waddell, M., Funk, K., & Clifford, J. (2014). *Social Emotional Assessment/Evaluation Measure (SEAM): Research edition*. Baltimore, MD: Brookes Publishing.

Squires, J. K., Waddell, M. L., Clifford, J. R., Funk, K., Hoselton, R. M., & Chen, C. (2012). A psychometric study of the infant and toddler intervals of the Social Emotional Assessment Measure. *Topics in Early Childhood Special Education*, *33*(2), 78–90.

Stevenson-Hinde, J. (2007). Attachment theory and John Bowlby: Some reflections. *Attachment & Human Development*, *9*(4), 337–342.

Suchman, N., DeCoste, C., & Mayes, L. (2009). The Mothers and Toddlers Program: An attachment-based intervention for mothers in substance abuse treatment. In C. H. J. Zeanah (Ed.), *Handbook of infant mental health* (pp. 485–499). New York, NY: Guilford Press.

Thomas, A., & Chess, S. (1977). *Temperament and development*. New York, NY: Brunner/Mazel.

Tomlin, A. M., & Viehweg, S. A. (2003). Infant mental health: Making a difference. *Professional Psychology: Research and Practice, 34,* 617–625.

Vedhara, K., Metcalfe, C., Brant, H., Crown, A., Northstone, K., Dawe, K., Lightman, S., & Smith, G. D. (2012). Maternal mood and neuroendocrine programming: Effects of time of exposure and sex. *Journal of Neuroendocrinology, 24*(7), 999–1011.

Velders, F. P., Dieleman, G., Henrichs, J., Jaddoe, V. W., Hofman, A., Verhulst, F. C., Hudziak, J. J., & Tiemeier, H. (2011). Prenatal and postnatal psychological symptoms of parents and family functioning: The impact on child emotional and behavioural problems. *European Child & Adolescent Psychiatry, 20*(7), 341–50.

Wheeler, R., Ludtke, M., Helmer, J., Barna, N., Wilson, K., & Oleksiak, C. (2013). Implementation of the piccolo in infant mental health practice: A case study. *Infant Mental Health Journal, 34*(4), 352–358.

Zeedyk, S. (2013). *Sabre tooth tigers and teddy bears: A brief guide to understanding attachment.* Aberdeen, Scotland: Aberdeen City Council.

Zentner, M., & Bates, J. E. (2008). Child temperament: An integrative review of concepts, research programs, and measures. *European Journal of Developmental Science, 2*(1–2), 7–37.

Zero to Three. (2001). *Definition of infant mental health.* Washington, DC: Zero to Three Mental Health Steering Committee.

PART 3

Early Childhood

Early Childhood: Physical and Cognitive Development

Nicole R. Hill, Brooks Bastian Hanks, Holly H. Wagner, and Torey Portrie-Bethke

Early childhood is a period of rapid growth during which the development that happened the first few years of a child's life provides a foundation to catapult profound physical and cognitive growth. Observing a 3-year-old child on a playground provides insight into the sheer energy that is reflective of this stage in life as well as the gross motor skills that are developing at a tremendous pace. A 3-year-old child can leap, swing on the monkey bars, climb up stairs rapidly, run around the playground while laughing and yelling, and many more things. Children are determined to try new feats physically, such as trying to reach higher, jump farther, run faster, and balance longer. Juxtaposed to where this child was two to three years ago, the physical engagement and expressiveness are testaments to the overall process of human development.

This chapter provides an overview of physical development and cognitive development of young children, with a critical focus on the ecobiodevelopmental paradigm. While understanding a developmental framework for early childhood, counselors must also recognize the impact of contextual factors on a child's ability to thrive. Around the world, most children experience significant challenges due to poverty, disease, and violence (Britto, Yoshikawa, & Boller, 2011; UNICEF, 2012). Poverty and malnutrition have been identified as the most profound factors negatively impacting over 200 million children under the age of 5 and contributing to them not achieving their "developmental potential" (Britto et al., 2011, p. 3; see also Engle et al., 2007). Early childhood development is situated in an ecological framework that highlights the impact of proximal and distal systems, such as the child's immediate caregivers and service providers, home environments, communities, clinics, schools, and local organizations, within country systems, national contexts, and international environments (Britto et al., 2011; Bronfenbrenner, 1979). As counselors who work with young children and their families, we must continually recognize the synergy and interactionality between individual children and their systems of influence. Poverty, nutrition, exposure to violence, and disease impact physical and cognitive development. Contextualizing a child's development is a critical counseling focus for all of us impacting young children directly or indirectly.

BOX 7.1 INDIVIDUAL REFLECTION

Frederick Douglass is quoted as saying: "It is easier to build strong children than to repair broken men [and women]." As you reflect on this quote, what are your thoughts about the role of counselors in contributing to the development of strong children? How is this quote applicable to children in early childhood? How do physical and cognitive development impact strong children? What are examples in your community of actions and initiatives that build strong children? Where are missed opportunities for such commitment? How can counselors cultivate strong children in their communities?

THE CASE OF ROSEY

Rosey is a 2-year-old Caucasian female. She is an only child, but her mother is currently pregnant and due in 2 months. Rosey lives with her mother, Carla, during the week and sees her biological dad, Paul, on the weekends when he is available. Rosey's mother is currently partnered with Raymond, who is the father of Carla's baby. Raymond is currently incarcerated on a drug charge, and Carla is hoping he will be released by the time the new baby turns 1 year old. Carla works full time at a grocery store, and Paul, Rosey's biological father, is currently seeking employment. Rosey attends a full-time daycare where she has interaction with other children similar to her age. Rosey is small in stature and has been consistently in the lower 10th percentile of growth during her regularly scheduled medical examinations. She does have many of her baby teeth, which have already started to turn yellow.

During a recent medical exam, her mother expressed frustration that Rosey does not talk yet, and when she does try to talk, Rosey's mother cannot understand what she is saying. Upon further examination, the pediatrician discovers that Rosey has yet another ear infection, the sixth one this year. The pediatrician refers Rosey to see an ear, nose, and throat specialist to discuss the possibility of eustachian tube surgery. The pediatrician continues to focus on Rosey's small stature and recommends that Rosey's mother consult a dietician. Rosey's mother becomes defensive and expresses frustration with these referrals. Carla tells the pediatrician that as a single mom she works full time and does the best she can with the food stamps she currently receives. She does not have the time off work to take Rosey to all the appointments that the doctor is recommending.

Overall, Rosey is an active child. She enjoys building and crashing her building blocks, making scribbles on paper with crayons, and taking care of her baby doll.

Rosey has interactions with other children at daycare, but she spends most of her time playing alone. Rosey often has tantrums, and her mother has noted that many of the tantrums are initiated when Rosey is trying to communicate with her mother and her mother does not understand what Rosey is saying. When Rosey becomes angry, she will throw herself on the floor and start screaming at the top of her lungs. Both Rosey and her mother are frustrated with one another, and there is a lot of yelling between the two. These tantrums are happening regularly—Carla reports that they happen at least once a day.

Consider your initial reactions to the case of Rosey. How much alignment is there between expected developmental processes and Rosey's development? What are your impressions of Carla and her parenting? What reactions do you have about Raymond and Paul? How do you envision Rosey's environment impacting her development? What else might you like to know about this family as you prepare to provide counseling?

PHYSICAL DEVELOPMENT IN EARLY CHILDHOOD

The physical development of early childhood decreases compared to infancy, but continues to have a steady growth pattern throughout early childhood. During early childhood, most children are becoming more independent in terms of their daily care and abilities. A young child is learning to become more self-sufficient in toileting, feeding, grooming, and dressing oneself. Physical development in early childhood encompasses body growth, brain development, gross and fine motor skill development, and handedness.

Body Growth and Development

One of the many physical changes during early childhood is head size. According to Santrock (2014), the head size at the age of 2 years old is one-fifth the size of the total body length. That fraction decreases by age 6, when the head size is about one-sixth of the total body length. By the end of the preschool years, most children have lost the top-heavy look associated with infancy and toddler years.

Early childhood is also a time when the trunk of the body lengthens (Santrock, 2014). You may notice that there is little physical variability between boys and girls during this time of their development compared with the adolescent years. Boys and girls are similar in their physical abilities and are able to challenge one another equally in terms of running, jumping, and other physical activities. Although their interests may differ between nurturing activities and more aggressive play, the physical abilities between sexes are comparable. Although the physical abilities of both sexes are comparable, individual differences are still present. There has been research that suggests other variables, such as ethnicity, socioeconomic status, prenatal care, and birth order may play a role in physical differences between children during this developmental stage (Santrock, 2014). Some children experience stunting, or low height-to-age outcome, based on the socioeconomic status of their family and community systems and parental engagement factors (DeBoer et al., 2012).

The Centers for Disease Control and Prevention (CDC) website is a helpful resource to review in terms of typical growth and development (http://www.cdc .gov/growthcharts/). The CDC publishes free growth charts from birth to 20 years old. These charts provide a series of percentile curves that demonstrate typical growth based on body measurements in children (CDC, 2010). These are similar to what one sees at one's physician's office during wellness checks. Growth charts have been used by health-care providers in the United States since 1977. The growth charts provided from the CDC (2010) for infants from birth to 36 months focus on length, weight, and head circumference of the infant. The charts for ages 2 to 20 focus on stature, weight, and body mass index (BMI) for those ages. Preschoolers, ages 2–5 years, have a chart specific to their weight and stature.

Although these charts are not intended to be used as diagnostic instruments, they can provide great information and help support the formation of an overall clinical impression of the child being measured (CDC, 2010). The data provided through these charts can also help contextualize where a child is at physically in comparison to a normative sample of children at the same chronological age. Height charts also help to identify concerns regarding stunting, which could mean that the child is not receiving adequate nutrients or is living in a disadvantaged home environment. Since these developmental charts are a common component of any well-child medical checkup, counselors should be aware of them because caregivers may reference them when discussing their child or important information about a child's physical development. Counselors can also use them as a quick reference if they are concerned about a child's physical development or stunting.

Brain Development and Neuroscience

When working with children during early childhood, it is important to have realistic expectations of what the child is capable of doing. Knowing more about the physical development of a child is important in understanding what a child is capable of doing and helps to reduce frustration of both the counselor and the client. If a counselor is working to engage a client in the counseling process and the specific intervention is beyond the child's ability, the child will become frustrated and disengage from the counseling process. An important aspect for counselors to be aware of is the development of the brain during early childhood.

Although the brain in early childhood is not growing as rapidly as it did during infancy, the brain and nervous system continue to develop significantly during childhood (Broderick & Blewitt, 2015; Santrock, 2014). The brain and head grow at a higher rate than any other physical aspect during childhood (Santrock, 2014). Within the brain, a number of neurons are making connections with one another, which allows the brain to more efficiently process information. A neuron is composed of a nucleus, dendrites, an axon, and terminal endings (Broderick & Blewitt, 2015). As neurons communicate with one another, various glial cells will insulate the axon to create a type of conduction that allows the message to move from one neuron more quickly to the next (Broderick & Blewitt, 2015). This process is called myelination. As children develop and gain more experience, more connections occur between neurons and the communication process between neurons quickens as well. In fact, myelination and an increase in dendrites account for much of the increased size of the brain from ages 3 to 6 years (Santrock, 2014).

As humans are born with an abundance of neurons, a process of neural pruning occurs over the next several years. Neural pruning occurs when a neural connection has been incorrectly formed, fails to make appropriate connections, or simply never connected with other neurons; these neurons and neural connections are selectively discarded, which allows the brain to continually reorganize itself (Broderick & Blewitt, 2015). According to Thompson et al. (2000), the overall size of the brain does not increase dramatically from ages 3 to 15 years; however, the patterns within the brain are what changes dramatically during this time.

During early childhood, the area of the brain with the most significant growth is found within the frontal lobe (Thompson et al., 2000). The frontal lobe is located at the top front part of the brain and is responsible for voluntary movements and higher level cognitive functioning such as planning, organizing, and maintaining attention (Broderick & Blewitt, 2015; Santrock, 2014). When a child is 6 years old through adolescence, the brain will develop most significantly within the temporal and parietal lobes (Santrock, 2014). The temporal lobe is found on the sides of the brain and is associated with auditory processing and language development (Broderick & Blewitt, 2015; Santrock, 2014). The parietal lobe is located at the top of the brain and is responsible for processing somatosensory information such as touch (Broderick & Blewitt, 2015). As the young child's brain develops, various functions such as cutting with scissors, throwing a ball, understanding language, and more abilities are improved upon because the child's brain structure has reached the requisite capacity for such skills.

The architecture of the brain for children can be negatively impacted by pervasive stressful situations and experiences (Garner et al., 2012). High levels of stress in early childhood that are not mediated by adaptive social supports can interrupt brain circuitry through the presence of increased stress hormones (McEwen, 2005). Prolonged and pervasive levels of stress hormones, such as cortisol, norepinephrine, and adrenaline, can generate long-term burdening of organs and the brain, thereby creating allostatic load concerns (McEwen, 2007). The plasticity of brains during early childhood makes them especially susceptible to the negative consequence of allostatic load emergent from ongoing stress. Chronic stress in children generates neural changes that can be permanent. For example, researchers have found evidence of hypertrophy in the amygdala and orbitofrontal cortex and a decrease of neurons and neural connections in the hippocampus and medial prefrontal cortex (McEwen, 2005). The change to the architecture of the brain contributes to increased mood disruption and decreased executive functioning, memory, and learning capabilities for children and their subsequent adult selves (McEwen, 2006; McEwen & Gianaros, 2011). Increased fear and anxiety responses have been associated with brain alterations due to exposure to chronic stress (Tottenham et al., 2010). Counselors must be aware of the negative impact of chronic stress on brain development, because it heightens the urgency of providing mediating supports for young children and fostering healthy families and communities.

Understanding which areas of the brain are developed and which areas are yet to be developed may assist the counselor in engaging the client in developmentally appropriate interventions. For example, asking a 5-year-old client to write in his or her emotions journal every night before bed would be unrealistic as children who are 5 years old generally do not have the ability to read. However, asking the child to draw how they felt at bedtime may be a more developmentally appropriate intervention. Brain development is inextricably tied to both physical and cognitive development and has synergistic relationships with both. Brain development affects components of physical and cognitive development and is also impacted structurally by developmental processes.

Gross and Fine Motor Skill Development

It is important to understand developmental milestones of the clients with whom one is working. By understanding these milestones, the counselor is able to appropriately refer clients and their families to other services that would best help promote the development of the client. Identifying a child client who is at risk for health or developmental problems can be difficult (Case-Smith & Clifford O'Brien, 2009). Many families who have had children with developmental delays will frequently reflect on knowing that something was not right (Fox, Vaughn, Wyatte, & Dunlap, 2002). By being aware of developmental milestones, a counselor will be able to be a better resource to these families and be better able to support and advocate for the child client. This section will provide an overview of some of the gross and fine motor skills typical of early childhood.

By the ages of 2 to 3 years, most children are able to walk, run, and jump with great joy. They are proud of themselves for being able to jump and may even be able to stand on one leg. The child's balance has improved, and he or she is able to kick a ball forward (Broderick & Blewitt, 2015). The child may be able to catch a large ball against his or her chest and will begin riding a tricycle as well (Case-Smith & Clifford O'Brien, 2009). At this point in their development, children should be able to navigate stairs and will use another's hand or handrail to help stabilize themselves.

By the age of 3, children have typically mastered the skill of using the pincer grip (the pinching of the thumb and index finger together) and are regularly able to pick up small objects between their fingers (Santrock, 2014). Children during this developmental time are working on dressing and feeding themselves (Broderick, 2010). These young children are also able to create block towers of six blocks high, one upon another, but generally the towers are not straightly aligned. Children who are 2 to 3 years old enjoy lining objects up and will often repeat this activity with a variety of objects (Case-Smith & Clifford O'Brien, 2009). The 2- to 3-year-old child may be engaging in simple puzzles that challenge his or her fine motor and spatial recognition. A child within this stage is now also engaging in turning pages in a book successfully (Broderick, 2010).

By the time children are 3 to 4 years old, they are typically able to engage in these same activities as the 2- and 3-year-olds, but with some added difficulty like a low level obstacle course. They may not be the fastest at completing the course, but they will enjoy engaging in the activity and will be proud of being able to complete the course. A 3- to 4-year-old child should also be able to navigate going both up and down stairs while alternating between which leg takes the step (Broderick, 2010; Case-Smith & Clifford O'Brien, 2009). A child within this age will have improved on his or her throwing ability, may be walking on his or her tiptoes, and will more successfully be eating with a spoon and fork. Children who are 3 to 4 years old continue to progress in their fine motor skills ability. The 3- to 4-year-old child will also continue to engage in building with blocks, but unlike earlier in his or her development, the 3- or 4-year-old child will focus on ensuring the blocks are lined up straight (Santrock, 2014). Children this age will appropriately grasp a pencil or crayon, copy simple shapes and letters, and begin to color within the lines(Case-Smith & Clifford O'Brien, 2009).

BOX 7.2   SUMMARY OF GROSS AND FINE MOTOR SKILL DEVELOPMENT

Age	Gross Motor Skills	Fine Motor Skills
2–3 years	Walk, run, jump, stand on one foot momentarily, kick a ball forward, catch a ball against the trunk of body	Build towers with six blocks, pick up small objects using pincer grip, starting to dress and feed self, turn pages of a book
3–4 years	Run through more complex situations, walk up stairs, walk down stairs, walk on tiptoes, throw ball with directionality	Build block towers that are straight, grasp a pencil, copy simple shapes, starting to color in lines
4–5 years	Skip for prolonged time, jump from elevated places, hop for a long time, throw and catch a ball	Draw stick figures, copy name, complete small puzzle, beginning to use scissors
5–6 years	Walk up and down stairs proficiently, can dress and undress easily	Can use scissors appropriately, can build more extensive objects with blocks, can color in the lines, able to button clothes

BOX 7.3 CLASS EXPERIENTIAL ACTIVITY: GROSS MOTOR SKILLS

Logistics: Before class begins, make a straight line on the ground with masking tape or something comparable. Have balls of various sizes and densities available.

Experiential Activity: Invite the students to perform the gross motor skills that would be expected during early childhood. As students act out the different gross motor skills, this playful activity showcases the developmental transitions in competence and skill during early childhood. Be mindful of varying physical needs and capabilities within the group of students. Provide a role for students who may not be able to participate physically in the activity, such as serving as the scribe or being the one to ask focused questions about cognitive development constructs. Start with the youngest developmental age group and move to the oldest.

Orientation: Have students spread out in the space around the line on the floor. Ask them to pick up some of the balls. Frame the activity as an opportunity for students to harness their inner child and act out some of the gross motor skills so central to early childhood. Transition to action by asking: what would you expect able-bodied 2- to 3-year-olds to be able to do with their bodies?

2- to 3-Year-Olds: After the class has brainstormed, share the following and encourage the students to act out the skills:

- Runs forward well
- Jumps in place with two feet together
- Walks on tiptoes
- Stands on one foot with help
- Throws ball *without* direction
- Kicks ball forward

3- to 4-Year-Olds: Transition to this age group by asking the students to identify the next developmental markers for physical development for 3- and 4-year-olds. Then encourage enactment of the following:

- Walks on line (use line on ground)
- Balances on one foot for 5 seconds (count out loud)
- Hops on one foot
- Throws ball *with* direction
- Catches ball *when bounced*

4- to 5-Year-Olds: Transition to this age group by asking the students to identify skills in physical development for 4- and 5-year-olds. Then encourage enactment of the following:

- Walks backward heel to toe
- Jumps forward 10 times without falling
- Does a somersault (some students do this one, though not all of them)
- Throws ball *with* direction and better accuracy
- Catches ball
- Skips

Children aged 3 to 4 years may now be able to button their shirts without the help from an older child or adult, will complete simple puzzles, will engage in the use of scissors, and are more cautious in their completion of drawing and coloring (Broderick, 2010).

Children who are 4 to 5 years old will continue to progress in their gross and fine motor skills. The gross motor development of a child aged 4 to 5 years includes jumping down from a high step, hopping in longer sequence such as four to six steps, throwing and catching a ball, and skipping for long distances (Case-Smith & Clifford O'Brien, 2009). The fine motor development of children within this stage includes the completion of puzzles up to 10 pieces, the use of scissors to cut out shapes, drawing stick figures, beginning to draw a body trunk with arms and legs, and copying their own name (Case-Smith & Clifford O'Brien, 2009).

By the ages of 5 to 6 years, children are now able to navigate steps efficiently and will engage in some more daring activities such as jumping off elevated surfaces or lengthening the space between landings from one object to the next (Santrock, 2014). The 5- to 6-year-old child is now possibly learning to tie knots and will help younger children button shirts or zip coats (Broderick, 2010). The 5- to 6-year-old has also progressed from simple building blocks to more involved creations such as a tower, building, or castle. Although their creations may still need some explanation, 5- to 6-year-old children demonstrate a greater command of their hand–eye coordination (Santrock, 2014). The 5- and 6-year-old child is more skilled in using scissors and is able to color within the lines most of the time (Broderick, 2010).

CONTEXTUAL FACTORS IMPACTING PHYSICAL DEVELOPMENT

An ecobiodevelopmental model provides a framework for conceptualizing the contextual factors impacting physical development in early childhood (Garner et al., 2012; Shonkoff, Garner, & American Academy of Pediatrics, 2012). As seen in Figure 7.1, the ecobiodevelopmental model frames development, health, and behavior across the lifespan as emergent from the interactionality of genetic predispositions, environmental influences, and early childhood experiences.

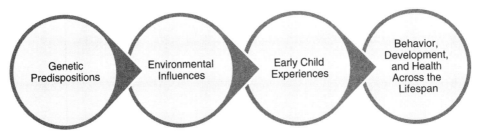

Figure 7.1 Factors of the ecobiodevelopmental model.

Ecological context interacts with genetic predispositions and can determine which genotype is expressed. Framing early childhood stressors from this model highlights the role that toxic stress has in negatively impacting physical development, especially brain development.

Toxic stress is differentiated from normal stress because it is prolonged and pervasive, thereby activating the physiological system without mediation by social support (Shonkoff, 2010). Toxic stress is typically created due to multiple stressors and can generate irreparable health and developmental consequences. Young children are especially vulnerable to permanent changes in their brain structure and functioning because of the level of plasticity of their brains. Researchers have found that maternal depression (Wachs, Black, & Engle, 2009; Walker et al., 2011), exposure to violence (Briggs-Gowan, Carter, & Ford, 2012; Dannlowski et al., 2013; Thabert, Karim, & Vostanis, 2006), poverty (Walker et al., 2011), and parental substance abuse negatively impact early childhood development. These toxic stressors have not only developmental but also biological disruptions and consequences (Shonkoff et al., 2012). Adult diseases and chronic health concerns have been rooted in early childhood exposure to toxic stress and adverse events (Shonkoff, Boyce, & McEwen, 2009). Researchers have identified the consequences of toxic stress in early childhood as liver cancer, cardiovascular disease, asthma, hepatitis, depression, dental issues, and autoimmune diseases. Shonkoff et al. (2012) summarized the debilitating impact by stating, "toxic stress in early childhood not only is a risk factor for later risky behavior but also can be a direct source of biological injury or disruption that may have lifelong consequences independent of whatever circumstances might follow later in life" (p. e238).

Another critical contextual factor related to physical development is child nutrition (DeBoer et al., 2012; Walker et al., 2011). Deficiencies in iron, zinc, riboflavin, iodine, and vitamins A, B12, D, and E can impact growth and health with asthma, eczema, or stunting occurring (Patelarou et al., 2011). Issues concerning nutrition also extend into the domain of obesity, which is rapidly becoming pervasive in many cultures and has long-term health and physical development implications (de Onis, Blossner, & Boghi, 2010). In the United States, statistics suggest that obesity rates have tripled in the last 20 years, with one in three children meeting the criteria for obesity. Children who are African American or Hispanic are disproportionately impacted, with over 40% of them being classified as obese. Obesity-related health concerns include diabetes, cardiovascular disease,

BOX 7.4   GLOBAL CONTEXTS FOR EARLY CHILDHOOD DEVELOPMENT

Britto et al. (2011) asserted that early human development initiatives are becoming a critical focus for international public policy as they are seen as the solution for mediating poverty and disease and generating equity within a global context. The Convention on the Rights of Children (CRC) provides an ecological framework for championing the rights of children to develop toward their optimal selves regardless of gender, age, ability status, socioeconomic status, ethnicity, or home space (Committee on the Rights of the Child, 2006). The CRC situates human rights for early childhood within the context of ecological systems that are proximal, such as family, and distal, such as national policies. Child development occurs through the intersectionality of child and context.

Reflective Questions

- What are your reactions to the ecological context of early childhood development? What are examples in which you have observed the profound influence of context on a child's developmental trajectory?
- As a counselor, in what ways do you need to consider global contexts for early childhood development?
- What would equity for young children look like on a global level? What do you consider to be nonnegotiable rights for children? How do you as a counselor work to advocate for such rights being honored for young children?

high blood pressure, and premature death. Counselors need to include issues of nutrition and consumption in their assessments of young children. They need to have a foundational understanding of how inconsistent access to necessary nutrients can negatively impact physical development. Because of the pervasiveness of childhood obesity and its negative correlation to health disruption, counselors should advocate for wellness-based priorities within treatment planning and community initiatives.

Infectious diseases are another contextual factor impacting young children in the United States and around the world. For example, over 2 million children in the world have HIV, which has been significantly correlated to motor and cognitive disruptions (Van Rie, Harrington, Dow, & Robertson, 2007). Whereas access to antiretroviral therapy in the United States has contributed to improvements in development, many children do not have access to such therapy (Lindsey, Malee, Brouwers, & Hughes, 2007). As another example, malaria has significant impact on development in early childhood with long-term consequences for physical health, language development, and cognitive development (Thuilliez, 2009). In addition to infectious diseases, the development of young children can be negatively impacted by environmental toxins such as pesticides, mercury, arsenic, and lead. Many children are exposed to such toxins in their food, water, house, or dust (Walker et al., 2011). Because of the potential impact on physical and brain development, counselors need to explore the conditions of a child's home and environment in the assessment process.

When considering the contextual factors of a child's development, counselors need to search for opportunities to optimize the family's, and subsequently the child's, support systems. Strengthening these supports will mediate the long-term impact of stress and generate decreased propensity for future poor health, substance abuse, poor nutrition and exercise behaviors, school failure, and economic concerns (Shonkoff et al., 2012). Counselors also need to be actively and continually screening for common catalysts for toxic stress such as parental depression, parental or domestic abuse, substance abuse in the home, community violence, lack of availability to nutritious food, and inadequate social relationships. Early identification of potential toxic stressors can help prevent the lifelong impact of stress on health and development.

KEY COUNSELING POINTERS FOR PHYSICAL DEVELOPMENT IN EARLY CHILDHOOD

As the physical development of young children with a critical focus on the eco-biodevelopmental paradigm has been presented, it is time to apply this information to the counseling process. When thinking about Rosey's physical and cognitive developmental issues as described in the beginning of the chapter, Rosey would benefit from a counselor who integrates a holistic approach. The following are some potential interventions that would help to facilitate Rosey's development and mental well-being. These interventions can be generalized to other children and families with adjustments made based on specific contextual and individual factors.

Engage caregivers. Due to Rosey's young age of 2 years, Rosey's mom, Carla, is going to be a key player in her development. As noted in the case scenario, Carla is a pregnant single parent who is working full time. When we consider the amount of stress and limited support Rosey's mom may have at this point, we can appreciate the level of exhaustion and frustration Carla may be experiencing. A key piece to working successfully with Rosey is to help her mom see the benefit of Rosey being engaged in the counseling process. Counselors have a variety of roles that we serve and advocating for our clients is one of those roles (ACA, 2014). If we help Carla understand that we are on Rosey's and her team, we can then optimize our relationship with Rosey's mom to ensure Rosey is receiving appropriate counseling that supports her development.

Referrals for the mother. If the counselor can help Carla be in a healthier place, mentally and emotionally, she will be able to attend to Rosey's needs more appropriately. As Carla seems to have a lack of support, providing Carla with individual counseling or connecting her with a young mothers' group would be beneficial. Individual counseling would help Carla receive the emotional support she may be needing, and the young mom parenting group would provide a support system and parental socialization. Another potential referral is to have Carla complete a parenting group to help her develop more appropriate parenting skills than yelling back at Rosey when Rosey has tantrums. Such parenting skills will have a long-term benefit as Carla will be adding a newborn into the family dynamic which will impact Rosey and her experience.

Assessments. When trying to assess young children, paper-and-pencil assessments are generally provided to the parent or caregiver of the young child. A biopsychosocial and sociocultural assessment would be beneficial to conduct at the time of intake with Rosey's mom. Information about Rosey's health, nutrition, exposure to violence, behaviors, culture, socioeconomic status, supports, and parent concerns are all valuable pieces of information to review when creating a holistic picture of Rosey and her current needs (DeBoer et al., 2012). Some parents will ask the intent of the questions and may become uncomfortable about providing personal information such as prenatal care, family medical history, and current economic status. The counselor can help alleviate some of these hesitations and concerns by explaining to the parent or caregiver that the counselor is coming from a holistic approach to be able to assist the child and the family in the best way possible.

Live observation. After completing an initial intake with Carla and gathering all of the necessary information and signing the necessary documentations (e.g., informed consent), it would now be appropriate for the counselor to engage in an observation of Rosey. The counselor may choose to watch Rosey and her mom interact in the waiting room or play room or to engage with Rosey in an activity to assess Rosey's overall development. When conducting a live observation, the counselor is attending to Rosey's ability to follow direction, speech, attention, listening skills, motor development, and even how Rosey responds to being redirected. If observing a child with a caregiver or other significant person, counselors can reflect on attachment behaviors within the relationship, type of discipline, communication styles, level of independence or dependence, and overall interactional dynamics. With such a young child, her attention span will be minimal, so the counselor should try to conduct the observation in a short amount of time. A general guide for attention span is about 5 minutes per age of the child, so a 3-year-old would have a 15-minute attention span and a 5-year-old would have a 25-minute attention span.

Identifying contextual factors. Counselors need to actively reflect on contextual factors that could be impacting the child. For example, Carla's baby is approaching full-term which means Rosey will need to adjust to have a new baby and sibling in the home. With Carla already working and single parenting, there may be even more stressors in the home as Carla is left to provide all the parenting to two young children instead of just one. Other contextual factors could include Rosey's relationship with her biological father and stepfather, her peer relationships, and her level of support and engagement at preschool.

Releases of information. As Rosey has already seen her medical provider, it would be beneficial to gain a release of information, so that the counselor can coordinate care with the physician. If other professionals were mentioned at intake by Rosey's mom, a release of information to coordinate care with the other professionals would be beneficial as well. By having these releases of information, the counselor is better prepared to provide a holistic treatment approach and act as an advocate for Rosey and Carla when needed.

Diagnosis. After completing all of the intake and observation procedures, the counselor should have a clear picture of Rosey and her current level of functioning. The counselor should then engage in the diagnosis process and refer to the *Diagnostic and Statistical Manual for Mental Disorders*, fifth edition (*DSM-5*; APA, 2013), for various diagnostic categories. Because Rosey is such a young child, it is important to keep in mind while diagnosing that diagnoses may follow a child across the lifespan. Careful attention should be spent when diagnosing young children and the counselor should explain the diagnosis clearly to the parent or caregiver of the young child. This process often helps validate the parent or caregiver while also educating that person on how best to support the child.

Treatment planning. After a diagnosis has been identified and explained to Rosey's mother, treatment planning may begin. Treatment planning is really like a road map of where you plan to take Rosey during counseling. It helps the counselor and client be focused and productive with the therapeutic time they have together (Zuckerman, 2008). In the case of Rosey, some elements the counselor may include are play therapy, filial play therapy, and a variety of referrals.

Play therapy. The use of play therapy with young children has been found to be one of the most effective modalities. Play therapy has been researched and shown to be effective with young children equally effective across age, gender, and presenting issue, especially when parents engaged in the play therapy with the young children (Bratton, Ray, Rhine, & Jones, 2005). Rosey's developmental capacity is not congruent with talk-based counseling, so the counselor needs to integrate play therapy or expressive arts into the counseling experience. It would also allow the counselor to model appropriate engagement with Rosey while her mom is allowed to observe. After some time observing the counselor and Rosey, the counselor would then invite Rosey's mom into the play therapy process and continue to work with both Rosey and her mom to further assist Rosey in developing healthy relationships and emotional regulation skills. These interventions would also engender protective factors to mediate the potentially chronic stress in Rosey's life.

Referrals. It is important that counselors work within their scope of practice (ACA, 2014). As the counselor works with Rosey, there may be a variety of referrals that come to mind that would further assist Rosey and her mom in their daily functioning. Some of those referrals may include medical, vocational, governmental, and financial referrals.

Supporting medical referrals. As the physician has already provided a referral for an ear, nose, and throat specialist and a dietician, it would be important for the counselor to show support of these referrals. As Rosey has had multiple ear infections and is delayed in her speech, attending to any and all medical issues is important to ensure optimal development of Rosey. It may also be helpful to validate Rosey's mom in her frustration with various appointments and obligations and that she is doing the best she can. After providing support and validation to Carla, the counselor should then provide encouragement to Carla that these other professionals are also there to help make sure that Rosey is developing appropriately.

Speech-language pathologist. As Carla has reported that Rosey has a difficult time communicating, a referral to a speech-language pathologist may be appropriate. Often times the medical provider will address one issue at a time, such as referring Rosey to an ear, nose, and throat specialist. If Rosey continues to demonstrate speech problems after working with the ear, nose, and throat specialists, a referral to have Rosey's speech and language development tested would be appropriate. Having a release of information to discuss various options with other professionals working with Rosey becomes even more essential as more professionals become involved.

BOX 7.5   REFLECTION QUESTIONS ON THE CASE OF ROSEY

Considering the case of Rosey, reflect on the factors that create anxiety and concern for you. Counselor self-reflection is an essential component to competent counseling practice. When conceptualizing Rosey's experiences and the presenting factors, describe what aspects may present as challenges for you as her counselor. Identify the personal biases you may experience.

- Describe how you would approach collaborating with other medical professionals who may not be familiar with the counseling profession, given that the appropriate releases of information have been signed.
- Considering that Rosey is a minor and both parents have custodial rights, how will you work to include Rosey's father in treatment? Describe how you would handle the situation if Carla is resistant or reluctant to have Rosey's father engage in the counseling process.
- From an ecobiodevelopmental perspective, identify additional information you would want to know about Rosey and her context. Consider other systems and community resources that would benefit Rosey and her family. Identify how you would communicate these options to her parents. Discuss potential advocacy strategies you would incorporate.

BOX 7.6   CASE STUDY AND CLASS DISCUSSION

Case Study

Hunter is a 5-year-old boy whose birthday is in late July. He is developmentally on par with his peers and often falls within the upper 25th percentile on the growth charts. Hunter has been in preschool for 2 years now and does well as reported by his preschool teachers. Hunter is currently able to count to 30, identify his ABCs, and print his own name without help. Physically, he tends to be very coordinated for his age and has been able to snap, whistle, and tie his own shoes for some time now. Although his parents believe he is developing at a typical rate and progressing well, Hunter's parents are struggling with the decision of whether or not they should enroll him into kindergarten this year or wait another year. The parents have noted that Hunter is extremely sensitive and will cry easily if his feelings are hurt. Hunter is also very shy and reserved when it comes to new experiences. His parents have enrolled him in a number of activities to work on his shyness, but Hunter's parents have come to accept that the first time Hunter attends the new activity, he will cry the entire first time and part of the second time attending the new activity. After attending the first couple activities, he will eventually engage with the other children. This has occurred during soccer, basketball, T-ball, and gymnastics.

Class Discussion

1. Knowing what you know about early childhood development, what would you do if you were Hunter's parents? Enroll Hunter in kindergarten this year or next year as a 6-year-old? What would be your reasoning for such a decision?
2. What are some pros and cons to holding a child back a year before introducing him or her into kindergarten? What other areas of development do Hunter's parents need to be considering as they make this decision? What is the potential long-term consequence of this decision for Hunter?

Government programs. There are various programs available for children who are struggling to thrive. One such program is the Head Start program. The Head Start program focuses on helping prepare children under the age of 5 years from low-income families for school (Office of Head Start, 2015). The Head Start program website (http://www.acf.hhs.gov/programs/ohs) provides information about the programs available to young children from low-income families and resources for both families and professionals.

Financial assistance programs. During your intake session with Carla, she addressed finances being an added stress for the family. Since Rosey's mom is a single, pregnant mother working full time at a grocery store, she finds it difficult to have the energy to spend quality time with Rosey and attend to Rosey's daily needs. As Carla also reports, she is currently receiving government aid through food stamps and other government programs. It is important for counselors to be aware of any potential supports for families within their communities. Often times there are housing agencies, free medical clinics, and food programs available to individuals beyond what is provided for them through government aid. Being aware of local resources and referring Rosey's mom to these various resources would be helpful in alleviating some of the stress Rosey's mom is experiencing which would allow her to spend more time and energy focused on Rosey.

COGNITIVE DEVELOPMENT IN EARLY CHILDHOOD

Children in the stage of early childhood are actively exploring and constructing their worlds. Young children begin by observing and describing events, which eventually gives way to their explanation of them. As children attempt to master cognitive challenges, there is a constant interchange between their abilities and their environment. Developmental theory aids in situating concepts of cognitive development within aspects of environment that shape and influence young children's courses of growth. This section highlights cognitive development theories by Piaget, neo-Piagetian theorists and Vygotsky and executive functioning constructs for young children.

Piaget: Preoperational Thought in Early Childhood

Jean Piaget was a Swiss biologist who studied child development during the 1920s. He explored how children think and learn, along with the characteristics associated with each stage of their development. Piagetian concepts such as schemes, assimilation, and accommodation prevail in this developmental theory (Ormrod, 2013). Schemes are groupings of thoughts or actions by which additional similar information can be more or less easily assimilated. However, when a child encounters information outside of a scheme, he or she must work to accommodate it. In essence, the child must somehow make sense of the new information. Piaget saw this as a basic process within child development. Piaget determined that children in early childhood belonged in the stage of development he termed preoperational. Preoperational refers to the idea that children have not yet learned to reason in logical ways which mirror adult reasoning (Ormrod, 2013).

Thinking in early childhood is associated with unidimensional focus, meaning that young children will center on a single feature of a situation. Children in this stage of development have difficulty taking into account multiple pieces of information. This process is referred to as centration (Hansen & Zambo, 2005; Ormrod, 2013). Thus, young children may have difficulty broadening their scope or seeing more than one side of an issue or concept. This developmental feature may apply to the concept of identity when a young child is unable to comprehend his or her teacher also being a mother (Vernon, 2009). Young children may also display egocentric thinking, as they have not yet learned that there are perspectives other than their own. Thus, taking on the perspective of another person may be challenging to the young child (Hansen & Zambo, 2005; Marion, 2010; Ormrod, 2013; Pallini & Barcaccia, 2014).

Young children also have limitations in distinguishing between appearance and reality. This developmental feature of cognition can be illustrated through the concept of conservation (Hansen & Zambo, 2005). The young child is not able to see how something changes or does not change, but is only able to perceive the result. For example, a child is presented two glasses of water, both containing equal amounts of water. Next, the water from one container is poured into a taller and thinner container. It appears to the child that this latter container now has more water, although no water has actually been added (Ormrod, 2013).

Children in early childhood are developing their abilities to pay attention and utilize memorization. They can become distracted by information that is not essential to the problem or issue at hand. For example, they may use transductive reasoning by assuming that two unrelated processes are the cause and effect of one another, such as the birds singing making the sun shine (Ormrod, 2013). They are able to recognize objects and imitate behavior; however, long-term memory and information processing are still developing. The ability to observe and imitate behavior, or deferred imitation, gives way to further cognitive development. For this reason, modeling is critical for young children's learning (Marion, 2010; Ormrod, 2013).

BOX 7.7 CLASS ACTIVITY

Preoperational Thinking in Action!

Ask students to form groups of four to five, depending on class size. Assign each group one of the following concepts from the preoperational stage of Piaget's theory of cognitive development: centration, conservation, egocentric thinking, transductive reasoning, deferred imitation, and symbolic thinking. Give students 5–10 minutes to come up with a role-play to demonstrate these concepts to the rest of the class. After students have conducted role-play, encourage the other students to identify the specific concept showcased and explain why the role-play exemplified such a concept. Before transitioning to the next group, ask the students who conducted the role-play to articulate how the role-play would be different if it were to be conducted with a child who is 5 years older.

Children in the stage of preoperational thought rely on concrete examples through seeing and hearing versus being able to understand concepts from logical or abstract perspectives. Abstract concepts such as death, divorce, and issues surrounding time and space may be arduous for young children to fully comprehend (Vernon, 2009). However, children in this stage may be able to logically conclude why characters in a storybook interact in certain ways and how that interaction affects the characters relationally. The visual and auditory presentation of a book may aid in concrete thinking processes and provide young children with a "cognitive boost" (Hansen & Zambo, 2005, p. 40), which leads to a richer comprehension of concepts (Hansen & Zambo, 2005; Vernon, 2009). Furthermore, children in the preoperational stage are also capable of symbolic thinking, meaning that they are able to think of an object that is not directly in front of them (Ormrod, 2013). In the case of the storybook, a young child would be able to think about the storybook characters after the story has been read, a notable cognitive process. Overall, Piaget emphasized that cognitive reasoning unfolds in successive stages that are structurally different.

Neo-Piagetian Contributions to Early Childhood Development

Neo-Piagetians are theorists who have focused on expanding or elucidating details in Piaget's theory (Green & Piel, 2013). Most notable of the neo-Piagetians are Robbie Case, Juan Pascual-Leone, and Kurt Fischer. Case's central conceptual structure and Pascual-Leone's structural capacity model extend Piaget's theory to more thoroughly explain the underlying processes at work, whereas Fischer's dynamic skill theory focuses more on specific domains of skill development.

In Case's central conceptual theory, he endorses the idea of stage-based development as espoused by Piaget, but he differs from Piaget by outlining four different stages of cognitive development: sensorimotor, interrelated, dimensional, and vectorial (Case, 1988, 1992). The interrelated and dimensional stages are most relevant for early childhood development. Children, typically ages $2\,1/4$ to 5 years old, are in the interrelated stage, during which they are experiencing increased mental control and the ability to anticipate relationships between behaviors and objects before the relationship happens. Thinking becomes interrelated, hence the name of the stage, as children interact with others and their environment. Words serve to help children obtain what they want, and words also provide instructions for them from others. Mental processes are acquired through social interaction. Around the ages of 5 or 6 years, children begin to enter the dimensional stage in which they can contextualize concepts such as distance, time, height, and weight. A child in this stage would understand that it will take longer time to drive longer distances. Multiple concepts can be understood concurrently (Case, 1988). Both of these stages of Case's model are similar to those of Piaget during the same age range, yet Case emphasizes the social interactionality of child and cognitive development and underscores culture and individual specificity over universality.

Pascual-Leone (1988) framed cognitive development in terms of M-capacity, the amount of mental processing and attention available to a child, and each child's M-capacity increases by one increment every other year from the ages of 3 to 15. In Pascual-Leone's conception of M-capacity, he asserts that attention is a discrete cognitive factor that adds explanatory power to how children increase their learning. Processing capacity, then, is slowly increasing across a young child's development, with a 5-year-old being able to add one independent item of information to processing compared with a 3-year-old peer. Pascual-Leone (1988) argued that the incremental increases in working mental attentional abilities are what explain the qualitative differences across Piaget's stages. For example, as a child gains in M-capacity, he or she is able to think about the world from a preoperational to an operational perspective. The shift to thinking about operations symbolically or abstractly, typically as children move into middle childhood, is because of their increased M-capacity.

The final neo-Piagetian overviewed in this chapter is Fischer and his dynamic skill theory. Fischer (1980) framed development around two organizing constructs, namely optimal levels and skill development. Every child has an optimal level of complexity that can be accessed and integrated into mental processes, and the development of optimal levels is qualitatively different as a child matures. Skills are the enactment of mental processes to address a problem or task, and skills can be learned and are more on a continuum of development. Children can perform tasks at a functional or optimal level in the representational tier, the stage most aligned with early childhood. For example, a 4-year-old who is learning to cut her food can do the task independently and evidence functional skill development. The food can be coarsely cut, fingers may hold the food and do more tearing of it than actual cutting with a utensil, and food can repeatedly fall off the plate. The same skill can be enhanced toward the optimal level when the environment positively contributes to the learning of the skill. Perhaps a caregiver can support the child as she cuts the food. An adult's hand and fingers can guide the child as she cuts her food. Fischer noted a continual process in which the optimal level becomes a functional level, whereby skills are integrated and coordinated to generate more complex and advanced future skills. For young children, Fischer (1980) championed the notion of transactions between child and environments as the child develops skills step by step through hierarchical stages. In recent years, Fischer (2008) translated neurocognitive research to further substantiate his ideas that cognitive development is an interwoven, complex, and fluid process.

Counselors can benefit from understanding the concepts of Case, Pascual-Leone, and Fischer because they help us frame the importance of a child's interaction with the environment and others in that context. The neo-Piagetian theories also clarify aspects of cognitive development that are more fluid and continuous, such as skill development. Optimal levels and M-capacity both showcase how cognitive development is a series of scaffolds between current functional performance and optimum potential. The notion of interactionality between child and context is further exemplified in Vygotsky's cognitive theory.

Vygotsky and the Sociocultural Perspective

While Piaget's work focused on the internal mental work that children are doing to develop cognitively, Lev Vygotsky's (1976) approach centered on society and culture's roles in facilitating development (Ormrod, 2013). Vygotsky found special importance in the arts, poetry, theatre, music, human experience, and creativity (Zittoun & Cerchia, 2013). He framed cognitive development through the context of children's social interactions, with both adults (i.e., parenting and education) and other children (i.e., play).

Further, Vygotsky saw imagination as the expansion of one's experience and as an avenue to facilitate development, specifically the zone of proximal development (Zittoun & Cerchia, 2013). Ormrod (2013) defined the zone of proximal development (ZPD) as "the range of tasks that children cannot yet perform independently, but can perform with the help and guidance of others" (p. 45). The term *scaffolding* refers to the specific guidance and support that adults provide to children to assist them in mastering tasks within their ZPD. Children of this age have vibrant imaginations and fantasies and often engage in make-believe play that involves role-playing and other creative expressive outlets (Hansen & Zambo, 2005; Vernon, 2009; Zittoun & Cerchia, 2013). Thereby, Vygotsky believed that children's zones of proximal development may be expanded through the guidance of adults and educators (scaffolding) and engaging in imaginative play and socialization. Play inspires imagination, which allows children to expand on what they already know. "Hence, imagination involves a specific process which always re-opens established (socially stabilized) forms of knowledge, into new combinations. Imagination is thus a complex thinking process, socially developed" (Zittoun & Cerchia, 2013, p. 311). Whereas the theorists overviewed so far in this section describe the series of developmental processes unfolding in early childhood, researchers examining executive functioning focus on the cognitive operations themselves.

Executive Functioning in Early Childhood

Executive functioning includes multiple cognitive processes that exemplify the goal-focused tasks of the prefrontal cortex, namely inhibition, working memory, task switching, and planning (Best, Miller, & Jones, 2009). Executive functioning develops in early childhood and continues its developmental trajectory into adolescence in a process that parallels the development of the prefrontal cortex. Many scholars believe that inhibition, or the capacity to suppress impulses, develops first and serves as the primary executive functioning task for younger children. For younger children, inhibition has been found by researchers to predict performance on a planning task, whereas for older children working memory predicted planning task performance (Senn, Espy, & Kauffmann, 2004). These results corroborate the idea that young children rely on inhibition to problem solve due to a lack of development of working memory (Isquith, Gioia, & Espy, 2004). As children develop, the executive functions available to them expand, thereby making the interrelationships among them more complex (Best et al., 2009).

Inhibition is the ability to overpower a powerful response, engage in management of interference, evidence emotional control, and engender targeted forgetting (Best et al., 2009; Nigg, 2000). Inhibition is a critical function for younger children due to their tendency to be distracted by factors within their environment. Children must master a level of inhibition in order to create the developmental pathway for other executive functions such as working memory and planning (Isquith et al., 2004). Researchers have found that inhibition significantly increases in early childhood and then continues to differentiate into middle childhood (Romine & Reynolds, 2005; Sabbagh, Xu, Carlson, Moses, & Lee, 2006). Inhibition in early childhood tends to be measured by tasks such as the day–night task, in which day must be said when seeing an image of a moon, and Luria's fist and finger task, in which a child must point a finger when the researcher makes a fist (Carlson, 2005; Luria, 1966). As children develop inhibition, they are poised to develop working memory.

Working memory, as a component of executive functioning, is the ability to retain and use information over a short duration of time (Alloway, Gathercole, & Pickering, 2006). The complexity of tasks related to working memory expands across development with younger children being able to retain smaller amounts of information and variability compared with their older peers. Development is scaffolded with easier working memory tasks being integrated before more demanding working tasks are mastered. Interestingly, brain imagery also evidences that the area of brain activated by working memory tasks changes across time, with younger children accessing the basal ganglia and thalamus more frequently than older children, adolescents, and adults who rely more on the prefrontal cortex (Scherf, Sweeney, & Luna, 2006).

Another executive functioning skill that emerges in early childhood is task switching, or shifting, which entails changing between operations or tasks (Best et al., 2009). Children in the early childhood phase of development can shift between two simple tasks in which the expectations are clear and easily identifiable. The ability to apply the same rules to new stimuli consistently emerges when children are age 5 to 6 (Hughes, 1998; Luciana & Nelson, 1998). As with working memory, increasing age is correlated to increasing skill in task switching (Huizinga & van der Molen, 2007).

The ability to plan and problem solve toward goal-oriented behavior requires the synergy of inhibition, working memory, and task switching. Planning as an executive function prepares children to navigate new and unexpected situations and to complete tasks in a structured and efficient way (Anderson, 2002; Best et al., 2009). Mastery of the planning skill for young children is mostly correlated with the level of complexity and challenge of the task or situation. Navigating tasks that require up to three moves, as in the Tower of London and Tower of Hanoi task of moving pegs to match a predetermined pattern (Baker, Segalowitz, & Ferlisi, 2001), are typically mastered by middle childhood with more complex task sequencing being mastered in adolescence.

Language Development in Early Childhood

The process of developing early childhood communication is fascinating and astounding. Language acquisition results from a complex system of anatomy, cognition, and behavior to produce and convey the intended message (Chomsky, 1959). From the moment of birth, children are immersed in an environment that fosters communication exchange and promotes the development of verbal expressive and receptive language. Developing language is a complex process that results from children learning to communicate as adults and as others do in their culture and environment (Hoff, 2014). According to Vygotsky (1976), children learn in an environment where observation of expressive language produced by a more competent and experienced communicator is challenging but not so difficult the child cannot comprehend the communication (Cogher, 1999). Behaviorists communicate a similar belief that children learn from observation and practice.

Behaviorists believe children learn the process for communication based on the consequences of prior behavior (Hoff, 2005). If an infant learns to babble in response to mother's "I love you" and the mother responds with compassionate communication, the baby has been rewarded and reinforced to continue language development meaningfully. In that same example, a child experiencing cognitive stimulation also learns how a person thinks, perceives, reasons, and accesses memory (Hoff, 2014).

Communication learning environments may be experienced by children in a variety of ways. For instance, a child developing expressive and receptive language may experience one to several communication models to observe and hear (Eisenberg, 2004). In these natural or structured moments, the child may experience opportunities to produce the target communication and receive responses from an adult based on the child's incorrect or correct target statement (Eisenberg, 2004). As infants and children respond to their caregivers' verbal and nonverbal interactions, the children learn to verbally express their intentions and gradually learn to refine communication skills through repeated interactions while adhering to the rule governed structures of language (Owens, 2005). The first behaviorist to denote language conditioning was B. F. Skinner. He strongly believed children developed language acquisition indirectly through conditioning of association, imitation, and reinforcement (Hoff, 2014).

Noam Chomsky strongly believed that infants have innate tendencies toward the complex and abstract system of language development (Chomsky, 1959). Chomsky intelligently argued that if Skinner was correct then children would only produce sentences that were already heard and memorized, resulting in limited communication. Chomsky believed if a child produced a statement that was incorrect, such as "I see rabbities," a parent would not directly correct the child; therefore, a reinforcement of correct language structure was not gained (Chomsky, 1959). In most cases the parent would express, "You see the rabbits in the field," or "I see the rabbits too." He shared that the rule-governed system of language development supports children's learning to produce sentences that were not previously heard (Chomsky, 1959).

BOX 7.8   VERBAL OR ORAL EXPRESSIVE LANGUAGE DEVELOPMENT

Type of Development	Categories of Development	Criteria of Developmental Indicators
Language	Expressive language	The output of verbal expression adhering to rule-governed order.
	Syntax	Sentence structure.
	Pragmatics	Social use of language within a social context.
	Semantics	The meaning of words.
	Receptive language	Auditory comprehension of messages.
Voice	Sound	Sound is produced as air moves from the lungs and is pushed between vocal folds into the larynx; the forceful movement creates the larynx to vibrate producing sound that we shape in our vocal tract, jaw, and lips to produce meaningful speech sounds known as phonemes.
Speech	Speech is the verbal way of expressing language.	Phonemes
	Phonology	The smallest unit of sound. The English language has approximately 44 units of sound. The phonological process of sound development.
	The study of sounds and the system of language	
	Articulation	Articulation is the movement of the speech organs and tongue, lips, and jaw to produce sound.

Language development may be acquired due to innate capabilities or through behavioral reinforcement. The process of language development is complex, and in some instances results in disordered communication. The National Institute on Deafness and Other Communication Disorders (NIDCD, 2010) estimates that some form of language impairment impacts 6 to 8 million people in the United States. In a large percentage of children and adults, communication deficits result in psychological impairments (Danger & Landreth, 2005). The NIDCD reported that 7.5 million people in the United States have trouble using their voices, and 8–9% of children have a speech sound disorder leading to an ongoing concern by the first grade, with an approximate 5% of children with a noticeable speech delay or disorder. The National Center for Educational Statistics (NCES, 2013) estimated that 21% of children protected under the Individuals with Disabilities Education Act had a speech or language impairment and 6–7% were diagnosed with an emotional impairment. Current literature and research support that emotional difficulties and impairments may be initiated and perpetuated by challenges in communication (Danger & Landreth, 2005; Irwin, 1974; Johnson, McCleod, & Fall, 1977). Because adult–child interactions often rely on the child's expressive and receptive communication abilities (Ray, 2011), when a breakdown in communication occurs between the child and parent, emotional impairment may be experienced. Play becomes an alternative communication modality that minimizes the reliance on children's verbalizations, which are still experiencing significant developmental growth.

Vygotsky identified play as the leading catalyst for development for children ages 2 to 6 years (Ray, 2011). During early childhood, children communicate through play while learning about the world without the pressure and need to use expressive and receptive language (Ray, 2011). Vygotsky noted that the use of play benefits the child in three distinct ways: child's zone of proximal development; self-regulation; and helping the child distinguish between thought and action (Hirsh-Pasek & Golinkoff, 2003; Ray, 2001). The premise that play was created by the child only for fun has been interpreted incorrectly as play provides the developing child a mental, emotional, and physical release while attempting to meet the demands of the world. For instance, a child may play out the pressure and demands of needing to brush teeth, get dressed, and find shoes upon the parent request in the morning before school. Play offers the child an opportunity to play out actions, thoughts, and emotions within the child's expressive and receptive capabilities. Play is the child's work, language, and tool for understanding the world and his or her role in it (Landreth, 2012).

Language and cognitive development significantly interact with each other, and counselors need to be cognizant of how verbal and expressive language is still undeveloped during early childhood. Play therapy becomes a meaningful therapeutic framework to optimize child development while harnessing the natural communication style of children.

BOX 7.9 VYGOTSKY'S FUNCTIONS OF PLAY AND ASSOCIATED PURPOSES FOR COUNSELORS

Vygotsky's Three Functions of Play	Purpose for Counselors
Child's zone of proximal development	Play offers a child free range of expression without the restriction of reality. As the child plays, the play therapist observes and tracks the child's play with verbalizations to match the child's play actions while creating for the child an ongoing narrative of the child's world (Ray, 2011). In this interaction the child is not required by the play therapist to mature in language development beyond the child's age. Children are considered to have the tools for expressive language by ages 11–12 years. If a child enters counseling at a young age and talk therapy is implemented, then the child is working beyond the child's zone of proximal development.
Self-regulation	A child spends time each day responding to demands of the world, parents, and others; these demands require the child to keep it together and exceed the child's capabilities and development. Play therapy offers the child a release of energy for free expression (Ray, 2011). Enhancing the child's sense of self and self-worth is achieved by the child's opportunity to play out private thoughts and self-talk while expressing struggles through toys and their actions.
Helping the child separate thought from action	Language development is not mastered by a child until later years. Later language development is one reason a child has a considerably difficult time verbally expressing how he or she feels or may have been affected by what he or she has experienced. Play therapy is an opportunity for the child to be in control of thoughts and feelings. This control empowers the child to express through play the symbolic language of self-expression to share what the child has experienced and the child's self-perception, feelings, and reactions (Landreth, 2012).

BOX 7.10   CLASS ACTIVITY AND DISCUSSION

Prepare the students to engage as 2-year-olds in a conversation. Designate one student to role-play the parent and the other student to role play a 2-year old child. Ask each student to take on a specific task in the day (e.g., getting dressed, brushing teeth, and combing hair; eating dinner; selecting a breakfast item; taking a bath; playing with toys). Have the students role-play the experience for about 3 minutes. After the role-plays, ask the students to write down a few of the questions and comments that were communicated. Collate all the material and present it in a central location—on a whiteboard or something comparable. Once the conversations are on the board, ask the students what stands out to them about the conversation between the parent and the child.

Discussion Questions

1. How are the parental demands developmentally appropriate? How could they be beyond a 2-year-old's cognitive and receptive language development?
2. Were the communications emergent from the students' role-playing developmentally congruent with expressive language skills?

Based on processing of the first role-play, discuss developmentally consistent responses of a 2-year-old child (two to three words and accurate production of sounds {p, b, t, d, m, n}). Ask the students to role-play the same scenarios as previously practiced by integrating the developmentally appropriate expectations of the parent into the parent's communication and the developmentally appropriate child's expressive responses.

Discussion Questions Following the Second Role-Play

1. How was the second conversation experienced differently by the parent and then the child? How do expectations placed on the child to communicate at an adult level impact the child's sense of self and the child's mental and emotional health?

CONTEXTUAL FACTORS IMPACTING COGNITIVE AND LANGUAGE DEVELOPMENT

Myriad contextual and environmental factors affect cognitive development within early childhood. Young children are inevitably influenced by the environment from whence they come. These factors include home environment, socioeconomic status, nutrition, parenting practices, and educational exposure (Brown & Lan, 2013; Christensen, Schieve, Devine, & Drews-Botsch, 2014; Frumkin, 2013; Gibbs & Forste, 2014; Jackson, 2015; Mollborn Lawrence, James-Hawkins, & Fomby, 2014; Tan, Yang, & Yang, 2014; Tucker-Drob & Harden, 2012). Developmental tasks concerning cognition may be complicated by environmental conditions both in home and educational contexts. However, there may be ways to mediate the effects of some negative environmental factors on cognitive development by the promotion of certain factors.

Roughly 25% of young children live in poverty (Jackson, 2015; Mollborn et al., 2014; Tucker-Drob & Harden, 2012). Children who are identified as coming from homes with lower socioeconomic status are at risk for delayed cognitive development and educational achievement (Tan et al., 2014). Socioeconomic advantage or disadvantage, including household income, assets, and parental education, establishes a pathway that influences children's cognitive achievement or difficulty, respectively. Mollborn et al. (2014) identified early childhood as the developmental time period wherein children are most sensitive to being disadvantaged socioeconomically. "Research investigating this path dependence has focused on early childhood as a period when environmental context is expected to enhance or constrain critical periods of development and growth. Because early childhood conditions have long-term consequences, every U.S. dollar invested in early childhood education is estimated to return $8–14 later on" (Mollborn et al., 2014, p. 56).

As such, the care and nurturance of young children is essential for their future educational achievement and success. Jackson (2015) found that living in poverty may affect early childhood nutrition, which is also directly linked to cognitive development. Women, Infants, and Children (WIC) is a federally funded supplemental nutrition program which has been shown to mediate the short- and long-term effects of lower socioeconomic environmental situations on children's cognitive development and early academic scores in math and reading, respectively (Jackson, 2015). Additionally, both prenatal and postnatal nutrition are essential in the process of healthy cognitive development (Christensen et al., 2014). WIC provides sustenance throughout these time periods (Jackson, 2015).

Christensen et al.'s (2014) findings corroborated that socioeconomic status negatively impacts cognitive development; however, child–home enrichment practices and other enrichment factors lead to higher cognitive test scores in both lower and higher socioeconomic populations. Children's cognitive development is influenced by their social relations with adults through an educational context and through the home environment. Home environment enrichment factors include parenting practices and processes. Parenting practices that are correlated with cognitive development include cognitive stimulation, sensitivity, and warmth (Gibbs & Forste, 2014; Tucker-Drob & Harden, 2012).

Cognitive stimulation is vital to the young child's mental development. "Parental cognitive stimulation, defined as 'parents' didactic efforts to enrich their children's cognitive and language development by engaging children in activities that promote learning and by offering language-rich environments to their children, has been identified as a predictor of children's cognitive abilities" (Tucker-Drob & Harden, 2012, p. 250). For example, reading to young children is a powerful method of cognitive stimulation and a home environment factor (Christensen et al., 2014; Gibbs & Forste, 2014). The frequency of reading is of particular importance. Daily reading sessions, along with parental sensitivity, were predictors of educational outcomes related to math and reading in early childhood. Promoting literacy interventions such as Reach Out and Read (http://www.reachoutandread.org/) and other parenting methods intended toward cognitive stimulation have been shown to have a positive impact on early childhood cognitive development. "Such interventions have encouraged parents to read together more often and have been associated with greater language outcomes in pre-school aged children. In particular, children from lower socioeconomic backgrounds with less educated mothers are less likely to read with parents, which undermine school readiness" (Gibbs & Forste, 2014, p. 492). Health-care providers and counselors would serve families from disadvantaged backgrounds well by providing preventative and educative procedures and resources (Christensen et al., 2014; Gibbs & Forste, 2014).

Frumkin (2013) determined that home learning environment and ethnic minority status effect assessment scores and cognitive achievement. However, among children from diverse ethnic backgrounds, the greatest impact factor was whether English was spoken in the home. Assessment scores were higher, regardless of ethnic background, when the home environment included members who spoke English with the children. Brown and Lan (2013) concurred that attention to children's cultural backgrounds is necessary in understanding their context and specific needs in regard to cognitive development.

It is evident that the home and the immediate surrounding environment significantly influence childhood cognitive development (Brown & Lan, 2013; Christensen et al., 2014; Frumkin, 2013; Gibbs & Forste, 2014; Jackson, 2015; Mollborn et al., 2014; Tan et al, 2014; Tucker-Drob & Harden, 2012). Other impactful factors, within an educational context, include the use of developmentally appropriate approaches in school and early intervention. Research has shown that attention to these aspects is critical when considering and facilitating early childhood cognitive development (Brown & Lan, 2013; Christensen et al., 2014). Brown and Lan (2013) emphasized that teachers' use of developmentally appropriate practice had a positive effect on children's cognitive development. Conversely, the absence of developmentally appropriate practice in early educational settings had negative repercussions on development. Early intervention with children who display developmental delays is essential to promote cognitive advancement, especially with children coming from populations that are disadvantaged. Early education interventions, such as Head Start and similar programs, can provide critical support in fostering cognitive development. Many developmental issues can be detected before children enter kindergarten. Thus, developmental screenings during early childhood are crucial in initially determining educational services for these children and promoting cognitive development (Christensen et al., 2014).

THE CASE OF JACKSON

Jackson is a 5-year-old Asian American male. He lives with his mother, father, and younger brother, Cameron, age 3 years. Jackson's mom is a full-time health-care worker, and his father is an electrical engineer. Jackson is preparing to enter kindergarten and currently attends a regular preschool. Jackson's parents enrolled him and his younger brother in preschool to help the boys develop their social skills and challenge their cognitive skills. Jackson enjoys testing out his physical abilities by challenging other children his age to foot races, pedal bike races, and seeing who can jump the farthest. Some of the games he currently engages in are hide-and-seek, Simon says, and duck, duck, goose. He enjoys games that challenge his physical and cognitive abilities. Although Jackson knows there is a difference between boys and girls, there is little notable difference in physical or cognitive abilities based on gender at this stage of development. For Jackson, girls have long hair and like the color pink, and boys have short hair and don't like the color pink. Since attending preschool, Jackson's parents have noticed a shift in his perceptions; he has recently been refusing kisses at drop off, uses phrases unfamiliar to the parents, and thinks any sentence can be made funny with the addition of *fart* or *butt* at the end. He identifies most of the children at his preschool as his friends, with an occasional child being identified as a bully. Jackson is able to write out his first name legibly and colors within the lines the majority of the time. He has recently begun to sound out some letter sounds and will often pretend to read to his brother at bedtime. Jackson is adept at feeding and dressing himself. Jackson will often help Cameron get his coat on and will make similar statements to Cameron that Jackson has heard his mother say, such as, "What a big boy. I'm so proud of you."

As you reflect on the case of Jackson, what areas of cognitive development emerge for you? How do you explain his recent changes in behavior? What else might you like to know about Jackson and his family to have a more thorough ecobiodevelopmental conceptualization?

KEY COUNSELING POINTERS FOR COGNITIVE DEVELOPMENT IN EARLY CHILDHOOD

Professional counselors are charged with integrating developmental theory and knowledge of developmental milestones and needs into our clinical treatment paradigm. To best serve clients' cognitive development, counselors are encouraged to engage clients in multiple counseling strategies to optimize cognitive development learning and attend to the clients' presenting cognitive developmental needs. Key counseling pointers highlight how a counselor can support clients from an ecobiodevelopmental perspective.

Individual counseling. Counselors need to be continually responsive to the cognitive complexities and skills of young children. Ensuring that vocabulary is developmentally appropriate is an important first step. Counselors mindfully consider how language and cognitive development during early childhood contribute to specific interventions being more developmentally appropriate than others. For example, expecting a young child to engage in talk-oriented counseling for 45 minutes would not be developmentally responsive. Engaging in play therapy or expressive and creative arts would provide young clients with opportunities to express themselves in a manner consistent with their cognitive and language development (Bratton et al., 2005; Landreth, 2012).

Engaging and educating caregivers. Cognitive development and language emerge as the child interacts with the environment. An important consideration for counselors is the role the child's caregiver plays in the child's development. Caregivers are useful and essential in the counseling process for many reasons. First, caregivers can provide valuable information about the context in which a child is functioning—at home, at school, and in the community. Caregivers and parents can also dictate how often and when a child is able to receive counseling services; therefore, building a collaborative relationship with caregivers and parents ensures a perceived benefit of the child receiving counseling. Third, caregivers and parents can positively impact the cognitive and language development of young children. Providing parents and caregivers access to resources may promote their willingness and knowledge of options to stimulate their child's cognitive and language development. Education for parents regarding the child's cognitive and language skills can enrich the home environment and provide more cognitive stimulation.

Promoting wellness at individual, family, and community levels. Because of the brain's susceptibility to the negative impact of toxic stress, counselors need to actively and continually promote wellness at the individual (child or caregiver), family, and community levels. Integrating wellness activities and strategies into counseling and sharing resources with families can enhance the protective factors that prevent stressors from becoming toxic. Teaching mindfulness, relaxation techniques, healthy coping strategies, anger management, conflict resolution, friendship skills, and emotional awareness to young children prepares them to navigate stressful situations with a repertoire of skills that either prevents stress or mediates stress. Counselors are uniquely prepared to have a similar impact at the family and community system levels as well.

Advocacy. Because cognitive and language development are deeply connected to stimulating and enriching early childhood environments, counselors can advocate on individual and community levels for these resources to be more readily available for children and families. At the individual level, counselors can identify potential community resources or early childhood programs that could enrich the child's cognitive and language development. After the identification phase, counselors can advocate to remove barriers and to build pathways that engender the engagement of such resources. At the community level, counselors can support initiatives for early childhood development and engage in consciousness-raising with local politicians and community members about the benefits of wellness and cognitively stimulating educational and communal efforts.

Assessment. Counselors need to continually assess for a child's cognitive and language development. Understanding expected developmental benchmarks prepares counselors to identify potential areas of concern and to identify resources to best support the child. Developmental screenings need to include ecobiodevelopmental factors so that issues of parental depression, exposure to violence, malnutrition, and lack of social supports can be addressed as early as possible. The experiences in early childhood develop a trajectory of health and well-being into adulthood, so counselors need to comprehensively engage in assessment of a child's functioning and lived experience.

BOX 7.11   TEACHING PHYSICAL DEVELOPMENT AND CONTEXT IN COUNSELING

Children in the cognitive development preoperational stage exercise their mental functions or semiotic mental functions to produce imaginary actions, symbolic encoding, and memory (Green & Piel, 2013). The mental manipulations of objects enable children to engage in thoughts over physical action. To assist caregivers in understanding the process of physical development for young children, a counselor may present a metaphor of planting a seed. This process supports the metaphor for growth and highlights how children are often growing in unnoticeable ways—similar to how a plant grows and changes daily in unnoticeable ways. Counselors can encourage caregivers to consider how they are nourishing their child on a daily basis to help facilitate the child's growth process.

If appropriate, an experiential activity of planting a seed can be done with a child and caregiver together to illustrate to both the child and caregiver the importance of nurturing development (see Figure 7.2). Counselors can use the expressive arts counseling intervention detailed next.

Figure 7.2 Taking care of seeds: a way to demonstrate nurturing.

Supplies	Instructions	Counselor Process
1. Planting bowl or clear cup 2. Seed 3. Soil 4. Shovel 5. Water 6. Sunlight	Discuss with the child the human growth process and what is required, connecting this to the metaphor of the planting process. Take the planting bowl and fill the bowl half way with soil. Then place in the seed and add ½ inch of the soil above the seed. Discuss the conditions for the seed to grow, and provide water and sunlight.	Discuss with the child and parent how a child grows; have the child give direct examples of what makes him or her grow. Discuss how growing a plant is similar and requires love, attention, food, and water, too. Have the child discuss how the planting bowl is similar to the child's house. Discuss how the child is the seed that is growing and changing. Discuss how the soil protects the seed and allows for growth to occur; discuss who the child perceives to offer protection and comfort to grow. Discuss how eating and drinking certain selections support the child's growth. Discuss the process of the sun and how this relates to the child.

BOX 7.12   CASE STUDY AND CLASS DISCUSSION

Case Study

Nadima is a 4-year-old girl who lives with her mom and dad. Her parents had an on-and-off relationship for most of Nadima's life but have recently married. Nadima is an only child and often makes comments similar to those of the adults she associates with regularly such as her parents, grandparents, aunts, and uncles. Besides being an only child, she is also the only grandchild on her mother's side and the only girl grandchild on her father's side. Needless to say, Nadima receives a lot of adult attention. Nadima's parents both work full time, and Nadima attends a preschool where she excels. One of Nadima's grandmothers is also a reading specialist in the local elementary school, and this grandmother picks Nadima up from preschool every day. Nadima stays with her grandmother after school until her parents get home a few hours later. Due to her extended stays at her grandmother's, Nadima has begun to sound out words and is able to read a number of introductory books. Nadima is often commended by others (even those outside of her family) on her ability to read and sound out words. In the last 3 months, Nadima has begun to focus on reading so much so that she doesn't want to go outside to play with her cousins or other neighbor children. Nadima's parents have been using her reading time as a reward or punishment to help modify various behaviors typical for a 4-year-old child. Nadima's parents have developed concerns for Nadima's preoccupation with reading and have recently enrolled her into a variety of activities such as soccer and cheerleading. Nadima will often cry when told she is going to soccer and will beg her parents to allow her to bring a book with her to the soccer field. She is a little more tolerant of cheerleading; she has told her mom that "the outfits are cute." But even with cheerleading, Nadima generally will ask to bring a book to cheerleading "in case I get bored," she tells her parents. At this point in Nadima's development, her parents are concerned that Nadima is preoccupied with books to the exclusion of other typical play.

Class Discussion

1. What are your initial reactions to the case of Nadima? How reasonable do you perceive Nadima's parents' concerns to be? If you were counseling Nadima's family, what are potential treatment goals?
2. What are potential contextual factors impacting Nadima's strong interest in reading?

SUMMARY

Competent counselors are cognizant of physical and cognitive developmental processes during early childhood, which enables them to match their counseling interventions with developmental capabilities, and they are able to identify areas of developmental need and unrealized potentiality. Early childhood is a time of substantial physical and cognitive development that has a long-term impact on a child's trajectory into adulthood. Given the counseling profession's position and commitment to conceptualizing human growth and development into the context of the client, counselors are uniquely positioned to contextualize children and families from a developmental paradigm, to integrate developmentally appropriate counseling theories and techniques, and to foster healthy development within their clients.

Given the plasticity of the brain during early childhood, counselors must recognize the level of vulnerability that young children have. The vulnerability is ecobiodevelopmental in that the presence of toxic stress and challenging environments can negatively impact the health and wellness of the child's future adult self. The cases of Rosey and Jackson highlight how the individual development is profoundly impacted by the family and community context. Just as counselors conduct assessment from a biopsychosocial perspective, they must integrate an ecobiodevelopmental paradigm when working with children.

USEFUL WEBSITES

Administration on Children and Families
http://www.acf.hhs.gov/
Bright Futures
http://brightfutures.aap.org/Family_Resources.html
CDC's "Learn the Signs. Act Early." Campaign
http://www.cdc.gov/ncbddd/actearly/index.html
Center for Parent Information and Resources
http://www.parentcenterhub.org/
Developmental and Behavioral Pediatrics Online
http://www2.aap.org/sections/dbpeds/
Let's Move
http://www.letsmove.gov/about
National Association for the Education of Young Children (NAEYC)
http://www.naeyc.org/
National Institute on Child Health and Development
http://www.nichd.nih.gov/Pages/index.aspx
The Whole Child
http://www.pbs.org/wholechild/

REFERENCES

Alloway, T. P., Gathercole, S. E., & Pickering, S. J. (2006). Verbal and visuospatial short-term and WM in children: Are they separable? *Child Development*, 77, 1698–1716.

American Psychiatric Association (APA). (2013). *Diagnostic and statistical manual of mental disorders* (5th ed.). Arlington, VA: Author.

Anderson, P. (2002). Assessment and development of executive function during childhood. *Child Neuropsychology*, 29, 161–173.

Axline, V. (1964). *Dibs: In search of self*. Boston, MA: Houghton Mifflin.

Baker, K., Segalowitz, J. A., & Ferlisi, M. C. (2001). The effect of differing scoring methods for the tower of London task on developmental patterns of performance. *Clinical Neuropsychologist*, 15, 309–313.

Best, J. R., Miller, P. H., & Jones, L. L. (2009). Executive functions after age 5: Changes and correlates. *Developmental Review*, 20, 180–200. doi:10.1016/j.dr.2009.05.002

Bratton, S. C., Ray, D., Rhine, T., & Jones, L. (2005). The efficacy of play therapy with children: A meta-analytic review of treatment outcomes. *Professional Psychology-Research and Practice*, 36, 376–390. doi:10.1037/0735-7028.36.4.376

Briggs-Gowan, M. J., Carter, A. S., & Ford, J. D. (2012). Parsing the effects violence exposure in early childhood: Modeling developmental pathways. *Journal of Pediatric Psychology*, 37, 11–22. doi:10.1093/jpepsy/jsro63

Britto, P. R., Yoshikawa, H., & Boller, K. (2011). Quality of early childhood development programs in global contexts. *Social Policy Report*, 25, 3–23.

Broderick, P. C. (2010). *The lifespan: Human development for helping professionals* (3rd ed.). Upper Saddle River, NJ: Pearson Education.

Broderick, P. C., & Blewitt, P. (2015). *The lifespan: Human development for helping professionals* (4th ed.). Upper Saddle River, NJ: Pearson Education.

Bronfenbrenner, U. (1979). *The ecology of human development: Experiments by nature and design*. Cambridge, MA: Harvard University Press.

Brown, C. P., & Lan, Y. (2013). The influence of developmentally appropriate practice on children's cognitive development: A qualitative metasynthesis. *Teachers College Record*, 115(12), 1–36.

Carlson, S. M. (2005). Developmentally sensitive measures of executive function in preschool children. *Developmental Neuropsychology*, 28(2), 595–616. doi:10.1207/s15326942dn2802_3

Case, R. (1988). The structure and process of intellectual development. In A. Demetriou (Ed.), *The neo-Piagetian theories of cognitive development: Toward an integration* (pp. 65–101). Amsterdam, The Netherlands: Elsevier.

Case, R. (1992). *The mind's staircase: Exploring the conceptual underpinnings of children's thought and knowledge*. Hillsdale, NJ: Erlbaum.

Case-Smith, J. & Clifford O'Brien, J. (2009). *Occupational therapy for children* (6th ed.). St. Louis, MO: Elsevier Mosby.

Centers for Disease Control and Prevention (CDC). (2010). *Growth charts*. Retrieved from http://www.cdc.gov/growthcharts/

Chomsky, N. (1959). A review of B. F. Skinner's verbal behavior. *Language*, 35(1), 26–58.

Christensen, D. L., Schieve, L. A., Devine, O., & Drews-Botsch, C. (2014). Socioeconomic status, child enrichment factors, and cognitive performance among preschool-age children: Results from the Follow-Up of Growth and Development Experiences study. *Research in Developmental Disabilities*, *35*(7), 1789–1801.

Cogher, L. (1999). The use of non-directive play in speech and language therapy. *Child Language Teaching and Therapy*, *265*, 6590–6599.

Committee on the Rights of the Child, United Nations. (2006). *Report of the Committee on the Rights of the Child (A/61/41)*. Retrieved from http://www.unhcr.org/refworld/docid/4725f1a82.html

Danger, S., & Landreth, G. L. (2005). Child-centered group play therapy with children with speech difficulties. *International Journal of Play Therapy*, *14*(1), 81–102.

Dannlowski, U., Kugel, H., Huber, F., Stuhrmann, A., Redlich, R., Grotegerd, D., Suslow, T. (2013). Childhood maltreatment is associated with an automatic negative emotion processing bias in the amygdala. *Human Brain Mapping*, *34*, 2899–2909.

DeBoer, M. D., Lima, A. M., Oria, R. B., Scharf, R. J., Moore, S. R., Luna, M. A., & Guerrant, R. L. (2012). Early childhood growth failure and the developmental origins of adult disease: Do enteric infections and malnutrition increase risk of metabolic syndrome? *Nutrition Reviews*, *70*, 642–653.

de Onis, M., Blossner, M., & Borghi, E. (2010). Global prevalence and trends of overweight and obesity among preschool children. *American Journal of Clinical Nutrition*, *92*, 1257–1264.

Eisenberg, S. (2004). Structured communicative play therapy for targeting language in young children. *Communication Disorders Quarterly*, *26*(1), 29–35.

Engle, P. L., Black, M. M., Behrman, J. R., DeMello, M. C., Gertler, P. J., Kapiriri, L., ... International Child Development Steering Group. (2007). Strategies to avoid the loss of developmental potential in more than 200 million children in the developing world. *The Lancet*, *360*, 229–242. doi:10.1016/S0140-6736(07)60112-3

Fischer, K. W. (1980). A theory of cognitive development: The control and construction of hierarchies of skills. *Psychological Review*, *87*, 477–531.

Fischer, K. W. (2008). Dynamic cycles of cognitive and brain development: Measuring growth in mind, brain, and education. In A. M. Battro, K. W. Fischer, & P. Lena (Eds.), *The educated brain* (pp. 127–150). Cambridge, UK: Cambridge University Press.

Fox, L., Vaughn, B. J., Wyatte, M. I., & Dunlap, G. (2002). "We can't expect other people to understand": Family perspectives on problem behaviors. *Exceptional Children*, *68*(4), 437–450.

Frumkin, L. A. (2013). Young children's cognitive achievement: Home learning environment, language and ethnic background. *Journal of Early Childhood Research*, *11*(3), 222–235.

Garner, A. S., Committee on Psychosocial Aspects of Child and Family Health, & Committee on Early Childhood, Adoption, and Dependent Care. (2012). Early childhood adversity, toxic stress, and the role of the pediatrician:

Translating developmental science into lifelong health. *Pediatrics, 129,* e224–e231. doi: 10.1542/peds.2011-2662

Gibbs, B. G., & Forste, R. (2014). Breastfeeding, parenting, and early cognitive development. *Journal of Pediatrics, 164*(3), 487–493. doi:10.1016/j.jpeds.2013.10.015

Green, M., & Piel, J. A. (2013). *Theories of human development: A comparative approach.* Boston, MA: Allyn & Bacon.

Hansen, C. C., & Zambo, D. (2005). Piaget, meet Lilly: Understanding child development through picture book characters. *Early Childhood Education Journal, 33*(1), 39–45. doi:10.1007/s10643-005-0020-8

Hirsh-Pasek, K., & Golinkoff, R. (2003). *Einstein never used flash cards: How our children really learn—and why they need to play more and memorize less.* New York, NY: Rodale Press.

Hoff, E. (2014). *Language development.* Belmont, CA: Wadsworth.

Hughes, C. (1998). Executive function in preschoolers: Links with theory of mind and verbal ability. *British Journal of Developmental Psychology, 16,* 233–253.

Huizinga, M., & van der Molen, M. W. (2007). Age-group differences in set-switching and set-maintenance on the Wisconsin card sorting task. *Developmental Neuropsychology, 31,* 193–215.

Irwin, R. B. (1974). Language of culturally deprived children. *Acta Symbolica, 3*(2), 129–132.

Isquith, P. K., Gioia, G. A., & Espy, K. A. (2004). Executive function in preschool children: Examination through everyday behavior. *Developmental Neuropsychology, 26,* 403–422.

Jackson, M. I. (2015). Early childhood WIC participation, cognitive development and academic achievement. *Social Science & Medicine, (1982),* 145–153. doi:10.1016/j.socscimed.2014.12.018

Johnson, L., McCleod, E. H., & Fall, M. (1977). Play therapy with labeled children in the schools. *Professional School Counselor, 1*(1), 31–34.

Landreth, G. (2012). *Play therapy: The art of the relationship.* New York, NY: Routledge.

Lindsey, J. C., Malee, K. M., Brouwers, P., & Hughes, M. D. (2007). Neurodevelopmental functioning in HIV-infected infants and young children born before and after the introduction of protease inhibitor-based highly active antiretroviral therapy. *Pediatrics, 119,* e681–693.

Luciana, M., & Nelson, C. A. (1998). The functional emergence of prefrontally-guided WM systems in four to eight year old children. *Neuropsychologia, 36,* 273–293.

Luria, A. R. (1966). *Higher cortical functions in man.* New York, NY: Basic Books.

Marion, M. M. (2010). *Guidance of young children.* Upper Saddle River, NJ: Prentice Hall.

McEwen, B. S. (2005). Stressed or stressed out: What is the difference? *Journal of Psychiatry and Neuroscience, 30,* 315–318.

McEwen, B. S. (2006). Protective and damaging effects of stress mediators: Central role of the brain. *Dialogues in Clinical Neuroscience, 8,* 367–381.

McEwen, B. S. (2007). Physiology and neurobiology of stress and adaptation: Central role of the brain. *Physiological Review, 87,* 873–904.

McEwen, B. S., & Gianaros, P. J. (2011). Stress and allostasis-induced brain plasticity. *Annual Review of Medicine, 62*, 431–445.

Mollborn, S., Lawrence, E., James-Hawkins, L., & Fomby, P. (2014). When do socioeconomic resources matter most in early childhood? *Advances in Life Course Research, 20*, 56–59.

National Center for Educational Statistics (NCES). (2013). *Fast facts*. Retrieved from https://nces.ed.gov/

National Institute on Deafness and Other Communication Disorders (NIDCD). (2010). Retrieved from http://www.nidcd.nih.gov/Pages/default.aspx

Nigg, J. T. (2000). On inhibition/disinhibition in developmental psychopathology: Views from cognitive and personality psychology and a working inhibition taxonomy. *Psychological Bulletin, 126*, 220–246.

Office of Head Start. (2015). *How do I apply for Head Start?* Retrieved from http://www.acf.hhs.gov/programs/ohs

Ormrod, J. E. (2013). *Educational psychology: Developing learners*. Upper Saddle River, NJ: Pearson Higher Ed.

Owens, R. E. (2005). *Language development: An introduction*. Boston, MA: Pearson Education.

Pallini, S., & Barcaccia, B. (2014). A meeting of the minds: John Bowlby encounters Jean Piaget. *Review of General Psychology, 18*(4), 287–292. doi:10.1037/gpr0000016

Pascual-Leone, J. (1988). Organismic processes for neo-Piagetian theories: A dialectical causal account of cognitive development. In A. Demetriou (Ed.), *The neo-Piagetian theories of cognitive development: Toward an integration* (pp. 25–64). Amsterdam, The Netherlands: Elsevier.

Patelarou, E., Giourgouli, G., Lykeridou, A., Vrioni, E., Fotos, N., Siamaga, E., Vivilaki, V., & Brokalaki, H. (2011). Association between biomarker-quantified antioxidant status during pregnancy and infancy and allergic disease during early childhood: A systematic review. *Nutrition Reviews, 69*, 627–641.

Ray, D. (2011). *Advanced play therapy: Essential conditions, knowledge, and skills for child practice*. New York, NY: Taylor & Francis Group.

Romine, C. B., & Reynolds, C. R. (2005). A model of the development of frontal lobe function: Findings from a meta-analysis. *Applied Neuropsychology, 12*, 190–201.

Sabbagh, M. A., Xu, F., Carlson, S. M., Moses, L. J., & Lee, K. (2006). The development of executive functioning and theory of mind: A comparison of Chinese and US preschoolers. *Psychological Science, 17*, 4–81.

Santrock, J. W. (2014). *A topical approach to lifespan development* (7th ed.). New York, NY: McGraw-Hill.

Scherf, K. S., Sweeney, J. A., & Luna, B. (2006). Brain basics of developmental change in visuospatial WM. *Journal of Cognitive Neuroscience, 18*, 1045–1058.

Senn, T. E., Espy, K. A., & Kaufmann, P. M. (2004). Using path analysis to understand executive function organization in preschool children. *Developmental Neuropsychology, 26*, 445–464.

Shonkoff, J. P. (2010). Building a new biodevelopmental framework to guide the future of early childhood policy. *Child Development, 81*, 357–367.

Shonkoff, J. P., Boyce, W. T., & McEwen, B. S. (2009). Neuroscience, molecular biology, and the childhood roots of health disparities: Building a new framework for health promotion and disease prevention. *Journal of American Medical Association*, *301*, 2252–2259.

Shonkoff, J. P., Garner, A. A., & the American Academy of Pediatrics Committee on Psychosocial Aspects of Child and Family Health. (2012). *Pediatrics*, *129*, e232–e246. doi:10.1542/peds.2011-2663

Tan, J. E., Yang, H., & Yang, S. (2014). A holistic intervention program for children from low socioeconomic status families. *Frontiers in Psychology*, *5*, 1–2.

Thabet, A. A., Karim, K., & Vostanis, P. (2006). Trauma exposure in pre-school children in a war zone. *British Journal of Psychiatry*, *188*, 154–158.

Thompson, P. M, Giedd, J. N., Woods, R. P., MacDonald, D., Evans, A. C., & Toga, A. W. (2000). Growth patterns in the developing brain detected by using continuum mechanical tensor maps. *Nature*, *404*, 190–193.

Thuilliez, J. (2009). Malaria and primary education: A cross country analysis on repetition and completion rates. *Review of Economy of Development*, *2*, 127–157.

Tottenham, N., Hara, T. A., Quinn, B. T., et al. (2010). Prolonged institutional rearing is associated with atypically large amygdala volume and difficulties in emotional regulation. *Developmental Science*, *13*, 46–61.

Tucker-Drob, E. M., & Harden, K. P. (2012). Early childhood cognitive development and parental cognitive stimulation: Evidence for reciprocal gene–environment transactions. *Developmental Science*, *15*(2), 250–259. doi:10.1111/j.1467-7687.2011.01121.x

United Nations Children's Fund. (2012). *Annual report 2012*. New York, NY: Author.

Van Rie, A., Harrington, P. R., Dow, A., & Robertson, K. (2007). Neurologic and neurodevelopmental manifestations of pediatric HIV/AIDS: A global perspective. *European Journal of Paediatric Neurology*, *11*, 1–9.

Vernon, A. (2009). *Counseling children and adolescents* (4th ed.). Denver, CO: Love Publishing.

Vygotsky, L. S. (1976). Play and its role in the mental development of the child. In: J. S. Bruner, A. Jolly, & K. Sylva (Eds.), *Play—its role in development and evolution* (pp. 537–554). New York, NY: Basic Books.

Wachs, T. D., Black, M. M., & Engle, P. L. (2009). Maternal depression: A global threat to children's health, development, and behavior and to human rights. *Child Development Perspectives*, *3*, 51–59.

Walker, S. P., Wachs, T. D., Grantham-McGregor, S., Black, M. M., Nelson, C. A., Huffman, S. L., Baker-Henningham , Chang, S. M., … &Richter, L. (2011). Inequality in early childhood: Risk and protective factors for early childhood development. *Lancet*, *378*(9799), 1325–1338. doi:10.1016/S0140-6736(11)60555-2

Zittoun, T., & Cerchia, F. (2013). Imagination as expansion of experience. *Integrative Psychological & Behavioral Science*, *47*(3), 305–324. doi:10.1007/s12124-013-9234-2

Zuckerman, E. L. (2008). *The paper office* (4th ed.). New York, NY: Guilford Press.

Early Childhood: Emotional and Social Development

Elsa Soto Leggett, Gail K. Roaten, and Kathy Ybañez-Llorente

The process of early childhood social and emotional development changes almost daily. The challenge of working with young children is in the interpretation of social and emotional stages according to the different ages. Counselors must have a sound knowledge of social and emotional development within the scope of normal human development (Henderson & Thompson, 2011). The study of human development from a scientific perspective began to emerge from Europe and the United States in the 19th century. This was set in motion by the emergence of biological science, growth in mass education, and the period of industrialization (Broderick & Blewitt, 2015). Prior to this time, the perception of childhood throughout the ages varied. Watson and Lindgren (1979) reported that the Greeks and Romans valued children as members of the family and as future citizens. During the Middle Ages, children were not seen as any different from adults. At the ages of 6 and 7 years, children took on adult responsibilities; males began learning trades and leaving home, whereas females married at age 10 or 12 years (Aries, 1962; Broderick & Blewitt, 2015; Orton, 1997). In the 17th century, John Locke believed that children required distinctive care, advising parents to spend time with them and to set good examples to influence child development. Charles Darwin fostered scholarly interest in children with his 19th-century study reporting daily changes in his young son, documenting differences in children's behaviors. During the 18th and 19th centuries, the Industrial Revolution produced a growth of occupations requiring an academic education. This included the education of children, which revealed the need to recognize that children were different from adults and how children change with age (Broderick & Blewitt, 2015; Orton, 1997). The 20th century ushered in many of the classic developmental theories, some of which we will review in this chapter.

Early childhood is the range from ages 2 to 6 years. In these preschool years, children increase skills needed to interact with, understand, and expand their world of people and things (Orton, 1997). This important developmental period lays the foundation for later competencies in many areas. Social and emotional development in early childhood is an essential building block to learn successful ways to

BOX 8.1 CULTURE AND THE DEVELOPING CHILD

From 2000 to 2010, the number of children in the United States who were non-Hispanic White decreased from 61% to 54%; it is projected to decline to 49% by 2020. During that same period, the number of Hispanic children has grown steadily and is projected to be 26% by 2020 (U.S. Census Bureau, 2014). Asian populations have grown slightly, whereas Black non-Hispanic and American Indian percentages remain static (U.S. Census Bureau, 2014).

Research suggests that children of color in early childhood are more likely to experience environmental factors that put them at risk for poor social and emotional development (Cooper, Masi, & Vick, 2009). Children of color, specifically African American children up to age 5 years, are overrepresented in the overall number of maltreated youth (21% vs. 14% in general population). In addition, 40% of preschoolers receiving specialized mental health services are children of color; African Americans comprise 24.8%, whereas 13.6% are Latino/a (National Child Abuse and Neglect Data System Child File, FFY, 2006). Correlations between culture and social-emotional well-being in children underscore that fact the negative early experiences may impair the developmental process (Cooper et al., 2009).

The majority of cultures in the United States emphasize individualism, whereas many groups who have or are currently immigrating to this country are from cultures that are more collectivist. Greenfield (1994) stated, "By these means, cultural ideals influence the trajectory of individual development" (p. 4). Beliefs, values, and worldview are all part of the developing child's experience, shaping each individual's social and emotional development. Children from traditionally White individualist cultures are encouraged to become self-sufficient and autonomous; behaviors such as sleeping alone, taking care of oneself, and making choices are encouraged, praised, and reinforced. Children from collectivist, or interdependent, cultures are socialized toward bidirectional responsibility within an extended family environment. In this type of culture, positive development values group goals over those of the individual (Greenfield, 1994). Children of color and those of collectivist cultures, along with their parents, enter a sociopolitical system grounded in an individualistic mindset. Basically, this leads to a collision of cultures; children from collectivist cultures do not fit the norm of their individualist counterparts within their collective social experiences. Training in cultural awareness, knowledge, and the skills to deal with this cultural dynamic is essential. This training is absolutely essential for mental health practitioners but is also important for anyone and everyone with whom the child might be in contact.

This includes preschool teachers, daycare administration and staff, religious educators, and social service workers. Barrera and Corso (2002) addressed this: "Practitioners can find it overwhelming and unrealistic to be familiar with cultural parameters for all the persons/children with whom they are asked to interact, especially when these children and families participate in multiple cultures" (p. 1). Early childhood services are often the "first point of contact with mainstream culture" for minority and immigrant families, so it is essential that these services be based on a deeper and better understanding of the cultural values and beliefs of the families in the dynamic, ever-changing culture (Maschinot, 2008).

reason, make decisions, solve problems, and experience well-being, leading to current and later successes (Ashdown & Bernard, 2011; Orton, 1997; Schroeder & Gordon, 2002). As preschoolers prepare to enter school, key social and emotional skills help them feel more confident and competent in developing relationships, building friendships, resolving conflicts, facing challenges, coping with feelings of anger and frustration, and managing emotions (Ashdown & Bernard). The Center on the Social Emotional Foundation for Early Learning (CSEFEL, 2010) defines social and emotional development as the developing capability of a young child to be confident, to have the capacity to develop relationships with peers and adults, to demonstrate concentration and persistence on challenging tasks, to effectively communicate emotions, to listen to instructions and be attentive, and to solve social problems.

THEORIES

Examining multiple theoretical perspectives allows us to better understand the contextual influence on theorists' approaches to viewing early childhood social and emotional development. Given the complexity of social and emotional development in early childhood, theorists understandably vary on the basic premise of what impacts social and emotional development. Table 8.1 provides a quick comparison of mid-20th-century theories of human development, providing the reader with an opportunity to consider which theory has had the greatest impact on his or her current understanding of social-emotional development. A review of psychosexual, psychosocial, and ecological systems theories follows the table.

Psychosexual Theory

Freud's psychosexual theory (1923, 1938) was one of the first theories to address social and emotional development in children. Underpinning Freud's theory is a structured personality made up of the id, ego, and superego; as a child interacts

Table 8.1   Theories Related to Social-Emotional Development for Early Childhood

Theory	Theorist	Basic Premise
Psychoanalytic	Sigmund Freud (1856–1939)	Focused on early emotional and social experiences and influence on later development.
Psychosocial	Erik Erikson (1902–1994)	Early experiences are determinants of personality; stage-related psychological conflicts must be resolved to move to next stage.
Behaviorism	Ivan Pavlov (1849–1936), John Watson (1878–1958), B. F. Skinner (1904–1990)	Behavior influenced by external rewards and punishments.
Social learning	Albert Bandura (1925–present)	Use knowledge of past experiences to determine consequences of future behavior; reciprocal learning experiences and self-regulation are important.
Cognitive-developmental/ constructivist	Jean Piaget (1896–1980)	Cognitive stages of development.
Sociocultural	Lev Vygotsky (1896–1934)	Emphasis on human relationships, historical cultural influences, and social experiences on development.
Ecological systems	Uri Bronfenbrenner (1917–2005)	Importance of considering bioecological influences on development in addition to family, community, society, and culture.

with parents and the world, these personality components become integrated in five developmental stages. The id is the source of individual's basic biological urges (needs, desires); this is the largest part of the child's mind. A child behaves in order to meet these pleasure-seeking energies, and this psychosexual energy, or libido, becomes the driving force behind behavior. The ego, which emerges in infancy, is the conscious, rational portion of the mind and personality. During early childhood, between the ages of 2 and 6 years, Freud proposed the emergence of the superego, or conscience, through communication and interactions between the parent and child. The superego's job is to mediate the demands of the id, the child's environment, and the conscience (Freud, 1938).

During early childhood, children move from the anal to the phallic stage of development. Toilet training is the major issue during the anal stage (ages 1–3 years), and how parents manage this issue of control of both urine and feces impacts the child's developing personality. Too many demands or shame might bring about a child who strives to control their world and, in later life, an adult who needs either extreme order or extreme messiness and disorder (Freud, 1938).

During the phallic stage, ages 3–6 years, Freud determined that children develop pleasure in genital stimulation and begin to feel a desire for the opposite-sex parent (Oedipus complex). As the child begins to avoid punishment for these feelings in their social world, they begin to align themselves with the same-sex parent (Electra complex). The superego forms as a result of this conflict and resolution.

According to Freud, children may develop maladaptive emotions and behaviors when they become overwhelmed during either of these stages. They may unconsciously act out to have their perceived needs met; Freud theorized that children can become fixated, or stuck, in one of these stages. Therapists working with children need to be thorough in assessing behavioral issues such as inappropriate thumb sucking or control of urine or feces, as these may be signals that the child needs intervention. Freud's theory has been criticized for its overemphasis on sexual feelings as well as the lack of a research base. In addition, Freud never actually studied children—only adults.

Psychosocial Theory

Erik Erikson, an early protégé of Freud who departed from Freud's emphasis on sex in the developing child, postulated that personality develops in a series of stages, but the social experience of the child over a lifetime has the greatest influence on personality development. Erikson's psychosocial theory (1950), also in the psychodynamic domain, has had a profound influence in explaining the social and emotional development of children.

Erickson proposed that individuals experience a psychological conflict during each of eight stages of psychosocial development. Each child seeks to resolve the conflict emotionally and socially at each stage, on a continuum from negative to positive; individuals emerge with psychological strengths or more negative and possibly maladaptive outcomes. How parents manage these psychological conflicts in early development will impact whether the child will attain a positive or negative outcome for each stage. Although this is not an all-or-nothing resolution, the resolution of the conflict at each stage will have an impact on succeeding stages.

From approximately ages 1½ to 3, children are in Erikson's second stage of development, autonomy versus shame and doubt. As children begin to gain independence, they begin to make choices such as what they like and what they want to wear. Through daily activities such as dressing, eating, and play, children discover they have abilities and skills; they develop a sense of personal control and self-reliance. Success at this stage is the virtue of will, the belief that they can act intentionally and independently, and is the foundation for self-esteem (Gross & Humphreys, 1992). Children who are allowed choices and some control by parents and caregivers develop a sense of autonomy. If parents and caregivers are patient, encouraging, and supportive when a child fails or becomes discouraged, the child feels competent and secure—the resolution is positive psychosocially for this child within this stage. If a parent or caregiver does not allow the child to choose or controls the child's daily activities (e.g., does everything for the child), then the child does not develop feelings of control or competence. Children who are overly criticized and never provided an opportunity to assert themselves may begin to feel a sense of shame and begin to doubt their abilities and competence. Early on, children who fall into the negative end of the continuum for this stage begin to lack self-esteem.

Initiative versus guilt is Erickson's third psychosocial stage. Children at this stage (ages 3–5 years) begin to assert control and power more frequently in their environment through self-directed play, planning activities, accomplishing tasks, and social interaction with other children. Imagination, make-believe play, and asking questions are significant and meaningful activities; positive cognitive and social-emotional development are dependent upon these behaviors. When adults reinforce a child's sense of initiative by giving the child freedom and encouragement to play or commending the child's efforts, the child begins to develop a sense of competence, feel more secure in his or her ability to make decisions, and lead others. Success at this stage leads to the virtue of purpose; purpose and initiative are positive attributes that will positively impact the child throughout the lifespan. Some parents and other caregivers (teachers, grandparents, others) may find these active behaviors and assertiveness to be aggression (Bee, 1992); they may try to protect the child through control or criticism. This type of reaction may lead the child to test the limits placed upon them (defensiveness) or withdraw and experience feelings of guilt. In addition, if parents ignore a child's questions, treat them as trivial, or even embarrass the child, the outcome might be feelings of guilt and possibly maladaptive behaviors.

Psychosocial theory focuses on feelings and emotions as well as the attitudes about self and others that children develop; it is an important theory when counselors are assessing childhood issues. Erikson believed that poorly resolved outcomes at these two stages could be resolved more adequately if conditions were right (Broderick & Blewitt, 2006). Interventions targeted at increasing autonomy and initiative by therapists may be useful in therapy. Since many children lack verbal skills and the cognitive ability to link thoughts, feelings, and behaviors, play therapy is often used as an effective form of intervention. In addition, counselors can assist parents and other stakeholders in their very critical roles in shaping children's social and emotional development; this would include filial therapy. Teaching parents, caregivers, teachers, and others about the dynamics of social-emotional development and the importance of using warm and nurturing behaviors is essential in positive social and emotional development in early childhood.

Case Study—Chloe

Chloe began having behavioral and physical problems at age 3 years. Chloe's immediate family consists of dad, mom, and older sister. At age 3, her father began working 2 weeks on and 2 weeks off. Chloe, who attended preschool 3 days a week, began to resist going to school at age 4 years. Her behavior worsened that year; she threw fits and fought with her mother and defied her teacher at school. She also developed severe constipation. Chloe's family moved later that year for her father's work; her behavior worsened. She fought with her mother often and refused to have a bowel movement using the toilet. A pediatrician confirmed

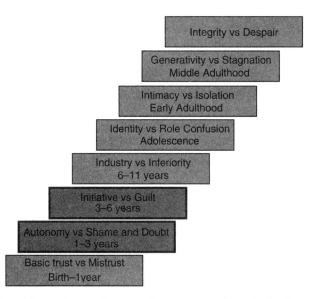

Figure 8.1 Erikson's psychosocial stages and period of development.

there was nothing physically wrong with Chloe and suggested counseling. Chloe received play therapy services for 8 weeks, and her behavior improved significantly. She began using the toilet for bowel movements again.

From a psychodynamic perspective, what was going on with Chloe? How and why did play therapy improve her behavior and toilet habits?

Ecological Systems Theory

In an effort to explain the complexities of development within the social context, Bronfenbrenner (1979) developed ecological systems theory. Ecological systems theory posits that individuals develop within a complex stratum of interconnected systems. The developing individual is engaged in some of these systems directly (e.g., family, school, work); some impact the person indirectly because of policies or resources (Newman & Newman, 2015, p. 52). Bronfenbrenner (2004) revised his theory, characterizing it as a bioecological model in which the child's genetic make-up and predispositions join with environmental factors at numerous levels to mold development. Additionally, Bronfenbrenner added that the environment not only shapes the individual's development but the developing person also influences his or her environment; he called this bidirectional influence (Bronfenbrenner & Morris, 2006). These layers include the microsystem, mesosystem, exosystem, and the macrosystem (refer back to Figure 2.1).

The microsystem, the innermost environmental level, is characterized by the numerous activities, roles, and interpersonal relationships experienced by the developing individual. In early childhood, there are multiple microsystems including family (including the extended family in collectivist cultures), preschool or childcare, neighborhood play areas, and social gatherings. Bidirectional influences during early childhood have an enduring influence (Collins, Macoby, Steinberg, Hetherington, & Bornstein, 2000). A child's behavior may affect an adult's behavior; a friendly and easygoing or obedient child is more likely to evoke positive parental response, whereas an irritable or cranky child may receive more a more negative response from parents. The third-party phenomena occur when an individual within the microsystem impacts a two-person relationship within that same system (one parent impacts the child–other parent relationship). This influence can be positive when parents are supportive and encouraging, but it can be detrimental when parents are in discord (Caldera & Lindsey, 2006). The mesosystem, the second level of Bronfenbrenner's model, represents the interrelationships among two or more of the settings in the microsystem. This could be an interaction between family and preschool or home and peer groups. In each of the interrelationships, there is bidirectional influence. Early parental involvement in preschool or daycare, or the lack thereof, will impact the developing the child in early childhood.

The exosystem, or third layer in ecological systems theory, consists of the settings that do not contain the developing individual, but these do affect the experiences of the person indirectly. These settings include the extended family, friends, and neighbors; they also include community organizations and services, religious institutions, and the workplace. An example of the influence on the developing child in such a setting might include the sick leave policy for the parent; if there is no paid sick leave, parents may have difficulty in adequately meeting the child's health-care needs. Settings may work together to offer positive influence in the developing child; the outcome for the developing child may be negative when families are isolated socially or do not engage in community activities (Coulton, Crampton, Irwin, Spilsbury, & Korbin, 2007).

The macrosystem, or the outermost layer of Bronfenbrenner's model, consists of culture (including values, beliefs, customs, and traditions), laws, economy, social policies, media, political, and other influential systems impacting the developing child. Priority given to meet the needs of the developing child affects the support he or she might receive at the inner levels of the model (Berk, 2010). Any shift at this outer level may impact the developing child. An example of a social policy (at both the federal and state levels) that impacts a child in early childhood is the Medicaid reimbursement for pediatricians and family practitioners. Only 11% reported that the reimbursement for developmental screenings during well-child visits covered the costs (Olson et al., 2002).

Bronfenbrenner posited that within his ecological systems model the environment is dynamic and ever changing. The developing individual may experience a change in role or settings; he called these shifts in context, or ecological transitions. During early childhood, the divorce of the child's parents would cause such an ecological transition. In their longitudinal study on the impact of divorce, Wallerstein, Lewis, and Blakeslee (2000) found that children may learn to cope with the divorce of their parents, but, as the children grow and develop, they might experience negative influences from the divorce as they embark on romantic relationships during

BOX 8.2 CLASS ACTIVITY: ADLERIAN EARLY RECOLLECTIONS

Adler believed that individuals all have a basic need to belong and to feel significant within a social context. He believed that early childhood social experiences, especially within the family constellation, would shape a child's worldview and attitude toward life and others. Adler thought that children who misbehaved were actually discouraged and that the discouragement may lead back to experiences during early childhood. By asking a client to determine their early recollections (ERs), therapists begin to determine how this client views himself or herself and the world, how he or she expects life to unfold, and what he or she expects of others (including the therapist). Use of early recollections can be used with clients of any age, and they provide a glimpse into the developmental process and the influence of early experiences in determining what Adler called the individual's style of life.

Activity

This activity can be done in pairs (students) in the classroom, and it takes about 15 minutes to complete. The instructor would want to leave about 5–10 minutes to discuss the activity and its application to early childhood social and emotional development and counseling interventions.

1. Ask one partner, the client, to close his or her eyes and to practice some deep breathing for a minute or two, trying to become grounded and clear his/her mind.
2. Ask the client to remember as far back as he or she can, particularly recollections, or memories, of specific incidents that occurred in early childhood—their very first memory. Ask the client to remember as many details as possible, including thoughts and feelings at the time. Ask, "If we took a snapshot when that happened, what would we see? How did you feel?" At least three ERs are needed to find an individual's pattern of behaviors or themes that appear in the recollections. The process should not be rushed. Counselors are suggested to pay attention to themes and elements such as context, content, people, and feelings.

   Counselors can even make ERs a memory game or an activity in which you ask the client to make up a story about when he or she was small. For nonverbal children or clients, ask them to produce drawings or some other type of artistic media (sand tray, clay, etc.).
3. Ask pairs to discuss the activity and their process. The instructor can link some of the shared memories to the importance of social experiences in early childhood and how they shape a person's personality.

adulthood. Other examples of ecological transition would include entering day-care, starting school, or moving. Each of these transitions brings some type of impact to the developing child, and these changes may have a longitudinal affect in the child's life.

Case Study—Alex

Alex, age 5 years, has been having difficulty in school since he started full-day kindergarten classes. His parents receive weekly teacher reports with descriptions of Alex's behavior: losing his temper easily, arguing with and actively defying the teacher and classroom aide, and deliberately distracting students sitting around him until they yell at him to stop, after which he becomes annoyed and angry until he does something to "get that kid back." Alex's family has moved numerous times in the last year due to his father's job loss and the need to be closer to treatment options to address the medical needs of Alex's younger brother, who was born prematurely. As you begin to think about what might be contributing to Alex's difficulty in school, what steps would be necessary to ensure all avenues are explored and assessed to determine Alex's current social-emotional development?

SCREENING AND ASSESSMENT

Researchers studying clinically significant social-emotional and behavioral problems of young children under the age of 5 years have reported prevalence rates between 9.1% (Lavigne, Lebailly, Hopkins, Gouze, & Binns, 2009) and 12.1% (Egger & Angold, 2006) and up to 19.8% (Weitzman, Edmonds, Davagnino, & Briggs-Gowan, 2014). With such high prevalence rates, one would think that a strong emphasis would routinely be placed on early screening and assessment for social-emotional problems during early childhood. Carter, Briggs-Gowan, and Davis (2004) stated that this is often not the case due to "societal nurturance of the myth that childhood, and especially early childhood, is a 'sacred,' happy time. Thus, parents, day care providers, teachers, pediatricians, and mental health care providers often avoid discussion of children's mental health needs" (p. 110). Lavigne et al. (2009) postulated that this dismissal of preschool aged children's mental health needs "may be related to (a) the belief that preschoolers 'grow out of' such problems; (b) the absence of psychometrically sound, developmentally sensitive assessments for this age group; and (c) the absence of effective treatments for some early-developing conditions" (p. 316). Further, Carter et al. (2004) pointed out additional complicating factors that must be considered when developing assessments: "(1) the rapid pace of developmental transitions and growth in early childhood; (2) a lack of guidelines for integrating data that are gathered from different sources and methods; (3) limited information for determining levels of impairment both within the child and within the family system; and (4) difficulty assessing child functioning within the relevant relational and cultural contexts" (p. 111).

This section examines the multidimensional factors that need to be considered when assessing social-emotional development in early childhood, along with examples of specific screening and assessment tools that could be adopted for use by counselors working with early childhood populations. For a comprehensive comparison of various screening tools, social-emotional assessment tools, and observational tools in relation to appropriate age range, administration, and psychometric data, see Squires (2012) and Tryphonopoulos, Letourneau, and Ditommaso (2014).

Developmental assessments used with toddlers and preschoolers often assess cognitive factors but should also include parent rating scales to assess adaptive behavior and social-emotional functioning of the child (McDevitt & Ormrod, 2013) as well as relational factors to gain a holistic picture of a child's social-emotional development. Wheeler et al. (2013) stressed the importance of examining relationship at this early age: "Observation of parenting interactions is critical because of the non-verbal nature of the parent–infant relationship during the time before the child has full mastery of verbal language" (p. 353). Examining the impact of prevention efforts with preschool-aged children, Hillen, Gafson, Drage, and Conlan (2012) asserted that this age group "has been found to benefit the most from early intervention" (p. 418). A proactive approach to screening and assessment can help identify social-emotional issues early, thereby mitigating potential long-term negative impact on a child's development.

In a study examining the social-emotional problems of children in foster care, Hillen et al. (2012) administered the Ages and Stages Questionnaire: Social-Emotional (ASQ:SE), a caregiver-completed questionnaire for use with children from 3 to 66 months of age to evaluate functioning across seven domains: self-regulation, compliance, communication, adaptive functioning, autonomy, affect, and interaction with people. Results revealed that 60.5% of children had unmet needs related to social-emotional functioning, and each was offered follow-up individual sessions where predefined interventions were conducted, including developmental advice to the caregiver to better understand the child's needs while in placement. The newest revision, ASQ:SE-2, has been normed on a large diverse population of 14,074 children and their families, has been translated into Spanish, and boasts ease of scoring for professionals.

Given the wide range of emotional and behavioral problems reflected in a child's social-emotional development, a parent questionnaire, the Infant-Toddler Social Emotional Assessment (ITSEA), was created to systematically evaluate one competence domain and three broad problem domains: externalizing, internalizing, and dysregulation (Visser et al., 2010). A benefit of this questionnaire is the diagnostic accuracy with which children are placed into groups: externalizing subscales (i.e., activity-impulsivity, aggression/defiance, peer aggression); internalizing subscales (i.e., depression-withdrawal, general anxiety, separation distress, inhibition to novelty); competency subscales (i.e., attention, compliance, imitation/play, prosocial peer interactions); and a dysregulation subscale (i.e., negative emotionality; Briggs-Gowan & Carter, 1998). Accurate assessment on a specific subscale allows a counselor to follow up with tailored interventions specific to the emotional or behavioral problem rated highest on the instrument.

The ITSEA has also been translated into Spanish. For more detail on the psychometric properties of the ITSEA, see Carter, Briggs-Gowan, Jones, and Little (2003).

Stressing the importance of identifying problems during early childhood, Wittmer, Petersen, and Puckett (2013) expressed concern regarding the use of valid screening instruments by qualified individuals to screen and diagnose. We are reminded of utilizing best practices related to multifaceted assessment through the "assessment of the *products* of children's work, the manner in which a child engages in work and play (*processes*), and the extent to which the child accomplishes expected goals or outcomes (*performance*)" (p. 323).

BOX 8.3   ASSESSMENT RECOMMENDATIONS

McDevitt and Ormrod (2013) prompted us to use the following recommendations when interpreting tests, assessments, and artifacts: "When evaluating children's responses to your own assessments, use explicit scoring criteria. Keep in mind both the advantages and limitations of paper-and-pencil tests. Interpret standardized tests cautiously. Remember that validity and reliability apply to all assessments. Watch for cultural bias in assessments. Assess environments to determine the extent to which they support children's well-being" (pp. 53–54).

Since parents and caretakers are often are the first to see potential developmental changes or delays in their children, including within the areas of social and emotional development, many are left asking the question: How do I seek out screening and intervention for my child when I think something is wrong? Accessing potential referral sources may assist caretakers in developing these answers quickly. One would expect that pediatricians, daycare centers, and early childhood centers like Early Head Start programs would have this type of information available. Parents are also able to directly contact early intervention programs within their communities and request a free evaluation to determine eligibility for early intervention services.

The reauthorized Individuals with Disabilities Education Act (IDEA) was signed into law in 2004, allowing for provisions to protect the education of children with disabilities. The act describes federal assistance provided to states to ensure the screening and evaluation of all children, along with requirements for educational intervention of qualified children ranging in age from preschool to grade 12. For more detailed information on the specific statutes, regulations, and documents related to IDEA, see the U.S. Department of Education website (http://idea.ed.gov).

BOX 8.4   CLASS ACTIVITY: BUILDING OBSERVATION SKILLS

Arrange for an opportunity to observe the interactions between preschool-aged children at a daycare center, early childhood development center, or preschool or elementary school. As you observe students in the class, listen for the quality of their storytelling and narratives, note how children interact with each other during times of cooperative play and during times of conflict, observe how they handle frustration, and describe how they interact with the adults present. Detail specific observations related to the following: eye contact, personal space, facial expressions, posture, and other nonverbal behaviors. Be sure to keep separate notes regarding what you observed and what you think the behavior means. As children grow out of early childhood, what differences would you expect to see in these observations?

INFLUENTIAL FACTORS IN SOCIAL AND EMOTIONAL DEVELOPMENT

Neuroscience

Neuroscience, or the science of the brain and its functions, has made huge strides in explaining brain–behavior relationships. Neuroscience informs psychological theories of emotional and social development; knowledge of compatible theories enhances therapeutic interventions with children.

Through modern technology, specifically magnetic resonance imaging (MRI) and functional magnetic resonance imaging (fMRI), researchers know that the brain is not simply one organ but is multiple systems that control every facet of human functioning, including emotions. Early on, MacLean (1970) proposed his theory of the triune brain, made up of the reptilian, limbic, and mammalian brains; each had specialized structure and function. According to his theory the limbic brain processed emotions; this idea still influences ideas about social-emotional development. Szalavitz and Perry (2010) discussed the idea of the triune brain, and particularly the importance of social experience, in the healthy and positive emotional development. A body of research also indicates that several emotional systems and chemical circuitry systems control emotions. LeDoux (1996) and Panskepp (1992) identified seven emotional circuits that operate integrally and semiautomatically when triggered, producing a wide range of emotions (Broderick & Blewitt, 2006, p. 116). The seven emotional circuits produce the emotional responses of seeking, fear, rage, lust, nurturance, sorrow, and play.

Szalavitz and Perry (2010) stated, "It is in our nature to nurture and be nurtured" (p. 3). These researchers and authors proposed that humans are genetically predisposed to be empathetic, but this requires experience and interaction with others. The foundation for the development of empathy is the ability to respond to and control stress. The development of multiple brain systems that have varying levels of conscious control regarding stress and its resulting emotions are interdependent but work simultaneously. Szalavitz and Perry focused on the interaction between the limbic system, the heart of emotions and relationships, and the cortex, the area of the brain in charge of abstract thought and reasoning. When a stressor is introduced, the response network literally takes over all parts of the brain, and the different regions and systems work together to respond to the perceived threat. As the authors stated, "It is impossible to actually separate rational thought from emotion" (p. 18). LeDoux (1996) believed that, in some instances, the limbic system may actually bypass the cortex, leading to emotional and less rational responses. His findings suggest that humans are wired to respond to some events emotionally. Szalavitz, Perry and LeDoux all agree that once the circuitry of stress is established from the limbic system to the cortex, emotions begin to take over much of the child's consciousness. This begets a repetition of negative emotions and poor emotional regulation.

Dopamine, an excitatory neurotransmitter in the brain, is connected with stress; early in mother–child relationship the release of this chemical literally pulls the mother and child together. This release of dopamine causes both the mother and child to crave affection (essential for bonding); the presence of this neurotransmitter puts child and mom in alert mode. Another chemical, oxytocin, is then released. This protein is known to be present when two intimate people interact, and it acts to calm and to help both parties feel pleasure (which comes from limbic part of the brain). This chemistry gets stronger and bonding becomes more intense when the interaction is one of nurturance between the two people. If the child is away from the caregiver, he or she may experience unpleasant feelings and go into stress mode. However, Szalavitz and Perry (2010) believe that small breaks in contact are essential and these small breaks followed by reconnection help children to learn to manage small and repeated doses of stress. This stress is not in and of itself a negative, and these early experiences enable the brain to manage and moderate stress. Social contact is necessary for children to develop resilience and healthy emotional development; without it the stress response system runs amok. When children get no pleasure or soothing from reciprocal social interactions, they often fail to develop empathy (Szalavitz & Perry, 2010). Similarly, during early childhood, children who have developed neural circuitry that is emotionally charged have a difficult time gaining rational control over these emotions.

Szalavitz and Perry (2010) outlined numerous preventive measures for the optimal social-emotional development of children as well as the development of empathy. Nurturing families are at the heart of healthy emotional development, so educating parents on the impact of nurturing quality time, the importance of play with children, teaching their children perspective taking, and use of reasoning when disciplining children are all important. Perry (2013) researched and wrote

BOX 8.5   PLAY THERAPY

Play is an intense sensory experience that provides physical stimulation. Furthermore, it is a developmentally appropriate means for building adult–child relationships; developing cause–effect thinking, which is critical to impulse control; processing stressful experiences; and learning social skills. It provides a sense of power and control, which can be used to solve problems and to master new experiences, ideas, and concerns. This in turn builds feelings of confidence and accomplishment (Drewes & Schaefer, 2010).

Play is a natural language for children and provides a medium for working out problems and communicating with others and is an appropriate modality for therapy. Play therapy is an active interpersonal relationship between a child and a counselor trained in this procedure. In play therapy selected play materials are provided and the development of a safe relationship for the child to fully express and explore self through play is facilitated (Landreth, 2012). A counselor uses toys and play as the primary vehicles to communicate with children (Kottman, 2009). Landreth explains that play is children's symbolic language, which offers a way to express experiences and emotions in a natural, self-healing process. The manipulation of toys allows children to show how they feel about themselves, people, and events in their lives more adequately than talking (Henderson & Thompson, 2011).

Filial therapy allows the parents to become therapeutic agents. Parents learn to conduct child-centered play sessions with their children to help overcome or prevent problems. Counselors train parents in basic child-centered play therapy skills. This approach allows the parent to become the primary agent of change in the child's life using the natural existing bond between the parent and child. Furthermore, parents become empowered, reducing feelings of guilt and helplessness. In addition, parents learn to interact with their children in more effective ways and have a greater potential for long-lasting changes as they continue to use acquired skills and attitudes with their children (Landreth & Bratton, 2006).

Filial therapy is most frequently used in early childhood but can also be used with children up to ages 10 to 12 years. The therapeutic goals for children are to (a) eliminate the presenting problems, (b) develop positive interactions between parents and their children, and (c) increase communication, coping, and problem-solving skills within families (Van-Fleet, 2005, p. 4).

Play therapy is used with a wide range of ages; however, it is most frequently used with children between the ages of 3 to 12 years. It is effective with children experiencing a wide variety of social, emotional, behavioral, and learning problems. As well, play therapy can be helpful with children struggling various life situations: abuse or neglect, adoption, divorce of parents, family violence, grief, hospitalization, chronic or terminal illness, parental deployment, severe trauma, and posttraumatic stress disorder brought on by such events as war, earthquakes, car accidents, and kidnapping (Vernon, 2009). It has been identified as the treatment of choice in school, mental health, agency, developmental, hospital, residential, and recreational settings (Carmichael, 2006; Reddy, Files-Hall, & Schaefer, 2005). The Association for Play Therapy (2015) purports that play therapy helps children:

- Become more responsible for behaviors and develop more successful strategies
- Develop new and creative solutions to problems
- Develop respect and acceptance of self and others
- Learn to experience and express emotion
- Cultivate empathy and respect for thoughts and feelings of others
- Learn new social skills and relational skills with family
- Develop self-efficacy and thus a better assuredness about their abilities

Play therapy allows children to be approached and understood from their appropriate developmental level. Children, especially in early childhood, often are inaccessible verbally and developmentally unprepared to express their feelings. The counselor assumes the responsibility to know how to communicate effectively with young children. Play therapy offers children the opportunity to respond and to bridge gaps between their experiences, thoughts, and feelings. It allows children to express these in concrete form (Leggett, 2012).

extensively on the use of play therapy, including his most recent neurosequential model of therapeutics, where he described play therapy as an effective therapeutic intervention to be used with children during early childhood to deal with maladaptive feelings and behaviors. Perry said that the sooner in the developing child's life the intervention is introduced, the more likely it is to be effective. Perry also advocated for filial therapy, described as parents engaging in guided interactions between themselves and their children, or participating in structured play therapy (Gaskill & Perry, 2014, p. 181). Numerous studies have shown such therapy to be effective with children who may have developed behavioral or social-emotional issues (Bratton, Ray, Rhine, & Jones, 2005; Landreth, 2012; Ray, Bratton, Rhine, & Jones, 2001). Ideally, early childhood, during ages 3 to 6 years, is an optimal time for effective intervention. Perry (2013) suggested that improvement can take place later through therapy, but it is a long, difficult, and frustrating process for families and children. LeDoux (1996) had similar thoughts, suggesting that "psychotherapy may be a long process because of the asymmetry in connections between the cortex and the amygdala" (p. 265).

Attachment

Attachment theory pulls together several threads to weave an integrated understanding about human emotions and social and emotional development. Furthermore, it addresses the organization of behaviors as an adaptive strategy of individuals to emotional and social experiences that strain coping capacities (Grossmann & Grossmann, 1991). John Bowlby (1969) introduced the concept of attachment when studying the bond between a mother and her infant. The early attachment forms the foundation for later relationships. This attachment stimulates pleasure, joy, and comfort in being near the loved one. These experiences give children expectations about other attachment figures and guide close relationships throughout early childhood, adolescence, and across the lifespan. Ainsworth (1989) went further to state that attachments beyond infancy transcend the caregiver's relationship to future relationships. For young children, this influences the relationships they are building with siblings and peers as well as other adults. For this group, those relationships outside of their parents or caregivers generally begin with those they play side by side with. The young children who form close friendships and relationships are able to further develop their social skills. They are able to interpret and understand the nonverbal clues given by their peers. They respond appropriately, use eye contact, use the names of their peers, and touch to get attention. When in disagreement with their peers, these young children will justify their actions, compromise, and even share their beliefs. When introduced to a new group, they will observe others until they develop a sense of their place in the group. However, young children without these skills can feel rejected, can appear withdrawn, and might be unable to listen to others or to express their wishes. They may have a negative sense of self (Henderson & Thompson, 2011). Therefore, it is evident that, despite the attachment being secured early in the child–parent bond, it is also reflected in the child's interpersonal relationships across the lifespan (Schneider, Atkinson, & Tardif, 2001). Erikson (1950) went further in his conclusions that this bond facilitates trust and sets the stage for young children's expectations that the world is a good and pleasant place to be.

Bowlby's (1969) theory of attachment begins with the first attachment relationship an infant has with the caregiver, generally the parent. This first relationship evolves into an attachment system between the infant and caregiver to serve the purpose of keeping the infant safe and ensuring survival. This attachment system serves three functions. First, it maintains proximity between the child and the caregiver, providing a nurturing emotional bond called proximity maintenance. It also provides the potential for protection that is ongoing, called secure base. Finally, it creates a safe haven during times of distress (Broderick & Blewitt, 2015). In infancy a baby cries and clings to convey need to the caregiver. In early childhood, the young child may call out, reach, or point to the caregiver to gain the same response. The caregiver may respond differently to different cries or calls, assessing the level and type of need, recognizing that the cry or call can serve multiple purposes. Mary Ainsworth and her colleagues' study of the different kinds of attachments to caregivers provided the identification of three patterns of infant response to changes in social situations (Ainsworth, 1989; Ainsworth, Blehar, Waters, & Walls, 1978). Later research identified a fourth category. These patterns represent attachments that infants need for proximity upkeep, a secure base, and safe haven. These styles of attachment are secure, anxious-ambivalent-insecure, avoidant-insecure, and disorganized-disoriented-insecure. See chapter 6 for more details about attachment theory in birth and infancy.

In young children, those who respond happily to interaction and reunion with caregivers characterize a secure attachment. They explore the environment knowing their caregivers are nearby or will be returning. During moments of distress they search for the caregiver and trust they will receive a response. With anxious-ambivalent-insecure attachment, children will search for their caregivers but then struggle to get away. They are reluctant to explore the environment, become upset easily, and display frustration with the response received from caregivers. In avoidant-insecure attachment, children avoid or ignore the caregivers' presence and show little response when the caregivers are close. They display few strong emotional outbursts and may avoid or ignore a caregiver's response to them. Children with disorganized-disoriented-insecure attachment can demonstrate unpredictable behavior. They appear unable to cope or to be comforted when stressed. They seem confused or fearful around caregivers (Brotherson, 2005).

This intense relationship characterizes a secure attachment, considered the basic building block for future socialization. Infants show their attachment to others by search for proximity or nearness to their caregivers and by crying when they are separated. The return of the caregiver is greeted with happiness. As young children grow, preschoolers seek help to accomplish tasks such as putting on clothes and tying shoes. In this stage of early childhood, their dependency will center more on striving for recognition and approval from caregivers and significant others (Broderick & Blewitt, 2015; Orton, 1997). In moderation, healthy signs of dependency are essential to socialization. Securely attached children feel free to grow increasingly independent. However, it is also developmental appropriate for certain situational factors or stresses to cause young children to regress to an earlier stage of development. An example of such fluctuation can been seen when a 3-year-old considers himself a "big boy" but wants to climb on his mother's lap and pretend he is a baby when his new sibling arrives. Likewise, a 5-year-old who has been attending preschool for 2 years may refuse to let go of her father's hand on the first day of kindergarten. Variations may occur in individual children and children from different cultures and family backgrounds. Some cultures and families may not express feelings as openly as other cultures or families. Furthermore, some cultures encourage children to be independent and therefore these children may demonstrate feelings of security differently (Wittmer, 2011).

Case Study—Jack

Jack, an African American 5-year-old boy, is the oldest child of a military family. Jack's stepfather is on active duty and was recently deployed for the second time. His mother cares for his three siblings at home. Jack's kindergarten teacher reports her concern that Jack withdraws from interaction with other students and pulls away from small groups. In some instances he becomes disengaged, and on occasion he crawls under the tables or desks. He refuses to respond to any requests. During these episodes Jack voices a concern for his mother's well-being and a request for her presence. Therefore, Jack's mother will come to school to help calm him.

Could the number of changes in Jack's life—military moves, stepfather replacing father, second deployment, and entry into kindergarten—create these episodes? Is this tied to separation anxiety, or is it an attachment issue? How can this be handled in a school setting?

Play

During early childhood, play serves an extremely important function. Play allows young children to rehearse behaviors similar to real work (i.e., nonplay context), thereby developing behaviors and skills that support social training (Lester & Russell, 2010). Various theorists suggest that play increases social development (Brunner, 1972; Flavell, Flavell, Green, & Moses, 1990; Lillard, 1993; Mead, 1934; Singer, 1973; Smilansky, 1968; Vygotsky, 1978). Parten's (1932) observation of social play identifies six categories of social play: unoccupied behavior, onlooker behavior, solitary play, parallel play, associative play, and cooperative play. Many consider the first two categories as nonplay behavior and the last three categories as indicators of social participation (Frost, Wortham, & Reifel, 2012). *Unoccupied behavior* is a form of observational play or watching others play. A small child might occupy him- or herself and take moments to observe a momentarily interesting play activity of those around. With *onlooker behavior*, the young child spends more time observing the play of others. The child will focus on a particular group of children, stand in proximity to the play, and talk to and ask questions of those in play. However, the child does not join in their play. *Solitary play* takes place when the child plays independently and alone. No effort is made speak to other children playing near or to move closer to others. In *parallel play* the play continues to be independent; however, the chosen form of play draws the child naturally closer to other children. The selection of toys is similar to those of the children around, but the play is not modified or influenced by those near. Instead the child plays beside others rather than with them. *Associative play* introduces play with other children including communication, borrowing and loaning, attempts to control which the child may or may not play in a group, and without play is not organized and does not have goals. *Cooperative play* ushers in a group that is organized for the purpose of making material products, attaining a competitive goal, dramatizing adult and group life situations, or playing formal games (Frost et al., 2012). The most advanced form of social play is *sociodramatic play*. Together children carry out imitation and drama as well as *fantasy play*. This form of play allows children to represent real-life events while including imagination in carrying out the roles. Sociodramatic play uses all of a young child's developmental attributes, combining physical, cognitive, and social play to carry out themes or events (Frost et al., 2012).

Preschool children are often not able to verbalize their feelings. Play allows them a safe means to express their full range of feelings through the activities they engage in; play can be used to express positive and aggressive feelings. It also helps children to reduce their anxiety and understand traumatic experiences. Through their play, children learn to cope with their feelings and develop mastery and control (Landreth & Homeyer, 1998).

Sociodramatic play provides a major contribution to emotional development. Taking on roles in dramatic play, children are able to act out relationships and experience the feelings of the people in the roles they are playing. Furthermore, they can express emotional responses to the roles and understand differences in feelings, thereby promoting emotional development, a greater feeling of power, a sense of happiness, and a positive feeling of self (Cohen & Stern, 1983; Piers & Landau, 1980; Singer & Singer, 1977).

Self-Regulation

Self-regulation generally refers to the capability to control or direct one's attention, thoughts, emotions, and actions. These intentional skills grow rapidly in early childhood and are critical to a healthy development and for early school success (McClelland & Cameron, 2012). Experiential and biological factors contribute to the development of these skills. Other contributing factors associated with self-regulation are the demographic characteristics of the child, parent, or household and parenting factors. The skills become apparent early in a child's life and increase in sophistication over time. Parenting practices and styles influence children's self-regulations skills (Piotrowski, Lapierre, & Linebarger, 2013).

The process of regulation depends on both cognitive and emotional advances with self-awareness and self-recognition. First, there is the representational thought and then the emotional response to wrongdoing. Young children construct internal accounts of standards and rules for everyday behavior. These standards or rules are somewhat different within families and cultures; however, every culture maintains them and reinforces them when they are violated. By the age of 2 years, children begin to develop the cognitive level of maturity to understand and remember some rules, and they begin to show signs of holding back or regulating behaviors. This demonstrates the important milestone of demonstrating the capacity for emotional response to wrongdoing and the beginning of conscience development. Children's emotional responses to rule violations are linked with how they perceive their parents' reactions. Furthermore, they will shape the development of morals (Broderick & Blewitt, 2015).

However, shame and guilt can lead to different consequences. The feeling of guilt has been associated with increase in empathy, positive reparative action, constructive problem solving, and low defensiveness and anger. Shame is connected to hiding or denial of wrongdoing, blaming others or situations, displaced aggression, externalizing behavior, low self-esteem, and psychiatric disorders (Tangney, Stuewig, & Mashek, 2007).

BOX 8.6   THE IMPACT OF POVERTY IN EARLY CHILDHOOD

According to data from the U.S. Census Bureau, 21.8% of U.S. children lived in poverty in 2012, with the percentage of those under the age of 5 years at 25.1%. The hardest hit are children of color, with 37.9% of African American children and 33.8% of Hispanic/Latino/a children living below the poverty line (below $23,492 for a family of four; Duncan & Magnuson, 2011). Although psychologists, sociologists, neuroscientists, and counselors all agree that children living in poverty experience detrimental consequences, they differ in the pathways and processes through which the impact on development occurs. What does appear clear is evidence that young children seem to suffer greater negative impact than their older counterparts. Poverty adversely affects academic outcomes of children, especially during early childhood (APA, 2013). Additionally, children living in poverty are at greater risk for developing behavioral problems including impulsiveness, poor social skills, aggression, and attention issues (APA, 2013). Approximately 9% of young children receive specialty mental health services, with prevalence rates doubling yearly from the ages of 2 through 4 years (Lavigne et al., 1996). Children from families living in poverty are at even greater risk for developing behavioral, emotional, and social problems (Knapp, Ammen, Arstein-Kerslake, Poulsen, & Mastergeorge, 2007). However, many of these young children who are on welfare are less likely than their peers to receive developmental services (Zimmer & Panko, 2006). To address these critical social and emotional needs of young children living in poverty, policy action is needed in all systemic levels. Beginning with the macro system (e.g., policies, laws) and working toward the micro system of the developing child, prevention services for all at-risk families are needed. An agenda is needed for social-emotional development in young children consisting of (a) access to services; (b) comprehensive screening, assessment, treatment, and support services; (c) research-based interventions with children and families; (d) increased and flexible funding for services and support; and (e) training and development for all providers in all settings so they may better know and understand the needs of young children (Cooper et al., 2009, p. 10).

Case Study—Anna

Anna, a 4-year-old Hispanic girl, was adjusting well to her new daycare with exception to her swimming class. Her father informed the swim teacher that they had discontinued swimming lessons during the summer because Anna had become so terrified of the water. Anna's father could not think of any reason for her fear. As a young child she commonly played in the wading pool with her older brother. She had never seen anyone get hurt in the water or drown. The swim teacher indicated that a counselor might be helpful in determining the root of Anna's fear.

Could Anna's reaction be based on comments or reactions of her family or her older brother's teasing? Would it be important to know if Anna had other fears? Due to her development level, what consideration should be given to the assessment and intervention process?

Social-Emotional Development and Bullying

Storey and Slaby (2013) pointed out a growing concern that adversely impacts the social-emotional development of today's children: bullying. We are cautioned to consider the fact that bullying can start in early childhood, despite the belief of many that bullying is a problem relegated to the experiences of older children. As such, it is imperative for educators and counselors to be aware not only of signs of bullying but also of ways to assist parents in addressing bullying with their children at home through the teaching of social skills. Storey and Slaby (2013) point out that counselors can incorporate the following social skills into counseling sessions or parent workshops and trainings:

> [Parents] can help their children develop **empathy** by labeling feelings, modeling helping behaviors and kindness, and encouraging their children to help others and show kindness. They can help their children develop **assertiveness** by encouraging them to ignore minor provocations, to keep cool during confrontations, and to say no to playmates' demands. Parents can help their children **solve problems** by encouraging them to think ahead about alternative responses to bullying and to anticipate the consequences. They can prepare their children to be helpful bystanders. (p. 54)

BOX 8.7   EMPATHY ACTIVITY: MODELING HELPFULNESS

Discuss the ways that bullying behavior leads both the child who bullies and the child who is bullied to disrespect each other and feel like enemies, rather than friends. Then use pictures, stories, puppets, or other concrete props to model examples of the many ways that children and adults can show that they care about others' feelings and can help each other. Discuss how caring behaviors make both the giver and the receiver feel happy and good (Storey & Slaby, 2013, p. 35; see also Adams, 2011).

KEY COUNSELING POINTERS FOR SOCIAL AND EMOTIONAL DEVELOPMENT IN EARLY CHILDHOOD

A counseling intervention plan bridges the gap between assessment and treatment. Traditional talk therapy alone is generally unsuccessful with this age group, especially within the development context of young children. As these children progress through developmental changes, even small age increments can translate into significant differences in behavior. Therefore counselors must be knowledgeable about child development and be able to distinguish between pathology and normal developmental deviation and minor crises (Peterson, 2009). Furthermore, a young child's ability to respond to counseling interventions may depend on his or her level of developmental function. To facilitate the verbal and nonverbal expressions of thoughts, feelings, and behaviors it will be necessary for counseling approaches be designed especially for preschoolers that use a combination of talk and play (Gladding, 2005; Leggett, 2009; Orton, 1997).

Landreth (2012) stated that play is children's work, toys are their works, and play is their language. Gladding (2005) stressed the importance of using expressive, creative arts to help young clients engage in the counseling process. He added that the combination of theory and practice in flexible ways will facilitate change and problem solving. Creative experiences such as painting, writing, dancing, or playing enhance counseling and encourage young clients to participate. The following list contains some strategies, interventions, and activities that counselors may consider using with preschoolers. It reflects only general categories and could include many others.

Art therapy
Bibliotherapy
Board games
Child–parent relationship therapy
Dance/movement therapy
Drama therapy
Drawing/art activities
Filial therapy
Music therapy
Play therapy
Puppetry
Role-playing
Sandtray therapy
Storytelling

In addition, consideration must be given to the young child's culture. Prior to entering school, young children may not have encountered other cultures, family structures, housing arrangements, or lifestyles. They reflect the culture in which they were raised. Therefore, the child's cultural frame of reference and mode of communication are crucial variables. Determining if any cultural variables are relevant should be assessed first. All treatment plans should be examined for cultural implication, and strategies that focus on cultural strengths should be considered when working with young children of diverse backgrounds (Henderson & Thompson, 2011).

BOX 8.8 BIBLIOTHERAPY WITH YOUNG CHILDREN

Counselors who work with young children may consider using bibliotherapy. This strategy may be used with individual clients, dyads, and small groups of children ages 4 to 6 years. It requires the selection of appropriate books for this development level. The best books for this strategy are generally picture books. These books combine visual and verbal narratives, telling a story with both words and pictures. Books selected do not have to be therapeutic books but can be general children's literature. They can be found easily in bookstores or libraries. The topics of the books can focus on feelings or match the needs of clients' situations. This may require that counselors spend time perusing libraries, bookstores, and the Internet and dialoguing with librarians, bookstore clerks, and others with knowledge of children's literature. Websites such as Picturing Books (http://www.picturingbooks.com), If the Book Fits…Read It (http://www.librarypatch.com/2013/10/if-book-fits-read-it.html), and Bibliotherapy Education Project (http://bibliotherapy.ehs.cmich.edu) provide picture book databases to guide counselors' selections. These explorations of literature will reveal books covering various topics, storylines, and feelings.

Cain's (2000) *The Way I Feel* may be a good book to begin with if there is some uncertainty about getting started. This book illustrates children experiencing a range of 13 emotions including frustration, shyness, jealousy, and pride. For young children this type of book creates a common vocabulary to begin a dialogue about feelings (Leggett, 2009). Begin by reading the book to the clients and exploring the various feelings described, and then ask them to identify two or three feelings they are dealing with along with an examination of each. Follow up with the young client by asking him or her to identify one feeling he or she would most like to change. This strategy allows clients to select the issue most important to them and allows counselors to understand the situation from the clients' perspectives (Leggett, 2009).

BOX 8.9   DRAWING WITH YOUNG CHILDREN

Often, counselors may want to consider drawing with young children ages 4 to 6 years to provide a means for them to respond to abstract questions and ideas in a concrete fashion. This activity is suited for early childhood and can be used with individuals, dyads, and small groups. Communicating through drawings is appropriate with clients who may have limited vocabularies, who may have difficulty expressing complex concepts, or whose primary language is not English. It should also be noted that the amount of time it takes for clients to progress through the counseling process might vary. Therefore, the counselor should provide adequate time for each client to fully complete his or her illustration and time to discuss the details of each drawing. Furthermore, it would not be unusual to have young clients progress through only one or two steps during one session (Leggett & Ybañez, 2009). Drawing materials can consist of simple art supplies such as plain paper or drawing paper of various sizes, pencils, crayons, markers, pastels, or colored pencils.

Invite young clients to draw a picture of their day or something they wish to share. Allow sufficient time for the clients to create their drawings. Counselors can utilize silence at this time to track or narrate actions, feelings, and intensity. Follow up with a discussion of the details in the drawings. Allow clients to provide the details and descriptions. The dialogue may be enriched with relationship questions and assessment questions (Degges-White and Davis, 2011, Leggett & Ybañez).

SUMMARY

The early childhood years are considered among the most important developmental periods, laying the foundation for later competences in many areas. During these preschool years, language, self-awareness, peer relationships, autonomy, and independence become apparent (Schroeder & Gordon, 2002). Social and emotional development in early childhood is multivariate, composed of skills and knowledge that are integrated across social, emotional, and cognitive development. Theorists vary on the basic premise of what impacts social and emotional development. Neuroscience explains emotional and social development in new ways that elaborate brain–behavior relationships in early childhood and neuroscience-enhancing therapeutic interventions. Since many important and critical steps occur during these early childhood years, attention and understanding should be given to social and emotional development of this group.

USEFUL WEBSITES

AbilityPath.org
http://www.abilitypath.org/areas-of-development/social-emotional/what-is-social-emotional.html
American Academy of Pediatrics
http://www.aap.org/en-us/about-the-aap/
Center on the Developing Child—Harvard University
http://www.developingchild.harvard.edu
Center on the Social and Emotional Foundation for Early Learning
http://csefel.vanderbilt.edu/
Child Development Institute
http://childdevelopmentinfo.com/child-development/erickson/
Child Trends
http://www.childtrends.org
Early Childhood Development Headstart Program
http://www.eclkc.acg.hhs.gov/hsla/tta-system/teaching/eecd
Early Childhood Research and Practice
http://ecrp.uiuc.edu/index.html
Early Childhood News
http://www.earlychildhoodnews.org
National Center for Children in Poverty—Columbia University
http://www.nccp.org
PBS: Social and Emotional Development
http://www.pbs.org/wholechild/abc/social.html
The Long Reach of Early Childhood Poverty—Stanford University
https://web.stanford.edu/group/scspi/_media/pdf/pathways/winter_2011/PathwaysWinter11_Duncan.pdf
Tools of the Mind
http://www.toolsofthemind.org
Zero to Three
http://www/zerotothree.org/

REFERENCES

Adams, E. J. (2011). Teaching children to name their feelings. *Young Children*, *66*(3), 66–67.

Ainsworth, M. D. (1989). Attachments beyond infancy. *American Psychologist*, *44*, 709–716.

Ainsworth, M. D., Blehar, M. C., Waters, E., & Walls, S. (1978). *Patterns of attachment*. Hillsdale, NJ: Erlbaum.

American Psychological Association (APA). (2013). *Effects of poverty, hunger, and homelessness on children and youth*. Retrieved from http://www.apa.org/pi/families/poverty.aspv?item=2

Aries, P. (1962). *Centuries of childhood: A social history of family life*. New York, NY: Knopf.

Ashdown, D. M., & Bernard, M. E. (2011). Can explicit instruction in social and emotional learning skills benefit the social-emotional development, well-being, and academic achievement of young children? *Early Childhood Education Journal*, *39*, 397–405.

Association for Play Therapy. (2015). *Play therapy makes a difference*. Retrieved from https://a4pt.site-ym.com/?PTMakesADifference

Barrera, I., & Corso, R. (2002). *Cultural competency as skilled dialogue: Strategies for responding to cultural diversity in early childhood*. Baltimore, MD: Brookes.

Bee, H. L. (1992). *The developing child*. London, UK: Harper Collins.

Berk, L. E. (2010). *Development through the lifespan* (5th ed.). Boston, MA: Allyn & Bacon/Pearson.

Bowlby, J. (1969). *Attachment and loss; Vol. 1. Attachment*. London, UK: Hogarth.

Bratton, S., Ray, D., Rhine, T., & Jones L. (2005). The efficacy of play therapy with children: A meta-analytic review of treatment outcomes. *Professional Psychology: Research and Practice*, *36*(4), 376–390.

Briggs-Gowan, M. J., & Carter, A. S. (1998). Preliminary acceptability and psychometrics of the Infant-Toddler Social and Emotional Assessment (ITSEA): A new adult report questionnaire. *Infant Mental Health Journal*, *19*(4), 422–445. doi:10.1002/imhj.21327

Broderick, P. C., & Blewitt, P. (2015). *The lifespan: Human development for helping professionals* (4th ed.). Upper Saddle River, NJ: Pearson.

Bronfenbrenner, U. (1979). *The ecology of human development*. Cambridge, MA: Harvard University Press.

Bronfenbrenner, U. (2004). *Making human beings human: Bioecological perspectives on human development*. Thousand Oaks, CA: Sage.

Bronfenbrenner, U., & Morris, P. A. (2006). The bioecological model of human development. In W. Damon & R. M. Lerner (Eds.), *Handbook of child psychology: Vol. 1. Theoretical models of human development* (6th ed., pp. 793–828). Hoboken, NJ: Wiley.

Brotherson, S. (2005). Understanding attachment in young children. *Bright Beginnings*, *6*. Retrieved from https://www.ag.ndsu.edu/pubs/yf/famsci/fs617.pdf

Brunner, J. S. (1972). Nature and used of immaturity. *American Psychologist*, *27*, 1–28.

Cain, J. (2000). *The way I feel*. Seattle, WA: Parenting Press.

Caldera, Y. M., & Lindsey, E. W. (2006). Coparenting, mother-infant interaction, and infant-parent attachment relationships in two-parent families. *Journal of Family Psychology*, *20*, 275–283.

Carmichael, K. D. (2006). *Play therapy: An introduction*. Upper Saddle River, NJ: Merrill.

Carter, A. S., Briggs-Gowan, M. J., & Davis, N. O. (2004). Assessment of young children's social-emotional development and psychopathology: Recent advances and recommendations for practice. *Journal of Child Psychology and Psychiatry and Allied Disciplines*, *45*(1), 109–134.

Carter, A. S., Briggs-Gowan, M. J., Jones, S. M., & Little, T. D. (2003). The Infant-Toddler Social and Emotional Assessment (ITSEA): Factor structure, reliability, and validity. *Journal of Abnormal Child Psychology*, 31(5), 495–514.

Center on the Social Emotional Foundations for Early Learning. (2010). *Handout 1.2 Definition of social emotional development CSEFEL Infant-Toddler Module 1.* Retrieved from http://csefel.vanderbilt.edu/resources/training_infant.html

Cohen, D. H., & Stern, V. (1983). *Observing and recording the behavior of young children*. New York, NY: Teachers College Press.

Collins, W. A., Macoby, E. E., Steinberg, L., Hetherington, E. M., & Bornstein, M. H. (2000). Contemporary research on parenting: The case for nature and nurture. *American Psychologist*, 55, 218–232.

Cooper, J. L., Masi, R., & Vick, J. (2009). *Social-emotional development in early childhood: What every policymaker should know*. New York, NY: National Center for Children in Poverty, Columbia University.

Coulton, C. J., Crampton, D. S., Irwin, M., Spilsbury, J. C., & Korbin, J. E. (2007). How neighborhoods influence child maltreatment: A review of literature an alternative pathways. *Child Abuse and Neglect*, 31, 1117–1142.

Degges-White, S., & Davis, N. (2011). *Integrating expressive arts into counseling practice: Theory-based interventions*. New York, NY: Springer Publishing Company.

DeNavas-Walt, C., Proctor, B. D., & Smith, C. (2012). *Income, poverty and health insurance in the United States: 2012* (U.S. Census Bureau, Current Reports, 60–245). Washington, DC: U.S. Government Printing Office.

Drewes, A., & Schaefer, C. E. (Eds.). (2010). *School-based play therapy* (2nd ed.). Hoboken, NJ: Wiley.

Duncan, G. J., & Magnuson, K. (2011). *The long reach of early childhood poverty*. *Pathways*, Winter, 22–27. Retrieved from https://web.stanford.edu/group/scspi/_media?pdf/pathways/wintern_2011/PathwaysWinter11_Duncan.pdf

Egger, H. L., & Angold, A. (2006). Common emotional and behavioral disorders in preschool children: Presentation, nosology, and epidemiology. *Journal of Child Psychology and Psychiatry and Allied Disciplines*, 47(3–4), 313–337. doi:10.1111/j.1469-7610.2006.01618.x

Erikson, E. (1950). *Childhood and society*. New York, NY: Norton.

Flavell, J. H., Flavell, E. R., Green, F. L., & Moses, L. J. (1990). Young children's understanding of fact beliefs versus value beliefs. *Child Development*, 23, 915–928.

Freud, S. (1923). *The ego and the id*. London, UK: Hogarth.

Freud, S. (1938). *An outline of psychoanalysis*. London, UK: Hogarth.

Frost, J. L., Wortham, S. C., & Reifel, S. (2012). *Play and child development* (4th ed.). Upper Saddle River, NJ: Pearson.

Gaskill, R. L., & Perry, B. D. (2014). The neurobiological power of play: Using neurosequential model of therapeutics to guide play in the healing process. In C. A. Maldiochi & D. A. Crenshaw (Eds.), *Play and creative arts for attachment problems* (pp. 178–194). New York, NY: Guilford Press.

Gladding, S. T. (2005). *Counseling as an art: The creative arts in counseling* (3rd ed.). Upper Saddle River, NJ: Pearson.

Green, E. J., & Drewes, A. A. (2014). *Integrating expressive arts and play therapy with children and adolescents.* Hoboken, NJ: Wiley.

Greenfield, P. M. (1994). Independence and interdependence as developmental scripts: Implications for theory, research, and practice. In P. M. Greenfield & R. Cocking (Eds.), *Cross-cultural roots of minority child development* (pp. 1–37). Hillsdale, NJ: Lawrence Erlbaum.

Gross, R. D., & Humphreys, P. (1992). *Psychology: The science of mind and behaviour.* London, UK: Hodder & Stoughton.

Grossmann, K. E., & Grossmann, K. (1991). *Attachment quality as an organizer of emotional and behavioral responses in a longitudinal perspective in attachment across the life cycle.* New York, NY: Routledge.

Henderson, D., & Thompson, C. (2011). *Counseling children* (8th ed.). Belmont, CA: Brooks/Cole.

Hillen, T., Gafson, L., Drage, L., & Conlan, L. (2012). Assessing the prevalence of mental health disorders and mental health needs among preschool children in care in England. *Infant Mental Health Journal, 33*(4), 411–420. doi:10.1002/imhj.21327

Knapp, P. E., Ammen, S., Arstein-Kerslake, C., Poulsen, M. K., & Mastergeorge, A. (2007). Feasibility of expanding services for very young children in the public mental health setting. *Journal of the American Academy of Child and Adolescent Psychiatry, 46*(2), 152–161.

Kottman, T. (2009). Play therapy. In A. Vernon (Ed.), *Counseling children & adolescents* (4th ed., pp. 123–146). Denver, CO: Love Publishing Company.

Landreth, G. (2012). *Play therapy: The art of the relationship* (4th ed.). New York, NY: Taylor & Francis Group.

Landreth, G. L., & Bratton, S. C. (2006). *Child-parent-relationship (c-p-r) therapy: A 10 session filial therapy model.* New York, NY: Taylor & Francis Group.

Landreth, G. L., & Homeyer, L. E. (1998). Play therapy behaviors of sexually abused children. *International Journal of Play Therapy, 7*(1), 49–71.

Lavigne, J. V., Gibbons, R. D., Christoffel, K. K., Arend, R., Rosenbaum, D., Binns, H., … Isaacs, C. (1996). Prevalence rates and correlates of psychiatric disorders among preschool children. *Journal of the American Academy of Child and Adolescent Psychiatry, 35,* 204–214.

Lavigne, J. C., Lebailly, S. A., Hopkins, J., Gouze, K. R., & Binns, H. J., (2009). The prevalence of ADHD, ODD, depression, and anxiety in a community sample of 4-year olds. *Journal of Clinical Child and Adolescent Psychology, 38*(3), 315–328. doi:10.1080/15374410902851382

LeDoux, J. (1996). *The emotional brain: The mysterious underpinnings of emotional life.* New York, NY: Simon & Schuster.

Leggett, E. S. (2009). A creative application of solution-focused counseling: An integration with children's literature and visual arts. *Journal of Creativity in Mental Health, 4,* 191–200.

Leggett, E. S. (2012). Play therapy. In J. Fox & R. Schirrmacher (Eds.), *Art & creative development for young children* (8th ed., p. 38). Stamford, CT: Cengage.

Leggett, E. S., & Ybañez, K. (2009). Expressive arts interventions: Draw a solution. In S. Degges-White & N. L. Davis (Eds.), *Integrating the expressive arts into counseling practice: Theory based interventions* (pp. 34–36). New York, NY: Springer Publishing Company.

Lester, S., & Russell, W. (2010). *Children's right to play: An examination of the importance of play in the lives of children worldwide*. Working Paper No. 57. The Hague, The Netherlands: Bernard van Leer Foundation.

Lillard, A. S. (1993). Pretend play skills and the child's theory of mind. *Child Development, 64*(2), 348–371. Retrieved from http://www.jstor.org/stable/1131255

MacClean, P. D. (1970). The triune brain, emotion, and scientific basis. In F. O. Schmidt (Ed.), *The neurosciences: Second study program* (pp. 336–349). New York, NY: Rockefeller University Press.

Maschinot, B. (2008). *The changing face of the United States: The influence of culture on early child development*. Washington, DC: Zero to Three.

McClelland, M., & Cameron, C. E. (2012). Self-regulation in early childhood: Improving conceptual clarity and developing ecologically valid measures. *Oregon State University Human Development & Families Studies, 6*, 136–142.

McDevitt, T. M., & Ormrod, J. E. (2013). *Child development and education* (5th ed.). Upper Saddle River, NJ: Pearson.

Mead, G. H. (1934). *Mind, self, and society*. Chicago, IL: University of Chicago Press.

National Child Abuse and Neglect Data System Child File, FFY. (2006). *Based on NCCP analysis on unduplicated cases*. Ithaca, NY: Cornell University, National Data Archive on Child.

Newman, B. M., & Newman, P. R. (2015). *Development through life: A psychosocial approach*. Stamford, CT: Cengage.

Olson, A. L., Kemper, K. J., Kelleher, K. J., Hammond, C. S., Zuckerman, B. S., & Dietrich, A. J. (2002). Primary care pediatrician's roles and perceived responsibilities in the identification and management of maternal depression. *Pediatrics, 110*(6), 1169–1176.

Orton, G. H. (1997). *Strategies for counseling with children and their parents*. Pacific Grove, CA: Brooks/Cole.

Panskepp, J. (1992). Toward a general psychobiological theory of emotions. *Behavioral and Brain Sciences, 5*, 407–467.

Parten, M. B. (1932). Social participation among pre-school children. *Journal of Abnormal and Social Psychology, 27*, 243–269.

Perry, B. D. (2013). *Bonding and attachment in maltreated children: Consequences of emotional neglect in children*. Houston, TX: Child Trauma Academy. Retrieved from http://www.childtrauma.org

Peterson, J. (2009). The individual counseling process. In A. Vernon (Ed.), *Counseling children & adolescents* (4th ed., pp. 81–146). Denver, CO: Love Publishing Company.

Piers, M. W., & Landau, G. M. (1980). *The gift of play*. New York, NY: Walker.

Piotrowski, J. T., Lapierre, M. A., & Linebarger, D. L. (2013). Investigating correlations of self-relation in early childhood with a representative sample of English-speaking American families. *Journal of Child & Family Studies, 22,* 423–436. doi:10.1007/s10826-012-9595-z

Ray, D., Bratton, S., Rhine, T., & Jones, L. (2001). The effectiveness of play therapy: Responding to the critics. *International Journal of Play Therapy, 10*(1), 85–108.

Reddy, L., Files-Hall, T., & Schaefer, C. E. (Eds.). (2005). *Empirically based play interventions for children.* Washington, DC: American Psychological Association.

Schneider, B. H., Atkinson, L., & Tardif, C. (2001). Child-parent attachment and children's peer relations: A quantitative review. *Development Psychology, 37,* 86–100. Retrieved from http://www.psy.miami.edu/faculty/dmessinger/c_c/rsrcs/rdgs/attach/schneider.peerAttach.dp2001.pdf

Schroeder, C. S., & Gordon, B. N. (2002). *Assessment & treatment of childhood problems: A clinician's guide* (2nd ed.). New York, NY: Guilford.

Singer, D., & Singer, J. (1977). *Partners in play: A step by step guide to imaginative play in children.* New York, NY: Harper & Row.

Singer, J. (1973). *The child's world of make-believe.* New York, NY: Academic Press.

Smilansky, S. (1968). *The effects of sociodramatic play on disadvantaged children: Preschool children.* New York, NY: Wiley.

Squires, J. (2012). Assessing young children's social and emotional development. In S. J. Summers & R. Chazan-Cohen (Eds.), *Understanding early childhood mental health: A practical guide for professionals* (pp. 99–123). Baltimore, MD: Brookes Publishing.

Storey, K., & Slaby, R. (2013). *Eyes on bullying in early childhood.* Waltham, MA: Education Development Center, Inc. Retrieved from http://www.promoteprevent.org/files/resources/Eyes%20on%woByllying%20in%20Early%20Childhood_1.pdf

Szalavitz, M., & Perry, B. D. (2010). *Born for love.* New York, NY: William Morrow/HarperCollins.

Tangney, J. P., Stuewig, J., & Mashek, D. J. (2007). Moral emotions and moral behavior. *Annual Review of Psychology, 58,* 344–372.

Tryphonopoulos, P. D., Letourneau, N., & Ditommaso, E. (2014). Attachment and caregiver–infant interaction: A review of observational-assessment tools. *Infant Mental Health Journal, 35*(6), 642–656. doi:10.1002/imhj.21461

U.S. Census Bureau, Population Division. (2014). *Annual estimates of the resident population by sex, age, race and Hispanic origin for the United States: April 1, 2010 to July 1, 2013.* Retrieved from http:www.census.gov/popest/data/national.asrh/2013/index.html

U.S. Department of Education. (n.d.). *Building the legacy: IDEA 2004.* Retrieved from http://idea.ed.gov

VanFleet, R. (2005). *Filial therapy: Strengthening parent–child relationships through play* (2nd ed.). Sarasota, FL: Professional Resource.

Vernon, A. (2009). *Counseling children & adolescents* (4th ed.). Denver, CO: Love Publishing Company.

Visser, J. C., Smeekens, S., Rommelse, N., Verkes, R. J., Van Der Gaag, R. J., & Buitelaar, J. K. (2010). Assessment of psychopathology in 2- to 5-year olds: Applying the Infant-Toddler Social Emotional Assessment. *Infant Mental Health Journal*, *31*(6), 611–629. doi:10.1002/imhj.20273

Vygotsky, L. S. (1978). *Mind on society*. Cambridge, MA: Harvard Press.

Wallerstein, J. S., Leves, J. M., & Blakeslee, S. (2000). *The unexpected legacy of divorce: A 25 year landmark study*. New York, NY: Authors.

Watson, R. I., & Lindgren, H. C. (1979). *Psychology of the child and the adolescent* (4th ed.). New York, NY: Macmillan.

Weitzman, C., Edmonds, D., Davagnino, J., & Briggs-Gowan, M. J. (2014). Young child socioemotional/behavioral problems and cumulative psychosocial risk. *Infant Mental Health Journal*, *35*(1), 1–9. doi:10.1002/imhj.21421

Wheeler, R., Ludtke, M., Helmer, J., Barna, N., Wilson, K., & Oleksiak, C. (2013). Implementation of the PICCOLO in infant mental health practice: A case study. *Infant Mental Health Journal*, *34*(4), 352–358. doi:10.1002/imhj.21395

Wittmer, D. (2011). Attachment: What works? 24. *What Works Brief Series*, Center on the Social Emotional Foundations for Early Learning. Retrieved from http://csefel.vanderbilt.edu/resources/what_works.html

Wittmer, D. S., Petersen, S. H., & Puckett, M. B. (2013). *The young child: Development from prebirth through age eight* (6th ed.). Upper Saddle River, NJ: Pearson.

Zimmer, M. H., & Panko, L. M. (2006). Developmental status and service use among children in the child welfare system: A national survey. *Archives of Pediatrics & Adolescent Medicine*, *160*, 183–188.

PART 4

Middle Childhood

Middle Childhood: Physical and Cognitive Development

Matt Glowiak and Mark Aaron Mayfield

Middle childhood is marked with many awkward stages. As children transition from one age to the next, their clothes become tighter, hormones run rampant, and some body parts are disproportionate to others. Similar to the stages of childhood explained in previous chapters, middle childhood is also met with significant change. As such, there are very specific developmental milestones that occur as a result of this typical lifespan development. Many of these changes are rapid and may arise seemingly unbeknownst to the child; hence, they are met with excitement by some children and with disdain by others.

It is important to recognize that development is a mix of both common and unique experiences. Santrock (2007) explained this well: "Each of us develops partly like all other individuals, partly like some other individuals, and partly like no other individuals. Most of the time our attention is directed to an individual's uniqueness. But as humans, we have all traveled some common paths" (p. 6). Everybody grows older. Everybody lacks fine motor skills at infancy. And everybody's brain and body continues to change throughout life. Not everybody has the same genetic makeup. Not everybody lives in the same environment (e.g., culture, neighborhood). And not everybody is exposed to the same opportunities and challenges.

Although professionals differ by about a year or so in defining precisely when middle childhood begins and ends, a general consensus, which will serve as the parameters within this book, is between ages 6 and 12 years (Croft & Smith, 2008). During this time a particular sequence of events occurs that is the product of human physiology. An infant's brain simply cannot grasp advanced algebra, just like children in middle childhood do not possess the brain anatomy to think critically (Palmer, 2007).

Physical and cognitive development during middle childhood do not occur in a vacuum; rather, they are impacted by a host of factors, including heredity, culture, gender, and nutrition (Croft & Smith, 2008). As such, contemporary literature has indicated the importance of viewing this development along the domains of the physical, cognitive, social, and emotional components of being (Cairns, 2000; Magnusson, 1985; Magnusson & Stattin, 2006). Zembar and Blume (2009) described middle childhood as

> both a stage and a pathway to future development. The metaphor of transition (i.e., the pathway) involves looking at markers (i.e., milestones) along the way in order to measure developmental progress. Developmental milestones in middle childhood can be classified into one of four broad domains—physical, cognitive, affective, or social development. (p. 19)

Each of these domains works independently and in combination with one another and responds accordingly. Success in one domain may contribute toward success in another, whereas shortcomings may contribute toward subsequent shortcomings, ultimately compromising growth and development (Office of Disease Prevention and Health Promotion, 2015). Deviations from the natural process may result in any variety of complications with implications lasting up to an entire lifetime (Schore, 1999). Therefore, it is essential that professional counselors have an understanding of middle childhood from each of these domains independently and in combination with one another.

This chapter provides specific information pertinent to the physical and cognitive development of children undergoing middle childhood, and the following chapter addresses the social and emotional components. You are encouraged to think back to your own middle childhood experience as each domain is further elaborated upon. Table 9.1 provides a brief summary of developmental milestones that will be discussed throughout the next two chapters.

Case Study

Keisha is an African American female who is quickly approaching 11 years old. She lives in a blue-collar suburb of a major midwestern city and attends the local middle school. Keisha lives with her biological parents and is the oldest of four siblings. Both of Keisha's parents work 40+ hours a week, and often Keisha is left to care for her siblings until her parents return home. Recently, Keisha has been acting out, refusing to help out around the house, often locks herself in her room, and has had significant mood swings. On several occasions, Keisha has physically aggressed against her siblings, which has caused her parents to seek out counseling. During the initial counseling session Keisha demonstrates some resistance, stating that she is "just fine" and "acts like any other kid" her age. She then goes on to explain how kids her age should not have the added responsibility of caring for their siblings when they already have schoolwork and other obligations.

Consider Keisha's story, along with your experience thus far as a counseling student. What are your initial assumptions? What more information might you need to develop a clearer conceptualization? (Note: The case of Keisha will be

Table 9.1	Developmental Milestones		
Physical	**Cognitive**	**Social**	**Emotional**
Increase in height and weight/loss of baby fat	Language is used for communication	Begin formal education	Self-conscious emotions of pride and guilt become clearly integrated by personal responsibility
Loss of baby teeth/emergence of permanent teeth	Preoperational: ages 2 to 7 Concrete operations: ages 7 to 11	Distance from the household setting and parents/caregivers	Shame is experienced when one violates a standard outside of one's control
Increased muscle strength and coordination/improved fine and gross motor skills	Ability to work beyond cognitive ability with assistance from MKO	Begin forming meaningful relationships	Pride motivates children to take on further challenges
More rapid neurological transmissions (myelinization)/improved motor and perceptual motor skills	Understand that someone else's perspective of direction may mirror their own	Can recognize that others may hold different perspectives, values, etc.	Guilt prompts children to make amends and strive for self-improvement
Increased stamina	Object permanence, decentration, reversibility, classification, seriation, spatial reasoning	Later middle childhood children begin to develop opposite and same-sex attraction	Explain emotion by referencing internal states
Hormonal changes	Understanding conservation of number, mass, length, and area		Awareness of the diversity of experiences
Early puberty begins (ages 10–12 for some children)	Scaffolding		Emotional expression does not necessarily correlate to one's true, current feelings Rise in empathy Gains in emotional self-regulation Development of self-efficacy

Source: Developed through resources cited by Ames, Ilg, and Baker (1988); Brooks (1999); Cole & Cole (1996); Croft and Smith (2008); Ozretich and Bowman (2001); Steinberg (1993); Institute for Human Services for The Ohio Child Welfare Training Program (2007); University of Kansas (2015).

discussed at different points throughout this chapter. We encourage you to keep notes on your thoughts and your assumptions concerning Keisha's case and compare them with our assertions during the final section of this chapter and the next.)

PHYSICAL DEVELOPMENT

Physical Changes

Physical development in middle childhood is a product of biological and neurophysiological development, the refinement of perceptual and motor skills, and physical health (Zembar & Blume, 2009). Although physical growth is not as rapid in middle as it is in early childhood, it is still substantial. In relative consideration, middle childhood is the second most significant period of growth in terms of physical structure and brain size development.

Growth Progression

Exiting the rapid growth progression of early childhood, middle childhood (ages 6–12 years) is a period of relative stability in preparation for the impending pubescent changes. Campbell (2011) suggested that middle childhood is defined by a uniquely specific set of biological characteristics that begin as early as age 5 years and as late as age 7 years:

- Eruption of permanent molars
- Development of adult locomotor efficiency (e.g., walking, running, balance)
- Rebound in adiposity (increase in body mass index [BMI])
- Near completion of growth in brain volume
- Onset of cortical maturation in the brain
- Development of axillary hair and odor

Along with these key developmental markers, middle childhood is an important transitional period, bridging early childhood to adolescence and then to adulthood. This stage brings an increase in cognitive development, an increase in emotional regulation, and an increase in relative social independence (Campbell, 2011).

Transition of Primary to Permanent Teeth

Middle childhood is also the period in which children's permanent (adult) teeth begin to push through the gums and replace primary (baby) teeth (Oswalt & Dombeck, 2015). Children generally lose their incisors (front teeth) around age 6 years and then their molars between ages 10 and 12 years. Between these ages their smiles resemble those of jack-o-lanterns, missing every other tooth or multiple teeth in a row. Although many young children are excited to lose their teeth so that the Tooth Fairy may exchange them for hard cash or another award, the pushing through of permanent teeth does cause discomfort and swelling of the gums. Because this is a critical period for the onset of permanent teeth, good oral hygiene is encouraged.

Bone Development

During middle childhood, bones continue to broaden and lengthen. The average child will grow anywhere from 2 to 3 inches per year throughout this stage, which is why 25–40% of children between ages 8 and 12 years experience what is most commonly referred to as growing pains (Oswalt & Dombeck, 2015). Such pains are real and are consequently the result of the bones growing at a faster rate than the surrounding muscles and tendons. It is typical for boys to enter middle childhood taller than girls but for the opposite to happen on the transition out. This awkward phase dies out during adolescence when most boys reclaim their taller frame.

Muscular Development

Similar to the aforesaid rapid bone growth is the substantial muscle and body mass growth of the prepubescent child. The average child gains in the area of 6–7 pounds per year (Oswalt & Dombeck, 2015). Boys are slightly heavier and taller than girls until the age of around 9 or 10 years, when girls begin their adolescent growth spurt. Boys will be more muscular in development (e.g., larger torso and bigger hands, feet, chest), whereas girls will begin to develop fat (e.g., buttocks, thighs; Campbell, 2011; Finkelstein, 2000). The additional fatty tissue prepares the girls for puberty. This difference becomes more pronounced throughout adolescence and adulthood.

Hormonal Changes

Along with the linear height and weight growth progressions, a significant hormonal event occurs within middle childhood. Andrenarche is marked by the increase of androgenic hormones produced by the adrenal glands (Finkelstein, 2000). The production of dihydroepiandrosterone (DHEA) becomes active in the middle child's circulation, thus making andrenarche "an endorcrinological marker of the juvenile transition" (Campbell, 2011, p. 328). The onset of andrenarche (typically around the age of 7 years) is paired with the somatic developments of permanent molars, rebound in adiposity, and the completion of growth in brain volume (Campbell, 2011). Though these stages can vary among individuals, each somatic stage is typically completed by the age of 7 or 8 years. Andrenarche can often be confused with the onset of puberty. Though there is no direct relation to andrenarche and puberty, "andrenarche is sometimes accompanied by the appearance of axillary and pubic hair, axillary odor, and increased secretion of sebum (sometimes causing acne)" (Finkelstein, 2000, p. 221), which falsely mirrors the beginning stages of puberty.

Sex Characteristics

Puberty is a period when primary and secondary sex characteristics undergo significant change. Primary sex characteristics include physical changes to the sex organs themselves (e.g., penis, testes, uterus, vagina), whereas secondary sex characteristics entail any visible changes that indicate adult maturation (Oswalt & Dombeck, 2010). The rate and extent of physical development of the gender-specific sexual body parts vary quite significantly from one child to the next. For instance, boys experience enlargement of the penis, prostate gland, seminal vesicles, and testes between the ages of 9 and 14 years. Spermarche occurs between ages 12 and 16 years, meaning that some boys will experience their first ejaculation during the final year of middle childhood. "For girls this includes the uterus starting to build a lining that will later be shed through the process of menstruation, and the vagina beginning to produce a mucus-like discharge" (Oswalt & Dombeck, 2015, para. 4). The first menstrual cycle typically begins between ages 10 and 15 years.

As children draw near to, and transition into, the earlier stages of puberty, they may "start feeling awkward or confused about their bodies" (Oswalt & Dombeck, 2015, para. 1). Responses may range anywhere from finding the changing of sex characteristics hilarious to becoming anxious to engaging in early sexual behavior. Because peers, teachers, parents, the media, and other key figures in their lives significantly influence children, it is imperative that they are educated on these sex characteristics and their transition accordingly.

BOX 9.1 SPECIAL DISCUSSION

As counselors, it is significantly important to pay attention to the potential irregularities present within our clients. The earlier appearance of secondary sexual characteristics presents concern inasmuch as it causes parents to discuss sexual development earlier than previously thought. Counselors must conceptualize and prepare for specific ways support can be given to families during this time (Finkelstein, 2000). Early menarche (8 years or younger) has been linked to familial conflict, stressful home life, paternal absences, and poor attachment (Boynton-Jarrett et al., 2013).

Case Study

Reflecting on Keisha's case it is important to note that Keisha, though almost 11 years old, is already 5'6" and close to 120 lb. Furthermore, Keisha's mom indicated that she has already entered puberty, as evidenced by starting menstruation several months earlier. How does this information expand your initial understanding of Keisha and her potential struggles therein? What challenges might Keisha be facing as an almost 11-year-old facing puberty?

LGBT Youth

Biology and social factors weigh significantly on children's gender identity. Consequent to hormonal changes that occur throughout middle childhood and early puberty, boys are driven toward a primarily masculine identity, whereas girls are driven toward a primarily feminine identity (Oswalt & Dombeck, 2010). Most children are comfortable with this and progress throughout their development with minimal to no distress. Lesbian, gay, bisexual, and transgender (LGBT) youth experience incongruence in that they may be physically one gender but experience themselves as the other or find themselves attracted to same-sex partners. Research exploring the biological factors associated with gender identity has already demonstrated how hormonal differences do exist between LGBT and heterosexual youth (Osmundson, 2011). As such, the *Diagnostic and Statistical Manual of Mental Disorders (DSM)* no longer cites homosexual identity as a diagnosable psychological disorder. The social and emotional implications for LGBT youth are discussed further in chapter 10.

MOTOR DEVELOPMENT

Gross Motor Skills

Gross motor development "refers to physical skills that use large body movements, normally involving the entire body" (Oswalt, 2015, para. 1). Development occurs as a result of the bone and muscle growth previously described in addition to a combination of other factors (e.g., brain development, cognitive development, experience). This period is a continuance from early childhood, wherein children continue to refine their large-scale body movements (e.g., walking, running). That is, they run faster and jump farther and higher. With the exception of balance and precise movements (e.g., hopping, jumping, skipping), boys develop these particular skill sets slightly faster than girls (Oswalt & Dombeck, 2015).

Middle childhood is a period when children also continue to refine their control over gross motor skills. According to Oswalt and Dombeck (2015), "they are able to gain this improved control and coordination due to increases in their flexibility (e.g., their range of movement in joints and muscles), balance, and agility (e.g., their ability to change their body's position, which requires a combination of balance, coordination, speed, reflexes, and strength)" (para. 3).

Further, they learn how to synchronize movements of their entire body. This allows them to participate in more advanced physical activities such as soccer karate, dancing, baseball, basketball, flag football, and diving. "First, I focus on one spot on the ball, Second, I plant my feet. Third, I wind back my right leg. Fourth, I swing forward. Fifth, I follow through past the focal point on the ball. The soccer ball flies forward." Individual and team sport training typically begin here, which is the start of competitive participation—where children may integrate a combination of cognitive, motor, and social skills.

Fine Motor Skills

Fine motor skills differ from gross motor skills with regard to the need for more advanced hand–eye coordination. According to Oswalt (2015), "Fine motor skills are necessary to engage in smaller, more precise movements, normally using the hands and fingers. Fine motor skills are different than gross motor skills which require less precision to perform" (para. 7). In this case, girls develop skills slightly faster than boys. Improvements during middle childhood may be witnessed in various tasks including handwriting (e.g., print, cursive), artistic ability (e.g., beading, building models, drawing, scrapbooking), playing a musical instrument, learning to touch type, playing complicated games (e.g., computer games, skill games, video games), and mastery of communication tools (i.e., computers, smartphones; Oswalt & Dombeck, 2015). With maturity and experience, children continue to further refine their skills.

THE IMPORTANCE OF A HEALTHY ENVIRONMENT

The environment in which middle childhood is experienced is extremely significant. A positive, nurturing environment is more likely to lead to positive outcomes, whereas a negative, threatening environment is more likely to lead to negative outcomes (Santrock, 2007). Depending on the child's internal ability to cope with stress and the severity of negative risk factors, consequences may result in which the brain may be physically altered while physical, social-emotional, and cognitive growth and development are compromised (Sander, 1987). Research with adult participants has revealed that predisease pathways leading toward various adult health and medical conditions have their roots in early and middle childhood (Schore, 1999).

THE IMPORTANCE OF GOOD NUTRITION AND PHYSICAL ACTIVITY

Nutrition and physical activity weigh heavily on middle childhood development. A world-renowned athlete may give birth to a child with exceptional athletic ability, but if that child partakes in unhealthy behaviors there is a great chance that another child who inherited less superior genes might actually demonstrate superior athletic ability over the child born with the genetic predisposition. Given the impact that the middle childhood experience has over one's life, it is important that good habits begin early (HealthyPeople.gov, 2015).

Nearly 15% of children ages 6–11 years are classified as obese (Croft & Smith, 2008). This percentage is on the rise and is the result of a variety of factors. The physical harm caused by this medical condition may include the following (Obesity Society, 2010):

- Insulin resistance
- Type II diabetes

- Asthma
- Hypertension
- High total and LDL cholesterol and triglyceride levels in the blood
- Low HDL cholesterol levels in the blood
- Sleep apnea
- Early puberty
- Orthopedic problems
- Nonalcoholic steatohepatitis

Each of these conditions, if untreated, may result in pervasive lifelong conditions that threaten the child's quality of life. Beyond these consequences are those that pose psychological harm. These will be discussed further in the next chapter.

At this age caregivers are primarily responsible for the healthy or unhealthy development of young children. Teachers, family members, family friends, and others may also do their part in helping (HealthyPeople.gov, 2015). It is not reasonable to assume that a 6- or 7-year-old will understand the difference between adequate and inadequate nutrition. If anything, children typically want to eat what tastes good regardless of how unhealthy it is. Sweets, soda, and salty snacks are only a few of many potentially harmful foods that children enjoy eating. Even more dangerous is the recent epidemic of fast food restaurants. Although a convenient alternative to cooking, fast food contains multiple times more calories and fat grams than most foods purchased from the grocery store (Santrock, 2007). McDonald's may call their kid's meal a "happy meal" because of the special toy in the box, but it should really be called the "unhappy meal" when the options selected are high in calories, fat, cholesterol, trans fats, carbohydrates, sugar, et cetera. Fortunately, many fast food restaurants are now offering healthier options that still appeal to children.

Before the advent of computers and video games, it was quite common for children to play outside all hours of the day and come in for bed late at night. Recent trends demonstrate that today's children prefer playing video games or watching television rather than participating in healthy, cardio-vascular activities (Santrock, 2007). By not promoting healthy eating habits and allowing children to remain stagnant for a vast majority of the day, parents are really giving their children a disadvantage in life (HealthyPeople.gov, 2015).

The benefits of diet and exercise are plenty. These include "stronger muscles and bones, a leaner body, and a lowered risk for type 2 diabetes" (Croft & Smith, 2008, p. 6). Programs such as NFL Play 60, the Presidential Youth Fitness Program, and Let's Move! are great ways to encourage children to engage in physical fitness. Activities offered through the school district, park district, YMCA and YWCA, and Boy and Girl Scouts provide great opportunities for the children to engage in various physical activities. They also offer opportunities for children to meet friends and enhance their social skills and emotional regulation. Children are not only physically healthier but also may experience elevated self-esteem, which improves social interactions (Santrock, 2007).

Case Study

Keisha lives in a very supportive environment, but her parents' work schedules do not (and cannot) allow them to be physically present most of the week. Subsequently, Keisha is tasked with caring for her siblings (ages 4, 6, and 8 years). Furthermore, Keisha and her siblings rely heavily on television, computers, and iPhones for entertainment and rarely get outside. Based on the information thus far, how would you evaluate Keisha's case?

COGNITIVE DEVELOPMENT

The physical changes experienced in middle childhood are nothing short of extraordinary; however, the changes experienced cognitively are oftentimes even more pronounced and noticeable. "Children's ability to consciously, thoughtfully and pro-actively choose to pursue goals (instead of simply reacting to the environment) appears during this developmental period" (Oswalt & Dombeck, 2015, para. 1). Those components contributing to cognitive development include intellectual and language development reasoning abilities and memory capacities (Zembar & Blume, 2009). During the middle childhood years, children continue to progress in each of these areas. For instance, children improve their consolidation of primary academic skills (e.g., reading, writing) while increasing logical thinking through concrete examples. Memorization and related skills also continue to improve during this time. As abilities in each of these core areas gradually increase, children become more apt to engage in more complicated, intricate activities.

The Nervous System

The nervous system is the central processing center by which people function. It is extremely complex and is composed of all the body's nerve tissues (Ophardt, 2003). These nerves transmit, receive, and initiate responses to various stimuli. Neurotransmitters allow such travel from one neuron to the next through synapses, the small gaps between cells, thereby taking on a domino-like effect where one signal triggers the next, et cetera. Central to the entire nervous system, then, is the central nervous system (CNS), which is composed of the brain and spinal cord. As a collection point for nerve impulses, it controls most functions of the body and mind. "Like a central computer, it interprets information from our eyes (sight), ears (sound), nose (smell), tongue (taste) and skin (touch), as well as from internal organs such as the stomach" (Christopher & Dana Reeve Foundation, 2013). The CNS is also the center of emotion, thought, and memory (University of Pittsburgh, 2013). As children continue to grow, additional neural pathways develop, allowing for a more rapid transmission and reception of information. The following section describes this process in further detail.

Neurobiology of Cognition

Taking the time to fully explain the neurobiology of a growing child could easily take an entire book. Similar to the previously discussed physical changes, the middle child's cognitive growth is substantial as they move on the continuum from childhood interdependence to the independence of adulthood (Santrock, 2007). The development of the central nervous system is anatomically complete, though there is a continued explosion of growth in the neural pathways (Finkelstein, 2000). Campbell (2011), referencing Chugai (1998), stated:

> Glucose utilization rates by the cortex and subcortical structures rise from birth to reach their peak at twice the adult rate at about eight years of age and then begin to decline. From eight to eleven years of age, glucose utilization remains elevated at about one and a half the adult rate and then declines more strongly at the end of puberty, when they reach adult levels. (pp. 334–335)

Simplistically, these developmental patterns of cortical glucose utilization point to what is typically know as synaptic pruning, thus increasing the capacity for the impending cognitive growth of adolescence and later adulthood (Campbell, 2011).

BOX 9.2   CONCEPTUALIZING SYNAPTIC PRUNING

Synaptic pruning during middle childhood is similar to rose pruning a gardener does in preparation for spring, which typically happens between the months of January and April. Though it seems counterintuitive, the gardener will prune the rose bush back to two-thirds the original size. Bushes that have been appropriately pruned will explode in growth during the growing season and will typically be one to two times the size of bushes that were not pruned.

While the synaptic pruning is happening, the brain is also increasing in size, reaching maximum thickness by the age of 10 years (Dionne & Cadoret, 2013). Though the prefrontal cortex is not fully developed (this does not fully develop until approximately 25 for men and 23 for women), strides are made toward the use of higher order thinking. Although the emotional center of the brain (e.g., the limbic system, consisting of structures such as the amygdala, the hypothalamus, the hippocampus) is the primary function of early childhood, the prefrontal cortex begins to increase in usage in middle childhood (Dionne & Cadoret, 2013). As it grows in strength, the middle child begins to develop the capabilities for insight, forethought, and inhibitory control, thus buffering the purely emotional responses (Campbell, 2011).

Notable Developmental Changes

Research continues to demonstrate how it is around age 6 years or so when children develop the cognitive ability to "actually 'reason' in the commonsense meaning of the world" (Eccles, 1999, p. 32). Because key thinking and conceptual skills are generally developed between ages 6 and 7 years, schools across the globe generally begin formal educational instruction during these years. Children continue to refine and consolidate these skills throughout the rest of middle childhood. Two classic theorists who contributed toward the field's knowledge of middle childhood development are Jean Piaget and Lev Vygotsky. Originally introduced in chapter 2, the following sections discuss Piaget's and Vygotsky's theories as they relate to middle childhood.

PIAGET'S THEORY OF COGNITIVE DEVELOPMENT

Piaget's (1936) theory of cognitive development focuses on cognitive development in relation to physical development. At younger ages the brain is still developing and is only capable of so much cognition until a point of maturation. From a developmental standpoint, Piaget (1936) believed that all children go through four stages of cognitive development: (1) sensorimotor (birth to age 2 years); (2) preoperational (ages 2 to 7 years); (3) concrete operations (ages 7 to 11 years); and (4) formal operational (ages 11 to 15 years through adulthood).

Each stage represents a major milestone in cognitive development that takes place in sequential order for every child regardless of genetics, temperament, culture, gender, and ability (Piaget, 1973). Although the stage-by-stage sequence of development does occur in a particular order within a typical age range, children will develop uniquely and at their own pace. Some children will demonstrate mastery within a particular stage sooner than others. Other children may demonstrate skills and abilities within specific situations, with certain people, or in particular contexts but not in others (Oswalt & Dombeck, 2015). It is typical for peak performance to occur in familiar environments and situations with familiar people. The more novel the experience, the more likely children are to become confused and underperform.

Piaget's Stages During Middle Childhood

Three of Piaget's (1936) four stages occur during middle childhood: preoperational, concrete operational, and formal operational. The preoperational stage lasts from about ages 2 to 7 years and is when language development begins. At this stage children represent the world by way of words, images, and drawings. Children are no longer limited to simple physical actions as a means of discovering the world. Egocentrism is also a key feature of this stage, whereby children are capable of viewing the world only through their own, egocentric lens. That is, they are unable to comprehend the perspectives of others. This is why shows like *Kids Say the Darndest Things* are full of obliviously candid and funny statements that children make. The concrete operations stage takes place around age 7 years and lasts until age 11 years or so. Concrete operations spans most of middle childhood and will be explained in further detail. During this stage children may perform concrete operations, and logical reasoning begins to emerge over intuitive reasoning. The formal operational stage begins somewhere between ages 11 and 15 years and lasts into and throughout adulthood. Here, children are finally able to move beyond concrete thought and start thinking in abstracts. With this comes the ability to manipulate ideas in one's head. With middle childhood ending somewhere around age 12 years, most children in this age range do not experience or comprehend abstract thoughts.

Piaget's Concrete Operations

Mental operations in Piaget's concrete operations stage are essentially the beginnings of more complex thought. "A mental operation," according to Oswalt and Dombeck (2015), "is the ability to accurately imagine the consequences of something happening without it actually needing to happen" (para. 2). As such, thoughts become more proactive than reactive. Children in middle childhood may think through and make predictions regarding events and scenarios that are yet to occur.

The defining feature of concrete operations is that children's logic is bound to what is concrete, or tangible. That is, thoughts are specific to persons, places, and things they may have seen, touched, smelled, heard, or tasted (Piaget, 1936). These children may understand how not brushing their teeth may lead to cavities but struggle to think about all of the other consequences that may occur if their teeth go untreated and are lost (e.g., social implications, dietary complications, concerns about self-image). Unless they have directly experienced or witnessed someone else experience all of these negative consequences, they struggle to comprehend them. It is not until adolescence that they develop the ability to abstract formal operations representative of intangible and abstract persons, places, or things (Oswalt & Dombeck, 2015).

Conservation

It was Piaget's contention was that younger ages could not comprehend a particular cognitive level at an age younger than the milestone age. To understand conservation, a child must possess the ability to cognitively preserve something (Piaget, 1936). This ability develops around ages 5–7 years. The principle of conservation relies on an amount of a particular something remaining constant across two or more conditions despite a change in shape or appearance (Oswalt & Dombeck, 2015). As explained by Dewey (2007), "That 'something' is an awareness of quantity, mass, number, area, or some other abstract characteristic of reality" (para. 9). As children progress through middle childhood, they become able to quickly and easily recognize that the actual mass of the object remains constant. Age ranges for children in Western cultures to attain various types of conservation are as follows: (a) conservation of number, age 7 years; (b) conservation of mass, age 7 or 8 years; (c) conservation of length, age 7 or 8 years; (d) conservation of area, age 8 or 9 years. Again, each of these age ranges is dependent on a multitude of factors. It was through these experiments (and some others) that Piaget came to recognize that conservation depends on two fundamental cognitive abilities: decentration and reversibility (Oswalt & Dombeck, 2015).

Decentration

Decentration is integral to conservation. According to Oswalt and Dombeck (2015), "Decentration involves the ability to pay attention to multiple attributes of an object or situation rather than being locked into attending to only a single attribute" (para. 2). Successful responses to the beaker experiment, for instance, require the child to conceptualize the dimensions of height and width at the same time. Decentration also requires the ability to hold a particular something in short-term memory while shifting to another aspect of that something without losing the original content. This is also something that occurs during middle childhood. As the overlapping memories are combined, the child develops an integrated perspective of that particular something. This ability significantly helps with mathematics and reading comprehension as children continue to build on a particular formula, find meaning in symbols, or follow a particular story.

Reversibility

As heightened memory and awareness continue to develop in middle childhood, children become capable of reversibility. Reversibility is the recognition that a particular something changed from one true form to another and may return to its original form (Oswalt & Dombeck, 2015). With the beaker experiment, then, reversibility is demonstrated when children recognize that liquid is poured from the short, wide beaker to the tall, slender beaker and back without any actual amount of liquid itself changing. The actual mass remains constant the entire time.

Classification

Classification entails the ability to simultaneously sort things into general and more specific groups using a particular type of comparison (Oswalt & Dombeck, 2015). According to Piaget, this ability begins between ages 7 and 10 years and is mastered throughout middle childhood. This is particularly important in school as children are expected to know different classifications of plants, animals, literature genres, colors, physical activities, and occupations (Piaget, 1936). Children may then take a primary classification and break it down further. For instance, the classification of *animal* may be further categorized to include *vertebrates* and *invertebrates*. Vertebrates are then categorized as *warm-blooded* or *cold-blooded*. Warm-blooded can be divided into *mammals* and *birds*. The classifications for persons, places, things, and thoughts are virtually limitless.

Seriation

Piaget also identified middle childhood as a period when the seriation ability is developed. Children capable of seriation are able to place things in order based on quantity or magnitude (Oswalt & Dombeck, 2015). In a classic experiment, Piaget (1936) demonstrated this by having children arrange sticks of varied lengths from smallest to largest. Another simple example is having students line up from shortest to tallest. This fundamental ability is critical toward achievement in core subjects including math (e.g., number sequences) and science (e.g., elements contained in the periodic table).

Spatial Reasoning

According to Piaget (1936), middle childhood is also the period when children develop spatial reasoning. Development of this ability allows children to understand and to reason using environmental cues that convey information about direction or distance (Oswalt & Dombeck, 2015). A basic principle of this is that objects in the distance appear small while ones closer appear larger. Although young children may understand that far-away objects are small, they do not recognize their size relative to the actual distance. As such, middle childhood is when it becomes possible to recognize that what appears as a bunny hill some 25 miles away is actually a gigantic mountain, tiny people from the top of the Willis Tower are actually full size, and bright lights in the sky are stars that dwarf planet Earth.

Middle childhood is a period when children are better able to comprehend maps and directions while developing their own cognitive maps. They can relate relative distance from one point or landmark to another. Further, children are also capable of providing directions from the vantage point of others. For instance, if two people are directly facing one another, they could recognize that "right" to the other person appears as "left" from his vantage point. Younger children struggle to create sophisticated maps and are easily confused by the appearance of contrasting direction.

PSYCHOLOGICAL DISORDERS IN MIDDLE CHILDHOOD

To this point this chapter has discussed typical cognitive middle childhood development. Although the majority of children will develop along this typical progression, some will face a variety of complications such as a diagnosable psychological disorder. Recognition and appropriate treatment of such disorders may minimize or even fully eliminate associated complications. As such, this section addresses several common psychological disorders as experienced during middle childhood. This section is by no means comprehensive, and readers are encouraged to engage in further review of those most common within their particular population.

Dealing with a psychological disorder can be a daunting task. It is difficult enough to deal with the disorder on a daily basis, and continual negative societal stigma associated with the disorder can only add to the stress. Costello, Mustillo, Erkanli, Keeler, and Angold (2003) suggested that at any given time one in five children struggle with some form of psychological disorder (e.g., attention-deficit/hyperactivity disorder [ADHD], anxiety, conduct disorder, depression). When working with children, diagnosis should be a slow process, and every avenue should be explored. Therefore, it is significantly important that counselors have a basic understanding of the main diagnoses that have the potential to disrupt middle childhood.

Costello et al. (2003) indicated that children with a history of mental illness are three times more likely to develop a disorder in middle childhood and adolescence than children with no childhood diagnosis. Many disorders peak in prevalence at the age of 9 or 10 years, falling to their lowest manifestation at the age of 12 years and then slowly increasing into adulthood (Costello et al., 2003). Though there is still, and there will continue to be, debate surrounding the diagnosis of children, the counselor must be keenly aware of the behavioral issues, the familial influence (behavioral and genetic), and the extraneous variables that can contribute to the child's diagnosis. For the purpose of this chapter we will explore only the most commonly diagnosed disorders in middle childhood: depression and anxiety disorders (DAS), ADHD, and disruptive disorders (oppositional defiant disorder [ODD] and conduct disorder [CD]).

Depressive and Anxiety Disorders

DAS within childhood and middle childhood can often be categorically lumped into one common etiology. According to Côté et al. (2009), there is a relationship between generalized anxiety and depression in both pre-adolescents and adults whereby one actually precedes the other, demonstrating how the two disorders feed into one another. Côté et al. (2009) alluded to one study where parental reports, combined with diagnostic criteria, showed a strong relationship between depression and anxiety, thus suggesting the two could be combined into a single distress disorder. Though there is significant crossover between depression and anxiety, it is still important for counselors to become aware of the potential differences between the two.

Depression

In the not too distant past, depression was thought to be a distinctly adult disorder inasmuch as children were considered to be developmentally incompatible (Maughan, Collishaw, & Stringaris, 2013). This view has slowly changed, as approximately 1–2% of preadolescent children struggle with depressive symptoms (Maughan et al., 2013). Diagnostic criteria suggest that symptoms could consist of persistent sadness, loss of interest, low self-esteem, excessive guilt, suicidal thoughts or behaviors, sleep and appetite disturbances, and psychomotor agitation (APA, 2013).

The risk factors of depression are thought to be bivariate, consisting of both environmental and biological components. Maternal depression, low education, low socioeconomic status, inadequate parenting, and high rates of conflict are thought to contribute to the onset of depression (Côté et al., 2009). Combined with these environmental factors, Patten (2013) reported that "30–40% of major depression is heritable. Gene–environment interactions may explain some of the heterogeneity in the way people respond to stressful life events, as may epigenetic changes occurring during development" (p. 927). It must also be noted that comorbidity may be high, as nearly two-thirds of individuals struggling with depression demonstrate a comorbid disorder (typically anxiety, ADHD, conduct disorder, or oppositional defiant disorder; Maughan et al., 2013). Furthermore, clinical studies indicate that youth who struggle with depression are 50–70% more likely to have a recurrent episode within 5 years (Maughan et al., 2013).

Anxiety

Characterized by excessive worry, restlessness, feeling on edge, being easily fatigued, difficulty concentrating, irritability, muscle tension, and sleep disturbance, anxiety can be a pervasive disorder within middle childhood (APA, 2013). The onset of anxiety varies from age 7 years for separation anxiety (309.21) to age 11 years for general anxiety (300.02) (Kessler et al., 2005). Anxiety disorders represent one of the highest, most dominant forms of psychopathology among middle childhood, with manifested impairments in psychosocial functioning, peer relationships, and academic performance (Feng, Shaw, & Silk, 2008).

Though little is known about the symptom trajectory of anxiety in middle childhood (Feng et al., 2008), it is important to understand the etiology of anxiety: "Anxiety disorders emerge from multiple developmental pathways that reflect the dynamic interplay between characteristics of children, and their environment over time" (p. 32). Personal characteristics (e.g., child's personality and epigenetics), interpersonal characteristics (e.g., social and familial), and familial history of psychopathology all contribute to the onset of anxiety within middle childhood (Feng et al., 2008).

BOX 9.3 HELPING CHILDREN MANAGE ANXIETY

A good place to start is by teaching children how to eliminate those unnecessary persons, places, and things that lead toward stress. Second, children may attempt to alter those stressful situations they cannot avoid. Third, figure out what they can do to change things so the problem doesn't present itself in the future. Fourth, if children cannot change the stressor, they may try changing their cognitions or behaviors in some healthy way.

Posttraumatic Stress Disorder

One significant traumatic event or continued exposure to stressors within childhood and middle childhood may lead to a state of internal crisis. During this state, feelings of restlessness, fear, confusion, anger, despair, anxiety, depression, and hopelessness are common (James, 2008). In more extreme reactions to crisis events—generally the result of more severe scenarios—individuals may actually develop a full-blown psychological disorder in posttraumatic stress disorder (PTSD; Marotta, 2000). PTSD is a mental health condition caused by either directly or indirectly (vicariously) experiencing such an event or events. Some events that might lead to PTSD may include but are not limited to abuse (i.e., domestic, sexual, emotional), war, bullying, and school shootings. Chapter 10 will go into further detail describing the social aspects of some of these events. Because the symptoms and their severity vary from person to person, so do the approaches necessary to address them. Two appropriate evidence-based approaches are cognitive-behavioral therapy (CBT) and interpersonal therapy (IPT).

BOX 9.4 COGNITIVE-BEHAVIORAL THERAPY

Childhood PTSD generally occurs from a very traumatic experience that may entail abuse, parental drug use, bullying, rape, or neglect. To treat such severe trauma, it is important to respond in a comprehensive manner. Cognitive-behavioral therapy (CBT) involves the "concepts and methods for understanding and treating individual and relationship problems in terms of behavioral patterns, individual's cognitions about themselves and other people, and emotional responses associated with those behaviors and cognitions" (Hecker & Wetchler, 2003, p. 243). By treating the cognitive pathology, the child may refocus on appropriate behavior and may resocialize with family, friends, and others (James, 2008).

Attention-Deficit/Hyperactivity Disorder

ADHD is characterized by inattention, hyperactivity, and significant impulsivity before age 7 years (Mulligan et al., 2013). Heritability (e.g., the extent to which genetic individual differences contribute to individual differences in observed behavior), delineated from several twin family and adoption studies, suggests that ADHD has a value of .76. This means that on average about 76% of the individual differences observed in ADHD can be attributed to genetic difference (Mulligan et al., 2013). Simply, the mention of heritability means that there is a genetic component to the development of ADHD in children (though more research needs to be done to explore this assertion further).

Adoption studies have shown the impact of early childhood influences on the development of ADHD (Mulligan et al., 2013). Adopted children had consistently higher rates than non-adopted children thus showing a potential causal relationship to early attachment and the onset of ADHD (Milligan et al., 2013). Furthermore, studies have determined that environmental factors such as marital discord, paternal psychopathology, maternal psychiatric disorders, large family size, fostered children, and low social status have the potential to predict psychological disorders (including ADHD) in middle childhood (Mulligan et al., 2013).

Disruptive Disorders

ODD and CD continue to be heavily researched as these disorders continue to grow in frequency among preadolescent children. Researchers suggest that ODD is a preliminary diagnosis to CD suggesting that approximately 25% of children who demonstrate consistently disruptive or defiant behaviors or have a diagnosis of ODD have a greater risk of a CD diagnosis (Valle, Kelley, & Seoanes, 2001). Therefore, counselors must be mindful that a comorbid diagnosis of ODD and CD is categorically impossible.

Oppositional Defiant Disorder

The symptoms of ODD are grouped into three types: (1) angry/irritable mood; (2) argumentative/defiant behavior; and (3) vindictiveness (APA, 2013). The *Diagnostic and Statistical Manual of Mental Disorders*, fifth edition (*DSM-V*; APA, 2013), also indicates that counselors must be mindful to recognize the difference between normal developmental behavior and associated symptoms of ODD. Therefore, the *DSM-V* has added criteria to indicate the symptom frequency and severity of the ODD (APA, 2013).

Similar to depression, anxiety, and ADHD, the etiology of ODD is multi-faceted and dependent on genetic factors, peer groups, familial interactions, and environmental factors (Valle et al., 2001). The parent–child interaction (if negative) can increase the child's defiant attitude. The more frequent a negative command is given, the greater the defiant response. This coercive cycle becomes a way for the child to escape responsibilities and consequences. If left untreated (from a familial standpoint), the behavior could lead to bigger issues such as conduct disorder in adolescence, delinquency, criminality, and possibly antisocial personality disorder in adults (Valle et al., 2001).

Conduct Disorder

CD is characterized by pervasive behavior that violates the rights of others or major societal norms (APA, 2013). To diagnose CD three symptoms must be present within the past 12 months with one recurring symptom in the past 6 months (APA, 2013): (1) aggression to people and animals; (2) destruction of property;

(3) deceitfulness or theft; and (4) serious violation of rules (APA, 2013). (Note: For a more detailed explanation please consult your *DSM-V*.)

BOX 9.5   CREATIVE ACTIVITY

For over a century, counselors have "recognized fantasy play as a rich, complex and multifunctional component of healthy child development" (Rubin & Livesay, 2006, p. 18). By taking a child's love and familiarity with superheroes and villains and infusing it into role-play, counselors may potentially reach children in ways not previously possible. The primary goals of superheroes and villains role-plays are to help children: (a) express their anger in a manner that is safe to themselves and others; (b) explore feelings they may keep hidden or are unaware of; (c) connect characters and their special abilities to the client's personality or condition; and (d) strengthen rapport with the therapist by having fun. This intervention is an intentional strategy to help increase self and other awareness, improve interpersonal communication skills, curb maladaptive behaviors, and displace anger from a real-life to imaginary setting.

KEY COUNSELING POINTERS FOR PHYSICAL AND COGNITIVE DEVELOPMENT DURING MIDDLE CHILDHOOD AND IMPLICATIONS FOR COUNSELING

Have you ever taken the time to think about what makes the role of a counselor different from that of a psychologist, psychiatrist, or social worker? Understanding what it means to be a counselor is essential to the desired therapeutic outcomes of our clients and the avenues we chose to take therein. As the counseling professional identity continues to strengthen it is important to think about how your own contribution might enhance the questions of what it means to be a counselor. Being a counselor is so much more than simply providing assessments, understanding pharmacokinetics and psychopharmacology, or providing casework. Though these things are important and beneficial to the bigger picture of counseling, it is about the establishment of a therapeutic relationship wherein the client is able to explore the idiosyncrasies and nuances of life, receive insight and support, make the necessary changes, and be empowered to successfully navigate life.

Understanding the bigger picture provides insight into the specifics of what it means to be a counselor, and this is why it is so important to explore the unique cognitive and physical growth patterns within middle childhood.

By understanding what typical development looks like, the counselor is able to develop a more comprehensive picture of the client and how he or she functions within his or her environment (e.g., home, family, school, church, peer group). By gaining specific knowledge of these milestones, the counselor is able to then develop appropriate therapeutic goals, thus enhancing the therapeutic outcome.

The remaining portion of this chapter will be spent discussing and exploring the various content and case conceptualizations in relation to what it means to be a counselor. We will provide our insight and draw from our experiences, yet it must be noted that these are our perceptions of each case and must not be considered absolute truth. Proper case conceptualization should not happen in a vacuum, but rather it should take place in the context of community with the collaboration of fellow counselors, psychologists, psychiatrists, and primary care doctors.

Conceptualizing Keisha

As counseling has progressed, Keisha has disclosed that she has a difficult time focusing at school and often gets in trouble for talking out of turn, not finishing homework, and getting into fights. Furthermore, Keisha has stated that she has a hard time finding something she enjoys and is often confused about who she is. Keisha appears to have a great support system, and she is a vibrant and enthusiastic middle school student and presents as a normal preteen. Nevertheless, Keisha shows signs of struggling with this transition from childhood to adolescence.

Hopefully you have been able to develop an ongoing conceptualization of Keisha throughout this chapter. We would encourage you to take out your notes and compare them to our conceptualization. (Remember: Often there is not a right or a wrong when it comes to conceptualizing a case, but there are different sides of the same coin. Make sure that you continue to develop your case conceptualization skills by collaborating with fellow counselors, thus gaining priceless perspectives on the same case.)

First, it would be extremely important to gain a better understanding of Keisha's culture. What does it mean to be a member in Keisha's family? What are the stated expectations of the family, and what are the psychological expectations of the family? How do Keisha's race, ethnicity, and gender influence her development? Exploring these key components will enhance the overall therapeutic interpretation and subsequently guide the future therapy. Second, it appears that due to Keisha's parents' work schedules, she has a lot of responsibility thrust upon her. It would be important to gain both her and her parents' perceptions of this. Third, Keisha has already entered puberty and is physically more mature that the majority of her peers. Fourth, she is transitioning between Piaget's concrete operational stage to the formal operational stage. Finally, it appears that Keisha could be struggling with either depression or ADHD. Therefore it would be imperative to explore whether or not she might have a diagnosis, as a formal diagnosis and subsequent treatment could also alleviate the rest of the aforementioned symptomatology.

SUMMARY

This chapter provides an overview of normal and abnormal physical and cognitive developmental factors as they occur throughout middle childhood. Biological and neurophysiological development and the refinement of perceptual and motor skills are primary components of physical growth throughout ages 6–12 years, thus preparing children for impending pubescent changes. Outside of one's biological predisposition, nutrition and physical activity weigh heavily on development. Notable changes experienced cognitively include advanced intellectual and language development reasoning abilities and memory capacities. With key thinking and conceptual skills appearing between ages 6 and 7 years, most children begin school at this time and continue to refine and consolidate these skills throughout the duration of middle childhood. Positive, nurturing environments are more likely to lead toward positive outcomes while negative, threatening environments lead toward negative ones. Although the majority of children will develop along this typical progression, some children will face a variety of complications. As such, counselors are encouraged to be knowledgeable of these complications and their appropriate treatment modalities.

USEFUL WEBSITES

Centers for Disease Control and Prevention
http://www.cdc.gov
HealthyPeople.gov
https://www.healthypeople.gov/2020/topics-objectives/topic/early-and-
   middle childhood
Mental Health Net
http://www.mentalhelp.net
National Institutes of Health
http://www.nih.gov
National Institute of Mental Health
http://www.nimh.nih.gov/index.shtml

REFERENCES

American Psychiatric Association (APA). (2013). *Diagnostic and statistical manual of mental disorders* (5th ed.). Washington, DC: Author.

Ames, L. B., Ilg, F. L., & Baker, S. M. (1988). *Your ten-to-fourteen-year-old*. New York, NY: Delacorte Press.

Anderson, M. (n.d.). *Discussion of Piagetian conservation experiments*. Retrieved from http://web.cortland.edu/andersmd/piaget/a3.html

Boynton-Jarrett, R., Wright, R. J., Putnam, F. W., Lividoti Hibert, E., Michels, K. B., Forman, M. R., & Rich-Edwards, J. (2013). Childhood abuse and age at menarche. *Journal of Adolescent Health: Official Publication of the Society for Adolescent Medicine, 52*(2), 241–247. doi:10.1016/j.jadohealth.2012.06.006

Brooks, J. B. (1999). *The process of parenting*. Mountain View, CA: Mayfield Publishing Company.

Cairns, R. B. (2000). Developmental science: Three audacious implications. In L. R. Bergman, R. B. Cairns, L.-G. Nilsson, & L. Nystedt (Eds.), *Developmental science and the holistic approach* (pp. 49–62). Mahwah, NJ: Erlbaum.

Campbell, B. C. (2011a). Adrenarche and middle childhood. *Human Nature, 22*(3), 327–349. doi:10.1007/s12110-011-9120-x

Campbell, B. C. (2011b). An introduction to the special issue on middle childhood. *Human Nature, 22*(3), 247–248. doi:10.1007/s12110-011-9118-4

Christopher & Dana Reeve Foundation. (2013). *What is the central nervous system?* Retrieved from http://www.christopherreeve.org/site/c.dJFKRNoFiG/b.4452157/k.3E9D/What_is_the_Central_Nervous_System.htm

Cole, M., & Cole, S. R. (1996). *The development of children*. New York, NY: W.H. Freeman and Company.

Corey, G. (2005). *Theory and practice of counseling & psychotherapy* (7th ed.). Belmont, CA: Brooks/Cole-Thompson Learning.

Corkville Briggs, D. (2010). *The mother of all toddler books: An All-Canadian guide to your child's second and third years*. Hoboken, NJ: Wiley.

Costello, J. E., Mustillo, S., Erkanli, A., Keeler, G., & Angold, A. (2003). Prevalence and development of psychiatric disorders in childhood and adolescence. *Archives of General Psychiatry, 60*, 837–844.

Côté, S. M., Boivin, M., Liu, X., Nagin, D. S., Zoccolillo, M., & Tremblay, R. E. (2009). Depression and anxiety symptoms: Onset, developmental course and risk factors during early childhood. *Journal of Child Psychology and Psychiatry, 50*(10), 1201–1208. doi:10.1111/j.1469-7610.2009.02099.x

Croft, C., & Smith, J. (2008). *Middle childhood: Physical growth & development*. Chicago, IL: Magna Systems.

Dewey, R. A. (2007). *The conservation experiments*. Retrieved from http://www.intropsych.com/ch10_development/conservation_experiments.html

Dionne, J., & Cadoret, G. (2013). Development of active controlled retrieval during middle childhood. *Developmental Psychobiology, 55*(4), 443–449. doi:10.1002/dev.21034

Eccles, J. S. (1999). The development of children ages 6 to 14. *Journal Issue: When School Is Out, 9*(2), 1–6.

Encyclopedia of Mental Disorders. (2012). *Interpersonal therapy*. Retrieved from http://www.minddisorders.com/Flu-Inv/Interpersonal-therapy.html#b

Feng, X., Shaw, D. S., & Silk, J. S. (2008). Developmental trajectories of anxiety symptoms among boys across early and middle childhood. *Journal of Abnormal Psychology, 117*(1), 32–47. doi:10.1037/0021-843X.117.1.32

Finkelstein, J. W. (2000). Middle childhood: Physical and biological development. In A. E. Kazdin (Ed.), *Encyclopedia of psychology* (Vol. 5, pp. 220–225). Washington, DC: American Psychological Association. doi:10.1037/10520-102

HealthyPeople.gov. (2015). *Early and middle childhood*. Retrieved from https://www.healthypeople.gov/2020/topics-objectives/topic/early-and-middle-childhood

Hutchinson, L. (2010). *Study guide for the NCMHCE* (5th ed.). Winter Park, FL: Licensure Exams, Inc.

Institute for Human Services for The Ohio Child Welfare Training Program. (October 2007). Developmental Milestones Chart adapted from Rycus, J., & Hughes, R. C. (1998). *The Field Guide to Child Welfare Volume III: Child Development and Child Welfare*.

James, R. K. (2008). *Crisis intervention strategies* (6th ed.). Belmont, CA: Brooks/Cole.

Kessler, R. C., Berglund, P., Demler, O., Jin, R., Merikangas, K. R., & Walters, E. E. (2005). Lifetime prevalence and age-of-onset distributions of *DSM-IV* disorders in the national comorbidity survey replication. *Archives of General Psychiatry, 62*, 593–602.

Knapp, C. (2011). *Appetites*. Berkeley, CA: Counterpoint Press.

Magnusson, D. (1985). Implications of an interactional paradigm for research on human development. *International Journal of Behavioral Development, 8*, 115–137.

Magnusson, D., & Stattin, H. (2006). The person in context: A holistic-interactionistic approach. In R. M. Lerner & W. Damon (Eds.), *Handbook of child psychology: Theoretical models of human development* (Vol. 1, 6th ed., pp. 400–464). Hoboken, NJ: Wiley.

Marotta, S. A. (2000). Best practices for counselors who treat posttraumatic stress disorder. *Journal of Counseling and Development, 78*(4), 492–495.

Maughan, B., Collishaw, S., & Stringaris, A. (2013). Depression in childhood and adolescence. *Journal of the Canadian Academy of Child and Adolescent Psychiatry, 22*(1), 35–40.

Mayer, S. J. (2005). The early evolution of Jean Piaget's clinical method. *History of Psychology, 8*(4), 362–382. doi: 10.1037/1093-4510.8.4.362

Moran, V. (2012). *Main street vegan: Everything you need to know to eat healthfully and live compassionately in the real world*. Danvers, MA: Tarcher—Penguin Random House.

Mulligan, A., Anney, R., Butler, L., O'Regan, M., Richardson, T., Tulewicz, E. M., … Gill, M. (2013). Home environment: Association with hyperactivity/impulsivity in children with ADHD and their non-ADHD siblings. *Child: Care, Health and Development, 39*(2), 202–212. doi:10.1111/j.1365–2214.2011.01345.x

Obesity Society. (2010). *Childhood overweight*. Retrieved from http://www.obesity.org/resources-for/childhood-overweight.htm

Office of Disease Prevention and Health Promotion. (2015). *Early and middle childhood*. Retrieved from https://www.healthypeople.gov/2020/topics-objectives/topic/early-and-middle-childhood

Ophardt, C. E. (2003). *Nervous system—overview*. Retrieved from http://www.elmhurst.edu/~chm/vchembook/661nervoussys.html

Osmundson, J. (2011). I was born this way: Is sexuality innate, and should it matter? *LGBTQ Policy Journal at the Harvard Kennedy School*. Retrieved from http://isites.harvard.edu/icb/icb.do?keyword=k78405&pageid=icb.page414413

Oswalt, A. (2015). *Early childhood physical development: Gross and fine motor development*. Retrieved from http://bhcmhmr.org/poc/view_doc.php?type=doc&id=12755&cn=462

Oswalt, A., & Dombeck, M. (2010). *Primary physical changes associated with puberty*. Retrieved from http://www.mentalhelp.net/poc/view_doc.php?type=doc&id=38406&cn=1276

Oswalt, A., & Dombeck, M. (2015). *Middle childhood development*. Retrieved from http://www.sevencounties.org/poc/view_doc.php?type=doc&id=37673&cn=1272

Ozretich, R. A., & Bowman, S. R. (2001). *Middle childhood and adolescent development*. Corvallis: Oregon State University.

Patten, S. B. (2013). Childhood and adult stressors and major depression risk: Interpreting interactions with the sufficient-component cause model. *Social Psychiatry and Psychiatric Epidemiology*, *48*(6), 927–933. doi:10.1007/s00127-012-0603-9

Piaget, J. (1936). *Origins of intelligence in the child*. London, UK: Routledge & Kegan Paul.

Piaget, J. (1973). *Memory and intelligence*. New York, NY: BasicBooks.

Rubin, L. (2012). Superheroes on the couch: Exploring our limits. *Journal of Popular Culture*, *45*(2), 410–431.

Rubin, L., & Livesay, H. (2006). Look, up in the sky! Using superheroes in play therapy. *International Journal of Play Therapy*, *15*, 117–133.

Sander, L. W. (1987). A 25-year follow-up: Some reflections on personality development over the long term. *Infant Mental Health Journal*, *8*(3), 210–220.

Santrock, J. W. (2007). *A topical approach to life-span development* (3rd ed.). New York, NY: McGraw-Hill.

Schore, A. N. (1999). *Affect regulation and the origin of the self: The neurobiology of emotional development*. Florence, KY: Psychology Press.

Sharf, R. S. (2008). *Theories of psychotherapy and counseling: Concepts and cases* (4th ed.). Belmont, CA: Brooks/Cole, Cengage Learning.

Steinberg, L. (1993). *Adolescence*. New York, NY: McGraw-Hill.

Valle, P. D., Kelley, S. L., & Seoanes, J. E. (2001). The "oppositional defiant" and "conduct disorder" child: A brief review of etiology, assessment, and treatment. *Behavioral Development Bulletin*, *10*(1), 36–41. doi:10.1037/h0100481

Vygotsky, L. S. (1978). *Mind in society: The development of higher psychological processes*. Cambridge, MA: Harvard University.

Wood, D., Bruner, J., & Ross, G. (1976). The role of tutoring in problem solving. *Journal of Child Psychology and Child Psychiatry*, *17*, 89–100.

Zembar, M. J., & Blume, L. B. (2009). *Middle childhood development: A contextual approach*. Boston, MA: Allyn & Bacon.

Middle Childhood: Emotional and Social Development

CHAPTER 10

Matt Glowiak and Mark Aaron Mayfield

Around age 6 years, children develop the key cognitive abilities (Eccles, 1999) that mark the point at which most children begin their formal educational experience. Depending on whether the child attended preschool, this may be the first time that the child has been exposed to same-age peers in a formal educational setting. During infancy and early childhood, children spend a vast majority of their time with their parents and caregivers. Upon enrollment in school they are exposed to new people (e.g., children, teachers, other authority figures), new places (e.g., the classroom, gymnasium, library), and new challenges (e.g., homework, exams, artistic activities, sports, social competitions). Although each child's individual experience is unique, the general progression is similar.

Most of us can think back to middle childhood and the drastic changes experienced throughout. Early on we learned how to tie our shoes, read, perform simple arithmetic, and skip rope. By the end we were sneaking staying up late, feeling cool when we received a phone call, and going to middle school dances. Middle childhood marks a period of significant social and emotional development. In addition to progressing through the physical and cognitive milestones outlined in chapter 9, these children are also exposed to novel social and emotional experiences that will ultimately influence the rest of their lives. Social and emotional development are composed of a variety of key components.

Components of social development include social skills, interpersonal understanding, moral development, ethical development, and maintaining close relationships (Zembar & Blume, 2009). In its simplest unit, a social skill is a skill that facilitates communication and interaction with others. A simple social skill, for instance, may involve waving when saying hello from a reasonable distance. Interpersonal understanding involves the ability to recognize and comprehend what another is communicating. For instance, when one child gives another a high five, it is generally a sign that something positive and worthy of celebration just occurred. Moral development is the emergence and change of morality throughout one's lifetime. Middle childhood moral development, as will be explored in this chapter, changes drastically and is significantly influenced by one's psychosocial environment. Ethical development is the emergence and development of how one engages in various scenarios involving human rights, basic needs, and social justice. Finally, close relationships are those in which two or more people share a "connection involving strong and frequent cognitive, behavioral, and affective interdependence" (Smith & Mackie, 2007, pp. 417–419). During middle childhood these individuals range from one's parents and siblings to best friends, coaches, teachers, boyfriends, girlfriends, and beyond.

In terms of emotional development, key components include personality, emotions, motivation, and self-esteem (Zembar & Blume, 2009). "Personality refers to individual differences in characteristic patterns of thinking, feeling and behaving" (APA, 2015). Alongside the physical and cognitive growth discussed in chapter 9, personality characteristics rapidly develop and become more ingrained. Emotions are instinctual; arise spontaneously; are influenced by one's mood, relationships, or situation; and may be accompanied by physiological changes— hence the word *feeling*, which is many times used interchangeably with emotion. With age, middle childhood–aged children generally learn to better control, express, and understand their emotions. Motivation in this respect involves the child's general desire or willingness to do something. Highly motivated children are generally those who succeed, while those who lack motivation struggle across many dimensions—academics, relationships, athletics, work. Then, self-esteem entails the level of confidence a child has in his or her own abilities or worth. For children in middle development, major influences acting on them are their parents and caregivers, teachers, peers, and other close individuals in their immediate environment (micro system). How the child responds to these influences significantly impacts the way the influences respond back.

As children continue to develop and refine each of these social and emotional components, they enhance core skills and abilities. These core skills and abilities include fundamental skills considered important to one's culture, reading and arithmetic skills, self-awareness skills, and an ability to take the perspective of others (Eccles, 1999).

Consequent to these skills and abilities children in middle childhood are capable of heightening their learning experiences, retrieving new information, solving novel problems, coping with novel situations, reflecting on what they are doing, recognizing what they want to accomplish, consciously planning, coordinating actions, evaluating progress, modifying plans based off reflection and evaluation, and understanding that others have a different point of view and knowledge (Eccles, 1999). As children progress through each succeeding age of middle childhood, their interactive environments typically become larger, contain more stimuli, and offer more experiential opportunities.

This chapter serves as an exploration of the social and emotional development experienced by school-aged children in middle childhood. Take particular note of how this development parallels the physical and cognitive development previously discussed.

Case Study—Franklin

Reflecting on the content of chapter 9, take some time to practice your skills by exploring the following case study. Franklin is an energetic 10-year-old boy who was referred to you, and your mental health agency, by his school. The referral indicates that Franklin deals with explosive anger and that it has gotten to the point that he has started to become a danger to himself and to others. Franklin is approximately 4′ 2″ tall and weighs approximately 68 lb., and he is dressed appropriately for his age. During the initial session it was noticed that Franklin walked by shuffling his feet and seemed to struggle with balance. When asked whether or not he wanted his parents to stay in the session, Franklin was insistent that they both stay and participate. Franklin's parents reported that he struggles to maintain pace at school and has a hard time with reading comprehension and handwriting. Furthermore, his parents stated that his explosive outbursts started several months ago and seem to come out of nowhere and without warning.

Conceptualizing Franklin

Franklin is firmly rooted in middle childhood, as evidenced by his age; however, there are several key issues that are immediate cause for concern. First, Franklin's safety must be thoroughly assessed, and an effectual plan needs to be developed and implemented with Franklin, his parents, and the leadership and teachers of his school. Second, from the initial assessment it appears that Franklin is delayed in the development of his locomotor efficiency as evidenced by his poor posture, inability to take normal strides (shuffling feet), and inadequate balance. Third, Franklin has potentially stalled in his physical growth, thus delaying the rebound in adiposity that happens prior to puberty. Fourth, Franklin presents as behind in the cortical maturation of his brain. (Note: The fourth factor could be an issue; however, his struggles in school could be linked to the aforesaid somatic symptoms, thus developing psychological effects).

So where do you go from here? What are your first steps with Franklin? Hopefully, you have been able to recognize the same concerns as we have, but the question is, what are the next steps? It appears that Franklin might be struggling with a couple of different things. Within the first couple of sessions it is important to build the therapeutic rapport with Franklin and his parents, and if possible it would be beneficial to spend individual time with Franklin to experience him apart from his parents. The initial assessment suggests that Franklin is internalizing his somatic struggles, and this is subsequently presenting as explosive anger. An assessment for childhood depression and anxiety would be beneficial in an effort to confirm or rule out underlying symptomology. Furthermore, it is important to advocate for Franklin's support system and to help develop a strong structure system that will intentionally engage in his success.

EMOTIONAL DEVELOPMENT

As children socially interact with the persons, places, and things in their external environments, they experience corresponding emotional responses. "During middle childhood, children make great strides in terms of their ability to recognize emotions in themselves and others, control their own emotions, and communicate about emotions, both expressively and with language" (Oswalt & Dombeck, 2010, para. 1). At this point most children have developed the ability for emotional regulation. They are able to self-sooth, utilize basic coping skills during distress withhold punching someone when angry, and can stop themselves from throwing embarrassing tantrums.

Social-Emotional Development

These children also possess the ability to recognize, respect, and demonstrate their culture's rules for emotional display. Here is where differentiation by culture becomes pronounced. Further, middle childhood–aged children develop the ability to recognize complex emotional content while socializing. They can decipher layers of emotions and recognize when there is a mismatch between one's displayed affect and underlying emotion. As they become better at doing this, they are also able expand their perspectives of others and develop deeper empathy skills. This ability continues to develop throughout middle childhood into adolescence, adulthood, and beyond.

Biological Factors

With the increased growth in the prefrontal cortex and the subsequent improvement of the child's higher order thinking, emotional regulation also matures. Colle and Del Giudice (2011) indicate that the "ecology of middle childhood suggests that change should be especially pronounced in two areas: the understanding of complex social emotions (e.g., shame, pride, embarrassment) and the deliberate, self-aware employment of emotional regulation strategies"

Table 10.1 Eight Basic Emotional Skills
1. Awareness of one's emotions
2. Ability to recognize others' emotions
3. Use of emotional vocabulary
4. Capacity for empathy and sympathy
5. Distinction between internal feelings and external expression
6. Adaptive coping through self-regulatory strategies
7. Awareness of the role of emotion in relationships
8. Emotional self-efficacy

Source: Developed through resources cited by Saarni (1999).

(p. 52). Though research continues to uncover the developmental aspects of emotional regulation, little is still known about the cultural and individual nuances therein (Colle & Del Giudice, 2011). Nevertheless, there must be an understanding that emotional competence is not a singular entity (Saarni, 1999). Saarni (1999), in her book *The Development of Emotional Competence*, suggests that emotional development is a process identified by eight basic emotional skills (Table 10.1).

PERSONAL IDENTITY AND SELF-ESTEEM

Middle childhood is a period where personal identity becomes "more complex, multi-faceted and abstract in nature" (Oswalt & Dombeck, 2010, para. 1). Rather than identify themselves according to physical, observable characteristics (e.g., gender, size, eye color), they identify more so by personality characteristics and psychological being. Further, they are able to differentiate between positive and negative qualities. For instance, rather than describing oneself as a 7-year-old girl with blond hair and blue eyes, a young lady might describe herself as a nice girl who enjoys helping people but is incapable of carrying the younger boys' heavy book bags. It is through this identity recognition of strengths and weaknesses that children begin to compare themselves to others.

As middle childhood–aged children become more influenced by social factors, their identities become entangled in the perceptions of others—especially their peers: Why is D.J. good at throwing a football when I can't even toss it 3 yards? Why is Megan so pretty when I'm stuck wearing these nerdy glasses? These personal perceptions may either be reinforced or discounted by others. As time goes on, these perceptions continue to become more ingrained into one's personal identity. That is, if others perceive a child as a loser, uncool, or any other negative connotation, he or she begins to self-identify in that light. On the other hand, if the child receives positive feedback from peers and others, then his or her self-identity may become inflated.

Throughout development, one's self-identity may continue to shift and take varied shapes. The same is true for self-esteem. Because external forces significantly impact these perceptions, the influence that positive individuals may place upon the child is extremely significant. Parents, teachers, coaches, and other positive adult role models may assist in the development of positive identity and self-esteem. One important theme is for children to understand that there are multiple means toward achieving success. Oswalt and Dombeck (2010) identified the following as these means: basic skill or ability, effort, practice and perseverance, maintaining a positive optimistic attitude, and asking for help when necessary. Recognition of these means helps children understand that although some peers may have a natural tendency to perform better in one domain, they might possess abilities to outperform other children elsewhere, especially with effort, practice, and perseverance. As children continue to make improvements and receive recognition for them, their self-esteem becomes boosted. This boost may continue to serve as the drive that propels them to succeed above others in their class. Without this boost, however, children may become unmotivated, lose their drive, and give up.

Attachment Styles

Emotional growth (or the lack thereof) happens in the context of culture and relationships and, thus, could be viewed through the lens of attachment. Colle and Del Giudice (2011), referencing Shaver and Mikulineer (2002) and Mikulineer, Shaver, and Pereg (2003) indicated that secure children have healthy primary strategies for affective regulation. These strategies are initially based on the mirrored coregulation with children's primary caregivers. As children enter middle childhood these regulation strategies provide them with stable, autonomous, independent ways of coping and regulating with the world around them (Colle & Giudice, 2011). When an insecure attachment with the primary caregiver is present, the aforementioned secure strategy is absent and one of two alternative strategies develop: 1) the *hyperactivating* strategy of the ambivalent child and (2) the *deactivating* strategy of the avoidant child. The hyperactivating child is characterized by continuous and sustained proximity seeking, constant monitoring of caregivers, and a preoccupation with the threat of abandonment (Contelmo, Hart, & Levine, 2013). Conversely, the deactivating or avoidant child dismisses his or her attachment needs, redirects focus and feeling of negative emotions, and develops maladaptive coping strategies based on the innate desire to avoid and a hypervigilance to suppress any resemblance of an emotion (Colle & Del Giudice, 2011; Contelmo et al., 2013).

With this brief understanding it must be realized that as the child enters middle childhood, the relationship between emotional regulation and attachment has the tendency to become more multifarious. The child's emotions are less reliant on the reciprocal interaction with the primary caregiver, internalized models begin to take on generalized representations, and friends take on more of a prominent role as the child's interdependence moves toward independence (Colle & Del Giudice, 2011).

Hormonal Changes Leading Toward Social Changes

For those boys and girls who experience early-onset puberty toward the end of middle childhood, there are social ramifications to consider. The physical and also the psychological, social, and emotional changes in puberty are equally profound. It is during this stage that boys become interested in relations with the opposite sex, which leads toward the sudden importance of physical attractiveness. Unfortunately, this could cause significant severe emotional strain. For instance, some females may develop anorexia or bulimia as an attempt to attract males. Another aspect of puberty that is more stressful for females than males comes by way of girls who progress through puberty more rapidly than others. Girls who fall into this group are more vulnerable to becoming sexually active at an earlier age and to beginning to participate in activities, such as substance abuse, which contribute to difficulties later in life (Santrock, 2007). Children who do not dress as stylish, or who cannot afford nicer amenities, are more vulnerable to harassment by peers. This is also a period where the more popular children begin to tease the less popular ones. Due to such social pressures, the onset of depression, anxiety, and other psychological dysfunctions becomes more prevalent. The impact of treatment received by peers during this stage of life may ultimately result in behaviors and emotions that will last the rest of the individual's life.

MORAL DEVELOPMENT

Moral development can often be an overlooked concept in exploring the developmental progression of middle childhood. Conventionally, focus is placed on the cognitive, emotional, and physical paradigms of development. Though these paradigms are supremely important it is imperative to understand how moral development is woven throughout the growth progression. We will not spend an exorbitant amount of time disseminating the specific nuances of moral development, yet beginning this conversation with counselors is tremendously important for several reasons. First, middle childhood is where the transition from Piaget's concrete operational to formal operational reasoning occurs (e.g., progression from concrete operational thinking to abstract logical thinking). Second, middle childhood is a pivotal stage, laying the foundation for Erikson's identity versus role confusion stage as the child transitions to adolescence. And third, middle childhood becomes a place where moral absolutes, values, and faith constructs are explored, tested, and eventually solidified.

Overview

Historically, moral development has been viewed as a structured cognitive progression espoused by theorists such as James Fowler and Lawrence Kohlberg. Within the context of these cognitive progressions, Kohlberg indicates that the individual progresses from the preconventional stage to the conventional stage, finally arriving at the postconventional stage (Passini, 2010). Though this cognitive paradigm has been predominant in the understanding of moral development, it does not fully capture the reciprocal multicultural complexities of the current culture.

It must be understood that individuals do not grow up in a societal vacuum, naïve to the world around them (Passini, 2010). Moral reasoning develops through the intentional interactions between the individual and the society through which she or he lives (Passini, 2010). Subsequently, moral knowledge is constructed within the context of the child's societal representations and simultaneous exchanges with her or his moral community (e.g., friends, family, neighborhood, church). Therefore, as the middle child develops, her or his moral judgments transition from a structured representation (e.g., black and white) to a more contextual framework (e.g., gray; Passini, 2010).

Key Concepts

Viewing moral development along the span of an individual life illuminates the progression from the egocentric perspective to the integration of multiple competing yet legitimate perspectives (Jambon & Smetana, 2014). Emerging from the egocentricity of Piaget's preoperational stage, the 7- to 8-year-old begins to develop a formal, concrete, logical conceptualization. Though lacking in intuition, the transitioning child is able to morally understand black-and-white concepts. Within the moral interaction with these black-and-white concepts, the child begins to recognize the externalized impact of his or her actions (e.g., if I hit Judy, Judy will cry and I will get in trouble). Though similar to the preoperational, egocentric way of thinking (e.g., I don't want to get into trouble), the child is able to concretely understand the moral blunder of hitting, if only by Judy's reaction of crying. Thus middle childhood moral development begins as an externalized response to a bounded stimulus (e.g., I won't do _____ because I don't want to get in trouble).

Middle childhood is a pivotal developmental stage as the child progresses toward adolescence. Though initially concrete, development shifts into the more abstract formal operational stage. The child begins to view the world through an abstract lens, thus developing her or his perspective-taking abilities (Jambon & Smetana, 2014). Perspective-taking abilities play an important role in the growth of moral reasoning and maturity (Jambon & Smetana, 2014). As the child is able to empathically take the perspective of another, she or he is better equipped to make an informed moral choice. This is where the moral influences transition from a predominantly familial construct to a broader societal integration of competing stimuli. As the middle child is able to explore differing societal influences, she or he begins to build up and solidify the moral self established in early childhood (Krettenaur, Campbell, & Hertz, 2013; Thompson, 2012).

Conclusion

Moral development within middle childhood is a critical transition. A gradual yet distinct shift from an egocentric vantage point to the ability to integrate differing viewpoints into her or his schemas begins to form (Jambon, & Smetana, 2014; Passini, 2010). These new perspective-taking abilities have the potential to create disequilibrium within the moral growth progression. Therefore, it is tantamount that the child relies on her or his moral community for stability, guidance, and affirmation within this transition (Passini, 2010).

SOCIAL DEVELOPMENT

Theorists who hold a belief in the social cognitive theory believe that development is a product of behavior, the environment, and person or cognition (Santrock, 2007). That is, all three of these components work in conjunction with one another to help develop the human being. Under this theory, an individual is capable of holding his or her own belief, yet the behaviors of other individuals are also motivating factors toward internalized behaviors. Here we see individuals actually adapting to behaviors represented by others in the environment.

Vygotsky and Middle Childhood

Vygotsky (1978) believed that middle childhood–aged children extramentally develop higher psychological functioning through interactions with the environment. As children internalize these interactions over time, they develop the means by which they may function intramentally. To support this theory, Vygotsky captured the structure of this relationship by creating experiments in which an external mediator would help a child perform a particular task (Wagoner, 2009). What Vygotsky (1962) found was an important link between language and cognitive and social development.

When very young children are trying to problem solve or perform some novel task, it is common for them to speak their thoughts out loud. They speak their needs and wants, ask questions, and provide answers to those questions out loud to where anyone else in the child's presence may hear. Vygotsky's (1962) experiments revealed that middle childhood is when children shift from the external dialogue to internalized thoughts. Externalizing dialogue helps guide young children through various tasks. Children in middle childhood are able to internalize this dialogue because they have developed to a point of being more efficient and skilled at various mental operations (Oswalt & Dombeck, 2010). A 3-year-old boy wanting to play with his fire truck might say out loud: I want to play with my fire truck. Where is it? Oh, it's in the toy box. Each step of the thought to find the fire truck is spoken out loud. The process for an 8-year-old boy wanting to find the truck would occur internally. The boy might think to himself: Where did I put my fire truck? Oh yes, it's under my bed.

The thought process and subsequent actions for both the 3- and 8-year old boys might be similar, but the 8-year-old does not speak his thoughts out loud. Vygotsky noted that when younger children partake in private speech (thinking out loud), they become more socially competent in middle childhood because it allows children to better guide themselves through their behaviors (Santrock, 2007). As children progress into and through middle childhood, internalized thought continues to reinforce one's learning and better commit it to memory. Consequently, this is essential for academic achievement, making friends, and participating in various activities.

An extremely important concept of Vygotsky's (1978) social development theory is the more knowledgeable other (MKO). MKO is an individual who is more knowledgeable or skilled in respect to a particular idea, process, or task (Vygotsky, 1978). This individual may offer direct or vicarious instruction through teaching or demonstration. A father demonstrating to his 6-year-old son how to throw a football by throwing the football himself is an example of this. Such a relationship may be extended to that of mentorship or apprenticeship. Then again, there may be no relationship at all past the initial instruction. It is important to note, however, that social development theory does not require the MKO to be a living person and is open to include all relevant variations of artificial intelligence (AI). Contemporary technology has contributed heavily to this form of MKO. Desktops, laptops, tablets, smartphones, and other devices that allow Internet access or interactions with software and other programs allow children to learn and reinforce that learning with various forms of practice.

Erikson and Middle Childhood

Erikson defined middle childhood as the period when children expand their social context from the home base to broader environments that strongly influence their social development (Eccles, 1999). He described the ages of 7 to 11 years as being those in which children develop a *sense of industry* and learn to cooperate with others (Eccles, 1999). During the *conflict of industry versus inferiority stage*, children are introduced "to new social roles in which they earn social status by their competence and performance" (Hamman, 2014, p. 39). Continued failures in an attempt to successfully meet social and academic challenges results in a "sense of inferiority" and increase the likelihood that a child will enter adolescence without the basic life skills needed to behave appropriately in varied social settings, build meaningful relationships, and achieve academic success. Should the child enter into adolescence without the proper support and guidance needed to address these challenges, myriad even more severe issues (e.g., academic, social, emotional) may continue into young adulthood and beyond (Sharf, 2008).

Bronfenbrenner and Middle Childhood

Children live and interact within multiple environmental systems. According to Bronfenbrenner (1979), there are five environmental systems by which individuals are influenced: microsystem, mesosystem, exosystem, macrosystem, and chronosystem. Significant influences during middle childhood most often occur within the microsystem and include family, school, and peers. As they progress through middle childhood, mass media and the attitudes and ideologies of culture increase in importance. Beyond these traditional systems is the Internet—a relatively new influence in relation to traditional ecological systems theory.

Given the influence of contemporary technology on society, it is important to note its impact on social development. Johnson (2010) explored the concept of the *techno-subsystem* (Johnson & Puplampu, 2008)—a newer concept that adds an additional layer to Bronfenbrenner's ecological system theory. The techno-subsystem is "a dimension of the microsystem which includes child interactions with both human (e.g., communicator) and nonhuman (e.g., hardware) elements of information, communication, and recreation digital technologies" (Johnson, 2010, p. 34). Accordingly, interactions with the Internet ultimately affect the child's microsystem. This virtual environment, in many respects, meets the experimental conditions upon which the classic developmental literature was built (Bandura, 1977; Erikson, 1968; Piaget, 1936; Vygotsky, 1978).

BOX 10.1   THE INTERNET AND MIDDLE CHILDHOOD

Middle childhood marks a period when the Internet has more of an impact on social development. Beyond the typical utilization, children are socializing with one another via instant messenger, email, chatrooms, and video conferencing applications. This virtual social environment mimics real social environments in that there are two or more entities (e.g., person–person, AI–AI, person–AI) communicating with one another. As such, children may declare their needs and wants, learn new information, share their knowledge, communicate with others, and so on while receiving the similar responses to those they would receive from the real social environment (e.g., feedback, rewards, consequences).

THE FAMILY SYSTEM

Children are raised in one of any variety of family systems. The concept of the traditional two-parent, heterosexual household is no longer the standard of the "normal" family. Contemporary family systems involve much greater variety. Although there is no one family system better than another, some still receive unwarranted criticism by less accepting members of society. Modern family systems include a two-parent, heterosexual household; a two-parent, gay, lesbian, bisexual, or transgender (GLBT) household; a single-parent household; a single- or divorced-parent household; an adoptive family household; a foster family household; and an extended family household. Despite all of these recent variations, the defining characteristics of family still remain intact. According to Thomlison (2007), the defining characteristics of family include (a) sharing a sense of history, (b) having some degree of emotional bonding, and (c) engaging in direction and goals for the future. Of important note is that they do not necessarily have to have legal ties or be biologically related. These characteristics, then, allow for much differentiation within the family demographic. As such, no two children experience an identical family dynamic during middle childhood or any other stage of development. It is also important to note how children living within the same household also share varied experiences.

More important than the actual makeup of members in the family is the parental style. As explained by Baumrind (1967), the actual parental style of the parent bares significant weight on the child's development. She described three types of parenting styles: authoritative parenting, authoritarian parenting, and permissive parenting. Though there are individual differences from one child to the next, the corresponding child qualities to parenting styles bear significant weight. Parents and caregivers are the primary authority figures over the child with whom they traditionally spend most of their time. As such, this influence impacts middle childhood physical, cognitive, social, and emotional development in unison.

BOX 10.2 PARENTING STYLES AND RESULTING CHILD QUALITIES

Authoritative Parenting

- Lively and happy disposition
- Self-confident about ability to master tasks
- Well-developed emotion regulation
- Developed social skills
- Less rigid about gender-typed traits (examples: sensitivity in boys and independence in girls)

Authoritarian Parenting

- Anxious, withdrawn, and unhappy disposition
- Poor reactions to frustration (girls are particularly likely to give up and boys become extremely hostile)
- Do well in school (studies may show authoritative parenting is comparable)
- Not likely to engage in antisocial activities (examples: drug and alcohol abuse, vandalism, gangs)

Permissive Parenting

- Poor emotion regulation (underregulated)
- Rebellious and defiant when desires are challenged
- Low persistence to challenging tasks
- Antisocial behaviors

SCHOOL

As children begin formal schooling around age 6 years, a substantial amount of changes occur (Eccles, 1999). This primarily occurs consequent with broadening their social arenas. Whereas infants and younger children spend a vast majority of their time at home or out with their parents, middle childhood–aged children begin their exposure to a variety of other individuals of varied ages, experiences, values, worldviews, and emotions. Each of these differences bears some influence over the child and continues to shape development. As the children progress in age, they begin to spend increasingly more time with other authority figures (e.g., teacher, coach, mentor, den leader, instructor, religious leader) until they reach a point of spending more time with them than their parents.

This is where a particularly influential adult role model becomes important. For those children who have grown up in abusive or neglectful households, this individual may serve as a life-changing positive influence.

Middle childhood–aged children also spend a lot of time with peers. Peers traditionally vary in age up to a few years at this point and are oftentimes in the same grade. They are with their peers in class, during recess, at extracurricular activities, and perhaps spend time at one another's houses or out in the community. Though adults maintain a significant influence over children, the children are oftentimes outside of the parents', caregivers', or other authority figures' range of control and are free to act as they feel (Eccles, 1999). Peer pressure becomes especially influential. Further, as children develop autonomy and increasing expectations, they are given more responsibilities, awarded more freedoms, and granted more rights. For some children this helps them mature while others use it as additional access toward deviant behaviors. Whether at the group or individual level, peer relationships are regulated by implicit and explicit rules that everyone is expected to follow. Adherence to these rules fosters harmony while failure to adhere to them leads toward discord. These experiences allow children to practice adjusting in society and adapting to work with others. Formal organizations such as school groups, sports teams, and Boy Scouts and Girl Scouts help set a standard of responsibility, respect, and teamwork. Rules established in these organizations may carry over into other relationships. When children join gangs or associate with social deviants, standards are lowered or nonexistent, making it acceptable or even admirable to partake in antisocial behavior. This may lead toward significant social and legal problems in the future.

BOX 10.3   KEEPING UP WITH TECHNOLOGY AND SOCIAL IMPLICATIONS

With new technological advancements seemingly popping up every month, it can be overwhelming for an individual to keep up with the status quo. As counselors, we must take into consideration the effects (positive or negative) technology has on the developmental trajectory. Hofferth (2010) conducted a large-scale longitudinal study from 1997 to 2003 and found that as time increased playing video games and computer games and watching television, time decreased in other nonscreen activities including time spent sleeping, reading for pleasure, and nonscreen study. Take some time to ponder what changes you have noticed since the dawn of the Internet.

SCHOOL LEADS TO A CAREER

Remember being asked what you wanted to be when you grew up? Career theorists posit that middle childhood is the period when children begin to recognize that their performance in school ties into what they become as adults.

Super (1953) identified a strong relationship between one's personal growth and career development. The theory takes into consideration life space, which entails life roles and how individuals play them out at each life stage. Each person experiences the world differently and will hold a unique pattern of development along the lines of personal (e.g., interests, needs, values) and situational factors (e.g., culture, family, gender, society). Gottfredson's (1981) theory of circumscription and compromise specifically focuses on the importance of childhood on career development. She demonstrated how vocational self-concept begins early in childhood and is defined through four orientations to work: size and power (ages 3–5 years), gender roles (ages 6–8 years), prestige and social valuation (ages 9–13 years), and the unique self (ages 14+ years). Two of these four orientations, gender roles and prestige and social valuation, occur during middle childhood. As such, this period is critical toward later career development.

Middle childhood–aged children recognize that higher achievement leads toward higher prestige careers and material goods. They also recognize that poor performance may lead toward lower end jobs, pay, and lifestyles. If any given occupation becomes unrealistic at any given time, however, the individual is more easily able to cope and compromise with another career within acceptable alternatives.

SOCIAL DEVELOPMENT THEORY IN RESEARCH AND LITERATURE

Impact of Divorce

A mere 40–50 years ago divorce was considered shameful; today most people would find these families as typical as any other. With over 45% of all first marriages in the United States ending in divorce, it is a special topic in family therapy that warrants attention (Hecker & Wetchler, 2003, p. 454). "Although divorce is a common event in today's families, it is an unscheduled transition that alters the traditional family life cycle and interrupts developmental tasks" (p. 456). The reality is that despite individual differences and reasons for divorce, "most divorcing families must address common issues and each spouse must face challenges" (p. 456). Additionally, if children are involved, they may get caught in the middle of this traumatic life event that may result in relatively severe repercussions if not addressed properly. The best results generally occur when the parents "focus on how to deal with the children's perceptions and responses, interpreting what is happening to them, and helping them express their fears, feelings, and hopes" (p. 460). Failure to consider children may lead to devastating results that may actually impact the individual for a lifetime.

The Impact of Deployment

Military trauma may result from any direct or indirect act that occurs during war (U.S. Department of Veterans Affairs, 2014). It is during these times that human beings are more likely to lower themselves to commit subhuman acts beyond injury and death, which include torture, rape, hostage situations, and indirect trauma (Crandall, Parnell, & Spillan, 2010). The impact of deployment on middle childhood–aged children cannot be understated. In an article by Songomonyan and Cooper (2010) written on the behalf of the National Center for Children in Poverty (NCCP), data revealed that

- Changes reported included changes in school performance, lashing out in anger, worrying, hiding emotions, disrespecting parents and authority figures, feeling a sense of loss, and symptoms consistent with depression.
- High levels of sadness were seen in children in all age groups.
- Depression was seen in about one in four children.
- Academic problems occurred in one in five children.
- Thirty-seven percent of children with a deployed parent reported that they seriously worry about what could happen to their deployed caretaker.
- Parents reported that one in five children coped poorly or very poorly with deployment separation. (p. 4)

Beyond the direct impact on the child is the indirect impact experienced by living with the other caretaker. Another study by Chandra, Burns, Tanielian, Jaycox, and Scott (2008) found additional evidence indicating that children "noted that deployment impacted their home caregiver's behavior" and "expressed greater worry about their home caregiver during deployment" (p. 54). When a caregiver's emotional state is impaired, it becomes difficult to adequately care for the child. Therefore, this additional stress may further compromise a child's psychosocial development.

The Impact of Returning Veterans

Depending on a variety of factors (e.g., length of deployment, physical and mental condition of returning veteran, experience with the primary caretaker), children may experience a variety of responses to a parent or caregiver's return from deployment. Chandra et al. (2008) explained how, although the children were excited to have the deployed parent return home, they were met with some notable challenges. One of these challenges entails confusion regarding who will now run the house. Further, the returning veteran struggles to reengage into what has become a new home routine. The same children also found it difficult to reacquaint with the returned veteran. During this time both the child and veteran have undergone a series of independent experiences that cause distance between the two individuals. Chandra et al. (2008) also revealed that around 30% of the children experienced issues dealing with parent mood change and stress. Each of these factors independently and in combination with one another lead toward a variety of complications (e.g., anxiety, depression, domestic violence, abuse, PTSD; Songomonyan & Cooper, 2010).

It is important to note that the impact of deployment and returning on children truly depends on the child and consideration of all other psychosocial factors. Though there are many examples of negative impacts on children, there are also positives. Songomonyan and Cooper's (2010) study actually revealed that negative consequences were less than predicted in their study. Children may better develop independent skills, be more disciplined, and engage in healthy living.

School Shootings

One of the most tragic incidents that may occur during middle childhood is a school shooting incident. Incidents reported in recent media have been alarming. "School Shooting" is a headline that no one ever wants to see, yet it continues to occur at an alarming rate. According to the latest statistics, there have been at least 109 school shootings in the United States since the Sandy Hook incident in Newton, Connecticut, in December 2012 (Everytown for Gun Safety, 2014). Of these shootings, 61 occurred at K–12 institutions with over 18 involving the death of at least one individual. Though some instances received more media attention than others, each left some level of devastating impact on the community.

School shootings result in physical, psychological, and economic trauma (Crandall et al., 2010). This trauma may result directly and indirectly. The most direct impact is experienced by those children who were either harmed or killed by the shooter. Other students directly involved are those who were onsite when the incident occurred. These students might have actually faced the shooter, been held hostage, hid, or were able to escape harm. Other children directly impacted are those who witnessed a close friend, classmate, or other person become harmed or killed. In some cases the assailant may actually be someone that victims know personally as a classmate or friend (Littleton, Kumpula, & Orcutt, 2011). Those who still suffer the same loss but were not witness to the incident are still directly impacted. An example of an indirect impact entails the responses of a society in mourning. Witnessing the pain and suffering that others are going through may lead to vicarious trauma. Further, children who see these incidents on TV may become worried that their school is next.

A child's reaction is dependent upon a host of factors. Direct or indirect involvement, the level of impact, and the individual child's ability to cope with stress will all weigh heavily on how the child responds. The National Child Traumatic Stress Network (2015) suggested the following as potential psychological challenges to consider: reactions to danger, posttraumatic stress reactions, grief reactions, traumatic grief, depression, physical symptoms, trauma and loss reminders, postviolent stress and adversities, consequences of these reactions, and coping after catastrophic violence.

As a clinician responding to a school shooting, it is important to utilize a crisis approach. In this case lower order needs must be satisfied before higher order ones (Best, Day, McCarthy, Darlington, & Pinchbeck, 2008), meaning that physiological and safety needs come first. It is important to first medically tend to those that have been injured. For those that were not injured but suffered from severe stress-induced shock, the first step is to provide immediate crisis intervention therapy that continues along into the next need of safety. Safety is further established by helping the children realize that the situation is atypical and that there is support available. Once further removed from the situation, higher-order needs including belonging and esteem continue to be established through the counselor's support, positive demeanor, and strategic intervention. These also continue to be established through the support of friends, classmates, teachers, family, and other members of the community.

BULLYING

Socialization in middle childhood can be a difficult task. "Pre-adolescents are acutely aware that pecking orders exist and that anything from and egregious offense to a classmate's whim can cause on to tumble down the status hierarchy" (Lease, Musgrove, & Axelrod, 2002, p. 509). The successful navigation of the peer system is an important developmental stage within middle childhood that can be disrupted due to bullying. Bullying is not a new problem, but over the past several decades it has nationally taken center stage due to the rise in mass school shootings such as Columbine in 1999.

Etiology of Bullying

According to Olweus (1993), bullying is defined as being "exposed, repeatedly and over time, to negative actions on the part of one or more other students" (p. 9). Within this framework, two types of bullying develop. First, direct bullying involves verbal and physical aggression, such as hitting, kicking, pushing, and name-calling (Klein & Kuiper, 2006). Second, indirect bullying involves discrete instances, such as starting rumors or forms of cyberbullying (e.g., social media; Klein & Kuiper, 2006). Eslea and Rees (2001) suggested that bullying is at its peak (33%) between the ages of 11 and 13 years.

To understand bullying, counselors must be aware of the differences between successful social development and unsuccessful social development. Successful social development is characterized by peer acceptance (e.g., the general sense of inclusion and belonging). This successful progression sets the stage for better communication skills; the greater capacity for sharing, helping, and cooperating; and the development of an easygoing temperament, greater sociability, and stronger self-control (Klein & Kuiper, 2006). The unsuccessful navigation through social development produces social isolation, social rejection, peer victimization, bullying, aggression, lack of communication skills, and the inability to construct appropriate responses in social situations (Klein & Kuiper, 2006). Several factors should be considered in the social development of middle childhood, and these can have either a positive or negative impact: relationships with parents and caregivers and peers, attachment model (e.g., secure or insecure), education, temperament, and social learning (Camodeca, Goossens, Schuengel, & Meerum Terwogt, 2003). The positive interaction with these factors allows the middle child to successfully navigate life, whereas the negative interaction with these factors has the potential to produce either the aggressor or the victim.

The Aggressor (Proactive Aggression)

Aggressors are not typically unregulated or overly emotional but display an organized behavior through which calculated aggression is used to strategically achieve intended goals, including peer domination (Camodeca et al., 2003; Schwartz, Dodge, Pettit, & Bates, 1997).

The Victim (Reactive Aggression)

Unlike aggressors, victims can sometimes display an emotional immaturity and social understanding, thus causing the potential for irrational, aggressive, and sometimes violent responses (Camodeca et al., 2003). Other types of victims will struggle with problems such as depression, low self-esteem, suicidality, and psychosomatic complaints (Carney, Hazler, Oh, Hibel, & Granger, 2010). Carney et al. (2010) suggest that a victim might also struggle with anticipatory stress reaction, which suggests that a victim's anxiety (e.g., the anticipation of a potential bullying event) is worse than the event itself.

BOX 10.4   CYCLE OF VIOLENCE SPAWNED BY CYBERBULLYING

Feelings of severe humiliation, degradation, and suicidal ideation are exemplary of the type of traumatic devastation inflicted by cyberbullies. In most cases, harassment online follows victims into the traditional school setting as well (Smith et al., 2008). Of important note is that victims of online bullying at home may seek retaliation against the bully the next time they meet at school (Hinduja & Patchin, 2007), creating a cycle of violence whereby bullies and their victims continually attack one another in and outside of school. As a counselor it is important to consider ways this cycle may be broken before it leads toward a myriad of consequences including psychopathology or even death.

Cyberbullying

Research conducted by Patchin and Hinduja (2007) revealed that approximately one-sixth of children aged 6–11 years have been subject to cyberbullying. Such harassment extends well beyond the computer itself and to various other electronic mediums such as cellular phones, PDA devices, portable video game systems, MP3 players, and any other device that may gain access to the Internet. Cyberbullying, as defined in a study conducted by Vandebosch and Van Cleemput (2008), has an intent to hurt the victim, is part of a repetitive pattern of negative interactions, and is performed within a relationship that is characterized by a power imbalance between the bully and victim. The bullying may occur through any variety of venues online including instant messenger, text messaging, emails, blogs, and chatrooms (Paulson, 2003).

BOX 10.5   CYBERBULLYING LAWS AND POLICIES

Currently, 49 states across the country (all but Montana) have bullying laws and policies, and 20 of them have already been amended to address cyberbullying (Hinduja & Patchin, 2014). As society moves further into the Internet age, more states will continue to adopt laws and policies while the laws and policies themselves continue to become more detailed and adapt to the virtual environment. Another way to help prevent victimization involves educating the children about cyberbullying, which "could take two formats: helping victims to understand the dangers and how to take simple steps to minimise any threat and educating those who believe that cyber-bullying is harmless" (Gillespie, 2006, p. 135). Think about ways that you as a counselor may help children make more informed decisions toward protecting themselves.

Social Implications of Bullying

Each victim will experience bullying differently. Social implications for victims may include being disliked or ignored by peers, being picked on by others beyond the original bully, experiencing social isolation, and compromised ability to socialize with others. By no fault of their own, victims are essentially punished for the actions that bullies inflict upon them. Though victims have options that may protect them, such as reporting the bullying, the social implications may far outweigh any punishment enacted upon the bully. Consequently, victims may engage in retaliation through various means (e.g., fist fighting, spreading rumors, cyberbullying). This feeds into the cycle of abuse further.

For bullies, social implications may entail the opposite, including being glamorized for the abusive behavior, being feared to the extent that others feel pressured to go along with the behavior, and inflated self-image built on abusing others. There are, of course, many cases where bullies are viewed unfavorably by peers and are either retaliated upon or reported. In these cases, the social implications are negative and result in bullies actually becoming victims of their own agendas. Ultimately, society may view them as social deviants, miscreants, and delinquents.

Impact of Bullying

Bullying tactics come in varying degrees of severity and are experienced by the victims differently. Although any form of bullying generally upsets the victim to some degree, some forms are just more inhumane than others.

Consequently, the emotional impact experienced may differ substantially. Common emotions experienced by victims include but are nowhere near limited to depression, inadequateness, fear, confusion, hurt, anger, and loneliness. Torment to a severe degree undoubtedly leads toward psychological distress (McKenna, 2007). If unaddressed, these feelings may develop into a diagnosable psychopathology (e.g., depression, anxiety, PTSD, panic disorder) of varied intensity and duration.

In terms of frequency of occurrences, less severe tactics are generally the ones that occur most often. Looking at traditional methods of bullying, students will call each other names much more often than they will initiate physical acts of violence such as punching and kicking. Katzer, Fetchenhauer, and Belschak (2009) found that most participants did not rate their experience of being attacked online as one that was severe. According to Paulson (2003), what makes Internet bullying more traumatizing for the victim is not necessarily how the victim is harassed but the large audience that witnesses these actions. One student that had been repeatedly harassed in both the traditional classroom setting and the Internet made the comparison, "But at least a relatively small group of people is there and aware of it. With wireless technology, that stuff is much more quickly spread, not only around school but it has the potential of being put up and shared around the world" (Paulson, 2003, p. 11). Victims become so surrounded by the bullying that they begin to feel trapped without any means of escape (McKenna, 2007).

CASE STUDY—TIM

Tim is a new client referred to you by his parents. Tim is a 12-year-old sixth-grade student who goes to the local middle school. Tim is 5'5" and 150 lb., wears large glasses, has braces, and is dressed in a polo shirt that is tucked into his khaki pants. Tim presents a flat affect and refuses to look you in the eye. Tim's parents report that over the past 3 months Tim has been complaining of migraine-type headaches that have persisted consistently. Initially, Tim's parents were concerned that there might be something seriously wrong and took him to see several different specialists. The EKGs, EEGs, blood tests, MRIs, and spinal taps all produced negative results, leaving Tim's parents and the doctors confused. It was only after Tim attempted to take his own life that his parents realized there might be more going on.

PAUSE: Do not read on until these two questions are discussed:

1. What information do you need to adequately help Tim?
2. What are your initial thoughts?

During the first couple of counseling sessions Tim's parents revealed that Tim was born 7 weeks premature and spent several weeks in an incubator, void of any skin-on-skin contact. Tim also reveals that he does not have very many friends and often feels like outcast. As you inquire further, Tim reveals he is terrified to go to school and often has to be coerced out of the car. As the sessions progress it becomes apparent that Tim is and has been bullied at school. Eventually, Tim reveals to you that for the past year an a half he has been pushed around, stuffed in lockers and trash cans, called names, and shunned at school.

Discussion Questions

1. As Tim's counselor where do you start? What would a treatment plan look like?
2. How do you advocate for Tim in his current position?
3. As a counselor, what is your response to bullying as a whole (e.g., on a community and social level)? Where do you begin?

DRUG USE

Social influences for drug use among middle childhood–aged children include parents, peers, and any other individual of influence (both in real life and in media). Parental influence is particularly significant, as there are hereditary and parental style components that factor into account. Evidence indicates that genetic predispositions may be passed from one generation to the next, therefore increasing the likelihood that succeeding generations will also suffer from substance-related disorders (Stevens & Smith, 2009). To build on genetics, substance-abusing homes increase the likelihood of children abusing drugs as well. First, modeling of such behavior may leave the child thinking it is acceptable to use. Second, substance abusing homes may not be as careful about securing substances of abuse in the household. Third, children may become resentful of their parents and use to spite them. Fourth, children may use as a coping mechanism to escape the pain experienced from their parents' issues. Stevens and Smith (2009) described the social consequences in the following statement:

> This makes the children in these families at high risk for the development of a variety of stress-related disorders, including conduct disorders, poor academic performance and inattentiveness. Children in substance-abusing families are socially immature, lack self-esteem and self-efficacy, and have deficits in social skills. (p. 257)

Although children coming from healthy households may also use drugs in an attempt to experiment or socialize with their peers, those coming from substance using households are much more likely to associate with other peers who use.

Unfortunately, drug use beginning in middle childhood is not uncommon. In fact, *The TEDS Report* (SAMSHA, 2014) revealed the following alarming statistics. First, in 2011, 10.2% of substance abuse treatment admissions aged 18 to 30 years with known age of initiation information initiated use at the age of 11 years or younger. Also, more than three-quarters (78.1%) of admissions that began substance use at the age of 11 years or younger reported abusing two or more substances at treatment entry. In addition, nearly two-fifths (38.6%) of admissions that initiated substance use at the age of 11 years or younger reported co-occurring mental disorder. As evidenced by these statistics, the potential impact of drug use on development is substantial. Early age onset of experimental use is the best predictor of substance abuse later (Sobeck, Abbey, Agius, Clinton, & Harrison, 2000). Social consequences for those who experimented before sixth grade include high susceptibility to peer pressure, poor decision-making skills, low confidence in skills, and negative perceptions of school. Therefore, early detection through being mindful of what children are doing, who they are associating with, and so on is critical toward minimizing early onset substance use disorders beginning in middle childhood.

Impact of Drug Use

The impact of drug use is substantial. During middle childhood children are still learning a lot about themselves, others, and the world and have not developed the necessary coping skills to handle the emotional impact of drugs. Many children who participate in drugging behavior are generally those facing some type of substantial conflict or issue including being the victim of physical, emotional, or sexual abuse; experiencing psychological disturbances (e.g., anxiety, depression, suicidal ideation); being the victim of bullying; experiencing GLBT sexual identity confusion; living in poverty or being of lower socioeconomic status; being raised by parents or caregivers who have substance abuse issues; experiencing a physical or mental disability; and being a minority within a predominantly dominant population.

For children who already suffer from emotional disturbances, the addition of drugs into the mix only makes everything worse. For those who started using without having any previous emotional disturbances, they are likely to start shortly after this point. Substance use compromises coping skills, which are learned throughout development. These are the skills described earlier that help children regulate emotions, read others, and make appropriate judgment calls. Children who use drugs become ill equipped at life skills and struggle to keep up as they progress through later stages of development.

BOX 10.6 FAMILY-INVOLVED SUBSTANCE ABUSE TREATMENT

Family-involved substance abuse treatment has two primary goals: (1) highlight and work with the family's strengths and available resources to assist the client's recovery; and (2) minimize the negative impact of the substance abuse on the identified client and the family system as a whole. This approach is particularly helpful as the interactions between and among family members contribute to the effectiveness or lack thereof within the system itself; when the family system is healthy the members may guide and support one another as appropriate.

KEY COUNSELING POINTERS FOR EMOTIONAL AND SOCIAL DEVELOPMENT DURING MIDDLE CHILDHOOD AND IMPLICATIONS FOR COUNSELING

As we pick up Franklin's story from the beginning of this chapter, consider the cognitive and physical factors that are currently impacting his development. Then reflect on and integrate the social and emotional factors as well. As previously stated, Franklin's explosive outbursts started several months ago and without warning. By session 3, Franklin revealed that he has been bullied at school for the past 6 months. Through the use of a kinetic drawing (e.g., house, tree, person), it was determined (and then later confirmed) that the bullying was more than just verbal, and on several occasions Franklin had been physically accosted. Finally, Franklin's parents also revealed that though Franklin is biologically related, he was adopted at the age of 2 years due to his mom's heroin overdose and his dad's incarceration.

Further Conceptualizing Franklin's Case

We determined that chronologically Franklin was firmly rooted in middle childhood; however, his developmental growth progression appeared to be delayed. This was evidenced by the lack of growth in fine motor skills, the current absence or delay in the rebound of adiposity, and the postponement in cortical brain maturation. It was also suggested that Franklin be initially assessed for depression and anxiety.

Through the progression of therapy Franklin revealed the presence of bullying, which has the potential of being the deliberate link to his outbursts. Franklin's response to the bullying could also be linked to his underdeveloped social skills. The delay in social skills could be connected to his biological mother's heroin use. It would behoove us to determine whether or not Franklin's biological mother was using heroin while pregnant with Franklin. Therefore, the collaboration with either his primary care physician (PCP) or a psychiatrist would be essential so that the proper tests could be ordered. Finally, Franklin's attachment bonds must be assessed as he could be struggling with an attachment-related disorder.

Therapeutically it would be important to focus on several key components. First, Franklin's safety plan should include input and collaboration from his parents, his PCP/psychiatrist, and the school (e.g., teachers, case workers, school counselors). Second, as his counselor it is imperative that Franklin have an advocate speaking out against the continued bullying. Third, Franklin would need to continue to meet with his PCP/psychiatrist to assess the possible need or management of medications. Finally, it is essential that Franklin develop his own toolbox of coping skills.

Conceptualizing Tim's Case

Tim's presenting problem is not a unique one; however the way it manifested somatically can be confusing. It is important to note that Tim's premature birth was quite traumatic and though he was eventually able to attach to his parents, the first several weeks in an incubator could have been developmentally disruptive. Furthermore, since there has been no physiological diagnosis to Tim's somatic symptoms it is important to look at the possibility of a psychological cause. Whether or not you agree with or like to diagnose, as a counselor it is important to utilize the *DSM-5* as an investigative tool. Exploring Tim's case through the lens of the *DSM-5*, he does not meet criteria for 313.89 Reactive Attachment Disorder, 309.81 Posttraumatic Stress Disorder, 308.3 Acute Stress Disorder, or 300.2 Generalized Anxiety Disorder. Rather, Tim appears to meet criteria for 309.21 Separation Anxiety Disorder. Criteria A suggests that there is a developmentally inappropriate and excessive fear or anxiety concerning separation from those for whom the individual is attached which is evidenced by at least three of the eight criteria (APA, 2013). Tim appears to meet at least three of the eight criteria: (1) recurrent excessive distress when anticipating or experiencing separation from home or from major attachment figures; (2) persistent reluctance or refusal to go out, away from home, to school, to work, or elsewhere because of fear of separation; or (3) repeated complaints about physical symptoms (e.g., headaches, stomachaches, nausea, vomiting) when separation from major attachment figures occurs or is anticipated. Tim's symptoms have lasted for at least 4 weeks and have caused clinically significant impairment.

As a counselor it is important to have as complete of a picture as you can prior to the start of the intervention process. With the aforesaid information it is crucial that Tim's therapy be done initially with the entire family, and then move toward a future goal of becoming individual prior to completion. Effectually it would be crucial that Tim learn to develop autonomy within the family structure, thus lessening his anxiety while strengthening his identity.

SUMMARY

Middle childhood is a period of substantial emotional and social development. Theorists who hold a belief in the social cognitive theory believe that development is a product of behavior, the environment, and person or cognition. Social development theory posits that middle childhood–aged children extramentally develop higher psychological functioning through interactions with the environment. As children internalize these interactions over time, they develop the means by which they may function intramentally. These functions extend toward Erikson's description of ages 5 through 12 being those in which children develop a sense of industry and learn to cooperate with others.

During middle childhood most children develop the ability for emotional regulation. They are able to self-sooth, utilize basic coping skills during distress withhold punching someone when angry, and stop themselves from throwing embarrassing tantrums. Middle childhood is a period where personal identity becomes more complex, dimensional, and abstract. Rather than identifying themselves according to physical, observable characteristics (e.g., gender, size, eye color), they identify more so by personality characteristics and psychological being.

Moral reasoning develops through the intentional interactions between the individual and the society through which she or he lives. Subsequently, moral knowledge is constructed within the context of the child's societal representations and simultaneous exchanges with her or his moral community. Therefore, as the middle child develops, her or his moral judgments transition from a structured representation to a more contextual framework.

USEFUL WEBSITES

Everytown for Gun Safety
http://everytown.org/article/schoolshootings/
Five Factor Personality Test
http://www2.wmin.ac.uk/~buchant/wwwffi/
Mental Health Net
http://www.mentalhelp.net
National Institutes of Health
http://www.nih.gov
National Institute of Mental Health
http://www.nimh.nih.gov/index.shtml
Substance Abuse and Mental Health Services Administration (SAMHSA)
http://www.samhsa.gov/
U.S. Department of Veterans Affairs
http://www.ptsd.va.gov/public/treatment/therapy-med/index.asp

REFERENCES

Almaas, A. H. (2000). *Being and the meaning of life (diamond heart, book 3)*. Boston, MA: Shambhala Publications.

American Psychological Association. (2015). *Personality*. Retrieved from http://apa .org/topics/personality/

Ames, L. B., Ilg, F. L., & Baker, S. M. (1988). *Your ten-to-fourteen-year-old*. New York, NY: Delacorte Press.

Bakhurst, D. (1990). Social memory in Soviet thought. In D. Middleton & D. Edwards (Eds.), *Collective remembering* (pp. 203–226). London, UK: Sage.

Bandura, A. (1977). *Social learning theory*. New York, NY: General Learning Press.

Baumrind, D. (1967). Child care practices anteceding three patterns of preschool behavior. *Genetic Psychology Monographs*, *75*(1), 43–88.

Best, D., Day, E. McCarthy, T., Darlington, I., & Pinchbeck, K. (2008). The hierarchy of needs and care planning in addiction services: What Maslow can tell us about addressing competing priorities? *Addiction Research & Theory*, *16*(4), 305–307.

Boynton-Jarrett, R., Wright, R. J., Putnam, F. W., Lividoti Hibert, E., Michels, K. B., Forman, M. R., & Rich-Edwards, J. (2013). Childhood abuse and age at menarche. *Journal of Adolescent Health: Official Publication of the Society For Adolescent Medicine*, *52*(2), 241–247. doi:10.1016/j.jadohealth.2012.06.006

Bronfenbrenner, U. (1979). *The ecology of human development*. Cambridge, MA: Harvard University Press.

Brooks, J. B. (1999). *The process of parenting*. Mountain View, CA: Mayfield Publishing Company.

Budd, B. E., Clance, P. R., & Simerly, D. E. (1985). Spatial configurations: Erikson reexamined. *Sex Roles*, *12*(5–6), 571–577.

Burton, T. (n.d.). *Tim Burton quotes*. Retrieved from http://www.brainyquote.com/quotes/quotes/t/timburton564597.html

Camodeca, M., Goossens, F. A., Schuengel, C., & Meerum Terwogt, M. (2003). Links between social information processing in middle childhood and involvement in bullying. *Aggressive Behavior*, *29*, 116–127.

Carney, J. V., Hazler, R. J., Oh, L., Hibel, L. C., & Granger, D. A. (2010). The relations between bullying exposures in middle childhood, anxiety, and adrenocortical activity. *Journal of School Violence*, *9*, 194–211.

Chandra, A., Burns, R. M., Tanielian, T., Jaycox, L. H., & Scott, M. M. (2008). *Understanding the impact of deployment on children and families: Findings from a pilot study of operation purple camp participants*. Retrieved from http://www.rand.org/content/dam/rand/pubs/working_papers/2008/RAND_WR566.pdf

Cole, M., & Cole, S. R. (1996). *The development of children*. New York, NY: W.H. Freeman and Company.

Colle, L., & Del Giudice, M. (2011). Patterns of attachment and emotional competence in middle childhood. *Social Development*, *20*(1), 51–72. doi:10.1111/j.1467-9507.2010.00576.x

Contelmo, G., Hart, J., & Levine, E. H. (2013). Dream orientation as a function of hyperactivating and deactivating attachment strategies. *Self and Identity*, *12*(4), 357–369. doi:10.1080/15298868.2012.673281

Cora, C. (n.d.). *Cat Cora quotes*. Retrieved from http://www.brainyquote.com/quotes/quotes/c/catcora442597.html

Crandall, W., Parnell, J. A., & Spillan, J. E. (2010). *Crisis management in the new strategy landscape*. Thousand Oaks, CA: Sage.

Croft, C., & Smith, J. (2008). *Middle childhood: Physical growth & development*. Chicago, IL: Magna Systems.

Eccles, J. S. (1999). The development of children ages 6 to 14. *Journal Issue: When School Is Out*, *9*(2), 1–6.

Erikson, E. H. (1950). *Childhood and society*. New York, NY: Norton.

Erikson, E. H. (1968). *Identity: Youth and crisis*. New York, NY: Norton.

Erikson Institute. (2013). *Erikson's institute namesake*. Retrieved from http://www.erikson.edu/about/history/erik-erikson/

Eslea, M., & Rees, J. (2001). At what age are children most likely to be bullied at school? *Aggressive Behavior*, *27*(6), 419–429. doi:10.1002/ab.1027

Everytown for Gun Safety. (2014). *School shootings in America since Sandy Hook*. Retrieved from http://everytown.org/article/schoolshootings/

Fireman, G., & Kose, G. (2002). The effect of self-observation on children's problem solving. *Journal of Genetic Psychology, 163*(4), 410–424.

Gillespie, A. A. (2006). Cyber-bullying and harassment of teenagers: The legal response. *Journal of Social Welfare & Family Law, 28,* 123–136.

Gottfredson, L. S. (1981). Circumscription and compromise: A developmental theory of occupational aspirations. *Journal of Counseling Psychology (Monograph), 28*(6), 545–579.

Grobman, K. H. (2008). *Diana Baumrind's (1966) prototypical descriptions of 3 parenting styles*. Retrieved from http://www.devpsy.org/teaching/parent/baumrind_styles.html

Hamman, L. P. (2014). *Exploring differentiated teaching in a grade 4 classroom*. Retrieved from http://scholar.sun.ac.za

Hecker, L. L., & Wetchler, J. L. (Eds.). (2003). *An introduction to marriage and family therapy*. Binghamton, NY: Haworth Clinical Practice.

Hinduja, S., & Patchin, J. W. (2007). Offline consequences of online victimization: School violence and delinquency. *Journal of School Violence, 6,* 89–112.

Hinduja, S., & Patchin, J. W. (2014). *State cyberbullying laws: A brief review of state cyberbullying laws and policies*. Retrieved from http://www.cyberbullying.us/Bullying_and_Cyberbullying_Laws.pdf

Hofferth, S. L. (2010). Home media and children's achievements and behavior. *Child Development, 81*(5), 1598–1619.

Institute for Human Services for The Ohio Child Welfare Training Program. (October 2007). Developmental milestones chart adapted from Rycus, J., & Hughes, R. C. (1998). *The Field Guide to Child Welfare Volume III: Child Development and Child Welfare*.

Jambon, M., & Smetana, J. G. (2014). Moral complexity in middle childhood: Children's evaluations of necessary harm. *Developmental Psychology, 50*(1), 22–33. doi:10.1037/a0032992

Johnson, G. M. (2010). Internet use and child development: The techno-microsystem. *Australian Journal of Educational & Developmental Psychology, 10,* 32–43.

Johnson, G. M., & Puplampu, P. (2008). A conceptual framework for understanding the effect of the Internet on child development: The ecological techno-subsystem. *Canadian Journal of Learning and Technology, 34,* 19–28.

Juvonen, J., & Gross, E. F. (2008). Extending the school grounds?—Bullying experiences in cyberspace. *Journal of School Health, 78,* 496–505.

Katzer, C., Fetchenhauer, D., & Belschak, F. (2009). Cyberbullying: Who are the victims?: A comparison of victimization in internet chatrooms and victimization in school. *Journal of Media Psychology: Theories, Methods, and Applications, 21,* 25–36.

Klein, D. N., & Kuiper, N. A. (2006). Humor styles, peer relationships, and bullying in middle childhood. *Humor: International Journal of Humor Research, 19*(4), 383–404. doi:10.1515/HUMOR.2006.019

Krettenauer, T., Campbell, S., & Hertz, S. (2013). Moral emotions and the development of the moral self in childhood. *European Journal of Developmental Psychology, 10*(2), 159–173. doi:10.1080/17405629.2012.762750

Larsen, R. (n.d.). *Rick Larsen quotes*. Retrieved from http://www.brainyquote.com/quotes/quotes/r/ricklarsen335010.html

Lease, M. A., Musgrove, K. T., & Axelrod, J. L. (2002). Dimensions of social status in preadolescent peer groups: Likability, perceived popularity, and social dominance. *Social Development, 11*, 508–533. doi:10.1111/1467-9507.00213

Lerner, M. (1959). *The unfinished country: A book of American symbols*. New York, NY: Simon and Shuster.

Liebman, J. L. (1966). *Hope for man—An optimistic philosophy and guide to self-fulfillment*. New York, NY: Simon and Schuster.

Littleton, H., Kumpula, M., & Orcutt, H. (2011). Posttraumatic symptoms following a campus shooting: The role of psychosocial resource loss. *Violence & Victims, 26*(4), 461–476; doi: 10.1891/0886-6708.26.4.461.

Malone, Y. (2002). Social cognitive theory and choice theory: A compatibility analysis. *International Journal of Reality Therapy, 22*(1), 10–13.

McKenna, P. (2007). The rise of cyberbullying. *New Scientist, 195*, 26–27.

Merton, R. K. (1968). *Social theory and social structure*. New York, NY: Free Press.

National Child Traumatic Stress Network. (2015). *Psychological impact of the recent shooting*. Retrieved from http://www.nctsn.org/sites/default/files/assets/pdfs/psychological_information_sheet_two_pager.pdf

Olweus, D. (1993). *Bullying at school: What we know and what we can do*. Oxford, UK: Blackwell.

Osmundson, J. (2011). I was born this way: Is sexuality innate, and should it matter? *LGBTQ Policy Journal at the Harvard Kennedy School*. Retrieved from http://isites.harvard.edu/icb/icb.do?keyword=k78405&pageid=icb.page414413

Oswalt, A., & Dombeck, M. (2010). *Primary physical changes associated with puberty*. Retrieved from http://www.mentalhelp.net/poc/view_doc.php?type=doc&id=38406&cn=1276

Oswalt, A., & Dombeck, M. (2015). *Middle childhood development*. Retrieved from http://www.sevencounties.org/poc/view_doc.php?type=doc&id=37673&cn=1272

Ozretich, R. A., & Bowman, S. R. (2001). *Middle childhood and adolescent development*. Corvallis: Oregon State University.

Pajares, F. (2002). Gender and perceived self-efficacy in self-regulated learning. *Theory Into Practice, 41*(2), 116–125.

Passini, S. (2010). Moral reasoning in a multicultural society: Moral inclusion and moral exclusion. *Journal for the Theory of Social Behaviour, 40*(4), 435–451. doi:10.1111/j.1468-5914.2010.00440.x

Patchin, J. W., & Hinduja, S. (2007). One of three teens and six preteens victims of cyberbullying. *New Social Worker, 14*, 30.

Paulson, A. (2003). Internet bullying. *Christian Science Monitor, 96*, 11.

Saarni, C. (1999). *The development of emotional competence*. New York, NY: Guilford.

SAMSHA. (2014). *The TEDS report*. Retrieved from http://www.samhsa.gov/data/sites/default/files/WebFiles_TEDS_SR142_AgeatInit_07-10-14/TEDS-SR142-AgeatInit-2014.htm

Santrock, J. W. (2007). *A topical approach to life-span development* (3rd ed.). New York, NY: McGraw-Hill.

Schwartz, D., Dodge, K. A., Pettit, G. S., & Bates, J. E. (1997). The early socialization of aggressive victims of bullying. *Child Development, 68*(4), 665–675. doi:10.2307/1132117

Sharf, R. S. (2008). *Theories of psychotherapy and counseling: Concepts and cases* (4th ed.). Belmont, CA: Brooks/Cole, Cengage Learning.

Smith, E. R., & Mackie, D. M. (2007). Chapter 11: Close relationships. *In Social psychology* (3rd ed). New York, NY: Psychology Press.

Smith, P. K., Mahdavi, J., Carvalho, M., Fisher, S., Russell, S., & Tippett, N. (2008). Cyberbullying: Its nature and impact in secondary school pupils. *Journal of Child Psychology & Psychiatry, 49*, 376–385.

Sobeck, J., Abbey, A., Agius, E., Clinton, M., & Harrison, K. (2000). Predicting early adolescent substance use: Do risk factors differ depending on age of onset? *Journal of Substance Abuse, 11*, 89–102.

Songomonyan, F., & Cooper, J. L. (2010). *Trauma faced by children of military families: What every policy maker should know*. Retrieved from http://www.nccp.org/publications/pdf/text_938.pdf

Steinberg, L. (1993). *Adolescence*. New York, NY: McGraw-Hill.

Stevens, P., & Smith, R. L. (2009). *Substance abuse counseling: Theory and practice* (4th ed.). Upper Saddle River, NJ: Pearson Education.

Super, D. (1953). A theory of vocational development. *American Psychologist, 8*(5), 185–190.

Taylor, J. G., & Baker, S. B. (2007). Psychosocial and moral development of PTSD-diagnosed combat veterans. *Journal of Counseling and Development, 85*(3), 364–369.

Thomlison, B. (2007). *Family assessment handbook* (2nd ed.). Belmont, CA: Thomson Brooks/Cole.

Thompson, R. A. (2012). Whither the preconventional child? Toward a life-span moral development theory. *Child Development Perspectives, 6*(4), 423–429.

University of Kansas. (2015). *Emotional and social development in middle childhood*. Retrieved from http://psych.ku.edu/dennisk/CP333/Emotional_Mid_Child.pdf

U.S. Department of Veterans Affairs. (2014). *PTSD: National center for PTSD*. Retrieved from http://www.ptsd.va.gov/public/treatment/therapy-med/index.asp

Vandebosch, H., & Van Cleemput, K. (2008). Defining cyberbullying: A qualitative research into the perceptions of youngsters. *CyberPsychology & Behavior, 11*, 499–503.

van der Veer, R., & Valsiner, J. (1991). *Understanding Vygotsky: A quest for synthesis*. Oxford, UK: Blackwell.

Van Wormer, K., & Davis, D. R. (2003). *Addictions treatment: A strengths perspective.* Pacific Grove, CA: Brooks/Cole.

Vogel-Scibilia, S. E., McNulty, K. C., Baxter, B., Miller, S., Dine, M., & Frese III, F. J. (2009). The recovery process utilizing Erikson's stages of human development. *Community Mental Health Journal, 45*(6), 405–414. doi:10.1007/s10597-009-9189-4

Vygotsky, L. S. (1962). *Thought and language.* Cambridge, MA: MIT Press.

Vygotsky, L. S. (1978). *Mind in society: The development of higher psychological processes.* Cambridge, MA: Harvard University.

Vygotsky, L., & Luria, A. (1994). Tool and symbol in child development. In J. Valsiner & R. van der Veer (Eds.), *The Vygotsky reader* (pp. 99–172). Oxford, UK: Blackwell.

Wagoner, B. (2009). The experimental methodology of constructive microgenesis. In J. Valsiner et al. (eds), *Dynamic Process Methodology in the Social and Developmental Sciences.* Springer Science + Business Media. doi: 10.1007/978-0-387-95922-1_5

Zembar, M. J., & Blume, L. B. (2009). *Middle childhood development: A contextual approach.* Boston, MA: Allyn & Bacon.

PART 5

Adolescence

Adolescence: Physical and Cognitive Development

Stephanie K. Scott and Kelli A. Saginak

The stage of human development commonly referred to as *adolescence*—and most commonly defined as ages 12–18 years—is a period of tremendous change as individuals transition from childhood to adulthood. It is of note, however, that the very concept of adolescence as a distinct developmental period is a relatively new concept historically. In fact, until the 20th century, little attention was paid to the unique developmental needs through this period. In ancient societies, the transition from childhood to adulthood was largely determined by biological maturity and readiness for reproduction. Children transitioned to adulthood with the support and mentorship of extended families and guided by the cultural influences of their societies. Toward the end of the 19th century, the Industrial Revolution was gaining momentum such that adult labor could not keep pace with demand. As a result, children were recruited in increasing numbers to provide inexpensive labor. There were few laws at this time restricting working hours or requiring children to attend school. Such spawned an activist movement to protect children from exploitation, geared at providing them some measure of safety and supporting their individual development.

This movement led to the enacting of child labor and mandatory education laws, which—in protecting individuals who were not young children but were not quite yet adults—were catalytic in the recognition of *adolescence* as being a distinct developmental stage. Moreover, during this historical period, the first textbook on adolescence was published by G. Stanley Hall (1904), eminent developmental researcher and proponent of children's rights. Even though much of Hall's original work has since been amended, revised, or even discredited, his influence on the recognition of adolescence as a distinct developmental stage changed the course of study of this period and has led to significant long-term changes in public policy and education.

Since the recognition of adolescence as a unique developmental stage, research efforts to better understand the processes, needs, and influences of individuals in this period have grown exponentially. In this chapter, the physical and cognitive considerations of this stage will be discussed, with specific attention given to the biological and cognitive changes adolescents experience, beginning with the onset of puberty. Implications for moral and identity development will also be examined, and cultural and contextual considerations be addressed. Last, implications for counselors working with adolescent clients will be noted, as will suggestions for further study.

PUBERTY: THE CATALYST FOR ADOLESCENCE

As a developmental stage, adolescence is preceded by puberty—a transitional period of rapid physical maturation and change. As such, puberty can be considered the marker for the beginning of adolescence and generally occurs between the ages of 9 and 16 years. Genetics account for 50–80% of observed variations in pubertal onset (Toppari & Juul, 2010), and whereas specific genes have been identified that are directly linked to the onset of puberty, just how and why these genes "switch on" when they do remain unclear (Palmert, & Boepple, 2001). Still, both heredity and environment appear to have influence on the onset and duration of puberty.

Hormonal Changes and the Endocrine System

The most notable changes in hormones occurring during puberty are seen in the systemic levels of sex hormones—estrogens and androgens. Although both estrogens and androgens are present in males and females, the relative levels of each vary significantly as puberty progresses. Increasing levels of testosterone—an androgen—in males are associated with a deepening of the voice, the maturation of penis and testes, and *spermarche* (first ejaculation of semen). By contrast, increasing levels of estradiol—an estrogen—in females are associated with breast development, maturation of the uterus and labia, and *menarche* (first menstrual period). In both males and females, increased levels of sex hormones are also associated with skeletal changes and the growth of body hair. Changes in sex hormones are controlled by the endocrine system, which is a network of glands throughout the body. This network affects almost every organ in the body and is responsible for system regulation—including growth and maturation, reproduction, metabolism, sleep, mood, and other important functions.

The parts of the endocrine system most directly involved with puberty are the hypothalamus, pituitary, thyroid, and gonads. Recent research suggests that the adrenal glands also play a role in puberty-related changes (Hiort, 2002; Santrock, 2007). The hypothalamus is a structure found in the forebrain that regulates eating, drinking, sex drive, and aggression. The pituitary is found just below the hypothalamus and is responsible for regulating other glands; it also produces growth hormones. The thyroid is located in the neck and is a butterfly-shaped gland that wraps around the windpipe; it interacts with the pituitary to stimulate growth during adolescence and is responsible for the regulation of metabolism. The gonads are sex glands, found in the testes in males and in the ovaries in females; they are responsible for the production of estrogens and androgens (Moore, Persaud, & Torchia, 2011).

The production and regulation of sex hormones—which directly contribute to the physical developments previously described—are controlled by a negative feedback loop. This means that if the levels of sex hormones get too high, the hypothalamus and pituitary reduce their action on the gonads, which in turn decreases the production of sex hormones. By contrast, if the levels of sex hormones are too low, the hypothalamus and pituitary increase their activity, stimulating the gonads to produce more androgens and estrogens (Nussey & Whitehead, 2001). Figure 11.1 summarizes the process of this negative feedback system.

The sexual maturation of puberty—called *gonadarche*—is preceded by a less evident prepubertal stage called *adrenarche*, which occurs 2–3 years before gonadarche. Adrenarche is marked by changes in secretions of the adrenal glands, located just above the kidneys. Throughout puberty, the adrenals produce androgens and are involved in the regulation of sexual development (Santrock, 2007). This change in activity of the adrenal glands is also associated with the emergence of sexual attraction and an increase in sexual awareness in both boys and girls (Collins & Steinberg, 2006; McClintock & Herdt, 1996).

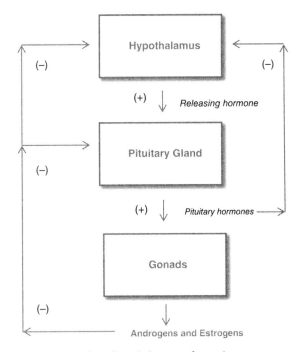

Figure 11.1 Negative feedback loop of sex hormone production and regulation.

Physical and Environmental Influences

Whereas genetic determinants clearly affect the onset of puberty, individual and environmental factors can influence pubertal timing as well (Euling, Selevan, Pescovitz, & Skakkebaek, 2008). For example, some research has supported a link between body weight and menarche, though this relationship appears to be influential rather than directly causal. Furthermore, the influence may be more related to percentage of body fat than to body mass. Studies have found that females with very low body fat—such as those who participate in certain sports or who have eating disorders—may experience delayed menarche, or a cessation of menstrual cycle (Palmert & Boepple, 2001) already begun (Fujii & Demura, 2003; Misra et al., 2004). By contrast, preadolescent weight gain in girls has been found to be associated with earlier onset of puberty (Addo, Miller, Lee, Hediger, & Himes, 2014; Davison, Susman, & Birch, 2003; Lee, Appugliese, Kaciroti, Corwyn, Bradley, & Lumeng, 2007). In males, poor nutrition has been linked to pubertal delays (Susman, Dorn, & Schiefelbein, 2003), though the correlation to body fat is less clear. Some studies have noted an inverse relationship between body fat and pubertal onset in males (Wang, 2002), whereas others stress a greater influence of body mass index (Lee et al., 2010).

Clearly, the relationship between body weight, body fat, and pubertal onset is not a simple one. One possible explanation for the interaction between these factors may be found in the hormone leptin, which is produced in fat tissue and appears to influence activity in the hypothalamus (Lassek & Gaulin, 2007; Misra, et al., 2004), thus affecting the onset of puberty (Sussman & Rogol, 2004). However, it is not solely the on switch it was once thought to be. Recent research has found that hormone kisspeptin, which a complex interaction of genetic and physiological controls, mediates leptin's influence. Kisspeptin acts as the signaling hormone, activating the production of gonadotropin releasing hormone by the hypothalamus, setting the process of sexual maturation into motion (Oakley, Clifton, & Steiner, 2009).

The role of this system on pubertal onset may help explain in part the continuing downward trend in mean pubertal age. Secular trends in mean pubertal age showed a rapid decline in the 19th and 20th centuries, mostly attributed to improvements in nutrition and general health of the population (Parent et al., 2003; Soliman, De Sanctis, & Elalaily, 2014). The observed decline slowed in the mid to late 20th century but has shown an increase over the past several decades. This may be due in part to the increasing incidence of childhood obesity, which—as has been noted previously—may affect the switching on of pubertal hormone systems. In addition, recent studies have shown a correlation between environmental chemicals and decreases in mean pubertal onset (Wang, Needham, & Barr, 2005). These chemicals function as endocrine disruptors, altering the process, flow, and efficacy of the endocrine system (Toppari & Juul, 2010). Because they are experiencing far more rapid developmental changes than adults, children are especially susceptible to the impacts of these chemicals, which are particularly abundant in more developed and industrialized areas (Euling et al., 2008).

Relational stressors in the environment can also affect pubertal timing. Poor parental attachment and conflictual family dynamics have been associated with precocious puberty in both males and females (Belsky, Steinberg, & Draper, 1991), although findings are less notable in males than in females (Walvoord, 2010). An *integrated evolutionary-developmental model* (James, Ellis, Schlomer, & Garber, 2012, p. 699) has been proposed to explain the variations observed in pubertal onset and puberty-driven behavioral changes in children who experience chronic stress in familial relationships and environment. In short, it is possible that observed precocious puberty is an evolutionarily advantageous response that facilitates alternative reproductive strategies.

BOX 11.1   AN EPIGENETIC PERSPECTIVE

Historically, the relationship between genotype (total information contained in the genome) and phenotype (expression of genetic information) was thought to be unilateral. That is, it was previously believed that genetic information gave rise to structure, which precipitated function. It is now known that trait expression is the result of an interactive collaboration between DNA and the environment. This *epigenetic* process is bidirectional across genetic activity, neural activity, behavior, and environment (Gottlieb, 2007). Though still a relative newer area of study, epigenetics offers promising insights into human development, including such timely topics as genetic predispositions to pathology and long-term effects of trauma and stress (Eaves, Silberg, & Erkanli, 2003; Essex et al., 2013; Guerrini, Quadri, & Thomson, 2014). Epigenetics may also enhance understanding of the interrelationship between genetics, physical development, and environment on the onset of puberty as well as subsequent developmental markers of adolescence.

PHYSICAL DEVELOPMENT IN ADOLESCENCE

Skeletal and Muscular Development

Puberty marks the beginning of the adolescent growth spurt—a period of rapid development in skeletal and muscular systems. Though the majority of physical changes occur over a period of 2–4 years, many adolescents experience multiple mini spurts of growth—observed, for example, in temporarily elongated legs, or torso or in disproportionate facial features. These periods of asynchronous development can be distressing for adolescents but are thankfully short-lived. Still, the awkward appearance often accompanying these rapid changes can contribute to increased anxiety and decreased self-esteem.

The adolescent growth spurt generally begins around age 12 years for girls and age 14 years for boys. During this time, girls gain about 6–7 inches in height and boys about 8–9 inches (Neinstein, 2007). There is also considerable growth in muscle tissue during this period and a markedly greater increase in males compared with females. By the end of adolescence, males are generally stronger than females of the same approximate size.

As noted previously, puberty marks the onset of noticeable physical changes at the beginning of adolescence; it also signals the beginning of sexual maturation. As adolescence progresses and physical development proceeds, secondary sexual characteristics become more distinct and developed in both boys and girls. Although the majority of this development occurs between puberty and middle adolescence, gender-related development may continue into early adulthood (Montgomery, 2005).

Impacts of Early or Late Maturation

There is considerable variation in adolescent development and sexual maturation—in fact, some children may only be on the cusp of their own growth spurts while their peers have finished theirs. Such variations, coupled with the social perceptions of maturity or immaturity, can have significant impacts on adolescent identity and self-concept and relational dynamics and interpersonal decision making.

BOX 11.2   CASE STUDY—MICHAEL

Michael is a 16-year-old African American male brought to counseling by his mother, who reports concern over her son's social withdrawal. Michael reports that he has experienced a great deal of bullying by his peers, who call him "girly man" and "sissy boy" and generally make fun of his smaller stature. Michael also shares that he used to be a decent football player in middle school and on his freshman team last year, but he did not make the cut this past fall—which he says is "just fine" because he was "dreading sharing the showers" with his peers anyway. Despite his minimizing the significance of these events, Michael is clearly struggling. As Michael's counselor, how can you help Michael cope with his later development and support a positive sense of self?

Research on the effects of early or late maturation has yielded some conflicting data. Most studies agree that early-maturing girls suffer higher rates or depression and anxiety (Walvoord, 2010), but others have found earlier development to be socially advantageous, positively affecting self-concept and confidence (Stattin & Magnusson, 1990). For boys, some research has found early maturation to be associated with higher rates of depression and anxiety (Reardon, Leen-Feldner, &

Hayward, 2009); however, far more data support the opposite (Walvoord, 2010). Still, as a general rule, early-maturing girls and late-maturing boys face more challenges than late-maturing girls and early-maturing boys (Graber, 2013).

A possible explanation for these differences may lie in the secondary social effects of early or late maturation. For example, early-maturing boys are often distinguished by taller height and more developed musculature. They are likely to be admired by their peers, perhaps even respected for their athletic or physical prowess. Such positive reinforcement may support feelings of confidence and security. By contrast, late-maturing boys may be teased by their peers for their smaller stature and more child-like features, which could directly contribute to feelings of insecurity and anxiety. Social reactions to girls' maturation tend to be the opposite, as early-maturing girls are more likely to be teased or bullied by peers (Copeland et al., 2010). Sontag, Graber, and Clemens (2011) suggested that complex interactions of gendered norms and psychosocial developmental expectations directly influence the experiences of and reactions to early or late maturation for both genders.

For both boys and girls, earlier puberty is associated with greater incidence of risk-taking behavior, including smoking, delinquency, and sexual activity (Copeland et al., 2010; Ostovich & Sabini, 2005; Van Jaarsveld, Fidler, Simon, & Wardle, 2007). However, as noted already, the social reactions to these behaviors may vary; thus, the net short- and long-term impacts on identity vary considerably as well. Furthermore, considerations must be given for the co-occurring neurological development during this time. It may very well be that the social implications of appearing older than one's peers create too much pressure on the cognitive development in process. In other words, perhaps adolescents who experience early physical development lack the cognitive maturity needed to effectively cope with these radical changes (Michaud, 2015).

BOX 11.3 PERSONAL REFLECTION: MATURATION AND SOCIAL IMPACT

Reflect on your own experience of physical development in adolescence, answering these questions:

- Was your physical development early, late, or in between? How did this compare with your peers?

- Did you experience a rapid growth period or a slower progression over several years?

- In what way did your development impact your self-concept and social interactions?

- As you consider your answers, think about how you might use your reflections to enhance your empathy for and understanding of adolescent clients.

The Adolescent Brain

Research over the past few decades has yielded previously unknown insights into the structural and functional differences in the adolescent brain. It is now widely accepted that the adolescent brain is fundamentally different from that of both children and adults (Keating, 2004). In fact, considerable change in neural pathways, neurotransmitter activity, and neural density occur well into early adulthood.

Myelination

During adolescence, several events take place that enhance the speed and effectiveness of neural connections in the brain (Blakemore, 2012). First, myelination increases, effectively enhancing the speed of neural impulses along axons, the part of the neuron responsible for transmission of information away from the nerve cell. Increased myelination improves the speed of neural transmission and continues into adulthood. Increasing myelination not only improves the speed of transmission, but also the amount and efficiency of connectivity between different regions of the brain (Steinberg, 2009). Thus, young adults have a much greater capacity to process emotional information and exercise self-control.

Synaptogenesis

This process—started in infancy—continues to progress through adolescence. Synaptogenesis is the creation of connections between neurons. However, because nearly twice as many synapses are created than are needed, a pruning process also occurs during this time. Neural pathways that are used and necessary will be strengthened, while those that are unused and unneeded will disappear or be replaced. The timing of this process varies in different regions of the brain. For example, a substantial amount of blooming and pruning occurs in the prefrontal cortex in early to middle adolescence, which corresponds to significant improvements in logical reasoning during this period (Steinberg, 2009).

Neurotransmitters

With the onset of puberty, levels of neurotransmitters change; these chemicals are responsible for transmission of impulses between neurons. Most notably, in the earlier part of adolescence, dopamine levels increase substantially in the prefrontal cortex and the limbic system. The prefrontal cortex is responsible for executive functioning and decision making, whereas the limbic system is the center of emotional processing. As such, increases in dopaminergic activity concurrently in these two regions directly affect sensation-seeking behavior, risk taking, and impulsivity (Spear, 2010).

Relative Development

The previously described processes occur in all regions of the brain; however, the relative amount of change in the different regions of the brain is asynchronous. Recent advances in technology have facilitated qualitative data collection and enhanced understanding of the growth spurts identified in each of the brain's four lobes. Although the overall size of the brain changes little over the course of childhood through adolescence, neural pathways and synaptic densities vary considerably. The net effect of these variations contributes directly to the patterns of processing and decision making seen in adolescents (Kelly, 2012; Steinberg, 2009; Wahlstrom, White, & Luciana, 2009). For example, although adolescents are highly capable of experiencing strong emotions, they often lack the ability to control or regulate their reactions. Until the prefrontal cortex catches up with the amygdala, and until myelination is more advanced and interconnectivity better developed, adolescents are—in a very real sense—at a cognitive disadvantage.

Implications

Although impulsivity and risk taking in adolescents are often attributed to hormonal changes, it seems evident that these behaviors are far more directly linked to developmental changes occurring in the brain. The question then becomes, how much responsibility should adolescents have for their behavior and decision making? Noted experts in adolescent development have long supported the notion that the developing adolescent needs to be considered *in context*—to include developmental and environmental considerations (Albert & Steinberg, 2011; Blakemore & Robbins, 2012; Smith, Chein, & Steinberg, 2013). The impact of adolescent impulsivity and risk taking within the context of developmental and environmental considerations on education, public policy, and health care is an ongoing discussion and beyond the scope of this chapter. For counselors, it is important to approach this topic from both a psychoeducational and a wellness perspective, encouraging responsibility and supporting proactive decision making, while also helping the adolescent client and family better understand the influences on the period of rapid development and change. For example, counselors can provide parents and adolescents with valuable awareness, knowledge, and skills regarding the myriad developmental changes, including neurological and hormonal, that teens experience during the adolescent years that influence decision-making and problem-solving abilities. Gaining an understanding of the general realities of adolescence could ease the storm and strife that families and adolescents experiences as they maneuver this stage of development (Spear, 2000a). Walsh (2014) emphasizes that with the amount of research continuing to emerge on brain development during adolescence, we are in a much better position to select parenting and prevention strategies that facilitate adolescent development instead of hinder it.

BOX 11.4 PERSONAL REFLECTION: SOCIAL ADVOCACY

Consider recent events in the news regarding adolescents and crime. What are your thoughts about the relative amount of individual responsibility these adolescents have in their decision making? Under what circumstances, if any, do you believe adolescents should be prosecuted as adults? How might you positively impact your community to better support adolescent development and minimize delinquency?

COGNITIVE DEVELOPMENT OF ADOLESCENCE

As discussed previously, adolescence is marked by a period of substantial physical development, including significant changes in brain structure and function. Concurrent to these physical changes are substantial advances in cognition, as evidenced by increasing complexity in thought and moral decision making. Adolescents begin this developmental stage with predominantly concrete thinking processes and high egocentricity; they end this period with abstract thinking skills and improved social perception and insight.

Piaget and Formal Operations

According to Piaget's theory of cognitive development, adolescents are in the developmental stage of *formal operations*. In this stage of intellectual development, individuals acquire the ability to think abstractly and hypothetically. This stage is qualitatively different from the previous one—*concrete operations*—which lasts through late childhood. In the concrete operational stage, children are able to think logically about concrete objects and to understand conservation. They are limited, however, by time and abstraction and struggle to fully understand future or hypothetical ideas. As they transition into the formal operational stage, adolescents develop the ability to consider what-ifs and can use their new hypothetical thinking abilities to support developing deductive reasoning skills. The latter is a particularly significant sign of more mature cognition, as from deductive reasoning emerges more complex problem-solving and logic skills.

The transition from concrete to formal operations is not a sudden one, but rather occurs over time concurrently with brain development. As children in the concrete stage become more adept at organizing thought and environmental stimuli, they begin to recognize relationships between information in a more complex manner than they had previously. In doing so, they are also able to begin to understand the potential holes in the concrete world—the what-ifs, maybes, and what about that had previously eluded them. Herein lies the beginning of the transition to abstract and hypothetical thought that is the hallmark of the formal operational stage.

It also is important to note that because this stage progression is dependent upon both neurological advances in the brain and experiential input which moves the developmental process forward, environment can affect both aspects of cognitive development. For example, poverty—which may adversely influence children's nutrition, health care, and education—can potentially interfere with both healthy neurological development and the stimuli needed for continued cognitive development. A counselor working with an adolescent client needs to consider not only the cognitive stage of the client but also the influences, such as cultural, which may be hindering or supporting continued development. For example, Kuwabara and Smith (2012) suggested that cognitive differences exist between Eastern and Western cultures in terms of relational and object attention. Whereas classical developmental theory tends to suggest development is universal across cultures, growing evidence suggests cross-cultural differences in development do exist (Kuwabara, & Smith, 2012; Saxe, 1999; Steinberg, 2005; Varnum, Grossman, Kitayama, & Nisbett, 2010).

Beyond Piaget

The most prominent criticisms of Piaget's theory are (a) that there is greater variation to the stage development than originally proposed, and (b) culture and context are far more relevant than Piaget suggested. For example, some adolescents remain very concrete in their thinking processes; in fact, many adults are not fully formal operational thinkers. In addition, certainly environment plays an important role in all aspects of development, a factor not well accounted for in Piaget's theory. Viewing intellectual development from a different angle, Vygotsky proposed a *social constructivist* theory, which emphasized a collaborative approach to learning and intellectual growth, stressing the role of social interaction and context. Vygotsky's theory accounts for cultural variations in both stage progression and skill acquisition and underscores the importance of opportunity in learning—thus taking into consideration the influences of parenting, schools, and peers on cognitive growth. Vygotsky's theory is not without its own criticisms, however, as some believe he overemphasized the responsibility of caregivers, teachers, and even peers on a child's intellectual development. Furthermore, neither Vygotsky nor Piaget accounted for substantial variations in rate of development, such as intellectual growth spurts. They also failed to fully acknowledge and explain how subcategories of intelligence may develop at different rates.

A more integrated theory may be better suited for explaining cognitive development in adolescence as well as across the lifespan. The *information processing view* is a theoretical framework of cognitive development built on the work of the neo-Piagetians in response to the criticisms and limitations of traditional theorists. However, unlike the majority of developmental theories, it is not a stage model, but rather a process model. The four primary mechanisms of cognitive functioning remain fairly consistent throughout development: encoding, automaticity, strategy construction, and generalization (Siegler & Alibali, 2005). Variation and development are directly impacted by available resources (nature) and opportunity (nurture). Thus, an information processing view may provide a more cohesive and diversity-oriented perspective of development.

Advanced Problem Solving

As they move through this developmental stage, adolescents acquire more complex problem-solving skills. These result from both continued neurological advances and life experience. Also in this stage, adolescents showed marked improvements in attention, processing speed, and memory and can organize ideas and topics in new and complex ways. Because they become more aware of the interrelationships between constructs and gain an ability to think more abstractly, they show significant advances in problem solving. They are able to effectively use scientific method—that is, they can identify patterns in information, create a hypothesis based on these patterns, test the hypothesis by gathering additional data, and modify the original hypothesis based on the new information. This is a significant advance in cognitive thought processes, as adolescents are able to consider multiple possibilities and abstractions and identify relationships between these.

This important cognitive advance influences educational and social realms for the adolescent. It informs academic programming and testing, as well as provides perspective for benchmarks and expectations. Further, this new pattern of thinking gives birth to the *adolescent philosopher*—the emerging aspect of adolescent identity that questions the status quo and rarely hesitates to propose improvements. It could also be argued that this cognitive development is an essential piece of what is often dismissed as a behavioral challenge: adolescent rebellion. Perhaps what adults perceive as a push back against rules and social policies is merely a process of evaluation, critique, and hypothesis testing from the adolescent's point of view. Therefore, adolescent "rebellion," so to speak, may be an essential aspect of the individuation process of development.

Metacognition and Egocentricity

As noted previously, a key feature of adolescent development is a more advanced and complex thought processes. During this stage, adolescents develop *metacognition*—literally, thinking about thinking—as evidenced by advanced reasoning and ability to consider multiple perspectives. They also develop increased insight, self-awareness, and analytical skills, all of which contribute to increasing introspection in adolescence. This introspection may appear ruminative to adults, most of who retain this skill but to not dwell in it. Increasing introspection is particularly evident in earlier adolescence.

These changes are also directly influential on the *egocentrism* seen in adolescence. Unlike the egocentrism of childhood, which is based in a cognitive inability to understand external points of view, the egocentrism of adolescence is founded in a preoccupation with the self. Though the adolescent is developing the ability to understand multiple points of view during this time, the initial focus is internal. Further, because they are transitioning from concrete to abstract thinking, adolescents may not always be able to consciously distinguish between internal and external constructs. In other words, through this transition, adolescents often assume that everyone thinks about them as they think about themselves. This phenomenon—dubbed the *imaginary audience*—can increase an adolescent's anxiety and self-consciousness as they mistakenly perceive heightened judgment in others. For example, an adolescent with common acne issues may be convinced that her peers are staring at her and making fun of her behind her back—to the point where she may find it difficult to focus in school, or she may even refuse to attend all together. In reality, it is far more likely that her peers have not noticed her skin problems to the degree she perceives they have. Still, such a belief can be very distressing for an adolescent and should be empathized with rather than denied.

Another consequence of the egocentrism of adolescence is the *personal fable* (sometimes called the *invincibility fable*). Like the imaginary audience, the personal fable is a direct result of the egocentrism of adolescence and an unfinished cognitive development. At the core of the personal fable is the belief that one's own experience of life is somehow unique and different from everyone else's. Further, many adolescents hold a fantasy-like belief that their uniqueness is tied to a great destiny, fame, or other grandiose fantasy and that they are somehow invulnerable to danger or even death. The personal/invincibility fable tends to appear in early adolescence and resolve itself by young adulthood as a direct result of continuing brain development and personal experience.

In addition to being a transitional aspect of cognitive development in adolescence, this egocentrism may serve additional functions. Elkind (1967) suggested that teenagers' egocentrism provides some explanation as to the increasing importance of peer relationships. The preoccupation with what friends think and increasing need for their approval may help explain why adolescents frequently engage in behaviors solely for the purpose of obtaining the attention of peers and reaffirming their own value. Lapsley (1993) proposed that adolescent egocentricity is the result of a developmental need to differentiate, and it helps to mitigate some of the reactive anxiety associated with these first steps toward individual identity. Additional studies (Arnett, 1990; Greene et al., 2000) investigated the influence of egocentrism and sensation seeking in relation to risk-taking behaviors. Whether the cause or the effect, it seems that egocentrism does serve an important developmental function in both individual and social identity development.

As adolescents evolve into adulthood, quite possibly egocentrism never truly resolves, manifesting differently across individual personalities, genders, and cultures (Kessler, Cao, O'Shea, & Wang, 2014). Interestingly, some believe that adolescent egocentrism is no different from adult egocentrism (Rai, Mitchell, Kadar, & Mackenzie, 2014). Egocentrism as a normal personality trait supports healthy development. When viewed along a continuum toward narcissism, egocentrism may hinder adolescents' abilities to see other perspectives or points of view. However, overly developed narcissism could prevent the adolescent from seeing the other person's point of view, and the adolescent does not care. In extreme cases, narcissism might manifest as anger or rage toward others that do not appreciate or accept the adolescent's point of view (Whitbourne & Halgin, 2014).

> # BOX 11.5 CASE STUDY—MARISA
>
> Marisa is a 13-year-old Hispanic female brought to counseling by her parents. Marisa had recently been caught sneaking out of the house to hang out with older kids in the neighborhood and had admitted to using alcohol and marijuana. Privately, Marisa also admits that she is sexually active with several boys in her neighborhood. Marisa does not seem to be worried at all about the risks of substance use, nor has she considered the possibility of becoming pregnant or contracting an STD. She laughs when you express concern about her decisions and how they might impact her health, responding, "Yeah, I know, but I'm fine. I'm just having fun." Knowing that Marisa may lack the ability to fully understand the impacts of her behavior, how can your support her development from a wellness perspective?

Historically, Freud (as cited in Sandler, Fonagy, & Person, 2012) believed that narcissism existed as a natural component of human nature and that only extreme narcissism provokes psychological dysfunction or disorder. Today, researchers propose a continuum of narcissism that resides between healthy, "normal" narcissism and a more dysfunctional form of narcissism (Hill & Lapsley, 2011). Although consensus is lacking as to whether healthy narcissism exists (e.g., Twenge & Campbell, 2003), normal narcissism might cushion adolescents from a variety of psychological issues, such as depressed mood or anxiety, and support psychological well-being while inspiring creativity, motivation, and achieving aspirations (Lapsley & Aalsma, 2006; Sedikides, Rudich, Gregg, Kumashiro, & Rusbult, 2004; Zeigler-Hill, Clark, & Pickard, 2008). In addition, Wink (1992) argued that healthy narcissism is necessary to support the developmental challenges common in late adolescence through emerging adulthood.

When healthy narcissism fails to support healthy psychological functioning and well-being, adolescents could be at risk of developing and experiencing a variety of challenges, such as unrealistic expectations, self-absorption, defensiveness, and relationship difficulties. In extreme cases, narcissism can manifest into narcissistic personality disorder. Some believe that today's society is ripe for producing a generation of narcissistic teenagers because of the barrage of attention on image, perfectionism, and fear of failure. Twenge (2006) argued that an increase in celebrity narcissism flooding reality television could be contributing to a rise in narcissism among adolescents. Parents may be contributing to this trend because of their own fears of judgment, image, and what the future holds for their adolescent. The literature clearly reports a generation of parents that are parenting based on fears regarding the future instead of what is realistic and perhaps best for their teen (Levine, 2006). Counselors are urged to help families support the development of a healthy sense of adolescent self-esteem that promotes internal happiness and life satisfaction versus external reward and recognition.

MORAL DEVELOPMENT IN ADOLESCENCE

Concurrent to the development of increasingly complex cognitive processes is the advancement of morality. Morality—in most basic terms—is the set of principles and beliefs upon which people perceive, contextualize, and react to situations. As adolescents' cognitive development advances, so do the intricacies of moral reasoning and the internalization of moral constructs. Moral development includes both an intrapersonal (core values and beliefs) and an interpersonal (manifestations of beliefs outside the self) component (Santrock, 2007). Intrapersonal morality influences an individual's behaviors and reactions independent of social input—in essence, it is who people are when no one is looking. Interpersonal morality affects behaviors in the social context—how people react to and resolve conflict and their reactions to the differing beliefs of others. During adolescence, morality transitions from the largely external process of childhood (beliefs based on what others have told them to believe) to an internalized process (beliefs that have been consciously chosen and accepted).

Kohlberg's Theory of Moral Development

According to Kohlberg, there are three levels of moral development, with two stages within each level. Moral development is a process that occurs over the lifespan, and not all individuals will reach the highest levels. Level 1 is the *preconventional level* and is marked by complete externalization of beliefs. Motivation is based on rewards and punishment; there is no internalization of constructs at this stage. Level 2 is the *conventional level* and is marked by the beginning of internalization. At this level, behavior is influenced by rewards and punishment, but with a deeper level of understanding—individuals now understand *why* they must follow certain rules, both for personal and societal benefit. Also at this level comes the emergence of internalized constructs such as trust, concern, honesty, loyalty, and similar concepts essential to the development of personal ideas and beliefs. However, most decision making is still motivated by conformity and duty. Level 3 is the *postconventional level* and is marked by complete internalization of constructs and ideals. At this level, decisions are made based on core beliefs of right and wrong—regardless of existing laws and rules. Although individuals at this level do understand and respect authority, they also recognize its fallible structure and take action based on their individual consciences. As with other areas of development, progression through these levels and their substages does not occur at exactly the same times for everyone. However—as a rule—progression is always in a forward direction and is influenced by biological and environmental influences (Eisenberg & Morris, 2004).

To better understand this transition, counselors need to bear in mind the client's chronological age as well as his or her cognitive developmental level; further, it is important to remember that chronological age, cognitive development, and moral development do not always occur as expected. As discussed previously, younger adolescents tend to retain some of the concrete processes of childhood and display greater egocentricity than do older adolescents. In addition, life experiences have a significant impact on all areas on development, and these can be instrumental in continued advancement or unsurpassable roadblocks. These considerations can affect the moral reasoning process in several ways. For example, younger adolescents may be expected to objectively understand the benefits to rules and social order; however, their cognitive development may still be at a more concrete level. Thus, their moral development is likely to be in the *conventional stage* where motivation for behavioral decisions is grounded in seeking approval or avoiding blame. In addition, because their brain development is at a stage in which the prefrontal cortex is still catching up to development in other areas of the brain, the children may appear much more impulsive than their older peers and may appear to disregard the consequences of their actions. Figure 11.2 provides a summary of key elements in Kohlberg's levels and stages.

Influences on Stage Progression

Morality develops concurrently with cognition and is strongly influenced by life experiences. Some of the factors that can directly influence moral development are modeling, problem solving, and influential relationships. Opportunities to learn about the more intricate decision-making processes beyond an individual's

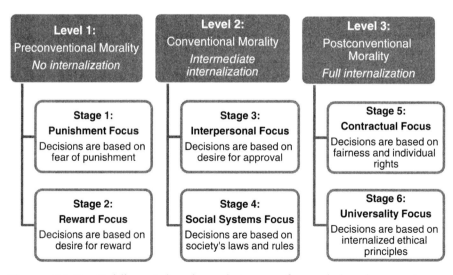

Figure 11.2 Kohlberg's levels and stages of moral development.

current developmental level can precipitate additional skill development and broaden perspectives. Similarly, engaging in thought-provoking, challenging discussion with peers or parents, which may require complex conflict resolution or analysis of hypothetical situations, also promotes progression toward higher levels of moral development. In short, new information—whether instructional or experiential—can facilitate enhanced moral development.

Beyond Kohlberg

There have been numerous critics of Kohlberg's theory since it was first proposed. Most of these have focused primarily on Kohlberg's objective and philosophical approach to moral thought and minimal attention given to moral behavior from an operational perspective. That is, while Kohlberg did effectively explain *how* people come to develop beliefs—and aligned these well with cognitive development—he did not account for *why* different behaviors are executed. Few would argue that most adolescents know right from wrong; this does not mean that their behaviors logically follow such knowledge. In addition, some critics have noted that Kohlberg's theory and stages do not hold up well in cultural context.

Social cognitive behaviorist Albert Bandura proposed an alternative perspective on morality, noting that *moral agency*—or the expression of moral beliefs—results from a "reciprocal interplay of personal and social influence" (Bandura, 2002, p. 101). As such, *moral reasoning* is contextual and is based both on an individual's beliefs and on the circumstances precipitating the decision-making process. Further, Bandura, Barbaranelli, Caprara, and Pastorelli (1996) also noted that rationalizations of actions are facilitated by situation-driven justification, particularly in retrospect. In an extreme example, an immoral action may be perceived as acceptable to the individual—or even to society—if it is viewed as being personally or socially beneficial. This is important for counselors working with adolescents to understand, as they may be more prone to rationalizing potentially destructive or even criminal behavior based on their perspectives of morality and circumstance and their tendency to make impulsive decisions.

Another criticism of Kohlberg's theory is in the lack of consideration for cultural influences and sensitivity to cultural values, traditions, and orientations (Walker & Snarey, 2004, as cited in Wood & Hilton, 2013). Notably, Kohlberg's stage progression assumes a Eurocentric, discrete process of internalization of moral constructs that favorably values individualism and a view of morality based on justice (Wainryb, 2006, as cited in Wood & Hilton, 2013). By contrast, collectivist cultures generally place high value on the common good; as such, moral behavior based solely on internalized, individual belief systems would not be considered developmentally advanced. Thus, it is important to overlay worldview and cultural orientation to moral development. Furthermore, Shweder (1991) proposed three general ethical perspectives which impact moral development and decision making: autonomy, community, and divinity. Understanding the client's primary ethical affiliation and influences is essential to understanding how he or she makes decisions. Furthermore, when working with adolescent clients, it would also be important to understand the moral and ethical orientation of the family of origin as well. It is not uncommon for generational differences across these considerations to be a source of stress and conflict in a family system.

Related to criticism based on a lack of cultural consideration is that grounded in the lack of gender consideration. Carol Gilligan (1996) stressed that relationships are an essential aspect of decision making as well as moral development as a whole. Her *care perspective* approach to morality contrasts Kohlberg's *justice perspective* by emphasizing the significance of concern for others. Research on the care perspective supported differences in the ways in which people make decisions as influenced by relational dynamics. Furthermore, differences have been noted in the ways in which males and females operationalize their moral constructs (Santrock, 2007). For example, before adolescence, girls are generally clear, objective, and perhaps even outspoken regarding what they see, hear, and experience. Interestingly, as girls approach adolescence, studies suggest differences in how girls use their voices. Eloquently noted by Gilligan (2005), girls begin "not to know what in another sense they knew" (p. 723) and "face a choice of having a voice or having a relationship" (p. 723). There is much debate over the consistency and meaning of these findings and over the potential rationale for the observed differences. However, these variations are important for counselors to bear in mind, as gendered differences and role socialization do seem to have an impact on moral development and moral agency.

Systemic Influences: Families, Schools, and Religious Institutions

Simone Weil (as cited in Browning, 2008) "define[d] morality as the silence in which one can hear the unheard voices" (p. 149). Thus, perhaps moral development involves more than the individual self and cognitive mind. Killen and Smetana (2013) viewed moral reasoning as a social process that assumes the role of socialization on moral development. Influenced by Piaget, Kohlberg, and Erikson, Selman (as cited in Nakkula & Toshalis, 2008) moved traditional moral development philosophy in a "relational direction" (p. 92), as did Gilligan in her studies of moral development from a gender specific perspective. Specifically, Selman sought to unravel the complex nature of social and moral cognition, which he referred to as *interpersonal understanding*. Through interactions with and toward others, and shaped overtime by the interpersonal environment, interpersonal understanding evolves from a state of infancy whereby there is no interpersonal perspective taking to a state of *reciprocal* interpersonal understanding, which characterizes more healthy adolescents and adults. Nonetheless, Selman believed that individuals have the capacity to grow to a higher level of interpersonal understanding, which he termed *mutual*. At this state of understanding, individuals interact with "genuine care and concern for others," which portrays "an understanding of another's needs and interests that is not contingent upon one's own interpersonal agenda" (p. 89). This complements Gilligan's concept of *ethic of care* (as cited in Browning, 2008), which views moral decision making as deeply entrenched in relationships with others.

Selman's theory of interpersonal understanding (as cited in Nakkula & Toshalis, 2008) evolved to include the actions that emerge or do not from interpersonal thought. In other words, what cognitive processes, or *interpersonal negotiation strategies*, mediate the actions that people take within relationships? Selman proposed a continuum of strategies from *impulsive* responses to the social environment to *cooperative* and *collaborative* responses, which involves the "giving up of the singular, independent self to an interconnected, relational self" (p. 90). Then again, relational cooperation and collaboration may not always align with one's moral reasoning and deduction of right or wrong. Not all relationships promote healthy moral development, as can be seen when adolescents begin exploring and risking. Deciphering healthy cooperation and collaboration from what is not healthy can be a complex process for adolescents, and even for adults. It is not always easy to say no when relationships are involved or at stake. Gilligan's concept of *care respective* and *voice* (as cited in Browning, 2008) is particularly resonant, especially for adolescent girls. If relationships play a role in moral reasoning and decision making, there exists the possibility for a moral relational paradox, as it portrays the cost of relinquishing a relationship in an attempt to do "what's right" and maintain voice, which holds the possibility for "heart break" (p. 141) and disconnection, a risk that adolescents seek to avoid.

Nonetheless, Selman viewed relationships as "developmental learning laboratories" for adolescents to experiment with interpersonal understanding, negotiation strategies, and orientations toward others (Nakkula & Toshalis, 2008, p. 92). Whereas various social contexts could influence adolescent moral development, such as community characteristics and socioeconomic status (Morris, Eisenberg, & Houltberg, 2011), the most fundamental learning laboratories studied include family, school, and religious institutions.

Modeling reciprocity and mutuality, healthy cooperation and collaboration, and developing voice while maintaining relational connections are key to promoting adolescent moral development. According to Nakkula and Toshalis (2008), as interpersonal understanding evolves to reciprocal orientation, the assumption of *fairness* sets the foundation for adolescent relationships. Families, schools, and religious institutions are in unique positions to influence adolescent moral development by engaging youth in conversations and discussions regarding fairness and challenging their often "righteous indignation" at assumed or perceived gaps in fairness (p. 89), which they often exhibit unconsciously. For example, youth will often defy authority in support of a peer or friend that they believe has been treated unfairly while also engaging in acts of teasing, bullying, and harassment of youth that are not included in their social network. When intervening in this moral development process, systems of influence are cautioned to avoid the do as I say, not as I do approach with adolescents as it generally results in power struggles and diminishes the learning of relational reciprocity (p. 89). Likewise, developing lists of rules or dos and don'ts is "fruitless outside of meaningful relationships" (p. 94). Gilligan, Selman, and others empowered systems of influence to be what they hope to see in others and to model relational understanding and strategies that scaffold adolescent moral development. Promoting and integrating volunteerism, community service, and civic engagement into adolescent development (i.e., school, family life, religious involvement) has been shown to enhance moral development (Morris et al., 2011). Equally, modeling disagreement and difference without disconnection is paramount to developing the voices of all youth, and this ultimately strengthens relationships. For example, Gilligan (as cited in Browning, 2008) credited Hirschman's visions of conflict resolution that connect, attach, and include people versus disconnect, detach, and exclude. Furthermore, Gilligan's contributions expand our understanding of morality as it relates to faith development (Nakkula, & Toshalis, 2008). Often the bigger, more challenging questions regarding values, ethics, and morals are precursors to deeper contemplations involving spirituality and religion. Families and religious institutions are encouraged approach these rich conversations and discourses with adolescents from a relational perspective that listens, hears, supports, and questions while nurturing and strengthening relationships.

An Integrative Perspective

In reflecting on the seminal works of the most respected researchers in cognitive and moral development, it is perhaps most efficacious for counselors to take an integrative approach to understanding and applying principal assertions relevant to adolescent moral development. Certainly, biological influences have a significant impact on cognitive functioning and in turn affect moral construction and agency (Paus, 2009). However, it is also true that environmental influences can affect these as well and may be both recursive and reciprocal in their impacts. Moshman (2011) noted:

> Development continues beyond childhood, but development beyond childhood is different from child development.... It is less predictable, less universal, less tied to age, and more a function of the individual's specific actions and experiences. The social context does not cause developmental change but does influence its likelihood and direction. We can encourage, promote, and facilitate development, but development by definition is not externally controlled. (p. 217)

Counselors must understand the underpinnings of their adolescent clients' cognitive development from an integrated perspective as it provides a frame of reference for identity development and for behaviors and decision making. Such understanding is essential for counselors' efficacy with adolescent clients and for facilitating connection and empathy in clinical practice.

BOX 11.6   CASE STUDY: PERSPECTIVES ON MORAL DEVELOPMENT

Jon is a 15-year-old male of Chinese descent. His parents emigrated to the United States when Jon was an infant, and they maintain strong cultural ties to their heritage. Jon, by contrast, embraces U.S. mainstream culture, which is often a source of conflict between him and his parents. Recently, Jon was suspended for fighting in school—an incident he reports was in response to his best friend being bullied by some older boys in his school. Though he regrets being suspended, Jon does not regret his choice to defend and protect his friend and tells you: "I'd do it again in a heartbeat." To better conceptualize this case, answer the following:

   Choosing a moral development theory, what considerations impact Jon's moral development?

   How does Jon's stage of moral development impact his moral agency?

   How might cultural influences impact moral perspective with Jon? With his parents?

IDENTITY AND SELF-CONCEPT IN ADOLESCENCE

Concurrent to the rapid physical and cognitive changes experienced during adolescence is a significant change in identity and self-concept. It might even be argued that physical and cognitive development *catalyze* the changes in identity and self-concept as adolescents experience broad sweeping changes in their physical appearance and thought processes. In this section, foundational theory of identity development in adolescence is offered, as are some considerations for application. In chapter 12, additional examination of systemic, cultural, and environmental influences on identity will be discussed.

Erikson, Marcia, and Identity Development

As has been discussed in previous chapters, Erik Erikson proposed a stage-based developmental theory that identified specific challenges—or crises—that need to be resolved in the process of healthy development. The adolescent years coincide with Erikson's fifth stage of development, for which the primary task is the search for identity. According to Erikson, adolescents are driven to figure out who they are and where they are going—that is, they have an inherent need to internalize their self-value and find their place in the world. During a relatively short period of human growth, adolescents transition from childhood to adulthood; along with this transition comes a multitude of changes in physical, emotional, and psychological processes.

Erikson (1968) described the challenge of this growth period as *identity versus role confusion*. Positive resolution of this developmental stage means an adolescent can transition to adulthood with a clear sense of *fidelity*—a foundational component in healthy relationships in all areas of life. The cohesive sense of self that emerges from this stage means the adolescent—now moving into adulthood—develops an ability to appreciate differences in others and within himself or herself. There is a clarity of one's own identity, direction, and purpose, which in turn supports transition to the next developmental stage, for which the primary challenge is intimacy. Negative resolution of this developmental stage can lead to role confusion—a state in which the individual is unsure about his or her place in society. Failure to effectively internalize identity and develop a firm sense of self can affect not only the young person's immediate developmental processes but also intimate relationships in the short and long term.

To navigate this important developmental stage, adolescents often explore aspects of self and others in ways they previously did not. Some of these behaviors may be misconstrued or dismissed as simply *adolescent rebellion*, when in fact they are important steps in personal development. For example, what may superficially appear as a rejection of parental or cultural values previously embraced may in fact be an important step to internalizing these very same beliefs. That is, before adolescents can commit to a set of principles and behaviors, they want to be sure these are what *they* want—what works for them and fits for them. This process of *internalization* of identity is an important aspect in empowering individual development and supporting the cohesive identity during adolescence.

During the exploration process, adolescents may try on different identities before finding one that fits well for them. There may be many starts and stops along the way, and perhaps even the appearance of regression as an adolescent readopts previous identity-based behaviors following rejection of a recent exploration. However, to assume such a pathway is regression would be incorrect. In fact, it has been suggested that this is, in fact, an important aspect of identity development. James Marcia (1966, 1980) suggested that the process of identity development can be subdivided into four statuses: diffusion, foreclosure, moratorium, and achievement. These statuses differ from *stages* with respect to their existence on a continuum, with each defined by the relative levels of exploration and commitment to identity—the depth and complexity of these increases with each status.

Diffusion is marked by low exploration and low commitment. Adolescents in this stage have not evaluated their opportunities or direction. The diffusion status is far more common in younger adolescents as they transition from the structured, concrete world of childhood. However, it may also be present in older adolescents who have yet to identify an occupational path or life goals. *Foreclosure* is marked by some level of commitment but a lack of exploration. Adolescents in this stage have accepted the likelihood of certain roles and values, but they have not yet explored options beyond those externally imposed by parents and other caregiving adults in their lives. They have not yet experienced *identity crisis*, during which they will

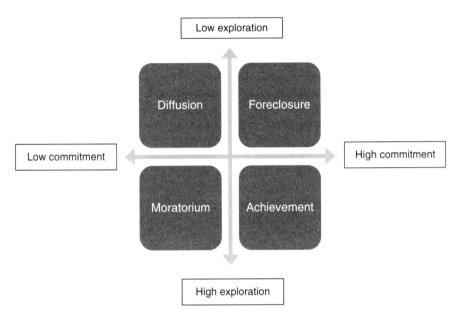

Figure 11.3   Marcia's four identity statuses of adolescence.

challenge preconceived notions and increase exploration. By contrast, *moratorium* is marked by low commitment and high exploration and is the time most often associated with the identity crisis of adolescence. During this time, options and alternatives are more actively explored, with little or no commitment to a single pathway. The last status—*achievement*—is the resolution to the crisis; it is when the adolescent has explored options and has made a commitment to the identity he or she has chosen. Figure 11.3 summarizes Marcia's four identity statuses of adolescence.

Although the overall progress does tend to move forward, adolescents may also find themselves in different statuses simultaneously as they pertain to different characteristics of self. In addition, life experiences often precipitate movement across the statuses that may or may not be in a forward direction. For example, traumatic experiences may precipitate a period of reevaluation, or perhaps even loss of options, which may cause the adolescent to disengage from commitment—effectively setting back identity development. Last, not all statuses are observed in every individual's development but rather should be seen as a way to better understand the complex processes and steps affecting the evolution of a cohesive identity.

Progression through identity exploration and development—whether viewed from the broad scope of Erikson's theory or from the more specific approach of Marcia—is supported or hindered by environmental influences. Parental and social reactions to adolescent exploration can have a significant impact on the manner in which the aspects of self are perceived, retained, and potentially incorporated. For example, in Western cultures—where individuality and personal choice are highly valued—an adolescent may move through exploratory aspects of identity and achieve a functional level of commitment with relatively less stress and conflict when his or her journey is supported and encouraged. Conversely, an adolescent whose primary cultural affiliation is collectivist in nature may experience greater difficulty progressing through exploration and commitment if he or she gravitates toward a more individualistic identity. A counselor must take into consideration both the external and internal influences on identity development during this pivotal time. Last, it is important to remember that *identity achievement* is a beginning, not an end; it provides a foundation for the transition to young adulthood, during which the internalized self is further examined and evaluated, and identity is tweaked in a conscious, deliberate manner. In essence, adolescent identity development provides the basis for continued healthy developmental processes.

Abnormal Identity Development

As discussed already, healthy identity development results from the successful navigation of both exploration and commitment during adolescence. Individuals who do not accomplish resolution of the crises and challenges associated with this developmental stage often carry forward weak ego identity into adulthood. Whereas this may cause future challenges in relationships, occupational commitment, and other important aspects of adult identity, these holes in development may also be filled in during the course of future development. However, it is also possible that more significant gaps in identity development through adolescence may be the underpinnings of personality disorders. The *Diagnostic and Statistical Manual of Mental Disorders*, fifth edition (*DSM-5*; APA, 2013), describes a personality disorder as "an enduring pattern of inner experience and behavior that deviates markedly from the expectations of the individual's culture" and "leads to distress or impairment" (p. 645). Though not generally diagnosed until adulthood, after identity is more consistent, characteristics of personality disorders are often recognized in adolescence. Marcia (2008) suggested that "different identity statuses may be related to particular personality disorders and that personality disorders, in general, impede identity formation by limiting the experience necessary to undergo meaningful exploration and maintain viable commitments" (p. 592). This proposal offers a helpful perspective in viewing both identity development as a whole as well as facilitating effective treatment plans in adolescent and young adult clients. Counselors can benefit from recognizing the potential impact of aberrations in standard processes when facilitating healthy growth and development.

Beyond Erikson and Marcia

The most consistent criticism of Erikson's theory has historically been that his research was initially based exclusively on European American males. As such, his progressive stage approach assumes the European American male identity development as the norm—and, by default, deviations from this standard to be abnormal and problematic. In addition, the premise that positive resolution of each developmental stage is necessary for successful progression through subsequent stages has not been well supported by research. Further, proponents of a more integrated, dynamic approach to development have argued that while there is value to Erikson's identified crises of development, progression is not necessarily linear; in fact, his stages might be better viewed as tasks that could potentially be achieved at any point in identity development. Still, Erikson's work was the first to recognize identity development as a lifelong process and has served as the foundation for contemporary developmental theories.

Marcia's work—which is a more contemporary theory built on Erikson's work—offered a more integrated, dynamic approach and has held up well in research testing its validity, including cross-cultural application. However, it has also been noted that Marcia's focus strictly on adolescent development may have been too short-sighted; in fact, there is support for the assertion that the described identity statuses exist well into adulthood (Hardy & Kisling, 2006). Furthermore, the characteristics of the statuses—*exploration* and *commitment*—are difficult to define and even more difficult to quantify.

It has also been suggested that the go-to identity development models lack the more inclusive considerations of race and ethnicity on identity. Similarly, the potential gender differences in the processes of identity development have been historically disregarded. More contemporary theories of identity development have utilized an integrative, systemically based perspective that incorporates the social and environmental influences on development in a much more cohesive manner (Collins & Steinberg, 2006; Cross & Fhagen-Smith, 2001; McFarland & Pals, 2005; Supple, Ghazarian, Frabutt, Plunkett, & Sands, 2006; Waterman, 1982). For counselors, a holistic, multidimensional approach to conceptualizing clients is arguably more efficacious and ultimately more meaningful when facilitating personal growth and development in the adolescent client.

Gender Identity and Sexual Orientation

The process through which individuals develop and express both gender identity and sexual orientation is multifaceted and involves strong influences from both biological and environmental factors. Chapter 12 explores some of social and emotional changes during adolescence that impact sexual behaviors. First, though, let's take a brief look at the biological and cognitive changes that impact gender identity and sexual orientation in adolescence.

Gender Identity

As was discussed previously, puberty generally signifies the onset of adolescence. With this change comes the development of primary and secondary sexual traits, which serve to significantly separate the genders. Prior to puberty, boys and girls—although certainly aware of their gender identities—assign less meaning to these differences. However, as puberty progresses, the gender differences become more prominent and meaningful.

According to evolutionary psychologists, gender role behaviors emerge as a consequence of the biological differences between males and females. During adolescence, as these differences increase, changes to behaviors and personalities become more evident (Buss, 2014). Like their ancient ancestors, males tend toward more competitive behaviors, while females tend toward more nurturing behaviors. Further, gender identity becomes associated with stereotypical traits—strength and assertiveness in boys and beauty and passiveness in girls. Critics of evolutionary psychology argue that these generalizations do not hold up well in large-scale studies, mostly because they do not account for the influences of culture or socialization.

By contrast, *social role theory* (Eagly, 2001) asserts that observed gender identity differences emerge as a result of differing roles males and females have in society. *Social cognitive theory* (Bussey & Bandura, 1999) goes a step further, noting that that male and female gender identities are the result of *gender scripts* which define and dictate gender-based behaviors and traits. These scripts are passed on to children by their environments; individuals are rewarded for their adherence to gender scripts through approval from their social network. Parents, peers, siblings, extended family, and cultural groups influence the both the gender scripts in an adolescent's life and the approval the teenager seeks. Adolescents are bombarded with influential messages about what it means to be male or female. The degree to which they adopt these constructs, as well as their comfort with how these messages may conflict with their inner beliefs or with those of other social influences, directly impact their comfort and integration—and ultimately define their gender identity.

Another important consideration regarding gender identity development is the concept of *losing voice* made popular by the research and publications of noted psychologist Carol Gilligan (1982). Gilligan has focused almost exclusively on the personality and behavioral changes that girls experience during adolescence. She described girls as silencing their different voice as they struggle against the influences of a male-dominated society. While many of her observations of changes in girls' self-concept, self-esteem, confidence, and other variables over the course of adolescence have been duplicated in others' research, critics have asserted that Gilligan and her contemporaries have overemphasized the significance of gender. In fact, other researchers have found similar declines in the same traits in boys as they traverse adolescence (Robins, Trzesniewski, Tracey, Potter, & Gosling, 2002). It may be that gender identity development emerges either along a concurrent pathway or as an aspect of an individual's core identity, and is therefore subject to similar challenges and processes previously described by Erikson's stage theory. Regardless, counselors working with adolescents would benefit from recognition of the struggles, questions, and narratives associated with gender identity development, as these are important aspects of the adolescent experience.

Sexual Orientation

Separate from, but related to, the concept of gender identity is *sexual orientation*, the consistent pattern of romantic and sexual attraction individuals feel for members of the opposite gender, the same gender, or a combination. Although some individuals may experience sexual attractions before puberty, most do not; rather, it is the onset of this developmental phase and the biological changes that accompany it that bring one's sexual orientation to light. Puberty catalyzes sexual awareness and drive in adolescents as individuals reach sexual maturity. Keeping in mind that adolescence is a period of exploration and identity development, it is not uncommon for boys and girls to engage in sexual behaviors with the same or opposite gender, independent of the orientation label that they may eventually settle into by adulthood.

Contemporary research has explored the etiology of sexual orientation; the current pervasive view is that sexual orientation is a complex combination of genetic, hormonal, and environmental factors—although the exact processes remain uncertain. There is much debate over pathways in the development of sexual orientation, but a few key points are consistent across respected domains—including the recognition that sexual orientation is not a choice, but rather a core identity trait. Furthermore, efforts to change sexual orientation can be extremely damaging; instead, individuals who are of minority sexual orientations should be offered support and acceptance (American Psychological Association, 2009).

Adolescents who are of minority sexual orientation may not openly disclose this during adolescence because being different is a significant social concern. Furthermore, depending on the family dynamics, the adolescent may feel pressured to present himself or herself as heterosexual as a means of gaining acceptance. Teenagers most often will confide sexual orientation in trusted peers first, perhaps testing the waters of approval and support before sharing the information with their family system. Counselors may also be among the first to whom the adolescent comes out (i.e., shares confirmation of minority sexual orientation); responding with unconditional regard and support is essential to the individual's comfort and confidence in the process. Sexual minority youth are at increased risk for depression, anxiety, and substance abuse, largely due to the social challenges associated with their minority status. Counselors should screen for these risk factors and adjust interventions accordingly. They should also consider integrating family therapy as needed to support cohesiveness and optimal development in the adolescent.

Whether addressing gender identity or sexual orientation, it is important to consider the individual in the context of his or her life experiences and worldview. Sexuality is a healthy aspect of human behavior; however, environmental influences and social conditioning can cause adolescents to develop negative views of themselves or others or to feel apprehensive about their desires. As with other aspects of identity development, counselors should support the individual's wellness and personal growth during this important developmental stage.

CONTEMPORARY ISSUES IN PHYSICAL AND COGNITIVE DEVELOPMENT

The Storm and Stress Debate

As was noted at the beginning of this chapter, adolescence as a distinct developmental stage was first identified by G. Stanley Hall (1904). It is in this same seminal work that Hall characterized adolescence as a period of *storm and stress*—primarily due to this period being associated with increasing conflicts between adolescents and parents, changes in mood and emotional regulation, and the emergence or risk-taking behavior. This concept persisted as a defining description of adolescence well into the late 20th century, spurred on in part by the research and writings of Anna Freud (1958), who asserted "To be normal in the adolescent period is by itself abnormal" (p. 257). Hall—whose views were strongly influenced by evolutionary theory—reasoned that the tumultuous period of adolescence was akin to turbulent and chaotic periods of evolutionary development and that such experiences were genetically encoded and passed to future generations. This particular application of *recapitulation theory* has since been discredited, and Hall's observations have been explained more reliably by the influences and effects of cultural and social systems. Further, anthropologists have noted that storm and stress seems to be a largely Western construct and not globally applicable. Some contemporary developmental researchers have gone so far as to assert that storm and stress is, in fact, not the norm of adolescence (Arnett, 1999; Susman, Dorn, & Schiefelbein, 2003). After a century of debate over the application and meaning of this concept, focus has shifted from critiquing the validity of the idea to enhancing the understanding of individuals' experiences of storm and stress and the cultural and systemic influences on its impact.

To this end, Hollenstein and Lougheed (2013) proposed a new model to describe adolescent change. Building on nearly a century of research on adolescent changes and challenges, the researchers proposed the following:

> Storm and stress is a vestigial developmental framework, and we propose a more comprehensive approach to understanding adolescent-typical changes based on six premises: (1) The biological changes of adolescence are inevitable and ubiquitous; (2) adolescent biological changes drive various mechanisms of adolescent behavior; (3) adolescent biological changes are shaped by environmental influences; (4) individual differences in adolescent emotional-behavior changes are domain specific and vary in intensity; (5) there are individual differences in the age of onset and duration of periods of adolescent change; and (6) individual differences in the duration and intensity of transitions in emotional arousal are functionally modulated by burgeoning emotion regulation skills. We conclude with the more comprehensive 4T (typicality, transactions, temperament, and timing) approach and suggestions to guide adolescent research in the 21st century. (p. 444)

The authors asserted that the 4T approach provides an in-context, systemic, adaptable, and individualized approach to the study of adolescent development. As such, considerations for the influences of biology and environment, as well as the reciprocal influences between the two, become part of the discussion and enhance overall understanding of the developing adolescent. This approach—while proposed as a means of improving the study of adolescence—offers promise in counseling application. That is, counselors who strive to view their clients from such a perspective, rather than from the limitations of the traditional "storm and stress" construct, are more likely to effectively integrate key aspects of development in clients—including physical, cognitive, systemic, cultural, emotional, and other significant impacts.

Emerging Adulthood

The concept of *emerging adulthood* is defined by a distinct period between adolescence and young adulthood—usually ages 18–25—and was first proposed by noted developmental researcher Jeffrey Jensen Arnett (2000). Jensen described individuals in this phase as being not fully independent from their parents or caregivers and not yet having achieved common developmental tasks of adulthood (such as marriage, children, owning a home, and having a set career path). Jensen described this stage as being characterized by five key elements: identity exploration, instability, self-focus, in-between feelings, and possibilities (Arnett, 2006). In many ways it is a bridge between adolescence and adulthood, and it has evolved in response to a changing society and economy. The need for advanced education, delayed marriage, and declining economic prospects are just a few of the many influences impacting emerging adulthood. Though highly influenced by context and culture (emerging adulthood is considered an almost exclusively Western construct), much attention has been given to this concept; a considerable amount of research over the past 15 years has sought to better understand the uniqueness of this group and how to best support its members' development. Emerging adults have been found to have unique perspectives on and experiences of their lives—including relationships, risk taking, self-concept, family relationships, and many other elements inherently vital to their health and wellness (DiDonato & Strough, 2013; King, Nguyen, Kosterman, Bailey, & Hawkins, 2012; Morris, McGrath, Goldman, & Rottenberg, 2014; Sandberg-Thoma & Kamp Dush, 2014; Syed & Seiffge-Krenke, 2013). Counselors working with emerging adults should bear in mind that they are a diverse and dynamic group whose identity development is likely to resemble both adolescents and young adults, depending on the developmental task at hand.

Another consideration in understanding emerging adulthood is to recognize the impact of the initiative on social policy. A key driving force in the validation and application of the concept of emerging adulthood has been the recognition that young people who reach the age of majority (18 years old in the United States) are not necessarily equipped to succeed as adults. Mental health and related services in place for minors often decline or are completely eliminated upon age of majority, leaving young people in transition without vital support resources

(MacLeod & Brownlie, 2014; Whitbeck, 2009). Social advocates continue to push for better transitional services for individuals transitioning through this critical developmental stage.

KEY COUNSELING POINTERS FOR: PHYSICAL AND COGNITIVE DEVELOPMENT IN ADOLESCENCE

- Adolescence is a time of rapid physical change. Counselors should be aware of the comparative physical development of adolescent clients and how this impacts their self-concept.
- Sexual maturation often precedes the cognitive development necessary to cope with its impact. Counselors should be prepared to help adolescent clients better understand their changing bodies.
- The adolescent brain differs from the brains of both children and adults. Counselors should educate parents on the impact of cognitive development on adolescent behavior and identity and should empower clients toward wellness and proactive decision making.
- Adolescents tend toward idealism and egocentrism. Rather than work against these concepts, counselors should acknowledge and integrate these perspectives into adolescent treatment, as they are essential components of identity development.
- Morality develops considerably during this stage, as adolescents internalize beliefs and move toward making decisions from a more broad perspective. Counselors must understand the level of moral development in clients in order to better facilitate personal growth and positive decision making.
- Risk taking behavior increases during this stage. Counselors should recognize potentially harmful risk taking versus developmentally supportive risk taking.
- A key goal of adolescence is the development of the foundation for a cohesive, consistent self. Not all adolescents will negotiate this developmental stage in the same manner, nor will they exhibit the same stages or levels of development. Counselors would benefit from understanding the point of identity development in their adolescent clients, giving consideration to gender, culture, religion, family, and other systemic influences.
- The foundations of identity are laid during adolescence, and they continue to be reviewed and refined into adulthood. These include not only key aspects of personality, but also gender identity and sexual orientation. Counselors should promote individual wellness and health during this critical developmental period.

SUMMARY

Adolescence is a period of rapid physical and cognitive development. Spurred by the onset of puberty, adolescence marks the transition from childhood to adulthood. During this period, individuals experience growth spurts, develop reproductive capacity, and show significant advances in cognition and morality. These changes, in turn, impact identity in profound ways, and young people move from an external to internal self. There is much variation to the developmental processes of adolescence, and consideration must be given for the impacts of cultural and systemic influences (to be further addressed in chapter 12).

Counselors working with adolescents are likely to see mostly social or emotional presenting issues. However, to effectively treat adolescents, counselors must understand not only the physical and cognitive growth in their clients, but also the impacts of these. Age of onset, rates of change, and relative developmental levels can all impact the experience of and adjustment to the roller coaster that is adolescence. Furthermore, the progression and achievement of key developmental milestones are essential aspects of successful navigation of this stage.

USEFUL WEBSITES

European Association for Research on Adolescence
http://www.earaonline.org
Society for Research on Adolescence
http://www.s-r-a.org
Developing Adolescents: A reference for professionals
http://www.apa.org/pi/families/resources/develop.pdf
Society for the Study of Emerging Adulthood
http://ssea.org
Changes in Cognitive Development During Adolescence
http://education-portal.com/academy/lesson/changes-in-cognitive-development-during-adolescence.html

REFERENCES

Addo, O. Y., Miller, B. S., Lee, P. A., Hediger, M. L., & Himes, J.H. (2014). Age at hormonal onset of puberty based on luteinizing hormone, inhibin B, and body composition in preadolescent U.S. girls. *Pediatric Research*, 76(6), 564–570.

Albert, D., & Steinberg, L. (2011). Judgment and decision making in adolescence. *Journal of Research on Adolescence*, 21(1), 211–224.

American Psychiatric Association (APA). (2013). *Diagnostic and statistical manual of mental disorders* (5th ed.). Arlington, VA: Author.

American Psychological Association. (2009). *Appropriate therapeutic responses to sexual orientation*. Retrieved from http://www.apa.org/pi/lgbt/resources/therapeutic-response.pdf

Arnett, J. (1990). Drunk driving, sensation seeking, and egocentrism among adolescents. *Personality and Individual Differences*, 11(6), 541–546.

Arnett, J. J. (1999). Adolescent storm and stress, reconsidered. *American Psychologist*, 54, 317–326.

Arnett, J. J. (2000). Emerging adulthood: A theory of development from the late teens through the twenties. *American Psychologist*, *55*, 469–480.

Arnett, J. J. (2006). Emerging adulthood: Understanding the new way of coming of age. In J. J. Arnett and J. L. Tanner (Eds.), *Emerging adults in America: Coming of age in the 21st century* (pp. 3–20). Washington, DC: American Psychological Association Press.

Bandura, A. (2002). Selective moral disengagement in the exercise of moral agency. *Journal of Moral Education*, *31*, 101–119.

Bandura, A., Barbaranelli, C., Caprara, G. V., & Pastorelli, C. (1996). Mechanisms of moral disengagement in the exercise of moral agency. *Journal of Personality and Social Psychology*, *71*(2), 364–374.

Belsky, J., Steinberg, L., & Draper, P. (1991). Childhood experience, interpersonal development, and reproductive strategy: An evolutionary theory of socialization. *Child Development*, *62*, 647–670.

Blakemore, S.-J. (2012). Imaging brain development: The adolescent brain. *NeuroImage*, *61*(2), 397–406.

Blakemore, S.-J., & Robbins, T. W. (2012). Decision-making in the adolescent brain. *Nature Neuroscience*, *15*(9), 1184–1191.

Browning, D. L. (Ed.) . (2008). *Adolescent identities: A collection of readings*. New York, NY: The Analytic Press.

Buss, D. M. (2014). *Evolutionary psychology* (5th ed.). Upper Saddle River, NJ: Pearson.

Bussey, K., & Bandura, A. (1999). Social cognitive theory of gender development and differentiation. *Psychological Review*, *106*, 676–713.

Collins, W. A., & Steinberg, L. (2006). Adolescent development in interpersonal context. In W. Damon & R. M. Lerner (Series Eds.), N. Eisenberg (Vol Ed.), *Handbook of child psychology: Social, emotional, and personality development* (6th ed., Vol. 3, pp. 1003–1067). Hoboken, NJ: Wiley.

Copeland, W., Shanahan, L., Miller, S., Costello, E. J., Angold, A., & Maughan, M. (2010). Outcomes of early pubertal timing in young women: A prospective population-based study. *American Journal of Psychiatry*, *167*(10), 1218–1225.

Cross W. E., Jr., & Fhagen-Smith, P. (2001). Patterns of African American identity development: A lifespan perspective. In B. Jackson & C. Wijeyesinghe (Eds.), *New perspectives on racial identity development: A theoretical and practical anthology* (pp. 243–270). New York: New York University Press.

Davison, K. K., Susman, E. J., & Birch, L. L. (2003). Percent body fat at age 5 predicts earlier pubertal development among girls at age 9. *Pediatrics*, *111*(4), 815–821.

DiDonato, L., & Strough, J. (2013). Contextual influences on gender segregation in emerging adulthood. *Sex Roles*, *69*(11–12), 632–643.

Eagly, A. H. (2001). Social role theory of sex differences and similarities. In J. Worrell (Ed.), *Encyclopedia of women and gender*. San Diego, CA: Academic Press.

Eaves, L., Silberg, J., & Erkanil, A. (2003). Resolving multiple epigenetic pathways to adolescent depression. *Journal of Child Psychology and Psychiatry*, *44*(7), 1006–1014.

Eisenberg, N., & Morris, A. (2004). Moral cognitions and prosocial responding in adolescence. In R. Lerner & L. Steinberg (Eds.), *Handbook of adolescent psychology* (pp. 229–265). New York, NY: Wiley.

Elkind, D. (1967). Egocentrism in adolescence. *Child Development, 38*, 1025–1034.

Erikson, E. (1968). *Identity, youth, and crisis*. New York, NY: Norton.

Essex, M. J., Boyce, W. T., Hertzman, C., Lam, L. L., Armstrong, J. M., Neumann, S. M., & Kobor, M. S. (2013). Epigenetic vestiges of developmental adversity: Childhood stress exposure and DNA methylation in adolescence. *Child Development, 84*(1), 58–75.

Euling, S. Y., Selevan, S. G., Pescovitz, O. H., & Skakkebaek, N. E. (2008). Role of environmental factors in the timing of puberty. *Pediatrics, 121*(Suppl. 3), S167–171.

Freud, A. (1958). Adolescence. In A. Freud, H. Hartmann, & E. Kris (Eds.), *Psychoanalytic study of the child* (pp. 255–278). New York, NY: International Universities Press.

Fujii, K., & Demura, S. (2003). Relationship between change in BMI with age and delayed menarche in female athletes. *Journal of Physiological Anthropology and Applied Human Science, 22*, 97–104.

Gilligan, C. (1982). *In a different voice*. Cambridge, MA: Harvard University Press.

Gilligan, C. (1996). The centrality of relationships in psychological development: A puzzle, some evidence, and a theory. In G. G. Noam & K. W. Fischer (Eds.), *Development and vulnerability in close relationships* (pp. 237–262). Hillsdale, NJ: Erlbaum.

Gilligan, C. (2005). From in a different voice to the birth of pleasure: An intellectual journey. *North Dakota Law Review, 81*(4), 729–737.

Gottlieb, G. (2007). Probabilistic epigenesist. *Developmental Science, 10*(1), 1–11.

Graber, J. A. (2013). Pubertal timing and the development of psychopathology in adolescence and beyond. *Hormones and Behavior, 64*, 262–269.

Greene, K., Krcmar, M., Walters, L. H., Rubin, D. L., Jerold & Hale, L. (2000). Targeting adolescent risk-taking behaviors: The contributions of egocentrism and sensation-seeking. *Journal of Adolescence, 23*(4), 439–461.

Guerrini, I., Quadri, G., & Thomson, A. D. (2014). Genetic and environmental interplay in risky drinking in adolescents: A literature review. *Alcohol and Alcoholism, 49*(2), 138–142.

Hall, G. S. (1904). *Adolescence: Its psychology and its relation to physiology, anthropology, sociology, sex, crime, religion, and education*. Englewood Cliffs, NJ: Prentice-Hall.

Hardy, S. A., & Kisling, J. W. (2006). Identity statuses and prosocial behaviors in young adulthood: A brief report. *Identity: An International Journal of Theory and Research, 6*(4), 363–369.

Hill, P., & Lapsley, D. (2011). Adaptive and maladaptive narcissism in adolescent development. In C. Barry, P. Kerig, K. Stellwagen, & T. D. Barry (Eds.), *Implications of narcissism and Machiavellianism for the development of prosocial and antisocial behavior in youth* (pp. 89–105). Washington, DC: APA Press.

Hiort, O. (2002). Androgens and puberty. *Best Practice & Research Clinical Endocrinology & Metabolism, 16*(1), 31–41.

Hollenstein, T., & Lougheed, J. P. (2013). Beyond storm and stress: Typicality, transactions, timing, and temperament to account for adolescent change. *American Psychologist, 68*(6), 444–454.

James, J., Ellis, B. J., Schlomer, G. L., & Garber, J. (2012). Sex-specific pathways to early puberty, sexual debut, and sexual risk taking: Tests of an integrated evolutionary-developmental model. *Developmental Psychology, 48*(3), 687–702.

Keating, D. P. (2004). Cognitive and brain development. In R. Lerner & L. Steinberg (Eds.), *Handbook of adolescence* (2nd ed., pp. 45–84). New York, NY: Wiley.

Kelly, P. (2012). The brain in the jar: A critique of discourses of adolescent brain development. *Journal of Youth Studies, 15*(7), 944–959.

Kessler, K., Cao, L., O'Shea, K. J., & Wang, H. (2014). A cross-culture, cross-gender comparison of perspective taking mechanisms. *Proceedings of the Royal Society B: Biological Sciences, 281*(1785). doi: 10.1098/rspb.2014.0388

Killen, M., & Smetana, J. G. (2013). *Handbook of moral development* (2nd ed.). New York, NY: Taylor & Francis.

King, K. M., Nguyen, H. V., Kosterman, R., Bailey, J. A., & Hawkins, J. D. (2012). Co-occurrence of sexual risk behaviors and substance use across emerging adulthood: Evidence for state- and trait-level associations. *Addiction, 107*(7), 1288–1296.

Kuwabara, M., & Smith, L. B. (2012). Cross-cultural differences in cognitive development: Attention to relations and objects. *Journal of Experimental Child Psychology, 113*(1), 20–35.

Lapsley, D. K. (1993). Toward an integrated theory of adolescent ego development: The "new look" at adolescent egocentrism. *American Journal of Orthopsychiatry, 63*, 562–571.

Lapsley, D. K., & Aalsma, M. C. (2006). An empirical typology of narcissism and mental health in late adolescence. *Journal of Adolescence, 29*(1), 53–71.

Lassek, W. D., & Gaulin, S. J. (2007). Menarche is related to fat distribution. *American Journal of Physical Anthropology, 133*, 1147–1151.

Lee, J. M., Appugliese, D., Kaciroti, N., Corwyn, R. F., Bradely, R. J., & Lumeng, J. C. (2007). Weight status in young girls and the onset of puberty. *Pediatrics, 119*(3), 624–630.

Lee, J. M., Kaciroti, N., Appugliese, D., Corwyn, R. F., Bradely, R. J., & Lumeng, J. C. (2010). Body mass index and timing of pubertal initiation in boys. *Archives of Pediatric Adolescent Medicine, 164*(2), 139–144.

Levine, M. (2006). *The price of privilege: How parental pressure and material advantage are creating a generation of disconnected and unhappy kids.* New York: Harper.

MacLeod, K. B., & Brownlie, E. B. (2014). Mental health and transitions from adolescence to emerging adulthood: Developmental and diversity considerations. *Canadian Journal of Community Mental Health, 33*(1), 77–86.

Marcia, J. (1966). Development and validation of ego identity statuses. *Journal of Personality and Social Psychology, 3*, 551–558.

Marcia, J. (1980). Identity in adolescence. In J. Adelson (Ed.), *Handbook of adolescent psychology* (pp. 159–187). New York, NY: Wiley.

Marcia, J. (2008). Ego identity and personality disorders. *Journal of Personality Disorders, 20*(6), 577–596.

McClintock, M. K., & Herdt, G. (1996). Rethinking puberty: The development of sexual attraction. *Current Directions in Psychological Science, 5*(6), 178–183.

McFarland, D., & Pals, H. (2005). Motives and contexts of identity change: A case for network effects. *Social Psychology Quarterly, 68*(4), 289–315.

Mendle, J., Harden, K. P., Brooks-Gunn, J., & Graber, J. A. (2010). Development's tortoise and hare: Pubertal timing, pubertal tempo, and depressive symptoms in boys and girls. *Developmental Psychology, 46*, 1341–1353.

Michaud, P. A. (2015). Pubertal timing, exploratory behavior and mental health: A view from a clinician and public health practitioner. In J.-P. Bourguignon, J.-C. Carel, & Y. Christen (Eds.), *Brain crosstalk in puberty and adolescence* (Vol. 13, pp. 45–56). Cham, Switzerland: Springer International Publishing AG.

Misra, M., Miller, K., Almazan, C., Ramaswam, K., Aggarwal, A., Herzog, D. B., ... Klibanski, A. (2004). Hormonal and body composition predictors of soluble leptin receptor, leptin, and free leptin index in adolescent girls with anorexia nervosa and controls and relation to insulin sensitivity. *Journal of Clinical Endocrinology and Metabolism, 89*, 3486–3495.

Montgomery, M. J. (2005). Psychosocial intimacy and identity from early adolescence to emerging adulthood. *Journal of Adolescent Research, 20*(3), 346–374.

Moore, K. L., Persaud, T. V. N., & Torchia, M. G. (2011). *The developing human.* New York, NY: Elsevier Health Sciences.

Morris, A. S., Eisenberg, N. & Houltberg, B. J. (2011). Adolescent moral development. In B. Brown & M. Prinstein (Eds.), *Encyclopedia of Adolescence.* Oxford: Elsevier's Academic Press.

Morris, B., McGrath, A., Goldman, M., & Rottenberg, J. (2014). Parental depression confers greater prospective depression risk to females than males in emerging adulthood. *Child Psychiatry & Human Development, 45*(1), 78–89.

Moshman, D. (2011). *Adolescent rationality and development: Cognition, morality, and identity* (3rd ed.). New York, NY: Taylor and Francis Group.

Nakkula, M. J., & Toshalis, E. (2008). *Understanding youth: Adolescent development for educators.* Cambridge, MA: Harvard Education Press.

Neinstein, L. S. (2007). *Handbook of adolescent health care: A practical guide* (5th ed.). Philadelphia, PA: Lippincott Williams & Wilkins.

Nussey S., & Whitehead, S. (2001). *Endocrinology: An integrated approach.* Oxford, UK: BIOS Scientific Publishers.

Oakley, A. E., Clifton, D. K., & Steiner, R. A. (2009). Kisspeptin signaling in the brain. *Endocrine Reviews, 30,* 713–743.

Ostovich, J. M., & Sabini, J. (2005). Timing of puberty and sexuality in men and women. *Archives of Sexual Behavior, 34,* 197–206.

Palmert, M. R., & Boepple, P. A. (2001). Variation in the timing of puberty: Clinical spectrum and genetic investigation. *Journal of Clinical Endocrinology & Metabolism, 86*(6), 2364–2368.

Parent, A. S., Teilmann, G., Juul, A., Skakkebaek, N. E., Toppari, J., & Bourguignon, J. P. (2003). The timing of normal puberty and the age limits of sexual precocity: Variations around the world, secular trends and changes after migration. *Endocrinology Review, 24,* 668–693.

Paus, T. (2009). Brain development. In R. M. Lerner & L. Steinberg (Eds.), *Handbook of adolescent psychology* (3rd ed., Vol. 1, pp. 95–115). Hoboken, NJ: Wiley.

Rai, R., Mitchell, P., Kadar, T., & Mackenzie, L. (2014). Adolescent egocentrism and the illusion of transparency: Are adolescents as egocentric as we might think? *Current Psychology*, 1–15. doi: 10.1007/s12144-014-9293-7

Reardon, L. E., Leen-Feldner, E. W., & Hayward, C. A. (2009). A critical review of the empirical literature on the relation between anxiety and puberty. *Clinical Psychology Review*, *29*, 1–23.

Robins, R.W., Trzesniewski, K. H., Tracey, J. L., Potter, J., & Gosling, S. D. (2002). Age differences in self-esteem from 9–90. *Psychology and Aging*, *17*, 423–434.

Sandberg-Thoma, S. E., & Kamp Dush, C. M. (2014). Casual sexual relationships and mental health in adolescence and emerging adulthood. *Journal of Sex Research*, *51*(2), 121–130.

Sandler, J., Fonagy, P., & Person, E. S. (2012). *Freud's on narcissism—an introduction.* London, UK: Karnac Books.

Santrock, J. W. (2007). *Adolescence* (11th ed.). New York, NY: McGraw-Hill.

Saxe, G. B. (1999). Cognition, development, and cultural practices. *New Directions for Child and Adolescent Development*, *83*, 19–35.

Sedikides, C., Rudich, E. A., Gregg, A. P., Kumashiro, M., & Rusbult, C. (2004). Are normal narcissists psychologically healthy?: Self-esteem matters. *Journal of Personality and Social Psychology*, *87*(3), 400–416.

Shweder, R. A. (1991). *Thinking through cultures: Expeditions in cultural psychology.* Cambridge, MA: Harvard University Press.

Siegler, R. S., & Alibali, M. W. (2005). *Children's thinking* (4th ed.). Upper Saddle River, NJ: Prentice Hall.

Smith, A. R., Chein, J., & Steinberg, L. (2013). Impact of socio-emotional context, brain development, and pubertal maturation on adolescent risk-taking. *Hormones and Behavior*, *64*(2), 323–332.

Soliman, A., De Sanctis, V., & Elalaily, R. (2014). Nutrition and pubertal development. *Indian Journal of Endocrinology and Metabolism*, *18*(Suppl. 1), S39–47.

Sontag, L. M., Graber, J. A., & Clemens, K. H. (2011). The role of peer stress and pubertal timing on symptoms of psychopathology in early adolescence. *Journal of Youth and Adolescence*, *40*, 1371–1382.

Spear, L. P. (2000a). The adolescent brain and age-related behavioral manifestations. *Neuroscience & Biobehavioral Reviews*, *24*(4), 417–463.

Spear, L. P. (2000b). Neurobehavioral changes in adolescence. *Current Directions in Psychological Science*, *4*, 111–114.

Stattin, H., & Magnusson, D. (1990). *Pubertal maturation in female development.* Hillsdale, NJ: Erlbaum.

Steinberg, L. (2005). Cognitive and affective development in adolescence. *Trends in Cognitive Sciences*, *9*(2), 69–74.

Steinberg, L. (2009). Should the science of adolescent brain development inform public policy? *American Psychologist*, *64*(8), 739–750.

Supple, A. J., Ghazarian, S. R., Frabutt, J. M., Plunkett, S. W., & Sands, T. (2006). Contextual influences on Latino adolescent ethnic identity and academic outcomes. *Child Development*, 77, 1427–1433.

Susman, E. J., Dorn, L. D., & Schiefelbein, V. L. (2003). Puberty, sexuality, and health. In R. M. Lerner, M. A. Eastbrooks, & J. Mistry (Eds.), *Comprehensive handbook of psychology* (pp. 295–324). New York, NY: Wiley.

Susman, E. J., & Rogol, A. (2004). Puberty and psychological development. In R. M. Lerner, & L. Steinberg (Eds.), *Handbook of adolescent psychology* (pp. 15–44). New York: Wiley.

Syed, M., & Seiffge-Krenke, I. (2013). Personality development from adolescence to emerging adulthood: Linking trajectories of ego development to the family context and identity formation. *Journal of Personality and Social Psychology*, 104(2), 371–384.

Toppari, J., & Juul, A. (2010). Trends in puberty timing in humans and environmental modifiers. *Molecular and Cellular Endocrinology*, 324, 39–44.

Twenge, J. M. (2006). *Generation me: Why today's young Americans are more confident, assertive, entitled—and more miserable than ever before*. New York, NY: Free Press.

Twenge, J. M., & Campbell, W. K. (2003). Isn't it fun to get the respect that we're going to deserve?" Narcissism, social rejection, and aggression. *Personality and Social Psychology Bulletin*, 29(2), 261–272.

Van Jaarsfeld, C. H., Fidler, J. A., Simon, A. E., & Wardle, J. (2007). Persistent impact of pubertal timing on trends in smoking, food choice, activity, and stress in adolescence. *Psychosomatic Medicine*, 69, 798–806.

Varnum, M. E., Grossmann, I., Kitayama, S., & Nisbett, R. E. (2010). The origin of cultural differences in cognition the social orientation hypothesis. *Current Directions in Psychological Science*, 19(1), 9–13.

Wahlstrom, D., White, T., & Luciana, M. (2010). Neurobehavioral evidence for changes in dopamine system activity during adolescence. *Neuroscience and Biobehavioral Reviews*, 34(5), 631–648.

Walsh, D. (2014). *Why do they act that way? A survival guide to adolescent brain and you*. New York, NY: Simon & Schuster.

Walvoord, E. C. (2010). The timing of puberty: Is it changing? Does it matter? *Journal of Adolescent Health*, 47, 433–439.

Wang, R. Y., Needham, L. L., & Barr, D. B. (2005). Effects of environmental agents on the attainment of puberty: Considerations when assessing exposure to environmental chemicals in the National Children's Study. *Environmental Health Perspectives*, 113(8), 1100–1107.

Wang, Y. (2002). Is obesity associated with early sexual maturation? A comparison of the association in American boys versus girls. *Pediatrics*, 110, 903–910.

Waterman, A. S. (1982). Identity development from adolescence to adulthood: An extension of theory and a review of research. *Developmental Psychology*, 18(3), 341–358.

Whitbeck, L. B. (2009). *Mental health and emerging adulthood among homeless young people*. New York, NY: Psychology Press.

Whitbourne, S. K., & Halgin, R.P. (2014). *Abnormal psychology: Clinical perspectives* (7th ed., with *DSM-5* update). New York, NY: McGraw-Hill.

Wink, P. (1992). Three narcissism scales for the California Q-set. *Journal of Personality Assessment, 58*(1), 51–66.

Wood, L. J., & Hilton, A. A. (2013). Moral choices: Towards a conceptual model of Black male moral development (BMMD). *Western Journal of Black Studies, 37*(1), 14–27.

Zeigler-Hill, V., Clark, C. B., & Pickard, J. D. (2008). Narcissistic subtypes and contingent self-esteem: Do all narcissists base their self-esteem on the same domain? *Journal of Personality, 76*(4), 753–774.

Adolescence: Emotional and Social Development

Stephanie K. Scott and Kelli A. Saginak

To truly understand the trials and tribulations of the social and emotional development associated with adolescence, it is helpful to first consider the intricacies of *adolescent culture*. Decades of research have shed much light on this complex and ever changing development, brought us closer to understanding the uniqueness of adolescence, and have attempted to ascertain and conceptualize adolescent behaviors, tendencies, and constructs. Whereas the tendency to associate adolescent culture with industrialized nations dates back to World War II and includes the emergence of the teenage market, adolescence as a culture has a long history in Europe and perhaps other preindustrial countries (Schlegel, 2000, p. 73). Historically, adolescent culture has generally been associated with a distinct expressiveness and magnetism toward festive activities (e.g., dances, parties) where opportunities unfolded for young people to "flirt, meet, and court" (p. 73), which set the stage for marriage and developing into young adulthood. While expressiveness and social gatherings continue to attract adolescents today, contemporary adolescents are distinguishable by a stronger connection with peers and materialistic consumerism than in the past.

Traditional visions of adolescence portray teens working alongside adults in factories, farms, and apprenticeships learning a trade or craft or preparing to take over the family farm or business. Intertwined were the lives of adolescents and adults within the home, school, and community. The lives of modern adolescents and adults paint a different landscape. Teens today are much more involved and connected with peers and activities outside the home such as athletics, service, and employment. Traditional family dinners have morphed into buffet- or diner-like atmospheres, and they occur at staggered times, in the car, in front of the television, or not at all. Although dependent on adults for basic needs, as Schlegel (2000) described, today's adolescents are "out of sight and out of mind most of the time" (p. 75). Furthermore, adolescents today are more apt to move out of the family neighborhood after high school and engage in post–high school opportunities that do not involve parents or family. Likewise, the traditional trajectory of marriage and starting a family, a widely anticipated social practice after high school for most adolescents, has stretched later into the 20s or even 30s.

Today's adolescents, although inspired to connect and attach, vary in their views and vision of relationship, marriage, and family.

Contemporary adolescence is a culture pursued by consumerism and mass marketing, which is reflected in the overabundance of media, technology, and product development specifically designed to target teenagers. Malls and shopping establishments abound with images, models, and fragrances designed to attract adolescents and seduce them into spending their money, or their parents'. Media, social networking, and technology devices are commonly used by adolescents and are increasingly used in schools as pedagogy shifts to meet the demands of educational reform and preparing youth for a technologically advanced global society. It is quite common for today's adolescents to be either plugged in, online, or both concurrently throughout the day. Whereas historically adolescents communicated verbally or through writing or telephone, today's youth are quite comfortable and competent with technological forms of communication, with texting being perhaps the most common. Observe adolescents communicating via texting and note the miraculous fine motor skill dexterity that characterizes a unique physical attribute of today's youth.

While modern adolescent culture reflects compelling shifts and variations from historical accounts, common rights of passage remain for many adolescents. For example, ages 13–16 years continue to mark significant developmental attainments. Within Jewish families, the ages of 12 and 13 years commonly mean that girls and boys become a bat or bar mitzvah. The age of 15 years symbolizes learning to drive and driving independently with an adult in the car; it is also associated with a *quinceañera* in Latino cultures. Age 16 years is most often associated with driving alone without supervision, although states are increasingly establishing stricter passenger regulations based on risk and safety data. Furthermore, religious practices, such as confirmation, a coming of age ritual, generally occur between ages 16 and 18 years. In most Western cultures, turning 18 equates with the developmental milestone of reaching adulthood. Choices abound as adolescents either enlist in the armed forces, go to college, or begin living independently and working. Likewise, many modern 18-year-olds continue to depend on the adults in their lives. Some will either live at home, in rentals, or on campuses while enrolled in postsecondary options as they transition into emerging adulthood (Arnett, 2007) in pursuit of degrees, technical training, and licenses and certificates in preparation for a career and the world of work.

These traditional—and to some extent, contemporary—milestones may reflect stereotypical and perhaps privileged assumptions of adolescent markers and milestones today. Cultural influences and variations, historically and in contemporary society, continue to influence adolescents today. For example, socioeconomic factors and inequities in education continue to be significant factors of adolescent health, in addition to safe and supportive families, schools, and peers (Viner et al., 2012). Whereas age 16 years might mark the age that adolescents gain the freedom to learn to drive, many adolescents will not experience this exciting event because of physical, social, and environment constraints, such as disabilities, poverty, lack of access, or family structure and dynamics. Adolescents with disabilities may not be physically able to drive or may lack the cognitive abilities to gain access to a driver's license. Likewise, many youth live in homes with one car, no car, or insufficient financial resources to afford an additional vehicle. These youth depend on alternative means of transportation that youth with privilege rarely experience. Furthermore, for many youth, turning 16 might mark entry into the workforce, particularly in families where adolescents are depended on to supplement the family income or when adolescents start families early. Whereas the rates of teenage pregnancy have decreased over the years (Kost & Henshaw, 2014), many adolescents give birth and begin families at an early age, which may or may not influence how they experience traditional adolescent milestones and markers. The array of trajectories that adolescents might experience as they move through this period of development is beyond the scope of this chapter. Nevertheless, it is paramount that counselors and helping professionals release traditional milestone assumptions and embrace a more contemporary diverse view of adolescence.

Stereotypical assumptions and media portrayal continue to constrict society's perceptions of adolescence and, as expressed by Painter (2013), tint "a flawed masterpiece of adolescence" (p. 2). Media and literature depict adolescence as a period of risky, stormy rebelliousness branded by slamming doors, loud explicit music, defiance, and no respect for authority. Whereas some of these descriptions might portray select adolescents, for many, or perhaps most adolescents, these descriptions are inaccurate (Arnett, 1999). Contemporary comparative analysis of adolescence suggest that stereotypical assumptions of adolescence are embedded in panoptical time and out-of-date and archaic paradigms, which are perpetuated by political factors and policy, media, sexuality, and schools (Lesko, 2012; Painter, 2013). Likewise, traditional linear stage theories perpetuate society's time bound and hierarchical view of adolescent development. Progressing, or advancing, to the top of the developmental trajectory preserves society's tendency to expect, evaluate, and judge development (Lesko, 2012). One of perhaps the most common stereotyped characteristics of development is gender.

Though studies suggest more similarities than differences (Hyde, 2005), gender stereotypes continue to influence male and female adolescent development. Conventional social norms, such as boys will be boys and girls will be girls, are deeply entrenched in traditional assumptions and a patriarchal lineage of what constitutes being a man and being a woman (Gilligan, 2011). A panoramic view of the contemporary culture of civilization uncovers gendered themes laced with society's expectations of masculine and feminine. The lyrics from the traditional nursery rhyme "What Are Little Boys Made Of?" continue to radiate throughout homes, nurseries, preschools, and the impressionable ears of girls and boys: "Snips and snails, and puppy dogs tails; That's what little boys are made of; What are little girls made of? Sugar and spice and all things nice; That's what little girls are made of" (Traditional, 1820). Socially preferred or acceptable images of what is male and what is female flood the media while larger social systems continue to write and promote policy that perpetuates society's perspective of gender, especially in relation to aggression, emotional expression, and more notably voice.

Whereas some studies (Lansford et al., 2012) suggest that boys are more aggressive, active, and less emotional than girls and girls are more relational, intimate, and helpful than boys, the influence of context on gender differences is compelling (Spencer, Steele, & Quinn, 1999), specifically in terms of aggression and helping behaviors (Hyde, 2005). Furthermore, boys' tendencies toward physical aggression, such as hitting, kicking, and using physical force, might suggest the influence of context (i.e., boys active involvement in sports, adventure activities, and physical experiences). Interestingly, as girls and boys age, tendencies toward physical aggression appear to decrease and relational aggression increases (Krahé & Busching, 2014). Nonetheless, both girls and boys appear to use relational and physical styles of aggression in relationships (James, Lawlor, Murphy, & Flynn, 2013; Juvonen, Wang, & Espinoza, 2013).

Within the study of development, the act of aggression is interesting to consider. What purpose might aggression serve in social-emotional development? What are boys and girls attempting to voice or reveal through aggression? Reasons why boys and girls resort to aggression could be uncovered in the study of how patriarchal gender norms continue to frame how we raise youth in contemporary society and the ways young people resist their loss of voice in relationships (Gilligan, 2011). By the age of 4 or 5 years, cultural messages and societal expectations that differentiate gender are clear. Whereas developmental theory emphasizes how important relationship is to development, boys and girls learn early that the act of relationship holds a different meaning for each gender. For example, girls immerse themselves in relationships, almost to the extent of losing themselves. The image of girls moving in groups of close proximity to and from a range of vicinities and locations, such as the bathroom, is widely accepted and perhaps even expected. Likewise, the image of the handsome athlete with the gorgeous cheerleader hooked on his arm is a persistent portrayal of girls' relational role of being seen but not heard. Although boys maintain close relationships during childhood and even through middle school, by high school they often begin detaching from relationships (Way, 2013) and conforming to the boy code (Comstock, 2005) that reflects society's view of masculinity and being a man. Around the age of 15 or 16 years, when most boys begin to drift away from their close friendships, is also the time at which suicide rates for boys increase significantly (Way, 2013). The culture of masculinity within society that negatively influences boys' close male friendships put boys at risk during a sensitive period of development when protection from peer group and other social pressures is most needed (Chu, 2005). Contemporary Western society socializes adolescent boys to establish distance in relationships by avoiding intimacy, emotions, and feelings, especially fear. However, Chu (as cited in Browning, 2008) argues that boys are caught between expressing their "full range of qualities and abilities" (p. 188) and obeying society's constrained masculine norms. The choice is either resist society's expectations in order to live more fully according to their "own sense of self" (p. 202) or maintain the masculine status quo. Chu (as cited in Browning, 2008) "questions models of development that focus on individuation and separation to determine maturity and health" and argues "boys are clearly capable of thoughtful self-reflection and deep interpersonal understanding" (p. 185). Furthermore, by resisting social norms and maintaining close male relationships, boys are more likely to circumvent peer group pressure (Chu, 2005).

Likewise, girls experience an oppressed expression of themselves within relationships, although it is different. What emerges throughout decades of studies (Browning, 2008; Gilligan, 2011) on adolescent girls' development is their dedication to the relationship and doing whatever it takes to maintain the relationship, even if it means sacrificing voice. For some girls, the relationship *is* identity and self-worth. Pleasing others, giving, helping and assisting, and sacrificing needs, expectations, and perhaps even dreams often provide the glue to adolescent girls' self-worth (Miller, 1984), which can put some adolescents in comprising or harmful situations or trigger other issues. In fact, Gilligan (2011) wondered if certain speech, learning, attention, and psychological issues that emerge during the school ages have a relationship with gender development. What is clear in the literature is that relationships, although challenging and complicated testing grounds for both genders, are pivotal social systems where adolescents can experiment, explore, and encounter possibilities.

BOX 12.1 CASE STUDY—ANSON

Anson, a 17-year-old Caucasian boy, has been brought to counseling by his parents because of their concern about Anson's mood, isolation, and distance from the family and friends. Anson's mom is quick to tell you how happy and spirited Anson was as a young boy: "He was always happy and had a lot of friends." Anson's dad interrupts, "I know teenagers are different, but this is ridiculous! I've got no time for this! He needs to grow up and be a man!" Anson shrugs and snaps, "I'm fine!" Later, when you see Anson alone, he shares, "My dad just doesn't get it. He doesn't get me. My mom, she tries, but dad's just too much. He doesn't hear me. I can't talk to him. He's always riding my back about being a man and acting tough." As Anson's counselor, conceptualize his development within the context of gender development and socially embedded gender norms. How might you proceed with Anson and support his development?

PEER RELATIONSHIPS AND ADOLESCENT SOCIAL SYSTEMS

The infinite interactions between biology and environment are uniquely different for each adolescent. Bronfenbrenner's ecological view of development proposes several environmental systems of direct and indirect influence on individuals, most notably family, peers, school, and community (Broderick & Blewitt, 2015). Peers and friendships comprise a vast and expanded social network of influences that extend beyond the home environment and include subsystems of relationships that extend across neighborhoods, schools, civic organizations, and religious institutions. The mini-society of a school is where adolescents generally spend a substantial part of their time and development. Comprised of a variety of peers, friendships, and adults, the system of school is an instrumental influence on adolescent development. Community can encompass a variety of subsystems of influence from narrowly defined neighborhoods and ethnic, religious or lifestyle groups, to more encompassing definitions that reflect entire cities or multiple communities (Reitz-Krueger, Nagel, Guarnera, & Reppucci, 2015). Collectively, these systems of influence play a role in the social-emotional development of adolescents.

Influence of Peer Groups

Adolescents spend most of their days immersed and enveloped within peer groups. Scan the social peer group scene of adolescents and you will generally observe a variety of small peer groups or adolescent cultural subgroups (Stearn, 2012) within the larger, school-wide peer culture (Lynch, Lerner, & Leventhal, 2013). Some peer groups are self-selected by adolescents, whereas adolescents might find themselves labeled or stereotyped into a peer group (e.g., jocks, nerds, preppy, popular, druggies). Adolescents may also find themselves placed into a particular peer group because of gender, race, religion, affection orientation, socioeconomic status, disability, and other types of cultural groupings. Furthermore, affiliation into a peer group can occur based on adult recommendation or assignment, such as ability grouping (e.g., gifted, talented; Nussbaum, Lucas, & McManus, 2012). Nonetheless, membership in or out of peer groups can have positive and negative consequences on adolescents' self-concept, self-esteem, and overall sense of self-worth (Nussbaum et al., 2012).

Through peer influence, a phenomenon characterized by the presence of both peer selection and peer socialization (Brechwald & Prinstein, 2011), adolescents come to know themselves. Within the peer group relational laboratories, adolescents experiment, risk, and learn about who they are in relation to others. Adolescents learn from peers and peer groups what is preferred, acceptable, and tolerated, and what is not. As youth individuate from adult values, peers serve as a social compass, a scope for modeling, imitation, comparison, and experimenting, each of which holds possibilities for positive and negative outcomes (Brechwald & Prinstein, 2011). In other words, involvement with peer groups can be as liberating as it is painful. Whereas peer groups serve as support for adolescents as they envision life beyond the family of origin, peer groups can also introduce adolescents to the harsh realities of judgment and how others view them. As Josselson (1992) described, "Never are people more unforgiving mirrors for each other than in youth" (p. 114). Through involvement in peer groups, "one finds oneself mirrored in another's eyes" (p. 210).

Peer groups can reflect negative influences of on adolescents, such as antisocial, deviant, and at-risk behaviors, in addition to internalizing behaviors, depressive symptoms, and issues with body image and eating (Brechwald & Prinstein, 2011). The desire to belong, be seen, and avoid rejection can motivate some adolescents to choose behaviors that they might not choose in other contexts. Threats and negative pressure to conform can be powerful forces on adolescents, who perceive the consequences of not belonging to be much greater than the outcomes of the proposed behavior, even if the consequences of the behavior are clear (Smith, Chein, & Steinberg, 2014). This could be the case involving adolescent gangs, whereby leaving the gang membership might result in harmful or dangerous circumstances; however, losing the friendships and connections is often the more devastating outcome (Carson, Peterson, & Esbensen, 2013). Additionally, peer group conformity might heighten adolescent vulnerability to negative affective outcomes such as mood or depressive symptoms. Joining peer groups where depressive symptoms are characteristic of the members could increase an adolescent's vulnerability to depression or mood issues (Conway, Rancourt, Adelman, Burk, & Prinstein, 2011). Likewise, vulnerability to eating and body image issues my increase for adolescents that associate with peer groups that emulate similar characteristics or behaviors (Goodwin, Haycraft, & Meyer, 2014). Remarkably, association with peer groups that reflect positive behaviors, attitudes, characteristics, and behaviors can buffer adolescents from vulnerabilities, external and internal, which suggests the important roles that positive peer groups can play in adolescent development (Conway et al., 2011; Linville, Stice, Gau, & O'Neil, 2011; Smith et al., 2014).

However, peer influence is difficult to reduce to specific individuals and groups. Different sources of peer influence exist, individually and collectively, and each exerts compelling influence on adolescent socialization, attitudes, and behavior. Romantic relationships (Connolly & McIsaac, 2011), close or best friends, and larger cliques and social networks comprise the more common sources of peer influence. Subsequently, adolescent friendships often nest within a larger friendship group or clique. Given the instability and variance of friendships during adolescence, although best friends may change quickly, the larger peer group generally remains relatively stable (Brechwald & Prinstein, 2011) and provides a buffer when negative social experiences occur. Interestingly, although peer groups can have a profound influence on adolescent behaviors and attitudes, peer groups outside of an adolescent's everyday social network can also exert influence (i.e., gangs, social media). Therefore, unraveling how youth reconcile the multiple influencing sources in their lives is important for promoting adolescent development across systems of influence.

How and why adolescents conform to peers continues to inspire inquiry and is critical for prevention programming efforts. Understanding the influence of peers and why adolescents conform to peers may inspire proactive developmental approaches that target peer group influence in ways that support positive youth development, individually and collectively. For example, as social learning theory and identity theory support, peer groups and success among peers are especially striking to adolescents' experiences of positive regard and belongingness (Davis, 2012). Adolescents invest in peers as primary sources of social and emotional support and rely on feedback and acceptance from their peers to support their developing self-concept and self-worth. Complying with peer influence can reinforce adolescents to behave in socially acceptable ways that positively influence their self-identity and peer relationships (Brechwald & Prinstein, 2011), all of which secures a sense of positive regard and belongingness.

Still, balancing and sustaining peer group membership is striking. For instance, consider the fine line between achieving high academic performance that might stereotype a youth into one group (e.g., gifted), only to feel the threat of being labeled into another (e.g., nerd; Nussbaum et al., 2012). Acceptance into one peer group can also mean rejection by another peer group. Likewise, adolescent girls are well aware of what is acceptable and not acceptable within peer groups, and they adamantly adjust their behavior accordingly. As described by Wiseman (as cited in Nussbaum et al., 2012), "They'll tolerate almost anything to stay in … and there's always the threat of being case out" (p. 309). The weight of feeling in or out can feel enormous during adolescence. Peer acceptance is a persuasive social reward for adolescents (Guyer, Choate, Pine, & Nelson, 2012), and the need to feel accepted might provoke some adolescents to make decisions that in a different social situation they might not make. Likewise, emotional reactivity to peer rejection, although a normal emotional developmental process, can heighten at-risk vulnerability for some adolescents, such as those at risk for depression (Silk et al., 2014). The threat of rejection can exaggerate adolescents' vulnerabilities to at-risk behaviors, such as experimentation, substance use, and other harmful or dangerous behaviors. However, positive peer relationships during adolescence may decrease sensitivity to negative social experiences (Masten, Telzer, Fuligni, Lieberman, & Eisenberger, 2012). Feeling connected to a peer group or significant peer relationship, even virtually or online (Davis, 2012), can cushion youth when social situations end in rejection.

BOX 12.2 CASE STUDY—RACHEL

Rachel, a 15-year-old biracial girl, has been brought to counseling by her father because of issues at school. Rachel and her family recently moved to a new region of the country, and not long after settling into their new home, Rachel started having problems at school. She had made a couple of friends, mostly boys, and joined the math club; however, recently Rachel started skipping school and staying in her room. Her grades have slipped dramatically. Rachel shared that some girls were calling her names and bullying her because of her accent, the music she listened to, her interest in math, and her male friendships. Rachel eventually got into a fight and received an in-school suspension. To avoid the embarrassment that in-school suspension creates, Rachel began skipping school. As Rachel's counselor, how might you conceptualize Rachel's development within the context of gender and peer influence? How might you move forward with Rachel and support her development?

Influence of School

Considering that adolescents spend approximately 14% of their time in school (Juster, Ono, & Stafford, 2004), the influence of the school experience on adolescent development should not be underestimated; schools are where adolescents spend most of their time besides their homes (Eccles & Roeser, 2011). Schools are rich with influential relationships, culture, and activities where options, choices, and opportunities abound. Whereas most adolescents move through school with ease and transition into emerging or young adulthood seamlessly, some adolescents do not and instead leave school completely (Eccles & Roeser, 2011). Gaining a deeper understanding of what connects adolescents to schools and what repels them is a key factor in adolescent development.

Contemporary schools are as diverse as the students who attend them. Many of today's schools reflect a college-like campus atmosphere with large class sizes, crowded hallways, and distant, impersonal relationships with staff and teachers. Class choices are as vast as the co-curricular and athletic opportunities. Youth have options to lead, participate, and join in an array of clubs, organizations, councils, and teams designed to resonate with all interests and abilities. Smaller private or lower enrollment schools provide adolescents with similar opportunities yet on a smaller scale, which some adolescents prefer as it provides closer contact with teachers and smaller, more intimate peer groups (Elkind, 1984).

Relationships within schools provide diverse sources of feedback, perspective, and modeling that inspire changes or turning points as adolescents begin to envision future roles in the world (Sadowski, 2008). Within these turning points or transitions, adolescents' identities expand to reflect meaning and purpose, a process that adolescents would prefer not to do alone (Toshalis, 2008). Whereas parents and peers are noted to be influential, external supports during transitions, identity formation processes, and the development of purpose (Malin, Reilly, Quinn, & Moran, 2014), likewise, schools play an instrumental role. As adolescents develop a sense of their place in world, work, career, and vocational aspirations begin to emerge. The emphasis on college and career readiness (Conley, 2012) in today's schools increases the opportunities for schools to influence the adolescent's transition beyond high school. Schools, specifically teachers and other professional educators, such as school counselors, coaches, and paraprofessionals, provide important relationships for adolescents that illuminate the importance of multiple influences on development for today's adolescents.

Bernstein-Yamashiro and Noam (2013) revealed that supportive relationships with teachers help youth navigate and cope with the emotional challenges they face as adolescents (p. 27). Likewise, studies reveal that having at least one "confiding relationship is the single best predictor of psychological and social risks for adolescents "(Browning, 2008). Furthermore, adolescents are more apt to share experiences with the adults in school that might prove to be "shocking" at home (p. 28). Teachers, much like peers, can provide objective feedback to adolescents that families cannot. However, positive experiences with teachers are not always the case. Perspectives from youth suggest that teacher assumptions and actions can hinder teacher effectiveness and negatively influence adolescents' abilities to cope with anxiety and difficult academic and school challenges (Wentzel, 2012). For example, adolescents quite often do not feel confident approaching a teacher. Viewed as an authority person in a position of power, a lack of confidence will prevent an adolescent from reaching out to a teacher for support or assistance. Likewise, if an adolescent avoids approaching or reaching out to a teacher, teachers might assume that the teen does not care about school. Teachers are encouraged to view adolescent behavior developmentally, use developmentally adaptive approaches (Flum & Lavi-Yudelevitch, as cited in Browning, 2008), and move toward youth in growth-fostering ways that strengthen relationships as adolescents balance the emotional energy that often accompanies identity development.

Achievement

The influence of school on adolescent identity development goes beyond social relationships. The ability to learn and achieve in school in the presence of peers inspires a sense of competence that has a significant influence on the adolescent self-concept (Bong & Skaalvik, 2003), particularly the academic self-concept (Shavelson, Hubner, & Stanton, 1976). For example, achieving in school increases adolescents' academic self-concept, which positively influences ensuing achievement and other educational experiences (Marsh & Martin, 2011). However, cultivating an academic self-concept can be challenging for some adolescents, such as racial or ethnic minority adolescents who are, negotiating social environmental factors while nurturing fragile racial identities. For example, when adolescents perceive achieving academically as a threat to peer group acceptance, some adolescents might discard the idea of academic achievement in order to maintain connections with peers. These types of mitigating factors (e.g., self-esteem, well-being, racial identity) place minority adolescents in a double-bind conflict as they protect one component of their developing self-concept at the cost of sacrificing another. The consequence is often lower academic self-concept, as reflected in GPA and overall academic achievement (Cokley, McClain, Jones, & Johnson, 2012).

Schools are social institutions and microcosms of the larger community, region, and nation—and therefore, they influence achievement. For many adolescents, school feels familiar in relation to social expectations and values. Scanning the school, these adolescents have a sense of commonality with other youth that look somewhat similar (skin color) and sound comparable (language). Perhaps these adolescents live in residential communities together where families interact and communicate regularly or they have grown up on citywide sports teams. These adolescents enter school with a calmer sense of what to expect, who they will encounter, how to behave, and perhaps more important, how they will be treated. How adolescents think and feel about themselves in relation to others and their environment can have a profound effect on how they will experience, achieve, and develop in school (Marsh & Martin, 2011).

Unfortunately, for many adolescents, school does not feel familiar, comfortable, or even safe. Walking the halls feels as threatening as walking through neighborhoods that are off limits or taught to be dangerous. Safety, security, and a sense of acceptance and belonging in school cross over socioeconomic status, race, ethnicity, sexual orientation, and other defining demographics. Even though well-meaning educators and professionals, such as school counselors, endeavor to change the culture of schools, schools do not always accept or celebrate being different. This is contrary to the developmental tasks of adolescence that speak to this period of development as being a time to explore, experiment, and risk as paths toward discovering identity. Schools often project conflicting messages that, on one hand, invite adolescents to be themselves yet, on the other hand, judge them for being too different. Minority and marginalized adolescents, such as lesbian, gay, bisexual, transgender, and queer (LGBTQ) youth, perhaps feel these conflicting messages more than any other adolescents do because of society's continued judgment and lack of acceptance toward sexual orientations other than heterosexual. During a time of self-discovery amidst the demands and expectations of school, some LGBTQ youth experience schools as unsupportive places where they feel unsafe disclosing their sexual orientation and expressing their identities (Jones, 2012), which undoubtedly influences learning and academic achievement. For example, the 2011 National School Climate Survey reveals the influence of harsh school environments on the academic achievement of LGBTQ youth (Kosciw, Greytak, Bartkiewicz, Boesin, & Palmer, 2012).

The influence of racial stereotypes and a negative school climate on achievement gaps and the underperformance of minority groups and marginalized youth surpasses intelligence and capacity to succeed academically. Likewise, Noguera (2008) noted that "understanding the process through which young people come to see themselves as belonging to particular racial categories is important because it has tremendous bearing on the so-called achievement gap" (p. 27). Long held assumptions and "stereotype threats" (p. 28) whereby teachers *and* students believe that "if you're White, you'll do better in school then if you're Black, or if you're Asian you'll do better in school than if you're Latino" (p. 29) continue to oppress the educational experiences of many minority and diverse youth. However, achieving in school is not always favorable within some racial and ethnic peer groups. For some ethnic minority adolescents, particularly African American adolescents, academic achievement mimics acting White, which creates a double-bind conflict between acting White enough to succeed and Black enough to survive (Carbado & Gulati, 2013). To protect their peer group membership and secure belongingness, some ethnic minority adolescents may live up to social stereotypes and assumptions by sabotaging their academic achievement and school success by skipping school, dismissing homework, and dissociating during class (Sadowski, 2008).

In terms of school experience, school success, and academic achievement, contemporary adolescents face one of three scenarios according to Bradley and Renzulli (2011): "in school, pushed out or pulled out" (p. 521). Whereas a number of theories (see Rumberger & Lim, 2011) offer potential influences that motivate an adolescent to drop out of school, the two most compelling reasons are individual and institutional. As the one institution where adolescents spend the most time, schools are in a unique position to support, nurture, and enhance adolescent social-emotional development. Educators, coaches, specialists, and other professionals in schools are important adults in the lives of adolescents and can make important contributions to their development. Nakkula and Toshalis (2009) believed that adolescent development is "promoted interactively within all of the relational and opportunity contexts within which we live" (p. 39). An interactive relational role summons adults in schools to reach out and invite adolescents to share their experiences while listening with curiosity through a developmental ear. In a sincere relational role, adults can listen for their passions and dreams and flesh out their deeper desires. Contrary, listening with a judgmental ear and slipping into the role of "unilateral advisor" and declaring to youth "what to do or how to act" (p. 33) will most likely create distance between adolescents and adults and further endorse the current generational divide. Whereas adults might be inclined to share their youthful experiences, which for some adolescents is refreshing, comforting, and possibly humorous, adults are cautioned not to project their experiences onto adolescents as standards or ideals that radiate a "When I was your age ..." paradigm, which can perpetuate outdated paradigms and stereotypical assumptions. Instead, adults that share their adolescent experiences as a route toward empathetic connection with youth provide a channel for the expression of mutual empathy within a growth-fostering relationship (Comstock, 2005; Flum & Lavi-Yudelevitch, as cited in Browning, 2008).

Embedding identity theory (Marcia, 2014) into youth development opportunities may also support positive identity status and dissuade the negative effects of peer pressure on adolescent development. Research (Dumas, Ellis, & Wolfe, 2012) implies that identity commitment and identity exploration buffer adolescents from both negative at-risk behaviors and peer pressure. Adolescents with greater identity commitment were observed to participate in less risky behavior than teens with lower identity commitment status. Likewise, studies (Crocetti, Jahromi, & Meeus, 2012) support a relationship between adolescent identity formation and civic engagement. Adolescents that attained an achieved status appear to be more involved in service and civic activities and reflect a stronger and deeper sense of self-worth and purpose than diffused adolescents. Clearly, adolescent identity development has the potential to thrive within intentional growth-fostering, interactive, service-oriented engagement with individuals and larger social systems.

Adults within schools can intervene in the identity development of adolescents by making positive changes in the culture and climate of schools. Changing the cultures of schools to ones that promote a growth-fostering culture and climate where *all* adolescents have access to quality academic curriculum that reflects the cultural diversity of the school can have a positive influence on identity development (Sadowski, 2008). For example, schools can foster identity development of adolescents with disabilities by supporting the growth in "self-definition, self-concept, and self-image, self-efficacy and perceptions of control, and self-determination" (Wehmeyer, 2008, p. 170). Likewise, gifted and talented students excel when they have access to high, rigorous curriculum opportunities within a supportive social and teaching environment. Jensen (2012) stressed the importance of integrating more of a cultural-developmental approach that is malleable to universal adolescent development. Clearly, approaches within schools that embrace the diversity of development within growth-fostering, relational, and engaged opportunities could ultimately promote the development of *all* adolescents.

BOX 12.3   CASE STUDY—CARLOS

Carlos, a 14-year-old Latino boy, has been brought to counseling by his mother. Carlos's mother shares that Carlos's appetite has decreased, he is not sleeping, and he appears very tired and fatigued. Likewise, Carlos's teachers have expressed concern, stating that Carlos has been withdrawn, uninterested in his schoolwork, and has been tardy for numerous classes. He is failing three required subjects. Carlos received two detentions in the past 3 months for excessive tardiness and not completing assignments. If Carlos does not change his behavior, his promotion to ninth grade might be in jeopardy. Carlos's mother works, and his father work two jobs to make ends meet. Carlos's mother expressed that Carlos would have to quit basketball so that he can take care of his sister at night while they are working. What are some of the social factors interfering with Carlos's ability to achieve at school? As Carlos's counselor, how might you work with Carlos and collaborate with the family and school to support Carlos's development and achievement in school?

FAMILY RELATIONSHIPS AND ADOLESCENT DEVELOPMENT

The traditional view of parental influences on adolescent development has been grounded in the notion that parents *train* their children—in essence, children are the products of their parents, socialization and instruction. This view was particularly popular through the mid-20th century, when adolescence was often viewed as a period of rebellion and an intentional pulling away from parental mores (recall the concept of storm and stress discussed in chapter 11). More contemporary views of parent–child relationships support a *reciprocal socialization* view; that is, it is now recognized that while parents do have significant impact on their children's development, children are also impacting parental development and behaviors. This *systemic approach* to understanding parenting and adolescent development offers a more comprehensive view of family processes and a better understanding of relational dynamics and dysfunctional family patterns.

To better understand the implications of reciprocal impacts and a systemic view, it would be helpful to consider a few examples. It is widely known that interparental relationships significantly impact the adolescent's development.

In fact, the effects of marital discord on adolescent processes and behaviors are well documented (Baril, Crouter, & McHale, 2007; Cui & Conger, 2008; Doyle & Markiewicz, 2005; Fosco & Grych, 2008; Lucas-Thompson, 2012). In one particular study, marital discord was found to be correlated with the development of eating disorders (Blodgett-Salafia, Schaefer, & Haugen, 2014). Though a direct mechanism was not immediately evident, the researchers proposed that both the marital conflict and the secondary adverse effects on the mother–child and father–child relationships played a role in the observed correlation. Marital discord has also been linked to depression, anxiety, peer conflicts, poor school performance, and other adjustment-related issues (Amato & Cheadle, 2005; Davies & Windle, 2001). Further, marital conflict has been associated with adolescents' poor responses to treatment (Amaya, Reinecke, Silva, & March, 2011). Clearly the marital relationship is an important factor for counselors, who need to consider both the direct and indirect impacts of family dynamics on adolescent development and treatment.

Marital discord and conflictual parental relationships may also impact the individual in the long term. For example, as adolescents progress into adulthood, marriage becomes an increasingly significant element in their perceptions of life satisfaction (Willoughby, 2010). However, adolescents who are raised in an environment of high marital conflict are less likely to have a positive view of marriage, and they may struggle with maintenance of healthy adult relationships (Miga, Gdula, & Allen, 2012). These data underscore not only the importance of a systemic developmental perspective but also the importance of parents as relationship role models.

In keeping with the reciprocal socialization view, it should also be considered that adolescents may significantly impact the development and relationships of their parents and caregivers. For example, adolescent delinquency behaviors can affect both the probability and stability of marriage (Doherty, Green, & Ensminger, 2012), as well as reported marital satisfaction and self-perceptions of parental efficacy (Downing-Matibag, 2009). Further, Cui, Donnellan, and Conger (2007) found that marital discord adversely impacted adolescent adjustment, and that adolescent maladjustment correlated with increasing marital discord. Too often, little consideration is given to the impacts of adolescent development and behaviors on the parents and caregivers in their lives. While it is logical that adolescent behaviors and processes may be stressful to parents and therefore impact their own lives and relationships, such consideration is often not emphasized in treatment of adolescents in counseling.

Reciprocal influences are not limited to parent–child dynamics. Studies have found correlations between sibling conflict and adolescent development that are also bidirectional (Kim, McHale, Crouter, & Osgood, 2007; Stocker, Burwell, & Briggs, 2002; Tucker, McHale, & Crouter, 2003; Yeh & Lempers, 2004). However, it is also of note that parental relationships may be mitigating or exacerbating to sibling conflicts, thus adding yet another dimension to the impact of relational dynamics on adolescent development (Campione-Barr, Greer, & Kruse, 2013). Figure 12.1 summarizes the reciprocal influences across family systems. For counselors working with adolescent clients, the impacts of familial

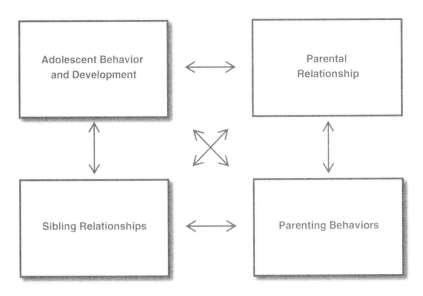

Figure 12.1   Reciprocal socialization influences in family systems.

influences must always be a consideration, even if an individual—rather than a systemic—treatment approach is used.

Parenting Styles and Adolescents

A key task of adolescent development is internalizing a locus of control and developing an individual identity (see chapter 11). Parents play a significant role in this process as they mentor, manage, and monitor their adolescent's behaviors and relationships. More specifically, the quality and type of parenting behaviors can have lasting impact on adolescents. Based on Baumrind's (1991) identification of four distinct parenting styles, the following is summary of these parenting behaviors as applied to adolescents:

1. *Authoritative parenting*: encourages adolescent input on decisions and processes, taking a democratic approach to rules and boundaries; supports individual development and identity; exemplified by high warmth and responsiveness. Supports adolescents' social competence and responsibility.
2. *Authoritarian parenting*: discourages adolescent input on decisions and processes; discourages individual identity, emphasizing strict adherence to parental rules; display low levels of warmth or responsiveness. Often leads to adolescent insecurity and poor social interaction.
3. *Neglectful parenting*: neither encouraging nor discouraging of adolescent input on decisions or processes, as style is marked by lack of parental involvement; displays low levels of warmth or responsiveness; lack of both rules and monitoring. Often leads to poor self-regulation and impulse control, as well as lower self-esteem.

4. *Indulgent parenting*: encourages adolescent input on decisions and processes; high levels of parental involvement, though lacking in rules and boundaries; high in warmth and responsiveness. Often leads to poor self-control and persistent egocentricity, with adverse effects in relationships.

Authoritative parenting is generally considered to be the best approach to child development throughout adolescence, and its relative efficacy has been researched across a wide range of cultures and contexts (Steinberg & Silk, 2002). Adolescents raised by authoritative parenting tend to develop autonomy and independence and higher degrees of social competence.

However, it is also important to note that while authoritative parenting *is* associated with positive outcomes, the reverse is not necessarily as predictable. Some researchers have found positive outcomes associated with aspects of authoritarian style within a specific cultural context. For example, while the vast majority of Asian American child-rearing practices would fit under the category of authoritarian based on Baumrind's categories, the predicted poor outcomes are the exception, not the rule (Choi, Kim, Kim, & Park, 2013). One explanation for this discrepancy may be found in the parenting *in context*—that is, behaviors that are labeled *controlling* in the Eurocentric view are viewed as *training* in the context of Asian-influenced culture (Chao & Tseng, 2002). Parental training is an essential aspect of support and guidance and is associated with positive outcomes (Lau & Fung, 2013).

African American parents also tend to use parenting strategies more inclined to fit under the authoritarian approach, and they often include corporal punishment as a means of behavioral control and a consequence to bad behavior. While corporal punishment is not associated with *positive* behavioral outcomes, there is a less negative impact in African American families than in European American families (Simons, Simons, & Su, 2013). Latino American parenting is also often categorized as authoritarian and is marked by high control and expectations of obedience. However, such parental behaviors are not consistently associated with poor outcomes (Dixon, Graber, & Brooks-Gunn, 2008). Thus, there appear to be mitigating factors in context and circumstance not accounted for in Baumrind's original research.

BOX 12.4   PERSONAL REFLECTION: PERCEPTIONS OF PARENTING STYLES

Think about the type of behaviors of your parents or guardians during your adolescence. Based on Baumrind's four styles *only*, how would you categorize the overall parenting style you experienced during this stage? Was it different from the parenting you experienced in childhood? What variables impacted the behaviors of your parents or guardians? Last, in what ways do you believe the parenting style you experienced affected your development?

Additional Considerations

One potential influence not consistently accounted for in culturally driven research on parenting practices may be the environmental influence of socioeconomic status. For example, in economically disadvantaged neighborhoods, where crime rates are higher and personal safety is lower, parents may be more likely to utilize controlling tactics to monitor and protect their children. In other contexts, they may appear to be rigid and domineering; however, within the context of their immediate environment, they are making the best decisions for their children. Considering the disproportionate number of minority children living in impoverished and unsafe environments, it is quite possible that authoritarian behaviors observed in these parents are in response to environmental stressors. This may also account for some of the differences in outcomes seen in parenting style studies across racial and ethnic groups.

Another mitigating factor that challenges the predicted outcomes of the traditional four parenting models may be seen in adolescents' *perceptions* of parenting practices. Context, circumstance, and individual personality can significantly affect the efficacy of parenting practices. In keeping with the example noted previously, adolescents raised in economically depressed environments where personal safety is a concern may be more accepting of parental control and demandingness, compared with adolescents raised in more affluent neighborhoods. In addition, the observed authoritarian practices of minority parents may be received more positively by their children, who must face the harsh realities of racism and prejudice (Brown & Bakken, 2011). In such circumstances, rigid boundaries and control may be viewed as unifying and protective, and may even be a contributory factor in ethnic identity development.

Last, the four-style parenting model is unidirectional and linear and does not incorporate considerations for reciprocal socialization nor developmental adaptation. Kerr, Stattin, and Ozdemir (2012) stressed that "parenting style cannot be seen as independent of the adolescent" (p. 1540), noting the bidirectional relationship between parenting behaviors and adolescent adjustment. Parenting experience, adolescent behaviors, and environmental factors influence parenting behaviors in a dynamic and continuous manner. Similarly, Vazsonyi, Hibbert, and Snider (2003) noted that specific parenting behaviors were employed by parents in response to adolescent adjustment and challenges. This evolving and dynamic process is an essential part of understanding adolescent clients in counseling and supports the need for parents or guardians to be consistently involved with the treatment process.

Developmentally Adaptive Parenting

Given the conflicting research on impacts of parenting styles and the variety of influences that shape the parent–adolescent dynamic, counselors may find themselves overwhelmed in the quest to find a foothold in counseling adolescents and their parents. To perhaps simplify this daunting task somewhat, it may be most prudent to conceptualize these relationships through an integrated, developmentally adaptive lens. Considerations should be given for the age, maturity, and personality of the adolescent, as well as the context and circumstances of presenting situations. Environment, culture, and parental goals must also be taken into account. Furthermore, characteristics of traditional parenting styles—such as warmth and monitoring—should also be recognized as important aspects of effective parenting. Together these components can help define *what works* in parent–adolescent relationships, which is fundamental to a wellness approach for counseling teenagers. Rather than focusing on authoritative versus authoritarian, for example, counselors should instead identify the aspects of parenting *behaviors* that are contextually effective and should support parental development concurrent to adolescent development. Such an approach can maximize the benefits of parental guidance and support while positively contributing to the adolescent's health and wellness.

Attachment and Autonomy

Research on the profound developmental impact of attachment has traditionally focused on early childhood. While first relationships certainly do have lasting impact, it is now recognized that attachment impacts identity and development well into adulthood. Furthermore, attachment in adolescence is associated with the development of autonomy, differentiation, and individuation as well as the ability to form healthy relationships in adulthood. Building on the theories of Bowlby and Ainsworth, contemporary developmental theorists recognize secure attachment in adolescence to be an extension of positive parenting practices and essential in successful navigation of the challenging journey of adolescence.

Secure attachment in adolescence has been found to be negatively associated with both depression and anxiety (Jokobsen, Horwood, & Fergusson, 2012) and suicidal ideation (Sheftall, Matias, Furr, & Doughter, 2013). Conversely, insecure attachment has been linked to depression and conduct problems in adolescence (Scott et al., 2013) and to increased risk of suicidality (Sheftall, Schoppe-Sullivan, & Bridge, 2014). Researchers have suggested that attachment quality in adolescence may be a *protective factor* and is a promising focus for treatment of adolescents.

Parent–adolescent attachment quality can impact social competence as well. Van Petegem, Beyers, Brenning, and Vansteenkiste (2013) found that insecure attachment was associated with less consistency in autonomy and increased interpersonal anxiety. Conversely, Mikulincer and Shaver (2013) noted that securely attached adolescents display greater confidence in decisions and comfort in interpersonal relationships and generally develop healthier romantic attachments. Hershenberg et al. (2011) also found a positive correlation between secure attachment and healthy interpersonal relationships, noting that securely attached adolescents had better emotional regulation and affect consistency. The researchers further suggested that secure attachment in adolescence may provide a buffer for common developmental challenges.

As in childhood, secure attachment in adolescence still holds the parental figures—particularly mothers—as a *secure base*. However, for the adolescent, the secure base is defined differently; parents serve a more supportive and guiding role for teenagers. Attachment is strengthened through positive, supportive interaction and may actually increase during adolescence (Ruhl, Dolan, & Buhrmester, 2014). Unlike the very young child who needs to *see and touch* the parent to feel secure, adolescents need to *know and feel* they have parental support. This internalization helps facilitate adolescent identity development, decision making, and social competence.

Sibling Relationships

Although constructs of attachment and recognition of impact generally pertain to parent–child relationships, similar concepts can apply to the influences of sibling relationships as well. The vast majority of adolescents have at least one sibling; these familial relationships can serve as sources of conflict and stress, but quite often they are sources of support, guidance, companionship, and modeling. In some ways, siblings may even be more influential on developmental processes than parents. Younger siblings, in particular, are attracted to the perspective of older siblings, whose stage-related experience is fresh, and who can empathize more effectively with the developing adolescent. For example, a 14-year-old boy struggling with the social challenges of being a freshman in high school may be more likely to seek counsel from his 17-year-old brother, the senior who has already survived the perils of high school. Similarly, the 16-year-old girl, who has her first serious boyfriend, may prefer to discuss sexual decision making and birth control with her older sister. In both cases, the older siblings' development can also be impacted as they are called upon to consider their own experiences and guide their siblings, stimulating their own moral and ethical development.

In addition to reciprocal socialization, siblings can also provide protective developmental factors for each other (Yeh & Lempers, 2004). Healthy sibling relationships may serve as a buffer for parent–child conflict or as a safe haven during family crises such as death or divorce. Conversely, conflictual sibling relationships may adversely affect adolescent development (Kim et al., 2007), particularly when combined with ineffective parenting and insecure parental attachment (Bank, Burraston, & Synder, 2004).

The Role of Conflict

Contrary to the assertions of traditional developmental theorists, adolescence is not rife with high degrees of conflict, nor is it defined by teenage rebellion. Conflicts between parents and adolescents are generally manageable and related to more mundane aspects of life—keeping a bedroom clean, coming home before curfew, participating in family functions, and similar day-to-day concerns. Though parent–adolescent conflict increases at the front end of this stage, by late adolescence conflicts have decreased in frequency (Santrock, 2007). Factors contributing to both the rise and decline of conflict in may be associated with both physical and cognitive developmental influences, as well as ongoing social development in both the adolescent and the parent.

Regardless of specific contributory factors, conflict is considered a normative part of adolescent development, and it is not necessarily a cause for concern. In fact, conflict may actually serve a *purpose* in adolescent development. For example, shifting roles and expectations may contribute to increased arguments between parents and adolescents. Likewise, many parents are entering middle adulthood and encountering their own developmental peaks and valleys, which can increase sensitivity and emotional reactivity in the home. However, these same arguments may create opportunities for enhanced mutual understanding, clarifications of rules and boundaries, and additional role modeling. In addition, conflict may serve as a *testing ground* for adolescents, who are actively exploring aspects of identity. A clash with parents might show the adolescent that a chosen direction does not meet parental approval. By the same token, the manner in which parents handle the clash—for example, communicating disapproval for the behavior while stressing love and support of the teenager—can have a significant impact on the manner in which the adolescent processes the outcome of the conflict. In learning to fight fair, parents and adolescents can work together to foster healthy individuation and differentiation.

BOX 12.5   THE COUNSELOR AS A CATALYST

Individuation and systems differentiation—as viewed within the context of the person—are important developmental tasks of adolescence, and they support identity and autonomy. Considering the influences of parent and family systems discussed thus far, it is not difficult to recognize the integral role parents and families have in the healthy development of the adolescent. Counselors can play an important part in supporting adolescent wellness and more fluid differentiation by integrating these systemic considerations into clinical interventions and psychoeducation:

- Improving communication and connection
- Enhancing warmth and responsiveness
- Increasing mutual understanding and empathy
- Supporting navigation of conflict and fostering growth

Contemporary Adolescents in Context

Most researchers agree that the optimal family structure includes two parents, under the same roof, who are both involved with raising children and running the household. However, in the United States, less than half of all children live in a "traditional" household, when defined as two heterosexual, married parents (Livingston, 2014). Contemporary family structures include parents who are cohabitating/unmarried, gay or lesbian parents (married and unmarried), grandparent guardians, extended family guardians, single parents, foster and adoptive parents, and more. In all forms, families have parent–child dynamics to consider, even if the parent is neither biological nor custodial. All adult members of family systems can play important roles in adolescent development.

In working with adolescents in counseling, it is important to understand both the present and past family structures and influences on the adolescent. For example, adolescents whose parents are divorced may have fewer supporting resources in their lives, as divorce generally adversely impacts parental finances, free time, and emotional availability. Furthermore, the marital discord that precipitated the divorce may remain between the divorced parents, causing stress for the adolescent who continues to feel torn between parents. In fact, particularly contentious divorces and continued animosity between parents can impact adolescent social development and attachment patterns well into adulthood (Afifi & Denes, 2012).

Though a large body of research indicates that adolescents from divorced families are far more likely to develop significant issues—including depression, anxiety, academic problems, and substance use—it would be inaccurate to assume that *all* adolescents who experience divorce face these challenges, or that the divorce itself is the *cause*. Constance Ahrons (1998), noted family therapist and author of *The Good Divorce*, suggests that it is the residual animosity that so often persists between divorced parents that is the biggest stressor for children and most directly impacts developmental outcomes. Divorced parents who strive to create a *binuclear* family system, continue to consult with each other over decisions affecting their children, and treat each other with respect and kindness will often find themselves with happy, well-adjusted teenagers.

Adolescents whose parents divorce may end up living with single parents or perhaps will soon find themselves in a stepfamily. Both circumstances have their unique challenges, including issues of *boundary ambiguity* and changing relational dynamics. While these issues can certainly have an adverse impact on adolescent development, negative outcomes are not foregone conclusions—in fact, many navigate the adjustments successfully. Counselors working with adolescent clients and their families through this period would be wise to help enhance communication and mutual understanding in relationships, as both are essential to healthy social and emotional development in adolescents.

Another increasingly common nontraditional family is that headed by gay or lesbian parents who are single, cohabiting, or married. Adolescents with gay or lesbian parents experience stage-related trials and tribulations with the same rates and outcomes as their peers raised by heterosexual parents (American Psychological Association, 2004; Goldberg, 2010). There are some unique developmental stressors for these teenagers, however—including facing prejudice based on assumptions by a heteronormative society (Robitaille & Saint-Jacques, 2009). Counselors may need to integrate such topics into treatment with these adolescents to ensure healthy identity development and social adjustment.

The key take away, as we discuss the impacts of family relationships and structure on adolescent development, is the quality of the relationships in an adolescent's life. Adolescence is a challenging time, filled with rapid changes and exploration. Teenagers who have loving, consistent role models and healthy, supportive relationships in their lives will have optimal outcomes through this stage. In the next section, we will look at the role of romantic and intimate relationships in adolescents' lives and how these impact development.

ROMANCE, INTIMACY, AND SEXUALITY

One of the most promising shifts in adolescent research has been the recognition of adolescent sexuality as a normative aspect of development. Historically, adolescent sexual activity has been grouped with risky behaviors such as substance use, perhaps because the two can unfortunately go hand in hand at times. Another contributory factor to the stigmatizing of adolescent sexuality has been concerns over teenager pregnancy rates and sexually transmitted infections (STI). While these are still relevant and timely issues in adolescents' lives, developmental research has moved away from a purely pathological view of adolescent sexuality. In fact, the paradigm shift has even included a distinction between *sexual development* and *sexuality development* (Tolman & McClelland, 2011), with the former being grounded in the biological and the latter being grounded in the behavioral. Such a shift has allowed for a deeper understanding of the *experience* of sexuality development as individuals transition from children to adults.

An important piece to remember in the effort to better understand adolescent sexuality is the role of cognitive and moral development. While biological changes give rise to the awakening of sexuality, conscious decision making still undergirds adolescents' behaviors. That is to say, though adolescent desires, urges, thoughts and feelings related to sexuality are *normal and expected*, we cannot—and should not—dictate the moral processes involved in sexual decision making. Instead, in matters relating to sexuality, adolescents should be considered in the context of their developmental, cultural, and contextual influences and empowered to make decisions that support wellness and optimal development.

There are many cultural and contextual influences that influence adolescent sexuality development. For example, adolescents may be more likely to be sexually active if they come from homes where there is less parental monitoring (Deptula, Henry, & Schoeny, 2010). Parental monitoring, in turn, may be related to a specific parenting style, cultural influences, stressors of low socioeconomic status, or a combination of factors. Furthermore, adolescents' choices regarding sexuality, dating, and intimacy may be strongly influenced by religious mores or by role modeling from older siblings and adults in their lives.

One of the strongest influences on adolescent sexuality development is the peer group. As has been discussed previously, adolescence is marked by exploration and identity development. This is often reflected in the adolescent's peer group, which tends to define what is "normal" to the individual during this time. This applies to sexuality as well; adolescents whose sexual behaviors fall within the norm of the immediate peer group tend to be better adjusted and less anxious than those whose sexuality development—whether comparatively early or late—falls outside the norm (Vrangalova & Savin-Williams, 2011). Still, many other factors can affect adolescent sexuality and perceptions, including parental knowledge and reaction and stage of moral development. Counselors must keep in mind that sexuality and intimacy are complex developmental processes for adolescents—systemic influences, behavioral motivation, and explorations of intimacy are just some of the areas to assess when addressing this topic with teenagers.

Contemporary Courtship

Beliefs and practices associated with courtship have changed dramatically over the past several decades. Descriptive language and narrative constructs have also evolved—and continue to—and are driven by sociological patterns and trends in society. Words such as *going steady* and *dating* are rarely used by adolescents today, perhaps driven in part by the perceived commitment associated with such concepts. Adolescent attitudes associated with courtship practices are arguably more liberal and open than in their parents' generation; however, they have also witnessed half of their parents' marriages end in divorce and may be understandably reticent when it comes to matters of the heart. As such, it is important for counselors working with adolescents to keep in mind the power behind the narratives and descriptions and understand their adolescent clients within the context of their experiences and perspectives.

Adolescents use varying descriptions to indicate levels of connection, interest, and exclusivity in intimate relationships. For example, talking to someone may indicate romantic or sexual interest but does not equate to a relationship or exclusivity. Hanging out is a phrase often used early in a relationship, when emotions are generally not shared and apprehension is high. Seeing someone is similar to the concept of dating used by past generations and indicates an ongoing connection; exclusivity may be part of this relationship, though is not always. Clearly, the language used to describe adolescent intimate relationships has evolved such that emotion and commitment are minimized, at least early in relationships. Adolescents will still use more common labels such as *boyfriend* and *girlfriend*—or the current trendy term *bae*—but generally not until an exclusive relationship is clearly established.

Another common label used in adolescent (and some adult) relationships is *friends with benefits* (FWB). This phrase describes sexually intimate relationships without a romantic or exclusive component. FWB relationships are far more common among today's youth than they were a generation ago, and while adults may disagree with the appropriateness of such relationships among minors, they can serve a positive role in adolescent sexuality development (Erlandsson, Jinghede Norvall, Ohman, & Haggstrom-Nordin, 2013). For example, FWB relationships can offer an opportunity for adolescents to explore intimacy and sexuality without the pressures associated with normative dating practices. However, since adolescents are generally not friends with dating partners prior to starting to date (Kreager, Molloy, Moody, & Feinberg, 2015), it is perhaps also true that FWB relationships are unlikely to evolve into more typical, exclusive dating relationships. There is also generally less emotional risk to FWB relationships, as boundaries are set from the beginning. On the negative side, adolescents in FWB relationships may find themselves developing emotional connections despite initial desires or expectations, increasing the risk of feelings of pain or rejection. In working with adolescents in FWB relationships, counselors should consider the developmental purpose of the arrangement and what need the adolescent is seeking to fill.

BOX 12.6 CASE STUDY—RHEE

Rhee is a 16-year-old African American female who presents with symptoms of anxiety and depression. Rhee shares that a classmate she thought was her girlfriend denied their relationship to another mutual friend, saying that they "were just talking." Rhee tells you that she has been sexually intimate with this girl and thought their relationship was exclusive. Through tears, Rhee adds that she feels stupid and embarrassed and doesn't want to face her classmates or the girl again. She also believes that something must be wrong with her if the girl denied their relationship. How can you support Rhee's challenges to her self-concept as they relate to her perception of the relationship? How might her sexual minority status affect the perceived impact of the circumstances? What might be some additional cultural and racial considerations for this client?

Dating and Social Development

Although there is not a great body of research focusing on the developmental purpose of dating practices in adolescents, some consistent themes have emerged from the extant literature. Grounded in developmental theory of Erikson, Sullivan, and Bowlby, adolescent romantic relationships can serve important developmental functions as teenagers explore identity, intimacy, and attachment (Steinberg, 2013). For example, the experiential elements of dating and intimacy may facilitate identity development by providing reflective opportunities; adolescents can learn more about themselves, who they are, and what they want through romantic relationships. In addition, dating practices can help lay the foundation for adult intimacy as adolescents explore a new dimension to interpersonal connections beyond the developmental catalysts offered by peer relationships (Santrock, 2007). Learned patterns in interpersonal relating and attachment are operationalized in adolescent dating and may offer an opportunity for deeper emotional exploration and can highlight potential concerns that could carry over into adulthood (Riggs, Cusimano, & Benson, 2011).

Dating in adolescence may also serve the purpose of mate selection, though in contemporary U.S. society, it is rare for adolescents to select a permanent lifetime partner. In fact, one of the criticisms of adolescent dating from a developmental perspective lies in the often transient nature of couplings, combined with emotional and cognitive immaturity that categorizes adolescence; detractors assert that encouraging dating behaviors in adolescents reinforces superficiality and lack of depth in intimacy (Steinberg, 2013). Another potentially negative developmental outcome from dating in adolescence lies in the aftermath of a broken heart. Just as a healthy adolescent romantic relationship can support positive identity development, an unhealthy one can adversely impact it. Adolescents who suffer emotionally from unhealthy or harmful intimate relationships may experience more challenges in positive identity development and experience lower self-esteem, higher anxiety, or even depression (Soller, 2014). Furthermore, dating behaviors in adolescents have been tied to increased risk behaviors, including substance use, delinquency, and sexual activity; however, dating has also been associated with greater peer acceptance and social capital (Santrock, 2007). Although these are not directly causal associations, they do need to be considered when conceptualizing adolescent clients and understanding them within context.

Another potential drawback to adolescent dating that can impact identity development lies in the catalytic role it may have in the exposure of prejudice, oppression, and marginalization. Romantic relationships in adolescence are normative; however, if adolescents choose to date partners who do not fit with common parameters of their dominant peer group, they may experience friction with peers—or in extreme cases, bullying and harassment. Dating partners of different religions, races, ethnicities, or socioeconomic statuses, for example, may not be accepted by peers or by parents, causing stress for the adolescent. Furthermore, sexual minority adolescents who do not live in diverse and supportive environments may feel pressured to hide their romantic behaviors and relationships. They may also find significantly fewer opportunities to engage in dating behaviors due to their minority status (Diamond & Lucas, 2004). These stressors on adolescent dating can vary in severity and impact adolescents in several ways—ranging from inconveniences to significant trauma. Regardless, when present, these challenges need to be assessed and considered as the impact on social and emotional development can be substantial.

Love

There are many different kinds of *love*, and by adolescence most individuals have some concept of what love feels like for them (Williams & Hickle, 2010). However, adolescence is often the first developmental stage during which concepts of love expand to include romantic attachments. The constructs and foundations of *intimacy* are laid by the nonromantic attachment relationships adolescents experienced during development—most influentially by those associated with parents, guardians, and caregivers, but also to a lesser extent by siblings and peers. These early attachments set examples for how close relationships function, how connection is forged and deepened, and how love is defined. For example, an adolescent who was raised in an encouraging, loving, and supportive family environment is likely to have the expectation that romantic relationships will be positive and satisfying. By contrast, an adolescent raised in an unaffectionate, critical, and cold family environment is likely to have negative expectations of romantic relationships, and may even gravitate toward partners who would fulfill such an expectation. The old adage is true—children do learn what they live. In fact, numerous studies have found clear correlations between parental–child and parent–parent attachment patterns and the beliefs, behaviors, and outcomes associated with adolescent romantic relationships (Santrock, 2007).

Another essential element in understanding adolescents' conceptualizations of love is the cultural variations of how love is defined (Williams & Hickle, 2010). In some cultures, such as traditional Asian cultures, romantic love is not considered a vital element in successful relationships. By contrast, most Western cultures highly value love and consider it an important part of healthy, long-term pair bonding. Culturally bound discussions about defining love and assessing its importance can range from the biological to the psychological to the philosophical. In order to fully grasp the relevance and meaning of love to an adolescent client, the counselor must consider all of these aspects from the cultural vantage point and to understand the influences on the adolescents' narratives of love.

Attachment patterns and cultural influences contribute significantly to how the adolescent defines love; however, perhaps the most crucial element influencing how love is experienced and its impact on subsequent development lies in how adolescent love is perceived by the most central adults in the adolescent's life. As previously noted, romantic love is fairly new notion to an adolescent, and its meaning evolves over time, aided by the foundations created in childhood. However, too often adults minimize the significance of this experience for the adolescent and may inadvertently do harm to the social and emotional development of this period by belittling, diminishing, or even forbidding the adolescent's experience and perceptions. Adolescents often hear "it's just puppy love" or "you don't know what real love is" or "you're too young." There are many possible reasons for this, including beliefs by parents or caregivers that romantic love endangers the adolescent as it may increase the risk of sexual activity. Adults may also believe that adolescent love is superficial and less meaningful, as they perhaps define love from their own more advanced and complex perspective. Regardless, it is vital for adults to recognize that love can be profound *to the adolescent*; validating and empathizing with this viewpoint are essential to maintaining connection and fostering guidance throughout the adolescent's experience.

Sexual Activity

Adolescence is not the beginning of an individual's sexual exploration or the start of a sexual identity—in fact, very young children will often explore their own bodies and each other's as they discover similarities, differences, and pleasurable sensations. However, adolescence *is* generally the beginning of genuine sexual desire, which starts at or around the time of puberty. Changes in hormones and the emergence of secondary sexual characteristics coincide with an increased interest in sexual activity, which may be expressed as masturbation, heterosexual sex play, homosexual sex play, intercourse, oral stimulation, or other sexual behaviors. The types of behaviors adolescents engage in vary widely and are influenced by social, moral, religious, and systemic factors. It is important for counselors working with adolescent clients to remember that sexuality is normative; however, it is also often frowned upon, discouraged, or forbidden by adults in the adolescent's life. As such, adolescents may not be entirely forthcoming about their sexual behaviors until they trust they will not be judged by the adult.

Adolescents may become sexually active out of curiosity, pressure, or desire, but more often it is a combination of factors. Sexual activity may also be an aspect of romantic relationships in adolescents' lives, though this is not always the case. Still, even though the percentage of adolescents engaging in intercourse is relatively low in grade 9 (approximately 30%), it steadily climbs throughout high school years to over 60% by grade 12 (Eaton et al., 2012). Rates of sexual activity also vary with ethnicity, socioeconomic status, and religious engagement (Santrock, 2007). Still, one of the most significant influences on adolescent sexual activity is the peer network. Brakefield and colleagues, (2014) found that the peer group can influence both sexual activity and the desire to be involved in intimate relationships. Adolescents may also be influenced by older siblings and friends, who can be valuable resources for questions and advice (Secor-Turner, Sieving, Eisenberg, & Skay, 2011).

As noted previously, adolescents may engage in a wide variety of sexual behaviors depending on context and influences. Adolescence is a time of great exploration, and sexuality is no exception. Though many adolescents are aware of their sexual orientation, some are not; experimenting with pleasure of various types with partners of the same or opposite gender is fairly common. These behaviors do not necessarily indicate a fixed sexual orientation at this stage or later (Santrock, 2007). Furthermore, contrary to a common misconception, same-sex attractions and sexual intimacies do not spread across peer groups (Brakefield et al., 2014). Any appearance of such is likely due to the emotional and psychological intimacy between friends who are comfortable exploring their sexuality together.

Adolescent sexual activity is often categorized as a risk behavior due mostly to the secondary issues that may be associated with the behavior. Sexual activity at any age can put people at risk for unintended pregnancy and for sexually transmitted infections and diseases. Understanding the influences on and incidences of adolescent sexual behavior are important elements to effectively supporting adolescent health and development. Another key consideration in understanding adolescent sexual activity is the potential relationship to other risk behaviors. Though some studies have found a direct correlation between early sexual debut and subsequent risk behavior (Armour & Haynie, 2007), others argue that the links between these are not that direct (Wheeler, 2010). It may be that peer norms, parental reactions or coping, religious and moral beliefs, and other factors mitigate the correlations between various types of risk behavior, including sexuality. Such potential influences may also be important considerations in the design and implementation of sex education programs.

> ## BOX 12.7 PERSONAL REFLECTION: SEXUAL LITERACY AND SEX EDUCATION
>
> Despite the endorsement of children's health organizations, not all schools provide comprehensive sex education for adolescents. In fact, many continue to provide only abstinence-based educational programs, which are often funded by religious organizations outside the school systems. Criticisms exist of both types of programs, including assertions regarding their outcomes and efficacies. One fairly consistent belief across both camps is that adolescents benefit from some type of education related to their developing sexuality. What types of sex education did you receive growing up? How did the information impact your decision making? Also, what type of sex education currently exists in public high schools in your area? How does this differ from the education you received?

CONTEMPORARY ISSUES IN SOCIAL AND EMOTIONAL DEVELOPMENT

Adolescent Risk Behaviors

As was discussed in chapter 11, adolescent risk-taking behaviors result from multiple influences, including neural development and egocentrism. It is also important to note that risk-taking behaviors are strongly influenced by social and emotional development. Adults often trivialize such influences as peer pressure and encourage adolescents to make more proactive decisions. Whereas the latter is good advice, the former misses the point of the behavior. First, it is important to remember that younger adolescents in particular often lack the self-regulatory skills necessary to reason through and consider their decisions; instead, they tend to be far more impulsive than older adolescents and young adults (Dahl, 2004). In addition, neurological changes during this stage predispose adolescents to increased thrill-seeking behavior (Steinberg, 2007). Furthermore, adolescents may associate risk-taking behaviors with independence and personal control (Broderick & Blewitt, 2015; Santrock, 2007). In fact, adolescents often do not view these behaviors as "risky" at all, but rather integrate their choices into a narrative of personal development and locus of control. For example, although pregnancy may be an unintended outcome of sexual activity, an adolescent may view the experience as a hallmark of adulthood and embrace the situation as proof of maturity. Similarly, adolescents may believe that the *choice* to consume alcohol or use drugs shows that they are in charge of their lives and make their own decisions. These are important considerations when adolescents are straddling the gap between being controlled by parents and being independent adults—it is very possible that the risk behavior is actually serving an important developmental purpose (Broderick & Blewitt, 2015). Counselors working with adolescents need to take a broad view of risk and understand not only the perceived function of the behaviors in the adolescent's life but also as the environmental, systemic, and social influences at hand.

Many of the most concerning adolescent risk behaviors—such as substance use, pregnancy, and sexual transmission of diseases—have been on the decline in recent years (CDC, 2011b, 2011c, 2011d). Such trends are likely due to increased education and access to preventive health services, both of which support adolescents making informed, healthy decisions. However, one very concerning risk behavior that appears to be increasing is bullying. Great strides have been made in recent years to combat environmental and institutionally based bullying, and electronic victimization has increased considerably (CDC, 2011a). In fact, recent research has found that *almost all youth* have experienced some form of cyberbullying (Mitchell, Finkelhor, Wolak, Ybarra, & Turner, 2010). This is a sobering consideration, as contemporary adolescents are firmly entrenched in social media and electronic communication. The ubiquity of electronic media makes cyberbullying easily accessible to many adolescents, and the anonymity and emotional dissociation make the impact seem less severe. In reality, the effects of electronic aggression can be as detrimental, if not more so, than those experienced in real-time interactions.

Developing Pathologies

Despite the challenges associated with adolescence, most individuals navigate this developmental stage with few substantial issues. Still, some teenagers will struggle with the social and emotional aspects of this stage; without consistent support and guidance, they may find themselves on the threshold of significant psychological disorders. For example, the incidence of depression in adolescence is more than double that seen in childhood, and girls are almost twice as likely to experience depression in adolescence as boys (Santrock, 2007). Furthermore, expression of depressive symptomology in adolescence can vary with age, gender, and context, and even cultural and familial perspectives can influence how depression is expressed and interpreted (Butler, 2014). Adolescents are also at an increased risk for eating disorders, substance abuse, and conduct problems (Santrock, 2007), which may or may not co-occur with depression. Even though health professionals should not be overly eager to burden adolescents with psychological diagnoses that may stay with them into adulthood, it is also imperative that unhealthy symptoms and harmful behaviors are addressed in a timely manner, as rarely do the underlying issues work themselves out without intervention.

Resiliency and Wellness

Just as certain systemic, biological, and environmental factors can put adolescents at higher risk for problems and pathologies, the same is true for decreasing these risks. In fact, studies have found some fairly consistent resiliency factors in adolescents that—when present and nurtured—can support long-term wellness and development. Individual traits such as intelligence, sociability, and spirituality are associated with resiliency in adolescents, as are systemic traits such as close family relationships and low systemic conflict (Oshri, Rogosch, & Cicchetti, 2013; Santrock, 2007). These resiliency factors exist across cultural groups (Trask-Tate, Cunningham, & Lang-DeGrange, 2010), though relative influence may vary. Regardless, resiliency is a key wellness trait for adolescence, and it is inversely associated with both risk-taking and pathologies previously discussed (Martel et al., 2007). As such, it is vital for counselors and other supportive professionals in an adolescent's life to identity strengths and to foster resiliency as a means to reinforce healthy short- and long-term development.

BOX 12.8   SOCIAL ADVOCACY: PREVENTION AND INTERVENTION

The most effective prevention and intervention programs are those that provide early identification of problematic behaviors and issues and that offer prompt support and resources. What local, state, and federal programs are available in your area to provide such services and to foster adolescent resiliency, wellness, and healthy development? Is the outreach of these programs sufficient? Where are the gaps and what steps might be taken to improve services?

KEY COUNSELING POINTERS FOR SOCIAL AND EMOTIONAL DEVELOPMENT IN ADOLESCENCE

- Adolescents are a unique cultural group—they are straddling the gap between childhood and adulthood, are easily influenced by their environments, and are struggling to develop individual identities. Counselors can best support their healthy development by understanding them within context of their various environmental and systemic influences.
- Although gender differences do exist in male and female emotional development, counselors should avoid making broad generalizations. These differences can vary widely, and they are influenced by both environmental and biological factors.
- Adolescent conformity should not be dismissed as peer pressure, nor should its significance be minimized. Counselors should explore the hows and whys of adolescents' desires to align with their peer groups and understand the developmental significance of these choices.
- School environments influence multiple areas of adolescent development, including social systems and individual identity. Adolescents who struggle to fit in, do not perform well in school, or do not have consistent academic

opportunities are less likely to be successful. Counselors should support adolescent achievement and facilitate successes in the school environment whenever possible.

- Emotional and social development are strongly influenced by family systems, including parents and guardians, siblings, and extended family. Adolescents with strong systemic supports will often have a much easier time of this developmental stage. Counselors should consider integrating family into treatment whenever possible, with a focus on strengthening relational dynamics and communication.

- Sexuality is a common developmental aspect of adolescence. Though behavioral decision making is a complex integration of personality, morality, spirituality, and culture, counselors can support healthy development in this area by fostering a sense of comfort and normalcy.

- Risk behaviors may be indicative of underlying issues and associated with pathologies, but they are often no more than personal exploration and expression of individuality. The counselor would do well to understand the role, function, and beliefs associated with the behaviors of concern to better support healthy decision making and development.

SUMMARY

Adolescence is marked by increasingly complex emotional expression and social behaviors. Development through this period is influenced strongly by environment and culture, which serve to shape, mold, challenge, and revise adolescents' constructs about self and self in relation to others. Understanding an adolescent means to conceptualize him or her *within context*, which includes physical, cognitive, social, and emotional developmental influences. The intense changes occurring in these areas and their mutual influences on each other can sometimes cause adolescents to appear overly impulsive, inconsistent, unpredictable, or even unstable. Although these may be true from time to time, such observations are generally transient and situational; the vast majority of adolescents traverse this period successfully.

Most adolescents are highly dependent on their peers and are firmly immersed in the social systems of their peer group, both in school and in their communities. Individual personality does influence the degree to which adolescents seek peer approval and crowd membership, though some level of these behaviors is considered normative. Social norms—including those related to gender, achievement, and relationships—are strongly influenced by peers.

During this stage, adolescents generally move away from the more direct influences of parents as relationships with peers, friends, and other adults expand. However, parenting is still a vital part of supporting healthy adolescent development; involved parenting, consistent monitoring, and healthy communication are all associated with positive outcomes for adolescents. Finding balance is a key. Still, parenting behaviors and parent–child dynamics often change dramatically during this period as teenagers transition from children to adults. Counselors can be valuable resources and supports during this time as both parents and adolescents negotiate changes and transitions. In many cases, counselors can help parents and teenagers hear each other and perhaps empathize with the developmental trajectories unfolding for each individual. As we have discovered, adolescent egocentrism often prevents teens from being able to walk in another's shoes, most definitely the shoes of parents. Likewise, parents often forget what it was like to be a teenager or grasp that their teenager is much different from them at their age. Counselors can facilitate conversations, interactions, and resolutions that can potentially strengthen parent–adolescent relationships and enhance adolescent development.

USEFUL WEBSITES

European Association for Research on Adolescence
http://www.earaonline.org
Society for Research on Adolescence
http://www.s-r-a.org
Developing Adolescents: A Reference for Professionals
http://www.apa.org/pi/families/resources/develop.pdf
MIT Raising Teens Project
http://hrweb.mit.edu/worklife/raising-teens/index.html
National Institutes of Health: Adolescent Development
http://www.nlm.nih.gov/medlineplus/ency/article/002003.htm
Society for the Study of Emerging Adulthood
http://ssea.org

REFERENCES

Afifi, T. D., and Denes, A. (2012). Divorced and single parent families: Risk, resiliency, and the role of communication. In A. L. Vangelisti (Ed.), *The Rout-ledge handbook of family communication* (2nd ed., pp. 145–161). New York, NY: Routledge.

Ahrons, C. (1998). *The good divorce*. New York, NY: HarperCollins.

Amato, P. R., & Cheadle, J. (2005). The long reach of divorce: Divorce and child well-being across three generations. *Journal of Marriage and the Family*, *67*, 191–206.

Amaya, M. M., Reinecke, M. A., Silva, S. G., & March, J. S. (2011). Parental marital discord and treatment response in depressed adolescents. *Journal of Abnormal Child Psychology*, *39*(3), 401–411.

American Psychological Association. (2004). *Policy statement on sexual orientation, parents, and children*. Retrieved from http://www.apa.org/about/governance/council/policy/parenting.aspx

Armour, S., & Haynie, D. L. (2007). Adolescent sexual debut and later delinquency. *Journal of Youth and Adolescence*, *36*(2), 141–152.

Arnett, J. J. (1999). Adolescent storm and stress, reconsidered. *American Psychologist, 54*(5), 317.

Arnett, J. J. (2007). Emerging adulthood: What is it, and what is it good for? *Child Development Perspectives, 1*(2), 68–73.

Bank, L., Burraston, B., & Snyder, J. (2004). Sibling conflict and ineffective parenting as predictors of adolescent boys' antisocial behavior and peer difficulties: Addictive and interactive effects. *Journal of Research on Adolescence, 14,* 99–125.

Baril, M. E., Crouter, A. C., & McHale, S. M. (2007). Processes linking adolescent well-being, marital love, and coparenting. *Journal of Family Psychology, 21,* 645–654.

Baumrind, D. (1991). Effective parenting during the early adolescent transition. In P. A. Cowan & E. M. Hetherington (Eds.), *Advances in family research* (Vol. 2, pp. 111–163). Hillsdale, NJ: Erlbaum.

Bernstein-Yamashiro, B., & Noam, G. G. (2013). Relationships, learning, and development: A student perspective. *New Directions for Youth Development,137,* 27–44.

Blodgett-Salafia, E. H., Schaefer, M. K., & Haugen, E. C. (2014). Connections between marital conflict and adolescent girls' disordered eating: Parent-adolescent relationship quality as a mediator. *Journal of Child and Family Studies, 23*(6), 1128–1138.

Bong, M., & Skaalvik, E. M. (2003). Academic self-concept and self-efficacy: How different are they really? *Educational Psychology Review, 15*(1), 1–40.

Bradley, C. L., & Renzulli, L. A. (2011). The complexity of non-completion: Being pushed or pulled to drop out of high school. *Social Forces, 90*(2), 521–545.

Brakefield, T. A., Mednick, S. C., Wilson, H. W., DeNeve, J. E., Christakis, N. A., & Fowler, J. H. (2014). Same-sex sexual attraction does not spread in adolescent social networks. *Archives of Sexual Behavior, 43*(2), 335–344.

Brechwald, W. A., & Prinstein, M. J. (2011). Beyond homophily: A decade of advances in understanding peer influence processes. *Journal of Research on Adolescence, 21*(1), 166–179.

Broderick, P. C., & Blewitt, P. (2015). *The life span: Human development for helping professionals* (4th ed.). Boston, MA: Pearson.

Brown, B. B., & Bakken, J. P. (2011). Parenting and peer relationships: Reinvigorating research on family-peer linkages in adolescence. *Journal of Research on Adolescence, 21*(1), 153–165.

Browning, D. (Ed.). (2008). *Adolescent identities: A collection of readings*. New York, NY: Analytic Press.

Butler, A. C. (2014). Poverty and adolescent depressive symptoms. *American Journal of Orthopsychiatry, 84*(1), 82–94.

Campione-Barr, N., Greer, K. B., & Kruse, A. (2013). Differential associations between domains of sibling conflict and adolescent emotional adjustment. *Child Development, 84*(3), 938–954.

Carbado, D. W., & Gulati, M. (2013). *Acting White?: Rethinking race in post-racial America*. New York, NY: Oxford University Press.

Carson, D. C., Peterson, D., & Esbensen, F. A. (2013). Youth gang desistance: An examination of the effect of different operational definitions of desistance on the motivations, methods, and consequences associated with leaving the gang. *Criminal Justice Review*, *38*(4), 510–534.

Centers for Disease Control and Prevention (CDC). (2011a). *Electronic aggression*. Retrieved from http://www.cdc.gov/violenceprevention/youthviolence/electronicaggression/index.html

Centers for Disease Control and Prevention (CDC). (2011b). *Reproductive health: Teen pregnancy*. Retrieved from http://www.cdc.gov/TeenPregnancy/index.htm

Centers for Disease Control and Prevention (CDC). (2011c). *Trends in the prevalence of alcohol use*. Retrieved from http://www.cdc.gov/healthyyouth/yrbs/pdf/us_alcohol_trend_yrbs.pdf

Centers for Disease Control and Prevention (CDC). (2011d). *Trends in the prevalence of marijuana, cocaine, and other illegal drug use*. Retrieved from http://www.cdc.gov/healthyyouth/yrbs/pdf/us_drug_trend_yrbs.pdf. September 15, 2015.

Chao, R., & Tseng, V. (2002). Parenting of Asians. In M. H. Bornstein (Series Ed.), *Handbook of parenting: Social conditions and applied parenting* (2nd ed., Vol. 4, pp. 59–93). Mahwah, NJ: Erlbaum.

Choi, Y., Kim, Y. S., Kim, S. Y., & Park, I. J. K. (2013). Is Asian American parenting controlling and harsh? Empirical testing of relationships between Korean American and Western parenting measures. *Asian American Journal of Psychology*, *4*, 19–29.

Chu, J. Y. (2005). Adolescent boys' friendships and peer group culture. *New Directions for Child & Adolescent Development*, *2005*(107), 7–22.

Cokley, K., McClain, S., Jones, M., & Johnson, S. (2012). A preliminary investigation of academic disidentification, racial identity, and academic achievement among African American adolescents. *High School Journal*, *95*(2), 54–68.

Comstock, D. (Ed.). (2005). *Diversity and development: Critical contexts that shape our lives and relationships*. Belmont, CA: Thomson, Brooks/Cole.

Conley, D. T. (2012). *A complete definition of college and career readiness*. Educational Policy Improvement Center (NJ1). Retrieved from http://files.eric.ed.gov/fulltext/ED537876.pdf

Connolly, J., & McIsaac, C. (2011). Romantic relationships in adolescence. In M. K. Underwood and L. H. Rosen (Eds.), *Social development: Relationships in infancy, childhood, and adolescence* (pp. 180–203). New York, NY: Guilford Press.

Conway, C. C., Rancourt, D., Adelman, C. B., Burk, W. J., & Prinstein, M. J. (2011). Depression socialization within friendship groups at the transition to adolescence: The roles of gender and group centrality as moderators of peer influence. *Journal of Abnormal Psychology*, *120*(4), 857–867.

Crocetti, E., Jahromi, P., & Meeus, W. (2012). Identity and civic engagement in adolescence. *Journal of Adolescence*, *35*(3), 521–532.

Crone, E. A., & Dahl, R. E. (2012). Understanding adolescence as a period of social–affective engagement and goal flexibility. *Nature Reviews Neuroscience*, *13*(9), 636–650.

Cui, M., & Conger, R. D. (2008). Parenting behavior as mediator and moderator of the association between marital problems and adolescent maladjustment. *Journal of Research on Adolescence*, *18*(2), 261–284.

Cui, M., Donnellan, M. B., & Conger, R. D. (2007). Reciprocal influences between parents' marital problems and adolescent internalizing and externalizing behavior. *Developmental Psychology*, *43*(6), 1544–1552.

Dahl, R. E. (2004). Adolescent brain development: A period of vulnerabilities and opportunities. *Annals of the New York Academy of Sciences*, *1021*, 1–22.

Davies, P. T., & Windle, M. (2001). Interparental discord and adolescent adjustment trajectories: The potentiating and protective role of intrapersonal attributes. *Child Development*, *72*(4), 1163–1178.

Davis, K. (2012). Friendship 2.0: Adolescents' experiences of belonging and self-disclosure online. *Journal of Adolescence*, *35*(6), 1527–1536.

Deptula, D. P., Henry, D. B., & Schoeny, M. E. (2010). How can parents make a difference? Longitudinal associations with adolescent sexual behavior. *Journal of Family Psychology*, *24*(6), 731–739.

Diamond, L. M., & Lucas, S. (2004). Sexual-minority and heterosexual youths' peer relationships: Experiences, expectations, and implications for well-being. *Journal of Research of Adolescence*, *14*(3), 313–340.

Dixon, S. V., Graber, J. A., & Brooks-Gunn, J. (2008). The roles of respect for parental authority and parenting practices in parent-child conflict among African American, Latino, and European American families. *Journal of Family Psychology*, *22*(1), 1–10.

Doherty, E. E., Green, K. M., & Ensminger, M. E. (2012). The impact of adolescent deviance on marital trajectories. *Deviant Behavior*, *33*(3), 185–206.

Downing-Matibag, T. (2009). Parents' perceptions of their adolescent children, parental resources, and parents' satisfaction with their parent-child relationship. *Sociological Spectrum*, *29*(4), 467–488.

Doyle, A. B., & Markiewicz, D. (2005). Parenting, marital conflict, and adjustment from early- to mid-adolescence: Mediate by adolescent attachment style? *Journal of Youth and Adolescence*, *34*, 97–110.

Dumas, T. M., Ellis, W. E., & Wolfe, D. A. (2012). Identity development as a buffer of adolescent risk behaviors in the context of peer group pressure and control. *Journal of adolescence*, *35*(4), 917–927.

Eaton, D. K., Kann, L., Kinchen, S., Shanklin, S., Flint, K. H., Hawkins, J., … Weschsler, H. (2012). Youth risk behavior surveillance—United States, 2011. *Centers for Disease Control Morbidity and Mortality Weekly Report: Surveillance Summaries*, *61*(4), 1–162.

Eccles, J. S., & Roeser, R. W. (2011). Schools as developmental contexts during adolescence. *Journal of Research on Adolescence*, *21*(1), 225–241.

Elkind, D. (1984). *All grown up and no place to go: Teenagers in crisis?* Reading, MA: Addison-Wesley.

Erlandsson, K., Jinghede Norvall, C., Ohman, A., & Haggstrom-Nordin, E. (2013). Qualitative interviews with adolescents about "friends with benefits" relationships. *Public Health Nursing*, *30*(1), 47–57.

Fosco, G. M., & Grych, J. H. (2008). Emotional, cognitive, and family systems mediators of children's adjustment to interparental conflict. *Journal of Family Psychology, 22*, 843–854.

Gilligan, C. (2011). *Joining the resistance*. Cambridge, UK: Polity Books.

Goldberg, A. E. (2010). *Lesbian and gay parents and their children: Research on the family life cycle*. Washington, DC: American Psychological Association.

Goodwin, H., Haycraft, E., & Meyer, C. (2014). Sociocultural risk factors for compulsive exercise: A prospective study of adolescents. *European Eating Disorders Review, 22*(5), 360–365.

Guyer, A. E., Choate, V. R., Pine, D. S., & Nelson, E. E. (2012). Neural circuitry underlying affective response to peer feedback in adolescence. *Social Cognitive and Affective Neuroscience, 7*(1), 81–92.

Hershenberg, R., Davila, J., Yoneda, A., Starr, L. R., Miller, M. R., Stroud, C. B., & Feinstein, B. A. (2011). What I like about you: The association between adolescent attachment security and emotional behavior in a relationship promoting context. *Journal of Adolescence, 34*(5), 1017–1024.

Hyde, J. S. (2005). The gender similarities hypothesis. *American Psychologist, 60*(6), 581–592.

James, D., Lawlor, M., Murphy, N., & Flynn, A. (2013). "It's a girl thing!" Do boys engage in relational aggression? Exploration of whether strategies to educate young people about relational aggression are relevant for boys. *Pastoral Care in Education, 31*(2), 156–172.

Jensen, L. A. (2012). Bridging universal and cultural perspectives: A vision for developmental psychology in a global world. *Child Development Perspectives, 6*, 98–104.

Jokobsen, I. S., Horwood, L. J., & Fergusson, D. M. (2012). Childhood anxiety/withdrawal, adolescent parent–child attachment and later risk of depression and anxiety disorder. *Journal of Family Studies 21*(2), 303–310.

Jones, R. (2012). *Managing the self: A grounded theory study of the identity development of 14–19 year old same-sex attracted teenagers in British Schools and Colleges*. Doctoral dissertation, University of Southampton, UK.

Josselson, R. (1992). *The space between us: Exploring the dimensions of human relationship*. Thousand Oaks, CA: Sage.

Juster, F. T., Ono, H., & Stafford, F. P. (2004). *Changing times of American youth: 1981–2003*. Ann Arbor: University of Michigan.

Juvonen, J., Wang, Y., & Espinoza, G. (2013). Physical aggression, spreading of rumors, and social prominence in early adolescence: Reciprocal effects supporting gender similarities? *Journal of Youth and Adolescence, 42*(12), 1801–1810.

Kerr, M., Stattin, H., & Ozdemir, M. (2012). Perceived parenting style and adolescent adjustment: Revisiting directions of effects and the role of parental knowledge. *Developmental Psychology, 48*(6), 1540–1553.

Kim, J.-Y., McHale, S. M., Crouter, A. C., & Osgood, D. W. (2007). Longitudinal linkages between sibling relationships and adjustment from middle childhood through adolescence. *Developmental Psychology, 43*, 960–973.

Kosciw, J. G., Greytak, E. A., Bartkiewicz, M. J., Boesen, M. J., & Palmer, N. A. (2012). *The 2011 national school climate survey: The experiences of lesbian, gay, bisexual and transgender youth in our nation's schools*. New York, NY: Gay, Lesbian and Straight Education Network (GLSEN).

Kost, K., & Henshaw, S. (2014). *US teenage pregnancies, births and abortions, 2010: National and state trends by age, race and ethnicity*. Retrieved from http://www .guttmacher.org/pubs/USTPtrendsstate10.pdf

Krahé, B., & Busching, R. (2014). Interplay of normative beliefs and behavior in developmental patterns of physical and relational aggression in adolescence: A four-wave longitudinal study. *Frontiers in Psychology, 5*, 1146. doi: 10.3389/fpsyg.2014.01146

Kreager, D. A., Molloy, L. E., Moody, J., & Feinberg, M. E. (2015). Friends first? The peer network origins of adolescent dating. *Journal of Research on Adolescence*. doi:http://dx.doi.org/10.1111/jora.12189

Lansford, J. E., Skinner, A. T., Sorbring, E., Giunta, L. D., Deater-Deckard, K., Dodge, K. A., & Chang, L. (2012). Boys' and girls' relational and physical aggression in nine countries. *Aggressive Behavior, 38*(4), 298–308.

Lau, A. S., & Fung, J. (2013). On better footing to understand parenting and family process in Asian American families. *Asian American Journal of Psychology, 4*(1), 71–75.

Lesko, N. (2012). Adolescence and development-in-time. *Journal of Human Growth and Development, 11*(1), 59–67.

Linville, D., Stice, E., Gau, J., & O'Neil, M. (2011). Predictive effects of mother and peer influences on increases in adolescent eating disorder risk factors and symptoms: A 3-year longitudinal study. *International Journal of Eating Disorders, 44*(8), 745–751.

Livingston, G. (2014). *Less than half of U.S. kids today live in a "traditional" family*. Retrieved from http://www.pewresearch.org/fact-tank/2014/12/22/less-than-half-of-u-s-kids-today-live-in-a-traditional-family/

Lucas-Thompson, R. G. (2012). Associations of marital conflict with emotional stress and psychological stress: Evidence for different patterns of dysregulation. *Journal of Research on Adolescence, 22*(4), 704–721.

Lynch, A., D., Lerner, R. M., & Leventhal, T. (2013). Adolescent academic achievement and school engagement: An examination of the role of school-wide peer culture. *Journal of Youth Adolescence, 42*(1), 6–19.

Malin, H., Reilly, T. S., Quinn, B., & Moran, S. (2014). Adolescent purpose development: Exploring empathy, discovering roles, shifting priorities, and creating pathways. *Journal of Research on Adolescence, 24*(1), 186–199.

Marcia, J. E. (2014). From industry to integrity. *Identity, 14*(3), 165–176.

Marsh, H. W., & Martin, A. J. (2011). Academic self-concept and academic achievement: Relations and causal ordering. *British Journal of Educational Psychology, 81*(1), 59–77.

Martel, M. M., Nigg, J. T., Wong, M. M., Fitzgerald, H. E., Jester, J. M., Puttler, L. I., … Zucker, R. A. (2007). Childhood and adolescent resiliency, regulation, and executive functioning in relation to adolescent problems and competence in a high-risk sample. *Development and Psychopathology, 19*(2), 541–563.

Masten, C. L., Telzer, E. H., Fuligni, A. J., Lieberman, M. D., & Eisenberger, N. I. (2012). Time spent with friends in adolescence relates to less neural sensitivity to later peer rejection. *Social Cognitive and Affective Neuroscience*, 7(1), 106–114.

Mitchell, K. J., Finkelhor, D., Wolak, J., Ybarra, M. L., & Turner, H. (2010). Youth Internet victimization in a broader context. *Journal of Adolescent Health*, 48(2), 128–134.

Miga, E. M., Gdula, J. A., & Allen, J. P. (2012). Fighting fair: Adaptive marital conflict strategies as predictors of future adolescent peer and romantic relationship quality. *Social Development*, 21(3), 443–460.

Mikulincer, M., & Shaver, P. R. (2013). The role of attachment security in adolescent and adult close relationships. In J. A. Simpson & L. Campbell (Eds.), *The Oxford handbook of close relationships* (pp. 66–89). New York, NY: Oxford University Press.

Miller, J. B. (1984). The development of women's sense of self. *Women's Spirituality: Resources for Christian Development*, 165–184.

Nakkula, M. J., & Toshalis, E. (2009). *Understanding youth: Adolescent development for educators*. Cambridge, MA: Harvard Education Press.

Noguera, P. A. (2008). "Joaquin's dilemma": Understanding the link between racial identity and school-related behaviors. In M. Sadowski (Ed.), *Adolescents at school* (2nd ed., pp. 23–34). Cambridge, MA: Harvard Education Press.

Nussbaum, J. F., Lucas, A., & McManus, T. (2012). Educational contexts and intergroup communication. In H. Giles (Ed.), *The handbook of intergroup communication* (pp. 306–318). New York, NY: Taylor & Francis.

Oshri, A., Rogosch, F. A., & Cicchetti, D. (2013). Child maltreatment and mediating influences of childhood personality types on the development of adolescent psychopathology. *Journal of Clinical Child and Adolescent Psychology*, 42(3), 287–301.

Painter, J. (2013). Nancy Lesko: Act your age: A cultural construction of adolescence. *Journal of Youth and Adolescence*, 42(7), 1108–1111.

Reitz-Krueger, C. L., Nagel, A. G., Guarnera, L. A., & Reppucci, N. D. (2015). Community influence on adolescent development. In T. P. Gullota, R. W. Plant, & M. A. Evans (Eds.), *Handbook of adolescent behavioral problems: Evidenced-based approaches to prevention and treatment* (2nd ed., pp. 71–84). New York, NY: Springer.

Riggs, S. A., Cusimano, A. M., & Benson, K. M. (2011). Childhood emotional abuse and attachment processes in the dyadic adjustment of dating couples. *Journal of Counseling Psychology*, 58(1), 126–38.

Robitaille, C., & Saint-Jacques, M.C. (2009). Social stigma and the situation of young people in lesbian and gay stepfamilies. *Journal of Homosexuality*, 56(4), 421–442.

Ruhl, H., Dolan, E. A., & Buhrmester, D. (2014). Adolescent attachment trajectories with mothers and fathers: The importance of parent–child relationship experiences and gender. *Journal of Research on Adolescence*, 25(3), 427–442. doi:dx.doi.org/10.1111/jora.12144

Rumberger, R., & Lim, S. A. (2011). *Why students drop out of school: A review of 25 years of research*. Santa Barbara: California Dropout Research Project, University of California.

Sadowski, M. (2008). Understanding "acting White": What educators need to know. In M. Sadowski (Ed.), *Adolescents at school* (2nd ed., pp. 35–41). Cambridge, MA: Harvard Education Press.

Santrock, J. W. (2007). *Adolescence* (11th ed.). New York, NY: McGraw-Hill.

Schlegel, A. (2000). The global spread of adolescent culture. In L. J. Corckett & R. K. Silbereisen (Eds.), *Negotiating adolescence in times of social change* (pp. 71–88). Cambridge, UK: Cambridge University Press.

Scott, L. N., Whalen, D. J., Zalewski, M., Beeney, J. E., Pilkonis, P. A., Hipwell, A. E., & Stepp, S. D. (2013). Predictors and consequences of developmental changes in adolescent girls' self-reported quality of attachment to their primary caregiver. *Journal of Adolescence, 36*(5), 797–806.

Secor-Turner, M., Sieving, R. E., Eisenberg, M. E., & Skay, C. (2011). Associations between sexually experienced adolescents' sources of information about sex and sexual risk outcomes. *Sex Education, 11*(4), 489–500.

Shavelson, R. J., Hubner, J. J., & Stanton, G. C. (1976). Self-concept: Validation of construct interpretations. *Review of Educational Research, 46*(3), 407–441.

Sheftall, A. H., Matias, C. W., Furr, R. M., & Doughtery, D. M. (2013). Adolescent attachment security, family functioning, and suicide attempts. *Attachment & Human Development, 15*(4), 368–383.

Sheftall, A. H., Schoppe-Sullivan, S. J., & Bridge, J. A. (2014). Insecure attachment and suicidal behavior in adolescents. *Crisis: The Journal of Crisis Intervention and Suicide Prevention, 35*(6), 426–430.

Silk, J. S., Siegle, G. J., Lee, K. H., Nelson, E. E., Stroud, L. R., & Dahl, R. E. (2014). Increased neural response to peer rejection associated with adolescent depression and pubertal development. *Social Cognitive and Affective Neuroscience, 9*(11), 1798–1807. doi:10.1093/scan/nst175

Simons, L., Simons, R., & Su, X. (2013). Consequences of corporal punishment among African Americans: The importance of context and outcome. *Journal of Youth & Adolescence, 42*(8), 1273–1285.

Smith, A. R., Chein, J., & Steinberg, L. (2014). Peers increase adolescent risk taking even when the probabilities of negative outcomes are known. *Developmental Psychology, 50*(5), 1564–1568.

Soller, B. (2014). Caught in a bad romance: Adolescent romantic relationships and mental health. *Journal of Health and Social Behavior, 55*(1) 56–72.

Spencer, S. J., Steele, C. M., & Quinn, D. M. (1999). Stereotype threat and women's math performance. *Journal of Experimental Social Psychology, 35*(1), 4–28.

Stearn, A. M. (2012). *Subcultural theory, drift and publicity: How a contemporary culture of adolescence relates to delinquency.* Doctoral dissertation, Northeastern University, Boston, MA.

Steinberg, L. (2007). Risk taking in adolescence: New perspectives from brain and behavioral science. *Current Directions in Psychological Science, 16*(2), 55–59.

Steinberg, L. (2013). *Adolescence* (10th ed.). New York, NY: McGraw-Hill.

Steinberg, L. D., & Silk, J. S. (2002). Parenting adolescents. In M. Bornstein (Ed.), *Handbook of parenting* (2nd ed., Vol. 1, pp. 103–134). Mahwah, NJ: Erlbaum.

Stocker, C. M., Burwell, R. A., & Briggs, M. L. (2002). Sibling conflict in middle childhood predicts children's adjustment in early adolescence. *Journal of Family Psychology, 16,* 50–57.

Tolman, D. L., & McClelland, S. I. (2011). Normative sexuality development in adolescence: A decade in review, 2000–2009. *Journal of Research on Adolescence, 21*(1), 242–255.

Toshalis, E. (2008). A question of "faith": Adolescent spirituality in public schools. In M. Sadowski (Ed.), *Adolescents at school* (2nd ed., pp. 189–206). Cambridge, MA: Harvard Education Press.

Traditional. (1820). *What are little boys made of?* England.

Trask-Tate, A., Cunningham, M., & Lang-DeGrange, L. (2010). The importance of family: The impact of social support on symptoms of psychological distress in African America girls. *Research in Human Development, 7*(3), 164–182.

Tucker, C. J., McHale, S. M., & Crouter, A. C. (2003). Conflict resolution: Links with adolescents' family relationships and individual well-being. *Journal of Family Issues, 24,* 715–736.

Van Petegem, S., Beyers, W., Brenning, K., & Vansteenkiste, M. (2013). Exploring the association between insecure attachment styles and adolescent autonomy in family decision making: A differentiated approach. *Journal of Youth and Adolescence, 42*(12), 1837–1846.

Vazsonyi, A. T., Hibbert, J. R., & Snider, J. B. (2003). Exotic enterprise no more? Adolescent reports of family and parenting processes from youth in four countries. *Journal of Research on Adolescence, 13*(2), 129–160.

Viner, R. M., Ozer, E. M., Denny, S., Marmot, M., Resnick, M., Fatusi, A., & Currie, C. (2012). Adolescence and the social determinants of health. *Lancet, 379*(9826), 1641–1652.

Vrangalova, Z., & Savin-Williams, R. C. (2011). Adolescent sexuality and positive well-being: A group-norms approach. *Journal of Youth and Adolescence, 40,* 931–944.

Way, N. (2013). Boys' friendships during adolescence: Intimacy, desire, and loss. *Journal of Research on Adolescence, 23*(2), 201–213.

Wehmeyer, M. L. (2008). The impact of disability on adolescent identity. In M. Sadowski, (Ed.), *Adolescents at school* (2nd ed., pp. 167–179). Cambridge, MA: Harvard Education Press.

Wentzel, K. R. (2012). Teacher–student relationships and adolescent competence at school. *Interpersonal Relationships in Education, 3,* 19–35.

Wheeler, S. B. (2010). Effects of self-esteem and academic performance on adolescent decision-making: An examination of early sexual intercourse and illegals substance use. *Journal of Adolescent Health, 47*(6), 582–590.

Williams, L. R., & Hickle, K. E. (2010). "I know what love means": Qualitative descriptions from Mexican American and White adolescents. *Journal of Human Behavior in the Social Environment, 20*(5), 581–600.

Willoughby, B. J. (2010). Marital attitude trajectories across adolescence. *Journal of Youth and Adolescence, 39,* 1305–1317.

Yeh, H., & Lempers, J. D. (2004). Perceived sibling relationships and adolescent development. *Journal of Youth and Adolescence, 33,* 133–147.

PART 6

Young Adulthood

Young Adulthood: Physical and Cognitive Development

Janet Froeschle Hicks and Brandé Flamez

Young adulthood refers to individuals between adolescence and middle age (All Psychology Careers, 2014; Levinson, 1978). Despite fewer physical and cognitive changes occurring than previously seen during adolescence, gradual transitions in physical and cognitive development continue throughout the 20s and 30s. Physical and biological factors become evident through changes in appearance, strength, joints, bones, lung and heart functioning, as well as sexuality. Cognitive health habits during early adulthood correlate with later life memory and brain functioning. Given the connection between physical and mental health (Collingwood, 2010; Russell-Chapin & Jones, 2014) and the importance of self-care on future development, counselors are in optimal positions to assist early adults with decisions that affect quality of life. As a result, this chapter offers information on physical and cognitive changes for those in early adulthood as well as information counselors need to improve clients' current and future mental health.

BOX 13.1   IMPROVING CLIENT HEALTH

Carmela is a 20-year-old African American female who comes to you for counseling. She states that she has been told by her medical doctor that she is overweight and headed for health issues if she doesn't change her diet and start exercising. When asked if she is making these changes, Carmela states, "I am not worried about it now. I will worry about it when I get old—you know, when it really affects me." As Carmela's counselor, what is your ethical responsibility? What might you say to Carmela?

DEFINITION OF TERMS

To understand physical and cognitive development, a distinction must be made between several terms. Biological changes include the physical functioning of the human body whereas cognitions refer to brain- and memory-related aspects. Each term is described as follows.

Physical Changes

Physical development involves biological factors such as height and weight and is fully attained by age 25 years. Females tend to reach maximum height by age 18 years, but males often grow into the early 20s. Once both genders reach age 21 years, maximum height has been attained and growth stops. Muscle mass and body fat continue to develop, however, and the average male and female gain 15 pounds between ages 17 and 25 years (All Psychology Careers, 2014).

This stage of full physical development tends to be a time of vitality and health. Early adults typically have healthy skin, maximum strength, coordination, reaction time, and motor skills. Further, the five senses (taste, touch, smell, hearing, sight) are optimal, sexual response is fully functional, and no age-related physical deterioration is evident. With the exception of death by homicide, suicide, eating disorders, and motor vehicle, death rates are low and disease is rare (All Psychology Careers, 2014).

By age 30 years, however, a progressive decline in health and strength begins. One of the first signs of aging is noticed in the musculoskeletal system. Lowered levels of growth hormone and testosterone along with fewer and less efficient muscle fibers eventually lead to a 10–15% reduction in strength and mass over the lifespan, lowered caloric needs, and reduced ability to compete athletically or exercise vigorously (Merck, 2014). For example, the maximum speed and duration for which a person can run, row a boat, or ride a bicycle decreases.

Other declines in physical health that begin around age 30 years include calcium loss, lowered kidney functioning, reduced reproductive capacity, and cardiovascular decline. Calcium loss in the bones can lead to osteoporosis later in life if the young adult does not have a proper diet including sufficient calcium. Physical activity has also shown the ability to offset decreased bone density in both men (Bolam, van Uffelen, & Taafe, 2013) and women (Andreoli, Celi, Volpe, Sorge, & Tarantino, 2012).

The third decade of life also affects the urinary system. Around age 30 years, the kidneys decline in their ability to filter blood and remove waste. As a result, the body becomes more easily dehydrated after age 30 (Merck, 2014). Proper intake of fluids is important especially when active in extreme temperatures.

Maximal oxygen consumption is reduced by 5–15% and maximal heart rate decreases by 6 to 10 beats each decade after age 25–30. This phenomenon explains the fact that most Olympic and professional athletes are under age 40 years. According to the American College of Sports Medicine (n.d.), regular physical activity can offset many of the negative aspects attributed to aging and contributes to a better quality of life. Counselors must motivate young adults to participate in regular exercise, eat a healthy diet, maintain optimal body weight, and avoid activities and substances that contribute to decline in wellness.

Motivating early adults to participate in healthy eating and exercise may be easier if specific age is taken into consideration, however. Quindry, Yount, O'Bryant, and Rudisill (2011) concluded that while fitness is a factor in promoting exercise engagement across the lifespan, exercise motivation for those aged 35 to 49 differs from those in adolescence or young adulthood. For example, fitness and interpersonal factors motivate those aged 20–34 years, whereas body image, psychological, and health factors motivate those ranging in age from 35 to 49 years. Further, young adults may need help transitioning from a time during their 20s where sports were an all consuming school passion to a new phase where family and career must take priority. This is helpful information for counselors to consider when seeking individualized ways to encourage healthy exercise behaviors.

BOX 13.2 THE CASE OF LLOYD

Lloyd is a 35-year-old African American single male who has been drinking several cans of beer on Friday and Saturday nights since he left home to attend college 12 years ago. He also eats junk food for meals because (as he states), "I like it, and I don't want to cook." Lately, Lloyd notices he has less energy, itchy skin, and his physician has told him he is dehydrated and his blood pressure is elevated. Why might Lloyd be experiencing these side effects? As Lloyd's counselor what information would you share with him?

Gender Issues

Regardless of gender, reproductive capacity declines with age. Fertility problems increase after age 35 years, affecting both ova in females and sperm production in males. For women, aging affects not only fertility but also pregnancy, postpartum functioning, and health of offspring.

Pregnancy and postpartum issues are significant milestones for women in early adulthood. For example, excessive weight gain during and after pregnancy is becoming more common. Of the weight gained during pregnancy, most women maintain approximately 5 pounds long term (Stotland et al., 2010). This weight gain can lead to obesity and associated health issues as well as lowered self-image. Support from family and friends during this time can influence increased physical activity levels and eating habits that correlate with weight loss (Keller, Allan, & Tinkle, 2006).

BOX 13.3 THE CASE OF BEN AND FRAN

Ben and Fran have been trying to conceive a child for 7 years without success. Fran recently found out she has a medical condition making it unlikely she will be able to conceive a child without medical intervention. Ben explains that Fran's emotions fluctuate from anger to tears over her inability to conceive and he is left feeling devalued and anxious. Fran wants to try in vitro fertilization, a procedure where her eggs will be surgically removed, fertilized with Ben's sperm, and reimplanted into her uterus. Ben is concerned about the expense, medical risks to Fran, and the possibility of a multiple birth. How might counseling help Ben and Fran?

Another developmental issue experienced during the postpartum stage is depression. New mothers may not anticipate the normal anxiety and depression experienced up to two weeks after birth, often termed the *baby blues*. This phase is characterized by mild sadness, anxiety, and mood swings. Should depressive symptoms become more severe and present within the first 3 months following childbirth, a more serious diagnosis of postpartum depression may be in order. Postpartum depression includes symptoms such as inability to sleep, lowered affect, and inability to function adequately. Postpartum psychosis, an even more severe diagnosis, is experienced by up to 0.3% of women and is characterized by hallucinations, delusions, and other psychotic symptoms. Clients experiencing the latter diagnoses are often treated with cognitive behavioral therapy, group counseling, and antidepressant medications (Association of Reproductive Health Professionals, 2013). For those experiencing baby blues, counselors can help normalize the experience, encourage healthy eating and sleep habits, and promote exercise to boost beta-endorphins (Association of Reproductive Health Professionals, 2013; Ko, Yang, Fang, Lee, & Lin, 2013).

Aging can also affect a person's offspring. The odds of delivering a baby with chromosomal abnormalities such as Down's syndrome increase as women age (Dotinga, 2014). Further, women over the age of 35 years are more likely to give birth to low birth weight or premature babies and have a greater chance of miscarriage or multiple births. Some studies infer a man's age at conception also affects the health of his biological children but more studies are needed to arrive at a definitive conclusion (Mayo Clinic, 2015).

Cognitive Changes

Cognitive growth involves development and changes in thought processes as promoted by major life issues, brain growth, memory, and environment. This cognitive growth typically peaks around age 35 years (Boundless, 2014).

Many researchers suggest that the prefrontal cortex (brain portion that controls self-judgment, problem solving, risk taking, planning, and prioritizing) remains underdeveloped until approximately age 25 years (Donald, 2001; Giedd, 1999, 2004; Simpson, n.d.). Jean Piaget's (1896–1980) theory of cognitive development, as mentioned in chapter 2, concurs with this stance in that adolescents use formal operational thinking until age 25 years (Boundless, 2014). At this time, cognitions become relativistic, that is, more flexible and less absolute. The early adult can now consider multiple options including a variety of ways to solve problems (All Psychology Careers, 2014). This postformal operational thinking results in reasoned argument and dialectical thinking between ages 20 and 40 years (Boundless, 2014).

Not surprisingly, this brain and cognitive development affects transition stages and decisions made as the young adult matures. Several theories have been written to describe these life stages that involve brain development, cognitions, and decision making in early adulthood, and these are described in the next section.

THEORETICAL BACKGROUND AND EARLY ADULTHOOD

Life Stages and Transition Theories for Early Adulthood

The early adulthood stage is built on numerous processes, rites, and passages that reciprocally influence physical and cognitive development. A thorough understanding of these processes and the theories that guide them assists counselors as they empathize with and take client diversity into account. Following are descriptions of transition theories that are applicable when working with clients in early adulthood.

Levinson's Seasons of a Man's Life

Levinson (1978) described five main stages whereby a person's life structure or pattern of relationships develops. The first adult stage, *era of early adulthood*, encompasses the ages between 17 and 45 years and consists of three substages: *early adult transition* (ages 17–22); *midlife transition* (ages 40–45); and *late adult transition* (ages 60–65). Within the *era of early adulthood*, three substages are described: *entry life structure for early adulthood* (ages 22–28); *age 30 transition* (ages 28–33); and the *culminating life structure for early adulthood phase* (ages 33–40). Levinson also discussed *mid-life* and *late life adult transition* stages. More emphasis will be given to these phases in later chapters.

Early adult transition marks the beginning of adult independence. The adolescent leaves home and must make responsible choices regarding personal and financial issues. This stage is pivotal because it marks the end of childhood and the beginning of adulthood. Counselors help young adults in this life stage by offering information on personal finances, educational choices, college financial aid assistance, career counseling, and other adjustment issues of living independently. Discouragement of drug use and encouragement of sexual responsibility may also be appropriate at this stage.

Entry life structure for early adulthood marks the time when early adults choose a life path. For example, the young adult ponders future family life, financial and career success, and begins to set goals for the future. The successful selection of mentors at this stage may be crucial to achieving future success. Early adults in this stage need help via career testing and counseling, assistance with goal setting, as well as personal counseling to overcome prior setbacks and consequences of poor decisions.

Age 30 transition is the stage where goals are attained or lost based on current and previous decisions. The young adult contemplates past successes and failures and forms new goals. A life structure is built around goals that have been accomplished. The person in this stage becomes interested in settling down, establishing a family, and finding a role in society. During this stage, the early adult may need career, premarital, relationship, or family counseling. Around age 30, the early adult must learn to maintain personal and career life balance as well as to manage family transitions.

The culminating life structure for the early adulthood phase requires a shift to adult and parental thinking. Young adults in this phase face demanding roles and expectations and feel pressure to find a niche within society. Many clients feel failure if they do not achieve career goals during this stage. Fortunately, as one matures, relativistic thinking develops allowing the ability to conceptualize ideas through others' perspectives (Perry, 1970). Counselors can help early adults transition to this form of adult thinking by pointing out differing viewpoints that help clients overcome feelings of failure.

Reinke's Turning Points

Although Levinson's work offered valuable information and stages to explain early adult transitions, it was missing a major component. The research was conducted on—and therefore could be generalized only to—males. As a result, Reinke, Holmes, and Harris (1985) built upon Levinson's work by studying early adult stages with females.

BOX 13.4   GENDER BIAS AND FEMALE LIFE TRANSITIONS

Barbara Reinke stated that females experience transition between the ages of 27 and 30 years marked by personal disruption, life reassessment, and reorientation. Reinke also discovered that the family system, geographical moves, career issues, and child-rearing all contributed to female transition (Reinke et al., 1985). How might gender bias have influenced these issues among females in the 1980s? Do you think results would change if the same study was done today? Why or why not?

Regardless of whether the transition was experienced by males or females, however, one commonality was evidenced. Transitions required decision making, which was affected by cognitive development and mature thought. For this reason, brain development and cognitive development are embedded within any discussion on life stages, transitions, and problem solving. Let us discuss these cognitive processes as based on brain functioning, cognitions, and developmental theories.

The Brain, Cognitions, and Development

A number of theories support the premise that from around age 18 years, until the third decade of life, mature thought and brain structures develop. For example, the adolescent entering young adulthood now considers multiple options when solving problems (All Psychology Careers, 2014). This postformal operational thinking results in reasoned argument and dialectical thinking between ages 20–40 (Boundless, 2014). Postformal relativistic and dialectical thinking require more insightful thought processes and are described, along with brain mapping and development, as follows.

Brain Mapping

Neuroscience is changing the way mental health professionals diagnose and treat client issues. For example, brain mapping is increasingly used to compare emotion regulation and decision making without the need for invasive surgery. Collura, Bonstetter, and Zalaquett (2014) advocated the use of electroencephalogram (EEG) technology to better understand client experiences based on emotional responses. For example, a client whose brain shows right hemisphere activity when given a phrase such as *body fat* is indicating negative emotion. This knowledge assists counselors as they empathize with clients and attempt to understand the degree for which certain issues affect emotions and accompanying emotional responses. Particular counseling micro skills can then be used to address concerns that might otherwise be unknown.

Brain Development

To further understand how to use and interpret brain mapping, let us examine the parts of the brain.

As young adults approach their mid-20s, the prefrontal cortex is undergoing vast changes that affect behavior. The prefrontal cortex, or executive suite, is affected by two factors: myelination and synaptic pruning. Myelination refers to the insulation of nerve fibers by a substance called myelin. This insulating process allows efficient transmittal of signals from the brain to the body (Simpson, n.d.). Synaptic pruning first occurs at puberty and continues throughout the 20s (Zukerman & Purcell, 2011). Pruning describes the process whereby patches of nerves are snipped allowing adept transfer of signals and communication with other parts of the brain. This enhanced communication between brain regions allows for improved emotion regulation, planning, problem solving, judgment, preparation, and calculation of risk (Simpson, n.d.). Not surprisingly, this improved brain functioning results in more mature and logical thought processes.

BOX 13.5 EXAMINE THE PARTS OF THE BRAIN

The occipital lobes are active in vision and the temporal lobes process hearing, language, and memory. The parietal lobes assist with spatial location, attention, and motor control. The frontal lobes are responsible for thinking, personality, and movement (Simpson, n.d.). The prefrontal cortex (pole) is active in decision making and is an especially relevant portion of the brain when considering young adult development. Why would counselors be advised to understand parts of the brain?

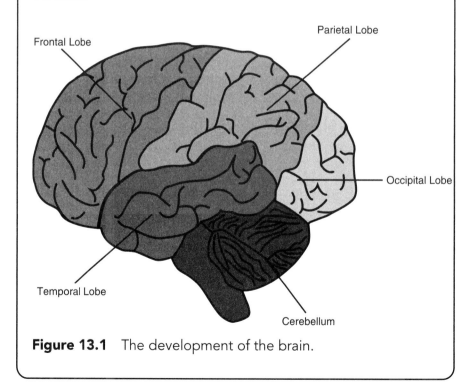

Figure 13.1 The development of the brain.

BOX 13.6 RISK TAKING AND THE PREFRONTAL CORTEX

The legal age in which a person may drink alcohol in most cases is 21 years. Thirty-five states, however, allow underage drinking provided it occurs on private, non-alcohol-selling premises and with parental consent (Procon.org, 2014). Based on the discussion in this chapter regarding the prefrontal cortex, why do you think many states allow this? Using the ACA Code of Ethics (2014; http://counseling.org/Resources/aca-code-of-ethics.pdf) as a guide, what stance should counselors ethically take on this position, or should they have an opinion at all? What ethical codes would support your stance?

Postformal and Logical Thinking in Early Adulthood

As adolescents move toward early adulthood, their brains and cognitive abilities reciprocally develop. This development creates the ability to focus on greater abstractions and the inherent organization of these abstract thoughts. This post-formal or logical thinking has been described as part of growth and development by numerous theorists as follows.

Piaget's Cognitive Development

Piaget described four stages of cognitive development: sensorimotor (ages 0–2 years); preoperational (ages 2–7 years); concrete operational (ages 7–11 years); and formal operational (ages 11–adulthood). During these stages, cognitive thinking evolves from reflexive, instinctual action in the sensorimotor stage to symbolic thinking in the preoperational stage. The concrete operational stage is noted as the child begins to understand logic about concrete events, including the concept of conservation. Formal operational thought is characterized by abstract thinking and logical hypotheses (Piaget, 1952, 1954).

Some theorists suggest the presence of a fifth stage transcending beyond Piaget's theory of cognitive development. This fifth stage, the postformal stage, is thought to evolve in young adulthood as adolescents mature and begin to accept ambiguity. For example, adolescents tend to look for correct answers whereas young adults are comfortable brainstorming multiple solutions to a problem. Further, disagreement is accepted in the postformal developmental stage and is viewed as the means to better understanding (Siobhan, 2007). Postformal thought is only observed in the adult population and some never reach this stage of reasoning (Freberg, n.d.).

Dialectical Thinking

Dialectical thinking involves cognitions in the form of process, context, relationship, and transformation. Process describes how changes occur whereas context describes the existence of pieces that fit within the entire structure. Relationship describes thinking about how things are related and what they have in common, while transformation is the formation of thoughts about the dissolution of previous systems, the consequent evolution of new developments, and the constant change that is part of the process (Boundless, 2014). Not surprisingly, dialectical thought has been referred to as the most advanced form of cognition. This is because the person is able to compare numerous angles and possibilities of a problem including advantages, disadvantages, beliefs, and experiences resulting in a new level of truth (Riegel, 1979; Rowan, 2000).

Relativistic Thinking

Perry (1970) found changes occur in cognitive processes as undergraduate college students mature. Sequential stages within Perry's model include dualism, multiplicity, relativity, and commitment. Younger students tend to think dualistically. That is, they divide ideas dichotomously and judge ideas as either right versus wrong or good versus bad.

As undergraduate college students age, they move into the multiplistic stage. During this stage, students sort problems into those that are solvable and those that cannot be solved. When evaluating these problems, equal credibility is given to all sources.

The third stage, relativity, is where solutions are evaluated within their own context. For the first time, the validity of various viewpoints is weighed. Nonetheless, determining which sources are credible is still a source of contention.

BOX 13.7   RELATIVISTIC THINKING

Bethany is an 18-year-old college freshman who comes to you, the counselor, to discuss the behavior of her roommate, Kara. Bethany explains that Kara is unreasonable and insists on inviting friends over on the weekends when she is trying to study. After arguing with Bethany for some time, Kara is willing to allow a quiet study day on Sundays but insists she needs to socialize "at some time." Bethany feels this is unreasonable and states that "weekends are for studying" and Kara is wrong to ask for any accommodation. Bethany also states she is failing her philosophy class because the instructor will not "just tell the class the right answers." What type of thinking is Bethany exhibiting? What might a counselor do to help Bethany learn to compromise? How does this apply to Bethany's grade in philosophy class?

The final stage, commitment in relativism, is where uncertainty is accepted and both experience and evidence are used to arrive at conclusions. This form of thinking looks at concepts from others' perspectives and angles and requires logic to analyze and problem solve (Perry, 1970). This relativistic thinking is the highest form of reflective judgment and results in creativity and even expertise if utilized fully (Boundless, 2014; Johnson, 1994).

Pragmatic Thought

LaBouvie-Vief (1980) stated that as individuals go through early adulthood they gain in cognitive-affective complexity. For example, LaBouvie-Vief refers to pragmatic thought experienced in adulthood as the transition from idealistic ideas to practical and realistic possibilities. Logic is the tool used to narrow down unlimited possibilities and transform them into usable practical choices. For example, success in a career requires the person to narrow choices such that a person's skills and aptitudes lead to expertise and success.

Schaie's Developmental Theory of Adult Cognitive Adjustment and Early Adulthood

K. Warner Schaie has studied how health, demographic, personality, and environmental factors influence individual differences in successful cognitive aging. Schaie's (2005) and Schaie and Willis's (2000) developmental theories divide the lifespan into several stages: acquisitive, achieving, responsibility and executive, reorganizational, reintegrative, and legacy leaving. These stages describe cognitive phases throughout the lifespan. Since this chapter focuses on early adulthood, let us discuss the stages falling within this phase of life.

The achieving stage begins in early adulthood. This substage depicts early adulthood as the time when the individual uses cognitive skills to acquire success in life situations such as on the job, in marriage, and in raising children. Previously learned skills are strengthened and decisions are considered with regard to how they affect other life issues.

The responsibility stage occurs once a family is established and decisions require a consideration of others. For example, the person in the responsibility stage must consider family needs and make decisions accordingly. Knowing that one's decisions affect others in the family or community creates a need for open mindedness and thoughtfulness in choices.

The executive stage affects approximately 25% of early- and middle-aged adults. These adults are those who attain professional positions requiring high levels of leadership and who must make responsible executive decisions affecting numerous people's lives and careers (Schaie, Willis, & Caskie, 2014). People at this level must learn skills related to societal hierarchies, conflict resolution, diversity, and loyalty.

As part of his studies on cognitive aging, Schaie also stated that four of six intellectual abilities (inductive, spatial, vocabulary, and verbal) are highest in the mid-40s to early 50s. Perceptual speed declines in the 20s and numerical ability falls in the 40s (Lyons et al., 2009). More studies are needed to determine exactly how intellectual and cognitive abilities decline after early adulthood. One thing that is certain, however, is that degeneration and memory loss are factors associated with aging.

Cognitive Degeneration and Memory

Just as the brain becomes fully developed, degenerative changes begin occurring. The brain shrinks with increasing age, memory impairment increases, and cognitions are affected (Muller-Oehring, Schulte, Rohlfing, Pfefferbaum, & Sullivan, 2013). This brain shrinkage is especially evident in the prefrontal cortex. For example, between the ages of 30 and 80 years, the brain loses up to 14% of frontal lobe gray matter and 24% of frontal lobe white matter (Balter, 2011). Other brain areas are also affected including the cerebellar hemispheres and hippocampus (Chang, Nien, Chen, & Yan, 2014).

Reductions in neurotransmitters such as acetylcholine and gamma aminobutyric acid (GABA) also make the brain less productive in memory retrieval and signal transmission. Reductions in acetylcholine may be responsible for memory loss associated with Alzheimer's disease, whereas decreases in GABA, the entity responsible for ensuring efficient transmission of signals, affect precision between neurons. Fortunately for young adults, the accompanying losses in cognitive performance and memory are not noticed until much later in life. Outcomes can be improved with physical activity, intellectual engagement, proper diet, and social interactions beginning in early adulthood (Chang et al., 2014).

Special Developmental Issues in Early Adulthood

While the average person achieves the stages discussed in the previous sections, it is important to remember that many adults have a wider range of experiences or never reach these milestones at all. For example, a person's outlook on midlife decline and available social supports influence the propensity to develop mental health disorders, use drugs, and experience good or bad physical health (Kim, Tiberio, Pears, Capaldi, & Washburn, 2013; Umberson & Montez, 2010). Early adulthood development is, therefore, influenced by both genetics and environment. Following is a description of some of the developmental issues that may impair normal early adulthood development as well as a discussion on the influence of both environment and genetics on the early adult's development of disorders.

Mental Health Disorders

Counselors who work with early adults must be willing to work with diverse clients on a wide range of problems. Because those in their 20s and 30s can face both typical and atypical developmental issues ranging from mental and physical health disorders to exceptional abilities, counselors need a wide range of skills and expertise to be of assistance. Because this chapter focuses on physical and cognitive development, discussion will focus on topics related to these areas. Later chapters will go into more detail on emotional and relationship issues faced by early adults.

Up to 75% of diagnosable mental health disorders are evident by age 24 years (Murphy, 2014), and many are related to physical and cognitive development leading up to and during early adulthood. For example, disorders typically treated in early adulthood include anxiety and panic disorders, depressive disorders, addictions, eating disorders, schizophrenia, acute stress disorder, posttraumatic stress disorder, and self-injury (Lyons & Barclay, 2014; Murphy, 2014). A description of some common disorders emerging in young adulthood and reciprocally influencing development follows.

Panic disorder is one of the most common fear and anxiety disorders emerging in young adulthood. It typically begins between adolescence and the mid-30s and affects up to 5% of the population (APA, 2013; Lyons & Barclay, 2014). Those experiencing panic disorder experience frequent and unexpected panic attacks characterized by the feeling one is having a heart attack or stroke or is going to die. These attacks cause such fear the person often makes lifestyle changes to avoid additional panic attacks, including avoiding places, social events, and other normal developmental parts of life. Biologically, panic attacks affect the amygdala and other parts of the brain involved in the regulation of fear and emotional arousal. Many theorists also believe those who experience panic attacks developed an overly sensitive fear network in the brain. Other theorists contend that a lack of GABA, which also inhibits anxiety, causes the disorder (Lyons & Barclay, 2014). Fortunately, many with panic disorder respond positively to caffeine avoidance, medications, and cognitive therapy (National Institute on Mental Health, n.d).

Major depressive disorder is the most frequently diagnosed disorder among young adults and co-occurs with physical issues such as cancer, diabetes, and heart conditions (Lyons & Barclay, 2014; Mayo Clinic, 2012). Further, depression shows comorbidity when diagnosing anxiety, substance abuse, eating disorders, and anxiety disorders. Approximately 15% of those diagnosed with a depressive disorder commit suicide (APA, 2000).

People between the ages of 18 and 24 years are at highest risk for substance use disorders (APA, 2013). Johnston, O'Malley, Bachman, and Schulenberg (2009) studied drinking trends for early adults (aged 19–28 years) and stated that 5.3% drank daily with 42% of those aged 21–22 years reporting having consumed at least five drinks in a row within the past 2 weeks. Drugs and alcohol impede development with consequences such as heart disease, stroke, cancer, hepatitis, lung disease, liver damage, kidney damage, neurological impairment, stunted growth, hormone imbalances, and inflammation of the stomach (Chen et al., 2012; National Institute on Drug Abuse, n.d.).

Those at highest risk for anorexia nervosa and bulimia nervosa are White females in adolescence to early adulthood living in Western industrialized nations (Lyons & Barclay, 2014). Anorexia nervosa is typically seen in females aged 15-24 years and is defined by three major symptoms: fear of weight gain, altered perception of body size, and refusal to ingest sufficient calories to maintain healthy body weight (APA, 2013). Bulimia nervosa is an eating disorder affecting up to 1.5% of females, and onset is 5 years later than that experienced with anorexia nervosa (Lyons & Barclay, 2014). Both disorders result in physical deterioration and interruption of normal development. According to the Mayo Clinic (2012), heart problems, organ failure, bone loss, stunted growth, digestive problems, kidney damage, severe tooth decay, increased or decreased blood pressure, and death are the physical consequences of eating disorders. Studies suggest a strong genetic link in family members experiencing anorexia nervosa (Fairburn & Harrison, 2003) and heritability estimates between 50% and 83% for bulimia nervosa (Striegel-Moore & Bulik, 2007).

Self-injury is an increasingly common phenomenon for those between the ages of 18 and 35 years. Researchers contend that those who have been abandoned by parents or have been sexually or physically abused are at particular risk (Maniglio, 2011). Since self-injury is comorbid with substance use disorder, depressive disorders, and antisocial personality disorder and can result in accidental suicide, it is an impediment to normal growth and development in early adulthood.

Cognitive and Learning Disabilities

Most learning and cognitive disabilities affect young children or older adults but can also affect the functioning of many early adults. Learning disabilities affect up to 4% of the adult population, and many decisions made by adults between the ages of 20 and 40 years affect future cognitions. Choices made about substance use and physical activities that increase risk of head trauma can affect brain functioning and impairment in later years (Lyons & Barclay, 2014).

Giftedness

Gifted adults tend to exhibit high levels of self-monitoring, perfectionism, personal insight, and metacognition (Shore & Kanevsky, 1993). They demonstrate high levels of postformal, dialectical, and relativist thinking (Lewis, Kitano, & Lynch, 1992). Despite these positive traits, many gifted adults report feeling isolated, misunderstood, and shamed. In fact, many gifted adults feel less cognitively developed than their peers and report an inability to fit into society (Jacobsen, n.d.). Cognitive development among gifted adults is often unrecognized and can be greatly influenced by both their past and future environments. Whether a gifted person copes well with anxiety, spends time alone, or uses intellect to fulfill emotional needs has been linked to a supportive family environment (Olszewski-Kubilius, 2010).

Environment

Regardless of age, environmental conditions are linked to cognitive and physical health. Power, Manor, and Matthews (2003) found that low socioeconomic status predicted health risk at birth, ages 16, 23, and 33 years. According to Weaver

(2009), "sequelae of early life social and environmental stressors, such as childhood abuse, neglect, poverty, and poor nutrition, have been associated with the emergence of mental and physical illness (i.e., anxiety, mood disorders, poor impulse control, psychosis, and drug abuse) and an increased risk of common metabolic and cardiovascular diseases later in life" (p. 314). Early environmental influences can also alter brain development such that stress responsivity throughout life is altered. Even at later ages, however, high blood pressure, Alzheimer's disease, obesity, cardiovascular disease, and cognitive decline can be reduced through exercise, diet, stress reduction, and counseling (Collins & Bentz, 2009).

Some environmental influences are directly related to personal decisions made throughout the lifetime. For example, a person's career choice impacts exposure to physical labor, chemicals, and for those in the armed forces, even violence and death.

Career-Related Issues

Negative developmental environments are often consequences of particular occupations. For example, some young adults choose jobs requiring demanding physical labor resulting in early physical deterioration. Others choose careers such as serving in the armed forces. This military career often means winding up in the midst of war as well as exposure to live images of death and violence. This, along with required participation in these violent acts, has an effect on an early adult's cognitive development.

BOX 13.8   MILITARY EXPERIENCES AND DEVELOPMENT

Brad is a devoted father and husband who served as a sergeant in the Air Force. While serving a 6-month deployment in Afghanistan, Brad witnessed the deaths of other soldiers—including his roommate. Brad and his family were very excited the day he arrived home. It didn't take long to notice, however, that Brad had changed dramatically. Brad was extremely depressed, could not concentrate on work or hobbies, and was having nightmares. He was screaming at his son regularly because he couldn't tolerate the sounds of his son laughing and playing like a normal child. What might be causing Brad's problems?

Genetics

Although environment plays a role in the aging process, it is important to understand that, despite all efforts made, genes do influence every aspect of development (Harvard School of Public Health, 2015). Genetic theories posit that aging occurs as a result of biological programming, whereas nongenetic theories or error theories emphasize that environmental influences contribute to physical and mental decline. Following are synopses of a few of these theories.

The *genetic theory of aging* is a programmed theory whereby a person's life span and degeneration is believed to be controlled by biological genes given to the person at birth. For example, animals tend to have approximately the same lifespan as others within their species. The theory further posits that children are expected to live the same length of time as their parents and grandparents (Stibich, 2014a).

The *wear-and-tear theory* states that the body simply wears out over time. Metabolism, body temperature, and inherent genetic traits are believed to play a role in the process. For example, animals with slow metabolic rates and lower body temperatures tend to live longer than their counterparts. Exposure to radiation and toxins exacerbate the decline (Stibich, 2014b).

The *mutation theory* describes a process where the body develops genetic mutations with age. As one cell mutates, others follow suit through replication. The result is damaged DNA (deoxyribonucleic acid) and less efficient bodily functioning. While this process sounds primarily genetic, many believe exposure to radiation expedites the process (Stibich, 2013).

Nature or Nurture?

Although these theories offer possible understanding of the genetic aging process, no theory can definitively predict how much of the process is within the control of the individual. We do know that genetics is believed to account for up to 35% of the normal aging process for the population at large, with another 65% controlled by environmental factors and personal choices (Stibich, 2014c). These percentages illustrate the importance of making good choices and the positive impact those decisions can have on the aging process. As a result, counselors must offer accurate information to clients so they make personal choices that offer the best future outcome.

KEY COUNSELING POINTERS FOR PHYSICAL DEVELOPMENT DURING EARLY ADULTHOOD

Many of the boxes in this chapter contain case studies with counseling-related questions. Following are possible responses to these case studies based on counseling theory, standard of practice, and the American Counseling Association Code of Ethics (2014). Responses are given, but it is important to remember that numerous possibilities often exist. It may be helpful to compare your responses with those given here and evaluate the relevance of each.

Conceptualizing the Case of Carmela (Box 13.1)

Carmela clearly misunderstands the importance of prevention when it comes to the aging process. Should the counselor advise Carmela to change her unhealthy habits? First, let us consider the American Counseling Association Code of Ethics (2014), section A.1.a. Client Welfare: "The primary responsibility of counselors is to respect the dignity and promote the welfare of clients" (p. 4). Obviously, ignoring Carmela's poor choices is not in the client's best interest. Rather than offering advice to Carmela, however, a better approach is to give accurate information so she understands the connection between early behaviors, chronic disease, and physical decline. This might be stated as: "Research has been conducted inferring that the earlier a person engages in healthy eating and exercise behaviors, the great the likelihood they will avoid chronic disease and delay some effects of aging" (August & Sorkin, 2011). Confrontations may also play an important role in helping Carmela see the behavior through a different lens as well as motivate her to begin exercising.

Since Carmela is 20 years old and age of client affects motivation to exercise, the counselor may need specific techniques. Quindry and colleagues (2011) stated that adults in Carmela's age group are most likely to exercise as a result of fitness or interpersonal goals. This being the case, the counselor might confront Carmela with phrases such as, "You say you want to be fit, yet you do not participate in regular exercise." Interpersonal areas might be challenged by asking, "Who else would notice that you were more fit?" Counselors have the ability and responsibility to help clients such as Carmela make informed decisions and alter unhealthy habits.

Conceptualizing the Case of Lloyd (Box 13.2)

Lloyd just turned 35 years old, and his body no longer repairs itself as efficiently as it did when he was younger. This degeneration is exacerbated by his drinking and poor diet. Alcohol consumption dehydrates the body, leading to dry skin, enlarged blood vessels, and, over time, high blood pressure. Heavy drinking is defined as consuming more than two drinks daily for males under age 65 years (Sheps, 2015). It is not surprising, therefore, that, when combined with the natural aging process, Lloyd is experiencing effects from his drinking.

Lloyd's consumption of sugar further harms his body. Large quantities of sugar decrease collagen production in the skin, contribute to weight gain, and can eventually lead to chronic illness. The earlier in life Lloyd adopts healthy eating habits, the less likely he will be to develop cardiovascular disease, diabetes, and some cancers. This is especially crucial for Lloyd since research infers that, as an African American, he is more likely to adopt unhealthy dietary and sedentary behaviors than non-Hispanic Whites (August & Sorkin, 2010).

Lloyd's counselor must offer information to alleviate confusion about the harm he is doing his body. Even though this sounds much like Carmela's case, a couple of differences exist. First, Lloyd's age places him in the middle-aged adult category and therefore alters motivational factors. Quindry et al. (2011) stated that middle-aged adults such as Lloyd are primarily motivated to exercise for body-related reasons. For this reason, Lloyd might be reminded that fitness improves appearance and alcohol causes weight gain, which diminishes attractiveness. Another important consideration involves the aging impact of Lloyd's drinking. Chen and colleagues (2012) stated that impaired liver functioning, a consequence of heavy drinking, is correlated with brain shrinkage and cognitive decline in later life. The counselor may need to confront Lloyd about his drinking, determine if he has an addiction, and help him understand how it may be impeding socialization (Borelli, 2014; MedicineNet, 2015).

Conceptualizing the Case of Ben and Fran (Box 13.3)

Ben and Fran have been trying to conceive a child for many years without success, and it seems apparent Fran is suffering from a medical condition referred to as infertility. Infertility can cause depression, anxiety, relationship problems, mood swings, changes in appetite and sleep, sexual difficulties, and even suicide ideation. Fran and Ben would be wise to see a couples' counselor specializing in fertility issues. This counselor will educate Fran and Ben about infertility by suggesting they read informative books, Internet sites, and brochures. The counselor might also suggest group counseling sessions with other couples experiencing similar difficulties. These sessions can offer support to Ben and Fran, as can sharing with their family and friends.

Counseling sessions should focus on Fran and Ben's fear of the medical procedures, possibilities of failure as related to treatment continuation or termination, possibilities for a fulfilling life without children or adoption, and relationship issues including sexuality, intimacy, and finances. Couples often experience relationship difficulties due to the scheduling of sexuality as well as blame and guilt experienced by both parties.

Ben and Fran might consider personal counseling to manage the distress caused by feelings of grief, frustration, pressures from family and society to conceive, failure at conception despite treatment, and emotions influenced by waiting for results. Theories suggested as beneficial to clients dealing with infertility include cognitive behavioral therapy, psychodynamic therapy, solution focused brief therapy, crisis intervention, and process-experiential grief counseling (Strauss & Boivin, n.d.). Both Ben and Fran need help establishing new methods of coping and specific techniques such as guided imagery and relaxation, Gestalt's empty chair technique, and future goal setting despite outcome.

KEY COUNSELING POINTERS FOR COGNITIVE DEVELOPMENT DURING EARLY ADULTHOOD

Conceptualizing the Case of Bethany (Box 13.7)

It is not surprising Bethany has difficulty compromising since, at her age, she is probably exhibiting dualistic thinking. This dualistic thinking is hindering Bethany in her philosophy course, which requires an analysis of several points of view. Students often exhibit strong emotions when being challenged to move to multiplistic thinking because additional frames of reference challenge familiar concepts. To help Bethany advance to a more multiplistic way of thinking, the counselor or instructor must ask open-ended thought provoking questions such as, "Tell me what it would be like if you had to do this differently." The counselor might ask Bethany to explore her friend's viewpoints by switching roles or even having her act out the part of her friend. This requires Bethany to recognize that several viewpoints and options are possible rather than simply adopting a single "correct" or dualistic stance. It will also be important to monitor Bethany's emotions, reflect, and reframe as needed. Counselors must recognize that relativistic thinking does not always occur in perfect sequence and, as a result, Bethany may gravitate to dualistic thinking even after previously exhibiting multiplistic levels (Carnegie Mellon, n.d.). Bethany's counselor must therefore have the patience to challenge Bethany and use immediacy as she recognizes her own frustrations in accepting differing views.

Conceptualizing the Case of Brad (Box 13.8)

Brad is a young soldier who is probably experiencing acute stress disorder. First listed in the American Psychiatric Association's (1994) *Diagnostic and Statistical Manual of Mental Disorders*, fourth edition, *(DSM-IV)*, in 1994, acute stress disorder is similar to posttraumatic stress disorder but must occur within and last no longer than 1 month after exposure to the traumatizing event.

Clinicians can validate Brad's possible ASD diagnosis through appearance and behavior, interviews, and testing. First, the counselor must determine when Brad's traumatizing event occurred and how long the symptoms have been evident. Interviewing Brad and his family (with Brad's permission) can help distinguish between acute stress reaction (ASR), a nondiagnosable condition; ASD; and posttraumatic stress disorder (PTSD). If Brad demonstrates signs of ASR, he will describe symptoms occurring minutes to hours after the traumatizing event and disappearing hours to a few days later. ASD may be present if symptoms last up to 1 month, whereas PTSD lasts beyond a month (U.S. Department of Veteran's Affairs, 2014). Instruments such as The Acute Stress Disorder Interview (ASDI) or the Acute Stress Disorder Scale (ASDS) are valid and reliable instruments that might be used to further confirm Brad's diagnosis.

If it is determined Brad has ASD, he needs an effective intervention. Treatments that have shown promise and might be used to treat Brad's ASD include: cognitive behavioral therapy, psychological debriefing, and eye movement desensitization and reprocessing (Gibson, 2014). Along with the aforementioned treatments, Brad's counselor should offer education about his disorder and help him manage his symptoms with techniques such as relaxation. Brad should be encouraged to take any prescribed psychotropic medications given to him by his doctors and to create a supportive network with others. This supportive network might include other soldiers suffering from ASD, his family, and friends (U.S. Department of Veteran's Affairs, 2014).

Family and career counseling may also benefit Brad and his family. Family counseling will teach Brad's wife how to support him as he struggles through this challenge. Brad may also need help with career-related issues such as applying for disability since ASD causes cognitive and emotional problems that can impede his work performance.

Counseling Tips for Stage Transition in Early Adults

The information presented in this chapter discusses relevant issues related to counseling-specific issues faced by early adults. The following information is given to guide counselors working with early adults as they transition through normal developmental stages. Because many of the developmental issues faced by early adults involve personal choices, counselors are in optimal positions to assist young adults as they explore unforeseen territory and chart life's path. Table 13.1 depicts early adulthood through three distinct transitional stages (ages 18–24 years, ages 24–35 years, and ages 35–40 years) and offers specific suggestions counselors can use to help clients functioning within each level. As always, consult the American Counseling Association Code of Ethics (2014) and other relevant codes when choosing strategies to work with clients.

Table 13.1 Transitional Stages

Developmental Level (Age)	Developmental Tasks	Suggested Counseling Strategies
18–24 years	Transition to academic or career world; adjust to new freedoms and independence; accept financial responsibility	Give information about consequences of drug use, sexuality, financial options, study skills, career information; empathize with the client as he or she faces consequences of mistakes; suggest mentorships as appropriate Teach stress management skills Help clients balance time and energy Make referrals to group or career counseling as needed
24–34 years	Accept first signs of drop in physical stamina; develop relationships; establish a career and goals; balance career, relationship, and family needs	Empathize Encourage mentorships Teach stress management skills Encourage career passion Make referrals to groups or career counseling as needed Encourage a balance between family, relationship, career, and personal time
35–40 years	Accept signs of physical decline; maintain career; accept realization that goals may be unfulfilled	Suggest fulfillment through social interest activities including career mentorship; normalize and empathize with the client's experience Discern the value of what has been accomplished and what is left to do Make referrals to group or career counseling as needed

SUMMARY

Early adulthood is typically a time of optimal physical and cognitive development. The body is at its strongest, and age has not yet affected appearance. The brain fully develops and logical, postformal thought evolves. Decreases in physical stamina and appearance do not appear until after age 30 years. With proper exercise, diet, environment, and life choices, early adults can offset the negative impacts of aging that come during middle and late adulthood. Counselors can help early adults through normal developmental issues as well as atypical developmental disorders using numerous counseling theories and techniques as well as information aimed at promoting client health and wellness.

USEFUL WEBSITES

American Counseling Association Code of Ethics (2014)
http://counseling.org/Resources/aca-code-of-ethics.pdf
Association of Reproductive Health Professionals
http://www.arhp.org/publications-and-resources/quick-reference-guide-
     for-clinicians/postpartum-counseling/mental-health
American Society for Reproductive Medicine
http://www.reproductivefacts.org
Early Adult Career Assistance
http://www.allpsychologycareers.com/topics/early-adulthood-development
     .html
Mental Health America
http://www.mentalhealthamerica.net/conditions/post-traumatic-stress-
     disorder
National Institutes on Mental Health
http://www.nimh.nih.gov/health/publications/anxiety-disorders/index
     .shtml#pub8
Understanding Mental Illness
http://www.thekimfoundation.org/html/about_mental_ill/by_population-
     youngadult.html
Young Adult Development Project
http://hrweb.mit.edu/worklife/youngadult/brain.html#cortexTables

REFERENCES

All Psychology Careers. (2014). *Early adulthood developmental psychology*. Retrieved
     from http://www.allpsychologycareers.com/topics/early-adulthood-
     development.html
American College of Sports Medicine. (n.d.) *Exercise and the older adult*. Retrieved
     from https://www.acsm.org/docs/current-comments/
     exerciseandtheolderadult.pdf

American Counseling Association. (2014). *Code of ethics*. Retrieved from http://www.counseling.org/Resources/aca-code-of-ethics.pdf

American Psychiatric Association (APA). (1994). *Diagnostic and statistical manual of mental disorders* (4th ed.). Washington, DC: Author.

American Psychiatric Association (APA). (2000). *Diagnostic and statistical manual of mental Disorders* (5th ed.). Washington, DC: Author.

American Psychiatric Association (APA). (2013). *Diagnostic and statistical manual of mental disorders* (5th ed.). Washington, DC: Author.

American Counseling Association Code of Ethics. (2014). *ACA Code of Ethics*. Accessed: *6/17/14*.

American Society for Reproductive Medicine. (n.d.). *Fact sheet: The patient education website of the American Society for Reproductive Medicine*. Retrieved from http://www.reproductivefacts.org/uploadedFiles/ASRM_Content/Resources/Patient_Resources/Fact_Sheets_and_Info_Booklets/Counseling-Fact.pdf

Andreoli, A., Celi, M., Volpe, S.L., Sorge, R., & Tarantino, U. (2012). Long-term effect of exercise on bone mineral density in post-menopausal ex-elite athletes: A retrospective study. *European Journal of Clinical Nutrition, 66*, 69–74.

Association of Reproductive Health Professionals. (2013). *Postpartum mental health*. Retrieved from http://www.arhp.org/publications-and-resources/quick-reference-guide-for-clinicians/postpartum-counseling/mental-health

August, K. J., & Sorkin, D. H. (2011). Racial/ethnic disparities in exercise and dietary behaviors of middle-aged and older adults. *Journal of General Internal Medicine, 26*(3), 245–250. doi:10.1007/s11606-010-1514-7

Balter, M. (2011). *The incredible shrinking brain*. Retrieved from http://news.sciencemag.org/brain-behavior/2011/07/incredible-shrinking-human-brain

Bolam, K. A., van Uffelen, J. G. Z., & Taafe, D. R. (2013). The effect of physical exercise on bone density in middle-aged and older men: A systematic review. *Osteoporosis International, 24*, 2749–2762.

Borelli, L. (2014). *What not to eat: Five food habits that ruin your skin*. Retrieved from http://www.medicaldaily.com/what-not-eat-5-food-habits-ruin-healthy-skin-make-you-age-faster-303474

Boundless. (2014). Cognitive development in adulthood. *Boundless Psychology*. Retrieved from https://www.boundless.com/psychology/textbooks/boundless-psychology-textbook-human-development-14/adulthood-74/cognitive-development-in-adulthood-288-12823

Carnegie Mellon. (n.d.). *Recognize who your students are*. Retrieved from http://www.cmu.edu/teaching/designteach/design/yourstudents.html

Chang, Y., Nien, Y., Chen, A., & Yan, J. (2014). Tai Ji Quan, the brain, and cognition in older adults. *Journal of Sport and Health Science, 3*, 36–42.

Chen, C.-H., Walker, J., Momenan, R., Rawlings, R., Heilig, M., & Hommer, D. W. (2012). Relationship between liver function and brain shrinkage in patients with alcohol dependence. *Alcoholism, Clinical and Experimental Research, 36*(4), 625–632. doi:10.1111/j.1530-0277.2011.01662.x

Collingwood, J. (2010). The relationship between mental and physical health. *Psych Central*. Retrieved from http://psychcentral.com/lib/the-relationship-between-mental-and-physical-health/0002949

Collins, J. C., & Bentz, J. E. (2009). Behavioral and psychological factors in obesity. *Journal of Lancaster General Hospital, 4*, 124–127. Retrieved from http://www.jlgh.org/Past-Issues/Volume-4--Issue-4/Behavioral-and-Psychological-Factors-in-Obesity.aspx

Collura, T. F., Bonnstetter, R. J., & Zalaquett, C. (2014). Seeing inside the client's mind. *Counseling Today, 57*(6), 24–27.

Donald, M. (2001). *A mind so rare: The evolution of human consciousness*. New York, NY: Norton.

Dotinga, R. (2014). *Babies born to moms over 35 and birth defect risk*. Retrieved from http://www.webmd.com/baby/news/20140203/babies-born-to-moms-over-35-may-have-lower-risk-for-certain-birth-defects

Enzinger, C., Fazekas, F., Matthews, P. M., Ropele, S., Schmidt, H., Smith, S., & Schmidt, R. (2005). Risk factors for progression of brain atrophy in aging: Six-year follow-up of normal subjects. *Neurology, 64*, 1704–1711.

Fairburn, C. G., & Harrison, P. J. (2003). Eating disorders. *Lancet, 361*, 407–416.

Freberg, L. (n.d.). *Beyond Piaget: Postformal reasoning*. Retrieved from https://www.psych.answers.com/developmental/beyond-piaget

Gibson, L. (2014). *Acute stress disorder*. Retrieved from http://www.ptsd.va.gov/professional/treatment/early/acute-stress-disorder.asp

Giedd, J. N. (1999). Development of the human corpus callosum during childhood and adolescence: A longitudinal MRI study. *Progress in Neuro-Psychopharmacology & Biological Psychiatry, 23*, 571–588.

Giedd, J. N. (2004). Structural magnetic resonance imaging of the adolescent brain. *Adolescent Brain Development: Vulnerabilities and Opportunities, 1021*, 77–85.

Jacobsen, M. (n.d.). *Arousing the sleeping giant. Giftedness in adult psychotherapy.* Retrieved from http://talentdevelop.com/articles/ATSG.html

Johnson, D. D. (1994). *Dualistic, multiplistic, and relativistic thinking as it relates to a psychology major*. Retrieved from https://www.opensiuc.lib.siu.edu

Johnston, L. D., O'Malley, P. M., Bachman, J. G., & Schulenberg, J. E. (2009). *Monitoring the future: National survey results on drug use, 1975–2008*. Bethesda, MD: National Institute on Drug Abuse.

Keller, C., Allan, J., & Tinkle, M. (2006). Stages of change, processes of change, and social support for exercise and weight gain in postpartum women. *Journal of Obstetric, Gynecologic & Neonatal Nursing, 35*(2), 232–240. doi:10.1111/j.1552-6909.2006.00030.x

Kim, H. K., Tiberio, S. S., Pears, K. C., Capaldi, D. M., & Washburn, I. J. (2013). Growth of men's alcohol use in early adulthood: Intimate partners' influence. *Psychology of Addictive Behaviors, 27*(4), 1167–1174. doi:10.1037/a0033502

Ko, Y. L., Yang, C. L., Fang, C. L., Lee, M. Y., & Lin, P. C. (2013). Community-based postpartum exercise program. *Journal of Clinical Nursing, 22*, 2122–2131.

LaBouvie-Vief, G. (1980). Beyond formal operations: Use and limits of pure logic in life-span development. *Human Development, 23*, 141–161.

Levinson, D. J. (1978). *Seasons of a man's life*. New York, NY: Random House.

Lewis, R. B., Kitano, M. K., & Lynch, E. M. (1992). Psychological intensities in gifted adults. *Roeper Review, 15*(1), 25–31.

Lyons, C. A., & Barclay, M. (2014). *Abnormal psychology: Clinical and scientific perspectives*. Reading, CA: BVT.

Lyons, M. J., York, T. P., Franz, C. E., Grant, M. D., Eaves, L. J., Jacobson, K. C., … Kremen, W. S. (2009). Genes determine stability and the environment determines change in cognitive ability during 35 years of adulthood. *Psychological Science, 20*(9), 1146–1152. doi:10.1111/j.1467-9280.2009.02425.x

Maniglio, R. (2011). The role of child sexual abuse in the etiology of suicide and non-suicidal self-injury. *Acta Psychiatrica Scandinavica, 124*(1), 30–41. doi:10.1111/j.1600-0447.2010.01612.x

Mayo Clinic. (2012). *Eating disorders: Complications*. Retrieved from http://www.mayoclinic.org/diseases-conditions/eating-disorders/basics/complications/con-20033575

Mayo Clinic. (2015). *Pregnancy after 35: Healthy moms, healthy babies*. Retrieved from http://www.mayoclinic.org/healthy-living/getting-pregnant/in-depth/pregnancy/art- 20045756

MedicineNet. (2015). *The alcohol debate: Should you or shouldn't you*. Retrieved from http://www.medicinenet.com/script/main/art.asp?articlekey=56016

Merck. (2014). The changes in the body with aging. *Merck home health manual*. Retrieved from http://www.merckmanuals.com/home/older_peoples_health_issues/the_aging_body/changes_in_the_body_with_aging.html

Müller-Oehring, E. M., Schulte, T., Rohlfing, T., Pfefferbaum, A., & Sullivan, E. V. (2013). Visual search and the aging brain: Discerning the effects of age-related brain volume shrinkage on alertness, feature binding, and attentional control. *Neuropsychology, 27*(1), 48–59. doi:10.1037/a0030921

Murphy, S. N. (2014). College disorientation. *Counseling Today, 57*(2), 38–43.

National Institute on Drug Abuse. (n.d.). *Medical consequences of drug abuse*. Retrieved from https://www.drugabuse.gov

National Institute on Mental Health. (n.d.). *Anxiety disorders*. Retrieved from http://www.nimh.nih.gov/health/publications/anxiety-disorders/index.shtml#pub8

Olszewski-Kubilius, P. (2010). The transition from childhood giftedness to adult creative productiveness: Psychological characteristics and social supports. *Roeper Review, 23*, 65–71. doi:10.1080/02783190009554068

Perry, W. G. (1970). *Forms of intellectual and ethical development in the college years*. New York, NY: Holt, Rinehart, & Winston.

Piaget, J. (1952). *The origins of intelligence in children*. New York, NY: International Universities Press.

Piaget, J. (1954). *The construction of reality in the child*. New York, NY: Basic Books.

Power, C., Manor, O., & Matthews, S. (2003). Child to adult socioeconomic conditions and obesity in a national cohort. *International Journal of Obesity, 27*, 1081–1086. doi:10.1038

Procon.org. (2014). *Forty-five states that allow underage drinking*. Retrieved from http://drinkingage.procon.org/view.resource.php?resourceID=002591

Quindry, J. C., Yount, D., O'Bryant, H., & Rudisill, M. E. (2011). Exercise engagement is differentially motivated by age-dependent factors. *American Journal of Health Behavior, 35*(3), 334–345. doi:10.5993/AJHB.35.3.7

Reinke, B. J., Holmes, D. S., & Harris, R. L. (1985). The timing of psychosocial changes in women's lives: The years 25 to 45. *Journal of Personality and Social Psychology, 48*, 1353–1364.

Riegel, K. F. (1979). *Foundations of dialectical psychology*. New York, NY: Academic Press.

Rowan, J. (2000). *Dialectical thinking and humanistic psychology*. Retrieved from https://society-for-philosophy-in-practice.org

Russell-Chapin, L., & Jones, L. (2014). Three truths about neurocounseling. *Counseling Today, 57*(3), 20–21.

Schaie, K. W. (1990). Intellectual development in adulthood. In J. E. Birren & K. W. Schaie (Eds.), *Handbook of the psychology of aging* (3rd ed., pp. 291–309). New York, NY: Academic Press.

Schaie, K. W. (2005). *Developmental influences on adult intelligence: The Seattle longitudinal study*. New York, NY: Oxford University Press.

Schaie, K. W., & Willis, S. L. (2000). A stage theory model of adult cognitive development revisited. In. R. L. Rubenstein, M. Moss, & M. H. Kleban (Eds.), *The many stages of aging* (pp. 174–193). New York, NY: Springer.

Schaie, K. W., Willis, S. L., & Caskie, G. I. L. (2014). The Seattle longitudinal study: Relation between personality and cognition. *Aging, Neuropsychology and Cognition, 11*, 304–324.

Shephard, R. J. (1998). Aging and exercise. In T. D. Fahey (Ed.), *Encyclopedia of sports medicine and science*. Toronto: Canada: Internet Society for Sport Science. Retrieved from http://www.sportsci.org/encyc/agingex/agingex.html

Sheps, S. G. (2015). *High blood pressure: Does drinking alcohol affect your blood pressure?* Retrieved from http://www.mayoclinic.org/diseases-conditions/high-blood-pressure/expert-answers/blood-pressure/faq-20058254

Shore, B. M., & Kanevsky, L. (1993). Thinking processes: Being and becoming gifted. In K. A. Heller, F. J. Monks, & A. H. Passow (Eds.), *International handbook for research and development on giftedness and talent* (pp. 133–148). London, UK: Pergamon.

Simpson, R. (n.d.). Brain changes. *Youth development project*. Retrieved from http://hrweb.mit.edu/worklife/youngadult/brain.html#cortex

Siobhan, C. (2007). Formal-operational vs. post-formal thinking: Brains grow up. *Educational Learning, Psychology, & Teaching, 3*, 1. Retrieved from https://www.siobhancurious.com/2007/09/08/formal-operational

Stibich, M. (2013). *The somatic mutation theory of aging*. Retrieved from http://longevity.about.com/od/researchandmedicine/p/age_mutations.htm

Stibich, M. (2014a). *The genetic theory of aging*. Retrieved from http://longevity.about.com/od/researchandmedicine/p/age_genetics.htm

Stibich, M. (2014b). *Wear and tear theory of aging*. Retrieved from http://longevity.about.com/od/researchandmedicine/p/wear_tear.htm

Stibich, M. (2014c). *Why we age: Theories and effects of aging.* Retrieved from http://longevity.about.com/od/longevity101/a/why_we_age.htm

Stotland, N. E., Gilbert, P., Bogetz, A., Harper, C. C., Abrams, B., & Gerbert, B. (2010). Preventing excessive weight gain in pregnancy: How do prenatal care providers approach counseling? *Journal of Women's Health, 19*(4), 807–814. doi:10.1089/jwh.2009.1462

Strauss, B., & Boivin, J. (n.d.). Counselling within infertility. *Guidelines for Counselling in infertility (2.1).* Retrieved from http://www.eshre.eu/~/media/emagic%20files/SIGs/Psychology/Guidelines.pdf

Striegel-Moore, R. H., & Bulik, C. M. (2007). Risk factors for eating disorders. *American Psychologist, 62,* 181–198.

Umberson, D., & Montez, J. K. (2010). *Social relationships and health: A flashpoint for health policy.* Retrieved from http://www.ncbi.nlm.nih.gov/pmc/articles/PMC3150158/

U.S. Department of Veteran's Affairs. (2014). *VA/DOD evidence based practice for the management of posttraumatic stress.* Retrieved from http://www.healthquality.va.gov/guidelines/MH/ptsd/CPGSummaryFINALMgmtofPTSDfinal021413.pdf

Weaver, J. B., (2009). The duration and timing of exposure: Effects of socio-economic environment on adult health. *American Journal of Public Health, 87,* 314–326. doi:10.1002/bdrc.20164.

Willis, S. L., & Schaie, K. W. (1999). Intellectual functioning in mid-life. In S. L. Willis & J. D. Reid (Eds.), *Life in the middle: Psychological and social development in middle age,* (pp. 234–247). San Diego, CA: Academic Press.

World Health Organization. (2015). *Genes and human disease.* Retrieved from http://www.who.int/genomics/public/geneticdiseases/en/index3.html

Wu, L. T., Pilowsky, D. J., Schlenger, W. E., & Hasin, D. (2007). Alcohol use disorders and the use of treatment services among college-age young adults. *Psychiatric Services, 58,* 192–200.

Zuckerman, W., & Purcell, A. (2011). *Brain's synaptic pruning continues into your 20s.* Retrieved from http://www.newscientist.com/article/dn20803-brains-synaptic- pruning-continues-into-your-20s.html#.VIMu0f90x1s

Young Adulthood: Emotional and Social Development

Brian Hutchison, Katheryne T. Leigh, and Holly H. Wagner

Young adulthood is a time often perceived as the prime stage of life when one is free from both the chains of adolescence and the stigmas that come with more advanced age. As individuals emerge from adolescence, their dependence on family lessens as they begin to establish autonomy, careers, and intimate relationships throughout the ensuing two decades of life (Seiffe-Krenke, 2006). During young adulthood, social-emotional development intertwines with that of identity, moral, and career in dynamic ways that portend one's future attitudes and lifestyle. Fresh from perceived travails of late adolescence, those navigating young adulthood often strive to establish homeostasis while navigating new environments and ongoing personal growth. It is the juxtaposition of (a) feelings of freedom from newfound autonomy (e.g., in determining personal identity, moral choices, and career directions) and (b) experiences of restriction as environmental challenges such as oppression, making moral decisions in a globalized world, and the economic realities of the world of work collide to create the hardships and rewards found in social-emotional development during this stage.

This chapter explores social-emotional development for young adults as it relates to the prolific questions of: Who am I? What do I value? And what do I want to accomplish? To help us answer these essential questions, we will present three people's stories to help guide the reader to deeper understanding. Let's begin with Ivan.

PSYCHOSOCIAL DEVELOPMENT DURING EARLY ADULTHOOD

Ivan's Story

Ivan is a 20-year-old Native American male activist who has participated in a recent protest in Canada. He has been back at university for 2 weeks and comes to counseling because he is struggling with transitioning back into his "normal" routine.

During intake Ivan reports difficulty in finding fit and balance within his relationships. His experience as an activist has "changed" perspectives, creating conflict within his old relationships. Most recently, Ivan has gotten into heated debates with friends and family members who are not as understanding of his new perspectives. He has begun to withdraw from these once close relationships. Ivan is also still in contact with activists whom he met on his trip and struggles to balance his moral call to activism and his personal goals of graduating college.

Ivan presents a complex case of young adult identity development in action. It is easy to see how his social and emotional development are impacted by his expanded life experiences and resulting worldviews. How might Ivan think about his social relationships with family and friends as he navigates this normal developmental task? What questions will Ivan have about perception of self, or self-identity, as he negotiates these experiences and relationships within his internal world? Finally, how will Ivan's Native American identity interact with these developmental tasks?

These are the types of complex questions that developmental thinkers and theorists have been struggling with for millennia. When considering Ivan's case, we first turn to the work of Erik Erikson to help ground our understanding of and thinking about Ivan.

Erickson's Psychosocial Theory of Human Development: Intimacy Versus Isolation

An ego psychologist and leading developmental theorist, Erik Erikson was one of the first to include young adulthood as its own developmental stage in the lifespan. Importantly, this stage focuses upon how the identity crisis within adolescence transitions into the crisis of intimacy during young adulthood (Erikson, 1968). According to Erikson (1968), young adults experience a time of increased need and desire to form close intimate relationships. These relationships should not be construed as sexually intimate relationships only; rather, intimacy is viewed as a spectrum ranging from light interpersonal dialogue to sexual intimacy (Erikson, 1968; Horst, 1995). Though a young adult may have a positive sense of identity, his or her social-emotional issues during this stage may stem from trying to find social fit or having aspects of identity challenged. Erikson noted that intimacy only promotes healthy relationships when individuals share other aspects of self, rather than just focusing on the sexual intimacy and ego fulfillment (Erikson, 1968; Horst, 1995). The nature of relationships shifts as young adult individuals confront relational differences, and at times challenges, that spur on new insight about them and others. This cauldron of relational experience occurs as a young adult grapples with the new responsibilities, ambiguity, and meaning-making tasks of living more autonomously. New life tasks and relationships can offer excitement along with anxiety as individuals navigate social interactions to find their niche (Azmitia, Syed, & Radmacher, 2013).

It is important to note that this developmental theory is not a strictly linear model and individuals can transition through the stages out of sequence, or simultaneously. For instance, identity development during the fifth stage can still be taking place during the sixth stage, intimacy versus isolation (Erikson, 1968; Hamachek, 1990; Horst, 1995). Though Erikson's stage theory is limited to its description of the White heterosexual male, it still remains distinct from previous Freudian human development theory because of the emphasis placed on relational needs for not only healthy identity but also social-emotional development (Horst, 1995). According to Eriksson's stage theory, healthy development occurs when one is open to sharing self with others emotionally and physically, while also being willing to be challenged by difference (Erikson, 1968; Hamachek, 1990). By contrast, poor social-emotional development can manifest when one is struggling to engage intimately with others, which then threatens the person's self-concept and ability for positive growth and change (Burt & Paysnick, 2014; Erikson, 1968; Tesch & Whitbourne, 1982).

In summary, the basic task of Erickson's intimacy versus isolation stage is to answer the question: Can I find relationships and love as the self identified person I am becoming? This question is illuminated in the case of Ivan because of the easily identified extremes within which he attempts to answer this question. Ivan has two distinct sets of relationships in three different geographically defined realities (i.e., protest space, university space, home space). In considering this conflict we will now consider two essential elements of this struggle.

Finding Niche

Positive identity development in late adolescence becomes a moderator for handling the stressful situations and obstacles that occur during the early adult life stage (Burt & Paysnick, 2014; Tesch & Whitbourne, 1982). However, having a high self-concept, or answering the question of who am I without social relationships that share enough common ground to be perceived as accepting, can threaten homeostasis and the ability for young adults to move through stressful life obstacles (Azmitia et al., 2013; Burt & Paysnick, 2014; Tesch & Whitbourne, 1982). Accordingly, healthy social-emotional development occurs when young adults (a) have a positive sense of identity that includes commitment to values, beliefs, and lived experiences; (b) remain open to exploring perspectives and experiences that counter their identities; and (c) successfully develop relationships where they share common experiences with others. Essentially, they find their niche (Azmitia et al., 2013; Burt & Paysnick, 2014).

When someone is struggling to find his or her niche, this person runs the risk of becoming isolated, developing what Erikson called identity crisis. In an identity crisis, individuals relinquish positive aspects of their identities to gain relationships, no matter how superficial (1968). Ivan displayed one common example of this. Many young adults struggle during college when they are exposed to new senses of autonomy and desire to explore their own interests along with the challenges of navigating interpersonal differences that can foster growth (Azmitia et al., 2013; Burt & Paysnick, 2014).

Identity Crisis

According to Erikson (1968), social-emotional issues in young adulthood develop from isolation. Isolation is multidimensional and can present as a range of symptoms, such as a client's fear of being intimate because it may challenge strongly held beliefs, values, experiences; fear of being rejected because of race, ethnicity, and sexual orientation; and the lack of ability to share oneself for the benefit of others in place of self-fulfillment (Burt & Paysnick, 2014; Erikson, 1968 Tesch & Whitbourne, 1982). This tendency of creating relationships only based on self-fulfillment rather than intimacy can lead to distantiation, when one becomes unwilling to engage in relationships that are with people who hold different values, beliefs, or experiences because they are perceived as dangerous to one's self-identity (Erikson, 1968). Distantiation leads to the development of prejudice, which left unchallenged can perpetuate interpersonal relationships that are only one-sided, rather than fostering deep mutual growth, intimacy, and positive identity development (Lehnart, Neyer, & Eccles, 2010). Isolation can also led to depression and anxiety when emerging adults struggle to find fit as they develop new senses of self and expression (Azmitia et al., 2013). Some behavioral characteristics of intimacy are (a) firm sense of own identity; (b) tolerant and accepting of differences in others; (c) able to form close emotional bonds without losing own identity; (d) can be close with others but also comfortable alone; and (e) able to express caring feelings and empathy (Hamachek, 1990, p. 678). Conversely, isolation is associated with the following characteristics: (a) no established sense of identity; (b) no acceptance of differences in others; (c) hesitancy to form close relationships for fear of losing identity; (d) development of competitive relationships rather than cooperative ones; and (e) difficulty expressing empathy (Hamachek, 1990, p. 678).

Though Erikson's intimacy versus isolation stage was progressive for its time, it remained closely aligned with his psychoanalytic background, which emphasized the separateness of self from relational identity (Erikson, 1968; Horst, 1995; Tesch & Whitbourne, 1982). One major critique was attributed to his studies including predominately White males during a time when racism and sexism were more overt within our society, and it remains a limitation that other theories sought to expand (Horst, 1995; Tesch & Whitbourne, 1982). The following theory, relational cultural theory, is one counseling model that expands on social-emotional development to include identities beyond White males with an increased emphasis on relational identity development.

Relational-Cultural Counseling Theory and Young Adulthood: Addressing Issues of Difference

Relational cultural theory (RCT) is a feminist theory that counters the separateness of ideological self, presented in theories like Erikson's intimacy versus isolation. It emphasizes the role interpersonal relationships have in positive identity and social-emotional growth while exploring the influence of female gender identity (Deanow, 2011; Jordan, 2010; Miller & Stiver, 1997). Relational cultural theory has seven concepts (Jordan, 2010, p. 24):

1. People grow through and toward relationships throughout the life span.
2. Movement toward mutuality rather than separation characterizes growth.
3. Relationship differentiation and elaboration characterize growth.

4. Mutual empathy and mutual empowerment are at the core of growth-fostering relationships.
5. Authenticity is necessary for real engagement and full participation in growth-fostering relationship.
6. In growth-fostering relationships, all people contribute and grow or benefit. Development is not a one-way street.
7. One of the goals of development from a relational perspective is the development of increased relational competence and capacities over the lifespan.

According to Erikson (1968), one of the most important goals of early adulthood development is the formation of intimate relationships. Once achieved, these growth-fostering relationships produce Miller's (1986) five good things: a sense of zest; better understanding of authentic self, other, and the relationship; sense of worth; enhanced capacity to act; and an increased desire for more connection (Miller & Stiver, 1997). Similarly to Erikson's theory, RCT characterizes young adulthood as the authenticity–voicelessness stage and includes the development of intimate relationships where one can exercise the authentic self (Deanow, 2011). Authentic self is determined by relational experiences when one is either accepted by others, similar to finding one's niche social group, or is rejected and subsequently hides aspects of his or her identity from relationships (Jordan, 2010; Miller & Stiver, 1997). Counter to authenticity and akin to isolation, voicelessness is when a young adult runs the risk of rejection and losing one's sense of self through pressure to conform (Deanow, 2011). When young adults keep themselves from engaging in authenticity within relationships, they can become trapped in a cycle of voicelessness and isolation.

Authentic Self

Authenticity is the ability to form relationships where one can share one's true self with others, including personal values, beliefs, interests, and experiences (emotional, cognitive, and physical; Jordan, 2010; Miller & Stiver, 1997). Exercising authenticity in relationships becomes even more salient when discussing voices that are often silenced such as the voices and experiences of people of color (Jordan, 1997). Our lived experiences are influenced by how others interact with us based on our personal identities as well as how effectively we are able to find fit within social groups while still holding true to our self-identities (Azmitia et al., 2013; Ellemers, Spears, & Doosje, 2002). Along with acknowledging the influences our identities have in our interpersonal experiences, it is important to understand that identities can come with both privileges and marginalization. Layering of multiple identities is called intersectionality and is the reason for the existence of diverse experiences even amongst groups of individuals with similar cultural backgrounds. For example, two people can witness the same event but are affected in extremely different ways. Intersectionality is important to understand if empathy is to exist within a relationship, and empathy can become a determining factor as to whether relational connections or disconnections occur (Jordan, 2010). Empathy, as defined by RCT theorists, is the acceptance of differences and acknowledgment that one can never fully understand another's experience.

Like Ivan, identifying as a person of color influences the way people interact authentically within relationships, find their niche social group, and navigate challenges created by racism along with other oppressive ideologies that manifest in both external as well as intrinsic ways, at both institutional and interpersonal levels (Jaret & Reitzes, 2009; Kiang, Yip, & Fuligini, 2008; Neblett, Banks, Cooper, & Smalls-Glover, 2013). Daily harms such as micro aggressions, covered in chapter 4, can negatively affect self-concept, especially if the individual is struggling to find a social group to connect with where he or she feels accepted and understood. When experiences are silenced by microaggressions and other -isms, individuals are left to toil with the images of those interactions and determine whether it is good to take a risk, to be one's authentic self with others, or to remain silent to stay safe (Jordan, 1997).

BOX 14.1   CODE SWITCHING

One strategy of navigating -isms is code switching, when individuals adapt to different situations based on dominant cultural norms such as language, dress, or mannerisms. This is not a false representation of self or identity but rather a cultural tool used to buffer the effects and harm of discrimination. However, if an individual has to code switch too often, this can keep him or her from expressing himself or herself fully with others, which again can lead to silencing and isolation and can impact social-emotional development.

Discussion Questions

1. What are some aspects of identity that might precipitate the use of code switching in your community?
2. Identify strengths and assets that you might elicit from a client who shares that he or she code switches.

Relational Paradox

When authenticity and mutual empathy are absent or inhibited in relationships, isolation and disconnection occur (Jordan, 1997, 2010). Social-emotional issues concerning isolation and disconnection occur in the form of relational paradox (Jordan, 1997, 2010; Miller & Stiver, 1997). Consequently, relational paradox is a cyclical pattern of wanting to be in authentic, mutually empathetic relationships with others, but instead disconnecting from such relationships out of fear of rejection or harm. This disconnection often leads to increased isolation, poor self-concept, and social-emotional issues (Jordan, 2010; Miller & Stiver, 1997). This paradox can manifest in ways that relate to an oppressive environment in the form of intrinsic racism (Jordan, 2010). Similar to Erikson's identity crisis, relational paradox is not often easy to identify and can present itself in many behaviors, emotional states, and so forth. The cycle is broken through a combination of both the development of positive self-concept along with establishment of a truly genuine authentic relationship (Jordan, 2010). Individuals who develop their balance of how to take risks in being authentic in relation with others will, in turn, gain an increased awareness, self-acceptance, and willingness to form more relationships where they can be vulnerable and share their lived experiences with others (Jordan, 2010; Miller & Stiver, 1997). Ultimately, positive social-emotional development in relation to identity is a balance between appreciating one's authentic experience with the willingness to share and accept the experience of another.

Counseling Application: Power-Over Relationships

Social-emotional issues stemming from identity are not absent from counseling and can in fact supersede other issues that come about while transitioning into adulthood. Social-emotional issues are especially important to address in counseling relationships where differences in identity between counselor and client are significant (Jordan, 1997, 2010). Power-over dynamics are defined as relationships in which there is a power differential based on one person's privileged status (e.g., cultural, profession, social class, gender, age) compared with the oppression experienced by another (Miller & Stiver, 1997). The emphasis on power within relationships is due to the identities of those involved. For instance, a White, heterosexual, male counselor tends to have more power within a counseling relationship (professional status; dominant gender, sexual orientation, and race), especially if his client is a woman, non-White, or a sexual minority (Jordan, 1997).

Depending on past relational schemas, counseling can either disrupt the relational paradox that has kept the client in a cycle of isolation or perpetuate it by ignoring or discounting the client's authentic experience, which can be counter to the counselor's values, beliefs, and experiences. If the counselor's cultural awareness is low, he or she may unknowingly perpetuate relational schemas that silence clients (voicelessness). The safety that comes from counselors remaining in dominant ideologies (e.g., counselor as expert) can create inauthentic relationships where counselors decide not to be vulnerable with their clients by recognizing what they do not know or struggling to understand a client's experiences or worldviews. Therefore, it is imperative when incorporating development frameworks to include populations and identities that offer counternarratives to the dominant ideologies.

When Erikson originally created his developmental framework, defining young adulthood as intimacy versus isolation, his population of study was White male college students (Tesh & Whitbourne, 1982). Relational-cultural theory focuses strongly on the female experience and in-depth exploration of how intersectionality influences the developmental processes of individuals along with their abilities to moderate the effects of relational paradox. Social-emotional growth occurs mutually when both participants exhibit empathy and evolve as a result of the relationship (Jordan, 2010; Miller & Stiver, 1997). This action of engaging in mutual empathy is a core element of RCT and expands previous developmental models like Erikson's through exploring the actions of compromise and giving self to other.

Authentic Dialogue Within Counseling

From an RCT perspective, it is vital that culture be part of the session dialogue and that the young adult client understands that the counseling relationship is a space where authentic dialogue about differences can occur. This dialogue may include experiences with oppression and past relationships (Jordan, 2010). Negative oppressive experiences faced by the client can be a marker of how internalized the effects of those experiences have become in impacting his or her self-concept and social-emotional growth. Additionally, understanding how an individual's cultural identity has impacted his or her ability to form relationships can be a marker of disconnections that might occur during counseling. For example, if the counselor disconnects because he or she fails to believe, accept, or listen to the client's story, it can create emotional harm to the young adult client and impact his or her outside social relationships. Conversely, if the client disconnects from the counseling relationship, it becomes important that the counselor exercises a high level of acceptance and mutually work with the client to move through his or her disconnection of differences toward connection and growth.

This working-through phase can become the most meaningful aspect of the counseling relationship because it interrupts the cycle of isolation and demonstrates to the client that authentic relationships, even with differences in identity, are positive and meaningful. As the counselor engages in authentic dialogue and mutual empathy with a young adult client, the client begins to offer more of his or her authentic self within the relationship, becoming comfortable with autonomy and working toward ending the counseling relationship more willing to act in engaging authentic relationships with others. Ultimately, the client is interrupting the relational paradox (Jordan, 2010; Miller & Stiver, 1997).

Returning to Ivan's Case

Ivan is currently on the verge of experiencing relational paradox as a result of his struggle to form intimate relationships with others. Though he has a positive self-concept and identity, he is struggling to find fit within his old relationships while concurrently finding ways of balancing his new sense of self within his life as a student. Ivan is experiencing voicelessness and isolation as he struggles to find others who can accept his new interests and values, specifically his experience as a young adult Native American involved in the activist movement.

One technique that can be used to alleviate the power-over relational dynamic is sand tray therapy. Ivan would use the sand tray to tell his experience to the counselor while also physically representing his relational conflicts that are causing his social-emotional issues. The sessions may begin with talking about how the sand tray is a tool to help depict current experiences and work through differences that exist within his relationships. Through Ivan telling his story using

BOX 14.2 DIALOGUES ABOUT DIFFERENCE

Learning How to Engage in Dialogue About Cultural Differences

As counselors we often talk about the need for more culturally conscious dialogue with clients, but often absent are the tools to develop ways of directly addressing our differences within our counseling sessions. This activity is a way to practice those tools while also learning more about your peers. Find a partner, preferably a classmate you do not know much about, who will join you in this activity. Take turns and ask each other the following questions while listening to the responses. Note that for some these questions may be difficult to answer, so make sure to leave enough time for this activity as to not rush each other.

Discussion Questions

1. When did you first become aware of your race?
2. What do you think is important for others outside of your race to know about your race?
3. Hold someone you have worked with recently in your mind: If you were to guess, what question would they like to be asked?
4. What would happen if you asked? How would it change your working relationship?
5. What prevented you from asking? What needs to change in the relationship order for you to feel comfortable to ask?

Share your answers with your partner and provide feedback on ways to increase mutual empathy.

his own symbolism, he experiences power in the counseling relationship. The counselor gives him voice in defining the various figures in the sand tray, which represent his unique experiences. As he continues to use the sand tray, Ivan can talk more authentically about relational conflicts that keep him disconnected and isolated. Questions that might be asked are: What does this sand tray scene mean to you? What would you change about your experiences represented here? These types of questions allow for the opportunity to explore the possible disconnections Ivan is experiencing in his friendships. As Ivan becomes more open to sharing his experience and working through disconnections in the here and now, he can make progress toward connection and establishment of authentic relationships outside of counseling. Working through disconnections experienced in the counseling relationship is an important step toward forming authentic relationships and demonstrating mutual empathy.

From the counselor's perspective, change in RCT is mutual and the counselor must be open to being changed and affected by the relationship and hearing the client's authentic experience (Jordan, 1997, 2010; Miller & Stiver, 1997). This occurs particularly when we explore how our own differences in identity (e.g., gender, ethnicity) may affect Ivan's level of comfort to be emotionally vulnerable within the counseling relationship. We have experienced cases like Ivan's while using sand tray therapy with diverse clients active in protest movements in response to events in Ferguson, Missouri. Months later, we continue to be humbled by the impact of this work on us as counselors in relation to the growth and healing of our clients, who in many ways are similar to Ivan.

MORAL DEVELOPMENT IN EARLY ADULTHOOD

Laura's Story

Laura is a 22-year-old Caucasian female who was raised Catholic within a predominately Catholic geographical region. Her family attended church regularly, at least once a week, closely followed the liturgical calendar, celebrated the sacraments regularly, and prayed the Rosary daily. Laura comes to you in a state of existential crisis because she claims to have "lost her religion" and along with it her sense of purpose and meaning in life. Previously, Laura based her sense of morality on the teachings of her church, without applying these values to her own developing beliefs and philosophies. She is currently in a state of confusion and disorientation and looks to you to help her reset her "moral compass" as she is facing some big decisions regarding her social-emotional trajectory.

When young adults are faced with a conflict regarding values, how do they reason through what is right or wrong and fair and just? Furthermore, how do they respond to such existential questions as: Who do I want to be? How do I want to act? (Hallam et al., 2014, p. 1167). Young adults are transitioning into a phase of life where their worldviews, meaning systems, and conceptualizations of morality may be shifting and changing. Dunlop, Walker, and Matsuba (2013) declared young adulthood as a pivotal point regarding moral motivation. During this stage of development, young adults may experience increasing pressure toward committing themselves to social roles and lifestyles that advance agency (self-interest) or communion (interest of others). Similarly, the developmental stage of young adulthood may elicit either a hedonic (pleasure focused) or eudemonic (value focused) position regarding what living a good life means (Hallam et al., 2014). Two main theories of moral development have emerged, both being influenced by factors such as gender, sex, and culture. These theories are presented for the reader to critically ponder how this aspect of social and emotional development potentially impacts a client like Laura.

Kohlberg's Theory of the Development of Moral Reasoning During Young Adulthood

Lawrence Kohlberg, through his theory of moral reasoning (Kohlberg, 1976, 1984), purported that the highest forms of moral thinking are influenced by the forces associated with a person's sense of justice. Kohlberg's phases or levels of moral reasoning, discussed in chapter 3, were based on the importance that individuals placed on answering the following questions: How do I behave according to external forces put upon me? How do I behave according to my internal expectations related to what society expects of me? How do I behave based on my own philosophies and beliefs regarding society's expectations? The significance one places on responding to any of these three questions may determine from which level of moral reasoning he or she is functioning: preconventional, conventional, or postconventional. Kohlberg purported that the cognitive and intellectual advances brought forth through young adulthood will ultimately influence advances in moral thinking and development. Thus, moral reasoning may be elevated during this developmental transition (Kohlberg, 1976, 1984).

Kohlberg used the famous dilemma referred to as the Heinz dilemma to conceptualize an individual's development and corresponding levels of moral reasoning. The Heinz dilemma described a scenario that involved a man named Heinz who was faced with the decision of whether to steal a drug to save the life of his dying wife. Heinz did not have enough money to pay for the drug, and the druggist refused to lower the price. The conflict that Heinz struggled with was based on the values to which he must adhere, the preservation of life or the maintenance of property and law. Refer to Table 3.1, which outlines the three levels of moral reasoning, the six stages within the levels, and the corresponding expected response from Heinz, based on his stage of moral development.

Kohlberg's theory of moral development was well researched and supported and thus became quite influential in regard to understanding how an individual comes to develop moral reasoning (Çam, Çavdar, Seydoogullari, & Çok, 2012). However, Kohlberg's theory came under scrutiny by other social psychologists, as his original research was based solely on the morality of men. Carol Gilligan (1982) asserted that the distinctive perspectives from women's life experiences were not given voice through Kohlberg's work, thereby disputing his claims of having created a universal theory of moral reasoning (Woods, 1996).

BOX 14.3   CONSIDERING THE HEINZ DILEMMA

What would *you* do if you were Heinz? Allow the class to form small groups and discuss their individual answers to this question.

Discussion Questions

1. What reasoning motivates their answers?
2. Accordingly, what level and stage of moral reasoning are they in?
3. Come back together to discuss and reflect as a class.

Gilligan's Theory of Moral Development and Young Adulthood

Carol Gilligan's (1982, 1988) theory of moral reasoning asserted that higher levels of moral thinking are related to one's sense of care, contrasting Kohlberg's previous assertions that advanced moral reasoning was associated with one's sense of justice. Gilligan discovered that females spoke of morality in terms of their responsibilities to themselves and others rather than focusing on individual rights. Moral decisions were based on caring for others as well as fairness. Gilligan found that the female identity was influenced by connections to and relatedness with others. Therefore, the themes of separation and connection impacted various approaches to moral decision making. This proposed variance in perspective was thought to be influenced by the manner in which males and females are socialized within a gender-stereotyped society. Males are taught to value characteristics such as assertiveness, independence, achievement, and individuation, whereas females are encouraged to value sensitivity, connectedness, caring, and concern for others.

Gilligan's (1982, 1988) work highlighted another perspective from which young adults may base their moral reasoning. Young adults are traversing new moral terrain as they experience increased levels of freedom and autonomy while balancing moral decisions based on what is fair, as well as what upholds their sense of caring. Previous life stages may have not afforded them the opportunity to apply moral reasoning to this expanded worldview. As young adults transition from home and school settings to more independent living, new challenges emerge concerning relationships, intimacy, and responsibility (Hallam et al., 2014).

Refer to Table 3.3, which outlines Gilligan's three levels of moral reasoning, along with the significant transitions between levels 1 and 2 and 2 and 3. Level 1 is characterized by a focus on self, which alternates within level 2 to a focus on others. Finally, within level 3, a balanced focus on self and others is achieved. A developmental challenge for young adults may center on movement from level 2 to 3, wherein individuals experience a balanced focus on self and others, thereby enhancing their abilities to successfully address care-based relationships and roles (Dunlop et al., 2013; Gilligan, 1982, 1988; Lehnart et al., 2010).

Although Gilligan's (1982) research recognized the divergent patterns within the socialization of males and females, she clarified that "the different voice I describe is characterized not by gender but theme" (p. 2). In other words, Gilligan maintained that a person's approach to moral reasoning is based not on his or her biological sex or gender affiliation but rather an orientation toward the ethic of justice or the ethic of care. Gilligan believed that people choose one focus or concern on which to base their moral decision making. More recently, research has supported the idea that approaches to moral reasoning are much more adaptable, fluid, and contextual than previously thought (Juujärvi, Pesso, & Myyry, 2011; Skoe, 2010).

Ethic of Justice and Ethic of Care

Many studies have been conducted comparing both Kohlberg's and Gilligan's theories, with the majority of this research claiming that differences in moral reasoning based on sex were unsubstantiated (Woods, 1996). Further, Juujärvi et al. (2011) contended that the ethic of justice and the ethic of care are both used in moral decision making and that males and females may be conceptualized as developing within both sequences, rather than one or the other. "A large body of research has verified that both orientations are used in moral reasoning. The most important predictor of orientation usage is the content of a moral conflict, rather than gender: in particular, prosocial dilemmas concerning the needs of others tend to invoke care-based judgments among both genders" (Juujärvi et al., 2011, p. 419). For example, a young adult female who is pondering issues regarding human rights may draw from her moral ethic of justice and fairness. Further, a young adult male who is deciding how to proceed within an intimate relationship may refer to his ethic of care.

Çam et al. (2012) concurred that men and women both use the ethics of justice and care as bases for moral reasoning. In light of these more recent discoveries regarding Kohlberg's and Gilligan's work, perhaps a synthesis of both theories might be useful as a framework for approaching conceptualization of moral development in young adulthood. Further, as Wood (1996) purported, within modern society, there are many factors that influence an individual's approach to morality. Rather than solely focusing on sex differences, dialogue and research regarding moral development must integrate other cultural variables. The idea of culture being a significant influence on moral development was in fact one aspect upon which Kohlberg and Gilligan both agreed (Çam et al., 2012). Young adults are becoming aware of myriad cultural and contextual factors that may affect their moral development. As young adults expand their perspectives and awareness of these influences, they may discover what is truly of value to them (Hallam et al., 2014).

Bohlin and Hagekull (2009) broadly defined social-emotional development and adjustment as "the relation an individual establishes with respect to the environment, and as such it has positive and negative, social and emotional aspects" (p. 593). Positive aspects of social-emotional development are characterized by their contribution to successful functioning within an individual's social context and involve prosocial behaviors associated with eudemonic values. Eudemonic values include courage, openness, kindness, generosity, and fairness (Bohlin & Hagekull, 2009; Hallam et al., 2014). Meaning and purpose in life become paramount within the focus of an individual operating from a values based perspective. On the contrary, negative aspects of social-emotional development are characterized externally by aggression and antisocial behaviors, and internally by anxiety, depression, and psychosomatic complaints. These behaviors and conditions are associated with hedonic values (Hallam et al., 2014). Hedonism, in both Kohlberg's and Gilligan's theories, is associated with lower levels of moral development and reasoning. A eudemonic values system promotes interest and care for self, others, and the world and encompasses a sense of justice as well as concern for relationships. Through a eudemonic position, *both* ethics of justice and care may be honored and utilized within the young adult's orientation to prosocial values. This orientation would, in turn, elevate one to the higher levels of morality as defined by Kohlberg and Gilligan.

Dunlop and colleagues (2013) asserted that young adulthood is the prime period of time for individuals to determine their moral motivations, and they discussed three paths upon which young adults must choose to progress in regard to developmental shifts in morality. One path indicates an inclination toward agency and personal interest, a lifestyle that reflects hedonistic values. The second path leads to communion, focused on the interests of others and reflective of eudemonic values. These first two paths could be compared to levels 1 and 2 of Gilligan's model of moral reasoning, yet there is a third path that could provide a synthesis of the first two, thereby promoting an individual to level 3. "Individuals may feel as though they have to decide between lifestyles that advance the self and lifestyles that advance others, failing to yet grasp the possibility of integrating these orientations" (Dunlop et al., 2013, p. 287). Moreover, a young adult may achieve the most advanced stage of morality by choosing a lifestyle that promotes personal interest through attending to the interests of others and/or the world.

Further, Hallam et al. (2014) found that behavior associated with eudemonic values in late adolescence increased emotional competence in young adulthood. In turn, emotional competence in young adulthood decreased symptoms of anxiety and depression during this developmental stage. Thus, the transition regarding social-emotional development and adjustment in young adulthood is significantly influenced by an individual's orientation to morality (Bohlin & Hagekull, 2009; Dunlop et al., 2013; & Hallam et al., 2014). The way young adults develop socially and emotionally is intricately tied to their moral motivation. The connection between morality, social-emotional adjustment, and psychopathology provides significant implications for counselors who are working to facilitate optimal social-emotional development within their clients.

Counseling Application: Moral Development in Early Adulthood

Counselors work to meet the developmental needs of their clients through measures associated with prevention as well as intervention. Counselors can encourage young persons to engage in prosocial activities that involve experiential and service learning (Hallam et al., 2014; Skoe, 2010) and facilitate self-reflection (Juujärvi et al., 2011). Engagement though these experiences can serve as preventative measures prior to young adulthood but also as forms of intervention during young adulthood.

Skoe (2010) discussed the interconnection of empathy with moral development and asserted that skills related to empathy building and perspective taking should be taught in elementary schools. The association with eudemonic values from an early age would be impactful to positive moral development. School-based and higher education curricula should be focused on educating the whole person, including the sociomoral and emotional aspects (Skoe, 2010).

BOX 14.4   EMPATHY IN ELEMENTARY SCHOOL

Ask students to pair up to discuss how they would approach teaching empathy to elementary school students.

Discussion Questions

1. How would they engage students in learning about and experiencing this crucial developmental aspect?
2. What activities might you use to facilitate this learning?

Allow students to share their ideas with the rest of the class.

Additionally, Hallam et al. (2014) purported that moral development may be facilitated through "opportunities to explore personal meaning and clarify existential values" (p. 1173). Such opportunities can take place through service learning and other types of experience-based learning, whereupon individuals may discover a meaningful connection to others (Skoe, 2010). Examples of prosocial involvement in young adulthood include recycling, fundraising, advocating for special needs within special populations, visiting the elderly, and volunteering for a cause of interest. These experiences can take place within both local and global contexts (i.e., organizing and participating in community events or working in developing countries; Hallam et al., 2014). In conjunction with self-exploration and opportunities geared toward facilitation of meaning and values, Juujärvi et al. (2011) discussed the importance of self-reflection and understanding ethical reasoning through relationships to facilitate a balance of fulfilling the needs of self, others, and the world.

Through connecting and engaging meaningfully with their environments, young adults may develop an intrinsic source of self-determination, which has been connected with emotional resilience and positive social adjustment (Hallam et al., 2014). Eudemonic values, when cultivated in early childhood, can influence behaviors that facilitate this connection and engagement. Both Kohlberg's and Gilligan's theories align with the idea that the eudemonic values of courage, openness, kindness, generosity, and fairness are associated with the highest levels of moral reasoning. Counselors serve their clients well when they find ways to preventively address the social-emotional aspects of moral development, as well as design interventions based on facilitating growth and development within this domain.

Returning to Laura's Case

With Laura, a counselor could begin assisting her in resetting her moral compass by developing insight regarding her moral development. It would be important to examine how Laura's moral development had thus far been influenced by cultural and societal expectations related to her gender, sex, and religion. What religious and societal assumptions had she previously been taking for granted that might be causing her current dissonance related to her morality? Through this exploration, Laura could come to understand her values and beliefs in light of her current stage of moral development.

Laura could be conceptualized as moving from Kohlberg's conventional to postconventional levels of moral reasoning. Her adherence to following the rules established by her Catholic upbringing is wavering, and she is attempting to align herself with standards that she sets for herself, based on her personal belief systems, philosophies, and experiences in life. According to Gilligan's model, Laura may also be transitioning to level 3, as indicated by her awareness of responsibility to both self and others. She is no longer solely considering her parents' desires regarding her involvement with the church but is taking into account her own need to question her worldview and values. Laura's counselor can pose crucial existential questions to explore the depiction of Laura's intrinsic vision of herself. Discussing how this aligns with society's (and her family's) expectations may be helpful toward clarifying and differentiating her emerging moral trajectory versus these former expectations to which she had adhered. Laura could benefit from engaging directly in activities and interactions surrounding aspects of life that hold meaning for her. A counselor might encourage her to explore what living a purposeful life means to her in light of her developmental transition. Additionally, a focus on career goals and development, as discussed in the following sections, could prove beneficial toward Laura's continued social-emotional development.

CAREER DEVELOPMENT IN EARLY ADULTHOOD

Adelina's Story

Adelina is a 19-year-old Latina first-generation college student living away from home for the first time on a residential campus. She is referred to her academic counselor shortly after returning from her hometown in Texas during the holiday break. "College just might not be for me," she reports with hesitation. "I am studying to be a clinical psychologist someday and will have many more years away from home for school and then am unlikely to get that kind of work in my hometown." With further probing by the counselor she shares, "It has only been 5 months since I left for college, and already I feel so different from my friends who stayed at home." Adelina spent much of her high school career and first semester diligently deciding that becoming a clinical psychologist is her passion, yet now she has doubts about whether or not it fits her self-concept.

Young adults have little choice in regard to career decision making; they must make such decisions as they transition from high school to the world of work or postsecondary training and education. In fact, many youth feel as though they have been directed on a career path throughout primary and secondary school to arrive at high school graduation carrying the weight of expectations (e.g., family, peers, and community) with little usable knowledge about themselves as they might fit into the world of work.

Even if a young adult has a clear career identity it may, as in the case of Adelina, conflict with previous developmental progress. What does it mean to leave one's hometown, including family, friends, and institutions, for work or postsecondary education? How will career choices (i.e., military, college) interact with one's community of origin, particularly if they fall outside the scope of that community? Will there be unintended consequences such as ridicule, isolation, or simply growing apart if the person leaves or chooses a certain job? For young adults, few things are more novel yet personal than making autonomous career choices for the first time.

Career development can be defined as "the lifelong psychological and behavioral processes as well as contextual influences shaping one's career over the lifespan." As such, career development involves the "person's creation of a career pattern, decision-making style, integration of life roles, values expression, and life-role self-concepts" (Niles & Harris-Bowlsbey, 2009, p. 12). Within a developmental context, this opens the doors for counseling practitioners to focus on age appropriate issues of culture (e.g., power, gender, social class; Gottfredson, 2005), personality, and career fit (Holland, 1997) and relationship within a complex matrix of life positions and tasks (e.g., worker, homemaker, community member; Super, 1990).

Although there are various theoretical approaches to career development over the lifespan, there are two predominant theories that help describe the intricate process for all developmental stages of life, but particularly the time spanning late adolescence and early adulthood. These are presented in chronological order as Super's lifespan, life space career theory, and Gottredson's theory of circumscription and compromise.

Super's Life Span, Life Space Career Theory and Young Adulthood

During the early stage of theory development, Super (1969) described it as a differential-developmental-social-phenomenological approach, but today it is largely viewed as the preeminent developmental theoretical approach to career counseling. Before we begin to focus on the specific developmental tasks of this age range, it is important to understand the essence of Super's theory. This is best accomplished by understanding 7 of his 14 core assumptions that most aptly apply to this age group (Super, 1990, p. 206):

1. People differ in their abilities and personalities, needs, values, interests, traits, and self-concepts.
2. People are qualified, by virtue of these characteristics, each for a number of occupations.

3. Vocational preferences and competencies, the situations in which people live and work, and, hence, their self-concepts change with time and experience.
4. Success in coping with the demands of the environment and of the organism in that context at any given life career stage depends on the readiness of the individual to cope with these demands.
5. The process of career development is essentially that of developing and implementing occupational self-concepts.
6. The degree of satisfaction people attain from work is proportional to the degree to which they have been able to implement their self-concepts.
7. Work and occupation provide a focus for personality organization for most men and women, although for some persons this focus is peripheral, incidental, or even nonexistent.

To capture the essence of these seven tenets of Super's work, one might describe the importance of viewing a young adult as unique in his or her career worldview and thus career tasks and goals (#1). Within this uniqueness, a person will find within the complex world of work that there are multiple good yet no perfect choices (#2). In fact, if a perfect choice were to exist, this perfect fit would eventually expire as career development, like human development, is adaptive and thus changes as needs and circumstances do over time (#3). For persons within the late adolescence and early adulthood stages of development, it is important to assess their decision-making skill development and coping mechanisms during the course of career counseling.

A study of genetics and biology suggests that the career decision-making point attributed to this time in the human lifespan (e.g., college major choice, work field) is either arbitrary or socially constructed (#4). This means that counselors must assess personal development and plan interventions accordingly to best benefit their clients' needs. Because of social pressure to make choices that students may be unprepared for, it is also important to not allow young adults to proffer a choice without thorough introspection. This may result in regrettable choices later in one's development because the choice was made without being rooted in "true," informed choice (#5).

Career choices are very personal decisions that represent to the world one's private ideas of self (i.e., self identity), fit in the social milieu (i.e., interests in others, expectations of status), and moral perspective (i.e., ethics behind career choices or life role activities). Particular to self-identity, career choices are very personal because they represent our current understanding of self and offer predictions of who we wish to become in the future. In other words, our career choices are often conscious and unconscious projections of our self-concept and therefore are not to be taken lightly, lest we end up dissatisfied later in life (#6). Finally, career is no longer considered a *point-in-time* choice but an ongoing developmental process spanning the birth through death lifespan while creating one's preferred lifestyle within contextual constraints such as social class and the labor market (#7).

It is within this complex tableau that young adults such as Adelina present for counseling regarding early adult career issues. Digging deeper into Super's theory provides several key concepts that will aid counselors to appropriately consider early adult developmental in a career specific context.

Self-Concept

The inclusion of ideas about self-concept is among Super's most important contributions to career counseling theory. Similar to Erikson's self-identity, self-concept is defined as, "a picture of the self in some role, situation, or position, performing some set of functions, or in some web of relationships" (Super, 1963, p. 18). Self-concept describes both subjective and objective phenomena. Subjectively, people are empowered to understand their career lives via the career stories they construct as they strive to make meaning of their lives. This includes personal ideas about work, leisure, family, and community. Objectively, one has the power of comparison to others as an aide to self-understanding while assessing abilities and capacities. We see this aspect today in the various approaches to assessment ubiquitously found in educational settings (e.g., I am in the 70th percentile of those who took the SAT).

Self-concept is essential to understanding clients through the lens of Super's lifespan, life space theory. Self-concept can be viewed as a common thread that pulls throughout each life stage and all developmental tasks. As a common reference point, attention to the self-concept aids counselors in planning interventions, monitoring progress, and evaluating the clarity of career decisions. Because it incorporates both subjective and objective phenomena, practitioners may find it seamless to incorporate it into their conceptualization of clients to plan career counseling interventions.

Super's Life Span

Like most developmental theories, Super's lifespan, life space theory outlines stages by which one's individual journey unfolds over time. When looking at career development, there is much more fidelity to the developmental tasks of each stage earlier in life than later when one's trajectory becomes much less uniform, shaped more by one's adapting to individual and contextual circumstances than a strict developmental progression of task completion. While persons in late adolescence and young adulthood typically span only two of Super's five stages, each is depicted in Table 14.1 to provide complete context.

It is most likely that early adults will be working through the exploration stage for the first time in their lives. This stage is marked by the tasks of crystallizing, specifying, and implementing occupational choices. Crystallizing describes the process by which people begin to focus on gathering more information about the preferences developed in the growth stage. Once enough information is gathered to specify occupational preferences (e.g., I want to work in the construction field), people will begin to make choices ranging from ones that include more information gathering (e.g., applying for an internship) to direct entry into an occupation (e.g., taking a job as an apprentice at a construction company). The exploration stage is often very dynamic for a person, as it is

Table 14.1 Super's Five Stages	
Stage	**Description**
Growth	Early in life, children progress through the growth substages of fantasy, interest, and capacity to prepare themselves for future stages.
Exploration	The process of exploration occurs each time a person wishes to gather information to determine a new career direction.
Establishment	A person decides that his or her chosen career matches his or her self-concept, and thus he or she wishes to further establish himself or herself in this career.
Maintenance	This active stage is designed to stave off career stagnation by choosing to update skills or innovate within a chosen career.
Disengagement	All good things, including careers, must come to an end. This may mean retirement or the development of a second or even third career.

filled with exploration of the unknown, new information, difficult decisions, and consequences for choices made.

Life Space

Super (1980) suggested that a career is characterized by the total constellation of life roles played out over the course of a lifetime. He identified four basic theaters in which we play nine major life roles. More specifically, he proposed that we play the roles of (1) son or daughter, (2) student, (3) leisurite, (4), citizen, (5) worker, (6) spouse or partner, (7) homemaker, (8) parent, and (9) pensioner within (1) home, (2) school, (3) the workplace, and (4) our community.

BOX 14.5 PIE OF LIFE

Take a piece of paper and draw a circle. List the life roles that you currently play and represent each in your life role pie chart such that the size of each life role slice represents the salience of that role in your life at this time. Share your life space pie with a partner.

Discussion Questions

1. How would you describe the current distribution of your life roles? Are there any in conflicts with one another?
2. Discuss what your life role pie looked like in early adulthood (if you are currently not in this stage) or how you expect this to change in middle adulthood (if you are currently a young adult).

Although this characterization of life space seems simple on the surface, it is important to note that it provides a more expansive, holistic approach to conceptualizing work than any career theory that had come before it. When work had only been conceptualized as that of paid labor or employment, it meant that many meaningful contributors to our society had been left behind when honoring the contribution of effort to society; an example apropos for the period when Super first proposed this theory is the homemaker parent who chooses to raise a child with no paid compensation.

To this end, it is equally important to note that although many or most life roles are present throughout the lifespan, each differs in its salience or magnitude at any given stage of development or life circumstances. For example, one's life space might be consumed with the role of worker until the point of a workplace accident that requires significant recovery time and prohibits engagement in work. If the role of worker inevitably contracts during this recovery time, other life roles (e.g., if on disability, that of pensioner in addition to parent, citizen, or any other role) would magnify and come to the fore. Coping with this change can be very difficult, but the ideas of life roles, life space, and lifestyle all help describe one's situation within a context of work.

Gottfredson's Theory of Circumscription and Compromise: A Rejoinder to Super and Early Adulthood

As stated previously in this chapter, the ontology of many early developmental theories found them held hostage by the time in which they were developed. Most often, this resulted in the perpetuation of White male norms at the expense of historically marginalized groups such as women and persons of color. Just as relational cultural theory was presented as a counterweight to this phenomenon in Erikson's theory and Gilligan was Kohlberg's, we present Linda Gottfredson's (2005) theory of circumscription and compromise to compensate the privileges inherent in Super's theory.

Like Super, Gottfredson (2005) believed that each person has a developmental trajectory that unfolds over time and that personal interest plays a key role in determining one's ultimate career path. Instead of seeing this trajectory being determined by human growth and flourishing, Gottfredson instead focused on the ways socialization and culture limit or eliminate career choices for individuals. Like self-concept, Gottfredson did identify a construct similar to self-identity but her assumption was that this social identity is formed as one interacts within four prime social domains: power, masculine–feminine expectations, personal interest, and prestige.

Early in life, the concept of power is learned as children come to understand that large, powerful adults work, whereas children (and others without power) do not. This basic understanding of power lays a foundation over the early lifespan to include an understanding of gender while in elementary school (e.g., the types of jobs men do versus those that women do), an understanding of personal interest and aptitude in middle school, and an understanding of social prestige via workplace participation (e.g., my mother is a factory worker, and yours is a doctor) that is developed during adolescence. This social learning occurs before the early adulthood stage of development, and it has framed the *zone of acceptable occupational choices* of those making career decisions during this stage (Gottfredson, 1981).

The creation of acceptable occupational choices is unique to each individual, derived from social learning experiences through two processes: circumscription and compromise. Circumscription occurs during developmental experiences in each of the four social domains. Early ideas about power and work are reinforced by socially and culturally bound messages about gender and work. This is often seen as the reason for gender and race/ethnicity gaps in the science, technology, engineering, and mathematics (STEM) fields (Charleston, George, Jackson, Berhanu, & Amechi, 2014; Smeding 2012; Szelenyi, Denson, & Kurotsuchi Inkelas, 2013). This has been found in many studies including a qualitative study about the experiences of African American women in the computing science field (Charleston et al., 2014). Several of the participants struggled with the stereotypes inflicted because of their intersectionality as Black woman along with feelings of isolation and subordination (Charleston et al., 2014). Personal interest is then influenced by these understanding of power and gender as they apply to the workplace. Finally, early adolescence brings increased social interest and perspectives on occupational prestige, particularly within the context of one's family of origin. All these factors provide the context for an ongoing process of compromise as young people and adults strive to place themselves into the optimal position within the world of work, as defined by the zone of acceptable occupational choices (Gottfredson, 2005).

BOX 14.6 SOCIAL STATUS AND THE GOOD LIFE

Take 5 minutes and consider how you would define a *good life* for yourself. Jot down some notes, and share this definition with a partner.

Discussion Questions

1. Describe your socioeconomic status (SES) or social class or origin (when you were in middle school).
2. Describe your definition of a *good life* to your partner.
3. How do you think your SES or social class of origin impacted your current definition of a *good life*?

An understanding of the forces that determine one's occupational preferences allows a counselor working with a client in early adulthood to explore the genesis of occupational preferences, push for a more authentic understanding of self, choose a career outside one's *zone*, and possibly find a greater sense of purpose and happiness through one's career. In our experience, it is difficult to find someone who does not know someone between the ages of 20–40 years who has not reset their career trajectory and found a second, more meaningful career after a significant life event, period of deep reflection, or counseling.

Counseling Application for Young Adulthood

Counselors often find themselves balancing clients' career concerns with issues of wellness, relationships, and mental health. The interplay between various facets of the whole client as he or she navigates away from the primary loyalties of his or her parents, what Erikson (1968) called the normative developmental crisis, is most dynamic during late adolescence and early adulthood. This crisis is often embedded in the intersectionality of social-emotional developmental tasks including those pertaining relational, moral, and career development. One of the great strengths of developmental theories is that they aid the counselor in identifying the stage and tasks at hand for a client. This allows the counselor to name what the client is experiencing in consistent ways.

Normalizing the narrative is described as such: "It is normal for clients to have problems, and it is normal to have difficult situations. Your task [as counselor] is to point out to clients that while we all have issues, our concerns are solvable" (Ivey, & Zalaquett, 2010, p. 418). Although this technique is often described as being focused on the fact that we all share concerns, normalizing can be focused more accurately when operating within a developmental framework such as that of Super or Gottfredson. In other words, identifying the developmental stage and tasks at hand allows the counselor to assist the client in developing perspective about what is happening in his or her life, how it is happening within the context of his or her human development, and what to expect in the future as the client resolves the current crisis, task, or conflict. How this unfolds is largely up to the counselor's theoretical orientation. For example, this process can be conceptualized as psychoeducation, cognitive schema work, mapping out a developmental journey, writing a future narrative, or hope building. The effective counselor uses knowledge of developmental theory and his or her theoretical orientation to conceptualize clients' presenting concerns and select appropriate counseling interventions.

Returning to Adelina's Case

Adelina presents in a normative developmental crisis as her career decisions to date (i.e., to move away from home, attend college, and aspire to be a clinical psychologist) have created a chasm between her primary loyalties (e.g., to family, friends, and community). The dissonance, or inconsistency between two held beliefs or experiences, clashes with the self-concept she had developed during earlier developmental stages. She seems to feel hopeless in her attempts to reconcile her preconceived self-concept with the impact her career decisions are making on her long-standing relationships. Given the complexity of human development and the specific cultural context (i.e., first generation college student, Latina, female), it is not incumbent on the counselor to educate or advise Adelina. Instead, it is the role of the counselor to help Adelina understand her experience in context and make choices she thinks best suits her needs (i.e., empowerment).

The counselor must establish a working alliance by listening to Adelina's story for the purpose of understanding from her perspective. What questions or prompts might you use as you attempt to understand Adelina's crisis through her eyes?

As you think about Adelina's career development, which career theory might inform your practice? Super would suggest that she is struggling in the transition from the exploration to the establishment stage. More importantly, Adelina is questioning her self-concept as she reconfigures the salience, or degree of importance, in her life roles of daughter, friend, and citizen. A counselor might describe this role conflict and self-concept dissonance as a normal developmental task for someone in Adelina's position (i.e., first-generation college student) before using his or her preferred theoretical orientation to help (e.g., psychoeducational and resource sharing, bibliotherapy, cognitive restructuring). Using a counseling approach with which the counselor is comfortable allows for more effective monitoring and addressing of other types of issues that might arise as these career concerns are addressed.

In summary, career-focused counseling is simply counseling within a specific array of presenting problems. Career concerns will at times be just as salient to a client as other concerns such as familial relationships, peer group interactions, and personal perception and worth. The genesis of the problem that might bring a client to counseling can often be conceptualized within a developmental framework such as career theory to more effectively understand and address concerns.

KEY COUNSELING POINTERS FOR SOCIAL-EMOTIONAL DEVELOPMENT DURING EARLY ADULTHOOD

Developmental theory is a useful guidebook of human development specific to each theory. This said, it is a loose approximation of normal developmental tasks and stages within which there is much variation; therefore, an effective counselor must adequately connect with (working alliance) and thoroughly assess each client's developmental journey before drawing conclusions.

An understanding of developmental theory allows a professional counselor to conceptualize client problems, behaviors, and tasks within the context of normal human development, thus facilitating the effective technique of normalizing client concerns.

When considering client concerns from a developmental perspective, it is important to be informed about the ontology of the theory so that diverse groups are fully considered in the therapeutic process. For example, Super's life span theory has lacked inclusion of women and people of color, a limitation that was answered by Gottfredson's circumscription and compromise theory, which includes an ontological perspective with a focus on how social and cultural factors influence the development of self-concept.

As counselors, we must develop a high level of empathy to demonstrate belief and acceptance of the different lived experiences of clients. This includes admitting what we do not know or understand and a willingness to engage in authentic dialogue with clients about their cultural differences.

While thinking about client concerns, it is important to consider all aspects of social-emotional development and that identity, relational, moral, and career development may intertwine for the client because of their deep connection to one another.

SUMMARY

Young adulthood approximately spans the ages 20–40 years. Though developmental theorists like Erikson, Kolhberg, Gilligan, Super, and Gottfredson came from different realms of ontological thought, they all find fit within the social-emotional development of young adults and contribute to counseling practice with this population. By tuning in to normal developmental issues pertinent to young adulthood, counselors often become important contributors to an individual's success in navigating this phase in the lifespan. The anchor questions in this chapter that help guide young adults, as well as counselors, in exploring the existential questions are who am I, what do I value, and what do I aspire to become?

Erikson taught us that, even when we understand who we are, the juxtaposition of individual autonomy, developmental growth, and evolving relationships continues to present challenges. Kolhberg and Gilligan emphasized the role that ethics of justice and care play as we develop moral reasoning capacity, a capacity that defines our ability to adapt to changes that cause us to question our identities or impedes the development of empathy toward others. Super and Gottfredson advocate for the role career development and choice play as we project our self, relational, and moral understanding into the wider world of work.

We can conclude that young adulthood social-emotional development overlaps through these three anchors in its own streamline when (a) we have a sense of who we are we desire to share our experience with others and need relationships that confirm our existence; (b) we encounter experiences that counter our own and can challenge our values, challenge us to expand our perspectives, and at times cause us to question our experiences; and (c) we establish a flexibility that leads to accepting the diversity of values and experiences while balancing new relationships. The progression through these anchors is not linear and can occur in any sequence or even simultaneously. As young adults, individuals gain freedom from the chains of a structured adolescent world. They now face a vast world that brings with it tremendous challenges to self along with the beautiful opportunity to constantly evolve, contribute to the lives of others, and make meaning out the unknown future. Therefore, we have a responsibility and privilege as counselors to walk with young adults on their journeys with empathy and authenticity.

USEFUL ASSESSMENTS FOR YOUNG ADULTS

Career Maturity Inventory
http://www.vocopher.com
Career Style Interview
http://www.vocopher.com
Defining Issues Test (DIT)
http://ethicaldevelopment.ua.edu

USEFUL WEBSITES

TED Talk by Niveen Rizkalla: "Intimacy Vs. Isolation"
http://youtu.be/ydTXf9zp7XE
TED Talk by Brene Brown: "Getting Intimate With Intimacy"
http://youtu.be/_UoMXF73j0c
Brene Brown: "Empathy Vs. Sympathy"
http://youtu.be/1Evwgu369Jw
Heinz's Dilemma Animated Description
https://www.youtube.com/watch?v=5czp9S4u26M
Donald Super's Theory Handout
http://www.careers.govt.nz/fileadmin/docs/career_theory_model_super.pdf
Vocopher Career Collaboratory for Counselors and Psychologists
http://vocopher.com/

REFERENCES

Azmitia, M., Syed, M., & Radmacher, K. (2013). Finding your niche: Identity and emotional support in emerging adults' adjustment to the transition to college. *Journal of Research on Adolescence*, *23*(4), 744–761. doi:10.1111/jora.12037

Bohlin, G., & Hagekull, B. (2009). Socio-emotional development: From infancy to young adulthood. *Scandinavian Journal of Psychology*, *50*(6), 592–601. doi:10.1111/j.1467-9450.2009.00787.x

Burt, K. B., & Paysnick, A. A. (2014). Identity, stress, and behavioral and emotional problems in undergraduates: Evidence for interaction effects. *Journal of College Student Development*, *55*(4), 368–384. doi:10.1353/csd.2014.0036

Çam, Z., Çavdar, D., Seydoogullari, S., & Çok, F. (2012). Classical and contemporary approaches for moral development. *Educational Sciences: Theory & Practice*, *12*, 1222–1225.

Charleston, L. J., George, P. L., Jackson, J. F. L., Berhanu, J., & Amechi, M. H., (2014). Navigating underrepresented STEM spaces: Experiences of Black women in U.S. computing science higher education programs who actualize success. *Journal of Diversity in Higher Education*, *7*(3), 166–176. doi:10.1037/a003662

Deanow, C. G. (2011). Relational development through the life cycle: Capacities, opportunities, challenges, and obstacles. *Affilia*, *26*, 125–138. doi:10.1177/0886109911405485

Dunlop, W. L., Walker, L. J., & Matsuba, M. (2013). The development of moral motivation across the adult lifespan. *European Journal of Developmental Psychology*, *10*(2), 285–300. doi:10.1080/17405629.2012.746205

Ellemers, N., Spears, R., & Doosje, B. (2002). Self and social identity. *Annual Review of Psychology*, *53*, 161.

Erikson, E. (1968). *Identity youth and crisis*. New York, NY: W.W. Norton.

Gilligan, C. (1982). *In a different voice: Psychological theory and women's development*. Cambridge, MA: Harvard University Press.

Gilligan, C. (1988). Adolescent development reconsidered. In C. Gilligan, J. V., Ward, J. M. Taylor, & B. Bardige (Eds.), *Mapping the moral domain*. Cambridge, MA: Harvard University Press.

Gottfredson, L. S. (2005). Using Gottfredson's theory of circumscription and compromise in career guidance and counseling. In Brown, S. D., Lent, R. W. (Eds.), *Career development and counseling: Putting theory and research to work*, (pp. 71–100). Hoboken, NJ: Wiley.

Hallam, W., Olsson, C., O'Connor, M., Hawkins, M., Toumbourou, J., Bowes, G., & Sanson, A. (2014). Association between adolescent eudaimonic behaviours and emotional competence in young adulthood. *Journal of Happiness Studies*, *15*(5), 1165–1177. doi:10.1007/s10902–013–9469–0

Hamachek, D. (1990). Evaluating self-concept and ego status in erikson's last three psychosocial stages. *Journal of Counseling & Development*, *68*(6), 677–683. doi:10.1002/j.1556-6676.1990.tb01436.x

Hoare, C. H. (2002). *Erikson on development in adulthood: New insights from the unpublished papers*. New York, NY: Oxford University Press.

Holland, J. L. (1997). *Making vocational choices: A theory of vocational personalities and work environments*. Lutz, FL: Psychological Assessment Resources.

Horst, E. A. (1995). Reexamining gender issues in Erikson's stages of identity and intimacy. *Journal of Counseling and Development*, *73*, 271.

Ivey, A. E., & Zalaquett, C. P. (2010). Psychotherapy as liberation: Multicultural counseling and psychotherapy (MCT) contributions to the promotion of psychological emancipation. *Diversity in Mind and in Action*, *3*, 181–199.

Jaret, C., & Reitzes, D. C. (2009). Currents in a stream: College student identities and ethnic identities and their relationship with self-esteem, efficacy, and grade point average in an urban university. *Social Science Quarterly*, *90*(2), 345–367. doi:10.1111/j.1540-6237.2009.00621.x

Jordan, J. V. (Ed.). (1997). *Women's growth in diversity: More writings from the Stone Center*. New York, NY: Guilford.

Jordan, J. V. (Ed.). (2010). *Theories of psychotherapy series: Relational-cultural therapy*. Washington, DC: American Psychological Association.

Juujärvi, S., Pesso, K., & Myyry, L. (2011). Care-based ethical reasoning among first- year nursing and social services students. *Journal of Advanced Nursing*, *67*(2), 418–427. doi:10.1111/j.1365-2648.2010.05461.x

Kiang, L., Yip, T., & Fuligni, A. J. (2008). Multiple social identities and adjustment in young adults from ethnically diverse backgrounds. *Journal of Research on Adolescence*, *18*(4), 643–670. doi:10.1111/j.1532-7795.2008.00575.x

Kohlberg, L. (1976). Moral stages and moralization: The cognitive developmental approach. In T. Lickona (Ed.), *Moral development and behavior: Theory, research, and social issues* (pp. 31–53). New York, NY: Holt, Rinehart & Winston.

Kohlberg, L. (1984). *The psychology of moral development*. New York, NY: Harper & Row.

Lehnart, J., Neyer, F. J., & Eccles, J. (2010). Long-term effects of social investment: The case of partnering in young adulthood. *Journal of Personality*, *78*(2), 639–670. doi:10.1111/j.1467-6494.2010.00629

Miller, J. B. (1986). *Towards a new psychology of women*. Boston, MA: Beacon.

Miller, J. B., & Stiver, I. (1997). *The healing connection: How women form relationships in therapy and in life*. Boston, MA: Beacon.

Neblett, E. R., Banks, K., Cooper, S. M., & Smalls-Glover, C. (2013). Racial identity mediates the association between ethnic-racial socialization and depressive symptoms. *Cultural Diversity And Ethnic Minority Psychology*, *19*(2), 200–207. doi:10.1037/a0032205

Niles, S. G., & Harris-Bowlsbey, J. (2009). *Career development and diverse populations*. Upper Saddle River, NJ: Pearson.

Seiffe-Krenke, I. (2006). Leaving home or still in the nest? Parent-child relationships and psychological health as predictors of different leaving home patterns. *Developmental Psychology*, *42*(5), 864–876. doi: 10.1037/0012-1649.42.5.864

Skoe, E. A. (2010). The relationship between empathy-related constructs and care-based moral development in young adulthood. *Journal of Moral Education*, *39*(2), 191–211. doi:10.1080/03057241003754930

Smeding, A. (2012). Women in science, technology, engineering, and mathematics (STEM): An investigation of their implicit gender stereotypes and stereotypes' connectedness to math performance. *Sex Roles*, *67*(11–12), 617–629. doi: 10.1007/s11199-012-0209-4

Super, D. E. (1963). *Career development: Self-concept theory.* (pp. 1–32) New York, NY: College Entrance Examination Board.

Super, D. E. (1969). Vocational development theory: Persons, positions, and processes. *Counseling Psychologist*, *1*(1), 2–9.

Super, D. E. (1980). A life-span, life-space approach to career development. *Journal of Vocational Behavior*, *16*(3), 282–298.

Super, D. E. (1990). *A life-span, life-space approach to career development*. San Francisco, CA: Jossey-Bass.

Szelenyi, K., Denson, N., & Kurotsuchi Inkelas, K. (2013). Women in STEM majors and professional outcome expectations: The role of living-learning programs and other college environments. *Research in Higher Education*, *54*(8), 851–873. doi: 10.1007/s11162-013-9299-2

Tesch, S. A., & Whitbourne, S. K. (1982). Intimacy and identity status in young adults. *Journal of Personality and Social Psychology*, *43*(5), 1041–1051. doi: 10.1037//0022-3514.43.5.1041

Woods, C. P. (1996). Gender differences in moral development and acquisition: A review of Kohlberg's and Gilligan's models of justice and care. *Social Behavior & Personality: An International Journal*, *24*(4), 375.

PART 7

Middle Adulthood

Middle Adulthood: Physical and Cognitive Development

Amy E. Ford and Leif A. Ford

AMELIA

Amelia is an African American who identifies as a lesbian woman. She grew up in a very poor neighborhood in Washington, D.C. As the oldest child of seven, she cared for her siblings while her parents worked. Amelia is very smart and excelled in school. She received a full scholarship to college, completed her baccalaureate degree, and then earned an MBA. She has had a very successful career in finance, managing a large, multimillion-dollar firm. Amelia has had a few relationships, but she has never found her life partner, which she blames on her 60 hours per week work schedule. As a result, Amelia put off having children, cryopreserving her eggs at the age of 35 years in hopes of a successful pregnancy when she found her partner. Now at age 46 years, Amelia has realized that her body and energy are changing. She has put on some weight and feels extreme fatigue. Three years ago she was diagnosed with type 2 diabetes. Last year, her father died from Alzheimer's disease, a deep source of grief for Amelia. Additionally, she has lost her concentration and is becoming forgetful. Last month she forgot to put a meeting with a major client on her calendar and stood up the client. The client was not happy about it and complained to the CEO of Amelia's company. Amelia has sought counseling, stating she is "depressed and tired all of the time." She says, "I am so proud of all that I have accomplished. I can kick any of those White guys' asses when it comes to making money. I raised my siblings, put myself through school, and now I'm wealthy. But I'm at a crossroads. I want to have a family and a partner that I love. I'm not in menopause yet, but I'm not sure my body can handle a pregnancy anymore. I'm worried that I'm starting to have some symptoms of dementia. I have the money to pay for a surrogate, but I always wanted my kids to have parents at home because I know what it's like to not have parents around when you're growing up. I'm not sure I want to be a single parent, and I don't even know if I could handle that right now with my work schedule and my health."

Middle adulthood, the period between ages 40 and 65 years, is a unique time of life! It is a time where most adults in the United States are working, raising families, or maintaining social and community relationships. Although changes in the body and signs of aging become noticeable, it also is a time where many adults begin to develop a deeper sense of self and a deeper connection with others.

Amelia represents the middle adulthood stage of life, and there are several considerations as we read her story. First, we notice a deep sense of identity and pride in what she has accomplished. She has overcome many barriers and is very successful in her vocation. Yet, at the same time, there is a sense of being

---

BOX 15.1 SMALL-GROUP DISCUSSION

Swiss psychiatrist Carl Jung believed that the task of middle adulthood and beyond was to successfully integrate the fractured pieces of the ego from the first half of life, essentially integrating them to find meaning and identity in the second half (Crain, 2000). Other major developmental theorists, such as Erik Erikson and Daniel Levinson, identified generativity and finding meaning as major developmental tasks during middle adulthood. However, these theories primarily were written through male, Eurocentric models and might not acknowledge the experiences of all middle adults. Both Erikson and Levinson acknowledged in their later work that external factors, such as oppression, racism, sexism, and workforce issues, do impact generativity (Levinson, 1996). Feminist writer and journalist Gail Sheehy, like male theorists, identified unique stages of adult development, but she also integrated critical factors related to gender, cultural influences, and biology (Sheehy, 1996). American psychologist Bernice Neugarten believed that adult tasks were based in social norms, and she argued against the idea of a social clock where adults are expected to achieve developmental milestones based on social expectations (Neugarten, 1996). Finally, Cornett and Hudson (1987) found that standard theories of middle adulthood development have "serious flaws" (p. 72) when applied to the experiences of gay men. These critiques give pause to the application of classic middle adulthood developmental theory, particularly in consideration of sociocultural factors and diverse populations. Given this controversy, discuss the following questions:

1. How do classic developmental theories of middle adulthood apply to Amelia? How do they not apply?
2. Which of Amelia's concerns seem like normal aspects of middle adulthood and an abnormal aspects of middle adulthood?
3. How might Amelia's sociocultural factors contribute to her health and cognitive concerns?

unfulfilled and wanting more in her life—perhaps a dream or goal that she has not yet accomplished. She recently lost her father and grieves over this loss. Alongside these social and emotional factors, Amelia reports some new challenges in her health and cognition. Amelia seems to be at an intersection; she is experiencing an inverse relationship between life mastery and life decline.

Does Amelia represent the norm for middle adulthood? And, although her social and emotional factors often are the first considerations for counselors, to what degree do her physical and cognitive issues impact her overall clinical presentation and treatment plan? This chapter discusses adult physical and cognitive developmental experiences that present significant implications for counseling.

PHYSICAL DEVELOPMENT IN MIDDLE ADULTHOOD

How many sociocultural clichés exist about aging in middle adulthood? Perhaps you yourself have attended an over-the-hill party, joked about someone's spare tire, or counted your own gray hairs! How about the classic stereotype of the middle-aged man who compensates for aging by running marathons, trading in his minivan for a sports car, and getting a younger girlfriend? (Perhaps Carl Jung would say that this gentleman is not integrating his fractured ego effectively.)

Although these stereotypes *might* represent some middle adults, they certainly do not represent all of them. The human body does begin to decline in middle adulthood, but most adults are healthy. A recent Centers for Disease Control and Prevention (CDC) study shows that most adults report good to excellent health, with only 17% reporting fair or poor health. According to the most recent CDC statistics, the most significant health issues in middle adulthood are obesity and inactivity. Only 28.6% of Americans aged 44–65 years reported a healthy body weight, whereas 36.8% were overweight and 33.7% were obese. Less than half of middle adults (46.9%) reported being sufficiently active, with over half moderately active or completely inactive (U.S. Department of Health and Human Services, 2014).

Other prominent health issues for middle adulthood were regular alcohol use and physical pain. Over half of middle adults reported regularly using alcohol. Although not a health condition per se, significant alcohol use can be a factor in health problems such as liver disease, diabetes, and increased risk of accidents. Physical pain included arthritis, joint symptoms, and localized body pain. Table 15.1 presents population percentages for common health conditions in adults aged 44–65 years.

Body Changes in Middle Adulthood

Beginning in their mid- to late 30s, adults begin to notice significant changes in their physical development. The most noticeable changes are a decrease in muscle and bone mass, decreased energy levels and longer recovery periods after an accident or strenuous activity, and changes in vision (presbyopia or farsightedness)

Table 15.1 Population Percentages for Health Conditions	
Health Condition	**U.S. adults Aged 44–65 Years**
Alcohol, regular use	51.8
Chronic joint symptoms	35.3
Pain in lower back	32.3
Arthritis	29.6
Smoker	19.5
Hearing trouble	19.2
Pain in neck	18.4
Migraines or severe headaches	13.6
Diabetes	12.7
Heart disease	12.1
Vision trouble	11.3
Cancer (any type)	9.3
Absence of all natural teeth	7.7
Pain in face or jaw	5.2
Liver disease	2.0

Source: U.S. Department of Health and Human Services (2014).

and hearing (hearing loss and tinnitus). Internally, the human body is slowing in systemic functioning; the heart rate slows and aortic walls become thicker, and the immune system declines (Kirasic, 2004). For men in middle adulthood, the reduction of muscle mass can be correlated with higher risks for weight gain, obesity, and high blood pressure (Murray & Lewis, 2014; Vimalananda et al., 2013). Men also have an increased risk of developing prostate cancer (Discacciati et al., 2011). Women also have an increased risk of obesity, diabetes, and high blood pressure (Ma & Xiao, 2010; Vimalananda et al., 2013). This is an inevitable part of the aging process, but adults might begin to notice many of these changes all at once or at a deeper intensity than during earlier developmental periods. Furthermore, adults can become aware of the cumulative effects of lifelong physical wear and tear that have resulted from earlier developmental periods and other risk factors (Gustafsson, Janlert, Theorell, Westerlund, & Hammarström, 2012). Recognition of these age-related changes can create more psychological distress for adults, although many anticipate these changes and negotiate them successfully.

Changes in physical development can be accommodated through minor adjustments, such as getting reading glasses or taking more recovery time after physical activity or illness. Although the majority of adults do not have significant health problems, this is the period of life where more serious health problems can begin. While hormonal and body changes attributed to aging factors do have an impact, many serious health issues can be altered through healthy lifestyle choices: healthy diet, regular exercise, limiting alcohol, and not smoking. For example, men who continue to engage in physical activity during middle adulthood can

BOX 15.2 CLASS ACTIVITY: ASSESSMENT OF CHRONIC PAIN

Chronic pain is any type of pain that lasts months or longer. Pain can create additional problems for adults, including depression and other emotional distress. It also can create severe fatigue if the pain interferes with sleep. Assessing pain levels in adults is imperative to their overall diagnosis and treatment. The mental status examination is particularly important in recognizing pain. Counselors should pay attention to the client's *appearance* (poor hygiene or inappropriate dress could be a result of problems with movement), *gait* (steady or unsteady, or requiring assistance such as a cane or wheelchair), and observed *discomfort* in sitting, standing, or moving. Counselors should assess *mood* and *affect*, particularly if the client's affect contains wincing or strained expressions when moving. Other considerations are *substance abuse* (both prescribed medications and illicit drugs) as well as feelings of *hopelessness* and *suicidal ideation*, which are common in clients that suffer from longstanding chronic and severe pain. Finally, counselors should ask outright about the client's pain level. Using a SUDS scale often is effective to get a measurable understanding of the client's pain. In the presence of chronic pain, the aforementioned symptoms should not be interpreted as hostile or uncooperative behavior on the part of the client. Empathizing with the client's pain is a very important part of validating the client, even if the pain appears to be more somatic.

In triads, practice giving an assessment of chronic pain through role play. There should be one counselor, one observer, and one client. The counselor should ask questions and make observations of the client, particularly around physical development and chronic pain. The observer should take notes and give feedback to the counselor. Switch roles after 10 minutes until everyone has functioned as the counselor at least once.

improve their heart and circulatory functioning (Kwaśniewska et al., 2014), which improves their overall health. Stress reduction strategies and improving sleep quality also can greatly improve health.

Certain factors can predict better overall health in middle adulthood for both men and women. Wellness practices during earlier developmental periods have a significant effect on adult health-related behaviors (Hampson, Edmonds, Goldberg, Dubanoski, & Hillier, 2013), which leads to improved health in middle adulthood. Providing a realistic self-assessment of exercise activities (Godino et al., 2014) and showing a willingness to participate in a variety of physical activities (Borodulin et al., 2012) also can play a significant role in maintaining good health in middle adulthood. Finally, engagement in religion, spirituality, or mindfulness can create a positive effect on both physical and emotional health of adults (Allen et al., 2013).

Physical Attractiveness

Changes in outward appearance become noticeable in middle adulthood. Skin begins to lose elasticity, which can cause sagging all over the body as well as on the face and neck. The outward appearance of the skin becomes thinner and more translucent, and skin sometimes develops dark patches from sun damage. Due to bone loss and loss of muscle mass, adults can lose height as they approach older age. Bone loss also can create dental problems, such as loss of teeth and a possible need for increased dental care.

Physical attractiveness is important to humans throughout the lifespan, but it is just as often determined individually than by sociocultural norms (Jæger, 2011). Body image also could play a factor in an overall sense of attractiveness; however, body image tends to be an issue throughout the lifespan. For example, Peplau and colleagues (2009) found that heterosexual men had the highest body image and that gay men tended to have lower body image than heterosexual males in a sample of middle-aged adults. However, Peplau et al. (2009) also found no difference in body image between heterosexual women and lesbian women. However, heterosexual men may begin to find more dissatisfaction with their bodies in middle adulthood due to body changes and weight gain (Murray & Lewis, 2014). Bybee and Wells (2006) found that, although attractiveness is important in middle adulthood, adults begin to think about other factors related to their bodies such as overall physical health, strength, and living a longer, disease-free life. Therefore, care for one's physical appearance in middle adulthood may be motivated more by maintaining good health rather than meeting a sociocultural stereotype of attractiveness.

Sexual and Reproductive Issues

Sex does not stop in middle adulthood! Although the frequency of sexual encounters may decrease due to hormonal and physical changes, most adults still find sex to be pleasurable (DeLamater & Koepsel, 2015). DeLamater and Keopsel (2015) also found that many adults begin to value emotional intimacy as much as penetrative sex, suggesting that meaningful sexual expression may vary among this population.

Sexual and genital responses also change in middle adulthood. Sexual changes for women usually occur earlier than for men, including the thinning of the vaginal walls, increased vaginal dryness, and hormonal changes due to menopause. Women also might experience fibroid tumors or cysts in the uterus, ovaries, or cervix, most of which are benign but can create bleeding irregularities during the menstrual cycle or during sex. Beginning as early as age 40 years, men experience a decrease in testosterone. This hormonal change reduces the frequency of their erections, and it also lengthens the time between arousal and orgasm during sexual activity. Men also may experience few erections, lower sperm count, less powerful orgasms, and less semen during ejaculation, with more recovery time needed in between orgasms.

Risky sexual behaviors also impact the middle adult population. Significantly larger numbers of middle age adults are currently living with HIV, AIDS, and STDs than in past generations (Jeffers & DiBartolo, 2011), which impacts the health of the global population at large. Child abuse and neglect have been found to predict risky sexual behavior during middle adulthood (Wilson & Widom, 2011) as well. In middle adulthood, adults may continue to negotiate sexually monogamous or nonmonogamous roles (MacDonald, 2001), and the termination of relationships has been associated with higher levels of sexual risk taking among men and women (Moreau, Beltzer, Bozon, & Bajos, 2011). Counselors should take care to assess attitudes toward higher risk sexual behaviors in their adult clients, including a sexual history and the diagnosis and treatment of STDs.

Sexual Dysfunction

Sexual dysfunction refers to anything that alters the human sexual response cycle of arousal through orgasm and includes lack of desire for sex, an inability for the body to respond during the phases of sex, or pain during sex. A common sexual dysfunction that occurs in men is erectile dysfunction, which is the inability to achieve or maintain an erection for desired sexual activity. Approximately 5–25% of men aged 40–65 years experience erectile dysfunction, which can impact self-esteem and the quality of intimate partner relationships.

In middle adulthood, sexual dysfunction more often occurs comorbid with other conditions rather than aging alone. For example, sexual dysfunction has been linked with depression (Boyarsky, Haque, Rouleau, & Hirschfeld, 1999), lymphoma recovery in men (Arden-Close, Eiser, & Pacey, 2011), and fibromyalgia (Rico-Villademoros et al., 2012). There also is a link between sexual dysfunction and psychosocial factors such as childhood sexual abuse (Easton, Coohey, O'Leary, Zhang, & Hua, 2011; Zwickl & Merriman, 2011), stressors related to military service (Wilcox, Redmond, & Hassan, 2014), and partner intimacy and attachment style (Burri, Schweitzer, & O'Brien, 2014; Stefanou & McCabe, 2012). Therefore, it is important for both counselors and medical professionals to take a thorough psychosocial assessment of adult clients prior to diagnosing a sexual dysfunction.

Menopause

Menopause is a gradual process that occurs in women over a period of years in middle adulthood (commonly between the ages of 45 and 55 years). Menopause is the cessation of fertility in women; more specifically, it is the changing of hormones that prompt the release of eggs from the ovaries. The uterus ceases to shed the lining of blood and mucus accumulated to nurture an embryo, and women's menstrual periods reduce and eventually stop altogether. Due to the hormonal changes, women might experience a myriad of symptoms including mood swings, vaginal dryness, irregularities in the menstrual cycle, and hot flashes. Common medical approaches to treat these symptoms are hysterectomy or hormone replacement therapy, although many women opt for a natural menopause with no surgical or chemical intervention.

Women cannot conceive naturally after menopause, which can add an element of grief or negative feelings about aging. Some research indicates that women with more negative attitudes toward menopause report greater menopausal symptomology (Ayers, Forshaw, & Hunter, 2010; Kĩsa, Zeyneloğlu, & Ozdemir, 2012). However, other research indicates that sociocultural factors also have a significant factor on women's negative experiences of menopause. Katz-Bearnot (2010) found that other factors such as previous psychological and medical problems, trauma, and the quality of women's interpersonal relationships were predictors of negative menopausal symptoms. Similarly, Hinchliff, Gott, and Ingleton (2010) found a positive association between interpersonal factors and menopausal symptomology. Although menopause normally is anticipated by women and their partners, an early menopause (40 or younger) can be traumatic. Women need support, primarily for grief and acceptance of the loss of fertility (Singer, 2012).

Sexual activity during and after menopause can be a common concern for adults. Sometimes, however, sociocultural factors might actually have a greater impact on sexual dysfunction than do menopausal symptoms. In a sample of 102 primarily Hispanic women, lower socioeconomic status and poor sleep quality were better predictors of sexual dysfunction than menopausal symptoms (Schnatz, Whitehurst, & O'Sullivan, 2010). Nappi et al. (2010) found that anxiety was just as significant a factor in sexual dysfunction as hormonal changes for menopausal women. Peri- and postmenopausal women still enjoy sex and have a normal sexual response cycle. Women might need to make some accommodations during sexual activity (e.g., use a secondary lubrication to compensate for vaginal dryness), but sexual functioning and satisfaction are not usually impaired by menopause alone.

Fertility

Fertility, which begins for both men and women during puberty, is the ability to reproduce through the procreation of children. For women, fertility peaks in the late 20s and then begins to decline until menopause. However, women can conceive and carry a fetus to term until they have completed menopause or have undergone a hysterectomy. Women who reach age 35 years are considered advanced maternal age, indicating lower chances of natural conception and a higher risk for birth defects. Men can remain fertile throughout their lifespan into old age, although this begins to slowly decline in middle adulthood. A variety of factors influence fertility for both sexes, namely, overall health and genetic predispositions toward infertility.

Many adults can experience infertility, especially if they have decided to delay having children until later in life. Some infertile couples may opt for assisted reproductive technology such as in vitro fertilization, artificial insemination, cryopreservation of genetic tissue (e.g., sperm, eggs, embryos), or surrogacy. Both men and women experiencing infertility can have additional psychological issues such as anxiety or low self-esteem. For example, a study on infertile Palestinian men revealed that their experiences of infertility were agonizing and a threat to masculinity (Birenbaum-Carmeli & Inhorn, 2009). Couples and individuals undergoing fertility treatments need psychosocial support (Dooley, Dineen, Sarma, & Nolan, 2014; Lykeridou, Gourounti, Deltsidou, Loutradis, & Vaslamatzis, 2009).

The Impact of Sociocultural Factors on Adult Physical Development

Several social and cultural components may influence physical development during the years of middle adulthood, specifically race and ethnicity, family relationships, and vocational and socioeconomic status.

Race and Ethnicity

Compared with the well-being of middle age adults belonging to ethnic majority groups, the measurable health levels of individuals belonging to racial or ethnic minority groups may be lower (Meyer, Castro-Schilo, & Aguilar-Gaxiola, 2014). African American women may experience menopause at an earlier age, on average, than White women; however, this observed difference may be due to differences in observed stress levels among various races or ethnic groups (Newhart, 2013). For many adults of racial or ethnic minority groups, exposure to various kinds of trauma is negatively related to self-related physical health (Klest, Freyd, Hampson, & Dubanoski, 2013). Other physical factors may not vary by ethnic and racial group; for example, similar factors may influence the health and weight management for White women and African American women (Capers, Baughman, & Logue, 2011). Minorities may be less willing to seek out medical resources or assistance (McGarrity & Huebner, 2014), which may lead to lingering physical problems and chronic health conditions.

Family Relationships

Family characteristics play a significant role in physical health during middle adulthood. Stressful environments or difficult transitions within the family life dynamic can trigger weight gain, poor sleep quality, and greater health stress for family members, which may contribute as a whole to lower levels of life satisfaction (Darling, Coccia, & Senatore, 2012). Although the physical well-being of middle age adults has been commonly evaluated by how frequently family members care for each other (Jianfang, Xiaomei, & Hearst, 2014), the act of providing care during this period of life may be accompanied by significantly negative physical affects for adults serving as caregivers for other family members (Mosher, Bakas, & Champion, 2013).

Vocational and Socioeconomic Status

Various occupational and economic factors can affect physical health in middle adulthood. One prominent psychosocial issue is that gaps in physical health among this population as a whole widen during middle age (Benzeval, Green, & Leyland, 2011). Adults in the workforce typically begin to experience losses of on-the-job

BOX 15.3 CASE STUDY AND CLASS DISCUSSION

Jeff is a 55-year-old, White, heterosexual male. His intelligence level is higher than average, and he has an outgoing, humorous personality. Jeff suffers from chronic pain due to a car accident that occurred in his early 40s. Three years ago, he underwent a back surgery to repair some of his damaged vertebrae. The surgery was botched, creating ongoing and excruciating back pain for Jeff. His back surgeon denied any responsibility for the pain issues and referred Jeff to a pain clinic, where he was prescribed Oxycodone. He quickly became addicted and was unable to function without it. Meanwhile, his marriage of 30 years began to crumble. According to Jeff, the marriage had always been difficult, but he stayed in it for his three children and to honor the values of his Christian faith. Now adults, his children were influenced by Jeff's ex-wife in the divorce, became hostile and alienated from him, and joined Jeff's ex-wife in the divorce litigation. Jeff lost everything in the divorce, including his cabinetry business. "But what pained me the most was losing my kids," Jeff says. "This is the whole reason I stayed with their mom, because I knew she would turn them against me. Now I'm a drug addict, I can't work, and I've had to relocate to get away from my ex. I would have thought at this point in my life I would have had extra money, a thriving business, and be enjoying my grandkids. I also thought my church would help me, but everyone there judged me when they found out I had a drug problem and was getting divorced."

Last year, Jeff reunited with his high school sweetheart and they soon married. He smiles when he talks about her. "She is the light of my life, the one I should have married the first time around. Without her, I would be dead—literally." One of the challenges Jeff and his new wife have had is dealing with his dependence on Oxycodone. At one point he checked himself into an inpatient rehab facility and was prescribed benzodiazepines to help wean him off the Oxycodone. Jeff says that getting off the benzodiazepines was the "most horrible experience of my life" because he did not titrate off. He was unable to sleep for 25 days at one point and had excruciating anxiety. His new wife took him to the emergency room several times, but the doctors didn't know what to do for him. "They just thought I was a drug addict and told me to go home." Jeff and his wife felt marginalized by the system and received no help for his recovery. It took 9 months of detoxing at home to finally feel normal again, during which Jeff could not work. Jeff now has reoccurring bouts of depression and hopelessness, which usually come when he has back pain or severe back spasms. He is reticent to take any medications for fear of becoming addicted again, which leaves him in chronic pain. Even though Jeff now can work minimally and is rebuilding his business, he faces some financial problems because he cannot work as long or as hard as he used to.

Class discussion: What is normal and abnormal about Jeff's physical development? What other mental health issues does Jeff present, and how are they connected to his physical problems? What is the influence of Jeff's sociocultural stressors on his physical and mental health? If you were Jeff's counselor, what would be some developmentally appropriate treatment goals or counseling interventions?

productivity due to physical or personal problems (Merrill et al. 2012), which can perpetuate socioeconomic inequity. Adults with better access to health care may display better overall physical functioning (Kim & Richardson, 2012). Decline in physical functioning is slower for adults who have private health insurance, which indicates that higher socioeconomic status and job stability may be factors in better health. Interestingly, Kim and Richardson (2012) also found that changes in economic status, such as decreases in income and assets, have a greater impact on women's physical functioning when compared with the functioning of men.

COGNITIVE DEVELOPMENT IN MIDDLE ADULTHOOD

What Is Cognition?

Cognition is the process by which humans construct and process their thoughts. However, this definition is actually quite simple. Cognition contains many domains of how humans receive, process, and communicate information—all in one gray matter space (the brain). Thus, adults could demonstrate impairment in one or more aspects of cognition but still have good cognition overall.

Given the multiple domains of cognition, it is essential for counselors to (a) determine the various domains of cognition in adults and (b) measure these domains in order to determine the level of functioning in each domain. One of the most common ways that counselors measure cognition is through assessment of a client's mental status. Counselors and medical professionals (e.g., psychiatrists) use the Mini-Mental State Examination (MMSE), initially developed in 1975 (Folstein, Folstein, & McHugh), to measure the cognitive functioning of adults on the domains of orientation, memory and recall, calculation, attention, language, repetition, and short commands via a scored method. Today, counselors often use modified versions of the MMSE, which they refer to as a mental status exam (MSE). Areas of cognition on the MSE usually assessed by counselors are concentration, attention, memory, thought processes, thought content, perception, insight, and judgment, but other domains can be included.

The *Diagnostic and Statistical Manual of Mental Disorders*, fifth edition (*DSM-5*; APA, 2013), also provides several domains to measure cognition: complex attention, executive function, learning and memory, language, perceptual-motor, and social cognition. This latter domain, which is defined as "recognition of emotions, theory of mind" (APA, 2013, p. 595), is a more contemporary idea in cognitive functioning, implying that cognition is more than just internal mental processes; it is also the method by which we interact with other humans.

Intelligence

Intelligence is the ability to learn and retain new information and then to use that information to acquire new information (Cattell, 1971). In other words, intelligence is how we know what we know and how we are able to learn new information and solve problems. However, intelligence has been studied widely with many varying definitions and its relevance to cross-cultural populations. For example, David Wechsler, the developer of the Wechsler Adult Intelligence Scale (WAIS), believed intelligence to be "the global capacity of a person to act purposefully, to think rationally, and to deal effectively with his environment" (Wechsler, 1939). Howard Gardner (1983) believed that intelligence was not just a single domain, but that it was comprised of multiple domains including musical, visual-spatial, verbal, logical-mathematical, bodily-kinesthetic, interpersonal, intrapersonal, and naturalistic. There is much criticism of standard definitions of intelligence since these definitions come from Eurocentric male perspective and might not adequately represent gender and culture.

Despite the difficulty in defining intelligence, the domains of fluid and crystallized intelligence emerged from Cattell in 1971. These two domains have remained a constant construct in the literature. Fluid intelligence is the ability to reason and solve problems in new situations, regardless of what has already been learned. Fluid intelligence includes the ability to solve problems by using logic. Crystallized intelligence is the use of one's acquired knowledge and skills to solve problems. One's personal experiences and wisdom also can play a role in crystallized intelligence. These two domains are particularly important in understanding intelligence in middle adulthood.

Cognition in Middle Adulthood

Cognition overall develops throughout the lifespan, primarily peaking during middle adulthood and then slowly declining as the adult approaches older age (Ghisletta, Rabbitt, Lunn, & Lindenberger, 2012; Verhaeghen & Salthouse, 1997). However, as previously mentioned, cognition should not be interpreted as the sum of its parts. The individual domains of cognition should be assessed individually since normal adult cognition might be stellar in some areas and weaker in others. Lack of cognitive functioning in one or two areas can be a sign of a separate problem rather than overall cognitive degeneration. An example of the latter might be an adult who is managing a full-time career with a high responsibility level, parenting adolescents, and caring for aging parents, who, due to all of these distractions, forgets to sign her daughter's permission slip for an outing at school. The problem here could be construed as a failure of memory or problems with attention, when in reality the larger issue is likely the individual's significant stressors using up cognitive energy.

Fluid intelligence peaks in early adulthood and then slowly declines throughout midlife into old age, whereas crystallized intelligence stays stable or actually improves in midlife (Botwinick, 1978; Cavanaugh & Blanchard-Fields, 2006; Kirasic, 2004). This inverse process is a great example of the interplay of how human cognition comes from natural abilities and life experiences. It also speaks to the idea that lived experiences become just as valuable (if not more valuable) in mid- to later life. Socioculturally, the ability to think and solve problems quickly (fluid intelligence) is strongly valued, but crystallized intelligence is just as valuable. It can be a source of meaning for the individual as well as a great mentoring tool for younger generations.

Memory may begin to decline in middle adulthood, and it is common for gaps to occur on all domains of memory (immediate, short-term, and long-term memory). Therefore, memory impairment, though potentially alarming to the middle adult (and perhaps frustrating—or even amusing—to those who live with them) is likely more a result of juggling increased stressors than a more significant problem like dementia. Severe memory problems such as Alzheimer's disease and other forms of dementia are not common in middle adulthood, but they can occur earlier than age 65 years on rare occasions. Genetic predisposition toward cognitive impairment and medical conditions such as Parkinson's disease or stroke are usually factors in these early cases.

Some factors actually can improve cognition in adulthood, and, not surprisingly, they have to do with good self-care. Stawski and colleagues (2011) found that adults that had normal cortisol patterns throughout the day reported better executive functioning. (Cortisol is a hormone that is greatly impacted by stress; the more stress experienced, the more the cortisol pattern is unbalanced, negatively impacting sleep quality and energy levels.) Scullin and Bliwise (2015) found that good sleep quality improved cognition in both young adulthood and middle adulthood and was a protective factor in cognitive declines later in life. Increased levels of physical activity and a healthy diet also have been associated with improving cognition in adulthood (Bielak, Cherbuin, Bunce, & Anste, 2014; Kesse-Guyot, Andreeva, Lassale, Hercberg, & Galan, 2014). These factors show a positive relationship between good cognition and a healthy lifestyle, which includes stress reduction, rest, regular physical activity, and a healthy diet.

Trauma, Mental Health, and Adult Cognition

Physical Trauma

A major factor that impairs adult cognition is physical trauma, including exposure to toxins. Although physical trauma can occur at any developmental level, adults have higher propensity for exposure due to work environment, frequent driving, or other high-risk situations. Physical trauma and toxin exposure can cause neurocognitive disorders such as traumatic brain injury (TBI). One adult population particularly at risk for TBI is veterans and/or actively enlisted service

BOX 15.4   NORMAL AND ABNORMAL COGNITIVE FUNCTIONING IN MIDDLE ADULTHOOD

Cognitive Domain	Normal Functioning in Middle Adulthood	Abnormal Functioning in Middle Adulthood
Orientation	Ability to identify one's self, location, and relevant environmental or social information	Wandering; getting lost in familiar places; unable to identify name or location; unable to identify current events
Immediate memory	Ability to remember information within a matter of a few minutes	Forgetting what one is doing in the middle of a task; forgetting what someone just said; small declines normal
Short-term memory	Ability to remember information within the matter of a short period of time (1 day to 1 week)	Forgetting a conversation from yesterday; forgetting concepts recently learned (e.g., passing a test last week and then forgetting all of the information); small declines normal
Long-term memory	Ability to remember details from the past; ability to perform tasks learned years ago	Forgetting children's names or birthdays; forgetting how to do tasks learned in one's primary vocation; small declines normal
Calculation	Ability to add, subtract, and do simple calculations	Failing simple calculation tasks, even when given assistance; failure to correctly use already learned basic math skills
Attention	Ability to hold attention to a task while filtering out other stimuli	Easily distracted by outside stimuli; cannot finish a task or conversation due to the distraction
Language	Ability to understand and communicate in one's primary language	Aphasia; apraxia of speech; mutism
Concentration	Ability to exert focus on a task or conversation for a sustained period of time	Easily distracted; requires prompts to stay on task; cannot finish a task or conversation within a sustained period of time

Cognitive Domain	Normal Functioning in Middle Adulthood	Abnormal Functioning in Middle Adulthood
Learning	Ability to retain and use new information; longer time required in learning new concepts, especially more difficult or new concepts (e.g., an adult graduate student struggling to learn online learning technology)	Slower processing times; inability to learn new concepts
Thought processes	Logical flow of thought, as evidenced through the individual's speech	Flight of ideas; poverty of thought
Thought content	Thoughts focus on real-life situations	Hallucinations, delusions, obsessions, perseveration, rumination
Perception	Oriented; understands what is real and what is not	Hallucinations, delusions
Insight	Ability to understand the nature of one's ailments or problems	Blames others for one's problems; fails to take appropriate responsibility for the resolution of one's problems
Abstraction	Ability to infer deeper meanings from common concepts	Extremely concrete thinking with little to no insight into deeper meaning or context
Judgment	Ability to make healthy choices in a variety of situations	Repeatedly makes unsafe or unsound decisions for self or others
Executive functioning	Ability to plan and execute decisions or desires	Failure to plan ahead; impulsive; poor reasoning; failure in memory
Perceptual-motor	Good coordination between body and sensory perceptions (e.g., vision)	Poor coordination between body and sensory perceptions (e.g., vision)
Learning	Ability to recall new information	Inability to recall information, either short term or long term
Social cognition	Sensitivity and adherence to appropriate social norms (e.g., speech, dress); can demonstrate empathy	Lack of empathy; refusal to conform to standards for health and safety; poor judgment in social interactions; aggression; extreme isolation

Cognitive Domain	Normal Functioning in Middle Adulthood	Abnormal Functioning in Middle Adulthood
Fluid intelligence	Ability to solve problems with reasoning skills or when given new information; may decline as age increases	Significant or immediate decline in previous level of functioning (but must account for normal decline due to age, such as slower processing times)
Crystallized intelligence	Ability to solve problems with common sense; stays stable or improves throughout middle adulthood	Decline in previous level of functioning

members, as; they are exposed to physical trauma more frequently than civilians. To give a comparison, Summerall (2014) estimated that 80% of TBIs in the civilian population are minor and resolve quickly without long-term symptoms, with only 10–15% of civilian TBIs developing chronic cognitive problems. However, among veterans, TBIs are much more common and significant. Veterans most typically experience TBIs from blasts (although they also experience TBIs from other means, such as motor vehicle accidents), with major cognitive problems that last 18–24 months after the trauma (Summerall, 2014). TBI cognitive decline symptoms are disorientation, memory impairment (immediate, short term, and long term), and difficulty learning new information. Other symptoms of TBI include personality change, especially an increase in irritability and aggression.

Mental Health Issues

Similar to physical health, most adults report good mental health, with only 3.9% reporting serious psychological distress (U.S. Department of Health and Human Services, 2014). The National Institute of Mental Health (NIMH, 2012) reported similar statistics, showing that 4.1% of adults, or 9.6 million adults aged 18 years or older, report serious mental illness (defined as a diagnosable mental, emotional, or behavioral disorder excluding substance abuse and developmental disorders).

The most common mental health issues for adults are anxiety and depressive symptoms, which, also according to U.S. Department of Health and Human Services (2014), approximately 1–2 of every 10 adults experience to some degree (Table 15.2).

Depression and anxiety symptoms often impair cognition, specifically concentration, memory, and thought content. For example, one of the diagnostic

Table 15.2 Population Percentages for Mental Health Conditions		
Condition	U.S. Adults Aged 44–65 Years: "All the Time"	U.S. Adults Aged 44–65 Years: "Some of the Time"
Sadness	3.5	8.0
Hopelessness	2.7	4.5
Worthlessness	2.3	3.9
Everything is an effort	5.7	8.7
Nervousness	4.5	11.4
Restlessness	5.4	11.5

Source: U.S. Department of Health and Human Services (2014).

criteria for generalized anxiety disorder is "difficulty concentrating or mind going blank" (APA, 2013, p. 222), and for a major depressive episode impaired cognitive symptoms include "diminished ability to think or concentrate, or indecisiveness" as well as "recurrent thoughts of death" (e.g., obsessive thinking) (APA, 2013, p. 161).

Psychological trauma also has a significant impact on cognition. The *DSM-5* recategorized posttraumatic stress disorder (PTSD) under its own category (trauma- and stressor-related disorders) with a new criterion set specifically addressing distorted cognition (APA, 2013). Criterion D, "Negative alterations in cognitions and mood associated with traumatic event(s), beginning or worsening after the traumatic event(s) occurred" (APA, 2013, p. 271), demonstrates the significance of setting apart cognitive distortions in the PTSD diagnostic criteria. Trauma-induced distorted cognition includes problems with memory and thought content as well as negative symptoms. Counselors should be careful not to assume a neurocognitive disorder without carefully ruling out PTSD and other stressor-related issues.

Impact of Sociocultural Factors on Adult Cognitive Development

Many of the same social and cultural factors that influence physical development also influence cognitive processes during middle adulthood. These factors include gender, ethnicity and race, sexual orientation, family and relationships, and vocational and socioeconomic status.

Gender

Similar to crystallized intelligence, emotional, psychological, and social health levels during the early middle-age years are remarkably consistent for both men and women (Kokko, Korkalainen, Lyyra, & Feldt, 2013) and may actually increase with age (Carstensen et al., 2011). Men and women may be inclined to reverse traditional male–female roles if men become more interested in home life and nurturing activities and women turn their attention to independent activities outside of the home (Rappoport, 1976). However, middle adulthood can lead to cognitive challenges by gender. For example, men who have held more traditional views of gender roles and have conflict with how these gender roles are enacted may be more inclined to consider self-harming behavior (Hunt, Sweeting, Keoghan, & Platt, 2006).

Research shows several interesting findings about adult women's cognitive development during middle adulthood. The personality of women may evolve over time as levels of psychological sensitivity and autonomy traits decrease, while willfulness traits increase (Edelstein, Newton, & Stewart, 2012). However, women may have less dramatic mood swings than men of the same age (Kokko et al., 2013). Age-associated changes in personal identity, intimacy, and activity level abilities may influence a renewed psychological commitment to personal hobbies (Cheek & Piercy, 2008) as well as social projects (Newton & Stewart, 2010). For women in middle adulthood transition, individual differences in one's openness to experience play the determining factor in self-efficacy and well-being (Weiss, Freund, & Wiese, 2012).

Ethnicity and Race

Differences in ethnic and racial identity among the middle adult population can influence the development of markedly different cognitive health processes, decision-making activities, and leisure activities (Herrera, 2011). Although participation in social activities is positively associated with reduced depression symptoms for adults of both Caucasian and minority backgrounds (Herrera, 2011), the ways that Caucasian and minority adults react to stress and depression may be markedly different (Jackson, Knight, & Rafferty, 2010). For example, minority women have been found to be more likely than Caucasian women to act as caregivers and to use the computer less often during their leisure time (Herrera et al., 2011). Counselors should take into consideration different expressions of stress management among diverse populations and their impact on cognition.

Sexual Orientation

For many lesbian, gay, bisexual, transgender, and queer (LGBTQ) individuals in middle adulthood, the processes of early sexual orientation identity development are continued or extended (Calzo, Antonucci, Mays, & Cochran, 2011). Lesbian women also may retain a more fluid sexual identity during middle age than heterosexual women within the same age group (Mock & Elbach, 2012). Mock and Elback (2012) also found that men who self-identify as heterosexual or gay have relatively stable identities when compared to men who identify as bisexual. Gay, lesbian, and bisexual adults have been found to carry a higher risk of developing mental health problems when compared to heterosexual men and women within the same age group (Fredriksen-Goldsen, Hyun-Jun, Barkan, Muraco, & Hoy-Ellis, 2013). Additionally, Fredriksen-Goldsen et al. (2013) found that gay, lesbian, and bisexual adults have a higher risk of disability, smoking, and excessive drinking during middle age than the comparable heterosexual population. Although lesbian women in middle adulthood report less psychological turmoil compared with heterosexual women, many lesbian women still reported psychologically negative feelings about the aging process (Howell & Beth, 2004). Counselors should be aware of historical marginalization of LGBTQ populations and give consideration to sexual orientation and sexual minority status in relationship to any cognitive issues.

Family and Relationships

For both men and women, middle adulthood brings changes in how close relationships are cognitively perceived and negotiated. Although healthy cognitive performance in middle age may be heavily influenced by one's biological inheritance (Stijntjes et al., 2013), many studies also provide evidence that justifies the importance of family or other connections in maintaining cognitive well being. Familial understanding and compassion regarding changes in adult cognition are essential. For example, adults may be more willing to practice forgiveness in day-to-day behaviors yet also be less likely to confront individuals who offend them (Ghaemmaghami, Allemand, & Martin, 2011), which might be a radical change from previous interpersonal relating.

The development of chronically poor-quality relationships may lead to the development of negative cognition patterns such as attention-deficit/hyperactivity disorder (ADHD), depression, and anxiety (Das, Cherbuin, Butterworth, Anstey, & Easteal, 2012). Adults who regularly provide more care and attention to their children than they receive may also be at a greater risk of developing depression and poor mental health (Perkins & Haley, 2013). Although cognitive well-being is influenced by how frequently family members care for each other (Jianfang et al., 2014), family members with middle-aged adults in ill health attach significantly negative emotional feelings to such caregiving (Mosher et al., 2013). For many adults, losses of relationship may be offset by certain practices. For example, divorced or widowed adults may cope better when friends make themselves available as confidants during the grieving or transition period (Bookwala, Marshall, & Manning 2014). Social networking tools may also have a positive effect upon emotional health of adults (Stephens, Noone, & Alpass, 2014).

Vocational and Socioeconomic Status

Cognition has a significant impact on the development of vocation. Employment associations and socioeconomic status play an important role in emotional health

BOX 15.5 CASE STUDY AND CLASS DISCUSSION

Judy is a 58-year-old heterosexual woman who lives in Nebraska. Judy describes her ethnicity as American. She has fair skin; long, brown hair; and brown eyes. She was referred to counseling by her mother, who is in her late 70s. According to her mother, Judy is "incompetent" and "needs to get her life together." Judy's mother brings Judy to her sessions, driving her in a large Cadillac. Judy never got a driver's license and relies on her mother and public transportation to get around. Judy is friendly but quiet. Her appearance is unkempt, with noticeable body odor and dandruff. Her clothes are too big, and she is dressed in an unattractive style (e.g., outdated glasses style, hairstyle). Judy appears much older than her stated age. In working with Judy, you learn that she has never been able to keep a job. Her vocational experience mostly has been in service work such as motel cleaning, but she has had a history of multiple terminations. As a result, she always has lived in a low socioeconomic bracket, barely making it on her husband's income (who also works service jobs). Judy has been married for 32 years to the same man. They had one daughter, who left the home at age 17 years and never returned. Judy has not had contact with her daughter for 12 years, although her daughter is in occasional contact with Judy's mother. Her husband is described as verbally abusive, but Judy minimizes the verbal abuse and denies that he has ever physically abused her.

As you continue to work with Judy, you notice that she presents the same way every session. She also seems to have little understanding of the questions you ask her, and she has a very concrete understanding of therapeutic concepts (e.g., self-esteem). She has very little insight into her problems, and you sense that she views counseling as more of a social outlet; she reports having no friends, so she really enjoys seeing you. She also seems forgetful of appointment times, sometimes arriving on a different day or time than scheduled. Her mother attends a session with her and expresses a great deal of frustration with Judy's forgetfulness. Judy comments to her mother's frustration, "I just need to get a job; then everything will be okay."

Class discussion: What cognitive issues do you observe in Judy? What seems normal or abnormal about her cognition given her developmental level? Are there any overlapping mental health issues, or sociocultural issues, that could be the etiology for her cognitive problems? What assessments would you administer as her counselor? Would you make any referrals, and, if so, to whom?

(Meyer et al., 2014). Individuals with poor employment histories may suffer from cognitive issues such as ADHD, depression, and anxiety (Das et al., 2012). Adults with lower than average cognitive abilities may have chronic problems with employment, such as lack of education, multiple terminations, and underemployment. As a result, these adults may suffer from low self-esteem, maladaptive coping (such as substance abuse), and lower socioeconomic status, all of which have implications for the counseling process.

KEY COUNSELING POINTERS FOR PHYSICAL AND COGNITIVE DEVELOPMENT

Let's return to Amelia's story. Counselors often first address the social and emotional factors in case conceptualization and treatment planning. However, we also see that Amelia has some significant physical and cognitive concerns. These concerns appear to be normal developmentally, but they do have implications for counseling.

For example, Amelia wants to become a parent but also has a strong value to co-parent with a loving partner. Her choice to delay childbearing is now impacted by her physical health. Failure on the part of the counselor to address Amelia's health concerns may not predict as favorable a treatment outcome nor provide a holistic approach to resolve her concerns around having a family. Moreover, her concerns about failing memory and concentration should not be overlooked. It could be easy for a counselor to minimize this concern in light of the other issues that Amelia presents. However, her vocational success is an important factor in her life, and, combined with losing her father to a neurocognitive disorder, the fear of her own cognition becoming impaired should be addressed. In this case, a more formal cognitive evaluation might alleviate some of Amelia's fears, which, in turn, might increase her self-efficacy in overcoming her grief and learning new strategies to improve her efficiency at work.

Taking Amelia's physical and cognitive developmental issues into consideration, the following are recommendations for a developmentally appropriate counseling process:

- *Rapport building.* Listening to all of Amelia's concerns is crucial. The counselor should be familiar with the physical and cognitive developmental issues presented in this chapter and have a high level of comfort with language surrounding Amelia's concerns.
- *Sociocultural assessment.* The counselor should be fully aware of the impact of sociocultural factors on physical and cognitive development. Sociocultural factors pertinent to Amelia are race and ethnicity, gender, sexual orientation, vocational issues and socioeconomic status, and family and relationship

issues. A recommended tool for assessment of the client's perspective is the Cultural Formulation Interview (APA, 2013, p. 749), which is a new tool in the *DSM-5* designed to assess the client's cultural context related to presenting problems.

- *Biopsychosocial assessment.* The counselor should perform a thorough biopsychosocial assessment. Data collection on physical development should include the following areas: current height, weight, and BMI; current physical activity level; medical history; sexual and reproductive history; appetite and eating patterns; body image satisfaction; substance abuse history; and contact information for current primary care doctor (with a possible release of information). Data collection on cognitive development should include (minimally) a mental status examination with a referral to a neuropsychologist if Amelia is demonstrating cognitive decline abnormal for middle adulthood.

- *Diagnosis.* Any mental health diagnosis for Amelia should be made after consideration of her sociocultural factors and clear identity of the presenting problem after physical and cognitive symptoms have been fully considered and ruled out. A recommended tool to clearly identify the client's symptomology is the Level 1 Cross-Cutting Symptom Measure (APA, 2013, p. 734), which can help the counselor identify general diagnostic categories. Prior to assigning a mental health diagnosis, the counselor also should note the ACA Code of Ethics section E.5 (ACA, 2014), which emphasizes proper diagnosis in consideration of sociocultural factors or populations that historically have faced oppression.

- *Treatment plan.* The counseling treatment plan should be developed collaboratively with Amelia, after careful assessment and explanation of the diagnosis. The treatment plan might include the following:
  - *Support for wellness practices.* The counselor can assist Amelia with developing daily wellness practices, including increasing physical activity levels, stress management, and strategies to increase her efficiency at work.
  - *Individual counseling.* Amelia would benefit from counseling related to her desire to have a family and grief over her father's death. The counselor also can assist Amelia in developing meaningful goals for the future, particularly encouraging Amelia to apply her crystallized intelligence, vocational skills and experience, and her self-efficacy developed from overcoming barriers to her success.
  - *Referrals.* In the event that Amelia did not perform well on the MSE, the counselor should consider a referral to a neuropsychologist to rule out a neurocognitive disorder. The counselor also can refer Amelia to a nutritionist to address her fatigue and weight gain. Finally, a referral to a fertility clinic would help Amelia to explore her options for having a family.

BOX 15.6 INDIVIDUAL REFLECTION

Spend some time reflecting on physical issues and health concerns, cognitive development, and sociocultural factors that impact middle adulthood. What are some of your biases surrounding these topics? For example, how comfortable would you be discussing a client's sexual functioning, such as erectile dysfunction or menopause, particularly if you are the opposite gender? How comfortable would you be empathizing with a client whose worldview was completely shaped by his or her experience of chronic pain or obesity? How confident would you be in assessing cognitive decline in a client? What steps can you take to increase your awareness, language, and competency around these topics?

SUMMARY

It is imperative that counselors look at all developmental aspects of clients, including physical and cognitive health. In middle adulthood, people usually experience good physical and cognitive health with small, yet normal, declines in many areas. The most significant physical issues facing adults today are being overweight or obese, chronic pain, and alcohol use. Most cognitive domains remain intact with minimal declines as adults age. Stress factors do impact cognitive areas, especially memory and processing speed. The cognitive domain that remains the most stable (or actually improves) is crystallized intelligence, which can be a great source of strength and meaning for adults. Sociocultural factors impact physical and cognitive health, which should be assessed prior to giving either a medical or psychological diagnosis. Like Amelia, many individuals in middle adulthood experience an intersection of life mastery and life decline. Counselors can honor their adult clients by helping them to find meaning in their lived experiences while simultaneously facilitating good physical and cognitive wellness strategies.

USEFUL WEBSITES

Harvard Diet Study "Middle-Age Spread"—Smart Health
https://www.youtube.com/watch?v=k9_8dKc9uJE
TED Talk by Laura Carstensen: "Older People Are Happier"
http://www.ted.com/talks/laura_carstensen_older_people_are_happier?
language=en

Middle Age Brains Are Awesome
https://www.youtube.com/watch?v=z08A_In0tcw
Middle Age Brains—NJN News Report
https://www.youtube.com/watch?v=lysdSn5EQVk

REFERENCES

Allen, R. S., Harris, G. M., Crowther, M. R., Oliver, J. S., Cavanaugh, R., & Phillips, L. L. (2013). Does religiousness and spirituality moderate the relations between physical and mental health among aging prisoners? *International Journal of Geriatric Psychiatry, 28*(7), 710–717. doi:10.1002/gps .3874

American Counseling Association (ACA). (2014). *ACA code of ethics.* Alexandria, VA: Author.

American Psychiatric Association (APA). (2013). *Diagnostic and statistical manual of mental disorders* (5th ed.). Arlington, VA: Author.

Arden-Close, E., Eiser, C., & Pacey, A. (2011). Sexual functioning in male survivors of lymphoma: A systematic review (CME). *Journal of Sexual Medicine, 8*(7), 1833–1840. doi:10.1111/j.1743-6109.2011.02209.x

Ayers, B., Forshaw, M., & Hunter, M. S. (2010). The impact of attitudes towards the menopause on women's symptom experience: A systematic review. *Maturitas, 65*(1), 28–36. doi:10.1016/j.maturitas.2009.10.016

Benzeval, M., Green, M. J., & Leyland, A. H. (2011). Do social inequalities in health widen or converge with age? Longitudinal evidence from three cohorts in the West of Scotland. *BMC Public Health, 11,* 947. doi:10.1186/1471-2458-11-947

Bielak, A. M., Cherbuin, N., Bunce, D., & Anstey, K. J. (2014). Preserved differentiation between physical activity and cognitive performance across young, middle, and older adulthood over 8 years. *Journals of Gerontology Series B: Psychological Sciences & Social Sciences, 69*(4), 523–532.

Birenbaum-Carmeli, D., & Inhorn, M. C. (2009). Masculinity and marginality: Palestinian men's struggles with infertility in Israel and Lebanon. *Journal of Middle East Women's Studies, 5*(2), 23–52.

Bookwala, J., Marshall, K. I., & Manning, S. W. (2014). Who needs a friend? Marital status transitions and physical health outcomes in later life. *Health Psychology, 33*(6), 505–515. doi:10.1037/hea0000049

Borodulin, K., Mäkinen, T. E., Leino-Arjas, P., Tammelin, T. H., Heliövaara, M., Martelin, T., ... Prättälä, R. (2012). Leisure time physical activity in a 22-year follow-up among Finnish adults. *International Journal of Behavioral Nutrition & Physical Activity, 9*(1), 121–126. doi:10.1186/1479-5868-9-121

Botwinick, J. (1978). *Aging and behavior: A comprehensive integration of research findings.* Berlin, Germany: Springer.

Boyarsky, B. K., Haque, W., Rouleau, M. R., & Hirschfeld, R. A. (1999). Sexual functioning in depressed outpatients taking mirtazapine. *Depression & Anxiety, 9*(4), 175–179.

Burri, A., Schweitzer, R., & O'Brien, J. (2014). Correlates of female sexual functioning: Adult attachment and differentiation of self. *Journal of Sexual Medicine, 11*(9), 2188–2195. doi:10.1111/jsm.12561

Bybee, J., & Wells, Y. V. (2006). Body themes in descriptions of possible selves: Diverse perspectives across the life span. *Journal of Adult Development, 13*(2), 95–101. doi:10.1007/s10804-006-9009-9

Calzo, J. P., Antonucci, T. C., Mays, V. M., & Cochran, S. D. (2011). Retrospective recall of sexual orientation identity development among gay, lesbian, and bisexual adults. *Developmental Psychology, 47*(6), 1658–1673.

Capers, C. F., Baughman, K., & Logue, E. (2011). Behaviors and characteristics of African American and European American females that impact weight management. *Journal of Nursing Scholarship, 43*(2), 133–144. doi:10.1111/j.1547-5069.2011.01393.x

Carstensen, L., Turan, B., Scheibe, S., Ram, N., Ersner-Hershfield, H., Samanez-Larkin, G.,…Nesselroade, J. (2011). Emotional experience improves with age: Evidence based on over 10 years of experience sampling. *Psychology & Aging, 26*(1), 21–33. doi:10.1037/a0021285

Cattell, R. B. (1971). *Abilities: Their structure, growth, and action.* New York, NY: Houghton Mifflin.

Cavanaugh, J. C., & Blanchard-Fields, F. (2006). *Adult development and aging* (5th ed.). Belmont, CA: Wadsworth.

Cheek, C., & Piercy, K. (2008). Quilting as a tool in resolving Erikson's adult stage of human development. *Journal of Adult Development, 15*(1), 13–24. doi:10.1007/s10804-007-9022-7

Cornett, C. W., & Hudson, R. A. (1987). Middle adulthood and the theories of Erikson, Gould, and Valillant: Where does the gay man fit in? *Journal of Gerontological Social Work, 10*(3–4), 61–73.

Crain, W. (2000). *Theories of development: Concepts and applications* (4th ed.). Upper Saddle River, NJ: Prentice-Hall.

Darling, C. A., Coccia, C., & Senatore, N. (2012). Women in midlife: Stress, health and life satisfaction. *Stress & Health: Journal of the International Society for the Investigation of Stress, 28*(1), 31–40. doi:10.1002/smi.1398

Das, D., Cherbuin, N., Butterworth, P., Anstey, K. J., & Easteal, S. (2012). A population-based study of attention deficit/ hyperactivity disorder symptoms and associated impairment in middle-aged adults. *Plos ONE, 7*(2), 1–9. doi:10.1371/journal.pone.0031500

DeLamater, J., & Koepsel, E. (2015). Relationships and sexual expression in later life: a biopsychosocial perspective. *Sexual & Relationship Therapy, 30*(1), 37–59. doi:10.1080/14681994.2014.939506

Discacciati, A., Orsini, N., Andersson, S., Andrén, O., Johansson, J., & Wolk, A. (2011). Body mass index in early and middle-late adulthood and risk of localised, advanced and fatal prostate cancer: A population-based prospective study. *British Journal of Cancer, 105*(7), 1061–1068. doi:10.1038/bjc.2011.319

Dooley, M., Dineen, T., Sarma, K., & Nolan, A. (2014). The psychological impact of infertility and fertility treatment on the male partner. *Human Fertility, 17*(3), 203–209. doi:10.3109/14647273.2014.942390

Easton, S., Coohey, C., O'Leary, P., Zhang, Y., & Hua, L. (2011). The effect of childhood sexual abuse on psychosexual functioning during adulthood. *Journal of Family Violence, 26*(1), 41–50. doi:10.1007/s10896-010-9340-6

Edelstein, R. S., Newton, N. J., & Stewart, A. J. (2012). Narcissism in midlife: Longitudinal changes in and correlates of women's narcissistic personality traits. *Journal of Personality, 80*(5), 1179–1204. doi:10.1111/j.1467–6494.2011 .00755.x

Folstein, M. F., Folstein, S. E., & McHugh, P. R. (1975). "Mini-mental state." A practical method for grading the cognitive state of patients for the clinician. *Journal of Psychiatric Research, 12*(3), 189–198.

Fredriksen-Goldsen, K. I., Hyun-Jun, K., Barkan, S. E., Muraco, A., & Hoy-Ellis, C. P. (2013). Health disparities among lesbian, gay, and bisexual older adults: Results from a population-based study. *American Journal of Public Health, 103*(10), 1802–1809. doi:10.2105/AJPH.2012.301110

Gardner, H. (1983). *Frames of mind: The theory of multiple intelligences*. New York, NY: Basic Books.

Ghaemmaghami, P., Allemand, M., & Martin, M. (2011). Forgiveness in younger, middle-aged and older adults: Age and gender matters. *Journal of Adult Development, 18*(4), 192–203. doi:10.1007/s10804-011-9127-x

Ghisletta, P., Rabbitt, P., Lunn, M., & Lindenberger, U. (2012). Two thirds of the age-based changes in fluid and crystallized intelligence, perceptual speed, and memory in adulthood are shared. *Intelligence, 40*(3), 260–268. doi:10.1016/j.intell.2012.02.008

Godino, J. G., Watkinson, C., Corder, K., Sutton, S., Griffin, S. J., & Van Sluijs, E. M. (2014). Awareness of physical activity in healthy middle-aged adults: A cross-sectional study of associations with sociodemographic, biological, behavioural, and psychological factors. *BMC Public Health, 14*(1), 1–19. doi:10.1186/1471-2458-14-421

Gustafsson, P., Janlert, U., Theorell, T., Westerlund, H., & Hammarström, A. (2012). Social and material adversity from adolescence to adulthood and allostatic load in middle-aged women and men: Results from the Northern Swedish Cohort. *Annals of Behavioral Medicine, 43*(1), 117–128. doi:10.1007/s12160-011-9309-6

Hampson, S. E., Edmonds, G. W., Goldberg, L. R., Dubanoski, J. P., & Hillier, T. A. (2013). Childhood conscientiousness relates to objectively measured adult physical health four decades later. *Health Psychology, 32*(8), 925–928. doi:10.1037/a0031655

Herrera, A. P., Meeks, T. W., Dawes, S. E., Hernandez, D. M., Thompson, W. K., Sommerfeld, D. H., … Jeste, D. V. (2011). Emotional and cognitive health correlates of leisure activities in older Latino and Caucasian women. *Psychology, Health & Medicine, 16*(6), 661–674. doi:10.1080/13548506.2011.555773

Hinchliff, S., Gott, M., & Ingleton, C. (2010). Sex, menopause and social context. *Journal of Health Psychology, 15*(5), 724–733. doi:10.1177/1359105310368187

Howell, L., & Beth, A. (2004). Pioneers in our own lives: Grounded theory of lesbians' midlife development. *Journal of Women & Aging, 16*(3–4), 133–147.

Hunt, K., Sweeting, H., Keoghan, M., & Platt, S. (2006). Sex, gender role orientation, gender role attitudes and suicidal thoughts in three generations. *Social Psychiatry & Psychiatric Epidemiology, 41*(8), 641–647. doi:10.1007/s00127-006-0074-y

Jackson, J., Knight, K., & Rafferty, J. (2010). Race and unhealthy behaviors: Chronic stress, the HPA axis, and physical and mental health disparities over the life course. *American Journal of Public Health, 100*(5), 933–939. doi:10.2105/AJPH.2008.143446

Jæger, M. M. (2011). "A thing of beauty is a joy forever"? Returns to physical attractiveness over the life course. *Social Forces, 89*(3), 983–1003.

Jeffers, L. A., & DiBartolo, M. C. (2011). Raising health care provider awareness of sexually transmitted disease in patients over age 50. *MEDSURG Nursing, 20*(6), 285–290.

Jianfang, Z., Xiaomei, R., & Hearst, N. (2014). Individual and household-level predictors of health related quality of life among middle-aged people in rural Mid-east China: A cross-sectional study. *BMC Public Health, 14*(1), 1970–1989. doi:10.1186/1471-2458-14-660

Katz-Bearnot, S. (2010). Menopause, depression, and loss of sexual desire: A psychodynamic contribution. *Journal of the American Academy of Psychoanalysis & Dynamic Psychiatry, 38*(1), 99–116.

Kesse-Guyot, E., Andreeva, V. A., Lassale, C., Hercberg, S., & Galan, P. (2014). Clustering of midlife lifestyle behaviors and subsequent cognitive function: A longitudinal study. *American Journal of Public Health, 104*(11), e170–e177. doi:10.2105/AJPH.2014-302121

Kim, J., & Richardson, V. (2012). The impact of socioeconomic inequalities and lack of health insurance on physical functioning among middle-aged and older adults in the United States. *Health & Social Care in the Community, 20*(1), 42–51. doi:10.1111/j.1365-2524.2011.01012.x

Kirasic, K. C. (2004). *Midlife in context.* New York, NY: McGraw-Hill.

Kisa, S., Zeyneloğlu, S., & Ozdemir, N. (2012). Examination of midlife women's attitudes toward menopause in Turkey. *Nursing & Health Sciences, 14*(2), 148–155. doi:10.1111/j.1442-2018.2011.00671.x

Klest, B., Freyd, J. J., Hampson, S. E., & Dubanoski, J. P. (2013). Trauma, socioeconomic resources, and self-rated health in an ethnically diverse adult cohort. *Ethnicity & Health, 18*(1), 97–113. doi:10.1080/13557858.2012.700916

Kokko, K., Korkalainen, A., Lyyra, A., & Feldt, T. (2013). Structure and continuity of well-being in mid-adulthood: A longitudinal study. *Journal of Happiness Studies, 14*(1), 99–114. doi:10.1007/s10902-011-9318-y

Kwaśniewska, M., Jegier, A., Kostka, T., Dziankowska-Zaborszczyk, E., Rębowska, E., Kozińska, J., & Drygas, W. (2014). Long-term effect of different physical activity levels on subclinical atherosclerosis in middle-aged men: A 25-year prospective study. *Plos ONE, 9*(1), 1–9. doi:10.1371/journal .pone.0085209

Levinson, D. J. (1996). *The seasons of a woman's life.* New York, NY: Knopf.

Lykeridou, K., Gourounti, K., Deltsidou, A., Loutradis, D., & Vaslamatzis, G. (2009). The impact of infertility diagnosis on psychological status of women undergoing fertility treatment. *Journal of Reproductive & Infant Psychology*, 27(3), 223–237. doi:10.1080/02646830802350864

Ma, J., & Xiao, L. (2010). Obesity and depression in US women: Results from the 2005–2006 National Health and Nutritional Examination Survey. *Obesity*, 18(2), 347–353. doi:10.1038/oby.2009.213

MacDonald, K. (2001). Theoretical pluralism and historical complexity in the development and maintenance of socially imposed monogamy: A comment on Kanazawa and Still. *Social Forces*, 80(1), 343–347.

McGarrity, L. A., & Huebner, D. M. (2014). Behavioral intentions to HIV test and subsequent testing: The moderating role of sociodemographic characteristics. *Health Psychology*, 33(4), 396–400. doi:10.1037/a0033072

Merrill, R. M., Aldana, S. G., Pope, J. E., Anderson, D. R., Coberley, C. R., & Whitmer, A. W. (2012). Presenteeism according to healthy behaviors, physical health, and work environment. *Population Health Management*, 15(5), 293–301. doi:10.1089/pop.2012.0003

Meyer, O. L., Castro-Schilo, L., & Aguilar-Gaxiola, S. (2014). Determinants of mental health and self-rated health: A model of socioeconomic status, neighborhood safety, and physical activity. *American Journal of Public Health*, 104(9), 1734–1741. doi:10.2105/AJPH.2014.302003

Mock, S., & Elbach, R. (2012). Stability and change in sexual orientation identity over a 10-year period in adulthood. *Archives of Sexual Behavior*, 41(3), 641–648. doi:10.1007/s10508-011-9761-1

Moreau, C., Beltzer, N., Bozon, M., & Bajos, N. (2011). Sexual risk-taking following relationship break-ups. *European Journal of Contraception & Reproductive Health Care*, 16(2), 95–99. doi: 10.3109/13625187.2010.547263

Mosher, C. E., Bakas, T., & Champion, V. L. (2013). Physical health, mental health, and life changes among family caregivers of patients with lung cancer. *Oncology Nursing Forum*, 40(1), 53–61. doi:10.1188/13.ONF.53-61

Murray, T., & Lewis, V. (2014). Gender-role conflict and men's body satisfaction: The moderating role of age. *Psychology of Men & Masculinity*, 15(1), 40–48. doi:10.1037/a0030959

Nappi, R. E., Albani, F., Santamaria, V., Tonani, S., Magri, F., Martini, E., … Polatti, F. (2010). Hormonal and psycho-relational aspects of sexual function during menopausal transition and at early menopause. *Maturitas*, 67(1), 78–83. doi:10.1016/j.maturitas.2010.05.008

National Institute of Mental Health (NIMH). (2012). *General format*. Retrieved from http://www.nimh.nih.gov/health/statistics/prevalence/serious-mental-illness-smi-among-us-adults.shtml

Neugarten, B. L. (1996). *The meanings of age: Selected papers of Bernice L. Neugarten*. Chicago, IL: University of Chicago Press.

Newhart, M. R. (2013). Menopause matters: The implications of menopause research for studies of midlife health. *Health Sociology Review*, 22(4), 365–376. doi:10.5172/hesr.2013.22.4.365

Newton, N., & Stewart, A. J. (2010). The middle ages: Change in women's personalities and social roles. *Psychology of Women Quarterly*, 34(1), 75–84.

Peplau, L. A., Frederick, D. A., Yee, C., Maisel, N., Lever, J., & Ghavami, N. (2009). Body image satisfaction in heterosexual, gay, and lesbian adults. *Archives of Sexual Behavior*, *38*(5), 713–725. doi:10.1007/s10508-008-9378-1

Perkins, E. A., & Haley, W. E. (2013). Emotional and tangible reciprocity in middle- and older-aged carers of adults with intellectual disabilities. *Journal of Policy & Practice in Intellectual Disabilities*, *10*(4), 334–344. doi:10.1111/jppi.12061

Rappoport, L. (1976). Adult development: Faster horses … and more money. *Personnel & Guidance Journal*, *55*(3), 106.

Rico-Villademoros, F., Calandre, E. P., Rodríguez-López, C. M., García-Carrillo, J., Ballesteros, J., Hidalgo-Tallón, J., & García-Leiva, J. M. (2012). Sexual functioning in women and men with fibromyalgia. *Journal of Sexual Medicine*, *9*(2), 542–549. doi:10.1111/j.1743-6109.2011.02513.x

Schnatz, P. F., Whitehurst, S. K., & O'Sullivan, D. M. (2010). Sexual dysfunction, depression, and anxiety among patients of an inner-city menopause clinic. *Journal of Women's Health*, *19*(10), 1843–1849. doi:10.1089/jwh.2009 .1800

Scullin, M. K., & Bliwise, D. L. (2015). Sleep, cognition, and normal aging: Integrating a half century of multidisciplinary research. *Perspectives on Psychological Science*, *10*(1), 97–137. doi:10.1177/1745691614556680

Sheehy, G. (1996). *New passages: Mapping your life across time*. New York, NY: Ballantine Books.

Singer, D. (2012). "It's not supposed to be this way": Psychological aspects of a premature menopause. *Counselling & Psychotherapy Research*, *12*(2), 100–108. doi:10.1080/14733145.2011.648202

Stawski, R. S., Almeida, D. M., Lachman, M. E., Tun, P. A., Rosnick, C. B., & Seeman, T. (2011). Associations between cognitive function and naturally occurring daily cortisol during middle adulthood: Timing is everything. *Journals of Gerontology Series B: Psychological Sciences & Social Sciences*, *66B*(Suppl. 1), i71–i81.

Stefanou, C., & McCabe, M. P. (2012). Adult attachment and sexual functioning: A review of past research. *Journal of Sexual Medicine*, *9*(10), 2499–2507. doi:10.1111/j.1743-6109.2012.02843.x

Stephens, C., Noone, J., & Alpass, F. (2014). Upstream and downstream correlates of older people's engagement in social networks: What are their effects on health over time? *International Journal of Aging & Human Development*, *78*(2), 149–169. doi:10.2190/AG.78.2.d

Stijntjes, M., de Craen, A. M., van Heemst, D., Meskers, C. M., van Buchem, M. A., Westendorp, R. J., … Maier, A. B. (2013). Familial longevity is marked by better cognitive performance at middle age: The Leiden Longevity Study. *Plos ONE*, *8*(3), 1–8. doi:10.1371/journal.pone.0057962

Summerall, E. L. (2014). *Traumatic brain injury and PTSD*. Retrieved from http:// www.ptsd.va.gov/professional/co-occurring/traumatic-brain-injury-ptsd.asp

U.S. Department of Health and Human Services, Center for Disease Control. (2014). *Summary health statistics for U.S. adults: National Health Interview Survey, 2012.* Retrieved from http://www.cdc.gov/nchs/data/series/sr\LY1\textbackslash_10/sr10\LY1\textbackslash_260.pdf

Verhaeghen, P., & Salthouse, T. A. (1997). Meta-analyses of age–cognition relations in adulthood: Estimates of linear and nonlinear age. *Psychological Bulletin, 122*(3), 231.

Vimalananda, V., Miller, D., Christiansen, C., Wang, W., Tremblay, P., & Fincke, B. (2013). Cardiovascular disease risk factors among women veterans at VA medical facilities. *Journal of General Internal Medicine, 28*(2), 517–523. doi:10.1007/s11606-013-2381-9

Wechsler, D. (1939). *The measurement of adult intelligence.* Baltimore, MD: Williams & Witkins.

Weiss, D., Freund, A. M., & Wiese, B. S. (2012). Mastering developmental transitions in young and middle adulthood: The interplay of openness to experience and traditional gender ideology on women's self-efficacy and subjective well-being. *Developmental Psychology, 48*(6), 1774–1784. doi:10.1037/a0028893

Wilcox, S. L., Redmond, S., & Hassan, A. M. (2014). Sexual functioning in military personnel: Preliminary estimates and predictors. *Journal of Sexual Medicine, 11*(10), 2537–2545. doi:10.1111/jsm.12643

Wilson, H. W., & Widom, C. S. (2011). Pathways from childhood abuse and neglect to HIV-risk sexual behavior in middle adulthood. *Journal of Consulting and Clinical Psychology, 79*(2), 236–246.

Zwickl, S., & Merriman, G. (2011). The association between childhood sexual abuse and adult female sexual difficulties. *Sexual & Relationship Therapy, 26*(1), 16–32. doi:10.1080/14681994.2010.530251

CHAPTER 16

Middle Adulthood: Emotional and Social Development

Dilani M. Perera-Diltz, Andrew J. Intagliata, and John M. Laux

What is middle adulthood? We know that it comes some significant time after being in the 20s. When you think of someone being in middle adulthood, what comes to mind? Write these thoughts on a piece of paper and see how it compares with what you read in the next several pages. Is middle adulthood defined by an established age range, by identifiable changes in the biological being, or by accomplishment of certain life tasks? Does what is considered middle adulthood change as life expectancy changes? Will life expectancy continue to rise? Is there a ceiling to life expectancy? Is middle adulthood a time of emotional and social development or merely a period through which we pass time in the aging process? This chapter provides you with information pertaining to emotional and social factors related to middle adulthood, including answers to the previous questions that are related to emotional and social factors.

Middle adulthood is a time when our influence on society peaks, and in turn society demands maximum social and civic responsibility. It can also be a time of doubt and despair depending on your developmental path and the decisions made through the previous years of life. For example, if you are successful in your career; are stable financially; live comfortably; have decent relationships with your significant other, family, children, and others; and have good health, then your middle adulthood years can be full of goals and responsibilities. Even securing a modicum combination of these achievements can provide future expectations and responsibilities. However, if life circumstances left you significantly lacking in one or more of these areas, then middle adulthood can be a time of turbulence.

Scholars studying the human passage from birth to death have theorized about lifespan development. Operating under the assumption that there are certain pathways and tasks to be accomplished along life's journey, theorists have proposed theories of adult development that recognize adulthood as a period of active physical, cognitive, social, and emotional development (Wortley & Amatea, 1982).

BOX 16.1 DOES WHAT IS CONSIDERED MIDDLE ADULTHOOD CHANGE AS LIFE EXPECTANCY CHANGES?

Life expectancy has almost doubled within the last century. Life expectancy in 1900 for males of all races was 46.3 years and for females it was 48.3 years (Center for Disease Control [CDC]/National Center for Health Statistics [NCHS], 2013). This expectancy was even lower for African Americans. In 1900, African American males' life expectancy was 32.5 years and females' was 33.5 years (CDC/NCHS, 2013). A century later, life expectancy had significantly increased for all races, with males at 74.1 years and females at 79.3 years. African American males' and females' life expectancies more than doubled, to ages 68.2 years and 75.1 years, respectively. By 2011, the American life expectancy continued to increase. Males of all races were expected to live to age 76.3 years and females to 81.1 years (CDC/NCHS, 2013). You can check your life expectancy at http://www.ssa.gov/planners/benefitcalculators.htm.

Discussion Questions

1. Will life expectancy continue to rise? Is there a ceiling to life expectancy? Support your answer. What factors do you think have contributed to the increase in the lifespan over the past century? What social and emotional outcomes are associated with increase in lifespan?
2. If age range is what determines middle age, then has what is classified as middle age changed from 1900 to 2015?
3. If life tasks determine middle age, then how might they have changed with the societal changes in the United States?

These theorists have postulated philosophies and notions about the aspects of change that occur during middle adulthood. These postulates rest on a second assumption that middle adulthood changes are a result of either internal genetic factors, external age-related life events, or a combination of both (Wortley & Amatea, 1982). Theorists have provided some guidance on the sequence of change, the catalysts for change, and how to adapt successfully to such changes in middle adulthood (Wortley & Amatea, 1982). Before we look at what theorists have provided to guide our understanding of middle adulthood and its advantages and challenges, let us introduce you to Rick, who is in his middle adulthood years.

Rick is a Caucasian male in his late 40s. He is working in a career of his choice. He has been at his present job for about 17 years and has recently been promoted to a managerial position. As a consequence of the promotion, he earns more, works longer hours, and manages others at work. Rick is remarried and has two biological children and two stepchildren. One child is from his current marriage. Out of all four children, the oldest child has been accepted to and attends university, and the youngest is in middle school. Rick's wife also works in a career of her choice. Her workplace is very stressful, and she often brings work stress home. Rick's current relationship with his first wife is volatile. His current wife's ex-spouse is supportive with the raising of their children and flexible in scheduling visits. Rick recently learned that his aging parents may no longer be able to live independently due to his father's failing health and his mother's deteriorating memory issues. Their failing health has made Rick aware of his own needs to save for his retirement and for some inheritance for his children. Rick does not want to burden his wife with his responsibilities to his work, his parents, or his children.

We will provide thought-provoking questions related to Rick's case at the end of each theory. Our hope is that you will read the theory a couple of times and understand what each theory has to offer for conceptualization and treatment planning with clients in their middle adulthood. We will provide our conceptualization of the various case vignettes presented throughout this chapter at the end of the chapter. Certainly, there is not a single method to conceptualize a case. It may benefit you to document some of your thoughts related to the vignette questions as you go along and see how those compare with our conceptualizations.

THEORIES ON EMOTIONAL AND SOCIAL DEVELOPMENT IN MIDDLE ADULTHOOD

First we turn to theory as it helps us decrease or manage uncertainty and make more responsible ethical decisions (Ettinger, 1991). There are a sufficient number of theories of adult development available to the reader. As you read the next couple of pages of theory, pay attention to the theorist's lifespan, provided within parentheses after the theorist's name, to grasp a better understanding of how the theory may have been influenced by the views of the theorist's time. For the ease of remembering, we have categorized theories as stage and task theories of development and provided only basic information that will help in client conceptualization and treatment planning options. Important theorists to consider include Jean Piaget, Lawrence Kohlberg, Erik Erikson, Daniel Levinson, Roger Gould, Bernice Neugarten, George Vaillant, and Robert Havighurst. The following sections are written based on the assumption that these theorists and their views have been explored earlier in this text. Consequently, only portions of the respective theories that are specific to persons in middle adulthood will be explored herein.

Let's start with someone most associated with being a seminal author about cognitive development: Jean Piaget. Piaget (1896–1980) provided a four-stage theory for cognitive development by observing and talking with children. Chapter 2 provides an in-depth discussion of his theory, so here we provide you some practical information so we can relate this information to the case of Rick. This theory proposes that from birth to 2 years is sensorimotor development; from

2 to 7 years is preoperational cognitive development; from 7 to 11 years is concrete operational development; and from 11 years onward is formal operational development (Atherton, 2013). What is of relevance to the middle adulthood period is concrete operational thought development (i.e, the ability to think logically about objects and events) and formal operational thought (i.e., the ability to think logically about abstract concepts). Although it is reasonable to assume from the given age ranges that by age 11 years a child will be moving to formal operational thought processes, Piaget's stages have been critiqued as being too rigid. For example, some children achieve concrete operational functions earlier than Piaget theorized, and some adults display an inability to perform formal operational thought (Atherton, 2013; Wood, Smith, & Grossniklaus, 2001). The value of formal operational thinking may be tied to Western cultural values to the exclusion of other cultures' focus on concrete operational thinking (Edwards, Hopgood, Rosenberg, & Rush, 2000). Finally, Piaget's methods on which his theory is based have received criticism as lacking scientific rigor (Edwards et al., 2000).

Piaget believed that we acquire knowledge through the use of certain skills, which he called schemas. What we call learning is the schema of adaptation. Adaption requires the ability to assimilate, use previous knowledge to incorporate a new object and accommodate, and adjust previous knowledge to incorporate knowledge about the new object. Piaget considered equilibrium as the balance between existing knowledge and new learning.

As we graduate through our stages of cognitive development, the schemas become more complex. During the concrete operational stage, for instance, we learn classification, the ability to group together objects that have similar characteristics. Another schema, conservation, is the ability to understand that initial quantity remains the same, even when objects of that quantity are rearranged. Reversibility is the ability to understand that when an object, such as clay, is changed in shape it can be changed back into its original shape in a different pattern or a different container. Seriation is the ability to put objects in order or in a pattern. During the formal operational stage, we are able to hypothesize about concepts that are not in our presence. The use of the above mentioned schemas become more multifaceted. For instance, the classifications are done at higher complexity. These terms aid in discussing our ability to perform certain cognitive tasks. (The section at the end of the chapter provides more information on the Jean Piaget Society, which contains great resources for students interested in learning more about his theory.)

Considering the case of Rick, what are the indicators that Rick is using either concrete or formal operational thought in processing his current life issues? Do you see where Rick may need to use formal operational thought? Which concepts would be helpful in communicating about what is cognitively occurring within Rick?

Lawrence Kohlberg (1927–1987) is best known as the stage theorist who offered a theory of moral development. In doing so, Kohlberg argued that moral reasoning is correlated with ethical behavior. His six stages fall under three levels: preconventional, conventional, and postconventional morality (Kohlberg, 1968, 1976). Preconventional morality includes stage 1 (obedience), during which behavior choices are based on avoiding punishment, and stage 2 (individualism), during which behavior is based on a self-interested exchange for personal ful-fillment. Conventional morality in stage 3 is related to maintaining individual relationships, such as conforming to social normatives, and in stage 4 it is related to adherence to law and order. Within level 3's postconventional morality, during stage 5 (social contract orientation) we engage in decision making based on fundamental rights of others. During stage 6, behavior is based on upholding a set of ethical principles that are applied universally, such as justice (Kohlberg, 1968, 1976). Although Kohlberg's model is heavily influenced by Piaget's views, it does not suppose that moral development is tied to a particular age range. Consequently, counselors should be prepared to work with middle adulthood persons whose moral reasoning falls into any of these six stages.

Let's apply Kohlberg's theory to the case of Rick. If Rick makes a decision to relocate closer to his parents, in what stage of morality would you consider he is engaging during his decision-making process? What conflict might he face when attempting to maintain all relationships in his current situation? What are some ways a counselor may help him recognize, evaluate, and address any conflicts that he experiences?

A lifespan stage theorist, Erik Erikson (1902–1994) proposed an eight-stage, age-normative developmental theory based on psychosocial development across the lifespan. After his death, his wife published the ninth stage of psychosocial development. Newman and Newman (2012) expanded this theory to 11 stages. Here we focus only on middle adulthood, during which we are faced with resolving the psychosocial crisis of generativity versus stagnation (Erikson, 1963). Erikson's theory considers middle adulthood to consist of ages 34–60 years. Generativity is defined as concern and well-being of future generations, whereas stagnation is the lack of such. Positive resolution of this psychosocial crisis leads to the prime adaptive ego quality of caring (Erikson). Caring is evidenced through a commit-ment and concern for the next generation. Core pathology emerges as a result of negative or ineffective resolution of this crisis, resulting in rejectivity or an willing-ness to include others in our generative concerns (Erikson, 1963). Further, Erikson viewed persons in this age range to be in one of two states of career development. Erikson expected workers to either be comfortable with and making progress in their careers or experiencing uncertainty about their career directions. Coping strategies most useful during this stage are flexibility, creative problem solving, and a sense of humor.

Using Erikson's psychosocial theory, what is Rick's status on the continuum between generativity and stagnation? If Rick came to see a counselor to discuss his placement on this continuum, how do you think his counselor could assist Rick to resolve his psychosocial crisis of generativity versus stagnation so that he could emerge with caring and concern for future generations?

BOX 16.2 THE STRUGGLE AGAINST STAGNATION IN MIDDLE ADULTHOOD

Middle adulthood can be a time when people have many different roles (Havinghurst, 1972). However, when the number of those roles starts to decrease due to impending retirement, job loss, or children moving out of the home, those in middle adulthood may need to find different avenues that could help against stagnation. Creative arts may be one option for individuals dealing with role changes in middle adulthood. An activity such as quilting has been shown to help resolve this crisis of generativity and stagnation, as it allows individuals in middle adulthood to contribute to family, friends, and younger generations (Cheek & Piercy, 2008). Although this activity may not be for all, it is an example of how those in middle adulthood can find new activities to combat the feelings of stagnation. Volunteering has also been found to be satisfying (Kulik, 2010), but it is important to remember that middle adulthood covers a number of years. Two adults in middle adulthood may have vastly different views and experiences. Those in middle adulthood with many roles and activities may find volunteering less substantial to well-being (Yunqing & Ferraro, 2006), and a study of individuals in this age group found middle-aged participants to perceive their volunteer contributions as less than younger-aged counterparts (Kulik, 2010).

Discussion Questions

1. How might your conversation about generativity versus stagnation with a 45-year-old parent differ from a discussion with a 60-year-old parent?
2. What techniques might you use with a middle-aged client who comes to you with concerns about stagnation?

Age-based sequential theorist Daniel Levinson (1920–1994) proposed a social psychological stage theory known as seasons of life, with four eras approximately 25 years in length each. The childhood and adolescence era lasts from birth to about age 20 years, early adulthood from about age 20–45 years, middle adulthood from 40 to about 65 years, and late adulthood from 65 years onward. Although Levinson studied men and women separately, he found that they went through the same eras and transitional periods of life, with the main difference being in the information of the dream or vision, goals, and aspirations for an ideal life (Brown, 1987). Males set the dream, which is often career related, between ages 22 and 28 years, but women struggle with the dream, with a dichotomy of identity between career woman and family.

Each of Levinson's eras includes a 3–6-year transitional period, which may be an unsettling time due to questioning, challenging, and adapting to new venues. Eras also include other stages. During the middle adulthood era, midlife transition occurs between ages 40 and 45 years, during which we typically evaluate our lives. Such evaluation may lead to crisis such as divorce or a change in career. Entering middle adulthood occurs between ages 45 and 50 years, when we may face further choices about our relationships, career, and possible retirement. Between ages 50 and 55 years, we enter age 50 transition. Depending on the dream, during this period we may even commit to new tasks while beginning to ponder about our legacy. This can be a stable period for some and transitional for others. Culmination of middle adulthood occurs between the ages of 55 and 60 years when we transition to late adulthood (Levinson, 1977, 1986).

Rick is in his late 40s and is considered in the middle adulthood era. He would be considered in the transition period labeled *entering middle adulthood*. What new tasks do you believe Rick may take on during this transition? What types of activities will help Rick adapt to his new challenges?

Another theorist who used the stages to conceptualize development in middle adulthood is Roger Gould (1935–present). Gould postulated that adulthood is a time to emancipate from childhood restraints and grow in personal identity. Gould (1978, pp. 39–40) challenged adults to address the following four assumptions:

1. We'll always live with our parents and be their child.
2. They'll always be there to help when we can't do something on our own.
3. Life is simple and controllable.
4. There is no real death or evil in the world.

Gould's (1978) theory provided a sequence of age-related levels of adult development beginning at age 16 years. Between ages 16 and 22 years, adolescents and young adults begin development by leaving their parents' world and questioning beliefs formed during their childhood. Gould (1978) believed this emancipation and belief examination is necessary to develop higher levels of consciousness of self. Then, between ages 22 and 28 years, we enter the adult world. Questioning and reexamination occur again between ages 28 and 34 years. Between ages 35 and 45 years, we begin to address midlife concerns such as health, loss of a loved one, changes in personal status, and the approach of our mortality. Interestingly, these years are called the midlife decade. Then from ages 43 to 50 years, reconciliation and mellowing occur, leading to finally achieving stability and acceptance around age 50 years (Gould, 1978).

Obviously Rick has challenged the first assumption and does not live with his parents. However, he may be facing the other three challenges due to his parents' failing health. How could a counselor use the knowledge of Gould's theory to facilitate acceptance and stability in Rick's life?

The stage theorists provide us with age ranges, conflicts that may arise related to an age range, and some solutions to proceed in our life's journey to the next stage. These theories are helpful to navigate what types of conflicts need to be explored within a certain life stage or era. This alone may not be adequate when attempting to conceptualize and facilitate changes in persons in middle adulthood.

Other theorists explained adult development through the achievement of life tasks. Bernice Neugarten (1916–2001) challenged views that adulthood should be viewed as a progression of stages that are tied to age ranges. She countered this age-based stage process through her social clock theory. Neugarten's theory proposed that we evaluated our progress through life based on the achievement of certain tasks, such as marriage and procreation, obtaining a first job, and retiring relative to our culture's social expectations. Social clock theory indicates age-related expectations for life events such as a first job, marriage, or retirement. Achieving these life tasks on time or off time influences our self-esteem (Wortley & Amatea, 1982). Neugarten was cognizant of the differences among cultures in setting the appropriate time frames within which these tasks were to be completed (Wortley & Amatea, 1982). Further, Neugarten's efforts dispelled commonly held beliefs about the difficulties of passing through midlife, menopause, and the experience of grief and loss when a parent's last child leaves the home. It is vital that counselors first explore the client's cultural expectations of life tasks prior to engaging in a course of action. Multicultural competencies require that counselors be knowledgeable about their culturally different client's world and its expectations. You can obtain a copy of the multicultural competencies from https://www.counseling.org/docs/competencies/multcultural_competencies.pdf?sfvrsn=5.

Let's think of the case of Rick again. Rick is a Caucasian male in his late-40s, is married, has children, and recently received a promotion at his job. Does this mean that he has accomplished all life tasks and he would have high self-esteem, or is there a possibility that his culture may require him to meet other life tasks at this stage of his life? What more about his Caucasian background would you need to explore to be culturally competent?

Life task theorist George Vaillant (1934–present) studied more than 800 men and women spanning 60 years and delivered the adult life tasks theory. Vaillant (1998) defined six tasks necessary to be completed to be a mature adult. These tasks begin with developing an identity separate from that of parents. This process begins around adolescence and is achieved by examining our values, passions, and beliefs. Next comes the development of intimacy through the development of reciprocal relationships. For such relationships to occur, we must be able to include another's identity. The third task is career consolidation. This can be achieved through personal career, career of a spouse, or as a stay-at-home parent. Vaillant (1998) promoted the idea that a job transitions to a career if and when we achieve contentment, compensation, competence, and commitment. The fourth task is generativity, which is the ability to give unselfishly. In the fifth task, we serve as the keeper of meaning, and we pass on traditions from the past to the next generation. Finally, as adults we will achieve integrity or a sense of peace and unity with others (Vaillant, 1998). Most of these life tasks presented by Vaillant can transpire during middle adulthood. (The Useful Websites section includes an interview with Vaillant.) If Rick from the case study seeks help from you, in which of the six tasks listed by Vaillant do you think Rick may be operating?

BOX 16.3   PERSONALITY IN MIDDLE ADULTHOOD: DO WE CHANGE AS WE AGE?

Leading proponents of the five-factor model of personality (Costa & McCrae, 1976) believed that personality is biologically based and fairly firmly established by around age 30 years. Recent evidence, however, suggests that personality is plastic and can be shaped by environmental factors well into middle adulthood. For example, in a study of over 132,000 persons, Srivastava, John, Gosling, and Potter (2003) demonstrated that conscientiousness and agreeableness increase throughout early and middle adulthood. Further, Srivastava et al. (2003) noted that neuroticism scores among women, but not among men, decreased as they aged into middle adulthood. Environmental correlates for personality change include support from life partners; significant life events, such as marriage and parenthood; and adaptation through social experiences (Branje, Lieshout, & Gerris, 2007). Others have pointed to the ways adults make sense out of life events (stressful events in particular), and not the events in and of themselves, as contributing to middle adult personality changes (Sutin, Costa, Wethington, & Eaton, 2010).

Discussion Questions

1. If the fixed-approach to personality is rooted in the view that personality is biologically based, what consequences do these findings that environmental factors are associated with personality changes over time have on nature theory of personality development?
2. You have access to a large sample of 21-year-old monozygotic twins and a grant to support a longitudinal line of research. Design a research study to answer the following question: How does time influence personality structure?
3. A 25-year-old client presents in your office and reports that he is the "son and the heir of a shyness that is criminally vulgar" (Marr & Morrissey, 1985). He asks if he is forever doomed to live in the shadows or if there is any hope that he might grow out of it or benefit from counseling. What are your responses to this young man?

The final theory we will consider in this section is Robert Havighurst's (1900–1991) developmental theory, based on age-related tasks. He identified three general tasks that arise from physical maturation (i.e., biological), from personal sources (i.e., psychological), and from living in a society (i.e., social; Havighurst, 1972). He proposed that the successful attainment of these tasks leads to happiness and lack of success leads to unhappiness, social disapproval, and difficulty with later tasks in life. Havighurst (1972) identified six major age-related stages that begin in infancy and early childhood, with middle adulthood identified as a period between ages 30 and 60 years. Havighurst considered middle age as the time most people enter into long-term significant other relationships, start families, and settle into their adult lives.

During middle adulthood, partners engage in many roles that are interdependent on their companion. A traditional male may have the role of provider, homemaker, father, partner, son, and friend, and similarly a traditional female may have the roles of provider, homemaker, mother, partner, daughter, and friend. As you can imagine, with the changes in the composition of family and societal demands, these roles can be even more complicated. Some tasks that need to be accomplished during the middle adulthood period include (a) engaging in adult civic and social responsibility; (b) establishing and maintaining an economic standard of living through a career or partnership; (c) guiding adolescent children to become responsible and secure adults; (d) engaging in adult leisure activities; (e) developing a relationship with spouses as separate entities; (f) finding ways to accept and adjust to the physiological changes; and (g) accommodating the needs of aging parents (Havighurst, 1972). For the last time, let's revisit the case of Rick. What roles does he play? In what middle adulthood tasks from Havighurst's considerations does he engage? What tasks may he be ignoring?

As you may realize, there are an adequate number of theories that can facilitate middle adulthood client conceptualization through a developmental lens. Middle adulthood appears to be a period between ages 34 and 60 years. During middle adulthood, the completion of certain life tasks and the initiation of others are expected. These tasks can encompass career, relationships, spirituality, or physical and cognitive areas. Issues related to physical and cognitive development are discussed in chapter 15. Now we highlight issues clients in middle adulthood may bring to counseling related to emotional and social development.

ISSUES COMMONLY EXPERIENCED IN MIDDLE ADULTHOOD

Prior to delving into the issues that may arise during middle adulthood, let's look at two overarching areas of interest throughout lifespan development: self-concept and individuality. Self-concept clarity has been shown to have a curvilinear relationship in respect to age: it goes up through young and middle adulthood but decreases in older adulthood (Lodi-Smith & Roberts, 2010). Middle adulthood may then be the time at which understanding of ourselves and our identities is at the highest (Lodi-Smith & Roberts, 2010). This conclusion makes sense because individuals in this age group may be in midcareer with a family. Those in young adulthood may still be trying to figure out an identity and develop socially, and individuals in older adulthood could be dealing with the loss of roles (e.g., worker, spouse, child). Dollinger and Clancy Dollinger (2003) measured individuality through the use of photo essays of adult participants aged 18 to 54 years. These photo essays required participants to use pictures to show who they were as individuals, and these were then given a score by trained raters. A comparison of the 20–25-year age group and the 45–50-year age group showed a significant difference in rated individuality, with the 45–50-year age group scoring higher (Dollinger & Clancy Dollinger, 2003). These results indicate that our personalities and our abilities to describe ourselves possibly develop throughout our adulthood. Think of the implications of these finding as you read the following sections.

The main areas that contribute to social and emotional development during middle adulthood are career, relationships, and spirituality. We provide vignettes at the beginning of each section to direct your attention to how you may provide counseling to someone experiencing these issues in middle adulthood.

Career

Career plays a significant role in our lives, and this role is prominent during middle adulthood. Employment is one of the most predominant daily engagements, with the highest number of hours of the day spent on work (Fleck, 2009). On average, Americans work 1,792 hours annually (U.S. Department of Labor, Bureau of Labor Statistics, 2014). This amount averages to about 34 hours per week or about 7 hours per 5-day week. The sex composition of the workforce has changed between 1970 and 2001. Smith and Mattingly (2014) reported that the number of males as sole breadwinners has decreased from 56% to 25% during this time period. This demographic decline indicates that within one generation there has been an increase in the number of women in the workplace, the number of two-income families, and the number of fathers taking stay-at-home duties.

Super's (1984) vocational development theory postulates the establishment of a stable career identity between ages 25 and 44 years and maintenance of that identity with small adjustments there onward. Although career development theories indicate gender-based occupational role salience in Westerners, research has produced mixed results across cultures. Although Bosch, de Bruin, Kgaladi, and de Bruin (2012) found similarities to Western context among Black African men and women, Rajadhyaksha and Bhatnagar (2000) found dissimilarities among Indian dual-career male and female partners. Statistics from the Bureau of Labor, career theorists' conceptualizations of the significance of work during middle adulthood, and researchers' findings indicate that career is a major task during middle adulthood. While engaging in a career during middle adulthood, we may experience promotion, requests to work in groups, a desire or pressure to change careers, an opportunity to return to school, a loss of employment due to workplace changes, and working in positions requiring lesser qualifications than we have. Before we dive into the discussion of how promotion affects an individual and his or her family, let's consider another vignette. Lloyd is a married African American male who is in his late 40s. He worked as an engineer for the past 15 years. Recently, he was promoted to be a senior managing engineer, which includes managing a small group of engineers as they complete their group projects. This promotion requires Lloyd to work more hours. What types of new challenges may Lloyd face due to his promotion?

BOX 16.4   THE EFFECT OF WORK ON MIDDLE ADULTHOOD DEVELOPMENT

In 2013, the average employed American person between the ages of 25 and 54 years living in a household with children under age 18 years spent an average of one-third (8.7 hours) of their day on work and related activities (U.S. Department of Labor, Bureau of Labor Statistics, 2014). It would not be surprising then to see work have an effect on development in middle adulthood. One study looking at changes in five-factor personality dimensions in more than 2 years found that for fathers, low work stress was related to emotional stability maturation and an increase in extraversion (van Aken, Denissen, Branje, Dubas, & Goossens, 2006). When one group of women physicians was retested on the California Psychological Inventory from their early 30s to mid-40s, participants increased in dominance, responsibility, self-control, good impression, and achievement via conformance, while at the same time they decreased in social presence and self-acceptance (Cartwright & Wink, 1994). This time period may be the peak of career involvement, and participants' responses indicated personality changes such as becoming more skilled leaders who had less desire for popularity, having greater acceptance of duties and responsibilities, and having better self-discipline (Cartwright & Wink, 1994). A longitudinal study found that over a period of 10 years, respondents with psychologically demanding jobs showed more extraversion, whereas those with hazardous working conditions decreased in agreeableness (Sutin & Costa, 2010).

Discussion Questions

1. Do you think that counselors would increase in extroversion over the course of adulthood? Why or why not? Have you noticed any changes in yourself?
2. You are a counselor who has a client come in reporting a dislike of her current job, which is having an effect on her well-being. How do you go about addressing this even though you may not be a career counselor?

Bobek and Robbins (2005) noted that recent financial events in this country produced a workforce that experiences a great many transitions. Whereas previous generations of workers could expect a relatively stable career path, today's middle-aged adults work in unsteady occupational and financial times. These circumstances have implications for career counseling with middle-aged persons. Savickas (2002) expanded on Super's (1984) theory and wrote that persons in this demographic are faced with two career directions: maintenance or management. Maintenance involves staying with a particular employer or within a certain career. The goal in maintenance is to continue an occupational role and solidify our self-concept (Savickas, 2002). Savickas projected that changes in the world of work would result in decreasingly fewer persons who are able to experience a career trajectory that allows for maintenance. Savickas augmented Super's theory by replacing the maintenance construct with the notion of management, a process that focuses on resilience and re-starting of work. Consequently, persons in this age group who are forced to initiate starts and who lived through forced stops to their world of work may experience negative self-esteem following job loss or extended periods of unemployment or underemployment. Interruptions in work may be associated with increased anxiety and doubt about future employability. Persons who lack the skills requisite to succeed in this fast-changing workforce may present for counseling feeling anxious about their finances and vulnerable about their abilities to meet their employers' demands (Bobek & Robbins, 2005). Let's look at how these changes affect career.

Promotion in Career

Middle adulthood is a time during which we are at a peak in career productivity. This often means a promotion to a leadership position. With a promotion we can experience both happiness and perhaps an increase in stress. Effective leadership requires good interpersonal skills with the ability to present ourselves competently to those above and below in hierarchy, to be open and flexible to others' ideas, and to read verbal and nonverbal cues of interpersonal interaction (Newman & Newman, 2012). Stressors may arise due to globalization of the work environments and the need for many styles of leadership to change to accommodate practices of employees outside our culture (Hoppe, 2007). Another stressor many face is the requirement to be more productive with fewer employees due to employers' budget cuts.

Managing subordinates may be stressful at times. It is necessary to achieve a balance between competitive and cooperative contribution among subordinates. The competitive nature brings innovation and drive while the cooperative nature brings successful completion of projects. Therefore, achieving a balance is productive. While managing people, managing social comparison is also necessary for productivity and effectiveness. In upward comparison we compare ourselves to others performing better than ourselves (Newman & Newman, 2012). Such comparison can bring happiness for others' accomplishments or jealousy for lack of self-achievement. With successful management a leader can encourage a person to strive to be like those who are excelling and support efforts toward such achievement. Downward comparison can bring positive feelings about our performance although at times it may bring frustration and unhappiness due to others' lack of accomplishments (Newman & Newman, 2012).

In the midst of learning a management style conducive to working with people from diverse cultures, working with a reduced workforce, and managing subordinates, leaders are expected to continue progress with personal accomplishments to maintain employment status and remain viable candidates for retention and promotion. Such positions require time that may infringe upon family life. Therefore, promotion brings the task of managing a modicum of balance between time at work and family wants and needs. Thinking back to the short vignette of Lloyd, what issues related to his career may he have to resolve as a result of his promotion to senior managing engineer?

Working With Groups

Middle-aged workers may be required to work either independently or in successful teams to promote and complete career-related projects. The process of working in teams has also been affected by the globalization of the work environment (Hoppe, 2007) and the concomitant need to understand people from diverse cultures across the world. Working in well-functioning teams provides the benefits of positive social relationships, increased abilities to achieve goals, and support for personal and professional development (Newman & Newman, 2012). However, at times, working in teams may challenge our interpersonal skills. Improved interpersonal skills and understanding of various cultural differences may facilitate better group interactions. If we are working in groups that are nonfunctional, then the stressors differ. Performance concerns, interpersonal relations, or company productivity demands may raise our discomfort. Let's consider how Lloyd might be affected if he had to work with a group that was in peak performance. What are some managerial concerns that may emerge? What may be some interpersonal concerns he may need to address? How should Lloyd proceed to promote positive interaction and a good balance between competitiveness and cooperation within his work group?

Career Change or Returning to School

Midlife is a time also for career transition. Such transition may imply a career change to a position that requires a different or new set of skills. It may require becoming more qualified in certain areas (or the worker may choose to improve his or her qualifications). Improving our employability may require a return to school to acquire academic or professional credentials. Alternatively, you may choose to leave an unstable employment situation and enter college to qualify for a field that is more stable. Whichever the choice, the improvement path may require a loss or reduction of income, loss of benefits, loss of familiarity, and a newness of identity. Returning to school may mean incurring expense and balancing an already full schedule. Depending on the reasons and circumstances of such change, you may engage in the change with enthusiasm or trepidation.

Let's consider a case vignette to understand the complexity of career change that features a return to school. Indira is an Asian descent woman in her mid-30s, and she is returning to school after a career in computer science and a recent divorce. Indira completed her degree in computer science under the directions of her parents, although she knew that she was not passionate about the field. Being of Asian descent, Indira believed it was important to follow her parents' directions while she lived under their roof. Indira completed her computer science degree and was married at age 27 years to a man of her choice from her own culture. Her parents approved of this partnership. She maintained part-time employment during her marriage. Her lack of ability to conceive children led to her recent divorce. Once divorced, Indira decided to go back to school and earn a degree in the field of her choice. What issues and stressors of returning to school will Indira face? What cultural stressors may she also experience?

Loss of Employment, Underemployment, or Unemployment

Other social-emotional concerns during middle adulthood is loss of employment, underemployment, and unemployment. The year 2008 was been dubbed the Great Recession, a period of time during which 7.5 million jobs were eliminated (Zuckerman, 2011). With such a large number of people losing jobs, unemployed (i.e., unable to find a job), or underemployed, the 2001 economic crisis was experienced across wide swaths of groups. Those who were once able to comfortably raise families suddenly were unable to even support themselves. Those planning retirement found themselves renegotiating their financial futures. Some who held jobs their entire lives found themselves unemployed. Skilled and educated workers found themselves underemployed. Recovering from such an economic disaster is a slow and long process. Feelings of insecurity due to what happened are common even for those who were able to secure jobs, were promoted to more palatable employment, or returned to previous held positions.

Let's look at the case of Alethea, a mixed ethnic origin female in her late 50s. Alethea has recently learned that she has early onset dementia. Her life has been a roller coaster. As a child, she was neglected and was placed in foster care. Foster care was adequate but nothing spectacular. After completing high school, she put herself through college to become an educator. Although she was able to maintain employment, secure a home, and even put away some money toward retirement, due to budget cuts and various other reasons she recently found herself without a job. What aforementioned theory gives you the most understanding of Alethea's case? What is another theory that provides you with a conceptualization of Alethea's case?

Retirement

Thinking of retirement in middle adulthood? Although actual retirement for most occurs during later adulthood, retirement immediacy occurs during middle adulthood. Most have been told to begin saving for retirement upon securing their first job in their 20s. Although some follow such direction and begin saving toward retirement, and others do not, the concept of retirement is a remote idea when you are in your 20s. However, in middle adulthood, people begin to plan career accomplishments they want to achieve prior to retirement, including their career legacy they want to leave behind. Some who have been privileged to work in jobs that allowed them the capacity of being able to secure retirement or save financially to supplement Social Security may look to retirement with anticipation. Others with less fortunate circumstances may be dismayed with the thoughts of imminent retirement and worrying about how to manage finances. Let's consider the case of Alethea again. What may be some retirement concerns she has due to unemployment? How does her early onset dementia complicate her retirement planning?

Relationships

Another area of socioemotional concern during middle adulthood is relationships. During middle adulthood thoughts of our legacy for our families may emerge. This legacy does not necessarily have to be financial in nature. This is a time that we are involved in numerous roles as employer, employee, spouse or significant other, parent, child, or friend. With several prominent roles to manage, it is not unrealistic to experience role overload. The rise in the number of dual income families has influenced the managing and balancing of the demands of other life roles for both women and men (Bosch et al., 2012). Some changes occur in relationships during middle adulthood. This section focuses on relationships with partners, children, and aging parents, but first let's consider the case of George.

George is an Italian descent male in his late 40s. George lost his wife to cancer a couple of years ago. He has two children, one a late teen and the other in early 20s. George and his wife were very involved in the community in which they resided. George has been dating a man since his wife's death. He has a career in medical technology and is happy with his employment. George would like to relocate to another area for a fresh start with his current partner. As you read the next couple of sections on relationships, consider what issues a counselor may need to address with George.

Partner Relationships

There are some theoretical contributions to understanding partner relationships. According to Erikson, our ego identity development influences intimacy (Beaumont & Pratt, 2011). Attachment theory (Bowlby, 1982) postulates that the parent–child attachment influences comfort and interdependence and that early attachment experiences contribute to our engagement with others across the life span (Wright, Crawford, & Castillo, 2009). Abusive early relationships may have an influence on later adult relationships. Women who experienced childhood maternal emotional abuse experienced daily emotional distress in middle to late adulthood (Poon & Knight, 2012). Such distress may contribute to unsatisfactory partner relationships.

Relationship satisfaction may be negatively influenced by stress. Adversity can vary in form and include sources such as daily stressors, chronic stressors, event stressors, and traumatic situations (Wheaton, 1994). Marital satisfaction has been associated with daily stressors such as the hassles of juggling our time among the various roles, overwhelming workload conveys the information adequately. Whisman (2006) indicated that 20% of current or formerly married persons experienced at least one major traumatic stressor as a child. Adults who experienced physical abuse, rape, or serious physical attack or assault were more likely to experience marital discord (Whisman, 2006).

Researchers disagree about sexuality and lifespan development. Some posit that there is decreased sexual activity and interest over the adult lifespan (Adams & Turner, 1985). Others argue that, at least in women, there is an increase in interest and incidence of heterosexual activity (Hite, 1976, as cited in Adams & Turner, 1985). Such issues related to sexuality may influence partner relationships during middle adulthood.

Reading the case of George, what type of partner relationship issues may he experience? How would you assess the salience and valence of his sexuality with the relationship issues that he presents?

Raising Children

Most children of middle adult parents are adolescents or older. One of Havighurst's (1972) tasks to be accomplished in middle adulthood is teaching teenage children how to become happy adults. During middle adulthood parents are helping their children think independently and make decisions for themselves. Some are assisting their children in choosing and enrolling in college. Neugarten's social clock theory indicated that there are age-related life tasks chosen from within a culture that we need to complete for better self-esteem (Wortley & Amatea, 1982). Therefore, for those middle-aged adults who are outside the common sociocultural expectations, such as being childless, having younger children, being divorced, widowed, remarried, or having never married or partnered with a life mate, middle adulthood may bring self-esteem concerns.

Another emerging group is the grandparents who are in their middle adulthood. In 2011, nearly 3 million children received their primary care from grandparents (U.S. Department of Commerce, 2009–2013). If you are a middle adulthood grandparent who was planning on a different future than raising

BOX 16.5 IS MIDDLE ADULT PSYCHOLOGICAL WELL-BEING RELATED TO PARENTHOOD?

Erikson (1963) viewed generativity to be evidence through one's concern and care for others. Although Erickson did not see parenthood as a necessary predicate to generativity, subsequent research established an empirical link between parenthood and generativity (e.g., Snarey, Son, Kuehne, Hauser, & Vaillant, 1987). The question about the role of parenthood in the experience of generativity and psychological well-being was addressed more recently by Rothrauff and Cooney (2008), who compared middle- and later-adult childless adults' and parents' well-being. Specifically, Rothrauff and Cooney measured parents' and nonparents' generativity, as measured by the Loyola Generativity Scale, and then compared these two groups' scores across six domains of well-being (Ryff, 1989): (1) attitudes toward others; (2) self-acceptance; (3) autonomy; (4) personal growth; (5) environmental mastery; and (6) purpose in life. The findings included a positive association between generativity and well-being, but no differences were found in this association between parents and childless adults. Further, no within-sex differences were uncovered.

Discussion Questions

1. Do this study's findings support or challenge Erikson's theory of psychosocial development?
2. An early-stage middle-aged couple comes to your office to discuss the anxiety they are experiencing because they are childless and they are worried about whether they can have meaning in their later adult lives without children. How would you use this study's findings to help this couple?
3. How can middle-aged persons achieve generativity without having to experience parenthood?
4. Despite psychosocial losses and increased health risks associated with aging, subjective well-being and life satisfaction do not decline with age (Schilling, 2006). In what ways might generativity be associated with subjective well-being and life satisfaction?

grandchildren, then you have to renegotiate your goals. You may be faced with different emotional and social challenges than those of raising your own children because these grandchildren may be under temporary child care, you may have to provide visitation to a parent, or you may seek custody due to grandchildren who have been abandoned or abused (Tremblay, Barber, & Kubin, 2014).

Consider the case of Juanita, a Hispanic female in her early 50s who has never been married and is currently not in a relationship. Juanita has a successful career in higher education and is financially comfortable. Juanita has family ties and is attached to her family of origin. However, she lives in another state from where her family lives. Juanita is very social and has a large pool of friendships that she treasures. Juanita is also very active in her community. What are some family and relational issues that may be affecting Juanita's life?

Caring for Aging Parents

Middle adulthood brings not only career, parenting, and partnership issues but also sometimes the added role of caring for aging parents. In middle adulthood we find ourselves not only taking care of our immediate family but also needing to lend a hand to those we believed were able to take care of themselves, our parents. Go back and look over the four assumptions that Gould (1978) proposed we needed to address in adulthood. This transition is difficult for most and requires some planning and adjusting on the part of middle adulthood people, their families, and their parents. Middle adulthood can become a time of role overload due to the added responsibility of parenting our parents.

Spirituality

Finally, let's take a look at the relationship between spirituality and middle adulthood. The variety of meanings associated with the term *spirituality* contributes to the difficulties in understanding the relationship between religiousness and spirituality. The terms *religious dweller* and *spiritual seeker* (Wuthnow, as cited in Dillon, Wink, & Fay, 2003) may offer some clarity. A religious dweller is someone who is willing to follow the doctrines of an established religion through the acts of prayer and communal worship. A spiritual seeker takes a more independent path through seeking a path outside of traditional religion. At times the spiritual seeker may even blend both Eastern and Western religious traditions (Dillon et al., 2003).

From the results of a study spanning 60 years, Dillon et al. (2003) concluded that religiousness and spirituality were positively correlated with generativity. That means the more we were engaged in religious or spiritual conduct, the more we had concerns toward the welfare of the next generation. The association between spirituality and generativity remained stable during middle adulthood (Dillon et al., 2003). Interestingly, there were some differences within generative practice among the religious dwellers and spiritual seekers. Religiousness was more correlated with altruism and selfless giving, which the authors viewed as communally oriented. Spirituality was correlated with impact on others and the legacy this sample of people will leave behind (Dillon et al., 2003).

There is debate among sociologists about the influence of recent cultural transformations on generative practice as people move away from communal and traditional centered religious practices to more private, seeker-oriented individual spirituality. The concern is whether or not such changes will replace socially responsible individualism with a more self-centered and narcissistic individualism (Dillon et al., 2003).

Some psychological theories suggest that spiritual growth leads to self-actualization. Similarly, developmental theories also associate spiritual growth with maturation. For instance, during middle adulthood, developmentally we have concerns with generativity according to Erikson, Havighurst, Vaillant, and others. Erikson described middle adulthood as the stage to develop the legacy for the next generation, Havighurst considered it a time for reaching out to help aging parents, and Vaillant suggested that middle adulthood is a period in which there is a drive to unselfishly give to others. All these behaviors could be associated with our current spiritual practices. In essence, there is a reasonable hypothesis that spirituality or an awareness and sense of connectedness to all others will lead to generative performance.

Let's focus our attention on the case study of Abdulla. Abdulla was raised in a traditional Muslim family. When growing up, he went to mosque every Friday and attended to the rituals of the varying worship days and holidays of his faith. At 53 years of age, Abdulla finds himself questioning his beliefs, behaviors, and traditions. He has neither attended mosque in the past month nor engaged in his daily prayers. Aside from the change in his behavior related to his religious traditions, Abdulla's behavior seems normal. He still maintains his employment of 17 years and other professional practices. He takes care of his family. He attends family functions. He maintains friendships. He is saving money to send his children to college. What do you think is happening with Abdulla in respect to his sense of spirituality? Is Abdulla moving away from being a religious dweller and becoming a spiritual seeker? Is Abdulla becoming a more self-centered individual? Is he having a religious or spiritual crisis? How would you, as a counselor, conceptualize the internal turbulence Abdulla faces?

ASSESSMENTS

We have provided some assessments that may be useful for you to either verify your interview impressions or to begin a discussion on a topic. The support of data gathered through standardized and nonstandardized assessments is useful in harnessing further information and supporting hypotheses about an area of a client's life. At times, the use of an assessment may be time efficient in providing services. Another useful utilization of assessments is as a second opinion when working with a client who may not be fully aware of the issues that are facing him or her. At such times a second opinion, or the results of an assessment, may help beyond a counselor's professional assessment alone. At times, assessments are useful to verify a counselor's conclusions from a counseling session. Another useful way to use assessments is to utilize the information in the assessment as a launching pad for discussion into areas that the client may have been hesitant to share. As with any assessment, it is our recommendation that you check the usefulness of these instruments and their psychometric values prior to their use to abide by ethical guidelines (American Counseling Association, 2014; Association for Assessment in Counseling and Education, 2003).

Career

Buros Mental Measurement Yearbook (http://buros.org/mental-measure ments-yearbook): Facilitates you finding a variety of measurement instruments that may be helpful to you in assessing your clients.

Self-Directed Search (http://www.self-directed-search.com): Takes 15–20 minutes to complete and provides your career report and costs $10.

Kuder (http://www.kuder.com): Useful in finding one's career interests.

Relationship

Relationship Assessment Scale (http://fetzer.org/sites/default/files/images/ stories/pdf/selfmeasures/Self_Measures_for_General_Relationship_ Satisfaction_RELATIONSHIP.pdf): Seven-item scale that assesses the personal satisfaction with a relationship. The seventh question especially is related to middle adulthood when there are significant changes within a person's life. This questionnaire provides the opportunity to dialogue on areas of dissatisfaction in a person's relationship. (Read more at http://www .midss.org/relationship-assessment-scale-ras.)

The Parent–Child Relationship Inventory (PCRI; https://www.wpspublish .com/store/Images/Downloads/Product/PCRI_Manual_Chapter_1.pdf): A 78-item, fourth-grade-reading-level assessment that can be completed in about 15 minutes. This instrument may be useful when working with a couple in their middle adulthood who may have difficulties with their relationship with children. It provides information on aspects that are problematic in the relationship and the quality of the relationship. It measures attitudes of both parents. (Product and pricing information is available at http://www.wpspublish.com/store/p/2898/parent-child-relationship -inventory-pcri.)

Parenting Style Questionnaire (http://www.comprehensivepsychology.com .au/assets/pdf/PARENTING%20STYLE%20QUESTIONNAIRE.pdf): Based on parenting styles defined as authoritarian, authoritative, and permissive and includes 13 questions each for authoritative and authoritarian parenting styles and four questions for permissive parenting style. This may be helpful as a discussion tool in a counseling setting with middle adulthood parents who may need to change their parenting styles to accommodate the growing independence of their children.

Parenting Test (http://psychologytoday.tests.psychtests.com/take_test.php? idRegTest=3261): This is provided free of charge for administration and it contains brief report on needing to be a perfect parent. This questionnaire asks questions related to parenting children from birth to about 16 years. There are life-like scenario questions that may be helpful for parents to discuss after taking the test to determine how to handle certain situations and how each parent may have a differing opinion on the best course of action.

Spirituality

There are more than 25 scales that can be used to assess spirituality. We have provided ones reviewed by a counselor at: http://counselingoutfitters.com/vistas/vistas07/Brown.htm.

Spiritual Well-Being Scale (SWBS; http://www.lifeadvance.com/): Twenty item questionnaire with two subscales: 10 questions assess religious well-being (RWB) and 10 assess existential well-being (EWB). SWBS may be useful in assessing the quality of spiritual experience.

Index of Core Spiritual Experiences (INSPIRIT; http://www.scribd .com/doc/49945421/Index-of-Core-Spiritual-Experiences#scribd): A seven -question assessment that is appropriate to open a discussion about internal relationship with a higher power and how these beliefs play out in one's life. It asks questions about method and regularity of spiritual practice.

Spiritual Assessment Inventory (SAI; http://onlinelibrary.wiley.com/doi/10 .1111/1468-5906.00121/pdf): A 49-item self-report questionnaire designed to assess spirituality in the following five aspects: awareness of God, disappointment, grandiosity, realistic acceptance, and instability. SAI may be helpful in measuring a middle adulthood individual's spiritual maturity if he or she brings such concerns to counseling.

Other instruments can be found at http://www.chcr.brown.edu/pcoc/spirit .htm.

KEY COUNSELING POINTERS FOR SOCIAL AND EMOTIONAL DEVELOPMENT DURING MIDDLE ADULTHOOD AND SOME IMPLICATIONS FOR COUNSELING

Here we provide our case conceptualizations for the various cases and related questions provided throughout the chapter. Case conceptualization can occur in a variety of ways, and no conceptualization is deemed correct. Please consider what you conceptualized and how we conceptualized as you read the following pages. We hope we can bring you some additional insight on the cases by presenting how we would conceptualize the cases.

Conceptualizing Rick

Let us return to Rick, the very first case vignette in this chapter. Conceptualizing Rick through Piaget's cognitive development theory, he is seen as able to use concrete operational processing as he is able to classify his children's needs for college. Furthermore, Rick is able to also utilize formal operational thought in that he foresees that his parents will need assistance soon and is making some provisions to accommodate those needs. We would further investigate Rick's hesitance to involve his wife in his planning for his parents' future. Then we can determine if there are issues with the schema conservation, that is, if he believes that sharing such news with his wife will take away his responsibility for his parents.

When conceptualizing Rick through Kohlberg's moral development theory, we see him working in both conventional morality and postconventional morality. He wants to maintain relationships with his parents, his spouse, and his children. However, he is also engaged in postconventional morality when accepting the responsibility for his own parents' well-being. It is the universal principal of taking care of our elders. If relocation is a necessity, then attending to his parents needs without thoroughly consulting with his wife may give rise to conflict in his spousal relationship. We would investigate with Rick his reasons for hesitating to discuss with his partner an upcoming significant change in his life. We would actively listen for any thought distortions that may need to be challenged for Rick to make the necessary changes to meet his goals.

Using Erickson's psychosocial theory, Rick appears to be satisfied with his role in his career. However, Rick may have issues with his relationships related to generativity. Rick's uncertainty in sharing with his wife his impending additional responsibility to his parents would be considered an issue related to generativity. Although Rick has successfully achieved the adaptive ego quality of caring demonstrated by his caring for his parents, for his spouse, and for his children, he still struggles to include his wife in concern related to his parents. We will discuss with him his progress in developing the ego quality of caring but further investigate his thought process on his decision-making process related to his parents' future well-being.

According to Levinson's seasons of life, Rick is in his third era, the middle adulthood era. We would explore if the promotion Rick recently received aligns with his dream. We would explore what tasks he seeks to initiate during this decade of his life. We would further explore his family relationships and how his impending decision about his parents' needs relates to his evaluation of the quality of his other relationships.

Using Gould's four assumptions adults need to challenge, we conceptualize that Rick is grappling with the realization that not only will his parents not be present to always help him but also they need his help for daily living. This probably challenges the third belief about the simplicity and controllability of life. We would also explore how Rick is processing the mortality of his parents. We would address each of these issues with Rick in counseling.

Especially when utilizing Neugarten's social clock theory, it is necessary to investigate in-depth cultural norms as relevant to the client. In the case of Rick, labeling him as Caucasian really does not provide much information on cultural norms. Therefore, we would investigate his ethnic heritage, his family traditions and expectations, his personal goals, and his relationship goals. Such information would hopefully provide us the opportunity to determine with Rick if he still needs to pursue other goals. Once we have the information on Rick's cultural heritage, learning more about immigration patterns and related issues will be helpful to bring in knowledge to discuss how these apply to Rick's life.

Utilizing Vaillant's six tasks, we would address tasks 2–5 with Rick. That is, we would investigate intimacy concerns in his relationships, his beliefs and goals related to his career, his need to take care of his parents while he has his own family, and his feelings related to becoming the keeper of family traditions. We would be very aware that some of this process could be very emotional for Rick because he will need to face the fact of mortality of his parents.

If conceptualizing Rick using Havighurst, we would explore the roles that are central to Rick's identity. We would share the seven tasks that Havighurst proposed for middle adulthood and engage with Rick on the relevance of these tasks to his life. As an outsider, we see that Rick is able to establish and maintain a stable financial household, is engaged in raising his children, has a spouse (but we do not know the quality of that relationship), and is making plans to aid his aging parents with daily tasks. We will explore these and the tasks we do not know about, which are his leisure time engagements and how he is coping with physiological changes during middle adulthood.

Conceptualizing Lloyd

Now that we have thoroughly conceptualized Rick from every possible perspective, let's look at Lloyd. Lloyd is a stable employee with a 15-year history of employment. As an engineer, Lloyd probably is financially stable. The recent promotion has placed Lloyd in a position where he has to manage not only his but also others' productivity. Such a change can bring some stressors. We will explore Lloyd's interpersonal style, ability, and self-confidence in managing others; his competence for management; and his goals in his new position. We will discuss what we know from this chapter on the need to balance competitive and cooperative forces among his engineers to achieve efficient production. Furthermore, based on the information in the chapter about the magnitude of working hours in the United States, we would explore how this promotion has affected Lloyd's career and family relationships and support and assist him to gain a functional balance.

Conceptualizing Indira

First and foremost, cultural acclimation and adaptation will be discussed with Indira to get a sense of her personal values and beliefs along with her Asian cultural values and beliefs. We would explore in depth how entrenched she is in her cultural expectations and how those expectations are influencing her current life. Then we will explore the pressures of her current existence. That is, how she is coping with her losses (e.g., inability to have children, the divorce, possible cultural expectations, financial decline), her relationship with her family, the stressors of going back to school, and her adjustment to living alone. Depending on what we gather, we may find her a support system that will validate her choices.

Conceptualizing Alethea

One of the first theories from the chapter that comes to mind is Neugarten's social clock theory. If you recall, she debunked the myths of difficulties of passing through midlife, menopause, and the experience of grief and loss when a parent's last child leaves the home, and so on. Without assuming that the loss of career is a crisis for Alethea, we would first explore Alethea's goals, resilience, and plans. If we find that the loss of her career is a significant issue for Alethea, then another theory that would be useful to conceptualize Alethea's situation is Havighurst's developmental tasks. First we would gather more information on Alethea's personal relationships. We know a bit about her childhood and about her current career crisis. Then utilizing Havighurst's theory, we would explore how her childhood experiences and her recent loss of employment influence her present sense of civic and social responsibility. We would also explore her plans for maintaining her standard of living during the time of unemployment and ways to make herself marketable to efficiently resecure employment. We would explore how she manages stress during this difficult time. We would investigate if she also has to deal with midlife female changes that may exacerbate her current feelings.

Conceptualizing George

We would not automatically assume that George has issues related to his same-sex partnership. Instead, we would investigate with George his relationships with his wife, his current partner, and his children. We want to know if there are any issues between his current partner and his children. We would also explore his reasons for relocation and how that would impact his relationships and his career. If we find out that George's partner and children have some difficulties in their relationship, we would explore the salience and valence of the issues related to his same-sex partnership as well as the context in which such difficulties occur.

Conceptualizing Juanita

When working with Juanita, similar to working with Indira, we would first explore her cultural ties and how those cultural values and beliefs influence her life decisions. We would explore her values, beliefs, and goals about family. We would also explore further her relationship with her parents and how living away from them affects her daily life and the lives of her children.

Conceptualizing Abdulla

In conceptualizing Abdulla, we would also need to first learn about his culture, faith, and relationship with his family. We will also explore the congruence of Abdulla's spiritual beliefs and values and his current spiritual practice. If there are any conflicts related to Abdulla's current spiritual practice, then we would tailor counseling to explore and remedy such. If there are no conflicts but there are conflicts related to his practices and the pressures of his family, then counseling will be to investigate ways to find peace both within himself and with his family.

SUMMARY

Middle adulthood is an approximate time period between the mid-40s and 60 years of age during which active emotional and social development occur. During middle adulthood, our influence on society peaks, and in turn society demands our utmost responsibility. Such influence and demands can bring a range of emotions including happiness, contentment, doubt, and despair based on one's history and developmental path.

Theorists have provided philosophies and concepts to manage uncertainties on developmental concerns when working with adults in their middle adulthood. These theories are based on the two assumptions that certain responsibilities and tasks must be accomplished along life's journey and that changes are a result of either internal or external factors. Piaget, Kohlberg, Erikson, and Levinson provided sequential age-related stages and responsibilities. Others such as Neugarten, Vaillant, and Havighurst provided life tasks that must be completed as an adult.

In attending to emotional and social development in the middle adulthood, it is necessary to investigate the roles of career, relationships, and spirituality. Career can bring diverse issues such as promotion, working within groups, change, return to school, loss of employment, unemployment, and underemployment. Middle adulthood is also a period during which retirement planning and related issues may emerge. During this middle adulthood period, we may evaluate our relationships with our partners, children, and aging parents. Such examination may also bring about issues that need to be resolved as we continue on life's journey. Finally, spirituality is intertwined with generative concerns, which is the main theme during middle adulthood. Addressing these areas with people in their middle adulthood is necessary for emotional and social development during this stage.

USEFUL WEBSITES

Theories of Middle Adulthood
https://www.youtube.com/watch?v=whMins1sdVE
Jean Piaget Society
http://www.piaget.org
Eric Erikson's Stages of Development
https://www.youtube.com/watch?v=dGFKAfixHJs Middle Adulthood
http://www.youtube.com/watch?v=ZMGgx1Qswcs by Mike
Kohlberg's Theory of Moral Development
http://www.youtube.com/watch?v=O7pQJ0ptjk0
http://www.youtube.com/watch?v=5czp9S4u26M (Interactive)
http://www.youtube.com/watch?v=FRvVFW85IcU (CBS)
Does Intelligence Decline in Middle Adulthood?
https://www.youtube.com/watch?v=jgQCbR4f3Yw

Vaillant Interview
http://link.brightcove.com/services/player/bcpid1460906593?bctid=
    22804415001
http://www.cdc.gov/nchs/fastats/life-expectancy.htm
Career
http://www.stanford.edu/~jdk/
http://www.mbti.com
http://study.com/academy/lesson/job-performance-career-change-and-
    unemployment-in-middle-adulthood.html
http://www.self-directed-search.com
Relationships
http://www.midlife-men.com/#axzz3P9CH9v3Q
Research Network on Successful Midlife Development
http://midmac.med.harvard.edu/
Spirituality
http://www.ted.com/talks/jonathan_haidt_humanity_s_stairway_to_self_
    transcendence/transcript?language=en
http://www.spiritualassessment.com/Manual.html

REFERENCES

Adams, C. G., & Turner, B. F. (1985). Reported change in sexuality from young adulthood to old age. *Journal of Sex Research*, *21*(2), 126–141. doi: 10.1080/00224498509551254

American Counseling Association (ACA). (2014). *ACA code of ethics*. Alexandria, VA: Author.

Atherton, J. S. (2013). *Learning and teaching; Piaget's developmental theory*. Retrieved from http://www.learningandteaching.info/learning/piaget.htm

Association for Assessment in Counseling and Education. (2003). *Responsibilities of users of standardized tests (RUST)* (3rd ed.). Retrieved from http://aac.ncat.edu/Resources/documents/RUST2003\%20v11\%20Final.pdf

Beaumont, S., & Pratt, M. (2011). Identity processing styles and psychosocial balance during early and middle adulthood: The role of identity in intimacy and generativity. *Journal of Adult Development*, *18*(4), 172–183. doi: 10.1007/s10804-011-9125-z.

Bobek, B. L., & Robbins, S. B. (2005). Counseling for career transition: Career pathing, job loss, and reentry. In S. D. Brown & R. W. Lent (Eds.), *Career development and counseling: Putting theory and research to work* (pp. 625–650). Hoboken, NJ: Wiley.

Bosch, A., de Bruin, G. P., Kgaladi, B., & de Bruin, K. (2012). Life role salience among Black African dual-career couples in the South African context. *International Journal of Human Resource Management*, *23*, 2835–2853. doi: 10.1080/09585192.2012.671506

Bowlby, J. (1969/1982). *Attachment and loss (Vol. 1)*. New York: Basic Books.

Branje, S. J. T., Van Lieshout, C. F. M., & Gerris, J. R. M. (2007). Big five personality development in adolescence and adulthood. *European Journal of Personality, 21*, 45–62. doi: 10.1002/per.596

Brown, P. L. (1987, September 14). Studying seasons of a woman's life. *New York Times*. Retrieved from http://www.nytimes.com/1987/09/14/style/studying-seasons-of-a-woman-s-life.html?pagewanted=2

Cartwright, L. K., & Wink, P. (1994). Personality change in women physicians from medical student years to mid-40s. *Psychology of Women Quarterly, 18*, 291–308. doi: 10.1111/j.1471-6402.1994.tb00456.x

Center for Disease Control (CDC)/National Center for Health Statistics (NCHS). (2013). *Life expectancy at birth, at age 65, and at age 75, by sex, race, and Hispanic origin: United States, selected years 1900–2011*. Retrieved from http://www.cdc.gov/nchs/data/hus/2013/018.pdf

Cheek, C., & Piercy, K. (2008). Quilting as a tool in resolving Erikson's adult stage of human development. *Journal of Adult Development, 15*(1), 13–24. doi:10.1007/s10804-007-9022-7

Costa, P. T. Jr., & McCrae, R. R. (1976). Age differences in personality structure: A cluster analytic approach. *Journal of Gerontology, 31*, 564–570. doi: 10.1093/geronj/31.5.564

Dillon, M., Wink, P., & Fay, K. (2003). Is spirituality detrimental to generativity? *Journal for the Scientific Study of Religion, 42*, 427–442. doi: 10.1111/1468–5906.00192

Dollinger, S. J., & Clancy Dollinger, S. M. (2003). Individuality in young and middle adulthood: An autophotographic study. *Journal of Adult Development, 10*, 227–236. doi: 10.1023/A:1026003426064

Edwards, L., Hopgood, J., Rosenberg, K., & Rush, K. (2000). *Mental development and education*. Retrieved from http://ehlt.flinders.edu.au/education/DLiT/2000/Piaget/begin.htm

Erikson, E. H. (1963). *Childhood and society*. New York, NY: Norton.

Ettinger, J. M. (1991). *Improved career decision-making in a changing world*. Garrett Park, MD: Garrett Park.

Fleck, S. E. (2009). International comparisons of hours worked: An assessment of the statistics. *Monthly Labor Review*, May. Retrieved from http://www.bls.gov/opub/mlr/2009/05/art1full.pdf

Gould, R. (1978). *Transformations: Growth and change in adult life*. New York, NY: Simon & Schuster.

Harper, J. M., Schaalje, B. G., & Sandberg, J. G. (2000). Daily hassles, intimacy, and marital quality in later life marriages. *American Journal of Family Therapy, 28*, 1–18. doi: 10.1080/019261800261770

Havighurst, R. (1972). *Developmental tasks and education* (3rd ed.). New York, NY: McKay Company.

Hoppe, M. H. (2007). Adult development theory may boost global leadership. *Issues & Observations, 27*, 21–22. Retrieved from http://www.ccl.org/leadership/pdf/publications/lia/lia27_3Adult.pdf

Johnson, J. G., Cohen, P., Kasen, S., & Brook, J. S. (2005). Personality disorder traits associated with risk for unipolar depression during middle adulthood. *Psychiatry Research, 136*, 113–121. doi:10.1016/j.psychres.2005.02.007

Johnson, J. G., Cohen, P., Kasen, S., & Brook, J. S. (2006). Personality disorders evident by early adulthood and risk for anxiety disorders during middle adulthood. *Anxiety Disorders, 20*, 408–426. doi:10.1016/j.janxdis.2005.06.001

Katz, J., Monnier, J., Libet, J., Shaw, D., & Beach, S. R. (2000). Individual and crossover effects of stress on adjustment in medical student marriages. *Journal Marital Family Therapy, 26*, 341–351. doi: 10.1111/j.1752-0606.2000.tb00303.x

Kohlberg, L. (1968). Early education: A cognitive-developmental view. *Child Development, 39*, 1013–1062. doi: 10.2307/1127272

Kohlberg, L. (1976). Moral stages and moralization: The cognitive-developmental approach. In T. Lickona (Ed.), *Moral development and behavior: Theory, research, and social issues* (pp. 31–53). New York, NY: Holt, Rinehart and Winston.

Kulik, L. (2010). Women's experiences with volunteering: A comparative analysis by stages of the life cycle. *Journal of Applied Social Psychology, 40*, 360–388. doi:10.1111/j.1559–1816.2009.00578.x

Levinson, D. J. (1977). The mid-life transition: A period in adult psychosocial development. *Journal for the Study of Interpersonal Processes, 40*, 99–112.

Levinson, D. J. (1986). A conception of adult development. *American Psychologist, 4*, 3–13. doi:10.1037/0003–066X.41.1.3

Lodi-Smith, J., & Roberts, B. W. (2010). Getting to know me: Social role experiences and age differences in self-concept clarity during adulthood. *Journal of Personality, 78*, 1383–1410. doi:10.1111/j.1467-6494.2010.00655.x

Marr, J., & Morrissey, S. P. (1985). How soon is now? On *Hatful of Hollow* [CD]. London, UK: Rough Trade.

Newman, B. M., & Newman, P. R. (2012). *Development through life: A psychosocial approach*. Belmont, CA: Wadsworth.

Poon, C. Y. M., & Knight, B. G. (2012). Emotional reactivity to network stress in middle and late adulthood: The role of childhood parental emotional abuse and support. *Gerontologist, 52*, 782–791. doi: 10.1093/gerant/gns009

Rajadhyaksha, U., & Bhatnagar, D. (2000). Life role salience: A study of dual career couples in the Indian context. *Human Relations, 53*, 489–511. Retrieved from http://www.iimahd.ernet.in/assets/upload/faculty/deeptipdf2.pdf

Rothrauff, T., & Cooney, T. M. (2008). The role of generativity in psychological well-being: Does it differ for childless adults and parents? *Journal of Adult Development, 15*, 148–159. doi: 10.1007/s10804-008-9046-7

Ryff, C. D. (1989). Happiness is everything, or is it? Explorations on the meaning of psychological well-being. *Journal of Personality and Social Psychology, 57*, 1069–1081. doi: 10.1037/0022-3514.57.6.1069

Savickas, M. L. (2002). Career construction: A developmental theory of vocational behavior. In D. Brown & Associates (Eds.), *Career choice and development* (4th ed., pp. 149–205). San Francisco, CA: Jossey-Bass.

Schilling, O. (2006). Development of life satisfaction in old age: Another view on the "paradox." *Social Indicators Research, 75,* 241–271. doi: 10.1007/s11205-004-5297-2

Smith, K. E., & Mattingly, M. J. (2014). Husbands' job loss and wives' labor force participation during economic downturns: Are all recessions the same? *Monthly Labor Review*, September. Retrieved from http://www.bls.gov/opub/mlr/2014/article/husbands-job-loss-and-wives-labor-force-participation-during-economic-downturns-are-all-recessions-the-same-1.htm

Snarey, J., Son, L., Kuehne, V., Hauser, S., & Vaillant, G. (1987). The role of parenting in men's psychosocial development: A longitudinal study of early adulthood infertility and midlife generativity. *Developmental Psychology, 23,* 593–603. doi: 10.1037/0012-1649.23.4.593

Srivastava, S., John, O. P., Gosling, S. D., & Potter, J. (2003). Development of personality in early and middle adulthood: Set like plaster or persistent change? *Journal of Personality and Social Psychology, 84,* 1041–1053. doi: 10.1037/0022-3514.84.5.1041

Super, D. E. (1984). Career and life development. In D. Brown & L. Brooks (Eds.), *Career choice and development* (pp. 193–234). San Francisco, CA: Jossey-Boss.

Sutin, A. R., & Costa, J. T. (2010). Reciprocal influences of personality and job characteristics across middle adulthood. *Journal of Personality, 78,* 257–288. doi:10.1111/j.1467-6494.2009.00615.x

Sutin, A. R., Costa, P. T., Wethington, E., & Eaton, W. (2010). Turning points and lessons learned: Stressful life events and personality trait development across middle adulthood. *Psychology and Aging, 25,* 524–533. doi: 10.1037/a0018751

Tremblay, K. R. Jr., Barber, C. E., & Kubin, L. (2014). *Grandparents: As parents.* Retrieved from http://www.ext.colostate.edu/pubs/consumer/10241.html#top

U.S. Department of Commerce. (2009–2013). *American fact finder.* Retrieved from http://factfinder.census.gov/faces/tableservices/jsf/pages/productview.xhtml?pid=ACS_13_5YR_DP02&prodType=table

U.S. Department of Labor, Bureau of Labor Statistics. (2014). *American time use survey.* Retrieved from http://www.bls.gov/tus/charts/

Vaillant, G. E. (1998). *Adaptation to life.* Cambridge, MA: Harvard University Press.

van Aken, M. G., Denissen, J. A., Branje, S. T., Dubas, J. S., & Goossens, L. (2006). Midlife concerns and short-term personality change in middle adulthood. *European Journal of Personality, 20,* 497–513. doi:10.1002/per.603

Wheaton, B. (1994). Sampling the stress universe. In W. R. Alison and I. H. Gotlib (Eds.), *Stress and mental health: Contemporary issues and prospects for the future* (pp. 77–114). New York: Plenum.

Whisman, M. A. (2006). Childhood trauma and marital outcomes in adulthood. *Personal Relationships, 12,* 372–386. doi: 10.1111/j.1475-6811.2006.00124

Wood, K. C., Smith, H., & Grossniklaus, D. (2001). Piaget's stages of cognitive development. In M. Orey (Ed.), *Emerging perspectives on learning, teaching, and technology*. Retrieved from http://projects.coe.uga.edu/epltt/

Wortley, D. B., & Amatea, E.S. (1982). Mapping adult life changes: A conceptual framework for organizing adult development theory. *Personnel & Guidance Journal, 60*, 476–482. doi: 10.1002/j.2164-4918.1982.tb00700.x

Wright, M. O., Crawford, E., & Castillo, D. D. (2009). Childhood emotional maltreatment and later psychological distress among college students: The mediating role of maladaptive schemas. *Child Abuse & Neglect, 33*, 59–68. doi: 10.10.1016/j.chiabu.2008.12.007

Yunqing, L., & Ferraro, K. F. (2006). Volunteering in middle and later life: Is health a benefit, barrier or both? *Social Forces, 85*, 497–519. doi: 10.1353/sof.2006.0132

Zuckerman, M. B. (2011, February 11). The great jobs recession goes on: The recession is officially over but unemployment rate remains high. *U.S. News and World Report*. Retrieved from http://www.usnews.com/opinion/mzuckerman/articles/2011/02/11/the-great-jobs-recession-goes-on

PART 8

Late Adulthood

Late Adulthood: Physical and Cognitive Development

Melinda Haley, Juliana J. Forrest-Lytle, and Nazak Dadashazar

With recent advances in medicine and health, there has been notable growth in the population of older adults. This population is composed of individuals aged 65 years and older (Erickson, Gildengers, & Butters, 2013; Vance et al., & Ball, 2008). It is estimated that by 2030, 20% of the U.S. population will be composed of older adults (Chalé & Unanski, 2012). Late adulthood is a time when many transition from leading active lives to becoming less able-bodied and in some cases even sedentary (Erickson, as cited in Coon & Mitterer, 2013). Counselors working with this population need to understand the implications of the various physical and cognitive changes and challenges that individuals in this stage of life may experience.

This chapter starts with a discussion of physical development in late adulthood, with subtopics including physical activity versus nonactivity, changes in the immune system and chronic disease, quality of life, social roles, and physical ability and mobility. Next, the chapter will proceed with multiple facets of cognitive development within this group. These facets include neural plasticity; declines in language processing, working memory, and attentional control; decision making and conscientiousness; environmental effects; and social involvement on cognitive function. Then this chapter looks specifically at aspects of counseling and effective clinical practice related to older adults, including a discussion about assessment for both physical and cognitive issues in this population, followed by a brief synopsis of key points. This chapter also provides some recommendations regarding best practices for counseling the older adult. One caveat is that due to space constraints, this chapter cannot possibly cover every physical or cognitive issue of development for this age range. Therefore, it is recommend that counselors and other health-care providers who seek to work with this population do additional research to supplement what can be provide here.

PHYSICAL DEVELOPMENT

As individuals age, bodies change in a multitude of ways, and often decline is noticed in some of an individual's physical abilities. Older adults are the most sedentary demographic in the United States, which contributes to poor physical and mental health outcomes (Notthoff & Carstensen, 2014). Some noted changes for this population could include weight gain, changes in posture and balance, physical activity, body image, hormonal changes, physical activity, and disease. This section will discuss the topics of physical activity, body image, hormonal changes, and the impact of disease.

Physical Activity

Age-related declines in older adulthood could include changes in posture (Krampe, Smolders, & Doumas, 2014). Postural control refers to maintaining balance and posture in relationship to stimuli in the environment and internal processes from "somatosensory, visual, and vestibular systems" (Krampe et al., 2014, p. 95). Balance is needed for an array activities related to daily living (Aguiar et al., 2015; Motl & McAuley, 2014). Issues with balance and postural control via declines in sensory and motor systems can lead to falls for older adults. Such falls could cause severe medical issues such as broken bones (Aguiar et al., 2015). As a way to counteract these age-related declines, researchers have found that older adults can better maintain their balance by engaging in balance oriented sports like martial arts, aerobic exercise, yoga, or dance (Krampe et al., 2014; Tait, Laditka, Laditka, Nies, & Racine, 2012; Thurm et al., 2011). For older adults who cannot engage in the aforementioned activities, resistance training has also shown good results in terms of improving strength and overall quality of life (Benton & Schlairet, 2012).

In general, physical activity has also shown numerous benefits for older adults (Moore, Mitchell, Beets, & Bartholomew, 2012). These benefits include better flexibility and weight control, and reduced risk for type 2 diabetes (Petry, Andrade, Barry, & Byrne, 2013); more positive body image and higher self-esteem (Moore et al., 2012); reduced risk of osteoporosis and osteoarthritis (Notthoff & Carstensen, 2014; Tait et al., 2012); reduced negative effects from obstructive pulmonary disease (Tait et al., 2012); better ambulation and sleep (Kangas, Baldwin, Rosenfield, Smits, & Rethorst, 2015; Riesco, Choquette, Audet, Tessier, & Dionne, 2011); better posture and balance control (Krampe et al., 2014); increased bone density (Moore et al., 2012); increased positive affect, decreased negative affect, and increased cognitive processing (Krampe et al., 2014); lower blood pressure and lower risk of heart attack (Moore et al., 2012); greater physical endurance and strength (Benton & Schlairet, 2012; Hogan, Mata, & Carstensen, 2014); and increased executive functioning (Karr, Areshenkoff, Rast, & Garcia-Barrera, 2014). All these benefits lead to a higher quality of life (Benton & Schlairet, 2012; Motl & McAuley, 2014).

Benefits in improved affect and cognitive ability may be seen in as little as one exercise session (Hogan et al., 2014), and benefits can be gained solely through walking (Notthoff & Carstensen, 2014) as well as with seated exercise (Thurm et al., 2011) or with resistance training just two to three times per week (Benton & Schlariet, 2012).

Physical activity as an intervention impacts several age-induced declines such as executive functioning, which can be a result of either cognitive aging or dementia (Karr et al., 2014). Exercise may even serve as a preventative measure and reduce risk for dementia (Karr et al., 2014; Moore et al., 2012) and other neurodegenerative processes (Thurm et al., 2011). Physical exercise has been found to help increase both gray and white brain matter via task-oriented activities (Thurm et al., 2011). It goes without saying that exercise also helps control obesity and high blood pressure (Meisler, 2002).

Interventions for older adults that include exercise need to consider the older adult's self-efficacy for exercise (Moore et al., 2012). Therefore, there may also need to be an intervention to increase the older adult's self-perception that he or she can be successful at exercise for the older adult to profit from the benefits of exercise (Kangas et al., 2015). Nothoff and Carstensen (2014) found that when older adults received information about the benefits of exercise, they engaged in more exercise than those who did not. In addition, exercise needs to be concretely linked to the older adult's overall goals (Nothoff & Carstensen, 2014). Petry et al. (2013) noted that positive reinforcement worked in helping older adults incorporate more exercise into their lifestyles.

BOX 17.1   CASE STUDY—FRANCO AND ANITA

Franco is a 72-year-old American of Italian descent. He lives in a retirement village in New Mexico with his wife of 52 years, Anita. Recently, Anita fell and broke her hip, and Franco had back surgery to repair some ruptured discs. Anita and Franco have been paying for home nursing care to come in daily to help them while they both recover medically. Both Anita's and Franco's doctors want to move the couple into physical rehabilitation to facilitate this recovery. Franco has always been an active individual throughout his life, and up until his surgery he regularly played golf with his friends from the retirement village. However, Anita has always enjoyed more sedentary pursuits such as crafts, pinochle and bridge, and her favorite TV shows. Her doctor recently scolded her for her sedentary lifestyle, and Franco has now started pressuring her to become more physically fit and engaged. Anita is balking at adding exercise to her lifestyle. In her youth when she did try to engage in more physical activity, she never enjoyed the feeling of discomfort such as being out of breath or having burning muscles. As a counselor working with this couple, how might you approach Anita to increase her self-efficacy and enjoyment for exercise that will serve to enhance her quality of life?

Body Image

Body image includes the way that one perceives the self and is self-evaluative (Liechty, 2012). As individuals age, priorities change along with expectations, perceptions of appearance, status of health, and less dependence on appearance for self-esteem (Liechty, 2012). It has been found that negative outcomes related to body image issues (e.g., eating disorders) are much less likely for the older adult (Liechty, 2012). Many older adults incorporate overall perceptions of health into their body images, and most have come to accept themselves for who they are, flaws and all. They incorporate other features into their overall perception of their image such as career accomplishments, intelligence, physical ability, health, and fashion style. Older adults do not see body image on a continuum but rather as a complex set of perceptions (Liechty, 2012).

Although a lot of research has been conducted on body image on younger men and women, very little has been conducted on the older adult. The research that has been conducted has found conflicting emotions regarding the older adult's appreciation for some aspects of his or her body, while being concerned about other aspects. Research shows that what concerns the older adult is often categorically different from what concerns a younger adult or an adolescent (Liechty, 2012). Although it has been noted that all the aforementioned groups receive messages from society and the media regarding the value of being young and thin (Tait et al., 2012), much of the current research on older adults has been found compromised in terms of accurate measurement because most of the measures were developed for research on younger populations (Liechty, 2012).

Hormonal Changes

Both males and females undergo changes in their hormone levels in later years (Lee et al., 2010). Changes in hormones can cause a reciprocal affect in the function of a person's immune system and can lead to other age-related issues such as menopause for women and testosterone and androgen deficiency in men (Amore et al., 2012; Hogervorst, 2013; Tait et al., 2012). These issues extend into late adulthood (Lee et al., 2010). Amore et al. (2012) found that as many as 30% of men over age 40 years have significantly deceased testosterone, or hypogonadism, and of those individuals with hypogonadism, as many as 12% exhibited clinical symptoms such as depression. Research has indicated that low levels of testosterone, combined with high levels of gonadotropins, have been "associated with cognitive decline in dementia cases in men" (Verdilel et al., 2014, p. 70).

Androgen has also been linked to quality of life and feelings of well-being for men (Finas et al., 2006; Lee et al., 2010). Reduced androgen levels may lead to bouts of depression and physical inactivity (Finas et al., 2006; Lee et al., 2010). Androgen may also influence men's perceptions regarding their physical health and ability, particularly their perceptions of sexual performance and capability (Lee et al., 2010). Androgen has also been implicated in male cognitive functioning (Finas et al., 2006).

Diminished levels of both estrogen and testosterone have been linked to dementia and Alzheimer's disease, although the manner in which this happens is not yet well understood (Hogervorst, 2013). However, women have been found to be at greater risk for developing Alzheimer's than men (Hogervorst, 2013). We will discuss Alzheimer's disease in greater detail later in this chapter.

Similarly, the change in estrogen and progestogens in women has also been associated with changes in mood and blood pressure (Harsh, Meltzer-Brody, Rubinow, & Schmidt, 2009; Meisler, 2002). Estrogen plays a role in the regulation of the neurotransmitters of acetylcholine, serotonin, noradrenalin, dopamine, and glutamate, and some research indicates postmenopausal women have higher rates of anxiety and depression than premenopausal women (Asthana et al., 2009; Harsh et al., 2009). Changes in estrogen level have also been linked to a change in the health of a woman's blood vessels, which creates a greater risk for postmenopausal women to develop hypertension (Meisler, 2002).

Changes in estrogen level have also been associated with changes in women's perceptions, cognition, verbal learning, and memory, perhaps contributing to dementia, Alzheimer's disease, and osteoporosis (Asthana et al., 2009; Harsh et al., 2009; Hogervorst, 2013, Liu, Cai, Liu, Zhang, & Yang, 2015). However, more research is needed in this area as results have been mixed (Asthana et al., 2009; Harsh et al., 2009; Hogervorst, 2013). Asthana et al. (2009) reported a key finding relevant to the development of Alzheimer's disease, which is "the ability of estrogen to reduce formation of β-amyloid," which is "a hallmark biochemical marker" of Alzheimer's disease (p. 201). Progestogens have been implicated in the function of neurons (Asthana et al., 2009). However, a meta-analysis conducted by Hogervorst (2013) found several studies with results supporting that high levels of estrogen in older women were more related to cognitive decline than were low levels. Therefore, results are still inconclusive.

Disease

As individuals age, they become more susceptible to one or more chronic diseases (Ballantyne, Mirza, Zubin, Boon, & Fisher, 2011). Aging-associated biological processes such as cell deterioration and molecular damage routinely occur (Stanner & Denny, 2009). Diet, exercise, and lifestyle choices can mediate these processes to some extent (Stanner & Denny, 2009). Considering the expectation that the population of older adults will continue to increase as the Baby Boomers age, it has become important to understand the unique needs of this population (Chalé & Unanski, 2012). Some of the more common diseases for the older adult include cardiovascular disease (CVD), heart disease, high blood pressure, diabetes, obesity, affective disorders, arthritis, osteoporosis, and Alzheimer's disease (Benton & Schlairet, 2012). Due to space constraints, this chapter focuses on CVD, hypertension, erectile dysfunction (ED), osteoporosis, and Alzheimer's disease.

CVD

Cardiovascular disease includes hypertension, arrhythmia, and congestive heart failure (Ai & Carrigan, 2007). Cardiovascular-related diseases are the number one cause of death worldwide regardless of gender or ethnicity (Ai & Carrigan, 2007; Akintunde, Akintunde, & Opadijo, 2015). Deaths from these causes will remain the leading cause of death worldwide (Akintunde et al., 2015; Almeida et al., 2014). Health-care costs for just CVD are estimated to exceed $430 billion each year in the United States alone (Folta et al., 2009), and this disease greatly affects an individual's quality of life. Studies have indicated that individuals with CVD require more services (e.g., health care, social services, adult daycare, Meals on Wheels; Ai & Carrigan, 2007) than elderly adults who do not have this disease.

It is estimated that as many as 2,150 U.S. individuals aged 65 years and older die every day from CVD, with men having a statistical greater chance of contracting this disease and women having a greater risk of having a heart attack or dying from this disease (Novak, Sandberg, & Harper, 2014). This gender disparity increases significantly after age 75 years (Ai & Carrigan, 2007; Keyes, 2004; Rice, Katzel, & Waldstein, 2010). It is also estimated that 30% of all deaths worldwide are caused by CVD (Akintunde et al., 2015). This disease can lead to many negative outcomes including erectile dysfunction and cognitive dysfunction for men (Novak et al., 2014). For women, estrogen appears to be a protective factor against CVD, but after estrogen levels decline for postmenopausal women, risk of cardiovascular disease increases (Meisler, 2002).

There are recognized risk factors preceding the development of CVD: (a) age (prevalence increases significantly with age); (b) unhealthy diet (e.g., diets high in fat and salt and low in complex carbohydrates create greater risk; Stanner & Denny, 2009); (c) tobacco use; (d) obesity; (e) physical inactivity; (f) high blood pressure; (g) diabetes; (h) dyslipidaemia (e.g., high cholesterol; Akintunde et al., 2015; Chalé & Unanski, 2012); (i) being on antipsychotic medication (Foley et al., 2013); (j) depression; (k) dysregulation of the autonomic, endocrine, and immune systems; (l) metabolic syndrome (Rice et al., 2010); (m) alcohol abuse; (n) menopause; (o) low socioeconomic status; (p) being an African American woman (e.g., this ethnic and gender disparity has been increasing steadily since the 1980s; Ai & Carrigan, 2007); and (q) chronic stress (Douthit, 2007).

Hypertension

Approximately one of every five adults in the United States has high blood pressure (Meisler, 2002). It is estimated that as many as 9.4 million deaths worldwide are attributed to high blood pressure, with 80% of these taking place in underdeveloped and poor countries (Akintunde et al., 2015). Among elderly adults, women and African Americans have higher rates of high blood pressure than do men or other ethnicities (Meisler, 2002). African American women tend to develop hypertension 10 years earlier than do African American men or other ethnicities (Meisler, 2002). Women also have a higher risk for having a stroke than do men (Meisler, 2002).

A variety of secondary issues arise for individuals with CVD and hypertension such as (a) depression, (b) anxiety, and (c) cognitive decline (Keyes, 2004; Köhler et al., 2012; Rice et al., 2010; Stanner & Denny, 2009).

Prevention of CVD and hypertension includes addressing the risk factors such as implementing a healthy diet and an exercise routine (Akintunde et al., 2015; Folta et al., 2009) and stress reduction efforts (Douthit, 2007; Katsuhisa et al., 2014). Weight loss is particularly impactful because "each kilogram of weight lost is associated with decreased blood pressure, and high blood pressure impacts the development of CVD" (Folta et al., 2009, p. 1275).Counselors can aid in prevention with behavioral modification techniques and modification of lifestyle (Folta et al., 2009).

ED

Erectile dysfunction is a "persistent inability to achieve or to maintain an erection sufficient for sexual intercourse" (Abdo, Afif-Abdo, Otani, & Machado, 2008, p. 1720). There are two types of ED: the psychogenic or organic type, which is present at the beginning of a man's sex life and is experienced throughout his life; and an acquired type that has a later onset and usually begins after a man has had a number of successful sexual experiences (Michetti, Rossi, Bonanno, Tiesi, & Simonelli). Whether the cause of ED is organic or not, it usually carries with it a psychological response (Roy & Allen, 2004). Research has shown that 86% of men over age 80 years have some form of ED (Abdo et al., 2008). It is estimated that within the next 10 years, as many as 320 million men will suffer from it (Moore et al., 2014).

One of the biggest contributors to erectile dysfunction in men is vascular disease (VD), and in fact erectile dysfunction has become an early warning sign for VD (Moore et al., 2014). In addition, "men with ED are at a 65% increased relative risk of developing coronary heart disease and a 43% increased risk of stroke within 10 years" (Moore et al., 2014, p. 164). Other risk factors include (a) age; (b) psychological and emotional factors, such as mood disorders (studies have found a link between a man's inability to regulate or communicate his emotions and ED; Michetti et al., 2006); (c) interpersonal relationship problems (relationship issues can be both a contributor and a consequence of ED; Abdo et al., 2008); (d) organic factors (80% of men's ED had a physical cause; Roy & Allen, 2004); (e) sedentary lifestyle; (f) alcohol consumption; (g) loss of income (Rosen et al., 2006); (h) diabetes; (i) stress; (j) hypertension; (k) smoking; (l) trauma; (m) pelvic injury (Roy & Allen, 2004); (n) treatment of prostate cancer (as many as 90% of men who have had surgery for prostate cancer and 80% of men who have had radiation also have ED; Hamilton & Mirza, 2014; Wang et al., 2013); and (o) personality factors, such as having an "externally oriented cognitive style" and a submissive personality (Michetti et al., 2006, p. 170).

Erectile dysfunction can significantly impact a man's quality of life (Abdo et al., 2008; Hamilton & Mirza, 2014). It is well-known that psychological difficulties both precede and follow erectile dysfunction, which can impact the duration and severity of the disorder (Nobre & Gouveia, 2000; Rosen et al., 2006). Many men suffer from thoughts and emotions associated with ED such as feeling ashamed, embarrassed, emasculated, anxious, or depressed. In addition, men can suffer an impact to self-esteem and self-confidence (Abdo et al., 2008; Roy & Allen, 2004). It has also been reported that some men become self-blaming and make "attributions for negative sexual events," which can set up a self-fulfilling prophecy (e.g., the man believes he will fail and therefore does; Nobre & Gouveia, 2000; Rowland, Myers, Adamski, & Burnett, 2012, p. E103).

Treatment often includes a change in lifestyle such as a healthier diet and habits, counseling, medication, rehabilitation or enhancement apparatus (e.g., vacuum devices), and sometimes surgery (including the surgical inclusion of a penile prosthesis; Abdo et al., 2008; Hamilton & Mirza, 2014). Counselors can help in the treatment of ED. Studies have shown that counseling does help increase sexual satisfaction and can help reduce incidence of ED (Abdo et al., 2008). Research also suggests that cognitive behavioral counseling, focused on helping a man explore and express thoughts and emotions and change perceptions, automatic thoughts, and cognitive distortions while building more positive schemas regarding sexual functioning, can be beneficial in the treatment of ED (Michetti et al., 2006). Counseling to strengthen interpersonal relationships with sexual partners and to increase self-confidence and self-esteem has also been found effective (Rosen et al., 2006). Sexual partners may also benefit from counseling. Many can feel rejected or unattractive or think their partner is having an affair (Roy & Allen, 2004). So couples counseling is an important part of any treatment protocol.

Osteoporosis

Osteoporosis is the resorption of bone and "microarchitecture disturbance of bone tissue" (Safizadeh, Aminizadeh, & Safizadeh, 2015, p. 1). It is often identified by measuring bone mineral density (BMD) (Liu et al., 2015; Miller, 2009). The BMD test is a procedure that measures and then compares the bone density of an older adult with that of a normal young adult. A normal bone density reading is when the score falls within "one standard deviation of a normal young adult" (Miller, 2009, p. 157). Scores lower than one standard deviation indicate "low bone mass or osteopenia," whereas scores below more than 2.5 standard deviations indicate osteoporosis (Miller, 2009, p. 157).

Osteoporosis is often referred to as a *silent disease* until a fracture occurs (Safizadeh et al., 2015, p. 1). There are few overt symptoms to indicate to the older adult that he or she has osteoporosis before a fall ends up in a bone break (Dunniway, Camune, Baldwin, & Crane, 2012). When an individual has osteoporosis, it takes very little to break a bone. A person can sustain a fracture just by doing minor actions such as standing up or sitting down. Even though osteoporosis can impact the entire body, the bones most commonly broken include the "femur, vertebrae, and distal radius" (Safizadeh et al., 2015, p. 1). Osteoporosis can also be a very expensive disease as in terms of medical costs and reducing quality of life (Safizadeh et al., 2015).

It is estimated there are over 10 million people in the United States with osteoporosis, and this number is expected to triple by the year 2040 as the Baby Boomers continue to age (Dunniway et al., 2012; Safizadeh et al., 2015). Women contract this disease 80% more often than do men, and Caucasian women have a 50% chance of having a bone fracture by age 50 years (Dunniway et al., 2012; Liu et al., 2015). Asian individuals also have a higher risk for developing this disease over other ethnicities (Safizadeh et al., 2015).

The risk factors associated with osteoporosis include (a) age; (b) gender; (c) smoking; (d) three or more alcoholic drinks per day; (e) a parent with a hip fracture; (f) a history of rheumatoid arthritis; (g) a low body mass index; (h) prolonged glucocorticoid or corticosteroid exposure (Dunniway et al., 2012; Safizadeh et al., 2015); (i) sedentary lifestyle; (j) dietary factors (e.g., low calcium and vitamin D intake and high caffeine consumption); (k) type 1 diabetes; (l) celiac disease; (m) epilepsy; (n) long treatment protocols for epilepsy and depression; (o) adults who have a fracture after age 50 years (Miller, 2009); and (p) women who enter menopause before age 45 years (Safizadeh et al., 2015). The reason that the other diseases mentioned are risk factors is because the typical medications used to treat them contribute to bone loss (Miller, 2009). The risk for developing osteoporosis increases exponentially with steroid (e.g., prednisone) and tobacco use (Dunniway et al., 2012).

There appears to be a strong link between osteoporosis and depression, although researchers are not yet sure of the connection between the two (Cocchi, Tonello, Gabrielli, & Pregnolato, 2011). There may be some evidence to suggest that individuals who have been treated for depression via selective serotonin reuptake inhibitors (SSRIs) could be at great risk for developing osteoporosis (Cocchi et al., 2011; Miller, 2009). Cocchi et al. (2011) discussed how excessive serotonin in the brain can lead to an "insult on the bone" and potentially prevent bone homeostasis, which could then lead to osteoporosis over time (p. 4).

Other associations for osteoporosis include chronic pain, limitations on mobility, loss of independence, and isolation (Dunniway et al., 2012). Often a hip fracture due to this disease leads to the older adult to spending time in a nursing home. For some of these older adults, they remain in nursing care for the rest of their lives, and as many as 20% with such a fracture die from complications (Dunniway et al., 2010).

Osteoporosis is untreatable. Once an individual has it, he or she will have it for the remainder of his or her life. However, there are preventive measures that can be taken (Safizadeh et al., 2015), including screening (with a BMD test); lifestyle changes such as change in diet (e.g., increased calcium and vitamin D intake); cessation of smoking and alcohol use; and increased exercise, especially "weight bearing and muscle-strengthening exercises" (Dunniway et al., 2012, p. 3).

This is where counselors can play a large role. Behavioral change can lead to reduction of risks and more positive outcomes for the older adult (Dunniway et al., 2012; Miller, 2009). In addition, counseling can help with behavior modification that can be preventive (Dunniway et al., 2012). Untreated, this disease leads to poor quality of life, lack of mobility, psychological difficulties, and even death (Liu et al., 2015). Miller (2009) strongly advocated that mental health counselors should also help screen for risk factors for osteoporosis because of the link between SSRI antidepressants and anticonvulsants medications and bone loss.

Alzheimer's Disease and Dementia

Alzheimer's disease is the most common form of dementia for older adults, and it is currently incurable. It results from brain cell death from plaque build-up and neurofibrillary tangles, which lead to a wasting of the brain (Douthit, 2007; Granello & Fleming, 2008). It is a condition that can rob the individual of his or her memories, interpersonal relationships, and independence. Ultimately, Alzheimer's can take an individual's life in as few as 12 years (Douthit, 2007; Granello & Fleming, 2008). It is also an expensive disease. The estimated costs incurred for this disease for health care and caregivers are between $61 billion and $100 billion (Desai, Grossberg, & Sheth, 2004; Granello & Fleming, 2008; Stanner & Denny, 2009).

There are two types of memory loss for an older adult with Alzheimer's: (1) an inability to recall new information and (2) an inability to remember the past (Douthit, 2007). The disease is also characterized by multiple cognitive deficits that include "at least one of the following cognitive disturbances: aphasia, apraxia, agnosia, or a disturbance in executive functioning" (Douthit, 2007, p. 16). The incremental decline that is associated with this disease can affect both higher functioning skills (e.g., balancing a checkbook) and lower level skills (e.g., bathing or dressing oneself; Desai et al., 2004). In fact, it is usually the inability to perform higher order skills that is the first sign of the disease (Desai et al., 2004).

There are cognitive, behavioral, and functional elements of deterioration, and cognitive decline may be initially secondary to behavioral and functional elements of decline (Desai et al., 2004). Some of the common effects of this disease include (a) disruption in language ability, both written and spoken; (b) an inability to speak; (c) echolalia; (d) repetition of sounds; (e) impaired motor functioning; (f) an inability to recognize familiar things such as loved ones or possessions; (g) an inability to remember the names for common things (e.g., a couch or a table); (h) depression; (i) cardiovascular disease; (j) high levels of stress, anger, agitation, hallucinations, paranoia, screaming, and other verbal noises; (k) repetitive actions; (l) incontinence; (m) inability to perform daily tasks of living such as bathing, dressing, and eating; (n) disruptions in sleep; and (o) issues with vision (Douthit, 2007; Granello & Fleming, 2008).

Risk factors associated with Alzheimer's include (a) gender (cognitive decline is more prominent in women); (b) lack of mental stimulation and a sedentary lifestyle (each additional hour of daily television viewing increases the risk of developing Alzheimer's by a factor of 1.3); (c) tobacco use; (d) unhealthy diet (e.g., diets high in saturated and trans fat); (e) nutritional deficiencies; (f) low educational level; (g) genetics; (h) age (50% of adults over age 80 years contract this disease); (i) ethnicity (African Americans and Latinos have a higher risk than Caucasians, and some Native American tribes and the Japanese have lower incidence); (j) depression; (k) cardiovascular disease; (l) diabetes; (m) lack of social engagement; (n) estrogen replacement therapy, especially later in life; (o) other hormones taken besides estrogen; (p) gene mutations; (q) impaired cerebromicrovascular perfusion; and (r) death of a close loved one (Desai et al., 2004; Douthit, 2007; Granello & Fleming, 2008; Stanner & Denny, 2009).

Individuals with more than three risk factors have a 20% greater chance of contracting this disease (Granello & Fleming, 2008). Diagnosis for AD is made via evaluation of the individual's mental status and through neurological testing to evaluate "language, memory, reasoning, and physical condition" (Granello & Fleming, 2008, pp. 14–15). However, there is not a singularly definitive test for Alzheimer's (Granello & Fleming, 2008). Early diagnosis is the key to controlling this disease (Granello & Fleming, 2008).

Although there is no cure, there are methods for preventing this disease (Douthit, 2007). Prevention efforts focus on modifying health and lifestyle choices such as weight loss; effective treatment of diabetes, high blood pressure, and depression; increased psychical activity; cessation of tobacco use; increased education level (e.g., this has been projected to decrease the prevalence of AD by as much as 8.3%); stress management; and diets high in polyunsaturates, monounsatures, and omega-3 fatty acids (Douthit, 2007; Harrison, Ding, Eugene, Siervo, & Robinson, 2014; Stanner & Denny, 2009).

Research has also supported that helping older women develop and extend their social support networks can help mediate the impact of dementia (Crooks, Little, & Chiu, 2008). Crooks et al. (2008) reported findings from several studies that individuals with no social support had twice the risk of developing lowered cognitive functioning then those with social support. These authors hypothesize that social networks provides a protective factor by making it more likely the individual will seek medical care, engage in a healthier lifestyle, and offset incidences of depression and stress that might also impact brain functioning. In addition, Crooks et al. (2008) reported that social engagement may help keep important neural pathways intact or even strengthen them.

Treatment often includes medications such as cholinesterase, memantine, or aricept to slow the progression of Alzheimer's and to aid memory retention. In addition, personal counseling can help the individual with Alzheimer's to deal with the emotional turmoil that comes with understanding and dealing with the disease. For example, individuals can undergo myriad emotions ranging from feeling "useless, dependent, and burdensome" to feeling depressed, helpless, isolated, invalidated, hopeless, and having lowered self-esteem (Desai et al., 2004, p. 854). However, this population can be challenging for the counselor due to the changes in intellectual and verbal abilities (Granello & Fleming, 2008).

In terms of counseling, it can be beneficial to provide couples counseling to help preserve the interpersonal relationship. Research supports that the quality of the partner relationship can impact the progression of the disease (Epstein & Mittelman, 2009). In addition, the partner of the individual with Alzheimer's may have resentments toward the individual with Alzheimer's and may grieve the loss of the relationship or previous level of functioning (Auclair, Epstein, & Mittelman, 2009). Both people could be in denial of the disease, especially in the early stages (Auclair et al., 2009). There can also be confusion as the individual with Alzheimer's fluctuates between states of dementia and states of clarity (Auclair et al., 2009). In addition, the partner as a caregiver can experience burnout, and therefore support for the partner as a caregiver is essential (Desai et al., 2004).

BOX 17.2 CASE STUDY—JUANITA

Juanita is an 80-year-old retired Latina. She is single, having divorced 30 years ago. Her ex-husband died 10 years ago. She has three grown children, all professionals. Only her oldest son lives in the same city as she does, and the other two moved out of state because of their careers. Juanita is in relatively good physical and mental health. She has kidney disease and high blood pressure, but she is under medical care and is doing well. She is physically active. She bowls on three different bowling leagues and goes on long walks several times per month. She has a social support network of several close friends, many of whom she has known since grade school or high school, and she is a member of the Red Hat Society, which is an elderly women's group. She has had one serious relationship since her divorce; it lasted 3 years. She now prefers to remain single and no longer dates.

Juanita watches her weight and is height–weight congruent. She watches what she eats but also indulges periodically such as during holidays or when out with friends. However, once she gains 5 pounds, she will be careful with her eating habits until she loses the 5 pounds. Juanita does not drink or smoke or have any other health harmful habits. It is important to Juanita that she remain physically fit and active.

Her greatest worry for herself is related to witnessing the rapid physical and mental decline of her own mother. When Juanita's father died, Juanita's mother, Agatha, was very active in maintaining the house and yard until the burden became too heavy; then she moved into an assisted living facility. There she became sedentary and depressed. Rapidly, Agatha lost mobility and began having bouts of evening dementia where she would not recognize Juanita and would speak to relatives who had been long deceased as if they were in the room with her.

Now that you have read about Alzheimer's, evaluate what risk and protective factors Juanita has in relationship to that disease. If you were Juanita's counselor, what suggestions would you make to her in regard to lifestyle that could be additionally preventive? What would you suggest she eliminate or reduce?

In terms of working with the patient with Alzheimer's, it can be prudent to do a functional analysis of his or her abilities so that an appropriate treatment plan can be established that best meets his or her needs as well as determining response to therapy (Desai et al., 2004). Treatment of depression is also important, especially for women, who suffer depression in concordance with Alzheimer's at twice the rate as do males (Douthit, 2007).

Other counseling considerations include providing (a) developing stress management techniques, which have been implicated in the prevention of Alzheimer's; (b) incorporating healthy diet and exercise; (c) doing an inventory of life goals and values; (d) developing mindfulness and reducing excessive stimulation; (e) treating other psychological issues; (f) coordinating health care and other services; (g) increasing social skills and support; (h) increasing or developing a sense of spirituality; (i) helping with emotional expression and development of coping skills for declining functioning; and (j) helping to structure the environment to provide cues (e.g., putting labels on items), reduce clutter, and condense living space to help the person with Alzheimer's live more effectively (Douthit, 2007; Granello & Fleming, 2008).

Regardless of the illness or disease, older adults have more susceptibility of contracting one of the aforementioned. All of these diseases can lead to a lower quality of life for the older adult if not managed and controlled (Benton & Schlairet, 2012). In addition to disease, up to 50% of the older adult population suffers from chronic pain (Hadjistavropoulos, Hunter, & Fitzgerald, 2009). These issues can lead to adjustment issues and psychological difficulties, which will need to be treated as well. Older adults may need to learn new coping mechanisms as their lifestyles change in accordance to a disease (Douthit, 2007; Granello & Fleming, 2008). Counselors can assist in the treatment of these diseases to help the older adult live a more fulfilling and productive life.

COGNITIVE DEVELOPMENT

Another area of development and changes for the older adult occurs in the cognitive domain. There can be both gains and declines in cognitions for the age group. Cognitive gains can be enhanced by dedicated effort (Carretti, Borella, Zavagin, & de Beni, 2013). This section examines both gains and declines and includes the topics of neural plasticity, working memory, attentional control, dual task performance, decision making, and the effects of environment and social involvement.

Neural Plasticity

Successful aging can be described as having the cognitive attributes to explore, navigate, negotiate, and enjoy one's life (Vance et al., 2008). Therefore, to age successfully, individuals in late adulthood need mental stimulation. Mental stimulation is an individual's engagement in cognitive activities that trigger connections between neurons (Vance et al., 2008). Such stimulating activities promote neural plasticity in older adults. Neural plasticity is the brain's ability to make new neural connections throughout life (Bryck & Fisher, 2012; Couillard-Despres, Iglseder, & Aigner, 2011; Stepankova et al., 2014; Vance et al., 2008). The process begins with the initial exposure to a new stimulus or stimuli, followed by neuronal expansion, and then the establishment of new synapses between neurons (Stepankova et al., 2014; Vance et al., 2008). As experiences repeat, the new neural pathways and connections will strengthen. As the number of neural connections increases, resistance to age-related changes also increases (Vance et al., 2008). As previously mentioned, such mental stimulation can be effective in slowing down cognitive decline or diseases such as Alzheimer's (Douthit, 2007; Harrison et al., 2014; Stanner & Denny, 2009).

Numerous activities can provide mental stimulation for older adults. Of course, personal preference and levels of interest will vary from person to person. Krampe et al., (2014) found that musical experience offsets age-related delays in neural timing, and there is also extensive support for the use of physical activities or exercise to improve the potential for neural plasticity (Erickson, Miller, Weinstein, Akl, & Banducci, 2012; Erickson et al., 2013). Counselors working with this population can encourage older adults to engage in activities that intrigue them or challenge them to try something new. The introduction of novel and interesting stimuli can potentially help increase neural plasticity and connectivity (Erickson et al., 2013; Vance et al., 2008).

As individuals age, there is often some level of difficulty or decline that occurs. Most notably are difficulties experienced with language, working memory, and attentional control (Fandokova, Sander, Werkel-Bergner, & Shing, 2014; Mattys & Scharenborg, 2014; Riediger et al., 2014). Notably, the sensory-decline approach has gathered a great deal of empirical support over the years (Mattys & Scharenborg, 2014). Researchers have found that when adverse listening conditions such as noise, reverberation, and competing talkers are considered, complex interactions between peripheral auditory, central auditory, and cognitive abilities have to take place (Mattys & Scharenborg, 2014). Specifically, studies have shown enduring age effects on speech processing even after receptive abilities have been accounted for (Mattys & Scharenborg, 2014).

Decline of Working Memory

People often use the terms *working memory* (WM) and *short-term memory* (STM) interchangeably. However, working memory tends to refer to the theoretical framework of structures and processes used for the temporary storage and manipulation of information (Bayliss & Jerrold, 2015). Age is a central determinant of working memory (Riediger et al., 2014). For example, evidence abounds that older adults' performance in working-memory tasks, on average, is lower than that of younger adults (Riediger et al., 2014). Often individuals employ various strategies and tools such as chunking or mnemonic devices to retain information (Xu & Padilla, 2013). This process can be more difficult for individuals in late adulthood. Fandokova et al. (2014) affirmed the existing assumption that the mechanisms underlying the associative component of memory are mature by middle childhood and undergo senescent decline in late adulthood and old age. Additionally, there are age-related differences in memory performance due to decreased functionality of strategic operations that contribute to developmental changes (Fandokova et al., 2014).

Decline of Attentional Control

Attentional control is an individual's capacity to choose what to pay attention to and what to ignore (Eysenck, Derakshan, Santos, & Calvo, 2007). As we age, it becomes increasingly difficult to split our attention between tasks (Bugg, 2014; Mattys & Scharenborg, 2014). Bugg (2014) affirmed the difficulties in splitting attention but noted the assumption that there is a general decline in cognitive control is unsupported. However, it is wise to be mindful of the potential for cognitive decline and to work proactively to prevent such deterioration. As previously noted, adding mentally stimulating tasks to daily life can make a difference (Bryck & Fisher, 2012).

In addition to mental stimulation, older adults can employ cognitive strategies to compensate for such losses (Bryck & Fisher, 2012). Well-informed older adults can access information and tools online to help combat the aforementioned declines (Bryck & Fisher, 2012). For example, websites such as Lumosity, Brain Metrix, and Mind Games offer free methods to help test and train the brain. In some cases, individuals can choose to pay a fee to subscribe to the site in order to get a personalized brain-training program. Additionally, members of this population can engage in other activities that require mental acuity, such as playing Sudoku or crossword puzzles.

Dual-Task Performance

Closely related to attentional control, dual-task performance requires individuals to be able to focus and shift focus at will (Bherer, Kramer, & Peterson, 2008). According to Bherer et al. (2008), age-related differences are greater when the two tasks require similar motor responses, with older people being much more susceptible to input interference in some conditions and having a larger dual-task deficit (Bherer et al., 2008). Activities with the same input and output often resulted in significant age-related difficulties for dual tasks in older people. This difference was likely due to struggle in coordination and execution of two tasks at the same time (Bherer et al., 2008). Activities with different input, but the same output, resulted in a significant age-related difference for task-set costs in older people. This was likely due to difficulty in capacity to hold multiple stimuli and responses in memory (Bherer et al., 2008).

Bherer et al. (2008) found that both younger and older people benefited from dual-task training. Older people benefitted more than their younger counterparts. However, there was an equivalent increase in reaction times for both groups (Bherer et al., 2008). Older adults had notably larger increases in their accuracy and larger decreases in task-set costs (Bherer et al., 2008).

Decision Making

Decision making is another area where older adults see notable changes. Although decision making is an essential ability for successful living in later adulthood, changes in this skill can be precursors or symptoms of impending disease or cognitive decline (Boyle et al., 2012). Boyle et al. (2012) asserted that just when many important late life decisions must be made, many older adults begin to have a decline in their abilities to make effective decisions. Decision making is a higher order cognitive function and deterioration in this ability can impact choices related to health care, transfer of finances, or end-of-life decisions and make the elderly adult more susceptible to scams (Boyle et al., 2012).

However, it should be noted that a decline in decision-making ability is often a normal development due to the aging process and is not necessarily a symptom of Alzheimer's disease (Boyle et al., 2012). Mata, von Helversen, and Rieskamp (2010) affirmed that older adults performed poorer on decision-making tasks compared with younger adults. The authors went on to note differences in performance when the environment favored the use of cognitively focused strategies (Mata et al., 2010).

Conscientiousness

Conscientiousness stands out as a singularly striking predictor of health across the decades of life (Shanahan, Hill, Roberts, Eccles, & Friedman, 2014). Shanahan et al. (2014) noted associations between conscientiousness and diverse aspects of health and described constructs of conscientiousness that are indicative of deliberative, self-controlled, and goal directed behaviors, such as impulse control, planning, the delay of gratification, orderliness, and the propensity to follow social norms and rules (Shanahan et al., 2014). Shanahan et al. (2014) asserted that conscientiousness was associated with reduced risk for many illnesses as well as biomarkers indicative of health in adult populations. In older adults, specifically, decline in conscientiousness is associated with the onset of functional limitations and health-related quality of life.

Environmental Effects on Cognitive Changes in Later Life

Even though almost a third of individual differences in cognitive changes during late adulthood were attributable to genetic influences, the environment also plays a significant role in cognitive development and changes in later life (Tucker-Drob & Briley, 2014; Tucker-Drob, Reynolds, Finkel, & Pedersen, 2014). According to Christensen, Doblhammer, Rau, and Vaupel (2010), people are living longer and with less disability. It has been noted that older adults under age 85 years tend to remain more capable and mobile than in previous generations (Christensen et al., 2010). Unfortunately, the other side of this is that older adults also have a higher incidence of chronic illnesses, such as cancers and heart conditions, but are surviving longer because of early diagnosis and treatment (Burri, Maercker, Krammer, & Simmen-Janevska, 2013). We cannot mention physical and cognitive changes in late adulthood without mentioning changes that have both physical and cognitive links.

Alastalo et al. (2013) posited that early life stress (ELS) experiences often have long-term effects on late adulthood physiological and psychological health. The authors found that ELS increased the risk for impaired physical functioning in men in late adulthood (Alastalo et al., 2013). Similarly, posttraumatic stress disorder (PTSD) is a concern for individuals at any age who have survived a traumatic event (Burri et al., 2013). Burri et al. (2013) reported individuals with PTSD showed lower cognitive function across all age ranges. When PTSD was found to be comorbid with depression, it led to even greater declining cognitive function (Burri et al., 2013).

The Effects of Social Involvement on Cognitive Well-Being

Have you ever heard older people say spending time with their grandchildren keeps them young? Well, there is some truth to this saying. For individuals in late adulthood, participation in social activities has a stronger effect on subjective well-being than personality (Chang, Wray, & Lin, 2014; González-Herero & García-Martín, 2012). González-Herero and García-Martín (2012) affirmed social involvement as a key source of life satisfaction and positive affect in late adulthood. Levels of activity directly influence quality of life (González-Herero & García-Martín, 2012). There is a noted increase in quality of life and overall well-being resulting from the interactions older adults have with others in social settings and when participating in leisure activities (Chang et al., 2014). Chang et al. (2014) asserted that along with the social and cognitive implications of remaining socially active, there are also notable physical benefits.

ASSESSMENT RELATED TO OLDER ADULTS

Numerous assessments have been designed for the older adult (ABA & APA, 2008). However, since neurological disorders are the primary cause of disability in older adults over age 65 years (AANN, 2009), the majority of assessments we review in this section focus on assessing tasks of daily living and cognitive functioning. However, first we discuss some special considerations for assessment with older adults and issues related to diagnostic criteria.

Special Considerations for Assessment With Older Adults

According to the American Geriatric Society (n.d.), the main goal of assessment for older adults is to promote continued wellness, independence, and quality of life. Therefore, practitioners will want to assess for medical and psychosocial status and the individual's ability to function and perform activities of daily living. Allaire and Marsiske (2005) advocated that counselors must understand that within the same individual, both adaptive and maladaptive variability might exist as the individual ages. During the transitional period between what is considered normal and abnormal cognitive functioning, practitioners can see a great amount of fluidity and fluctuation (Gamaldo, Allair, & Whitfield, 2012). Therefore, it is important to assess the older adult more frequently than for other age groups, while understanding that there can be variability within the same individual in day-to-day scores on cognitive psychometric tests and that this is normal (Allaire & Marsiske, 2005; Gamaldo et al., 2012). Yet as Haslam et al. (2012) noted, "variable performance has significant diagnostic implications" and baseline measurements are rare (p. 778). Therefore, getting a baseline measure of functioning is essential and tracking scores over time can be helpful in understanding areas of decline.

Each older adult should be assessed for special needs. For example, some assessments may have to be modified to eliminate potential vision or auditory barriers such as (a) using bigger print or higher contrast printing; (b) using rooms with good lighting; (c) minimizing extraneous noise or numerous interruptions; (d) considering the length of time it takes to give the assessment; (e) considering the time of day the assessment is given; and (f) considering the older adult's perceptions of his or her abilities due to society's messages regarding ageism (American Geriatric Society, n.d.; Goncalves, Albuquerque, Byrne, & Pachana, 2009; Haslam et al., 2012). It has been noted that an older adult's perception of his or her health and abilities is one of the strongest "predictors of mortality" (Mora, Orsak, DiBonaventura, & Leventhal, 2013).

Further, Goncalves et al. (2009) cautioned about practitioners being cognizant of vocal tone, pacing, clarity of questioning, explaining psychological terms, and framing effects. Framing effects suggest that the way a question is framed might influence the answer that is given (Goncalves et al., 2009, p. 612). In addition, the American Geriatric Society (n.d.) suggested that counselors and other health-care workers start any interaction with older adults by greeting them by their last name as a sign of respect and by also introducing themselves.

Normal factors of aging that can influence assessment outcomes in older adults include blood pressure, reduced eyesight, insomnia, stress, emotionality, physical functioning, education level, reading ability, medication side effects, sensory deficits, unfamiliarity with psychological assessment, anxiety, and normal age-related decreases in perceptual speed (AANN, 2009; Gamaldo et al., 2012; Goncalves et al., 2009). Further Gamaldo et al. (2012) cautioned that some ethnic and gender groups tend to have higher frequencies of these types of factors that could skew testing results. Therefore, these factors must be taken into consideration when interpreting assessment results. In addition, Allaire and Marsiske (2005) noted that cognitive and behavioral change can be a function of the older adult modifying his or her modus operandi in terms of experience and learning in terms of how he or she copes with challenges. Therefore, change or intraindividual variability does not necessarily reflect developmental change, cognitive decline, or neurobiological compromise (Allaire & Marsiske, 2005, p. 390). All these considerations can make properly assessing and treating the older adult challenging.

Frequency of assessment is dependent on the individual issues related to the older adult. For example, some conditions such as mild cognitive impairment, dementia, or Alzheimer's disease will require more frequent assessment.

Further, Mungas, Reed, Farias, and DeCarli (2009) noted that it might be necessary for counselors to take demographics into consideration when evaluating the cognitive functioning of an older adult. For example, there can be fewer differences between early adulthood and late adulthood in cognitive functioning, but when variables such as education are considered, counselors could see an impact in score variations for ethnically and culturally diverse individuals. This can be especially true when such assessments were normed on nonminority populations (Mungas et al., 2009). If these variables are not taken into consideration under these circumstances, then minority individuals might show erroneous cognitive declines or false positives (Mungas et al., 2009). Mungas et al. advocated for adjusting scores to account for education when testing minority clients in order to improve diagnostic accuracy. However, these authors did note that the practice of doing so is controversial.

The main concern for many practitioners is that individuals with less access to education, or who are being evaluated with an assessment that is not normed for the individual's age range, may not be evaluated fairly. This can lead to a large amount of false positives or false negatives and greatly hinder the successful assessment and treatment of the individual (Goncalves et al., 2009; Mungas et al., 2009). Other suggested cultural considerations include "language, immigrant status, economical status, perceptions of institutions such as hospitals, as well as perceptions of disability and the role of family in care" (ABA & APA, 2008, p. 11).

It is also important to do a thorough assessment to understand causes, antecedents, and consequences of symptoms, because there can be multiple explanations even for cognitive decline, such as depression. In addition, apathy can be a symptom of Alzheimer's disease, Parkinson's disease is often associated with emotional lability, and aphasia can coincide with someone who has had a stroke (Goncalves et al., 2009). Therefore, careful assessment is needed with this age group. It can be important to integrate behavioral observation and reports from family members or caregivers into the assessment, and the assessment should include all aspects of the older adult's functioning, such as activities of daily living, mood and affect, negative life events, physical ability, behavior, access to health care, psychosocial development, and any changes in these areas (Goncalves, 2009).

Diagnostic Criteria

Historically, the *Diagnostic and Statistical Manual of Mental Disorders* (DSM) (APA, 2013) has based diagnostic criteria on younger individuals, and there has been a lack of differentiation between younger and older adults (Balsis, Gleason, Woods, & Oltmanns, 2007). This historical factor echoes the American Psychological Association's caution that older adults comprise a special cultural group that must be considered as an entity of their own and not lumped together into other categories. Per Balsis et al. (2007), without taking age, historical factors, and development into consideration, older adults are vulnerable to being misdiagnosed and improperly treated. As early as 2009, Balsis, Segal, and Donahue (2009) implored that the *DSM-5* consider the unique characteristics of older adults. They cautioned that not doing so would "result in the continued limited validity, reliability, and utility of the *Diagnostic and Statistical Manual of Mental Disorders* (*DSM*) system for this growing population" (p. 452).

There are additional considerations that counselors need to make when working with the age group. For example, Goncalves et al. (2009) stated that older adults often do not associate their symptoms with psychiatric or mental health issues; therefore, more psychoeducation may be needed to help them understand their health issues and put them into a developmental context. Gonclaves et al. further suggested the first time a counselor meets with an older client that the counselor do an extensive clinical interview and allow for both structured questions and open dialogue. For example, it can be important to let the older client tell his or her story in his or her own words. However, these authors also noted that there are vast individual differences between the older adult demographic and counselors should avoid stereotyping or overpathologizing due to preconceived notions related to age. The next section discusses some common assessments that are used for older adults, including those for both physical and cognitive characteristics as well as assessments for activities of daily living. In terms of physical assessments and wellness, the American Geriatric Society (n.d.) recommend assessing for physical ability, nutrition, vision, and hearing.

Global and Functional Assessment

Several mnemonics can be used for assessing activities of daily living (AANN, 2009). These can be used by any health-care provider to screen for areas that might need a method for more formal assessment. For example, the mnemonic DEATH can be used to remember to assess for "Dressing, eating, ambulation, toileting, habits." Another commonly used mnemonic is SHAFT, which stands for "shopping, housekeeping, able to use phone, food preparation/finances, transportation" (AANN, 2009, p. 9).

Activities of Daily Living (ADL) Scale

This is a more formal assessment that reviews criteria in six categories: toilet, feeding, dressing, grooming, physical ambulation, and bathing. The ADL scale was developed on the concept that levels of functioning are rated. Scores on the ADL indicate present level of functioning and counselors can maintain a record of changes of an individual's abilities over time. The ADL has a score range of 0 to 6. Only the highest level of functioning in each category receives a score of 1 (AANN, 2009).

Instrumental Activities of Daily Living Daily Living (IADL) Scale

This assessment looks at eight categories: ability to use telephone, shopping, food preparation, housekeeping, laundry, mode of transportation, responsibility for own medications, and ability to handle finances. The total score range is from 0 to 8 (AANN, 2009).

The Older Persons Counseling Needs Survey (OPCNS)

Developed by Myers (2010), the OPCNS has been developed for individuals aged 60 years or above to help counselors better evaluate counseling needs for this population. This 27-question assessment includes questions on personal, social, environmental, and physical concerns and activity. This assessment can also be used for screening purposes for groups (Myers, 2010). The OPCNS uses a 4-point Likert scale ranging from strongly agree = 4 to strongly disagree = 1. Higher scores indicate greater counseling need. This assessment can be accessed at http://libres.uncg.edu/ir/uncg/f/J_Myers_Counseling_1981.pdf.

Blessed Information Memory Concentration Test (BIMC)

This is a 33-question Likert scale that assesses the older adult on a variety of categories such as "orientation, personal information, current events, recall, and concentration" (ABA & APA, 2008, p. 164). As with other cognitive screening tests, this one can help the practitioner determine an overall level of functioning and whether additional assessment is needed. There is also a shorter version that contains only six items (ABA & APA, 2008).

Mini-Mental Status Exam (MMSE)

There are several versions of the MMSE, some more detailed than others. However, the one discussed by the American Bar Association and the American Psychological Association (2008) contains 30 items that assess "orientation, immediate registration of three words, attention and calculation, short term recall of three words, language, and visual construction" (p. 164). This is another useful screening tool to determine whether greater neuropsychological assessment is needed. Generally neuropsychological domains include appearance, sensory acuity, motor activity, attention, memory, expressive langue, receptive langue, math skills, reasoning, visual-spatial, executive functioning, and insight (ABA & APA, 2008). This type of assessment is often the first step in evaluating for disorders such as Alzheimer's disease (Granello & Fleming, 2008).

Framingham Risk Model

This is a model that can assess and predict an individual's chances of having a stroke or coronary heart disease within the next 10 years (Harrison et al., 2014). The model evaluates a number of risk and protective factors. This model is said to have "reasonable predictive accuracy" for cardiovascular disease events such as stroke or heart attack (Harrison et al., 2014, p. e114431).

Get Up and Go Test

This is both a qualitative and observational assessment that can be timed. The goal is to assess the older adult's gait, balance, and ability to walk. Individuals are assessed for risk of falling. Generally the older adult is asked to get up from a sitting position, walk a short distance, turn around, walk back, and sit down again. When timed, it is generally in 20-second intervals (Greenberg & Rader, n.d.).

Assess for Nutritional Status

An assessment for nutritional status would include such factors as the older adult's height, weight, and body mass index. Are there indicators for obesity or poor nutrition and unintentional weight loss? Unexplained weight loss of more than 10 pounds may indicate an underlying medical or psychological issue that may warrant further assessment and treatment (American Geriatric Society, n.d.)

SPICES

The acronym SPICES stands for sleep disorders, problems with nutrition or eating, incontinence, confusion, evidence that the individual has fallen or has had repeated falls, and skin issues. This assessment is used to determine some of most common ailments that impact older adults. This is a preliminary screening to determine whether more extensive assessment is needed (Greenberg & Rader, n.d.).

Pain Assessment

Chronic pain is impactful to older adults, and up to 50% of this population experiences frequent pain (Flaherty, 2012). There are several assessments to determine pain level in older adults. Flaherty (2012) listed several such as the Numeric Rating Scale (NRS), Verbal Descriptor Scale (VDS), and the Faces Pain Scale-Revised (FPS-R). These assessments work by asking the individual to either rate his or her pain level on a scale of 0 to 10 or asking him or her to pick out a picture of a facial expression representing his or her perception of his or her pain (Flaherty, 2012).

KEY COUNSELING POINTERS FOR PHYSICAL AND COGNITIVE DEVELOPMENT DURING LATE ADULTHOOD

Because the U.S. population continues to become older as Baby Boomers reach late adulthood, the need for adequate training in the treatment and assessment of older adults will become paramount (Hadjistavropoulos et al., 2009; Riesco et al., 2011). The population of older adults is expected to double by the year 2030 and reach a peak of 71.5 million, with those over age 85 years the fastest

BOX 17.3 MINIMUM ESSENTIAL COMPETENCIES FOR GERONTOLOGICAL COUNSELORS

The following nine guidelines have been paraphrased from the *American Counseling Association's for Adult Development on Aging*. These are the minimum standards that need to be in place for counselors working with older adults. Counselors need to:

1. Take care to demonstrate respect and affirmation for all aspects of this population's development and be aware and responsive to any sensory or physical changes in the older adult to provide proper accommodations to facilitate the counseling process.
2. Demonstrate understanding of the unique characteristics associated with the older population and how those characteristics impact the counseling process.
3. Be knowledgeable of the psychological theories that are applicable to the older population as well as what is considered normal versus dysfunctional development related to the physical, cognitive, emotional, and behavioral aspects of aging.
4. Understand the social and cultural aspects of older individuals including causes of stress such as ageism, and understand the impact of demographic characteristics (e.g., declining numbers of men, increasing number of older minorities) and how that impacts social and economic issues for older adults.
5. Be knowledgeable about the special needs of the older adult and how these might impact the techniques of counseling and group work with older adults.
6. Understand issues related to lifestyle, career trajectory, and retirement and the impact of age-related changes on the lifestyles of older adults.
7. Understand how to assess older adults in the domains of psychological, social, and physical development and understand the practical and ethical issues impacting assessment techniques for this population.
8. Be cognizant of the current research literature and ethics pertaining to the older population.
9. Be knowledgeable of the ethics related to working with other professionals in the care and treatment of the older adult and the appropriate referral networks available in the community.

Source: Myers (2010).

growing demographic (ABA & APA, 2008). Because special considerations exist for the developmental, cultural, and historical aspects of the older adult population, the American Psychological Association (APA, 2014) cautions practitioners to get training when working with this population (p. 35). Counselors and other health-care providers need to understand "later-life wellness" for this age group. Further, practitioners are cautioned to self-reflect on their perceptions and biases and the myths toward aging, as this population can be considered a special cultural group (APA, 2014). Therefore, education and preparatory work for providing services to this population are a must (APA, 2014).

The APA (2014) Guidelines for Psychological Practice with Older Adults provide several resources for mental health practitioners to obtain this needed training. For example, there is a national conference on training in professional geropsychology. Via this conference, the Pikes Peak Model for Training in Professional Geropsychology was developed (APA, 2014). In addition, the Council of Professional Geropsychology Training Programs (CoPGTP) was created in 2006 (APA, 2014). The National Board of Certified Counseling (NBCC) along with the Council for Accreditation of Counseling and Related Educational Programs (CACREP) created a certification in gerontological counseling, and the American Counseling Association (ACA) helped to develop curriculum to further training for counselors who work with older adults (Myers, 2010). In conjunction with funding by the ACA, a team of counselors and educators developed the minimum competencies for counselors who work with older adults (Myers, 2010).

Counselors provide mental health-care services to older adults in a wide range of settings, from in-home and community-based settings to long-term nursing care and inpatient settings. However, older adults experiencing mental health issues are less likely than younger adults to receive mental health counseling services (Frazer, Hinrichsen, & Jongsma, 2011). Trust is the first of Erik Erikson's virtues in his psychosocial model of development. If therapeutic progress is to be made, a client must develop trust in the counselor and the counselor must show genuine concern about the older client through patterns of behavior that demonstrate care.

Counselors working with older adults should establish and maintain culturally appropriate effective face-to-face communication by minimizing background noise. Other helpful practices are for the counselor to face the older adult and make sure his or her lips are at the same level as the client's. Counselors can also use appropriate visual aids as necessary to help clarify and convey key points, and they should avoid speech that may be viewed as patronizing. Counselors should always be aware and monitor and control nonverbal behavior.

In addition to the counseling services provided for late adulthood cognitive development issues, counselors are also called upon to address functional abilities, including the ability to perform activities of daily living (e.g., bathing, dressing) and independent activities of daily living (e.g., managing finances, preparing meals, managing health). Furthermore, counselors should be familiar with symptoms of various disabilities among older adults that are often due to age-related cognitive and physical changes (e.g., sensory system, cardiovascular system, musculoskeletal system; Saxon, Etten, & Perkins, 2010).

It is necessary for counselors working with older adults to become familiar with other individuals involved with their day-to-day care, including health-care professionals and family members. During counseling sessions, counselors should ask specific questions about the older adult and his or her living situation and social contacts, set counseling goals around the older adult's cultural beliefs and values pertaining to illness and death, engage all parties involved in shared decision making, and involve the older adult in the conversation at all times.

Given that older adults often have comorbid conditions and multiple chronic health conditions, it is important that counselors coordinate care with other health-care professionals so that best practices are followed and duplication of care is prevented. Integrated care has been shown to reduce symptomology and lead to better outcomes for patients (Johnston, 2013). This is especially important because psychological factors often comingle with physical disease. In fact, 88% of all hospitalizations for a physical condition also had a behavioral health component attached to it (Johnston, 2013).

Counselors need to keep in mind that cognitive changes in older adults are highly variable from one person to another. Dementia is a general term applied to a decline in mental ability severe enough to interfere with daily life. As previously mentioned, Alzheimer's disease is the most common form of dementia (Alzheimer's Association, 2012). Counselors working with older adults experiencing cognitive impairments should modify language use in order to communicate more effectively. Older adults with Alzheimer's disease and other forms of dementia pose considerable communication challenges. Reduced information processing speed and capacity lead to problems in understanding complex sentence structures, which place more strain on the older adult's declining working memory. Therefore, it is important to adjust communication styles to meet the changing cognitive levels of the aging older adult in counseling.

BOX 17.4   TIPS FOR COUNSELING THE OLDER ADULT

Counselors should:

- Be aware of what is normal development and what is not normal during this stage.
- Work toward developing and maintaining trust.
- Identify and learn about the individuals involved with the day-to-day care of the older adult.
- Focus on creating a therapeutic partnership with all parties involved.
- Modify language and communication style as necessary.
- Amend treatment objectives and goals in response to evolving needs and concerns.
- Provide ample time for counseling the older adult.
- Adjust counseling to support different learning styles.

Depending on the individual and the issue that brings him or her into counseling, it might be necessary to vary the emotional intensity of the counseling session so that the older adult does not get overwhelmed (Auclair et al., 2009). Due to generational or cultural effects, the older adult may have difficulty expressing intense emotion (Auclair et al., 2009). When the older adult does express emotion, it is important to validate him or her (Granello & Fleming, 2008). It is also important to consider that not many older adults grew up in a time when counseling was the norm, so they may have difficulty opening up to a stranger. Rather than asking a lot of questions, it can be more comforting to the older adult to collect information by just talking about his or her life (Auclair et al., 2009).

SUMMARY

This chapter covered the developmental domains of physical and cognitive growth and decline for late adulthood. Within it, readers were given concrete examples of best practices for working with this population. Special care was taken to provide useful assessment tools, procedures, and cultural considerations so that counselors could build a foundation of knowledge. However, readers are cautioned that additional information and training are needed if this is a new treatment population. Due to the space constraints of a chapter, only a minute amount of material could be covered in any depth.

USEFUL WEBSITES

Aging: Physical and Cognitive Changes in Later Years
https://www.boundless.com/psychology/textbooks/boundless-psychology-textbook/human-development-14/adulthood-74/aging-physical-and-cognitive-changes-in-later-years-291-12826/
Alzheimer's Society: Cognitive Assessment Tool Kit
http://www.alzheimers.org.uk/cognitiveassessment
Brain Age Games
http://www.freebrainagegames.com/
Brain Training
http://www.brainmetrix.com/
The Human Memory
http://www.human-memory.net/types_short.html
Late Adulthood Development
http://www.allpsychologycareers.com/topics/late-adulthood-development.html
Lumosity
http://www.lumosity.com/
Mind Games
http://www.mindgames.com/brain-games.php
Psychology Today: The Neuroscience of Vitality
https://www.psychologytoday.com/blog/vitality/201407/the-neuroscience-vitality-tip-1-neuroplasticity

wiseGEEK
http://www.wisegeek.org/what-is-neural-plasticity.htm
Cognitive Changes With Aging: What Can You Expect?
https://www.youtube.com/watch?v=r4Bb96gv6Ks
Healthy Aging of the Brain to Mild Cognitive Impairment
https://www.youtube.com/watch?v=s2uTPL5vmjI
Smarter Brains excerpt: "Beckman Institute and Cognitive Aging"
https://www.youtube.com/watch?v=ZhvmivNP3Nk
The Aging but Resilient Brain: Keeping Neurons Happy
https://www.youtube.com/watch?v=y5i3jBhxI4Q

REFERENCES

Abdo, C. H. N., Afif-Abdo, J., Otani, F., & Machado, A. C. (2008). Sexual satisfaction among patients with erectile dysfunction treated with counseling, Sildenafil, or both. *Journal of Sexual Medicine, 5,* 1720–1726.

Aguiar, S. A., Polastri, P. F., Godoi, D., Moraes, R., Barela, J. A., & Rodrigues, S. T. (2015). Effects of saccadic eye movements on postural control in older adults. *Psychology & Neuroscience.* Advance online publication. doi:http://dx.doi.org/10.1037/h0100352

Ai, A. L., & Carrigan, L. T. (2007). Social-strata-related cardiovascular health disparity and comorbidity in an aging society: Implications for professional care. *Health and Social Work, 32*(2), 98–105.

Akintunde, A. A., Akintunde, T. S., & Opadijo, O. G. (2015). Knowledge of heart disease risk factors among workers in a Nigerian university: A call for concern. *Nigerian Medical Journal, 56*(2), 91–95.

Alastalo, H., von Bonsdorff, M. B., Räikkönen, K., Pesonen, A-K., Osmond, C., Barker, D. J. P., ... Eriksson, J. G. (2013). Early life stress and physical and psychosocial functioning in late adulthood. *PLoS ONE, 8*(7), e69011–e69011. doi:10.1371/journal.pone.0069011

Allaire, J. C., & Marsiske, M. (2005). Intraindividual variability may not always indicate vulnerability in elders' cognitive performance. *Psychology and Aging, 20*(3), 390–401. doi:10.1037/0882-7974.20.3.390

Almeida, O. P., Hankey, G. J., Yeap, B. B., Golledge, J., Norman, P. E., & Flicker, L. (2014). Mortality among people with severe mental disorders who reach old age: A longitudinal study of community-representative sample of 37892 men. *PLoS ONE, 9*(10), e111882–e111882.

Alzheimer's Association. (2012). Alzheimer's disease facts and figures. *Alzheimer's Dement, 8,* 131–68. Retrieved from http://www.alz.org/alzheimers&uscore;disease&uscore;facts&uscore;and&uscore;figures.asp

American Association of Neuroscience Nurses (AANN). (2009). *Neurologic assessment of the older adult: A guide for nurses.* Glenview, IL: AANN Clinical Practice Guideline Series. Retrieved from http://www.aann.org/pdf/cpg/aannneuroassessmentolderadult.pdf

American Bar Association (ABA) and American Psychological Association (APA). (2008). *Assessment of older adults with diminished capacity: A handbook for psychologists.* Retrieved from http://www.apa.org/pi/aging/programs/assessment/capacity-psychologist-handbook.pdf

American Geriatric Society (AGS). (n.d.) *Assessment of the older adult.* Retrieved from http://www.ouhsc.edu/geriatricmedicine/documents/GRS5-Geriatric\LY1\textbackslash_Assessment.pdf

American Psychiatric Association. (2013). *Diagnostic and statistical manual of mental disorders* (5th ed.). Arlington, VA: Author.

American Psychological Association. (2014). Guidelines for psychological practice with older adults. *American Psychologist, 69*(1), 34–65. doi:10.1037/a0035063

American Psychological Association. (2015). *Guidelines for psychological practice with older adults.* Retrieved from http://www.apa.org/practice/guidelines/older-adults.aspx

Amore, M., Innamorati, M., Costi, S., Sher, L., Girardi, P., & Pompili, M. (2012). Partial androgen deficiency, depression, and testosterone supplementation in aging men. *International Journal of Endocrinology, 2012,* 1–17. doi:10.1155/2012/280724

Asthana, S., Brinton, R. D., Henderson, V. W., McEwen, B. S., Morrison, J. H., & Schmidt, P. J. (2009). Frontiers proposal: National Institute on Aging "bench to bedside: estrogen as a case study." *Age, 31,* 199–210. doi:10.1007/s11357-009-9087-2

Auclair, U., Epstein, C., & Mittelman, M. (2009). Couples counseling in Alzheimer's disease: Additional clinical findings from a novel intervention study. *Clinical Gerontologist, 32,* 130–146. doi:10.1080/07317110802676809

Ballantyne, P. J., Mirza, R. M., Zubin, A., Boon, H. S., & Fisher, J. E. (2011). Becoming old as a 'pharmaceutical person': Negotiation of health and medicines among ethnoculturally diverse older adults. *Canadian Journal on Aging, 30*(2), 169–184. doi:10.1017/S0714980811000110

Balsis, S., Gleason, M. E. J., Woods, C. M., & Oltmanns, T. F. (2007). An item response theory analysis of DSM-IV personality disorder criteria across younger and older age groups. *Psychology and Aging, 22*(1), 171–185. doi:10.1037/0882-7974.22.1.171

Balsis, S., Segal, D. L., & Donahue, C. (2009). Revising the personality disorder diagnostic criteria for the diagnostic and statistical manual of mental disorders-fifte edition (DSM-V): Consider the later life context. *American Journal of Orthopsychiatry, 79*(4), 452–460. doi:10.1037/a0016508

Bayliss, D. M., & Jarrold, C. (2015). How quickly they forget: The relationship between forgetting and working memory performance. *Journal of Experimental Psychology: Learning, Memory, And Cognition, 41*(1), 163–177. doi:10.1037/a0037429

Benton, M. J., & Schlairet, M. C. (2012). Improvements in quality of life in women after resistance training are not associated with age. *Journal of Women and Aging, 24,* 59–69. doi:10.1080/08952841.2012.638877

Bherer, L., Kramer, A. F., & Peterson, M. S. (2008). Transfer effects in task-set cost and dual- task cost after dual-task training in older and younger adults: Further evidence for cognitive plasticity in attentional control in late adulthood. *Experimental Aging Research, 34*, 188–219. doi:10.1080/03610730802070068

Boyle, P. A., Yu, L., Wilson, R. S., Gamble, K., Buchman, A. S., & Bennett, D. A. (2012). Poor decision making is a consequence of cognitive decline among older persons without Alzheimer's Disease or mild cognitive impairment. *PLoS ONE, 7*(8), e43647–e43647. doi:10.1371/journal.pone.0043647

Bryck, R. L., & Fisher, P. A. (2012). Training the brain: Practical applications of neural plasticity from the intersection of cognitive neuroscience, developmental psychology, and prevention science. *American Psychologist, 67*(2), 87–100.

Bugg, J. M. (2014). Evidence for the sparing of reactive cognitive control with age. *Psychology and Aging, 29*(1), 115–127.

Burri, A., Maercker, A., Krammer, S., & Simmen-Janevska, K. (2013). Childhood trauma and PTSD symptoms increase the risk of cognitive impairment in a sample or former indentured child laborers in old age. *PLoS ONE, 8*(2), e57826–e57826. doi:10.1371/journal.pone.0057826

Carretti, B., Borella, E., Zavagin, M., & de Beni, R. (2013). Gains in language comprehension relating to working memory training in healthy older adults. *International Journal of Geriatric Psychiatry, 28*, 539–546. doi:10.1002/gps.3859

Chalé, A., & Unanski, A. G. (2012). Nutrition initiatives in the context of population aging: Where does the United States stand? *Journal of Nutrition in Gerontology and Geriatrics, 31*, 1–15. doi:10.1080/21551197.2011.623924

Chang, P.-J., Wray, L., & Lin, Y. (2014). Social relationships, leisure activity, and health in older adults. *Health Psychology, 33*(6), 516–523. doi: http://dx.doi.org/10.1037/hea0000051

Christensen, K., Doblhammer, G., Rau, R., & Vaupel, J. W. (2010). Ageing populations: The challenges ahead. *PMC, 374*(9696), 1196–1208. Retrieved from http://www.ncbi.nlm.nih.gov/pmc/articles/PMC2810516/

Cocchi, M., Tonello, L., Gabrielli, F., & Pregnolato, M. (2011). Depression, osteoporosis, serotonin cell membrane viscosity between biology and philosophical anthropology. *Annals of General Psychiatry, 10*(9), 1–7.

Coon, D., & Mitterer, J. O. (2013). *Introduction to psychology: Gateways to mind and behavior* (Laureate Education, Inc., custom ed.). Belmont, CA: Wadsworth/Cengage Learning.

Couillard-Despres, S., Iglseder, B., & Aigner, L. (2011). Neurogenesis, cellular plasticity and cognition: The impact of stem cells in the adult and aging brain—A mini-review. *Gerontology, 57*, 559–564.

Crooks, V. C., Little, D., & Chiu, V. (2008). Social network, cognitive function, and dementia incidence among elderly women. *American Journal of Public Health, 98*(7), 1221–1227.

Desai, A. K., Grossberg, G. T., & Sheth, D. N. (2004). Activities of daily living in patients with dementia clinical relevance, methods of assessment and effects of treatment. *CNS Drugs, 18*(13), 853–875.

Douthit, K. Z. (2007). Averting dementia of the Alzheimer's type in women: Can counselors help? *Adultspan, 6*(1), 15–29.

Dunniway, D. L., Camune, B., Baldwin, K., & Crane, J. K. (2012). FRAX counseling for bone health behavior change in women 50 years of age and older. *Journal of the American Academy of Nurse Practitioners, 00*, 1–8.

Erickson, K. I., Gildengers, A. G., & Butters, M. A. (2013). Physical activity and brain plasticity in late adulthood. *Dialogues in Clinical Neuroscience, 15*(1), 99–108.

Erickson, K. I., Miller, D. L., Weinstein, A. M., Akl, S. L., & Banducci, S. E. (2012). Physical activity and brain plasticity in late adulthood: A conceptual review. *Ageing Res., 4*, 34–47.

Eysenck, M. W., Derakshan, N., Santos, R., & Calvo, M. G. (2007). Anxiety and cognitive performance: Attentional control theory. *Emotion, 7*(2), 336–353.

Fandokova, Y., Sander, M., Werkel-Bergner, M., & Shing, Y. L. (2014). Age differences in short-term memory binding are related to working memory performance across the lifespan. *Psychology and Aging, 29*(1), 140–149.

Finas, D., Bals-Pratschz, M., Sandmann, J., Eichenauer, R., Jocham, D., Diedrich, K., & Schmucker, P. (2006). Quality of life in elderly men with androgen deficiency. *Andrologia, 38*, 48–53.

Flaherty, E. (2012). Try this: Best practices in nursing care to older adults. *Hartford Institute for Geriatric Nursing, 7*. Retrieved from http://consultgerirn.org/resources

Foley, D. L., Mackinnon, A., Watts, G. F., Shaw, J. E., Magliano, D. J., Castle, D. J., … Galletly, C. A. (2013). Cardiometabolic risk indicators that distinguish adults with psychosis from the general population, by age and gender. *PLoS ONE, 8*(12), e82606–e82606. doi:10.1371/journal.pone.0082606

Folta, I. S. C., Lichtenstein, A. H., Seguin, R. A., Goidberg, J. P., Kuder, J. F., & Neison, I. E. (2009). The Strong Women-Healthy Hearts Program: Reducing cardiovascular disease risk factors in rural sedentary, overweight, and obese midlife and older women. *American Journal of Public Health, 99*(7), 1271–1277.

Frazer, D. W., Hinrichsen, G. A., & Jongsma, A. E. (2011). *The older adult psychotherapy treatment planner* (2nd ed.). Hoboken, NJ: Wiley.

Gamaldo, A. A., Allaire, J. C., & Whitfield, K. E. (2012). Intraindividual variability in psychometrically defined mild cognitive impairment status in older African Americans. *Psychology and Aging, 27*(4), 989–997. doi:10.1037/a0028557

Goncalves, D. C., Albuquerque, P. B., Byrne, G. J., & Pachana, N. A. (2009). Assessment of depressing in aging contests: General considerations when working with older adults. *Professional Psychology: Research and Practice, 40*(6), 609–606. doi:10.1037/a0017305

González-Herero, V., & García-Martín, M. A. (2012). Personality, activities, and well-being: A study based on women in late adulthood. *Journal of Women & Aging, 24*, 152–168. doi:10.1080/08952841.2012.639662

Granello, P. F., & Fleming, M. S. (2008). Providing counseling for individuals with Alzheimer's disease and their caregivers. *Adultspan, 7*(1), 13–25.

Greenberg, S., & Rader, C. (n.d.). *Module 4: Functional assessment.* Retrieved from http://search.yahoo.com/search?ei=utf-8&fr=aaplw&p=Module+4.++++Functional+Assessment

Hadjistavropoulos, T., Hunter, P., & Fitzgerald, T. G. (2009). Pain assessment and management in older adults: Conceptual issues and clinical challenges. *Canadian Psychology, 50*(4), 241–254. doi:10.1037/a0015341

Hamilton, Z., & Mirza, M. (2014). Post-prostatectomy erectile dysfunction: Contemporary approaches from a US perspective. *Research and Reports in Urology, 6*, 35–41. doi:http://dx.doi.org/10.2147/RRU.S39560

Harrison, S. L., Ding, J., Eugene, Y. H. T., Siervo, M., & Robinson, L. (2014). Cardiovascular disease risk models and longitudinal changes in cognition: A systematic review. *PLoS ONE, 9*(12), e114431–e114445. doi:10.1371/journal.pone.0114431

Harsh, V., Meltzer-Brody, S., Rubinow, D. R., & Schmidt, P. J. (2009). Reproductive aging, sex steroids, and mood disorders. *Harvard Review of Psychiatry, 17*(2), 87–102.

Haslam, C., Morton, T. A., Haslam, A., Varnes, L., Graham, R., & Gamaz, L. (2012). "When the age is in, the wit is out:" Age-related self-categorization and deficit expectations reduce performance on clinical tests used in dementia assessment. *Psychology and Aging, 27*(3), 778–784. doi:10.1037/a0027754

Hogan, C. L., Mata, J., & Carstensen, L. L. (2014). Exercise holds immediate benefits for affect and cognition in younger and older adults. *Psychology and Aging, 28*(2), 587–594. doi:10.1037/a0032634

Hogervorst, E. (2013). Effects of gonadal hormones on cognitive behavior in elderly men and women. *Journal of Neuroendocrinology, 25*, 1182–1195.

Johnston, D. (2013). What makes a difference to patients? *International Review of Psychiatry, 25*(3): 319–328. doi:10.3109/09540261.2013.782854

Kangas, J. L., Baldwin, A. S., Rosenfield, D., Smits, J. A. J., & Rethorst, C. D. (2015). Examining the moderating effect of depressive symptoms on the relation between exercise and self-efficacy during the initiation of regular exercise. *Health Psychology, 34*(5), 556–565.

Karr, J. E., Areshenkoff, C. N., Rast, P., & Garcia-Barrera, M. A. (2014). An empirical comparison of the therapeutic benefits of physical exercise and cognitive training on the executive functions of older adults: A meta-analysis of controlled trials. *Neuropsychology, 28*(6), 829–845. doi: http://dx.doi.org/10.1037/neu0000101

Katsuhisa, S., Koufuchi, R., Yoh, T., Ryoko, N., Ayaka, H., Ayako, T., … Ichiro, S. (2014). Possible benefits of singing to the mental and physical condition of the elderly. *BioPsychoSocial, 8*(1), 2–16. doi:10.1186/1751-0759-8-11.

Keyes, C. L. M. (2004). The nexus of cardiovascular disease and depression revisited: The complete mental health perspective and the moderating role of age and gender. *Aging & Mental Health, 8*(3), 266–274. doi:10.1080/13607860410001669804

Köhler, M., Kliegel, M., Kaduszkiewicz, H., Bachmann, C., Wiese, B., Bickel, M., … Wagneri, M. (2012). Effect of cardiovascular and metabolic disease on cognitive test performance and cognitive change in older adults. *JAGS, 60*, 1286–1291. doi:10.1111/j.1532-5415.2012.04032.x

Krampe, R. T., Smolders, C., & Doumas, M. (2014). Leisure sports and postural control: Can a black belt protect your balance from aging? *Psychology and Aging, 29*(1), 95–102. doi:10.1037/a0035501

Lee, A. M., Chu, L.-W., Chong, C. S.-Y., Chan, S.-Y., Tam, S., Lam, K. S.-L., & Lam, T.-P. (2010). Relationship between symptoms of androgen deficiency and psychological factors and quality of life among Chinese men. *Academy of Andrology, 33*, 755–763.

Liechty, T. (2012). Yes, I worry about my weight…but for the most part I'm content with my body: Older women's body dissatisfaction alongside contentment. *Journal of Woman and Aging, 24*, 70–88. doi: 10.1080/08952841.2012.638873

Liu, X.-D., Cai, F., Liu, L., Zhang, Y., & Yang, A.-L. (2015). MicroRNA-210 is involved in the regulation of postmenopausal osteoporosis through promotion of VEGF expression and osteoblast differentiation. *Biological Chemistry, 396*(4), 339–347.

Lukert, B., Satram-Hoang, Wade, S., Anthony, M., Gao, G., & Downs, R. (2011). Physician differences in managing postmenopausal osteoporosis: Results from the POSSIBLE US treatment registry study. *Drugs Aging, 28*(9), 713–727.

Mata, R., von Helversen, B., & Rieskamp, J. (2010). Learning to choose: Cognitive aging and strategy selection learning in decision making. *Psychology and Aging, 25*(2), 299–309. doi:10.1037/a0018923

Mattys, S. L., & Scharenborg, O. (2014). Phoneme categorization and discrimination in younger and older adults: A comparative analysis of perceptual, lexical, and attentional factors. *Psychology and Aging, 28*(1), 150–162. doi:10.1037/a0035387

McCarrey, A. C., Henry, J. D., & Luszcz, M. (2010). Potential mechanisms contributing to decision-making difficulties in late adulthood. *Gerontology, 56*, 430–434. doi:10.1159/000275060

Meisler, J. G. (2002). Toward optimal health: The experts discuss hypertension. *Journal of Women's Health and Gender-Based Medicine, 11*(2), 111–117.

Michetti, P. M., Rossi, R., Bonanno, D., Tiesi, A. & Simonelli, C. (2006) Male Sexuality and regulation of emotions: A Study on the association between alexithymia and erectile dysfunction (ED). *International Journal of Impotence Research, 18*, 170–174. http://dx.doi.org/10.1038/sj.ijir.3901386

Miller, M. J. (2009, October). The importance of screening for osteoporosis in mental health settings. *Clinical Schizophrenia & Related Psychoses*, 155–160.

Moore, C. S., Grant, M. D., Zink, T. A., Panizzon, M. S., Franz, C. E., Logue, M. W., …Lyons, M. J. (2014). Erectile dysfunction, vascular risk, and cognitive performance in late middle age. *Psychology and Aging, 29*(1), 163–172. doi:10.1037/a0035463

Moore, J. B., Mitchell, N. G., Beets, M. W., & Bartholomew, J. B. (2012). Physical self-esteem in older adults: A test of the indirect effect of physical activity. *Sports, Exercise, and Performance Psychology, 1*(4), 231–241. doi:10.1037/a0028636

Mora, P. A., Orsak, G., DiBonaventura, M. D., & Leventhal, E. A. (2013). Why do comparative assessments predict health? The role of self-assessed health in the formation of comparative health judgments. *Health Psychology*, *32*(11), 1175–1178. doi:http://dx.doi.org/10.1037/a0032044

Motl, R. W., & McAuley, E. (2014). Physical activity and health-related quality of life over time in adults with multiple sclerosis. *Rehabilitation Psychology*, *59*(4), 415–421. doi:http://dx.doi.org/10.1037/a0037739

Mungas, D., Reed, B. R., Farias, S. T., & DeCarli, C. (2009). Age and education effects on relationships of cognitive test scores with brain structure in demographically diverse older persons. *Psychology and Aging*, *24*(1), 116–128. doi:10.1037/a0013421

Myers, J. (2010). *Gerontological counseling*. Retrieved from http://wellness-research .org/jem\LY1\textbackslash_info/docs/gerontology.htm

Nobre, P., & Gouveia, J. P. (2000). Erectile dysfunction: An empirical approach based on Beck's cognitive theory. *Sexual and Relationship Therapy*, *15*(4), 351–366. doi:10.1080/14681990020007201

Notthoff, N., & Carstensen, L. L. (2014). Positive messaging promotes walking in older adults. *Psychology and Aging*, *29*(2), 329–341. doi:http://dx.doi.org/10 .1037/a0036748

Novak, J. R., Sandberg, J. G., & Harper, J. M. (2014). Older couples with and without cardiovascular disease: Testing associations between and among affective communication, marital satisfaction, physical and mental health. *Families, Systems, and Health*, *32*(2), 186–197. doi:10.1037/fsh0000015

Petry, N. M., Andrade, L. F., Barry, D., & Byrne, S. (2013). A randomized study of reinforcing ambulatory exercise in older adults. *Psychology and Aging*, *28*(4), 1164–1173. doi:10.1037/a0032563

Rice, M. C., Katzel, L. I., & Waldstein, S. R. (2010). Sex-specific associations of depressive symptoms and cardiovascular risk factors in older adults. *Aging & Mental Health*, *14*(4), 405–410. doi:10.1080/13607860903586185

Riediger, M., Wrzus, C., Klipker, K., Müller, V., Schmiedek, F., & Wagner, G. G. (2014). Outside of the laboratory: Associations of working-memory performance with psychological and physiological arousal vary with age. *Psychology and Aging*, *29*(1), 103–114. doi:10.1037/a0035766

Riesco, E., Choquette, S., Audet, M., Tessier, D., & Dionne, I. J. (2011). Effect of exercise combined with phytoestrogens on quality of life in postmenopausal women. *Climacteric*, *14*, 573–580. doi:10.3109/13697137.2011.566652

Rosen, R., Janssen, E., Wiegel, M., Bancroft, J., Althof, S., Wincze, J., ... Barlow, D. (2006). Psychological and interpersonal correlates in men with erectile dysfunction and their partners: A pilot study of treatment outcome with Sildenafil. *Journal of Sex and Marital Therapy*, *32*, 215–234. doi: 10.1080/00926230600575314

Roy, J., & Allen, P. (2004). Erectile dysfunction counseling and advice. *Practice Nurse*, *27*(1), 46–50.

Rowland, D. L., Myers, A. L., Adamski, B. A., & Burnett, A. L. (2012). Role of attribution in affective responses to a partnered sexual situation among sexually dysfunctional men. *BJU International*, *111*, E103–E109. doi:10.1111/j.1464–410X.2012.11347.x

Safizadeh, M., Aminizadeh, E., & Safizadeh, H. (2015). Awareness of osteoporosis among female employees in Kerman, Iran. *Russian Open Medical Journal, 4*(1), 1–4. doi:10.15275/rusomj.2015.0103

Saxon, S. V., Etten, M. J., & Perkins, E. A. (2010). *Physical change and aging: A guide for the helping professions.* New York, NY: Springer.

Shanahan, M. J., Hill, P. L., Roberts, B. W., Eccles, J., & Friedman, H. S. (2014). Conscientiousness, health, and aging: The life course of personality model. *Developmental Psychology, 50*(5), 1407–1425. doi: http://dx.doi.org/10.1037/a0031130

Stanner, S., & Denny, A. (2009). Healthy ageing: The role of nutrition and lifestyle—A new British Nutrition Foundation Task Force Report. *Nutrition Bulletin, 34*, 58–63.

Stepankova, H., Lukavsky, J., Buschkuehl, M., Kopecek, M., Ripova, D., & Jaeggi, S. M. (2014). The malleability of working memory and visuospatial skills: A randomized controlled study in older adults. *Developmental Psychology, 50*(4), 1049–1059.

Tait, E. M., Laditka, S. B., Laditka, J. N., Nies, M. A., & Racine, E. F. (2012). Use of complementary and alternative medicine for physical performance, energy, immune function, and general health among older women and men in the United States. *Journal of Women and Aging, 24*, 23–43. doi:10.1080/08952841.2012.638875

Thurm, F., Scharpf, A., Lieberman, N., Kolassa, S., Elbert, T., Luchtenberg, D., Woll, A., & Kolassa, I. T. (2011). Improvement of cognitive function after physical movement training in institutionalized very frail older adults with dementia. *GeoPsych, 24*(4), 197–208. doi:10.1037/a0035893

Tucker-Drob, E. M., & Briley, D. A. (2014). Continuity of genetic and environmental influences on cognition across the life span: A meta-analysis of longitudinal twin and adoption studies. *Psychological Bulletin, 140*(4), 949–979.

Tucker-Drob, E. M., Reynolds, C. A., Finkel, D., & Pedersen, N. L. (2014). Shared and unique genetic and environmental influences on aging-related changes in multiple cognitive abilities. *Developmental Psychology, 50*(1), 152–166.

Vance, D. E., Webb, N. M., Marceaux, J. C., Viamonte, S. M., Foote, A. W., & Ball, K. K. (2008). Mental stimulation, neural plasticity, and aging: Directions for nursing research and practice. *The Journal of Neuroscience Nursing, 40*(4), 241–249.

Verdilel, G., Laws, S. M., Henley, D., Ames, D., Bush, A. I., Ellis, K. A., … Martins, R. N. (2014). Associations between gonadotropins, testosterone, and β amyloid in men at risk of Alzheimer's disease. *Molecular Psychiatry, 19*, 69–75.

Wang, Y., Liu, T., Rossi, P. J., Watkins-Bruner, D., Hsiao, W., Cooper, S., … Jani, A. B. (2013). Influence of vascular comorbidities and race on erectile dysfunction and prostate cancer radiotherapy. *Journal of Sex Medicine, 10*, 2108–2114. doi:10.1111/jsm.12215

Xu, X., & Padilla, A. M. (2013). Using meaningful interpretation and chunking to enhance memory: The case of Chinese character learning. *Foreign Language Annals, 46*(3), 402–422.

CHAPTER 18

Late Adulthood: Emotional and Social Development

Ann Vernon and Darcie Davis Gage

According to an Association of American Retired Persons (AARP) report (Nelson, 2013), this country is experiencing one of the most dramatic demographic shifts in history, with over 40 million Americans age 65 years and older. In fact, the 65 and older age group has been increasing twice as rapidly as the rest of the population (Moody & Sasser, 2012), with 10,000 people a day turning 65, a trend that is expected to continue for the next 16 years (Jenkins, 2014). It is a projected that by the year 2030, the number of people over age 65 years will double (Ortman, Velkoff, & Hogan, 2014), and by the year 2060, this figure will rise to over 90 million, with older Americans outnumbering children under age 18. Not only is the aging population increasing rapidly due to greater life expectancy and advances in the medical field, but it is also becoming more diverse. Although presently the older population is not as diverse as the younger population, this is projected to change, with considerable increase in ethnic and racial diversity during the next four decades. By the year 2030, projections are that 72% of the population will be Caucasian, 10% African American, 11% Hispanic, and 5% Asian (Ortman et al., 2014), and this poses new challenges and opportunities as we attempt to address the needs of all aging populations. Clearly the dramatic increase in the aging population and the diversity factor will have far-reaching implications for how the major institutions of our society address the needs of those over age 65, as well as how we reconceptualize the concept of aging.

Moody and Sasser (2012) stressed that aging is a gradual process that begins earlier in life and that as we learn more about this process it will become imperative to reexamine traditional concepts and stereotypes about aging. Jenkins (2014) concurred, challenging us to "disrupt" aging (p. 32) and reimagine what it means to get older. We need to debunk the myths about what *old age* is and instead think in terms of aging as a good healthy process. We need to define people by who they are, not how old they are, since in many respects age is relative. In fact, just as there is a clear distinction between early and middle adolescence, there is also a distinct difference between *young old age* and *older old age*. Although this does not appear to be addressed in the literature, it seems important to make this designation to avoid the stereotypic notions associated with late adulthood.

BOX 18.1 REFLECTIONS ON LATE ADULTHOOD

Reflect on what adjectives come to mind when you think about people in late adulthood (over age 65 years). List 10. Once you have completed the list, put a plus sign (+) next to those you view as positive descriptors, a minus sign (–) next to those you think are negative, and a number sign (#) next to those you consider neutral. Look over the list to see what patterns emerged and how these adjectives reflect your attitudes about aging. Discuss your perceptions with three or four of your classmates.

Fortunately, our perception of aging is shifting from "a dreaded period of decline to one of dignity" (Rand, 2014, p. 38), where our lives and social expectations have been fundamentally transformed. Those who still cling to the stereotype of a gray-haired granny sitting in her rocking chair watching television or knitting are being forced to rethink this viewpoint, as the older adult population is by no means a homogeneous group defined by narrow-minded misconceptions of elderly people slowly easing out of life and passing time until their inevitable death. Instead, the meaning of aging is changing. As Rand (2014) noted, "America is in the midst of a second aging revolution as many of the children of that first-ever retirement generation-boomers-hold new and very different aspirations. They are realizing that their life experience has tremendous value. While many aspire to retire from work, they have no desire to retire from life" (p. 38). Given that many in this age group are in better health and live longer, their later years will look very different from generations past. Rand referred to this period as the freedom to do something different. "Instead of accepting decline, it celebrates discovery—a Life Reimagined" (p. 38).

Looking through this new lens on late adulthood, this second revolution that follows the first aging revolution, which was about freedom from work, is all about new possibilities. Referring to the Boomers, Rand (2014) noted that they created the Age of Possibilities because "they reject the notion that their possibilities are shrinking as they get older. They see their 50-plus years as a chance to grow in new and rewarding ways, to unleash their passions, to live the American dream, to make the world a better place" (p. 38).

This chapter explores the emotional and social aspects of late adulthood, generally defined as age 65 years and older. We address the notion of aging with dignity and growing more whole, not just older. The reader will be challenged to reframe the concept of aging in a more positive light, to examine the possibilities this stage of life brings, and also to learn about the challenges presented during this period, particularly in the emotional realm. In addition to understanding the emotional and social issues for older adults, the chapter also suggests how counselors can better serve this population that is increasing at a dramatic rate.

> ## BOX 18.2 CAN LATE ADULTHOOD BE REWARDING?
>
> After reading the introductory portion of this chapter, have your opin-
> ions about late adulthood changed? If so, in what ways? Do you agree
> with Rand (2014) that people during late adulthood can grow in reward-
> ing ways and embrace this period of development with optimism and
> enthusiasm for life? Discuss your opinions with three or four of your
> classmates.

FACTORS INFLUENCING EMOTIONAL AND SOCIAL DEVELOPMENT IN LATE ADULTHOOD

Clearly there are many factors that impact emotional and social development
in late adulthood. The following section discusses several of these, illustrating
through case studies how they significantly affect the way people navigate their
journeys through late adulthood.

The Baby Boomer Generation

We would be remiss if we did not reference the influence of the Baby Boomer
generation, defined as those born between 1946 and 1964, because they have been
the impetus for redefining the meaning of aging. Numbering nearly 77 million
(Jenkins, 2014), Boomers make up about a third of the population in the United
States, and for the first time the senior age group is the largest in terms of size and
percent of the population. It is expected that Boomers will live into their 80, 90,
and 100 (Whitbourne & Whitbourne, 2011), which will necessitate revising social
policies that affect older adults.

As young adults, the Boomer generation redefined normative behavior just,
as they are now redefining aging. According to O'Ryan, Rawlins, and Rawlins
(2005), they are "a force to be reckoned with" (p. 34). O'Ryan and colleagues
also noted that Boomers have transformed many of the preconceptions we
have regarding aging; they "remake each life stage and are rewriting what it
means to be a senior citizen" (p. 34). Boomers look at aging from a very different perspective that embraces individuality, self-expression, and youthfulness.
They value self-determination and have different developmental needs than
other cohorts.

Boomers are typically well educated and socially conscious. Many fought hard
for racial and gender equality and paved the way for gays, lesbians, and bisexuals to
be more empowered. Their generation was the catalyst for change in traditional
family structures, including dual-career families, as many Boomer women entered
the workforce to pursue meaningful careers, not just jobs. Boomers embrace
youthfulness—they do not want to "grow old gracefully" (O'Ryan et al., 2005,

p. 37), nor do they consider themselves old (Moody & Sasser, 2012). Many intend to stay active as long as possible, valuing their individualism and autonomy. Moody and Sasser noted that many Boomers have made a "fundamentally different life plan" (p. 458) from that of their parents and grandparents. They are not just drifting to the end of their lives—many are staying gainfully employed, at least part time, well past retirement age, either because they enjoy working or can't afford to retire.

Counselors working with adults in this stage of development need to remain cognizant of the fact that the Baby Boomer generation defies traditional assumptions about aging, and therefore, they need to reconceptualize how to best address the needs of this age group, which is also ethnically and racially diverse (Cavanaugh & Blanchard-Fields, 2011). O'Ryan and colleagues (2005) stated that counselors working with the Boomer population must be flexible, open-minded, creative, and culturally sensitive. They must create new paradigms that better address the emerging needs of this cohort, including advocating for changes in social policies that affect older adults. O'Ryan et al. also suggested that counselors will need to be prepared to help clients with wellness and preventive health-care practices and to initiate good working relationships with medical doctors to facilitate appropriate health care. They must be able to help individuals and couples deal with the transition to retirement and increase their awareness about how this will impact them socially, emotionally, and financially. Counselors need to be familiar with referral sources so their clients can get sound advice regarding financial and estate planning. If clients are raising grandchildren, counselors may need to set up support groups to help them deal with the stressors and issues associated with this new responsibility. Even if they are not raising their grandchildren, clients may need family education or communication skills to facilitate the relationship with either the grandchildren or their adult children.

Because of the unique needs of the Boomer cohort, counselors will need to assume an advocacy role with regard to health care and social security reform. Whitbourne and Whitbourne (2011) stressed the importance of this, noting that "new ideas are needed to revamp the current health care system for the aging baby boomers, whose numbers, lifestyles, and values will almost invariably lead to challenges of the status quo of care now being offered" (pp. 277–278). In addition to being advocates, counselors will also need to be collaborators, helping this cohort navigate transitions that present new challenges as different issues emerge.

Retirement

As Rand (2014) noted, the first aging revolution was about freedom from work, resulting in a new life stage called retirement. According to Butterworth and colleagues (2006), retirement is a "loosely defined construct" (p. 1180) that is, typically associated with age 65 years, although clearly there is great variation regarding the age at which people retire. Whitbourne and Whitbourne (2011) identified five phases of retirement: an anticipatory period which could last a long time; the decision to retire; the act of retirement; adjustments after retirement; and decisions about how to structure life postretirement. Wang and Schultz (2010, as cited in Whitbourne and Whitbourne) stressed that retirement should be thought of as an adjustment process because it is not just an event with a definitive beginning and ending.

Traditionally, retirement meant that people no longer went to work every day—they had their farewell party, claimed their gold watch or plaque, and went on their merry way. They may have marked off days on their calendar, waiting enthusiastically for the time to come when they could do whatever they wanted to do with no hard and fast commitments—they could sleep late, read, golf, or travel without time constraints. And because they didn't live as long as retirees do now, there was not as much need to look beyond leisure and find a new purpose for being. For many, this version of retirement was what they had been working hard to achieve all their lives, and they enjoyed their newfound freedoms, embracing their new lives with vigor.

For others, the picture might be quite different. As Schlossberg (2004) noted, retirement is "an enormous period of adjustment as people move into uncharted territory" (p. 5). She used the word *scary* to describe retirement because so many different aspects of our lives are in flux. Whereas during our working years there were generally strict schedules and routines, suddenly those change when the familiar structure of work is gone. Schlossberg likened retirement to setting sail in a storm, "with little sailing experience, toward a hoped-for destination" (p. 6).

Weiss (2005) described retirement as perplexing, noting that we have the freedom to do nothing and also to create a new legacy or contribute to society in different ways than we did when we were working. Deciding on that path is not always clear cut, and to a large extent, it depends on whether the retiree is relieved about not having to deal with the stressors associated with work and embraces the newfound freedoms or whether the end of work represents a huge deficit in one's life.

Redefining Retirement

According to Schlossberg (2009) and Weiss (2005), the image of retirement is changing, and the term *retirement* needs to be retired, or at least redefined. Schlossberg (2004) noted that even the language used to describe retirement is changing: "retirees and seniors are now rebounders or prime timers" (p. 6). Levine (2005) used the term *rewirement* as a replacement for *retirement*. Both Schlossberg and Weiss (2005) concurred that even for those who were counting down the days until retirement, this is still a period of tremendous adjustment in which people need to redefine their roles, routines, relationships, and identities (Schlossberg, 2004, 2009).

Freedman (1999) described retirement as "an interlude between stages … [because] more and more individuals are 'retiring' for a period—to catch their breath—before making the transition to a new chapter in life" (p. viii). In looking at retirement from this perspective, it is not the end but the beginning of the third stage of life, a term also referred to by Schlossberg (2009) and Lawrence-Lightfoot (2009). Unfortunately, many are caught off guard because they have not given careful thought to what this third stage of life will look like. Sociologist Phyllis Moen (as cited in Schlossberg, 2009) contended that people spend more time planning a wedding than they do retirement. Perhaps if there were more good retirement role models and more preparation for retirement, this third stage of life would be easier to figure it out.

So what is the new definition of retirement? Obviously it's more than sitting in a rocking chair just passing time. It's about starting on a new path that may merge into several, the longer we live. It's about the freedom to redefine the future, about new beginnings. It is a milestone that forces us to embark on a new phase of life. It's about letting go of who we were and answering the question, Who am I?

Letting Go

When we retire we let go of people, places, and things. We let go of the role that for so many years defined us through our work. If we identified strongly with this role, it is all the more difficult to let go, which results in a grieving process. As Schlossberg (2009) noted, a vacuum is created if you leave a role that was central to your sense of self and have nothing to replace it with. A poem titled "I Used to Be" (Claus, 2015) is a profound expression of this letting go process:

I walked into the office

Where I used to go every day

To see someone I used to know.

She wasn't there.

Walls had been removed

To make room for cubicles

Lots of them.

I used to be someone so important

Here.

No one looked up

No one called my name.

No one answered my silent questions.

Finally, a young lady glanced my way and said,

"May I help you, honey?"

I saw myself reflected in her face.

She thought I was lost

And she was right, I was.

BOX 18.3 REFLECTING ON I USED TO BE

After reading the poem "I Used to Be," what thoughts and feelings come to mind? Imagine that you are working with a client who has just retired and has shared this poem with you as a way of expressing how she feels about retirement. What first steps would you take in helping this person adjust to her new life?

Letting go and moving on can be challenging, although the degree of challenge depends on the individuals and their perceptions of the transition to retirement. Schlossberg (2009) referred to this transition process as involving a change in roles, routines, relationships, and assumptions about retirement, indicating that it takes time and patience to sort through these issues and create a new path. Furthermore, several changes are often involved in the retirement process—leaving work, selling a home, moving to a new location, leaving old friends and making new ones—resulting in additional challenges and adjustments. According to Schlossberg, "Retirement … forces us to reconsider almost every aspect of our life" (p. 27). For this reason, it is imperative that counselors be better prepared to help facilitate this phase of development for their adult clients.

Who Am I?

A quote from *Alice's Adventures in Wonderland* comes to mind as retirees ponder the question of who am I? To quote Alice, "Who in the world am I? Ah, that's the great puzzle." Those words can speak loudly to retirees. Weiss (2005) noted that it is not possible to retire without identity change since our feelings of worth are often connected to our occupations—so who are we without that identity? For those who defined their feelings of worth in terms of their employment, there will almost certainly be some nostalgia for who they once were and confusion about how to reinvent themselves. Once again, this is a process that takes time. Retirees knew who they had been, but many have no idea of who they are now. As Weiss (2005) said, "As far as the psychological definition of retirement goes, I am resistive. I do not want to think of myself as retired" (p. 3).

Schlossberg (2009), who interviewed many retirees to learn more about their experiences with the transition to retirement, found that "Many of those I interviewed said that the greatest issue in retirement resided in the assault on their identity" (p. 85). She maintained that when you are retired and no longer have a "real" job, "it is harder to know how to describe yourself to the outside world" (p. 85). She noted that although you could simply say that you were a retiree, it might be preferable to create a new identity that holds some meaning. The following case study exemplifies this search for a meaningful identity.

Case Study: Who Am I?

I (first author) have struggled significantly with the issue of a meaningful identity. When I retired, I not only left my jobs as therapist and counselor educator but also the home we had lived in for more than 20 years. We moved to an active adult community in a state far away from where I had lived my entire life. I knew from the outset that this would be a difficult transition, but I had not considered some of the difficulties that presented themselves as I attempted to redefine myself and my world. One of the first disturbing events was a conversation I was involved in shortly after moving into my new neighborhood. I was at a dinner party in which people were discussing where they had lived, how they ended up in this community, and what they had done prior to retiring. One woman commented, "What you did when you worked doesn't matter anymore.... Here we are all on an equal playing field." I was aghast, especially when I saw others agreeing with her. I immediately spoke up and said I vehemently disagreed, that being a therapist and counselor educator for more than 30 years played a central role in my life, shaping my values, attitudes, and outlook on life. I was proud of what I had done during my professional career and knew that many of the skills I had learned throughout the years were still invaluable to me now, even if retired. I said that I couldn't just throw out the most meaningful years of my life by saying that who I was then has no bearing on who I am now. Suffice it to say that there was uncomfortable silence around the table and the conversation moved to safer topics. Such was my introduction to my new environment!

But it didn't stop there. I needed to find a doctor, and when I went to fill out the new patient information I felt a bit like a deer in the headlights when I came to the line asking for occupation and work phone number. Like Weiss (2005), I did not want to think of myself as retired, but I didn't know who I was. Since I was still doing some consulting abroad, I decided I would now call myself a consultant. But what felt like assaults to my being kept coming. I attended a national conference because even though I was retired I wasn't dead, and I still felt a desire to keep up with the profession that had meant so much to me for so many years. I must say it came as an unwelcome surprise when a fellow professional saw me and said, "What are you doing here? I thought you were retired." I felt angry, sad, and marginalized—like a fish out of water.

Schlossberg (2009) advised that thinking about what matters to you is a good way of determining your new identity. She suggested imagining that you are writing a play about yourself in the future to help shed some light on "new ways of being when the old labels no longer work" (p. 86). As many have found, discovering this new identity takes time and may involve trial and error, but ultimately our new selves emerge as we continue our journeys through the late adult years.

Adjusting to Retirement

Retirement is a complex process that represents an extremely significant life transition (Cavanaugh & Blanchard-Fields, 2011). Cavanaugh and Blanchard-Fields identified several factors that influence the adjustment to retirement, including whether retirement was elected or a mandatory early retirement, physical health, financial resources, gender and ethnic differences, and feeling in control. Bjorklund (2011) noted that people who have several leisure time interests adjust more rapidly than those who retire without a clear vision of how they will spend their time. Individual differences must be taken into consideration given that there are so many personal variables that contribute to a person's ability to adjust to this major transition. Counselors can facilitate this by using expressive writing to help retirees write the next chapters of their lives, recommending nonfiction bibliotherapy to help clients clarify their issues and goals, or helping them work through grief and loss if this is a difficult transition.

Health and Health Care

Another major factor that impacts social and emotional well-being in late adulthood is a person's health and access to affordable and quality health care. Simply put, people are living longer because of the dramatic improvements in health care and advances in medical technology, but the question remains as to whether living longer will be characterized by good health or by health problems, which in turn will affect their quality of life. According to Cavanaugh and Blanchard-Fields (2011), "There have never been as many older adults as there are now, especially people over age 85" (p. 5). The average life expectancy continues to rise and has been steadily increasing since 1990, although there are ethnic and gender differences affecting this (Cavanaugh & Blanchard-Fields, 2011). Promoting healthy lifestyles for all people, but especially for older adults, must be a priority because as Aldwin and Gilmer (2004) noted, staying healthy is a major factor in decelerating the rate of aging.

The truth is, as we age we are more susceptible to certain types of infections and have a higher risk for cancer and autoimmune disorders. Furthermore, older adults are more likely to experience some common chronic conditions, such as arthritis, diabetes, hypertension, respiratory diseases, and incontinence, all of which affect the quality of life. Cardiovascular conditions can result in chronic disability and remain the number one cause of death (Whitbourne & Whitbourne, 2011). Diseases in later adulthood can be extremely disabling or fatal, although with increasing emphasis on prevention and medical advances, the outlook may be more optimistic. Another health-related concern is that there may be undesirable side effects from medications used to treat these conditions. Cavanaugh and Blanchard-Fields (2011) noted that older adults are more prone to adverse drug effects related to how the body absorbs the drugs.

Dementia is undoubtedly the condition that is most feared in the elderly population since the incidence increases with age and profoundly impacts so many aspects of an individual's functioning. Presently that there is no cure for dementia or Alzheimer's, and until there is, it is projected that by 2030, the number of people with dementia will increase by 50%, with 8 million people and their families being affected (Cavanaugh & Blanchard-Fields, 2011).

Access to quality and affordable health care is also an issue for many older adults, which in turn has a major emotional impact. Consider the following case study as an illustration of these points.

Case Study: Alberto

Alberto is 61 years old and has lived legally in this country most of his life. He and his wife Angela raised four children, who now all live independently. Alberto worked hard and supported his family by selling produce at local markets. Angela had a good job with health benefits for herself and Alberto until recently when her job was terminated.

Several years ago Angela developed multiple sclerosis but was able to control it quite successfully with medication. Without a job she could not afford the medication, and her condition worsened rapidly. Alberto himself was severely diabetic and also needed medical services. Although he worked, he did not earn enough money to make house payments, so the couple had to foreclose and move in with two of their adult children. This was a tremendous loss for the couple who had always prided themselves on being able to support their family, and they both experienced considerable stress.

Alberto sought counseling at a low-income clinic where services were free. The counselor explored options with him, which were limited because of his health and the fact that they no longer had medical insurance and were not yet eligible for Medicare. The counselor helped him apply for social security disability for his wife, but he was too proud to resort to that for himself at this point. The counselor encouraged him to control what he could, which was diet and exercise to keep his diabetes at bay, and helped him find ways to cope with his depression which began with his wife's job termination and other losses.

As this case exemplifies, one's health can significantly impact emotional well-being and quality of life for older adults and their families. As one becomes more vulnerable to more health issues, lack of good health care can be a major source of stress with far-reaching implications.

Financial Security

Saving for retirement is something that has been drummed into the heads of many, yet there is a lot of uncertainty about what retirement expenses will be, making it difficult to anticipate how much is enough to retire with. Most people over age 65 years will have social security income and, depending on the retiree, a pension plan. Cavanaugh and Blanchard-Fields (2011) contended that although social security was intended to be supplementary income, in fact it is the primary source of income for most retired Americans. According to Bjorklund (2011), although the number of retired people living below the poverty line has decreased considerably, many poor retired people are still not eligible for special programs that provide support. Poverty is more prevalent in older women, Blacks, and Hispanics than in older men or Caucasians. So despite the fact that those age 55 years and older control more than three-fourths of America's wealth (http://www.immersionactive.com/resources/50-plus-facts-and-fiction), the reality is that for many the financial constraints of retirement cause significant stress and negatively impact the quality of life for older adults.

People who retire with means have a very different life from those who have to lower their standard of living if they have less money in retirement. Those with money have less stress and anxiety because they don't have to worry as much about how to manage financially when they are no longer employed. For them, it is much easier to live the American Dream than for those who have nothing to rely on except social security.

EMOTIONAL DEVELOPMENT IN LATE ADULTHOOD

The years after retirement are often referred to as the Golden Years, although many older adults might not share this positive perspective, depending on their circumstances, social support systems, financial resources, physical and emotional health and resilience, and overall quality of life. As you read in the previous section, several factors impact emotional well-being in late adulthood: being part of the Boomer generation, retirement, health and access to affordable quality health care, and financial security. Depending on which side of the fence you are on, life in late adulthood can be as different as night and day, impacting emotional well-being.

Emotional Well-Being

In reality, emotional well-being in late adulthood is closely related to how we experience loss because as we get older, loss is inevitable. Depending on the individual, some of these losses are minor, and others are major; it is a matter of perspective, the significance of the loss, and the degree of importance associated with the loss. Many of these losses are health related, whereas others are associated with loss of privilege and independence. For example, my (first author) mother had to stop driving at age 92 years. This was a tremendous loss because it meant loss of independence and freedom and more social isolation. When she turned 95 and had had numerous falls and back fractures, she finally admitted that she might need to live in an assisted living facility where loss of dignity (needing help bathing and dressing) and having to rely on others became an issue. Leaving the home she had lived in for more than 30 years was another huge loss because she realized that this move represented another mile down the road to the end—the next to the last stop. Obviously her losses are our losses as a family. However, the up side of this picture is that until age 90 years she took her dog on long walks, played golf, went to book club, and had a good quality of life. Even now she watches basketball and can talk about game strategy and NBA trades better than many.

Emotional Health Issues in Late Adulthood

As we have stressed throughout this chapter, because life expectancy is so much higher than ever before and people are living well into their 80s and 90s and beyond, many in relatively good health, it is important to reconsider what aging really means. We have challenged the reader to stop thinking of older adults as weak and frail, with failing minds and bodies, and to recognize that older people are much younger than they used to be, due to a variety of factors. However, the reality is that the aging process cannot be reversed and that people will not live forever. As with any stage of development, there are changes, challenges, and new things to learn. However, as we age, these things take on new meaning. Whereas it was a challenge to learn to ride a bicycle when you were 5 or 6 years old, once you mastered the task it was fun, it opened up your world, and you could continue doing it for a long time. The same could be said for learning to read and write. Then you had an entire lifetime before you, and what you were learning was exhilarating. But the older you get, the faster the clock is ticking. The challenges that present themselves aren't necessarily intriguing and interesting; they are necessary for survival and safety. For example, it would probably be unlikely to find someone who thought learning how to operate a scooter when they were 90 years old to help decrease the risk of falling was exciting and exhilarating. Similarly, learning to tie your shoe or zip your sweater comes with a different sense of accomplishment for a child as opposed to an elderly adult who struggles with something so basic.

As older adults age and are forced to make more adaptations to stay healthy and safe, live with chronic pain, lose friends and partners to death or dementia or moving, and experience other losses such as mobility, memory, or physical stamina and agility, emotional well-being can become a major factor. Anxiety and depression are the two most prevalent emotions experienced by older adults.

Anxiety

As Cavanaugh and Blanchard-Fields (2011) reported, anxiety disorders are especially prevalent in older adults as they increasingly experience losses. As health issues become more prevalent for this population, as they become more dependent on caregivers, as they lose their independence or become more isolated as a result of relocating to an assisted living or nursing facility, the stress associated with these changes increases the likelihood of an anxiety disorder, described as intense anxiety, worry, or apprehension (Whitbourne & Whitbourne, 2011). According to Bjorklund (2011), anxiety disorders, including phobias, posttraumatic stress syndrome, and obsessive-compulsive disorder are the most typical anxiety disorders, and more women than men experience them.

Anxiety is often associated with fear of the unknown and is about what-if thinking. When my (first author) mother was hospitalized for severe cardiovascular problems, her what-if thoughts were: What if these medications don't work? What if I won't get better? What if I have to be bedridden for the rest of my life? What if I recover enough to go home? Where will I live and how will I manage?

Cavanaugh and Blanchard-Fields 2011 made an important point, which is that anxiety may be an appropriate response given the circumstances. As older adults lose control or mastery and feel more helpless, wouldn't it seem normal to worry about falling, forgetting, or dying? These scholars noted that because many older adults who have an anxiety disorder may have underlying health problems, those health problems may be responsible for the symptoms of anxiety. They listed physical changes associated with anxiety, including dry mouth, dizziness, sweating, insomnia, upset stomach or diarrhea, chest pain, choking, and headaches as common physical changes that can negatively impact social functioning.

Although anxiety disorders can be treated with medication, Cavanaugh and Blanchard-Fields (2011) cautioned that although drugs such as Valium or Paxil may be somewhat effective, the potential for side effects in this population is significant because they can't take high doses. Counseling is a much better alternative, with an emphasis on relaxation training, stress management, and rational thinking. However, it is often difficult for elderly people to access counseling services due to negative stereotypes about what counseling is and how it can help and lack of finances or transportation. Furthermore, hearing loss may make it difficult for them to benefit from counseling, which makes it imperative for counselors working with this population to use expressive arts techniques, which have been shown to be more effective than relying solely on verbal approaches (Vernon & Barry, 2014).

Cavanaugh and Blanchard-Fields (2011) discussed the concept of *death anxiety*, which is by no means restricted to the elderly. In fact, according to Thorson and Powell (2000, cited in Cavanaugh & Blanchard-Fields, 2011), older adults tend to have less death anxiety than younger adults, especially if they are realistic about this stage of life or are religious. Those older adults who experience more death anxiety also have greater physical and psychological problems. Interestingly, men have more death anxiety than women, but there were few differences across ethnic levels. Some contend that death anxiety may in fact be a good thing because if people are afraid to die, they may put more effort into practices that enhance their lives and keep them safe. Regardless, counselors working with older adults who experience this will want to help them guard against focusing on this type of anxiety that might interfere with their normal functioning. Instead, helping clients reduce anxiety about death by providing death education that includes factual information as well as emotional awareness and experiential activities can be very beneficial. Some clients may want assistance writing their own obituaries or planning their funerals or celebrations of life.

Depression

Although depression may increase as people age and have more physical illnesses and disabilities, it is a mistaken belief that aging inevitably results in depression. Many older adults are in fact quite resilient and cope with the increased challenges without experiencing serious depression. Moody and Sasser (2012) reported that major depression is less frequent among older adults than younger, but the rate of depression rises when older people require home health care or live in nursing homes or other types of care facilities. Fiske, Wetherell, and Gatz (2009) contended that depression during this stage of development is a public health problem because it is associated with increased risk of morbidity and suicide and with self-neglect and decreased social, physical, and cognitive functioning. Suicide is closely associated with depression, and according to Moody and Sasser (2012), older people are at higher risk for suicide than all other age groups.

They noted that there are a number of predictors for suicide in this age group, including intolerable psychological or physical pain and a feeling of hopelessness or helplessness.

Depression in later adulthood may be difficult to diagnose, in part because some of the changes associated with normal aging can be confused with depression. For example, as people age they often withdraw from activities, have difficulty concentrating, or may experience insomnia or fatigue, all of which are symptoms of depression. Moody and Sasser (2012) suggested that late-life depression, commonly referred to as late-onset depression, should be considered along a continuum that looks at the number of symptoms experienced during a defined period of time. In fact, older adults may report higher levels of symptoms associated with depression than younger adults, but they are less likely to adhere to the criteria for clinical depression. Another factor that makes it difficult to diagnose depression is that it may appear in conjunction with other problems, such as dementia. Furthermore, over half of adults presenting with late-onset depression have no previous history of depression, and this type of depression can be very different from early-onset depressive disorders.

It is also important for health-care professionals to assess depression from a broad perspective, including looking at psychosocial factors such as sensory impairments, the inability to provide self-care, or functional impairments. Changes in cognition and personality should also be noted.

Whitbourne and Whitbourne (2011) reported that older adults are less likely than younger adults to identify with common psychological symptoms of depression, including dysphoria, guilt, low self-esteem, and suicidal thoughts. Instead of seeking help for depression, they are more likely to present with physical symptoms. Consequently, it is imperative that health-care professionals are trained in recognizing symptoms of depression in their older clients and refer them for counseling. Accessing help may be complicated because many insurance companies do not reimburse for psychological problems, although that has improved with new Medicare guidelines.

Factors Contributing to Depression

Several factors contribute to depression in older adults, including loneliness, grief, and stressful life events. At this stage of life, individuals may not have adequate coping strategies and may become easily overwhelmed, which increases the risk of becoming depressed. Another major contributing factor includes various types of medical disorders, which result in limitations in one's activity level. Stroke, hypertension, arthritis, bone fractures, diabetes, and cognitive impairment all have potentially life-altering consequences that necessitate significant adjustment. Boyle, Porteinsson, Cui, King, and Lyness (2010) stressed that physical conditions increase the risk for depression, and if these conditions go untreated, individuals are more susceptible to physical and cognitive impairments.

Counselors working with depressed older adults need to be sensitive to the fact that life may not hold many promises for them at this stage of development, particularly if they are in their 80 and beyond, and that they may suffer from multiple physical or mental problems and lose their support systems via attrition. Rather than focus on the present and future, it may be helpful for counselors to help clients reflect on their lives and tell their stories. Engaging them in a lifeline intervention that encourages them to recall memorable events throughout their lifetimes can be very helpful. Another good strategy is to interview them, asking them key questions about various aspects of their lives that they would like to share with children or grandchildren. With the client's permission, this could be tape-recorded and copies can be made for family members. And as simple as it sounds, asking them to keep an I'm grateful jar, where each day they write something on a slip of paper that they are grateful for, is an effective way to help them focus on something positive when many things in their life are depressing. Naturally, counselors do need to address the depression and anxiety by listening to clients' concerns and helping them control what they feel is in their control, which could include doing something they like to do each day, if possible, eating well and staying hydrated, taking necessary medications, and having some social contacts. Depending on their level of cognitive functioning, rational-emotive and cognitive behavior therapy techniques can be helpful. For example, they can learn to avoid catastrophic thinking and focus more on the present, taking one day at a time. Thus, instead of dwelling on the worst-case scenario (I might die), the counselor can help the client see that although this is a possibility, what good does it do to dwell on it since it just increases the anxiety? Counselors can also help clients learn to distinguish assumptions (e.g., my son doesn't visit often because he doesn't want to see me) and facts (my son does not visit often). Although interventions of this nature seem minor in the overall scheme of things, they can help clients manage their distressing emotions.

BOX 18.4   HOW WOULD YOU HELP LATE ADULTHOOD CLIENTS WITH EMOTIONAL PROBLEMS?

Imagine that you are a counselor working with clients in late adulthood. Develop an intervention that you think would help address anxiety and one that would address depression, and describe what strength-based approaches you think would be most effective in working with this population.

SOCIAL DEVELOPMENT IN LATE ADULTHOOD

If we reflect on social development across the life span, it is clear that there are periods of expansion and reduction. As infants and young children, social networks were generally limited to parents, grandparents, siblings, and caretakers. During childhood and adolescence, friends also became an important part of that social network. As young adults, relationships with intimate partners developed and evolved into families with children for many couples. During late adulthood, social networks once again are reduced as friends and relatives die and people become more isolated.

One cannot underestimate the important connection between optimal aging and social relationships. Lansford, Antonucci, and Akiyama (2005) found that women in the United States and Japan have fewer depressive symptoms if they have a spouse, mother, and a best friend in their social network, and Antonucci, Ajrough, and Janevic (2002) noted that men who have less education but large social networks were as physically healthy as highly educated men. Studies also suggest that social relationships help buffer against stress, so it seems imperative that new research focuses on how to promote healthy social relationships in late adulthood in order to promote optimal aging (Ertl, Glymour, & Berkman, 2009).

Social Development Theories

It seems rather ironic that although people continue to develop throughout the lifespan, it has been only in recent years that attention has been paid to social development in late adulthood. Given the large cohort of people in this age group, it is critical that we understand more about the ways social relationships evolve and impact older adults. Several theories shed light on this process.

Erikson's Ninth Stage

Erik Erikson was a developmental psychologist whose comprehensive theory of development emphasized the importance of social relationships (Meece, 2002). He believed that human beings have similar basic needs, as well as societal and cultural expectations and personal relationships, which influence how people they respond to their basic needs. Although this famous theorist didn't deal exclusively with social development, his theory has significant implications for adults in late adulthood, particularly as it has been reconceptualized.

Erik Erikson died in 1994 at age 91 years, and his wife and collaborator Joan died 3 years later, at age 95 years (Gusky, 2012). While Erikson was in a nursing home, he and Joan did a videotaped interview in which Joan spoke about Erikson's last stage of development, integrity versus despair. She noted that this stage should be reconceptualized—that "they owed an apology to people for theorizing that wisdom and integrity were so great" (Gusky, 2012, p. 60). She stated that it is easy to theorize about something, but when you are actually there it is a different matter. Thus, a new stage—the ninth stage—was developed a year after Erikson's death. Joan described this final stage of development as a metaphor of a woven fabric. Titled the *woven cycle of life*, she described the warp, the lengthwise threads attached to a loom before weaving, "as a person's indomitable core" (p. 60) and that throughout the life cycle, "everything that was in utero is there—all our potential" (p. 60).

Gusky (2012) noted that the weft, which is the thread that is woven to complete the piece of fabric, represents a person's challenges and experiences in life. The fabric is less colorful when a person is weaker, but as he or she regains strength, the colors are brighter. According to Joan Erikson, the strength is always there because humans are resilient. She also shared that in old age, the order of Erikson's original stages is reversed. This is a relatively new concept and something that deserves careful attention because it is very helpful in understanding development in late adulthood.

Trust Versus Mistrust and Mistrust Versus Trust

During infancy, a critical task during the first year of life is to develop trust that our infants' basic needs will be satisfied. Generally this bond develops with parents or primary caretakers. If children are raised in a warm, supportive manner, they will develop trust, but if those primary caretakers are angry and aloof infants will learn to mistrust (Vernon & Clemente, 2005). In late adulthood, this first stage now becomes mistrust versus trust. According to Joan Erikson (Gutsky, 2012), as older adults become more aware of things they cannot, do they may become distrustful. The major task, then, is to revert to trust and forgive the weaknesses such as a failing memory or decreased mobility.

Autonomy Versus Shame and Doubt and Shame and Doubt Versus Autonomy

During this second stage of development, children ages 2–3 years need to learn how to become more self-sufficient. It is important for parents to allow them to do some things independently so that they learn to develop self-confidence in their abilities (Vernon & Clemente, 2005). As older adults reach the point of not being able to care for themselves, they lose their autonomy and feel ashamed that they have to rely on others to care for them.

Initiative Versus Guilt and Guilt Versus Initiative

The third stage, which occurs for children between ages 4 and 5 years is when they need to develop a sense of self by initiating activities and learning to be responsible for their actions. If they are punished when they take initiative, they feel guilty (Vernon & Clemente, 2005). For older adults, the process is reversed. For example, many older adults want to take on new challenges or projects but underestimate their physical or mental abilities to do this. Guilt results as they realize they should not have attempted this in the first place.

Industry Versus Inferiority and Inferiority Versus Industry

Between ages 6 and 12 years, young children's worlds expand as school becomes a primary place to develop a sense of self-worth, as they learn new things, and as they interact more with peers. If they are compared with others and criticized for their shortcomings, they develop a sense of inferiority. During late adulthood, this stage becomes inferiority versus industry as older adults are able to do less and less on their own and feel inferior as a result.

Identity Versus Role Confusion and Role Confusion Versus Identity

Stage 5, which occurs between ages 13 and 20 years, is a very important stage because this is when adolescents need to establish a strong sense of identity that will influence choices they make in their future. During this stage they clarify personal values and begin to shift from a here-and-now orientation characteristic of childhood to a future orientation (Bjorklund, 2011). If they struggle to develop a strong sense of identity, the result is role confusion, where they do not know who they are. In late adulthood, this stage becomes role confusion versus identity, as older adults question who they are and what they do as they increasingly become more dependent on others to take care of them.

Intimacy Versus Isolation and Isolation Versus Intimacy

During early adulthood, ages 19–25 years, individuals who have developed a strong sense of self are then able to form intimate relationships with others, not depending on others to help them find their identity. Those who are not able to experience intimate relationships are more isolated and lonely because their relationships are more superficial (Bjorklund, 2011). In old age, isolation becomes more and more prevalent as friends and relatives with whom they may have had intimate relationships die or move to be cared for.

Generativity Versus Stagnation and Stagnation Versus Generativity

This seventh stage of development, ages 25–65 years, revolves around establishing the next generation through childrearing. In addition, it involves being productive and creative, mentoring younger colleagues, and being a vital part of society. Adults who are not able to accomplish these tasks become self-absorbed and stagnate. Joan Erikson stressed that in this stage older adults need to ask themselves, "How far do you go along with the stereotype of yourself as an old lady or an old man?" (Gusky, 2012, p. 60). Furthermore, they need to determine how much longer then wish to be productive human beings who continue to contribute to society or at what point do they give this up. Much of this depends on how able they are but also the extent to which they have successfully moved through previous stages and are not prone to giving into old age and stagnating. At some point, however, they will experience more stagnation than generativity, but preferably not until later adulthood.

Ego Integrity Versus Despair and Despair Versus Ego Integrity

This is the eighth stage, for those over ages 65 years, individuals look back on their lives and determine whether they led productive lives that held meaning for them. According to Erikson's theory (Gusky, 2012), if they hadn't resolved previous conflicts, their lives may not have been as fulfilling and they may feel more despair, not only with regard to the past but also the future. Ultimately, adults in late adulthood have a diminishing life cycle and need to be prepared to deal with death. Counselors can be an important source of support and encouragement for elderly adults dealing with the last years of their lives. They can help them review their strengths and focus on how to help them live their final years with integrity.

Joan Erikson, who remained productive almost until the end of her life, believed that personality and identity continue to evolve until advanced stages of life (Gusky, 2012), but in the ninth stage older adults begin to look at things from the other point of view as emphasized in the aforementioned discussion. She revised Erikson's 1997 book, *The Life Cycle Completed*, focusing on the concept of *gerotranscendence*, a term developed by a Swedish sociologist. In essence, this term redefines consciousness in old age as well as self in relationship to others and offers a new understanding of several existential questions. Specifically, during late adulthood, there is decreased interest in material things and superficial social interaction, a redefinition of time and space, and a different way of perceiving life and death, with decreased fear of death. Clearly counselors need to help older adults explore their beliefs and feelings about aging, death, and dying and encourage clients to keep on becoming, which was Joan Erikson's advice to older adults (Gusky, 2012).

BOX 18.5   REVERSAL OF DEVELOPMENTAL TASKS

In your opinion, does the notion that Joan Erikson proposed regarding the reversal of developmental tasks in late adulthood make sense? Interview an older adult and share this information with him or her, contrasting it to the stages as originally conceived, and asking this person to reflect on how this concept of reversal does or doesn't apply to him or her.

Attachment Theory

One of the most familiar social development theories is attachment theory, originally described as the bond that develops between infants and their primary caregivers (Bjorklund, 2011). Just as infants rely on an attachment figure, so do adults who form new attachments with spouses or partners while at the same time maintaining attachment to their parents. According to Mikulincer and Shaver (2009), people of all ages want several things from people to whom they are strongly attached: proximity (close physical or psychological presence); a safe haven (support when they feel insecure or threatened); and a secure base (help in achieving goals). Bjorklund emphasized that older adults who have secure attachments feel safe and can generally deal with life's challenges, knowing they can call on others for support as needed.

The Convoy Model

Another theorist who specifically addressed social development in late adulthood was Toni Antonucci, who used the term *convoy* to "describe the ever-changing network of social relationships that surrounds each of us throughout our adult lives" (Bjorklund, 2011, p. 172). Convoy relationships are reciprocal and developmental in that as individuals change over time, so does the nature of their relationships. Antonucci, Akiyama, and Takahasi (2004) noted that convoy relationships "shape and protect individuals, sharing with them life experiences, challenges, successes, and disappointments" (p. 353). Research conducted by Antonucci, Burditt, and Hiroko (2009) revealed that older adults have smaller social networks than younger adults, consisting primarily of family members. Highly educated people had larger social networks than those who were less educated; African Americans had smaller social networks than Caucasians, and their social networks tended to be family members with whom they had frequent contact.

Socioemotional Selectivity Theory

Another way to look at social development in late adulthood is through the socioemotional selectivity theory, developed by Laura Carstensen and colleagues (Cartensen, Mikels, & Mather, 2006). In essence, this theory proposes that we seek more meaningful social relationships as we age, which means that although one's social network may be smaller it is likely to be more emotionally satisfying. Older adults spend less energy pursuing relationships that are not satisfying because their energy may be more limited and they see time as constrained. They value quality of relationships over quantity.

Relationships in Late Adulthood

As previously noted, relationships evolve over the human life cycle, as poignantly portrayed in Robert Munsch's (1986) book, *Love You Forever*, a story that chronicles a young boy's relationship with his mother from birth through adulthood and the ways she nurtured him. The book ends with the boy, now a man, caring for his mother when she is old and sick and singing the same song that his mother sang to him throughout the years as he gently rocks her. This role reversal characterizes many relationships that younger adults have with their aging parents.

In thinking about different types relationships older adults experience, the list often includes relationships with spouses or partners, adult children, grandchildren and great-grandchildren, siblings, friends, and, depending on circumstances, parents. At some point in time, caregivers are added to the list, including in-home care or caregivers in assisted living facilities or nursing homes. Bjorklund (2011) briefly summarized the following changes that occur from ages 65 to 74 years and age 75 years and older.

Relationship Changes Between Ages 65 and 74 Years

Bjorklund (2011) noted that between the ages of 65 and 74 years, those who are married generally experience high satisfaction, psychological intimacy, and much less conflict than in previous years. Divorce rates are generally low, but increasingly new intimate relationships may develop as spouses die. Remarriage or becoming involved in a new intimate relationship generally results in new relationships with each other's friends, relatives, and children and grandchildren from previous partnerships. It is also quite probable that social networks will not include parents, although increasingly adults who themselves are in the 65–74-year-old age range do have at least one parent still living. However, as Munch's book illustrates, the parent–adult child relationship roles are often reversed, with the adult children caring for aging parents.

As they retire, social relationships will most likely not include as many coworkers, and new relationships develop as older adults engage in volunteer activities or relocate in new communities. Also, adults in postretirement may develop new hobbies and interests, which in turn provide opportunities to network with others and nurture new social relationships.

Other changes during the 65–74-year period include relationships with siblings. When their aging parents are ill or die, siblings may grow closer for support. However, these relationships can also become contentious if there are conflicts over who will care for aging parents, what type of care they should receive, or when it is time to consider withdrawing life-sustaining measures. Sibling relationships may also be strained if there are disagreements over disbursement of property, possessions, and money. Counselors can play a critical role in facilitating family meetings to clarify roles and responsibilities, increase positive and assertive communication, and help family members cope with the emotional issues related to the end of their parents' lives.

Bjorklund (2011) also noted that as spouses, die relationships with the spouse's extended family members may change, particularly if it was a second marriage. Relationships can also become strained or stressful if adult children have financial or marital problems or if their grandchildren have financial or health problems, have problems with addictions or mental illness, or are in conflictual relationships with their parents and rely on their grandparents for support.

Relationship Changes at Age 75 Years and Older

After age 75 years, more people, particularly women, are widowed, and this can impact relationships in several ways. First, they may become more socially isolated, at least during the period of intense grief. Later, they many spend more time with close friends and family members, depending on proximity, health, and degree of mobility.

Perhaps the most significant change in relationships involves relationships with caregivers as older adults become increasingly dependent on others. There are many layers of loss involved in the transition to having to be cared for by others, and it is particularly stressful if an adult child or grandchild has this responsibility. Not only do they have to be responsible for day-to-day care, depending on need, but they also have emotional issues to deal with as they watch their parents age and become more debilitated and dependent. Needless to say, there is typically a great deal of stress as family caregivers juggle their own jobs and family demands with the needs of the aging parent.

BOX 18.6 COMMUNITY ASSESSMENT OF OLDER ADULTS' NEEDS

Find a partner and research older adults' social needs in your local community. Also identify what programs currently exist. Based on the data you gather, identify several different kinds of programs you think could be initiated to enhance social development of this population. Describe these programs in some detail and also how you would implement and advertise them.

Social Challenges for Older Adults

When working with older adults in counseling, social needs must be addressed to promote healthy development. These adults need to feel a sense of connection with friends and family and a feeling a mattering to others, and they need to continue to establish ways to contribute to society and to enjoy active leisure lives to the extent possible. As they age, connections can become more challenging due to mobility issues and access to transportation. Although older adults who reside in retirement communities, senior centers, or residential facilities have more opportunities for social interaction, many do not take advantage of these opportunities for social interaction because of hearing loss or physical limitations. Depression can also impact the degree to which they interact with others. In particular, individuals who are over the age of 80 years, live alone, have infrequent and fewer social contacts, have no family members who live nearby, or experience poor health or sensory or cognitive difficulties are most at risk for social isolation. Increased isolation results in greater loneliness, which negatively impacts physical and mental health (Riffin, 2010) and increases the likelihood of depression and cognitive decline (Luanaigh & Lawlor, 2008).

It is also important to remember that some groups of older adults have additional factors that affect them socially as well as emotionally. Those who identify as gay or lesbian have increased stressors such as exclusion from legal marriage in many states, decreased access to traditional family support, and exclusion and marginalization in health-care and residential facilities. Not being able to be open about their intimate relationships can result in more social isolation, particularly if the partner dies. It is important that counselors serve as advocates for this population of older adults and create innovative programs to address their needs.

Social Connections for Older Adults

Although it may be more challenging for older adults, particularly those in later stages of late adulthood, to maintain social connections, friendship seems to be a positive buffer against stress, depression, and isolation. Many programs and prevention strategies have been found to help older adults feel socially connected, contributing to society and living a life of mattering.

Befriending Programs

Research suggests that having a least one close friend later in life makes a positive contribution to well-being as one grows older because the two can become each other's confidants and sources of support (Ryff, 2014). In response to the increasing need for social support for older adults, befriending programs have developed. Befriending is defined as a relationship between individuals that is initiated and supported by a community agency and is designed to address unmet social relationship needs. These relationships are mutual, nonjudgmental, supportive, purposeful, and extend over a significant period of time (Dean & Goodlad, 1998). Community agencies also use such terms as friendly visitors and senior companions to describe befriending.

Often agencies work to match volunteer befrienders and older adults with similar interests, demographics, and life experiences. Cattan, Newell, Bond, and White (2003) suggested matching individuals in the same generation, noting that these relationships have more potential for positive outcomes because they honor older adults' needs for reciprocity. Davis (1990) found when matched on similar characteristics, individuals were more likely experience positive attachment and improved mental health.

Contact between the befriender and older adult is usually a combination of face-to-face contact and telephone contact. Although participants in a study conducted by Lester and colleagues (2012) preferred face-to-face contact, Cattan, Kime, and Bagnall (2010) found that telephone contact via befriending helped older adults increase self-confidence and social contacts, become more engaged in the community, and feel safer as a result of this positive bond.

To understand befriending programs, Lester, Mead, Graham, Gask, and Reilly (2012) completed a qualitative study, interviewing 25 individuals who participated in befriending programs across five different European agencies. The average age of participants was 83.5 years, with 17 females and 8 males. Themes emerged from the qualitative analysis and identified the important experiences and elements of the befriending relationships. First, participants acknowledged that many adults live in a context of loss, as they experience many losses such as death and loss of physical abilities on a daily basis. The befriending relationship helped them deal with these multiple losses. Some participants described feeling trapped and isolated in their own homes, which increased feelings of loss and loneliness. They often used the noise of radio or television for companionship, so the befriending relationship was a welcoming connection. Second, the participants reported that it was not important that the pair shared similar previous experiences, but the relationship was more beneficial when commonalities such as shared hobbies or similar opinions about popular media started to surface as the relationship progressed. Next, the predictability of the relationship seemed to be beneficial to many participants in that there were clear boundaries and reliable and resourceful contacts in the community. In addition, participants acknowledged they often ruminated and at times became self-absorbed. The befriending relationship interrupted some of these patterns and also provided a relationship with a low risk of rejection. Last, participants enjoyed sharing their knowledge and wisdom they had gained over the years, and this process increased positive feelings of self-worth, autonomy, and self-efficacy. Overall, participants were able to build social skills, share intimacies, and build trusting relationships in a safe context. Counselors need to be aware that befriending programs can help clients build connections and address older individuals' risks for isolation, in addition to numerous other positive benefits.

Programs at Senior Centers

Although most befriending programs take place in individuals' homes, many older adults find friendship and connection in various community centers and senior living facilities. Taylor-Harris and Zhan (2010) examined the third-age lifestyle of 15 African American seniors over age 55 years who had used multipurpose senior centers for at least 3 months. They represented a mixture of gender, socioeconomic status, education attainment, marital status, and type of residency. Qualitative analysis revealed that, in addition to physical benefits, participants increased their self-image through interaction with others and reported various positive aspects of aging. Participants reported that they no longer felt lonely since participating in activities at the center, they had more friends, and they were able to increase the depth of connections with the friends they had made. Participants also increased their social contact by volunteering at the center or assisting at the adult day programs.

Whether older adults live independently, in residential facilities, or within retirement communities, they can take advantage of senior programs such as nutritional meals, exercise classes, creative arts classes, and volunteer or paid work activities (Gelfand, 1999). Engagement in these types of activities can improve the quality of life, reduce social isolation, and increase life satisfaction, independence, and self-confidence. Participation in physical activities such as walking has positive health benefits, relieves depressive symptoms, and increases social connections if walking with a friend or in a group (Pennix et al., 2002). Strength training for those who are able creates a challenge and can increase confidence. This is especially beneficial if done in a group setting, which increases social contact and support and enhances life satisfaction (Rejeski & Mihalko, 2001).

Another activity that counselors might want to suggest to older adults is tai chi, which combines a mind and gentle body movement with meditation, relaxation, and social interaction. It is ideal for older adults and can be easily modified for various mobility levels. Numerous studies (Chung, Lo, & Fong, 2005; Irwin, Pike, & Cole, 2003; Wang, Collet, & Lau, 2004) cited many positive physical and emotional outcomes of tai chi. Older adults may also benefit from engaging in creative processes and leisure activities, joining classes such as painting, fiber art, or making pottery, stained glass, baskets, or jewelry. Serious leisure activities such as these promote mental well-being (Dieser, Christianson, & Davis-Gage, 2015).

Social Contributions and Mattering

As discussed previously, social connection is vital for healthy aging. Within those relationships, older adults need to contribute to society in meaningful ways and feel a sense of mattering to others. They can accomplish these tasks through being active in the community, nurturing meaningful connections, and creating opportunities to make a difference in their own and others' lives. Since suicide rates in people older than age 85 years are twice the national average, meaningful connections with others are essential (Dixon, 2007).

Mattering to others is the phenomenological experience that occurs when older adults are noticed by others and their contributions are appreciated. Interpersonal mattering involves mattering to specific individuals and has been studied more recently, whereas mattering to an organization or a larger entity is what has traditionally been studied. When older adults have found a greater purpose in life they have lower stress levels, higher self-esteem and personal strength, increase in overall well-being, and fewer episodes of depression and sadness. Essentially, having a purpose in life makes people feel good (Dixon, 2007).

Dixon (2007) acknowledged the importance of mattering in later life, exploring the relationships between older adults' levels of perceived mattering to others, purpose of life, depression symptoms, and overall wellness. She surveyed 39 men and 128 women in retirement communities ranging in age from 73 to 92 years. Instruments measured older persons' perceived interpersonal mattering to other people in general, to their friends, their children, their grandchildren, and their significant others; depth of meaning in their lives; depressive symptoms; and overall well-being. Dixon found that mattering to others is positively correlated to purpose in life and overall wellness and negatively correlated to depression. Purpose in life was negatively correlated to depression and positively correlated to overall wellness. Older adults perceived themselves to matter to their children most, followed by friends, grandchildren, significant others, and general others. The results of this study emphasize the need for counselors to explore mattering and life purpose with older adults. By addressing these topics, older adults might avoid depressive symptoms and improve overall well-being.

Case Study: Searching for Meaning and Mattering

Phillip is a 72-year-old African American male who lives with his wife in a small midwestern city. They, along with their extended family, moved to the Midwest after Hurricane Katrina destroyed their homes. In New Orleans, Phillip had been very active in his community and his church, and he worked as an electrician until he retired shortly before Hurricane Katrina hit. As a result of moving and being recently retired, Phillip is struggling to fill his time in meaningful ways. He had a rich social life with many meaningful connections in New Orleans, but he is having difficulty making those connections in this new community. At the urging of his pastor, he decided to speak with the counselor who has an office at their church. The counselor and Phillip agreed that his main issues were loneliness and lack of connection and that the goal of counseling would be to help him build new connections in the community. They brainstormed ways to meet others through senior centers and volunteer opportunities. After only a few sessions, Phillip was flourishing. He initiated movie nights at this house for his grandchildren, and it became so popular that other neighborhood children asked to attend.

He also noticed problems with bullying at the bus stop by his house, so he became a mentor to several children, chatting with them at the bus stop about better ways to treat others. He also started to attend the local senior center and connected with some men at the local barbershop. Both places allowed him to begin to build some relationships outside his family. Counseling was successful because the counselor was knowledgeable about older adults' needs and development.

KEY COUNSELING POINTERS FOR EMOTIONAL DEVELOPMENT DURING LATE ADULTHOOD

Counselors working with clients struggling with retirement could initiate a group titled Searching for Self in Retirement. The group format could encourage reflection and discussion about key issues participants are dealing with regarding this major transition. The facilitator could present some content to stimulate thinking using information from Nancy Schlossberg's books *Retire Smart, Retire Happy: Finding Your True Path in Life* (2004) and *Revitalizing Retirement: Reshaping Your Identity, Relationships, and Purpose* (2009).

Counselors working with clients will want to be well versed in grief counseling given the multiple losses older adults will begin to experience. Using expressive writing is very effective: have clients write a letter to the house they are leaving and what memories they have of their time there; write a letter to their disease and tell it how they feel about it invading their body; write a letter to their partner's dementia and talk about how it has robbed them of happier times.

Counselors working with clients with anxiety or depression will find that the creative arts are very effective. Suggest that clients draw what their depression looks like or make a word cluster in which they brainstorm words they associate with their anxiety or depression (Gladding, 2011). Both of these methods stimulate good discussion about the emotions the client is grappling with, and the counselor can help the client identify effective coping strategies.

Counselors working with anxious clients may want to use relaxation and mindfulness techniques. Another effective intervention is worry management (Vernon, 2009), an intervention that uses a sorting board to help clients categorize their worries as immediate (next 24 hours); not so immediate (within the week); longer term worry (within the next few weeks); and long-term worry (in the next month or longer). They also identify worries they have control over and can do something about and worries that they don't have much control over. This intervention helps clients manage their anxiety more effectively because they realize that they don't have to worry about everything at once.

KEY COUNSELING POINTERS FOR SOCIAL DEVELOPMENT DURING LATE ADULTHOOD

Counselors can support older adults' social development by being familiar with various community resources for this population, as well as state and national resources and service agencies, and direct older adults to these services. It is equally important to connect them socially in places such as senior and community centers and faith-based organizations, which can also help them find meaning and purpose, as well as support.

Gladding (2013) suggested that older adults participate in remotivation, reminiscence, and reorientation groups. Reorientation groups help members establish daily routines and orient them to time and place. Reminiscence and remotivation groups remind older adults about what was meaningful in their lives and how they can realign their current lives to new purposes and meanings. Social relationships develop through the group experience.

Counselors working with older adults can collaborate with local school counselors to address unmet needs of young students. Older adults could be matched with youth to provide tutoring and mentoring. The youth will benefit from this guidance and positive attention, and this may provide meaning and mattering to the older adults.

SUMMARY

Counselors play a critical role in helping individuals in late adulthood deal with the changes and challenges inherent in aging and can help them maintain a sense of meaning, mattering, and satisfaction with life. It is important that as counselors, we debunk many of the myths that are typically associated with aging, as we have attempted to highlight in this chapter. Although aging is often associated with sadness as physical and mental functions begin to decline, many older adults learn to cope quite successfully and would describe themselves as happy and resilient. Maintaining strong social connections and staying physically active as long as possible promote mental health and increase the likelihood that older adults will lead longer and healthier lives.

Developing a culturally sensitive counseling environment that focuses on strength-based approaches is recommended for counselors who work with an aging population. And rather than looking at this cohort as over the hill, we need to reconsider what aging is and focus on making this third chapter of life a quality life. Given the number of older adults in assisted living facilities or nursing homes, having counseling services on the premises would be an effective way to help them deal with emotional and social issues that arise at this stage of development.

USEFUL WEBSITES

AARP
http://www.aarp.org
Association for Adult Development and Aging
http://www.aadaweb.org
National Council on Aging
http://www.ncoa.org
Gerontological Society of America

http://www.geron.org
National Institute on Aging
http://www.nia.nih.gov
American Society on Aging
http://www.asaging.org/about-asa

REFERENCES

Aldwin, C. M., & Gilmer, D. E. (2004). *Health, illness, and optimal aging: Biological and psychosocial perspectives*. Thousand Oaks, CA: Sage.

Antonucci, T. C., Ajrough, K. J., & Janevic, M. R. (2002). The effect of social relationships on the education-health link of men and women aged 40 and over. *Social Science and Medicine, 56*, 949–960.

Antonucci, T. C., Akiyama, H., & Takahasi, K. (2004). Attachment and close relationships across the life span. *Attachment and Human Development, 4*, 353–370.

Antonucci, T. C., Burditt, K. S., & Hiroko, A. (2009). Convoys of social relations: An interdisciplinary approach. In V. I. Bengtson, D. Gans, & N. M. Putney (Eds.), *Handbook of the theories of aging* (2nd ed., pp. 247–260). New York, NY: Springer.

Bjorklund, B. R. (2011). *The journey of adulthood* (7th ed.). New York, NY: Prentice Hall.

Boyle, L. L., Porteinsson, A. P., Cui, X., King, D. A., & Lyness, J. M. (2010). Depression predicts cognitive disorders in older primary care patients. *Journal of Clinical Psychiatry, 71*, 74–79.

Butterworth, P., Gill, S. C., Rodgers, B., Anstey, K. J., Villamil, E., & Melzer, D. (2006). Retirement and mental health: Analysis of the Australian national survey of mental health and well-being. *Social Science & Medicine, 62*, 1179–1191.

Cartensen, L. L., Mikels, J. A., & Mather, M. (2006). Aging and the intersection of cognition, motivation, and emotion. In J. E. Birren & K. W. Scheie (Eds.), *Handbook of the psychology of aging* (6th ed., pp. 343–362). Amsterdam, The Netherlands: Elsevier.

Cattan, M., Kime, N., & Bagnall, A. M. (2010). The use of telephone befriending in low level support for socially isolated older people: An evaluation. *Health and Social Care in the Community, 19*, 198–206.

Cattan, M., Newell, C., Bond, J., & White, M. (2003). Alleviating social isolation and loneliness among older people. *International Journal of Mental Health Promotion, 5*, 20–30.

Cavanaugh, J. C., & Blanchard-Fields, F. (2011). *Adult development and aging* (6th ed.). Belmont, CA: Wadsworth.

Chung, B. M. Y., Lo, J. L. F., & Fong, D. Y. T. (2005). Randomized controlled trial of qigong in treatment of mild essential hypertension. *Journal of Human Hypertension, 9*, 697–704.

Davis, C. (1990). What is empathy and can it be taught? *Physical Therapy, 70*, 707–714.

Dean, J., & Goodlad, R. (1998). *Supporting community participation: The role and impact of befriending*. Brighton, UK: Pavilion Publishing and Joseph Rowntree Foundation.

Dieser, R. D., Christenson, J., & Davis-Gage, D. (2015). Integrating flow theory and the serious leisure perspective into mental health counseling. *Counseling Psychology Quarterly, 28*, 97–111.

Dixon, A. (2007). Mattering in the later years: Older adults' experiences of mattering to others, purpose in life, depression, and wellness. *Adultspan Journal, 6*, 83–95.

Ertl, K. A., Glymour, M. M., & Berkman, L. F. (2009). Social networks and health: A life course perspective integrating observational and experimental evidence. *Journal of Social and Personal Relationships, 26*, 73–92.

Fiske, A., Wetherell, J. L., & Gatz, M. (2009). Emotional health issues in late adulthood. *Annual Review of Clinical Psychology, 5*, 363–389.

Freedman, M. (1999). *Prime time: How baby boomers will revolutionize retirement and transform America*. New York, NY: Public Affairs.

Gelfand, D. E. (1999). *Aging network: Programs and services* (5th ed.). New York, NY: Springer.

Gladding, S. (2013). Group work: A counseling specialty *(7th* ed.) Englewood Cliffs, NJ: Merrill.

Gladding, S. T. (2011). The creative arts in counseling *(4th ed.)*. Alexandria, VA: American Counseling Association.

Griffin, J. (2010). *The lonely society*. London: Mental Health Foundation.

Gusky, J. (2012). Why aren't they screaming? A counselor's reflection on aging. *Counseling Today, 55*, 60–61.

Irwin, M. R., Pike, J. L., & Cole, J. C. (2003). Effects of behavioral interventions, tai chi chih on varicella-zoster virus specific immunity and health function in older adults. *Psychosomatic Medicine, 65*, 824–830.

Jenkins, J. (2014). Let's disrupt aging. *AARP Bulletin/Real Possibilities, 55*(8), 32.

Lansford, J. E., Antonucci, T. C., & Akiyama, H. (2005). A quantitative and qualitative approach to social relationships and well-being in the United States and Japan. *Journal of Comparative Family Studies, 36*, 1–22.

Lawrence-Lightfoot, S. (2009). *The third chapter: Passion, risk, and adventure in the 25 years after 50*. New York, NY: Sara Crichton Books.

Lester, H., Mead, N., Graham, C. C., Gask, L., & Reilly, S. (2012). An exploration of the value and mechanisms of befriending for older adults in England. *Ageing and Society, 32*, 302–328.

Levine, S. B. (2005). *Inventing the rest of our lives: Women in second adulthood*. New York, NY: Penguin.

Luanaigh, C., & Lawlor, B. (2008). Loneliness and the health of older people. *International Journal of Geriatric Psychiatry, 23*(12), 1213–1221.

Meece, J. L. (2002). *Child and adolescent development for educators* (2nd ed.). New York, NY: McGraw Hill.

Mikulincer, M., & Shaver, P. R. (2009). An attachment and behavioral systems perspective on social support. *Journal of Social and Personal Relationships, 26*, 7–19.

Moody, H. R., & Sasser, J. R. (2012). *Aging: Concepts and controversies* (7th ed.). Los Angeles, CA: Sage.

Munsch, R. (1986). *Love you forever*. Willowdale, Ontario: Firefly Books.

Nelson, B. (2013). Greater numbers, greater risks. *AARP Bulletin/Real Possibilities*, *54*(4), 38.

Ortman, J. M., Velkoff, V. A., & Hogan, H. (2014). *The aging nation: The older population in the United States: Population estimates and projections.* http://www.census.gov/prod./2014/retrieved

O'Ryan, L. W., Rawlins, M. E., & Rawlins, L. D. (2005). Baby boomers: Weaving a new tapestry for aging. *Illinois Counseling Association Journal*, *153*(1), 32–47.

Pennix, B. W., Rejeski, W. J., Pandya, J., Miller, M. E., Di Bari, M., Applegate, W. B., & Pahor, M. (2002). Exercise and depressive symptoms: A comparison of aerobic and resistance exercise effects on emotional and physical function in older persons with high and low depressive symptomology. *Journal of Gerontology: Psychological Sciences 57*, 124–132.

Rand, A. B. (2014). Our age of possibilities. *AARP Bulletin/Real Possibilities*, *55*(6), 38.

Rejeski, W. J., & Mihalko, S. L. (2001). Physical activity and quality of life in older adults. *Journals of Gerontology*, *56*, 23–35.

Riffin, J. (2010). *The lonely society*. London, UK: Mental Health Foundation.

Ryff, C. D. (2014). Psychological well-being revisited. Advances in the science and practice of eudemonia. *Psychotherapy and Psychosomatics*, *83*(1), 10–28.

Schlossberg, N. K. (2004). *Retire smart, retire happy: Finding your true path in life*. Washington, DC: American Psychological Association.

Schlossberg, N. K. (2009). *Revitalizing retirement: Reshaping your identity, relationships, and purpose*. Washington, DC: American Psychological Association.

Srode, M. (2003). *Creating a spiritual retirement: A guide to the unseen possibilities in our lives*. Woodstock, VT: Skylight Paths.

Taylor-Harris, D., & Zhan, H. J. (2010). The third-age African American seniors: Benefits of participating in senior multipurpose facilities. *Journal of Gerontological Social Work*, *54*, 351–371.

Vernon, A. (2009). *More what works when with children and adolescents: A handbook of individual counseling techniques*. Champaign, IL: Research Press.

Vernon, A., & Barry, K. L. (2013). *Counseling outside the lines: Creative arts interventions for children and adolescents*. Champaign, IL: Research Press.

Vernon, A., & Clemente, R. (2005). *Assessment and intervention with children and adolescents: Developmental and multicultural approaches*. Alexandria, VA: American Counseling Association.

Wang, C., Collet, J. P., & Lau, J. (2004). The effects of tai chi on health outcomes in patients with chronic conditions: A systematic review. *Archives of Internal Medicine*, *8*, 493–501.

Weiss, R. S. (2005). *The experience of retirement*. Ithaca, NY: ILR Press.

Whitbourne, S. K., & Whitbourne, S. B. (2011). *Adult development and aging: Biopsychosocial perspectives* (4th ed.). Hoboken, NJ: Wiley.

PART 9

End of Life

Generativity, Death, Dying, and Bereavement

Brandé N. Flamez, Ann M. Ordway, Javier Cavazos Vela, and Janet Froeschle Hicks

This book chapter is dedicated to Nate Cobb and his family with love.

INTRODUCTION

Death is a part of life. There is simply an anticipation that all life will one day come to an end and an acceptance that no one lives forever. Some rely on this understanding as motivation to live a full life and as an opportunity to leave a mark on the world so that others who come after them have some evidence that they were here. Others are satisfied with the impact their interactions have had on family and friends. Then there are those who face death with regret or with a wish that there was somehow an opportunity to wipe the proverbial slate clean to start over. A lifetime represents a set of opportunities, choices, and a culmination of experiences, but as one faces death, the chance to make up for the wrongs of the past or to revisit the roads not taken dwindle until those chances are extinguished, leaving the deceased only with their life lived. For some, there is satisfaction and little or no regret as they breathe their final breath, whereas for some there is an overwhelming sense of what was not accomplished, a dwelling on disappointment and unraveled relationships, and a lack of fulfillment over what will never be fixed and undone in the final days.

The circumstances of death are often relevant in terms of time to process for both the dying person and those most closely affected by their death. It seems that when we love someone, whether they are age 5 or age 95 years, death seems untimely. Those left behind wish they had more time—another year, another month, another hour. Mourning is the process through which we reflect on the life lost and the circumstances of death and come to terms with how to move on. Each person's grief is unique to him or her, and counselors are faced with meeting clients where they are in the context of their own personal grief experiences.

BOX 19.1 A YOUNG WIDOW'S JOURNAL

At age 36 years, Missy's husband, Nate, was diagnosed with acute myeloid leukemia. She decided to chronicle their journey through social media as she supported efforts and hopes for a full recovery, struggled through failed treatments and procedures, accepted the inevitability of death, and then navigated the personal pain of his final days and ultimate passing. The following are excerpts of Missy's letters on social media to Nate; the first reflects her commitment to support him and to be by his side during his illness, expressing love and hope about their future; the second expresses fear and heartbreak in his final hours over the impending loss she knows she will feel when he is gone; a third, days after his passing, reflects on love and a life together and the need to go on without him—sharing the pain and loneliness she feels as she tries to attend to everyday tasks; and last, a reflection, just 2 months later, on her need to feel connected to him, through love and memories and in spirit.

 Missy Cobb
November 7, 2013 · Houston, TX · 🔊

At our first outpatient clinic appt...holding back tears as I sit here with my sick husband...it's so overwhelming and there are so many sick patients everywhere. Other families/wives are trying to offer me support and share stories...some good and some bad. I just can't wrap my brain around this being our "new life"...it's so scary. Please pray for me and of course for Nate. Thank you all 🙏💜 — 😩 feeling overwhelmed.

 Missy Cobb
October 19, 2014 · 🔊

****Our sweet Nate is in his final hours... 🙏 please pray for peace beyond all understanding, courage, strength and love. We love him SO much and all of our hearts are breaking. 💔💔💔 — 😢 feeling heartbroken with Gale Evans Cobb Clarida at MD Anderson Cancer Center.

Like · Comment · Share

Missy Cobb
October 28, 2014 · Sienna Plantation, TX · 👥

I ventured out into the world alone today...to the bank and grocery store.
They're errands I used to run all the time alone but today it felt so much more
lonely. 😭

It's like my life was a record, playing so nicely...then it just stopped on Sunday,
10/19...and since that day...trying to get it to go again is like pushing it through
quicksand...like turning a steering wheel with no power steering...it's sooooo
difficult and so hard to explain. 😕💔

I don't want to be around families or couples or see a father and his son
together. It hurts...😞

I thank God for Pierce because if it weren't for him, I wouldn't be getting out of
bed every day.

Please continue to pray for me, for strength through my pain and how to learn
to live with the pain...a friend told me that the pain never goes away, but
neither does the love. 🤍🕯️

— 😥 feeling sad.

Like · Comment · Share

Missy Cobb
December 18, 2014 · Sienna Plantation, TX · 👥

TBT...this was May 28th, the day you got your "discharge ticket" after a long 2
months in the hospital having your transplant. I'll never forget that magical day
and thought we were going to have it again...but God had other plans. I wear
these pajamas of yours often. They are soaked in tears of love and heartache.
I wish we could be together physically for the holidays but since we can't,
please be with us spiritually. Make your presence known. I just want to feel
you, to see you in my dreams, to hug you & kiss you. I miss you every second
of every day my love 🤍 — 😥 feeling sad with Nate Cobb.

This chapter will provide a framework for conceptualizing generativity, death, the process of dying, and bereavement. The clinician who specializes in working with clients facing end-of-life issues and grieving families and friends will want to approach these issues and conditions in the context of developmental considerations. This chapter includes an overview of the historical context of death and death rituals, attitudes about death and dying in a changing world, cultural considerations, and the manner in which the circumstances of death impact the nature of grieving, mourning, and bereavement. In addition, the information in this chapter illuminates how the developmental process affects the manner in which a dying person receives end of life and how those left behind process their loss. Specific attention is dedicated to the contemporary influences on the experiences of death and dying for both those facing death and those left in the aftermath. The implications of significant recent historical events on grief will be reviewed.

HISTORICAL OVERVIEW OF DEATH AND DEATH RITUALS

Death is the final stage of the life cycle that creates physiological, psychological, and social implications (Craig & Dunn, 2007). Physiologically, irreversible cessation of life functions, such as brain activity, is part of the process (Craig & Dunn, 2007). Psychologically, death creates numerous psychosocial consequences for individuals who mourn the loss of a loved one. Socially, rituals must be carried out. Although people will grow old, become ill, and eventually pass, significant death events and life-threatening illnesses will impact some individuals. Regardless of how people die, the manner in which they are mourned and ritualized varies by culture (Shabanowitz, 2013). Table 19.1 highlights the 10 leading causes of death by age group in the United States as of 2012.

BOX 19.2   TOP 10 LEADING CAUSES OF DEATH

After reviewing Table 19.1, did any of the results surprise you? What are some counseling implications based on the different age groups?

Significant Death Events

Whereas some forms of death are natural (e.g., old age), other forms are premature and significant. Examples of significant death events include tsunamis, plagues, mass suicides, terrorist attacks, earthquakes, and war (Scanlon, McMahon, & van Haastert, 2007). These death events create an incredible number of deaths in a short amount of time. For example, an earthquake in Kobe, Japan, produced approximately 300 deaths, whereas an explosion in Texas City claimed 552 people (Nishimura, 1997, and Stephens, 1997, as cited in Scanlon et al., 2007).

Table 19.1 Ten Leading Causes of Death by Age Group, United States, 2012

Age Groups

Rank	<1	1–4	5–9	10–14	15–24	25–34	35–44	45–54	55–64	65+	Total
1	Congenital Anomalies 4,939	Unintentional Injury 1,353	Unintentional Injury 743	Unintentional Injury 807	Unintentional Injury 11,908	Unintentional Injury 15,851	Unintentional Injury 15,034	Malignant Neoplasms 48,028	Malignant Neoplasms 113,130	Heart Disease 477,840	Heart Disease 599,711
2	Short Gestation 4,202	Congenital Anomalies 501	Malignant Neoplasms 440	Malignant Neoplasms 472	Suicide 4,872	Suicide 6,216	Malignant Neoplasms 11,337	Heart Disease 35,265	Heart Disease 71,228	Malignant Neoplasms 403,497	Malignant Neoplasms 582,623
3	SIDS 1,679	Malignant Neoplasms 392	Congenital Anomalies 167	Suicide 306	Homicide 4,614	Homicide 4,342	Heart Disease 10,489	Unintentional Injury 20,394	Unintentional Injury 15,622	Chronic Low. Respiratory Disease 122,375	Chronic Low. Respiratory Disease 143,489
4	Maternal Pregnancy Comp. 1,507	Homicide 339	Homicide 138	Homicide 173	Malignant Neoplasms 1,574	Malignant Neoplasms 3,674	Suicide 6,758	Liver Disease 8,877	Chronic Low. Respiratory Disease 15,212	Cerebro-vascular 109,127	Cerebro-vascular 128,546
5	Unintentional Injury 1,169	Heart Disease 154	Heart Disease 67	Congenital Anomalies 160	Heart Disease 956	Heart Disease 3,231	Homicide 2,705	Suicide 8,862	Diabetes Mellitus 12,553	Alzheimer's Disease 82,690	Unintentional Injury 127,792
6	Placenta Cord. Membranes 1,018	Influenza and Pneumonia 93	Chronic Low. Respiratory Disease 63	Heart Disease 108	Congenital Anomalies 423	HIV 652	Liver Disease 2,469	Diabetes Mellitus 5,747	Cerebro-vascular 11,230	Diabetes Mellitus 52,881	Alzheimer's Disease 83,637
7	Bacterial Sepsis 566	Septicemia 62	Benign Neoplasms 47	Chronic Low. Respiratory Disease 56	Diabetes Mellitus 196	Diabetes Mellitus 646	Diabetes Mellitus 1,867	Cerebro-vascular 5,654	Cerebro-vascular 11,070	Unintentional Injury 44,698	Diabetes Mellitus 73,932
8	Respiratory Distress 504	Cerebro-vascular 56	Influenza and Pneumonia 44	Cerebro-vascular 51	Cerebro-vascular 183	Liver Disease 597	Cerebro-vascular 1,730	Chronic Low. Respiratory Disease 4,533	Suicide 6,929	Influenza and Pneumonia 43,355	Influenza and Pneumonia 50,636
9	Circulatory System Disease 492	Benign Neoplasms 55	Cerebro-vascular 34	Influenza and Pneumonia 41	Complicated Pregnancy 169	Cerebro-vascular 535	HIV 1,345	HIV 2,582	Septicemia 4,982	Nephritis 37,740	Nephritis 45,622
10	Neonatal Hemorrhage 422	Chronic Low. Respiratory Disease 51	Septicemia 26	Benign Neoplasms 40	Influenza and Pneumonia 147	Congenital Anomalies 401	Septicemia 757	Septicemia 2,340	Nephritis 4,765	Septicemia 27,022	Suicide 40,600

Data Source: National Vital Statistics System, National Center for Health Statistics, CDC.
Produced by: National Center for Injury Prevention and Control, CDC using WISQARS™.

CDC

Centers for Disease Control and Prevention
National Center for Injury Prevention and Control

Source: CDC (2012).

Pandemic illnesses also create mass deaths, including the Spanish flu (Scanlon et al., 2007), the black death of 1347, cholera hysteria, yellow fever, and the plague of Athens (Cohn, 2012). In addition to significant death events (e.g., plagues and tsunamis), life-threatening illnesses are important to consider given the significant threat to life.

Life-Threatening Illness

Life-threatening illnesses are typically undefined in the literature but can refer to a significant threat to life (Shields et al., 2015). There are numerous life-threatening illnesses, including cancer, diabetes, heart conditions, hypertension, chronic kidney disease, HIV, and strokes (Lyons & Levine, 2013; Shields et al., 2015). Bousso, de Souza Serafim, and Misko (2010) noted that "the experience of having a life-threatening disease causes suffering and immediate attempts to attribute meanings" (p. 157). Researchers examined gender and ethnic differences related to life-threatening illnesses. Shields et al. (2015) did not report gender differences on life-threatening conditions of cancer, chronic kidney disease, and HIV. Whereas Black individuals are associated with greater risk of life-threatening illnesses (Lyons & Levine, 2013), Hispanic individuals have the highest diabetes rates among ethnic groups in the United States. Although some researchers did not identify gender and ethnic differences, counselors and helping professionals might consider these factors in interventions.

Several factors impact survivors with life-threatening diagnoses. Survivorship refers to economic, physiological, and psychosocial ramifications of living with a diagnosis (Dow, 2003). In a systematic review of literature regarding psychosocial implications of living with a cancer diagnosis, Foster, Wright, Hill, Hopkinson, and Roffe (2009) examined physical problems, quality of life, psychological distress, sexual problems, social relationships, and financial concerns. Among psychological consequences, depression and posttraumatic stress disorder were reported among survivors of cervical and breast cancer. To survive and cope with psychological consequences, optimistic coping style was among the most frequently mentioned coping response. Less effective forms of coping included fatalistic mentality and emotive responses (Foster et al., 2009). Counseling and support groups are also effective means to cope with a life-threatening condition (Wenzel et al., 2002). To this end, counselors and other helping professionals can encourage survivors of life-threatening illnesses to develop positive coping responses and attend support groups.

In addition to individuals with diagnoses of life-threatening illnesses, it is helpful to consider caregivers or family members. These individuals see family members struggle and endure a range of emotions such as loss of hope, emotional exhaustion, frustration, and loss of meaning in life. One effective way to help caregivers cope with a family member's life-threatening illness is a support group. A semistructured support group can provide educational and supportive components to help family members learn how to cope. Family members who attended a support group showed improvements in preparedness, competence, and personal rewards related to caregiving (Henriksson, Arestedt, Benzein,

Ternestedt, & Andershed, 2012), providing evidence that support groups can provide guidance and resources. Additionally, an effective approach to help parents of children with life-threatening illnesses is acceptance and commitment therapy. This form of therapy focuses on subjective appraisal of a child's illness and helps parents with posttraumatic stress symptoms, psychological flexibility, and mindfulness (Burke et al., 2014). These findings suggest that family members can utilize positive self-talk and reframing to influence perceptions toward life-threatening conditions.

Mass Burials Due to Mass Death

Mass death events have numerous implications for death investigation officials and helping professionals. Mass death events include plagues, mass suicides, terrorist attacks, plane crashes, and tsunamis (Signoli, 2012). For example, the estimated number of deaths in Sri Lanka from a 2005 tsunami was 40,000 (Perera, 2005). Mass death events, such as tsunamis, create psychological, psychosocial, and financial concerns among survivors and family members. Also, death investigation officials must provide mass burial services for family members. A mass burial refers to "burying more than one deceased of a single or related incident in a single grave or multiple graves simultaneously" (Perera & Briggs, 2007, p. 1). Legal consequences of mass burials include issuing death certificates, identifying bodies, and finding storage facilities to store the deceased in hospitals (Perera, 2005). Other important issues include death investigations and preparations to manage massive disasters. Although mass death events and burials create complicated circumstances for death investigation officials, they need to provide adequate care to allow family members to maintain culturally appropriate burial procedures (Perera & Briggs, 2007).

Cultural Death Rituals

Death rituals refer to practices, ceremonies, or behaviors that provide meaning and sense of support (Reeves, 2011). Culture-based views of death rituals are common, with different cultures and subcultures displaying common and unique forms of experience (Craig & Dunn, 2007). Whereas every culture has unique cultural rituals, most cultures provide the deceased with a life review or remembrance (Cacciatore & Thieleman, 2014). Funerals and memorial services are common in Western cultures (Craig & Dunn, 2007), whereas other cultures and subcultures have unique means to honor the deceased. A common subculture is the Susquehanna motorcycle club. War veterans established this club to promote participation in motorcycle riding and motorcycle sportsmen's events (Shabanowitz, 2013). In an investigation on funeral and mourning rituals among club members, Shabanowtiz (2013) identified unique forms of rituals: missing man formation and memory patches. Similar to variations of the missing man formation in the military, deceased club members are honored with an empty space in front of a motorcycle procession. Club members also create memory patches to show respect and reverence (Shabanowtiz, 2013). The aforementioned example illustrates how death rituals in a subcultural context provide group members with significant and unique means to honor fallen members.

Other cultures also have unique ways to mourn, remember, and ritualize death. Walker and Balk (2007) investigated bereavement and death rituals among members of the Muscogee Creek tribe. Common rituals included: members conducted a wake service one night before burial services; members did not leave the body alone before burial services; members built homes over the grave; and members waited 4 days before initiating burial services. Muscogee Creek members also viewed death as part of a life cycle and not the end of a life journey (Walker & Balk, 2007). Additionally, Cacciatore and Thieleman (2014) investigated rituals, mourning, and death in a Hutterite colony. Two cultural rituals involved social enactments of death rituals and shared identity (i.e., they mourned the loss of a child as if he or she were their own; Cacciatore & Thieleman, 2014). Finally, Chen (2012) identified death rituals among Chinese Confucianists: notification, washing and preparing the corpse, setting up the preburial ritual area, assuming mourning status, providing offerings, and preparations for the spirit journey, the burial, the funeral feast, and postburial rites. Whereas the aforementioned culture shares some similar practices to Western cultures, they differ in several ways, such as the practice of toward the seven. Following the death of an individual, the seventh day and ensuing multiple days are regarded as special days. All families are expected to burn paper money and incense as part of a ceremony (Chen, 2012).

In conclusion, there are many benefits of grief rituals. Grief rituals can assist our clients in the expression of grief, stimulate recollections of the deceased, provide social support to the grievers, bring a sense of finality to the loss, and provide a sense of meaning to the loss.

BOX 19.3 CULTURAL RITUALS

Karina is a 75-year-old Mexican American female who comes to you for counseling. She has 5 children and 12 grandchildren. She states that she lost her husband 2 days ago to stomach cancer. She also explains that her Mexican American family has important traditions and rituals related to death and funerals. How might you work with Karina to learn about her cultural views toward funerals and rituals? How could you support Karina in her acceptance and practice of cultural-based rituals?

ATTITUDES TOWARD DEATH

All people will eventually die, and nearly all people have attitudes toward death. Factors that influence death attitudes include age and life cycle (e.g., ego integrity vs. despair). Some factors also impact the psychosocial path among elderly individuals.

Age

The ages of children and adults can impact the way they think about and conceptualize death.

Childhood

Most researchers suggest that children have different conceptualizations of death compared with adolescents and adults (Bonoti, Leondari, & Mastora, 2013). In a systematic review of literature on young children's understanding of death, Slaughter (2005) identified several components of death: irreversibility (i.e., the deceased cannot come back to life); universality (i.e., all living things eventually die); personal mortality; inevitability; cessation or nonfunctionality (i.e., bodily functions stop after death); causality (i.e., bodily breakdown creates death); and unpredictability (i.e., timing is unknown). Around late childhood, children shift from biological to metaphysical death explanations (Bonoti et al., 2013). Also, having a previous death experience might help children understand irreversibility and nonfunctionality aspects of death. For example, children with previous death experience drew pictures to ritualize death, whereas children without death experience depicted violent images (Bonoti et al., 2013). Given that researchers found children as young as age 4 years might understand death as a biological concept, helping professionals can talk to children about their theory of biology and folk theories about life (Slaughter, 2005). The aforementioned findings are also important for counseling professionals to learn about children's previous experiences with death of a relative or animal. Counselors can discuss the relationship among human bodily functions, life, and death with children and can explore irreversibility and nonfunctionality concepts (Bonoti et al., 2013).

Adolescence

Age and developmental level also influence how adolescents conceptualize death. There are three main periods of adolescence: early (ages 10–14 years); middle (ages 15–17 years); and late (ages 18–23 years). These stages of development consist of individuation, separation, and identity (Erikson, 1963). One of the most important components of how adolescents conceptualize death is meaning making (Muselman & Wiggins, 2012). Those adolescents who lose a loved one must make sense out of death, discover positive outcomes, and search for identity (Gillies & Neimeyer, 2006). Other important factors that impact death conceptualization include spirituality, faith, self-control, and emotional closeness. Chui and Chan (2013) identified a negative relationship between adolescents' self-control and fear of death. This means that adolescents who had low self-control (e.g., impulsive and volatile tempered) had greater fears of death. Finally, Servaty-Seib and Pistole (2007) found that emotional closeness contributed to adolescents' grief reactions. It is important to mention that adolescents' grief was stronger toward loss of friends compared with grandparents. Counselors and other helping professionals can use art therapy, bibliotherapy, and journal writing to encourage adolescents to identify meaning, develop self-control, and express emotions toward death of a loved one (Muselman & Wiggins, 2012). In summary, age, developmental level, self-control, and emotional closeness to the deceased will influence how adolescents conceptualize death.

Adulthood

There is a relationship among age, adulthood, and death attitudes. Researchers found that young adults experience greater death anxiety than older adults (Russac, Gatliff, Reece, & Spottswood, 2007). This concept, known as the *age effect*, refers to "the fact that young adults often report higher levels of concern over mortality issues than older adults" (Russac et al., 2007, p. 549). Jackson (2008) explored how gender and self-esteem impacted death anxiety among adults. Older adults with less death anxiety might develop positive coping responses to manage death attitudes (Jackson, 2008). Another important factor related to adults' conceptualization of death is search for meaning in life. Lyke (2013) found that search for meaning in life related to young adults' fear of death and dying. It is possible that because search for meaning in life and death are future oriented, young adults begin to worry about their futures (Lyke, 2013). The aforementioned findings are important for counseling professionals to learn about young adults' perceptions of meaning in life. Counselors can discuss the relationship among meaning in life, death, and dying with young and older adults (Lyke, 2013).

Older Adults

Age has been associated with resilient attitudes toward death. Although some researchers suspected that older adults might be susceptible to adverse consequences to death events (Knight, Gatz, Heller, & Bengtson, 2000), other researchers found older adults were resilient in the face of exposure to natural disasters. Shira, Palgi, Hamama-Raz, Goodwin, and Ben-Ezra (2014) investigated posttraumatic symptoms among older adults following Hurricane Sandy. Older adults were resilient, as indicated by a weaker association between exposure to human disaster and posttraumatic stress disorder symptoms. Other researchers reported similar findings in which older hurricane survivors reported lower psychological distress (Acierno, Ruggiero, Kilpatrick, Resnick, & Galea, 2006). Shira and others offered two hypotheses to explain resilience among older adults: maturation hypothesis and inoculation hypothesis. Maturation theorists (Diehl et al., 2014) contend that increased coping responses are the result of aging, whereas inoculation theorists (Eysenck, 1983) suggest coping responses are related to previous exposure to traumatic life events. Taken together, the aforementioned findings suggest that older adults might have resilient attitudes toward death as a result of increased quality of coping with aging and experience coping with previous traumatic events.

Elderly

Ego Integrity Versus Despair

The final stage of Erikson's human development theory is ego integrity versus despair (Erikson, 1986). Ego integrity refers to acceptance of one's life. To successfully progress through stages of life development, individuals must resolve issues to achieve healthy development, meaning in life, and personal satisfaction (Wang, 2008). Failure to reintegrate experiences and achieve ego integrity might contribute to depression (Erickson et al., 1986). Researchers suggest the following to help older individuals achieve ego integrity: reminiscing and life reviews. Reminiscing refers to helping individuals remember and reflect on life experiences and memories (Burnside & Haight, 1992), which helps reexamine and reintegrate past experiences (Wang, 2008). Wang (2008) examined the effects of reminiscence on depressive symptoms of older institutionalized adults. Reminiscing therapy helped older adults reduce depression by providing avenues for self-expression and reflection on memories. Therefore, counselors and other helping professionals are encouraged to use reminiscing therapy to help older individuals work toward ego integrity.

In contrast to reminiscing, which involves focus on positive events, life reviews involve evaluation of positive and negative events (Burnside & Haight, 1992). By self-reflecting and exploring positive and negative events, older adults identify meaning and purpose (Randall & Kenyon, 2001). Life reviews include three components: recontextualizing, forgiving, and reclaiming. First, recontextualizing refers to reframing previous negative experiences, mistakes, or failures. Recontextualizing helps older adults learn how to redefine memories and experiences (Jenko, Gonzalez, & Alley, 2010). Second, forgiving others and oneself creates positive thoughts and memories. And finally, reclaiming an unlived life focuses on earlier opportunities that were not taken. Binder and colleagues (2009) interviewed older women's perspectives on the impact of therapeutic life review activities. Older women identified the following benefits: enhanced ego integrity as a result of interaction with a home care worker; resolution of previous negative experiences; and reintegration of past feelings. Counselors and other helping professionals might also consider the use of reminiscing to help older adults achieve ego integrity.

Factors Influencing Attitudes Toward Death and Psychosocial Path

An essential concept related to death attitudes and psychosocial path is death anxiety, which refers to attitudes of fear, threat, or discomfort toward death (Neimeyer, 1998). Gender differences were examined in relation to death anxiety. Numerous researchers found that women exhibited higher death anxiety (DePaola, Griffin, Young, & Neimeyer, 2003), whereas other researchers did not identify gender differences (Missler et al., 2011). Azaiza, Ron, Shoham, and Tinsky-Roimi (2011) explored death anxiety among bereaved and nonbereaved elderly parents. Bereaved mothers had higher levels of death anxiety compared with bereaved fathers. In another investigation, Kaur Kang and Kaur Kang (2013) explored death anxiety among elderly persons. They identified significant differences between males and females on death anxiety. However, Missler et al. (2011) explored death anxiety among elderly participants in an assisted-living facility. Male and female elderly participants did not exhibit different levels of death anxiety. These contradictory patterns make it difficult to speculate what role gender might play among death attitudes. However, counselors are encouraged to explore possible gender differences when working with elderly individuals' attitudes toward death.

There also are positive psychology factors that influence death attitudes (Niemic & Schulenberg, 2011). Positive psychology focuses on strategies that promote happiness and well-being (Seligman, 2002). Other focal points of positive psychology are (a) how to come to terms with the past; (b) how to become optimistic about the future and the present; and (c) how to recognize and cultivate strengths (Seligman, 2002). Given positive psychology's focus on strengths and meaning, some factors impact death attitudes, including meaning in life, spirituality, and self-transcendence. Meaning in life refers to a process of self-discovery of meaning and purpose in life (Frankl, 1963). Steger and Shin (2010) proposed two components of meaning in life: presence of meaning in life and search for meaning in life. Presence of meaning in life refers to current attribution of meaning in one's life, whereas search for meaning in life relates to motivation toward finding meaning in life (Steger & Shin, 2010). Finding meaning can help individuals cope with death and identify positive aspects in suffering (Frankl, 1963). Niemiec and Schulenberg (2011) noted the importance of tragic optimism or ability to identify hope and meaning in difficult circumstances (e.g., death). Individuals, particularly the elderly, who display tragic optimism might be more likely to embrace each moment and identify meaning in life. As a result, counselors and other helping professionals should explore individuals' optimism toward death and aging.

Spirituality refers to individual awareness and perceptions of closeness to God or a higher power as well as connection to the universe (Myers, Sweeney, & Witmer, 2000; Underwood & Teresi, 2002). Peterson and Seligman (2004) conceptualized spirituality as beliefs about the universe. Given that elderly individuals might lose their significant others, the role of spirituality might influence death attitudes. Damianakis and Marziali (2012) highlighted how spouses in the grieving process used spirituality or religiosity to reframe thoughts toward loss and death: spirituality helped individuals identify and renew life purpose; spiritual rituals helped with the grieving process; and spirituality facilitated social reengagement. Another factor that might contribute to positive death attitudes is self-transcendence. Defined as commitment to participate in social activities, self-transcendence helped elderly individuals become resilient after a spousal death. Some elderly individuals used volunteer activities and social immersion to search for meaning in life following the death of a spouse (Chan & Chan, 2011). For older individuals who have not lost a spouse, it is also essential to consider how self-transcendence might facilitate self-fulfillment and meaning.

BOX 19.4   EGO INTEGRITY AND DEATH ATTITUDES

Roberto is a 70-year-old married man with a wife, two adult children, and five grandchildren. He has been a retired lawyer and judge for the past 4 months. For the past 3 months, he has been feeling scared and nervous about the aging process. Sometimes he feels as though life is not worth living as a result of his numerous physical complications. His physical complications include arthritis, diabetes, and increased heart rate. He also has not reached ego integrity. How would you work with Roberto? How would you help him reach ego integrity? What role might reminiscing and life review play in the counseling process?

INFLUENCES OF CIRCUMSTANCES OF DEATH

Anticipated Death

There are certain times in life when death is anticipated. For example, though it represents a loss, it is usually not a shock when an elderly family member dies. As adults, we fully expect that our grandparents and our parents will die during our lifetimes, and the older those family members become the more their death is expected. While supporting a loved one through a terminal illness can be a draining experience, the process also affords family members some opportunity to adjust to the inevitable, such that death represents a sense of peace for the person who had been suffering and even some relief for caregivers.

Unexpected Death

When death takes us by surprise, there is simply no time to prepare and little opportunity to adjust. It has been suggested that the often grueling emotional ordeal associated with waiting for death during a long, terminal illness is far more painful (Kaplow, Howell, & Layne, 2014). However, being blindsided by death leaves those left behind with no opportunity to say good-bye, to make amends, or to plan for the aftermath. Some people seem to have a genetic longevity, or predisposition for a long life. Others have a list of relatives who have died young and therefore assume they will as well. There is honestly no way of knowing for sure when we will die. Family background and premature death due to illness or health condition can cause some to engage in more diligent self-care and be more aware the possibility that issues such as heart disease or breast cancer might arise.

Terminal Illness

Diagnosis with a life-threatening illness, on one hand, can trigger an opportunity to reflect on life and prepare for death (Bousso et al., 2010). On the other hand, the notion that death is coming also triggers a focus on the premature termination of life and creates significant psychological and emotional distress (Foster et al., 2009).

The nature of the illness plays a role in the manner in which the illness is received and the level of support the dying individual receives. For example, family members and friends might rally around a patient diagnosed with cancer who is undergoing chemotherapy or radiation treatments (Shields et al., 2015). However, the historical stigmas attached to HIV/AIDS have triggered judgments of the suffering person and, in the past, have resulted in individuals being discriminated against, wrongfully terminated from employment, and ostracized by family and friends upon diagnosis.

There are different implications entirely when sudden, terminal illness affects a child. First, we are conditioned to expect that death will affect those who are older than us and that it will affect us personally in old age. Second, death preparation is not part of parenting training. Since parents are charged with the care of their children, the overwhelming feelings of helplessness and inability to redirect the course of the illness can be debilitating. When a child dies, it is not uncommon for parents and close family members to experience shock, intense grief, and posttraumatic stress symptoms (Burke et al., 2014).

Sudden Traumatic Death

Occasionally, a significant event such as a natural disaster or an act of terrorism results in a large number of lives lost in a short period of time (Scanlon et al., 2007). This type of death is distinguished from simple unexpected death because of the traumatic nature of the underlying causal event. Sometimes the death cannot be immediately confirmed, though it is known that a person was in the immediate vicinity of the event. Family members experience layers of denial and intense fear (Kristensen, Weisaeth, & Heir, 2012). Moreover, when bodies are not recovered, families are left without the ability to engage in their traditional death rituals, and there may never be a symbolic resting place, such as a grave or a mausoleum (Kristensen et al., 2012).

Acts of terrorism, such as the attacks on the World Trade Center and U.S. Pentagon on September 11, 2001, resulted in a significant loss of life as a result of the deliberate acts of a militant group in furtherance of a message and a cause. Loss ranged from individual life to widespread loss among first responders from the New York City police and fire departments who risked their own lives in an effort to save others. In the aftermath, U.S. citizens rallied to celebrate individual and collective acts of bravery with the flying of American flags to the rebuilding of a Trade Center monument. Such efforts represent a search for meaning in the wake of tragedy and support in numbers as those remotely affected by the tragic event rallied around those who experienced sudden, personal loss. However, commemorative events as many as 14 years later serve to stir up the kind of grief uniquely associated with mass, traumatic death, and the search for meaning often fails to prove fully satisfactory. Similarly, events of mass murder, such as the one that occurred when a lone killer at Sandy Hook Elementary School in

Newtown, Connecticut, gunned down children and their teachers, become foundations for change. As a society, we endeavor to make sense of the senseless and seek to derive lessons to effectuate change to prevent similar events in the future. Indeed, increased security and crisis preparedness training in elementary and high schools and universities and colleges nationwide have developed in response to events like Sandy Hook, Columbine, and Virginia Tech.

Accidents also are usually unexpected, triggering feelings of shock and devastation among those left behind. In many cases, an individual leaves home with the intent of living out his or her everyday responsibilities and then returning home. A car accident or a work-related accident carries similar connotation, but they often also trigger a search for someone to blame. Was the car accident alcohol related? Was the work equipment faulty or defective? Would my loved one still be here if not for the actions of some other negligent person? Similarly, a suicide also leads to complex grief-related symptoms, including a search for someone to blame, a questioning of whether something else could have been done to prevent the incident, shame, and even a conscious effort to hide the cause of death from public knowledge (Sveen & Walby, 2008).

BEREAVEMENT AND PATTERNS OF GRIEVING

Stages of Grief

Elizabeth Kubler-Ross (1969) was one of the first individuals to provide mental health professionals with an understanding for grief and loss. She identified her theory of five stages associated with grief in her seminal work, *On Death and Dying*. Table 19.2 highlights Kubler-Ross's stage model. Specifically, Ross opined that individuals navigate their way through a cycle or pattern of emotions as part of grief in five stages: denial, anger, bargaining, depression, and acceptance. According to Kubler-Ross, the stages were not intended to be a limiting definition of what grieving individuals experience and feel in connection with death and loss but rather were a recognition of key emotions commonly experienced by many. She further noted that the stages did not necessarily occur in a specific order and recognized the nuances of individual grief experiences. Kubler-Ross's theory has evolved as a widely accepted framework and foundation for the manner in which grief is manifested, but subsequent research and general studies of the grieving process have not served to provide concrete support for her theory.

The proposed stages can involve both literal and figurative interpretations. For example, someone might acknowledge the death of his or her father but might also occasionally think about his or her father walking through the door or subconsciously dial his phone number to share some news or ask a question. There is almost an automatic, reflexive behavior in response to being used to the now deceased person always being there. It is an adjustment and involves some reconditioning, and in time the person will likely cease making those phone calls. Other times, when a missing loved one is presumed to be dead due to his or her proximity to a tragic event, such as working in the World Trade Center on

Table 19.2	Kubler Ross's Stages of Grief
Stages	**Description**
Denial	First stage of dying, in which the person imagines a false or preferable reality or denies that the death is going to take place
	Clients may use adjectives such as disbelief, paralyzed, and numbness to describe this phase.
Anger	Numerous sources within the grief cycle:
	Anger at the loss; anger at ourselves (Did we cause it? Why my child? Why would God let this happen?); anger at doctors, nurses, parents; anger at ourselves for being angry; anger that we feel overwhelmed
Bargaining	An attempt to return to normal so the loss would not have to be experienced
	Neither the family nor the person can move past this stage without experiencing their inner pain.
	The individual sometimes makes promises to a higher power if the pain can be removed.
Depression	A normal response to significant disappointment, including dreams
	Can be a reaction to:
	Loss of perceived images and abilities of self; loss of expected or hoped for dreams; loss of abilities once possessed; loss of or impaired health; inability to fix or change that which is different; guilt or feelings of blame for disability
	Sometimes a combination of counseling and medication is needed to move beyond this stage.
Acceptance	Doesn't mean liking the loss or transition, but rather learning to live with it rather than suffering
	Recognizing anger and finding appropriate ways to deal with it
	Letting go of self-blame, guilt, and disappointment
	Accepting what cannot be changed and working to change what can be

September 11, 2001, or living in New Orleans during Hurricane Katrina, a family member might experience actual denial when a body isn't recovered.

Critics of Kubler-Ross have argued that there are no true stages associated with grief because resiliency essentially carries individuals through their losses (Bonnano, 2004). Current focus appears to be less on the strict adherence to a schedule of stages and patterns and more on the recognition of trends and commonalities shared and associated with specific grief experiences. In addition, individual coping skills, the circumstances of a death, the relationship to the deceased, the time available for preparation in advance, and a support system during and afterward will all likely play a role in how grief is experienced and whether or not the proposed Kubler-Ross stages apply.

Grief Response

Grief response is directly affected by our relationship to the person who died, the nature of that relationship, and the context of the death (Kristensen et al., 2012). For example, most people expect that they will experience the loss of their grandparents and parents during their lifetime, and it is certainly possible that one spouse will lose the other to death in the course of a long-term marriage (Randall & Kenyon, 2001). There are reported cases of one spouse dying almost immediately following or in proximity to the death of the other when the couple has been together for an extended period of their adult lives.

BOX 19.5   UNTIL DEATH DO US PART

Sadie and Henry married in 1940, following a brief courtship. She was 20 years old, and he was 25. The each came from Eastern European immigrant families with strong work ethics and blue-collar backgrounds. Each family of origin struggled through the Great Depression. Each came into the marriage with a trade—Sadie as a seamstress and Henry as a painter and paperhanger for the union. They had one child, who himself married much later in life. Sadie and Henry experienced minimal personal or family trauma during their life together, though they did struggle with infertility and spent time as joint caregivers for their respective elderly parents until death. Sadie and Henry survived their parents (all of whom died prior to age 85 years) and all of their respective siblings. There was minimal marital conflict and, though each worked outside the home, they assumed fairly traditional gender roles in their relationship.

In his late 80s, Henry developed genetic blindness and became hard of hearing. He gradually developed dementia but continued to know and recognize Sadie, who, also in her 80s, became his primary caregiver. Sadie died of natural causes at age 98 years, following 72 years of marriage. Though Henry was in reasonably good health, he missed his lifelong partner deeply. Though he was seemingly unaware of his surroundings or the identities of his caregivers, he cried mournfully for Sadie every day, until exactly 2 weeks following her death, when he also passed away from natural causes just shy of his 103rd birthday. There are many reported incidents of spouses dying within proximity to the other.

What psychosocial factors may have contributed to the longevity of Sadie and Henry, as individuals and as a couple? What role might the duration of their marriage and their relationship have played in their natural deaths in such proximity?

Death from natural causes, although painful, can be easier to process because it is expected. Nevertheless, Prigerson (2004) estimated that 10–15% of grieving individuals experience PTSD symptoms even when death is from natural causes. Death from terminal illness carries a layer of trauma, particularly when the death applies to a child or someone who society would generally view as too young to die. When death stems from a traumatic cause, ranging from suicide to accident to homicide or an act of terrorism, it is unexpected and tends to trigger more significant grief symptoms (Kristensen et al., 2012). Currier, Holland, and Neimeyer (2006) reported higher levels of PTSD and complicated grief among those who experience the death of a loved one as a result of a homicide more so than even with accident or suicide.

Mourning

Mourning is the process and sadness that accompanies the death of a loved one. It involves a sense of profound loss associated with the knowledge that the physical presence of the person who died is lost forever. It is the sense of permanency that, once realized, reinforces the loss and causes some to feel the loss more deeply over time. A sense of shock or numbness often accompanies the early news of death and the immediate aftermath, particularly when death is unexpected, as in the cases of suicide, homicide, and accident (Armour, 2006). Sometimes, the rituals associated with death serve to provide time for adjustment and acceptance (Reeves, 2011). Bonanno (2004) concluded that some individuals demonstrate a greater resilience to loss and noted that it is common for individuals to experience some distress over an extended period of time. In other words, grief associated with loss due to death doesn't just vanish. Feelings of loss persist over time but gradually are less dominant, such that individuals in mourning are able to go on with their lives. In contrast, those for whom grief does not dissipate at all or for whom grief is pervasive and prevents a resumption of ordinary functions exhibit more maladaptive patterns (Bonanno, 2004).

Complex Grief

Grief is an individualized process and everyone experiences and manages the related feelings in a unique way. Ordinary grief, or that associated with expected loss, can be similar to feelings associated with depression. Individuals often initially experience such a deep sadness that it becomes difficult to participate in normal, everyday events. However, grief varies in intensity over time, since sadness is often mingled in with positive reminiscing.

Additional layers of grief can be triggered for those facing the violent nature of the loss of their loved one. Prolonged grief disorder (PGD), also known as complicated grief, was proposed to be included in the *Diagnostic and Statistical Manual of Mental Disorders*, fifth edition (*DSM-5*; APA, 2013), but was not. Instead, the *DSM-5* distinguishes certain symptoms associated with a diagnosis of major depressive disorder when those symptoms are related to loss related to death and continue for more than 12 months. In the latter circumstance, a diagnosis of *persistent complex bereavement disorder* might be more appropriate to consider (APA, 2013).

Although described symptoms with complex grief are similar to those associated with PTSD, the symptoms are distinct because they are triggered by the sudden, violent death of a loved one (Prigerson, 2004). Kristensen and colleagues (2012) reported that violence more than the suddenness associated with death was likely to trigger symptoms that mirror PTSD symptoms. For some, witnessing a homicide will trigger PTSD reactions, just as imagining the horrific circumstances that might have been endured by a loved one prior to a traumatic death (such as in the context of war or for hostages and prisoners of war; Kristensen et al., 2012). There is evidence of prolonged grief among parents whose sons die in connection with active military service (Kristensen, Heir, Herlofsen, Langsrud, & Weisaeth, 2012). In fact, this experience is not limited to parents but also seems to apply to surviving friends, including those other soldiers serving alongside the soldier who was killed (Papa, Neria, & Litz, 2008).

It is never easy for a parent to lose a child under any circumstances. However, the cause of death may play a role in the nature of the grief and how that grief is processed (Murphy, Johnson, Wu, Fan, & Lohan, 2003). Some parents, after the violent death of a child, experience suicidal ideation or at least a desire to die to reunite with their child (Murphy, Tapper, Johnson, & Lohan, 2003). Still others rely on religion, spirituality, and faith in their personal search for meaning and as a source of support (Kristensen et al., 2012). Table 19.3 highlights some normal and abnormal grief reactions.

Culture and Context

As noted previously, culture is a key component for the processing of death, ranging from the death ritual to coping (Shabanowitz, 2013). The ritual practice offers

---

Table 19.3   Normal and Abnormal Grief Reactions

Normal Grief Reactions

- Protest, disbelief, and denial
- Sadness and survivor guilt
- Somatic symptoms
- Withdrawl
- Anger and irritability
- Disruption of normal patters
- Preoccupation with memories
- Identification with the deceased

Abnormal Grief Reactions

- Persistence of denial
- Suicidal ideation
- Acute organic disease
- Progressive isolation
- Hostility about medical care
- Continued disruption of behavior
- Preoccupation with the deceased
- Conversion symptoms (deceased)

time for those left behind to essentially process the death and adjust to the loss, yet the actual absence of the individual may not fully set in until after the ritual has come to an end and ordinary life resumes (Reeves, 2011). Circumstances matter. With homicide, reactions can vary depending on whether the victim was an intended and targeted victim or an accidental victim, such as in the case of a drive-by shooting. Moreover, when a homicide is isolated and an anomaly for the environment, shock and fear reverberate throughout the community. However, when homicide is more common, though still devastating, surrounding communities sometimes regard the new death as part of ordinary life. This seems to be particularly true in communities where gang violence and retaliation are manifested through drive-by shootings and where innocent people are gunned down in the streets incidental to gang aggression directed at a particular person.

Moving Forward

Ultimately, for those left behind in the aftermath of death, no matter what the circumstances, life must go on. While some survivors do emotionally shut down for a period of time following a significant loss resulting from death, most engage in death rituals and specific practices designed to celebrate the life of the person lost and to cope.

A Nonlinear, Nonstage Approach to Helping Clients

Now that we have discussed Kubler-Ross's stage model and the grief response, we would like to call attention to a nonlinear, nonstage approach. As counselors you will assist your clients in understanding and facilitating the four tasks of grieving: accepting the reality of the loss; experiencing the pain of grief; adjusting to a new reality; and letting go and reinvesting emotional energy. Grief is highly individual, and individuals grieve in their own ways. Some may respond to grief physically (e.g., aches and pains, changes in appetite, sleep disturbances); others may have emotional reactions (e.g., loneliness, sadness, guilt, anger); some may respond cognitively (e.g., reduced attention span, impaired self-esteem, idealization of the past); others respond behaviorally (e.g., acting out, withdrawing, lashing out); and others may have a sense of relief (e.g., when a person has been suffering for a long period of time).

As counselors it is important we understand our clients' grieving styles. Kenneth Dakota and Terry Martin described two main styles of grieving: the *intuitive griever* and the *instrumental griever*. According to Martin and Doka (2000), patterns of grieving occur on a continuum and those clients near the center demonstrate a blending of the two styles. These clients represent the *blended-style griever* and experience both patterns.

Intuitive griever

- *Feelings and emotions* are intensely experienced.
- Outward expressions such as crying mirror the inner experience.

- Griever may have difficulty regulating emotional expression and may experience prolonged periods of confusion, disorganization, inability to concentrate, and difficulty with daily functions.
- Griever may experience physical exhaustion or anxiety.

Instrumental griever

- *Thinking* is dominant over feeling and emotion, and grieving is cognitively focused.
- Emotional expression is kept private and the griever is reluctant to talk about specific feelings.
- Griever is helped by thinking and doing because mastery of oneself or environment is most important.
- Brief time periods of cognitive dysfunction (e.g., forgetfulness, confusion) are common.

Blended-style griever

- Griever shows characteristics of both the intuitive and instrumental grieving styles, although one style typically dominates.
- Griever is able to shift between styles as needed.

Humphrey (2009) discussed ways mental health professionals can counsel and approach those coping with loss based on these different grieving styles. Recall with the intuitive griever that feelings are intensely experienced. Humphrey (2009) recommended that counselors working with the intuitive-style griever normalize and validate the emotional response, help the griever with emotional regulation, and discuss successful strategies that facilitate the experience and expression of emotion. Counselors also help the intuitive griever investigate ways to lesson focus on the feelings. For example, you may engage the client in conversation about existential or spiritual meaning associated with coping with the loss of a loved one. With the intuitive griever you may need to help the client manage possible negative responses to others. It is important to encourage self-care with the intuitive-style griever and assess if there is a possibility of acting out or the possibility of substance use, overeating, or food restriction by your client in order to maintain emotional regulation. Counselors can also assist the clients with enhancing less familiar ways of coping such as asking for support and problem solving.

When counseling the instrumental-style griever, remember that your client may have a general reluctance to talk about feelings, but this does not mean your client does not feel. As a counselor you want to respect the reserved grieving experience of your client's grieving style and help the client express emotions to the extent possible. You may need to educate the instrumental griever on grieving styles and assist your client with managing the possibility of others that he or she is viewed as insensitive. Humphrey (2009) further recommended that the counselor assess any acting out, risk-taking behaviors, possibilities of substance use, and food restriction or overeating to evaluate if the purpose is to hasten the occurrence of the emotion. When working with the instrumental griever, Humphrey (2009) discussed the importance of facilitating effective decision-making activities and using his or her problem-solving skills to help others. It is further recommended that the counselor encourage membership in coping with loss support groups in addition to individual therapy.

With blended grievers, Humphrey (2009) recommended that characteristics from both intuitive and instrumental styles are combined while favoring one style. In other words, as the counselor you can use both styles but can adjust in the direction of your client's dominant style. Clients can also benefit from coping with loss support groups since they are able to relate to more than one grieving style. There are several approaches to grief counseling, including cognitive behavioral, narrative, and solution-focused methods; massage; meditation and mindfulness; yoga; nature walks; music; art; and poetry.

ETHICAL, LEGAL, AND MEDICAL CONSIDERATIONS WITH DEATH

Death brings with it a variety of legal implications. Though we will outline some key considerations associated with legal concepts, this section should not be construed as offering legal advice or legal interpretation. In the event of a death, it is best for those most closely affected to determine if the deceased left legal documents for guiding the processing of an estate and to consult with an attorney.

In the ordinary course of life, individuals work, save money, invest, and accumulate a variety of belongings and document events in the form of photographs, recordings, and other memorabilia. Many also have debt, which is sometimes dramatically increased in the course of a catastrophic illness. It is advisable for adults to, and most do, plan for the disposition of their property and belongings following their death by expressing intent for to whom specific items should transfer, how any debts should be satisfied, and even the means by which physical remains will be disposed of. Death rituals are often dictated by culture to include religious beliefs about burial, cremation, or forms of internment (Shabanowitz, 2013).

The purpose of having a plan for the aftermath of death is rooted in the desire to make matters easier to process for relatives or those left behind to address loose ends associated with the business of life. A directive from the deceased made during life can serve to spare families from disputes over who gets what of the personal property representing the estate of the deceased. Even close families sometimes argue over the distribution of property, entitlements to inheritance, and conflicting notions over what the deceased would have wanted. When there is no will or written directive, survivors are left to their own devices or to state or federal laws that otherwise dictate what must happen.

In addition to legal implications associated with death, there are layers of ethical implications associated with a suffering person's right to die and other components of end-of-life care. These topics can trigger personal value considerations for counselors, so much so that the ethical interaction with clients addressing end-of-life issues is clarified in the American Counseling Association Code of Ethics (ACA, 2014).

Euthanasia and the Right to Die

When a loved one is suffering with a debilitating condition or with a terminal illness, it can be emotionally draining to sit back and watch. Family members often feel despair and helplessness in the wake of an inevitable death experience. It is not extraordinary to hope for relief from suffering for the dying person, notwithstanding the competing hope for recovery. *Euthanasia* is a process of ending someone's life for the express purpose of ending the suffering associated with his or her incurable, often terminal, condition. When more overtly administered, euthanasia can include the administering of a lethal dose of prescribed medication or other means designed to end the patient's life. Euthanasia is illegal in many states and is viewed as a form of homicide. In some states, where the dying person expresses the wish to take his or her own life but lacks the physical capacity to do so without assistance, euthanasia takes the form of an *assisted suicide*, through which the third party essentially facilitates the wishes of the person who expresses the desire to die. Dr. Jack Kevorkian was a euthanasia activist who assisted in many patient suicides and faced related legal charges and medical ethics inquisitions. In contrast, *passive euthanasia* is a more commonly accepted practice through which medical treatment is gradually reduced or withheld to expedite the natural death process.

Responsibility for Death

Death involves far more than the physical process or circumstances through which one breathes his or her last breath. It triggers consideration of a multitude of questions. How will the individual's remains be disposed of? Will there be a funeral or memorial service of some kind? What will happen with the individual's belongings? Who will assume responsibility for any minor children left behind? How will debts be satisfied? Answering these questions can be complex. Some individuals choose to be involved in the planning of their own postdeath arrangements, ranging from purchasing a burial plot to selecting songs or readings that will be a part of any ceremonial ritual. Many take the time to prepare a last will and testament to express intent for the disposition of property and instructions for an *executor* or administrator for how to address unresolved issues postdeath. Some, however, avoid the preparation of a will—leaving successors with the challenging task of having to manage postdeath issues to the best of their abilities with little or no direction from the decedent.

  When death is a surprise, particularly when it occurs at an early time of life or due to tragic circumstances, there may be no time to plan and prepare. It is advisable for adults to engage in a practice known as *estate planning*, through which they make arrangements for their death and express intent regarding the handling of their postdeath affairs regardless of whether death is pending within an expected and semidefined time frame. The purpose of advanced preparedness is simply so those left behind are not caught completely off guard and without instructions as to how the decedent would have wanted matters handled. The discussion of concepts associated with end-of-life decision making and estate planning is not intended to provide legal advice of any kind. In fact, the nuances of laws and regulations related to estate administration postdeath will likely vary from state to state and may, in fact, also be impacted by federal laws and guidelines. Rather, this discussion is designed to highlight some of the key ethical and legal considerations associated with death and dying and the importance of estate planning well in advance of the actual death event.

BOX 19.6 ESTATE PLANNING AND COGNITIVE CAPACITY

Living wills are documents through which a living person makes known his or her wishes regarding life-saving medical treatment in the event of life-threatening circumstances. Often, individuals declare their desires to forego life-saving measures, such as a breathing apparatus or emergency cardiac intervention to prolong life—especially where outcome might include a decreased quality of life, such as a comatose state or other severe in capacitation. Through a power of attorney, an individual can also designate a third party to make end-of-life decisions on his or her behalf should he or she not be able to do so on his or her own. A last will and testament is a document through which a person identifies his or her intent for the management of debt and the distribution of his or her belongings and assets postdeath. It is legally binding and generally enforceable, absent a determination that the individual lacked or had diminished cognitive capacity at the time these documents were prepared or a showing of threat, duress, or undue influence on the writer, such that the documents reflect the intent of someone else who would benefit rather than the true intent of the person executing the legal documents.

Why is cognitive capacity a factor when considering the legality and enforceability of documents relating to end-of-life decisions and post-death distribution of property? Consider circumstances under which the lack of documents would be problematic for surviving family members.

Legal Preparation

The legal preparation for death includes planning for custody and guardianship of minor children and the disposition of property. It is customary for a surviving spouse to assume custody of minor children when one parent dies, even when parents are separated or divorced. Yet a will can include special circumstances under which the surviving parent would not assume custody and through which the deceased parent could designate a third party as a guardian for their children. These matters are most often left to the courts when the wishes of the deceased, as to care of their children, are challenged by a surviving parent or relatives.

State and federal laws speak to tax implications and layers of entitlement related to the disposition of property. For example, a spouse is, in many instances, entitled to assume full ownership of real property that had been titled in joint names as *tenants by the entirety* without the need for a last will and testament. Other properties, where someone is designated as a beneficiary, such as with a life insurance policy or certain pensions, can pass outside the estate and need not be addressed in a will. Inheritance left to a spouse or children of the deceased may not be taxable by the government, whereas the values of inheritances left to siblings or nieces and nephews or other third-party designees might be reduced by a tax implication.

In certain circumstances, family members believing they were unintentionally overlooked in the disposition of property challenge the intentions of the deceased, even when these intentions are expressed clearly in legal documents. Most often such challenges come in the form of a claim that the deceased lacked the cognitive capacity to fully know and understand the implications of their last stated intentions. For this reason, witnesses are required to attest to the decedent's sound mind at the time of their legal declarations and legal documents memorializing those declarations are most important.

Living Will

A *living will* is a legal document through which the signer makes known his or her wishes regarding the use of medical treatment and extraordinary measures to prolong his or her life in the event of catastrophic circumstances where the individual is incapacitated. The purpose of this document is to alleviate the burden placed on family members who, in times of crisis, are called on to make decisions about the use of life support to prolong the physical life of someone who has otherwise been medically determined to be *brain dead*, or without capacity for decision making or even interaction with others around him or her. Making a decision about when to utilize life support measures or to terminate them once they are already in use often involves balancing the juxtaposition of a practical analysis of what is best for the person whose life is being prolonged and the emotional challenges associated with making the choice to let a loved one go.

Last Will and Testament

A last will and testament is the legal document through which an individual makes known his or her wishes regarding the disposition of assets and belongings following death, including the management and handling of any debt. Properties previously owned by the deceased are collectively known as an *estate* and the distribution of an estate carries with it tax implications and a hierarchy of entitlement defined by both federal and state laws.

Death Without a Will

When someone dies without a will, he or she dies *intestate*. This means that there is no legal document outlining the deceased's wishes for the handling of his or her estate postdeath. Usually, a family member seeks to be officially appointed (sometimes through a surrogate court) as the designee for administering the remainder of the deceased's belongings and the payment of debt. Most often this person is a surviving spouse or an adult child but can be a third party agreed upon by the family. Certain laws govern the disposition of property when someone dies without a will to include protections for a surviving spouse and minor children. The purpose of such laws is to protect close family members, especially those who relied on the deceased for support or with whom the deceased's financial affairs were closely intertwined, from these parties swooping in and taking what is not rightfully theirs. Intestacy creates a whole host of additional complications for processing the death of a loved one.

DEVELOPMENTAL ISSUES AND NON-DEATH-RELATED GRIEF

Although grief typically is thought to be a response related to death, it can also accompany non-death-related developmental issues throughout the lifespan. For example, parents of children with disabilities experience feelings of grief regardless of the age of their child. Consider the case of Mark, a father of a child struck by a car at age 5 years. The child, Brandon, is now age 8 years and can no longer walk or talk clearly. Mark has been told that Brandon will never be able to feed himself, clothe himself, or perform routine life tasks. Although Mark loves Brandon, he often experiences feelings of anger, depression, and loss of hope, and he feels less bonded with his child since the accident. Mark clearly suffers grief from the loss of Brandon's functioning.

Another example of non-death-related grief might be a job loss. Consider the case of Frank, who was in the same job for 15 years when his supervisor told him he was fired. Upon hearing the news, Frank immediately feels shame and denigration. He avoids telling his wife about the job loss for several hours. Over time, Frank becomes more depressed and angry, refuses to ask for help, and becomes resentful of his former employer as well as others still employed. It seems clear Frank is experiencing grief even though he has not confronted death.

KEY COUNSELING POINTERS FOR GENERATIVITY, DEATH, DYING, AND BEREAVEMENT

Counselors can aid those suffering grief as a result of death, dying, bereavement, or non-death-related circumstances. In the preceding section, cases were described depicting non-death-related client grief situations and reactions. This section discusses possible techniques and responses a counselor might use to help clients such as Mark and Frank. Possible responses are discussed, but they must be considered as possibilities and not absolute answers.

Mark is experiencing the loss of typical childhood and adult experiences for Brandon. He clearly has little hope and optimism regarding his child's future. It will be important to acknowledge and affirm Mark's grief since he not only may have deep emotions but also may feel guilty for having such negative feelings. The counselor can validate Mark's feelings through paraphrasing. For example, if Mark says, "I hate knowing Brandon will never be able to take care of himself," the counselor could respond with, "It is difficult knowing Brandon will not fully recover." Simply listening without judgment is invaluable. It is also important to avoid pushing Mark to process his grief. Nontherapeutic responses of this type might be, "At least you still have your son," or "Someday everything will be okay." Other platitudes or advice that might also be avoided include responses such as, "The Lord works in mysterious ways," "In time you will understand the reason for this," or "You will be a stronger person because of this." These responses do not validate the true impact faced by Mark, and they minimize his feelings.

Helpful techniques might include helping Mark plan for the future and problem solve. For example, Mark can search for and help determine options to help with caregiving as Brandon ages. He may also need information on sources available to assist Brandon with educational possibilities and medical referrals. Support groups might also be suggested for both Mark and Brandon. This is especially important for Mark who needs to take care of himself while also taking care of Brandon.

Frank, who was recently fired from his job, may feel stigma due to gender-based cultural expectations and feel pressured not only to work but also to succeed financially. Because Frank may be unaware he is grieving, it might be helpful to educate Frank about the stages of grief. Once Frank understands that his moods are normal, he may experience greater optimism in the knowledge that acceptance is a later stage within the grieving cycle. The more involved Frank becomes in future planning through career counseling and assessment, the more optimistic he may become. Frank can be encouraged to participate in group counseling sessions so he understands he is not alone in his plight. Further, he needs encouragement to take care of himself through massage, meditation, yoga, nature walks, music, art, poetry, healthy eating, and other self-declared methods of stress management. The hope is that Frank will eventually freely ventilate his feelings, own the reality of the loss, ask for and accept help, and view the job loss as an opportunity for growth.

Frank and Mark experienced non-death-related grief, but the following considerations are important for those coping with death:

- Death develops over the course of lifespan, with small children (ages 3–5 years) seeing death as temporary, older children (ages 5–10 years) gradually accepting that death is both permanent and inevitable, and adolescents accepting permanency and inevitability but view death as something so remote that it does not really affect them directly.

- Significant death events (e.g., plague, mass suicide, terrorist attack, plane crash, tsunami) and life-threatening illnesses (e.g., cancer) will impact some individuals.
- Life-threatening conditions impact individuals and family members on physical, psychological, and psychosocial levels.
- Culture will be a factor in how individuals experience death and are able to cope with it.
- Culture-based views of death rituals are common, and different cultures and subcultures display common and unique forms of experience.
- Some older adults are resilient in the face of death events.
- Ego integrity refers to acceptance of one's life.
- Reminiscing and life reviews are effective ways to help elderly individuals achieve ego integrity.
- Meaning in life, spirituality, and self-transcendence might impact elderly individuals' psychosocial paths.
- Some individuals are better prepared to accept natural death in their final stages of life due to ego integrity and a sense of satisfaction over what they have accomplished during their lifetimes.
- Others experience fear or denial because they are painfully aware of missed opportunities and failures as time runs short.
- The circumstances of death are direct factors in how family and friends react to death and mourn the loss.
- Often, when death is expected, though the death still might represent a loss, family and friends are afforded some time to prepare for the inevitable.
- Sudden, unexpected death is frequently traumatic, leaving survivors with another dimension of loss, including a surreal experience as if the death didn't really happen, feelings of guilt and denial, and a keen awareness of unresolved issues.
- Some circumstances of death, even when survivors have an opportunity to anticipate and prepare, are controversial, due to social stigma (HIV/AIDS) or societal implications (e.g., terrorism, the mass killing of schoolchildren and their teachers at Sandy Hook Elementary School in Connecticut).
- Hospice is an end-of-life intervention through which trained professionals provide medical and emotional support for the dying individual and family members as they prepare for final moments.
- Euthanasia and other third-party interventions to hasten death are legally, morally, and socially controversial, with legal guidelines varying across the United States. In some states assisted suicide is illegal, whereas in other locations it is permissible when specified guidelines are followed.

SUMMARY

Generativity, death, the process of dying, bereavement, and grief are issues that require an understanding of developmental processes. Researchers such as Kubler-Ross describe key emotions commonly experienced by those facing death- and non-death-related grief, whereas others tout diversity as part of the process. For example, factors such as age, culture, values, beliefs, life stage, and whether loss is sudden or unanticipated all play a role in the grieving experience. Counselors can help clients experience grief in a mentally healthy manner by understanding ethical and legal considerations related to generativity, viewing death and grief as a developmental process, recognizing the difference between normal and complicated grief, learning crisis counseling skills, and enhancing clients' ego integrity and resiliency.

USEFUL WEBSITES

Association for Death Education and Counseling
http://www.adec.org/adec/default.aspx
Association for Adult Development and Aging
http://www.aadaweb.org/
Living Trust Network
http://livingtrustnetwork.com/estate-planning-center/applicable-state-laws/
   intestate-succession.html
PsychCentral
http://psychcentral.com/lib/the-5-stages-of-loss-and-grief/000617
Good Grief
http://www.good-grief.org
The Center for Complicated Grief
http://www.complicatedgrief.org/bereavement/
Euthanasia.com
http://www.euthanasia.com
Terri Schiavo Life and Hope Network
http://www.terrisfight.org/facts-about-euthanasia

REFERENCES

Acierno, R., Ruggiero, K. J., Kilpatrick, D. G., Resnick, H. S., & Galea, S. (2006). Risk and protective factors for psychopathology among older versus younger adults after the 2004 Florida hurricanes. *American Journal of Geriatric Psychiatry, 14*, 1051–1059. doi:10.1097/01.JGP.0000221327.97904.b

American Counseling Association. (2014). *ACA code of ethics and standards of practice.* Alexandria, VA: Author

American Psychiatric Association (APA). (2013). *Diagnostic and statistical manual of mental disorders* (5th ed.). Washington, DC: Author.

Armour, M. P. (2006). Violent death: Understanding the context of traumatic and stigmatized grief. *Journal of Human Behavior in the Social Environment, 14*, 53–90.

Azaiza, F., Ron, P., Shoham, M., & Tinsky-Roimi, T. (2011). Death and dying anxiety among bereaved and nonbereaved elderly parents. *Death Studies, 35*, 610–624. doi:10.1080/07481187.2011.553325

Binder, B. K., Mastel-Smith, B., Hersch, G., Symes, L., Malecha, A., & McFarlane, J. (2009). Community-dwelling, older women's perspectives on therapeutic life review: A qualitative analysis. *Issues in Mental Health Nursing, 30,* 288–294. doi:10.1080/01612840902753885

Bonanno, G. A. (2004). Loss, trauma, and human resilience: Have we underestimated the human capacity to thrive after extremely aversive events? *American Psychologist, 59,* 20–28.

Bonoti, F., Leondari, A., & Mastora, A. (2013). Exploring children's understanding of death: Through drawings and the death concept questionnaire. *Death Studies, 37,* 47–60. doi:10.1080/07481187.2011.623216

Bousso, R. S., de Souza Serafim, T., & Misko, M. D. (2010). The relationship between religion, illness, and death in life histories of family members of children with life-threatening diseases. *Rev. Latino-Am. Enfermagem, 18,* 156–162.

Burke, K., Muscara, F., McCarthy, M., Dimovski, A., Hearps, S., Anderson, V., & Walser, R. (2014). Adapting acceptance and commitment therapy for parents of children with life-threatening illness: A pilot study. *Families, Systems, and Health, 32,* 122–127. doi:10.1037/fsh0000012

Burnside, L., & Haight, B. K. (1992). Reminiscence and life review: Analyzing each concept. *Journal of Advanced Nursing, 17,* 855–862.

Cacciatore, J., & Thieleman, K. (2014). We rise out of the cradle into the grave: An ethnographic exploration of ritual, mourning, and death on a Hutterite colony. *OMEGA, 69,* 357–379.

Centers for Disease Control and Prevention (CDC). (2012). *10 leading causes of death by age group, United States 2012.* Retrieved from http://www.cdc.gov/injury/wisqars/pdf/leading_causes_of_death_by_age_group_2012-a.pdf

Chan, W. C. H., & Chan, C. L. W. (2011). Acceptance of spousal death: The factor of time in bereaved older adults' search for meaning. *Death Studies, 34,* 147–162. doi:10.1080/07481187.2020.535387

Chen, B. (2012). Coping with death and loss: Confucian perspectives and the use of rituals. *Pastoral Psychology, 61,* 1037–1049. doi:10.1007/s11089-012-0476-6

Chui, W. H., & Chan, H. C. (2013). Self-control and the fear of death among adolescents in Hong Kong. *Journal of Youth Studies, 16,* 70–85.

Cohn, S. K. (2012). Pandemics: Waves of disease, waves of hate from the Plague of Athens to A.I.D.S. *Historical Research, 85,* 535–551. doi:10.1111/j.1468–2281.2012.00603.x

Craig, G. J., & Dunn, W. L. (2007). *Understanding human development.* Upper Saddle River, NJ: Pearson.

Currier, J. M., Holland, J. M., & Neimeyer, R. A. (2006). Sense-making, grief and the experience of violent loss: Toward a meditational model. *Death Studies, 30,* 403–428.

Damianakis, T., & Marziali, E. (2012). Older adults' response to the loss of a spouse: The function of spirituality in understanding the grieving process. *Aging and Mental Health, 16,* 57–66.

Depaola, S. J., Griffin, M., Young, J. R., & Neimeyer, R. A. (2003). Death anxiety and attitudes toward the elderly among older adults: The role of gender and ethnicity. *Death Studies, 27*, 335–338.

Diehl, M., Chui, H., Hay, E. L., Lumley, M. A., Gruhn, D., & Vief, G. (2014). Change in coping and defense mechanisms across adulthood: Longitudinal findings in a European American sample. *Developmental Psychology, 50*, 634–648. doi:10.1037/a0033619

Dow, K. H. (2003). Seventh National Conference on Cancer Nursing Research keynote address: Challenges and opportunities in cancer survivorship research. *Oncology Nursing Forum, 30*, 455–469.

Erikson, E. H. (1963). *Childhood and society*. New York, NY: Norton.

Erickson, E H., Erickson, J. M., & Kinvick, H. Q. (1986). *Vital involvement in older age: The experience of old age in our time*. New York, NY: Norton.

Eysenck, H. J. (1983). Stress, disease, and personality: The inoculation effect. In C. L. Cooper (Ed.), *Stress research* (pp. 121–146). New York, NY: Wiley.

Foster, C., Wright, D., Hill, H., Hopkinson, J., & Roffe, L. (2009). Psychological implications of living 5 years or more following a cancer diagnosis: A systematic review of the research evidence. *European Journal of Cancer Care, 18*, 223–247. doi:10.111/n.1365-2354.2008.010001.x

Frankl, V. E. (1963). *Man's search for meaning: An introduction to logotherapy*. New York, NY: Washington Square Press.

Gillies, J., & Neimeyer, R. A. (2006). Loss, grief, and the search for significance: Toward a model of meaning reconstruction in bereavement. *Journal of Constructivist Psychology, 19*, 31–65.

Gintner, G. G. (2001). Sudden and violent loss: Clinical guidelines for screening and treatment of survivors. In D. Sandhu (Ed.), *Faces of violence: Psychological correlates, concepts and intervention strategies* (pp. 355–376). New York, NY: Nova Science.

Henriksson, A., Arestedt, K., Benzein, E., Ternestedt, B. M., & Andershed, B. (2012). Effects of a support group programme for patients with life-threatening illness during ongoing palliative care. *Palliative Medicine, 27*, 257–264. doi:10.1177/0269216312446103

Humphrey, K. M. (2009). *Counseling strategies for loss and grief*. Alexandria, VA: American Counseling Association.

Jackson, B. R. (2008). How gender and self-esteem impact death anxiety across adulthood. *Psi Chi Journal of Undergraduate Research, 13*(2), 96–101.

Jenko, M., Gonzalez, L., & Alley, P. (2010). Life review in critical care: Possibilities at the end of life. *Critical Care Nurse, 30*, 17–26.

Kaplow, J. B., Howell, K. H., & Layne, C. M. (2014). Do circumstances of death matter? Identifying socioenvironmental risks for grief-related psychopathology in bereaved youth. *Journal of Traumatic Stress, 27*(1), 42–29. doi: 10.1002/jts.21877

Kaur Kang, P., & Kaur Kang, T. (2013). Death anxiety (thantaphobia) among elderly: A gender study. *Indian Journal of Gerontology, 27*, 637–643.

Knight, B. G., Gatz, M., Heller, K., & Bengtson, V. L. (2000). Age and emotional response to the Northridge Earthquake: A longitudinal analysis. *Psychology and Aging, 15*, 627–634. doi:10.1037//0882-7974.15.4.62

Kristensen, P., Heir, T., Herlofsen, P. H., Langsrud, O., & Weisaeth, L. (2012). Parental mental health after the accidental death of a son during military service: A 23- year follow-up study. *Journal of Nervous and Mental Disease, 200*, 63–68.

Kristensen, P., Weisaeth, L., & Heir, T., (2012). Bereavement and mental health after sudden and violent losses: A review. *Psychiatry: Interpersonal & Biological Processes, 75*(1), 76–97. doi:10.1521/psyc.2012.75.1.76

Kubler-Ross, E. (1969). *On death and dying.* New York, NY: Macmillan.

Lyke, J. (2013). Associations among aspects of meaning in life and death anxiety in young adults. *Death Studies, 37*, 471–482. doi:10.1080/07481187.2011.649939

Lyons, B. P., & Levine, H. (2013). Physical symptoms, chronic and life-threatening illness trajectories among minority and aging populations. *Journal of Health and Human Services Administration, 36*(3), 323–366.

Martin, T., & Doka, K. (2000). *Men don't cry … women do: Transcending gender stereotypes of grief.* Philadelphia, PA: Brunner/Mazel.

Missler, M., Stroebe, M., Geurtsen, L., Mastenbroek, M., Chmoun, S., & Van Der Houwen, K. (2011). Exploring death anxiety among elderly people: A literature review and empirical investigation. *OMEGA, 64*, 357–379.

Murphy, S. A., Johnson, L. C., Wu, L., Fan, J. J., & Lohan, J. (2003). Bereaved parents' outcomes 4 to 60 months after their children's deaths by accident, suicide, or homicide: A comparative study demonstrating differences. *Death Studies, 27*, 39–61.

Murphy, S. A., Tapper, V. J., Johnson, L. C., & Lohan, J. (2003). Suicide ideation among parents bereaved by the violent deaths of their children. *Issues of Mental Health Nursing, 24*, 5–25.

Muselman, D. M., & Wiggins, M. I. (2012). Spirituality and loss: Approaches for counseling grieving adolescents. *Counseling and Values, 57*, 229–240.

Myers, J. E., Sweeney, T. J., & Witmer, M. J. (2000). The wheel of wellness counseling for wellness: A holistic model for treatment planning. *Journal of Counseling and Development, 78*, 251–266.

Neimeyer, R. A. (1998). Death-anxiety research: The state of the art. *Omega, Journal of Death and Dying, 9*, 3308–3316.

Niemiec, R. M., & Schulenberg, S. E. (2011). Understanding death attitudes: The integration of movies, positive psychology, and meaning management. *Death Studies, 35*, 387–407. doi:10.1080/07481187.2010.544517

Nishimura, A. (1997). Medical examination report on the Great Hanshin Earthquake. In C. Wakasugi (Ed.), *Advances in legal medicine* (pp. 234–238). Yoyodo, Osaka.

Paloutzian, R. F., & Ellison, C. W. (1982). Lonliness, spiritual well-being, and the quality of life. In L. A. Peplau & D. Perlman (Eds.), *Loneliness: A sourcebook of current theory, research, and therapy* (pp. 224–237). New York, NY: Wiley.

Papa, A., Neria, Y., & Litz, B. (2008). Traumatic bereavement in war veterans. *Psychiatric Annals, 38*, 686–691.

Perera, C. (2005). After the legal tsunami: Legal implications of mass burials of unidentified victims in Sri Lanka. *Policy Forum, 2*, 494–497.

Perera, C., & Briggs, C. (2007). Guidelines for the effective conduct of mass burials following mass disasters: Post-Asian tsunami disaster experience in retrospect. *Forensic Science, Medicine, and Pathology, 4*, 1–8.

Peterson, C., & Seligman, M. E. P. (2004). *Character strengths and virtues: A handbook and classification*. Washington, DC: American Psychological Association/New York, NY: Oxford University Press.

Prigerson, H. G. (2004). Complicated grief. When the path of adjustment leads to a dead end. *Bereavement Care, 23*, 38–40.

Randall, W. L., & Kenyon, G. M. (2001). *Ordinary wisdom, biographical aging and the journey of life*. Westport, CT: Praeger.

Reeves, N. C. (2011). Death acceptance through ritual. *Death Studies, 35*, 408–419.

Russac, R. J., Gatliff, C., Reece, M., & Spottswood, D. (2007). Death anxiety across the adult years: An examination of age and gender effects. *Death Studies, 31*, 549–561. doi:10.1080/07481180701356936

Scanlon, J., McMahon, T., & van Haastert, C. (2007). Handling mass death by integrating the management of disasters and pandemics: Lessons from the Indian Ocean, Tsunami, the Spanish flu, and other incidents. *Journal of Contingencies and Crisis Management, 15*, 80–94.

Seligman, M. E. P. (2002). *Authentic happiness: Using the new positive psychology to realize your potential for lasting fulfillment*. New York, NY: Free Press.

Servaty-Seib, H. L., & Pistole, M. C. (2007). Adolescent grief: Kinship category and emotional closeness. *Omega, 54*, 147–167.

Shabanowitz, R. B. (2013). Hog heaven: Funeral and mourning rituals of an independent motorcycle club. *International Journal of Motorcycle Studies, 9*.

Shields, L., Molzahn, A., Bruce, A., Schick Makaroff, K. S., Stajduhar, K., … Shermak, S. (2015). Contrasting stories of life-threatening illness: A narrative inquiry. *International Journal of Nursing Studies, 52*, 207–215.

Shrira, A., Palgi, Y., Hamama-Raz, Y., Goodwin, R., & Ben-Ezra, M. (2014). Previous exposure to the World Trade Center terrorist attack and posttraumatic symptoms among older adults following Hurricane Sandy. *Psychiatry, 77*, 374–385.

Signoli, M. (2012). Reflections on crisis burials related to past plague epidemics. *Clinical Microbiology and Infection, 18*, 218–222. doi:10.1111/n.1469–0691.2012.03787.x

Slaughter, V. (2005). Young children's understanding of death. *Australian Psychologist, 40*, 179–186. doi:10.1080/0005006050060500243426

Steger, M. F., & Shin, J. Y. (2010). The relevance of the Meaning in Life Questionnaire to therapeutic practice: A look at the initial evidence. *International Forum on Logotherapy, 33*, 95–104.

Stephens, H. W. (1997). *The Texas City disaster, 1947*. Austin, TX: University of Texas Press.

Sveen, C. A., & Walby, F. A. (2008). Suicide survivors' mental health and grief reactions: A systematic review of controlled studies. *Suicide and Life Threatening Behavior, 38*, 13–29.

Underwood, L. G., & Teresi, J. A. (2002). The Daily Spiritual Experiences Scale: Development, theoretical description, reliability, exploratory factor analysis, and preliminary construct validity using health-related data. *Society of Behavioral Medicine, 24*, 22–33.

Walker, A. C., & Balk, D. E. (2007). Bereavement rituals in the Muscogee Creek tribe. *Death Studies, 31*, 633–652. doi:10.1080/07481180701405188

Wang, J. J. (2008). The effects of reminiscence on depressive symptoms and mood status of older institutionalized adults in Taiwan. *International Journal of Geriatric Psychiatry, 20*, 57–62. doi:10.1002/gps.11248

Wenzel, L. B., Donnelly, J. P., Fowler, J. M., Habbal, R., Taylor, T. H., Aziz, N., & Cella, D. (2002). Resilience, reflection, and residual stress in ovarian cancer survivorship: A gynecologic oncology group study. *Psycho-Oncology, 11*, 142–153.

Author Index

Subject Index